THE COLLECTED ROBERT E. HOWARD

VOLUME 2

1930-1932

With Index

First Edition Edited by
Rob Roehm

Second Edition Edited by
John Bullard

Introduction & Annotations by
Rusty Burke

THE Robert E. Howard FOUNDATION PRESS

Special thanks to Glenn Lord and his wife Lou Ann, who provided access to the original Robert E. Howard typescripts, manuscripts or transcripts thereof.

Also grateful thanks to Texas A&M for allowing us to scan Howard's letters to Tevis Clyde Smith from their collection.

Published by the REH Foundation Press, LLC by arrangement with
Robert E. Howard Properties Inc.
http://www.rehfoundation.org

Cover design and artwork by Mark Wheatley.

2nd Edition, version 1.0

TABLE OF CONTENTS

1931

INTRODUCTION

By Rusty Burke

Wright recently sent me a letter from the W.T. author Robert E. Howard, praising my "Rats in the Walls" & giving incidental remarks on early Celtic Britain. Howard seems to be rather an erudite person - & I am dropping him a line. – H.P. Lovecraft

As 1930 began, Robert E. Howard's correspondents were chiefly those two stalwarts, Tevis Clyde Smith and Harold Preece. Smith, of course, was his friend of long standing, and with Preece he had been increasingly discussing Irish/Celtic subjects and developing his "Irish" persona. It was his study of British prehistory, and his dabbling in Gaelic, that led directly to what is perhaps the greatest correspondence cycle in the history of fantasy literature.

At the end of "The Rats in the Walls," H.P. Lovecraft (1890-1937) had his narrator gibber in increasingly archaic tongues to indicate his descent into madness and reversion to the primitive. *"Magna Mater! Magna Mater!... Atys... Dia ad aghaidh 's ad aodann... agus bas dunach ort! Dhonas 's dholas ort, agus leat-sa!... Ungl... ungl... rrlh... chchch..."* When the story was reprinted in the June 1930 issue of *Weird Tales*, Robert E. Howard wrote a letter of enthusiastic praise to the editor, in which he surmised that, because Lovecraft had his character speaking in Gaelic rather than Cymric, he held to an outdated theory of the settling of the British Isles. In fact, Lovecraft knew perfectly well that his character should have been speaking in Cymric, as he had noted to Frank Belknap Long in late 1923. He had simply lifted a phrase from "The Sin-Eater" by Fiona McLeod (William Sharp) thinking "Nobody will ever stop to note the difference."

Seven years later, Robert E. Howard did, and with Wright's forwarding of the letter to Lovecraft began the most important correspondence of Howard's short life. At last the young Texas writer had found a correspondent worthy of his outsize talents, one who would challenge him as none of his other friends ever had. "He's out of my class," Howard confided to Smith. "I'm game to go the limit with a man my weight, but me scrapping with him is like a palooka climbing into the ring with a champion." He had stepped up to the heavyweight class, but it would not be long before he showed he could slug it out in the same ring as Lovecraft, who was surely the epistolary champion of the world. There is no way of knowing how many letters Lovecraft wrote: S.T. Joshi estimates something between 80,000 and 100,000, of which "no more than 20,000 now survive." (For understatement, it's hard to beat "no more than 20,000"!) While the bulk of these may have been brief missives, one or two pages, the front and back of a single sheet of paper, a great many of them were lengthy: "30, 40, 50, and evidently in at least one instance... over 100 handwritten pages long," according to Joshi. "One can only wonder at the reaction of Lovecraft's correspondents at receiving novel-length letters of this sort. How did they answer them?" In the case of Howard, at least, the answer becomes clear in this volume: he wrote lengthy letters right back.

These letters make for fascinating reading, and not only for students of fantasy literature, as I have learned on more than one occasion when I have left copies on my desk and later found co-workers engrossed in them. The subject matter ranges so broadly -- beginning with Celtic language and cultures, moving into European prehistory, then into the history and lore of the South and of Texas, and on to other phases of history, literature, politics and current events, lengthy travelogues -- that even those with no interest in weird fiction can find them enthralling. For the student of the genre, though, the letters are a treasure trove of information about the writers and their work. In Howard's side of the correspondence can be traced the development of many of his stories, as well as general themes. Some are obvious, such as the letter in which he relates the plot-germ that later became "Pigeons From Hell." Some are more subtle, such as the plot-threads and much of the incidental material for "Old Garfield's Heart," which can be traced through letters from 1931 to 1933. In some cases, Lovecraft's own letters serve as the source of inspiration, as when his comments on the witch-cults and legends of "little people" work their way into "The Children of the Night" and "Worms of the Earth."

One cannot, of course, ever quantify the degree to which one writer has influenced another, but the effects of Lovecraft's encouragement were surely considerable, and as the correspondence continued and began to turn toward debate, one begins to see in Howard's fiction the crystallization of many of the ideas he advances in the letters.

The debating begins almost imperceptibly. For the first two years, the letters are mostly rather impersonal (if splendidly written) discussions of various historical and literary topics. Even when individual differences in preferences arise -- such as Howard's animosity toward Lovecraft's beloved Roman Empire -- they are discussed amicably. Two topics seem to strike the spark that leads to full-blown debate. When Howard says he finds himself more suited to physical than to mental pursuits, Lovecraft counters that the physical, while certainly a necessary part of life, is inferior to the mental, and represents a waste of energy that could be devoted to "superior" activities such as scientific or artistic efforts. And a discussion of "zones of physical violence" -- Lovecraft asserting that it was unknown among the essentially law-abiding citizens of the East (excepting, of course, the "foreign element") -- led gradually to a discussion of law enforcement, and that's when things hit the fan. But the debate really heats up in the next volume.

Two other correspondents appearing for the first time in this second volume of letters are worthy of a note. Wilfred Blanch Talman (1904-1986) had met Lovecraft while attending Brown University, and later became a member of the Kalem Club (a group of Lovecraft's correspondents in New York City, so called because all of the original members' names began with K, L, or M). Lovecraft had helped him with revisions to his story "Two Black Bottles," which was published in *Weird Tales* in 1927, and he had another published in 1928. His third and final story, "Doom Around the Corner," was published in November 1931. At the time he entered Howard's life, he was an editor of *The Texaco Star*, a magazine issued by the oil company, for which Howard would write the article "The Ghost of Camp Colorado" as well as at least two others that were not published.

In December 1932, at the end of the period covered by this volume, Howard began corresponding with August Derleth (1909-1971), a frequent contributor to *Weird Tales* who came to be well-regarded as a writer of regional fiction set in his native Wisconsin, and of course became best-known as co-founder and long-time publisher of Arkham House. Lovecraft had passed along some of Howard's letters with lengthy passages on Texas history to Derleth, whom he knew to be interested in regional histories, prompting Derleth to write Howard and strike up a correspondence. While the correspondence with Talman faded away, Howard and Derleth continued writing one another until the Texan's death.

The three-year period covered in this volume was the most prolific of Howard's life in terms of letter-writing, and may well have been his most fecund as a writer of fiction, as well, bookended as it is by the first of his contributions to *Oriental Stories* in 1930 and the publication, in December 1932, of "The Phoenix on the Sword." The fertile soil from which these stories sprang is contained in this volume.

FIRST EDITION ACKNOWLEDGEMENTS

The letters of Robert E. Howard are scattered all over the place, in private collections, historical societies, and universities. Before *The Collected Letters* could even get off the ground, I had to acquire copies of the actual documents. Many people helped me with this task: Glenn Lord, Leo Grin, Joe Marek, Rusty Burke, Edward Waterman, Patrice Louinet and Paul Herman — and I'm probably forgetting someone. Howard's letters to August Derleth are housed with the Wisconsin Historical Society; letters to Clark Ashton Smith are at Brown University, and the University of California at Berkeley is home to the Robert Barlow collection.

As the letters trickled in, I either had to prepare an electronic text (e-text), or check the letter against an existing e-text. Leo Grin, Dennis McHaney, Paul Herman, and Patrice Louinet were most helpful in providing e-text; the students of Eastside High School's class of 2009 helped prepare new e-text — for a bit of extra credit.

Once the e-text was prepared, the letters had to be arranged in chronological order. This could not have been done without the efforts of Rusty Burke, Patrice Louinet, and Glenn Lord, who have spent countless hours dating the letters.

When editing the letters, I sought advice and assistance from Rusty Burke, Paul Herman, Don Herron, and Leo Grin. Their patient, and sometimes heated, advice helped make the present collection what it is. Any praise for this work is shared by them, any criticism is mine.

FIRST EDITION NOTES ON THE TEXT

The letters have been sorted and are presented here in the best guess of the order in which they were written. Most of Robert E. Howard's letters after 1926 were undated, and we have had to rely on internal clues to establish approximate dates. In some cases, reference to news events allowed the establishment of a precise date (though sometimes Howard apparently worked on longer letters over the course of several days, or even weeks). Someone penciled dates on some of the letters to H.P. Lovecraft (it does not appear to have been Lovecraft himself), and several letters to Harold Preece were kept in their original envelopes, with postmark dates. By 1934 Howard had begun to date letters more often, though some were still left without. A very few of the letters to Tevis Clyde Smith contained no clues to help establish dating, and are collected at the end of the final volume.

Given the history of Robert E. Howard's works and editors, this three-volume collection of Howard's correspondence is essentially unedited: only minor changes to the original text have been made. The most obvious of these changes is the use of italics. Generally speaking, Howard put the titles of books, movies, and stories all in quotes, and only capitalized magazine titles. This practice has been changed to conform to current standards: movie, book, and magazine titles have been italicized. Also, any underlined words and most words typed in all capital letters have been italicized.

Howard rarely used apostrophes, especially early on, in words like "can't," and "don't"; these have been inserted. Obvious typos and misspellings have also been corrected, with the exception of words that Howard consistently spelled differently than the American norm—surprize and travelled, for example—which have been left alone. Some attempt has been made to standardize Howard's spelling of hyphenated and/or compound words.

For those researching such issues, the editors can provide exacting details of when Howard's various spelling/punctuation practices started or stopped.

The text for this second volume of collected letters was taken from copies of Howard's originals, with the following exceptions:

116. To Harold Preece, postmarked January 4, 1930: Text from *The "New" Howard Reader* #3, November 1998, poetry from typescript.
119. To *Weird Tales*, ca. January to Mid-February 1930: Text from the April 1930 issue.
147. To *Weird Tales*, ca. December 1930: Text from the January 1931 issue.
166. To Farnsworth Wright, ca. June-July 1931: Text from *The Ghost*, May 1945.
186. Mythical Dane Dream character: From *The Last Celt.*
190. To *Weird Tales*, ca. January 1932: Text from the March 1932 issue.
196. To *Oriental Stories*, ca. Spring 1932: Text from the Summer 1932 issue.
219. To H.P. Lovecraft, ca. mid-October 1932: "With a Set of Rattlesnake Rattles": From *Leaves* #1, Summer 1937.
223. To *Magic Carpet*, ca. November 1932: Text from the January 1933 issue.
230. To Unknown Recipient, ca. 1932:"Not much to say.": Text from a transcript provided by Glenn Lord.

SECOND EDITION NOTES FROM THE EDITOR

In updating the first edition of the *Collected Letters*, I have tried to make minimal changes to the original work, as Rob did such a fantastic job. The following are changes I did make. I chronologically inserted letters found since the first edition was published. During the long process of re-editing the books, Rob Roehm and Patrice Louinet suggested that some of the letters' dates be changed, or more fixed in date, which caused a general re-evaluation of the letters, especially the undated ones in Volume 3, trying to apply more certain dates on them. This of course caused the changing of letters from where they were in the first edition of the books to their current positions in this edition. I changed the footnotes to endnotes and placed them at the end of the applicable letter to make them easier to refer to, and changed the font-size to the same size as the text to make them easier to read. I also added some new notes by Rob Roehm, Patrice Louinet, and myself. To distinguish these new notes from Rusty and Rob's marvelous and voluminous work, I have added Rob's and Patrice's names, and my initials, "JB", at the end of the new notes to denote who made them. The biggest change starting in this volume and continuing in Volume 3 is the inclusion of all existing drafts of letters to H.P. Lovecraft. The drafts have been transcribed by Rob Roehm, Jeff Shanks, and myself from the typescripts. I have numbered the drafts and final letters with lower case alphabet letters after the letter number, with the final alphabet letter listed being the final letter as sent to Lovecraft. Finally, I added and updated the index that Bobby Derie made for the First Editions of *Collected Letters*. These indexes will now be split up between the various volumes as appropriate.

One final note, you will also find at the end of many letters "**TSS**", followed by a number or numbers. "TSS" stands for "Typescript", that is, an original page typed by REH, though in a few instances it will be a retype by someone else, when the original is not available. The numbers following are document numbers referencing digital scans of the original letters. These scans are part of a collection of digital items in the Foundation's collections. This notation has been added to make it easier for researchers and scholars who wish to review a scan of the original typescript to request access from the Foundation to look at the scan online. By having the TSS number, you will be able to quickly find the document among the thousands of items in the collection. You will also notice that many times the numbers are out of order. This is because in achieving his Herculean effort of scanning all the Howard items from Glenn Lord's collection and other sources, Paul Herman would often find the pages out of order and mixed up, requiring later identification, sorting, and indexing. The TSS numbers reflect his order of scanning of each page as he found it in the boxes and piles. The address to write to The Foundation to be given access to the TSS documents is:

info@rehfoundation.org

Researchers can also go view the original typescripts. The Foundation can also provide the information on where these are kept.

SECOND EDITION NOTES ON TEXT

Photograph of 1927 Regional Gathering of the Lone Scouts taken from 1927 Texicoma Yearbook.

List of First Edition Letter Numbers with Their New Second Edition Numbers

In updating the First Edition by adding in the letters found since the original publication, the numbers of the letters and their order has changed. In order to help scholars and researchers looking at research published using the original 1st ed. letter numbers, the below lists show the 1st ed. letter number paired with its new letter number in this edition. (V3) is *The Collected Letters Vol. 3*, and (V4) is *The Collected Letters Index and Addenda.* The drafts that Howard wrote before finalizing his letter and sending it to H.P. Lovecraft that weren't included in V4 are included and identified as "New".

1st Ed.#	2nd Ed.#
100	116
101	118
102	120
103	121
104	122
105	119
106	123
107	124
108	125
109	126
110	127
111	128
112	129
113	130
114	131
115	132
116	133
117	134
118	135b
119	136
120	137
121	138
122	139
123	140
124	141
125	142
126	143
127	144
128	146
129	148
130	149
131	150
132	145
133	147
134	152
135	153
136	155
137	154
138	156
139	157
140	158
141	159
142	160
143	161
144	162
145	163
146	164
147	165
148	166
149	167
150	168
151	169
152	170
153	171
154	172
155	173
156	174
157	175
158	176
159	177
160	178
161	179
162	180
163	181
164	182
165	183
166	184
167	185
168	188
169	189
170	191
171	192
172	190
173	193
174	194
175	195
176	196
177	197

1st Ed.#---2nd Ed.#		New	2nd Ed.#
178	198	Draft to HPL: Dec. '32	225a
179	199		
180	200		
181	201		
182	202		
183	203		
184	204		
185	205		
186	206		
187	207		
188	208		
189	210		
190	209		
191	211		
192	212		
193	213		
194	214		
195	215		
196	216		
197	217		
198	218		
199	219		
200	220		
201	221		
202	222		
203	223		
204	224		
205	225b		
206	226		
207	227		
208	228		
340(V3)	232		
341(V3)	187		
343(V3)	229		
353(V3)	230		
354(V3)	186		
359(V4)	231		
361(V4)	233		
365(V4)	151		
366(V4)	117		
367(V4)	135a		

SECOND EDITION ACKNOWLEDGMENTS

It's been a long, tough, exasperating road since that Summer of 2017, when while talking with Paul Herman about the work we were doing on some of Howard's oeuvre, he mentioned that the Foundation was going to bring out second editions of the *Collected Letters*, and was looking to find someone to take over the editing of them as Rob Roehm was looking for a break from his years of masterfully editing the Foundation's Howard books. I thought, "Hey, that sounds like it would be fun and interesting," and promptly volunteered myself. Never, ever volunteer!

But in all seriousness, it has been an incredibly enriching and frustrating job for me. Having never edited a book before, the learning curve was steep. Just when I thought I had the book finished, I'd notice an error, or have one pointed out to me by others looking over the book. Then, it was back to the drawing board. I hope my ideas on some of the changes I've made to Rob's original fantastic job will make it easier to read and use these books by both readers and scholars.

I want to thank the following people for their help in preparing these second editions: Rob Roehm for doing all the hard work first, and for his suggestions on correcting mistakes or dates; Bobby Derie for his hard work on creating the indexes first, and his help on my updating his work; Paul Herman for scanning all of the known Howard material, and answering my questions on the letters and working with Word; Rusty Burke for his help in answering my questions and giving suggestions; Patrice Louinet for his great knowledge on letter dates, Howard history, photographs, and helpful suggestions. And again, Paul and Rob for their kind and gracious help in tutoring me through learning to be an editor. To quote the eloquent Mr. Roehm: "Their patient, and sometimes heated, advice helped make the present collection what it is. Any praise for this work is shared by them, any criticism is mine." I would add that there was never any heated advice or remarks by any of these good gentlemen in dealing with a neophyte, me.

Also, I would also like to thank my Seventh grade Texas History teacher, Mrs. Carrico, for her Friday classes on teaching us researching, which during our free time after completing our assignments, allowed me to read my first actual Howard story getting me interested in Howard's writing; and my brother, Thomas, for letting me borrow his 2 Lancer Conan paperbacks, which got me fully hooked on Robert E. Howard.

And, finally, I would like to thank Robert E. Howard for a near-lifetime of entertainment, and meeting and making new friends through our shared love of his work and genius.

1930

116. To Harold Preece, postmarked January 4, 1930.

Yes, we fade from youth swiftly. Most of my school mates are married, long ago. Those with which I graduated from Brownwood High, I mean. You say you realize that no girl will ever fall in love with you. Well, you're lucky. As long as you only fall in love with them, it's alright; you can love them and leave them. When they fall in love with you, the Hell starts. Man was born to be the hunter, not the hunted.

I saw both pictures you mention, *The Loves of Casanova*, and *The Tempest* here in Cross Plains, nearly a year ago. I thought Ivan Mosjukine did rather well though like most foreign actors he over-acted. I rather liked *The Tempest*, even if the plot was rather thread-bare. At least it portrayed one truth: that an oppressed people exceed their oppressors in cruelty when they get the upper hand. It's no use for the reformers to howl about the brotherhood of man and all that stuff; whoever are the rulers are swine. You can't change men's nature by prating and canting about the new dawn, and all that much, regardless of the howls of Upty Sinclair. I admit the ruling class now are unspeakable hogs, but I maintain that if the oppressed classes were to get the upper hand, they'd be just as bad. They howl about their love for man-kind — that's a lie. What they want is privileges and special rights for their own particular gang and the rest can go to Hell. They'd abuse somebody else as much as the capitalists abuse them. Look at history: the pagans in Rome oppressed the early Christians. The Christians got control and began to maltreat the weaker sects. The Catholics in England oppressed the Church of England, then they got the upper hand and oppressed Catholics, Presbyterians and Puritans, who fled to America and oppressed the Quakers who would have oppressed anybody who might have been weaker than they.

I got the copy of the *Longhorn*[1] though I was a long time in acknowledging receiving it to Lenore. I enjoyed her poems very much. They stood out from the muck and drivel which characterizes all college magazines.

As for Nora Hopper's poem,[2] when I enjoy the theme and rhythm of a poem I do not trouble my brain overmuch about the psychic interpretation. I know that "dark man" is the Gaelic term for blindness and whether she meant this in a physical or spiritual way, I do not know nor am I overly interested. There is much latitude in Gaelic phrases and terms. It is a difficult language and very adaptable. The spelling and pronunciation is apt to trip the English speaking student. I imagine that a man, learning the language by word of mouth only, would find it almost impossible to write it correctly. Let us glance at an example: An cailin rua na ri. That means "The red girl of the king," and is pronounced, "An colleen roe na ree." Or take men's names: the name which is pronounced Mac Cool is spelled variously Mac Collum, Mac Cumhail, and so on. The very term Gael, is spelled Goidhel, though pronounced Gael. As you know, it comes from the great chief Goidhel who led his wanderers out of Scythia and into Egypt where he married pharaohs' daughter Mileta, whence comes the name Milesian, not as some erroneously attribute it to the Grecian Miletus. The De Danaan came from Greece — not the Gaels. The path of the Gael first crossed that of the children of Israel in Goidhel's time for as came into Egypt he met Moses coming out with the Israelites. And it's a pity old Goidhel couldn't have foreseen the future then and there. Goidhel's Celts remained in Egypt some time fighting as mercenaries and it might have been his son who married Mileta instead of himself. I don't remember. From Egypt they went to Spain where they fought the Celtiberians and from Spain they went to Ireland and for a long time it was customary for Irish historians to deny the Celtic origin of the Gael. I think that was the last drift of the Celt from the great central plains which were, theoretically the cradle of the Indo-European, or Aryan race. The Cymri and the Gauls had come earlier.

Just in the last few years historians have realized the vast extent of what might be called the Celtic epoch. Trusting to the biased and superficial accounts of their enemies, the Romans and Greeks, historians for long, failed to delve into the real sources of knowledge. That has been the work of the past decade.

The Celts were in Europe when history begins. A great semi-nomadic peoples, they were far from being the stupid savages many suppose them to have been. They built cities, they had advanced far in poetry and music, and they excelled all primitive peoples in metal work. They and they alone introduced the Bronze Age into Europe. They ranged from Scandinavia and the British Isles to the furtherest tip of Spain, Italy and Greece, and they had their colonies in Asia Minor. The names Walloon, Wallatchia and Galatia are remnants of their reign. In Spain they formed, with the aboriginal Iberians, the great nation of the Celtiberians who repelled later Gallic invasions and fought Rome so long and bitterly. The first Greeks, the Acheaens or however it's spelled, were Celts. You will note a striking resemblance between Greece's heroic age, sung by Homer, and the Red Branch Cycle of the Irish legends. Achilles, Patroclus, Ulysses, and Ajax were indubitably Celts in word, action and thought.

The great nation of the Celts were divided into two main groups which were sub-divided into many smaller groups, some of which seemed to have no connection with the others save as possessing a common root stock of language. This came, doubtless, of their mingling with other races — Iberians; aboriginal Greeks, that is Myceans; and Germans. More than any other Aryan race, they intermarried with other peoples. As a race, the Celts are passing swiftly. As an influence, they will be felt in the veins of a thousand generations to come, as they have been felt in the destinies of all European nations.

The two main groups of Celts were of course, Continental and insular. Of the Continental groups such few traces remain that history is barely able to distinguish the vague forms of the tribes in the mist of antiquity. It is like seeing great shadowy phantasms forever shifting in dim clouds. We know that the main branch was the Gauls. And there were the Belgae, who were strongly mixed with German and who had colonies in Britain and possibly in Ireland, since many claim that Firbolg, men with bags, is simply the Gaelic term for Belgae. It is possible. Then there were that strange fierce people who came suddenly and terribly into southern Gaul and Italy — the Cimbri, who because of their association with the Germanic Teutones, many historians, including Plutarch, supposed them to be Germans. With them came a strange old tribe called Ambrones, who possibly corresponded to the Picts in Britain, or might have been Iberians. At any rate, the Ligurians recognized a bitter kinship with them in that last fearful battle.

Some historians have said that Gaul is a form of Gael, therefore the dominant Continental Celts were the children of Goidhel. This is improbable. The legends of the Irish mention no division of their tribe. The Gauls were a branch of their own. Their language more nearly approached the Cymric, being of the "p" group, but their use of "s" differed from that of the Britons and marked them as a separate tribe. So few Gallic words have survived it is hard to form an estimate of the language. Present Breton is an Insular branch, having been transplanted from Britain to France. At any rate, old historians such as Plutarch and the like, tell us plainly that the Gauls were grey or blue eyed and yellow haired. So were the Britons, while the Gaels, who probably more nearly approached the original Celtic type, were generally grey eyed and dark, rather than blond, with dark brown or black hair. Some think that their darkness came from a mixture with an Egyptian or Spanish strain. This is a very prevalent Irish type today. Truett for instance, would be a typical Gael in appearance except for his rather fair skin which betokens a slight Germanic strain. He has the hair and eyes. On the other hand, I have the dark hair and skin of the Gael but my blue eyes are a heritage of the Danes. Blue eyes, dark skin and black hair, are an excepted Irish type but it comes from a Norse strain, which you know, runs strong in Ireland. My family were all grey eyed two generations ago until one of my ancestors married a Dano-Irish woman with red hair.

But I didn't start out to talk about myself. The Insular branch includes, as you know, the Gaelic and Cymri, which include, Gaelic: Irish, Highland Scottish, a Lowland dialect called more or less incorrectly, Erse, Manx, I believe, which is greatly corrupted by Norsk, and Cymri: Welsh, Breton, Cornish, now extinct, and possibly the original language of Ireland, though it is likely that the first Celtic conquerors were Belgic or Gallic rather than Cymric. At any rate, their language was absorbed, except possibly in County Antrim, by the flood of Gaelic invasion. It is possible, though no historian to the best of my belief has ever put forth such a theory, that the Belgic or Gallic natives of Ireland fled over into Scotland and became known as Picts. Of speech alien both to the Gael and the Cymri, their hands would be against all men. Understand, I do not put this forward as a belief of my own. I simply say it is possible. I believe the Picts to have been an aboriginal peoples who antedated both Gael and Cymri. No doubt they were deeply mixed with Celtic blood later. The difference between Gaelic and Cymric languages is very marked and the two have so little in common that it is hard to believe that they came from the same root stock. Yet a close study of the speech shows this to be the case. There are two branches, as I have said, called the "c" branch and the "p" branch. So called because of their treatment of the old Aryan "qu". Celtic comes from the same stock of the Italic, Grecian and Germanic languages and I think, though I may be wrong, that it most closely approaches the Italianate in its treatment. That it is closely akin to the ancient Greek is shown by the words, hippos, hikkos, meaning horse. I haven't time to go into that now, however. But the change from one form to the other is characteristic.

Let us return to the old original Aryan. Suppose, for the working out of the theory, that Maqu is son. The qu ending being changed to "p" in Cymric and Gallic, "son" becomes Map — which is the old Welsh term for the noun; now call Ap or App. "Son" in Gaelic becomes Macc, or Mac, as the "qu" termination in changed to "c" with the "k" sound. There is no "k" in the Gaelic language nor is there the soft sound of "c"; it is always pronounced "k". Nor is there a "v", though the "v" sound is common. For instance, lamh, meaning hand, pronounced lauv. I may be wrong, as I am certainly no authority on Gaelic and know very little about it, but I don't believe there is a "w", it being usually denoted by "mh." There is certainly no "j", at least in vocalization. "J" is given and spelled the "sh" sound, thus "John" becomes, "Shon", "Shone", "Shane", or "Shawn", the last usually being applied to a man of poorer class. "James" becomes "Shamus," "Seamas," "Shamas", or "Sheemas". The proper Gaelic spelling of John and James is "Seon" and "Seamas", the "e" denoting the sound of "sh", as "Joseph" spelled "Seosamh," and pronounced, I suppose, "Shosauv".

I think that by close application I could learn Gaelic but I despair of Welsh for it is undoubtedly the most bewildering Western language in the world. About all I know of it is that the frequent form of "dd" is usually pronounced "th", and that the "ll" sound is most musical, like smoothly flowing streams. I may have made a number of errors in what I have been saying about Gaelic, but I think in the main I am right. Gaelic has a number of dialects, on both sides of the channel which differ in many ways.

Well, the Celt is a fast fading symbol of the past. The race has fought oblivion savagely but it has been and is a losing fight. What arms and war could not do, intermarrying and the growth of the English language is doing. It is destiny. But it has been a fight of which to be proud. For centuries the Celt was the dominant figure in Europe and even Rome bowed to him. Forced to the western fringes of the world, he held his own for a thousand years and more. The story of the Saxon conquest of Britain is a stirring one. The Cymri were softened and weakened by centuries of peace and idle prosperity. When the tide burst they were harried by their own kin in the north and west. Yet it took the combined powers of the Anglos, Saxons and Jut, over a hundred and fifty years to gain control of the eastern half of what we call England. Thrust into the mountains of Wales, those Romanized Britons waged a back-to-the-wall war which for ferocity and reckless valor has never been surpassed. Early English historians denounced the Welsh as barbarians and spoke scathingly of their lack of culture and civilization. Well, when a people are fighting day and night for their lives, they have scant time to waste in the pursuit of higher knowledge.

When the Britons staggered westward, broken and bleeding, they carried with them the remnants of a civilization which has in some ways never been surpassed. The music and art of old Greece, flowing through the veins of Rome, crystallized in the poetic people of Britain. But Ebbracum fell, and Lundunium, and Aquae Sulis, and Corinium, and the ox-eyed red bearded Saxon replaced even the musical Roman-British names with his York, London, Bath, Winchester. Ah, well — pinned in the western mountains, harried on one side by the Saxons and on the other by the Irish pirates, the Welsh forgot their civilization. Culture languishes and dies in the mountains to the everlasting clamor of the war trumpet. From polished, educated citizens of the Roman empire, the Welshmen became shock headed, iron handed savages, who knew nothing of the arts of their immediate forbears, but in whose veins coursed hotly the fighting blood of their barbaric Celtic ancestors. What a nation gains in one way, it loses in another. Had the Saxons, leaping from their dragon-beaked galleys, found the same yellow haired giants that Caesar found, rushing down in their iron chariots, there had been no conquest, only windrows of slaughtered pirates, and the speech of Britain today would have been not English, but Cymric. As it was, by the time the weakened Britons had regained all their old savagery, they had been reduced to a remnant and their personal stature seemed to have permanently diminished. The Welsh who broke the armies of William Rufus were powerfully built men, deep chested and strong, but short in height. Admixture with the Silurian natives, doubtless of Iberian blood, or a strong strain may have been responsible for this loss of height, as well as the change in complexion. For Caesar found blond giants on the Ceanntish beaches and the accepted type of Welsh today is rather dark, with black hair and hazel eyes. A settling of Gaelic tribes in Wales may possibly have had something to do with this. The red Welshman, who occurs very often, is of course, a Celtized Dane; the Norse played a considerable part in the history of Wales, more often as allies than foes, for they found little but savage fighting when they harried the western coast. The Welsh suffered more from Irish freebooters than from Norse, because the Gael and the Cymri were ever at each other's throats, and the Irish fought less because of loot, which was mainly the Norseman's reason, but mainly for love of rapine. The blond Welshman is either a throwback to the original British strain or else is of mixed blood, sharing Welsh with Fleming. For as you know a great number of Flemings were brought from the Netherlands under the reign of the Angevin kings and were settled on the marches of Wales to form a bulwark of intermarrying between these two peoples. I think the Welsh language will live longer than any other Celtic speech. This extended life is due mainly to the efforts of the workers in the Celtic Renaissance, or however it's spelled, who have been working faithfully to revive the western languages. But like all other Celtic languages it will become submerged in English eventually. It is many and many a day since Cadwallon rode into Northumbria with Penda the Pagan, swearing to leave that kingdom only when no man, woman, or child remained alive. And it is many a day since that red day when Penda, wearying of slaughter, rode back to Mercia and left Cadwallon ravaging the land in the midst of his enemies — many a day since the East Angles came to the aid of the broken Northumbrians and Cadwallon and his North Welsh died like wolves in a closing ring of foes. Yet Cadwallon was the last great champion of the Cymri — attest the bleeding head of Guffa, king of South Wales, sent by his faithless vassals as a tribute to Harold the last Saxon king. The history of Wales is as the history of Ireland, Scotland, Brittany, Cornwall — the history of all Celtic peoples — full of oppression and violent retaliation, bravery and cruelty and treachery, unexpected timidity and unexpected valor.

I've been writing some verse lately. I haven't been devoting much time to it for some time. I've been too busy writing fiction. There's no money in rhyme and I can't afford to devote much time to it.

One thing, I can get good beer here which is what I need. I haven't tasted beer for six months and have been drunk only twice — once on wine elixir and once on corn whiskey. Outside of that I've had three small drinks of whiskey and one of wine, which is all the liquor that's passed my lips in six months.

I wrote a long narrative rhyme in the fassion of the old ballads some time ago which might interest you. Here are a few verses from it.

Before them all King Geraint rode,
White was the great steed he bestrode,
A gift from Ulster's king, Leoghaire;
Gold in the sun was Geraint's hair.
*****
Close there rode on the king's left side
Donal, the chieftain of Strathclyde.
Dark was he, and hard of hand,
As well befitted that desperate band
That held the hills of the Cumberland
Three hundred years from the Saxon horde.
There followed close with his great black sword,
Cormac of Cornwall, called The Hawk,
Savage branch on an ancient stalk.
More than half a pagan, he,
Ruling alone by the western sea.
*****
— A stunted giant, most strange to see —
A shape from the grisly past was he.
His people ruled, in the dark old days
The western isles, and their altar blaze
Lighted the land and they alone
Reigned in the grim old Age of Stone.
Now a scant remnant, hunted forth,
Lived like wolves in the misty north.
The Pict was banished, a lone exile;
God only knows what plot or guile,
What grisly crime, or what fell deed
Barred Dulborn from his own strange breed.
When they rebel who are strange and fell,
Surely the deed was born in Hell!
But Dulborn rode to Geraint's court
And followed him ever, life and morte.
His lips were locked and the heart inside
And with him his secret lived and died.
*****

They have locked their shields in a solid wall
Their spears a-bristle above them all.
Grimmest arm of the Saxon war,
Geraint sees his setting star.
He bunches close his thinning ranks,
An iron bolt for the iron banks.
Shoulder to shoulder, flying fast,
The Britons charge in a blinding blast.

* * * * *

Cormac struggled and tore him clear,
Rose through the rain of sword and spear.
He braced his feet and he smote once more,
Through iron and flesh the black sword tore.
Corpses rattled against his feet,
He scarcely felt the blades that beat
Hard on his helmet — once again
The black sword crashed and men were slain.
Battle and sky were growing black,
Misty dim swam the battle wrack.
He heard the clash of falling men
They fell at his feet like trees and then
As the sword flashed round in that deathly arc
The world wavered and all went dark.

* * * * *

They hewed at his corselet and crested crown,
They grappled his legs to wrestle him down.
But the spears were splintered, the brands were bent
And their eyes went dim when their strength was spent.
From every joint of his armor ran
The blood of the terrible Northern man.
A terrible harvest Angus mowed,
High heaped the corpses he bestrode.
They lay about in a ghastly ring
Leaving a space for his mace to swing.
He sought to sound his battle cry
As he saw his foes give way and fly,
He swung his iron mace on high
And sank on a heap of dead to die.

* * * * *

The standards reel and the riders rock,
The whole earth shudders at the shock,
And the charging Britons' desperate blows
Carry them into the heart of their foes.

* * * * *

And his Welshmen who were left to die
Rushed with a yell that ripped the sky.
Like a pack of grey wolves, gaunt and grim,

They tore chief Lodbrog limb from limb.
Leaped from their horses and made a wall
Where King Cadallon met his fall,
And around the corpse of their ancient king,
Died in a red unbroken ring.

* * * * *

With a blinding might that caught the breath
Like a triple thunderbolt of death
That bursts through clouds heaped dark and blue
The three great steeds came crashing through.
Under the hoofs that spurned the wold
Headlong horses and riders rolled.
Men saw the great white charger loom
Like a flashing thunder cloud of doom,
And the great red steed like a storm of hate
And the huge black horse like a wind of Fate.

* * * * *

Men groped like blind men through the tide
And no man knows how King Geraint died.
But sudden the mist was cleared away;
On a mighty heap of dead he lay,
Last great King of the British race
There on a kingly resting place,
On a mighty couch that was red and grim,
Nial of Ulster lay by him.

* * * * *

Who is the mistrel fit to sing
Of the last great fight of Britain's king?
The song of a race swift vanishing.

Well, it's a great life — maybe. Answer when you have time.

NOTES

1. Student literary magazine of the University of Texas, Austin, to which Lenore Preece contributed 1929-30.
2. "The Dark Man," from *Under Quicken Boughs.*

TSS: 15775, 15776; GR: 20563-20574

117. To Alvin P. Bradford, ca. January 1930, unsent

Dear Bradford:

You'll have to pardon my delay in answering your letter. I moved back to Cross Plains just before Christmas and have been very busy.

If I can help you any with the anthology, I'd be glad to do so. Just now I'm pretty busy, but I'm sending you a rhyme and will send others later.

I suppose you will receive contributions from Clyde and Truett soon.

Hope you have a happy New Year.

Bob

TSS: 92118

118. To Tevis Clyde Smith, ca. January 1930.

Many thanks for the letter you wrote Farnsworth. It appeared in the Eyrie this month. I sure appreciate it. Also appeared in this issue an illegitimate child of mine.[1] By that I mean I had no idea it was to be published this month as I never got any advance sheets for it. If you don't mind, I wish you'd read it. It's purely psychological; I've told you of it before. No other magazine except *Weird Tales* would publish such a story — I know because I tried most of them with this one.

Have you sold anything else lately? And by the way — I wish you'd give the address of *Ten Story Book* if you don't mind. I have some stuff I want to put into circulation, and I have no T.S.B. rejection slips in my collection as yet — a deficiency I must supply.

You are right about life and destiny and all. As you say, we may choose our road, but it is like a man selecting the road by which he will walk to the gallows. They're all alike in most respects.

I finally got back my rhymes from the *Scroll*. Scutto[2] surprized me after all. I expected tirades of righteousness, howls of orthodox wrath, scathing rebukes and trenchant remarks about the general absence of merit of my slop, but his criticism was as follows, to say: "—While excellent in many respects, they lack rhythm—"! Can you beat that? And he sent me a dinky little pamphlet page entitled "Rhythmic and Natural Accents," with a lot of primer stuff in it. Heh heh heh! The poor fish. Well, it's a new experience — I've had plenty of criticism before but nobody ever told me my verse was unrhythmic. Ah well — I know the reason — two reasons — some of my rhyme scheme was too intricate and complicated for his blunt musical — or rather unmusical ear to catch — and the rest was too brutal for him, and he didn't have the guts to say so. He couldn't have published it, consistently with the policy of the magazine. It would have been letting loose a wolf in a sheep fold. A lot of the old maids, artistic business men — heh heh heh — budding feminine sweet singers and gooey-gooey jinglers that smear their mush and saccharine over the pages of his juvenile abortion would leap convulsively clean out of their drawers with pure horror had they come upon my serpents coiled between the pages. Not attributing my stuff any particular power — for us it was mild and restrained. but you know how thin-skinned most pipple are. He asked me to send him some more stuff — with more rhythm! Heh heh heh! But that's a phase of my life I've outgrown. All I do is begrudge the money spent for subscribing to it. It's all right for dabblers — a damned good thing in fact, to a certain extent, though there's no room for real development in such a magazine. But it's good for kids who haven't yet seen their stuff in print, and for dabblers who'll never produce anything worth a curse anyhow. But it's bad in this respect, as are all such sheets — it's likely to mold a young versifier into narrow lines — but Hell, if a young poet lets himself be molded he's not worth a damn anyway. I'm going to keep Scutto's letter; I've gotten several big laughs out of it.

I've received the first of the usual cavalcade of rejections. Looks like I can't sell anything here. Got a letter from Fiction House. I'd written about "Iron Men." He said they hadn't seen it but would try to trace it. I'd told him I'd rewrite from the copy and send it to him, if he hadn't gotten it. He said to hold everything till he heard from me again. I hope he'll find it and take. I don't see how in Hell a carefully addressed letter gets lost in the mail. He also said — in response to my remark that I was preparing more Steve Costigan stories — "I am glad to hear that Steve Costigan is going to swashbuckle his way across more pages of *Fight Stories*. All of us here are for him." Now watch me get the next seventeen back. I'm not blaming the editors as much as I used to do. I write a good story, they enthuse about it, next time I fall so much below standard — whatever that is — they get discouraged about me and forget all about me. Oh well —

By all means come the 18th or any time. And answer soon.

Fir Dun

NOTES

1. "The Fearsome Touch of Death."
2. "Scutto" must be *The Poet's Scroll* editor, E. A. Townsend.

TSS: 82205

ଔଓଔଓଔଓ

119. To *Weird Tales*, ca. January to Mid-February 1930.

"Thirsty Blades" is fine. It moves like a cavalry charge, with an incessant clashing of steel that stirs the blood. Gigantic shadows from the outer gulfs fall across the actors of the drama, yet the sense of realism is skillfully retained.

❧❧❧

120. To Tevis Clyde Smith, ca. February 1930.

Well, here is the letter. I haven't much to add. Fiction House — *Fight Stories* — took another Steve Costigan story for $100. Also they finally located "Iron Men" and accepted it for $200. This is by far the best fight story I ever wrote. In many ways the best story of any kind I ever wrote. I guess my destiny is tied up with the Costigan family. I've never sold *Fight Stories* a story that didn't deal with them. The central figure of "Iron Men" isn't a Costigan but both Steve and his brother Iron Mike figure in the story. This tale isn't humorous like the others. It's harsh and brutal; I don't know whether the readers will like it or not.

The older I grow the more I sense the senseless unfriendly attitude of the world at large. I reckon it isn't that way everywhere but it seems so. The average man is such a fool he hasn't sense enough to keep his head out from under the axe. He goes out of his way to make trouble. The people in this town treat me in several manners; contemptuously ignore me, which doesn't bother me any; go out of their way to start trouble with me, which does; and assume a sort of monkey in a cage attitude. Those who deign to notice me at all, are forever on the lookout for some peculiarity, some difference that will stamp me as an eccentric. The infernal fools can't seem to understand that a man can make his living some other way besides dressing tools or selling stuff and still be an ordinary human being with human sensations. The more money I make at my trade the more strangely they eye me. I can feel their damned lousy stares on me every minute I'm on the streets; eagerly watching for me to do something that they can garble and chatter and jabber among themselves. It's the price a man pays for being any way different from the mob. Well, damn the mob. Let them stare and whisper behind my back, but let them do it, behind my back. Ninety nine men out of a hundred are brainless fools that were born to be failures. Fools. The cringing, crawling, blind, senseless reptiles. Damn the mob! There's only one way they can break me — and that's what I'm afraid of all the time. That some cursed slack jawed jackass-eyed damned fool will push me too far some day and I'll lose control of myself. If they'll let me alone, I'll get along alright. It's a cinch I'll let them alone.

Well, I'm not highly intellectual, but I realize that I have so much more brains than the average fool that if I fail I ought to be shot. Let these swine stare and snigger. Curse their empty skulls, I'll be a national figure with more money than they ever saw, when they're creeping about their dull narrow ways, half forgotten by their own generation in their own township. To Hell with them; all I ask is that none of them goes so far with me as to make me lose my self control. Ah well, the scum — they're not worth thinking about except when they intrude their slimy presence into one's sight.

Answer soon.

TSS: 82204

ଔଔଔଔ

121. To Tevis Clyde Smith, ca. February 1930.

Salaam; Fear Orghruagach;[1]

> Life is a cynical, romantic pig;
> Life is a jackass on a slender twig;
> Life is an elephant upon a fig;
> Life is a lobster with a yellow wig.
> Philosophy of Hoolyu Li Awn.

I owe Hink[2] a letter. I must answer him, before he thinks I've sunk into utter sotdom. Thenks very much for the nice thingels you said about my hooey. I'm just now trying to hammer out some junk for Farnsworth, as his supply of my muck is rapidly diminishing. I haven't seen this month's issue but know I haven't anything in it. Next issue appears my "A Song Out of Midian" for which I've already received the advance page; and he tells me he is going to give me the cover design for the June issue in which will appear the first installment of "The Moon of Skulls". I have sold him three rhymes lately, "The Song of a Mad Minstrel" for which he kindly offers me $8.00, "Black Chant Imperial", $6.00, and "Shadows on the Road" with which he seemed much pleased and offered me $11.50, considerably more than I ever got for any other poem. Pardon me for mentioning these mundane matters of cash; I know it is banal and inane, because you are like me, and scorn material dross. Farnsworth tells me that the company is going to publish another magazine[3] this summer, using stories of all sorts, so long as they are somewhat out of the ordinary. I gather that they don't have to be impossible, but just different from the general run of stories. I'm hoping to just about double my income from his company when that magazine comes out. Of course, I may not be able to sell them a blightin' thing.

Glad you like *The Satyricon.* Petronious was an utter wretch but he wasn't a hypocrite, anyway. I believe it is said that he was not a native Roman, but a Romanized Gaul. Well, if he was, he was so completely Romanized that all the Gaul had faded out of him.

I got the *Junto* and roared with much crude barbaric mirth at your delicate technique i.e. fencing with a sledge hammer. Keep up the good woik. Belabor the skulls of the Juntites with your shillailah until they howl.

Well, I seem to be unusually banal and inane today. I'll try to write you a better letter soon. I've been working rather hard lately and its sucked my scanty brain supply about dry. Answer soon.

Fear Dunn

NOTES

1. "Golden-Haired Man."
2. Harold Preece.
3. The proposed magazine, *Strange Stories*, was never published.

TSS: 82148

ೲೲೲ

122. To Harold Preece, ca. February 1930.

Go manee jeea git,[1]

You're in Kansas now, eh? Well, I imagine how you feel. I've never been to Kansas and I don't intend to be. To my mind it's the lousiest of all of Hell's backyards. Ah well, it's a great life.

I saw *The Virginian* not long ago and liked it fairly well. But Judas, it was full of hokum, though rather realistic. Why must people be such damned hypocrites? Sure, they hung cattle thieves — that is, those who stole them on small scale. But the big swine got by just as they're doing in business now. I know; I spent a good deal of my early childhood on ranches and in cow country. How many of the cattle kings didn't get their start by stealing cattle? Bah! They were all thieves. They hanged men for stealing cattle that they themselves stole from somebody else. Then they squalled about law, order, protecting honest business. A couple of bahs. Why didn't they admit that they were committing murder for their own interests? But hypocrisy is so burned into the grain that even primitively inclined people can't get away from it. I care nothing about the cattle thieves, large or small, but the ingrained hypocrisy nauseates me. — "The poor naturally hate the rich" — Webster.

So you've been reading MacPherson?[2] Well, don't take him too seriously. He's a damned fraud. I like his stuff because of their beauty and imagery — "The oaks of the mountains fall. The mountains themselves decay with years. The ocean shrinks and grows again. * * * * * Age is dark and unlovely. It is like the glimmering light of the moon, when it shines through broken clouds, and the mist is on the hills." " 'Who comes so dark from ocean's roar, like autumn's shadowy cloud? * * * * The people fall! see! how he strides like the sullen ghost of Morven!' "

Well, read him for his beauty but realize his junk's a hoax. It was the style then to "discover" new unpublished manuscripts. As for him denying the origin of his race, damn him for a red shanked gilley. Also, it was the custom to deny, in those days, all Celtic legends. Smart little English historians! Bah! Research has since proved many of those myths had a basis of truth. Gibbons,[3] than whom no more despicable pseudo-chronicler ever lived, pulled the same stuff. That the Irish came from Scotland. Why, that swine didn't even have guts enough to marry the woman he wanted, because it would mean losing his inheritance.

If the Irish stole Finn Mac Cumhail from the Scotch, why is it that it's rare you find a legend of Finn — or Fingal — in Scotland, while the most ignorant plough-boy in Ireland can spin tales of the Mac Cool? That is, they could until they got so damned civilized and Anglicized. Bah. History shows — proves — that the Gaels — Scots — Milesians — landed in Ireland and spread over the isles from that starting point. Listen, if the Irish originated in Scotland, why was it, that toward the last days of the British-Roman Empire, there were only a few Gaelic tribes in Scotland, while Ireland was full of them? And a few years later, the Picts have been subordinated, the people — Cymry — of Strath-Clyde and Cumberland are paying tribute to an ever growing Gaelic power known as the Dalriadian kingdom, which dynasty culminated in Malcolm Canmore, shortly before the Norman invasion of England. Did they all go to Ireland and then come back? Bah.

And if MacPherson says that Conaire ardri na Eireann was a Scotchman, he lies in his teeth. Conaire came out of the sea, naked and with a sling in his hand, to rule Ireland and he lived and died in Leinster.

Welsh bowmen broke the charges of the gallowglasses and won Ireland for Norman Henry. The Fitzgeralds were half Welsh. Maybe that's why they took up Irish customs so quickly. I don't blame the Welsh; if I'd been a Welsh soldier then I'd have probably taken service under de Clare myself. The Welsh owed nothing to the Irish. The nations had never been friendly. When the Cymry were fighting for their life against the Saxons, the Gaels were harrying them from the sea and carrying them off into slavery. It took the Germanic races hundreds of years to subdue Wales, whereas Welsh and Normans beat the Irish down in a comparatively short time. (However, of course, they didn't stay down.) But the reason for that was treachery. Out of any five Irishmen you can select, one's an active traitor and two of them are potential traitors. They fight much better for other races than their own.

By the way, the word Welsh in its present usage is not Celtic but Germanic. The German tribes first came into contact with a Celtic tribe named Walii, or Wealli, on the Danube — I think the word Volga came from them originally, though I may be wrong. The Teutonic tribes called all non-Germanic peoples, Wealli, Weallas, or Welsh. But the word lost its significance everywhere but in the Isles.

The Irish-Gaelic alphabet has only seventeen letters — formerly sixteen. The alphabet is called aibghitir, or formerly Beith-luis-nion, when it began with B rather than A as it now does, due to the introduction of Latin. The letters are named after trees or Feadha. Here is the alphabet.

A Ailm the palm-tree (O'Brien) or the fir-tree (O'Flaherty)
B Beith
C Coll the hazel-tree
D Duir the oak-tree
E Eabha the aspen-tree
F Fearnog the elder-tree
G Gort the ivy-tree
I Iodha the yew-tree
L Luir the quicken-tree
M Muin the vine
N Nuin the ash-tree
O Oir the spindle-tree
P Peith-bhog
R Ruir the elder-tree
S Rail the willow-tree
T Teine the furze-tree
U Urbhur the yew-tree

You might be interested in Irish names. I don't know much about them myself but here's a few original Irish first names with their English equivalent.

Gaelic	English	Scandinavian
Diarmid	Dermot	
Eochaid		
Nial	Neil	
Aongus	Angus	
Tadng	Teig	
Leabnar	Lever	
Murtagh		
Turlough	Terence	
Domnail	Donald	
Cuileahn		
Eamohn	Edmund	Eadmund

Some names adopted by the Gaels and changed in pronunciation or spelling:

origin	English	Gaelic
Hebrew	Patrick	Padraic or Padraig
Hebrew	John	Shane, Seann, Seon
Hebrew	Michael	Micaul, Mihul, Meehaul
Hebrew	Joseph	Seosamh
High German	Gerald	Gearoidh
Scandinavian Hrobjart	Robert (Norman)	Raibeard
Danish	Hugh Hugo	Aodh

These are just a few. Maybe I can give you some more data some other time. Answer soon.

Raibeard Eiarbhin hui Howard

NOTES

1. A phonetic rendering of Gaelic *go mbeannai Dia duit*, "May God bless you."
2. Probably *The Poems of Ossian* which James MacPherson (1730 – 1796) claimed were his translations of the legendary Scottish poet's work.
3. Historian Edward Gibbon.

TSS: 92081, 92080

ᘓᘐᘎᘓᘐ

123. To Tevis Clyde Smith, ca. March 1930.

Well, Fear Finn,[1] tell Cuchullain the Dutchess of Paddelpants rides green elephants across fertile plains impregnated with flying ostriches, and to examine the down on the off wing of a superannuated sea-gull. Do you recognize the artistic touch? Heh heh heh!

I remember the supercilious sentences pertaining to the type-writing junk. Kind of a glorified primer muck. Oh well, life is a pulchritudinous pair of pink panties. How's that for alliteration?

No, you didn't show me the *Nomad*,[2] but I have an idea of what it's like. Reginald Van Proudrear calls his valet: I say, me man, I'll think I'll rough it in the wilds of Dutch Guinea awhile. Have the hotel person to give me a suite of room overlooking the jungle. And bah Jove, I'll have the bally natives to do some of their dawnces foh me — I'm of old pioneer stock after all, you know. But cheer up; all the sophisticates between Brooklyn and Hell can't keep you from making a success. You've got something they haven't — power and hunger. They go together. It's hunger for success, money, power, that makes giants out of men. I don't believe that a bastard whose always had what he wants, can possibly have any real guts, brains or brawn. At least, not the power that drives a man through opposition and up through the ranks, so to speak.

I received a letter from Farnsworth today accepting my "Kings of the Night" — $120, on publication of course. I rather expected him to take it for the new magazine, as it's full of action but has no really weird touches. However he accepted it for *Weird Tales*; possibly because the central figure is Kull of Atlantis, featured in "The Shadow Kingdom" and "The Mirrors of Tuzun Thune." It was rather a new line for me, as I described a pitched battle. However, I think I handled it fairly well. The plot of the story is woven about the attempts of the Romans to extend their boundaries in Britain, about the time the Gaels were beginning to build the Dalriadian kingdom on the western coast of what now is Scotland.

You know, it's strange how the English language absorbs the other tongues with which it comes in contact. The English have a pig headed and perverse way of changing the spelling of foreign words to suit themselves. Take for instance Kaatskill, a Dutch word, now Anglicized to Catskill. On the other hand Cill Cinni, a Gaelic word, becomes Kilkenny. Also Cill Dara, the Cell of the Oak, is made Kildare. And Cill righ cill becomes Kilreekill. Why, do you know that there's scarcely a town or locality in Ireland which bears a pure Irish name. Well, I'll modify that. Most of the names or of Irish origin but the spelling is almost invariably English or Scandinavian. The very name of Ireland is Danish, as is Munster, Leinster, and Ulster. The Celtic names were, I think, Mumhain, Laigheann, and Ulahd. Only one province retains the Gaelic name — Conneda, Connacht or Connaught, named, I think, for Conn mac Connmor, thousands of years ago. The Irish alphabet goes like this: a b c d e f g i l m n o p r s t u. The sounds of h, w, and v are given, but not the letters themselves; the sound is generally denoted by a dot over the preceding letter. A great many letters are silent in the pronunciation, though they have a meaning. Let's see a sentence. I don't know whether the construction of this one is right but we'll see. An cailin gead ruadh mor na righ a Ebroch. This means, roughly, The girl with the big red buttocks of (belonging to) the king of York; the English pronunciation would be something like this: Awn colleen gead roe more naw ree aw Ebroch. The proper Gaelic spelling of ruadh, mor, righ and Ebroch would be: ruad·, mor', rig· and Ebroc·.

Well, the Gaelic is a rather impractical language. Formerly, not only did each section have its dialect, but the trades and professions had their jargon. One Irishman might be unable to meet on a common level with a close neighbor. English I consider the ideal language for literature. It is flexible, yet clear cut, combining the best features of Latin, Celtic and Scandinavian. I believe that Celtic forms a larger part of the language base than authorities will admit. Certainly it does in America; in the spoken speech at any rate. For instance, gumpshon, (Irish gomsh) muley cow, (Irish maol, blunt) dun, (Irish dunn or donn.) It's significant of the power of the Germanic tongues that most of our dictionary words are of Latin origin while the most of our spoken words, that is, every day words, are Germanic. But Hell, you knew that of course. A funny thing about the languages of Western Europe. Take the Norman Invasion of England for instance; this introduced the elegant Scandinavian-French tongue into the Isles but for a long time pure Saxon remained the speech of the common people — well, not pure Saxon either because it was mixed a great deal with Danish. But it went by the name of Saxon. So a hog was a Saxon while he lived and a Norman when he was served on the table. While had to be herded and fed and chased out of the cabbages, he was looked upon with considerable contempt, not to say scorn, and was roughly called hog, which is Saxon. Or was it swine? Well, anyway when he was served up on the lord's table, he was given the Norman name pork, which I supposed comes from porcine, Latin hog. The custom prevails in the English speaking countries to this day. We do not say: Chase the pork into that pen. Nor do we say: Serve me a slice of hog. Thus with ox — beef, and sheep — mutton, and deer — venison. Had it been the custom for the barons to eat their vassals I suppose the luckless Saxon would have been served up under some fancy Latin — French designation: Ho, Athelred, thou whoreson varlet, pass me a dish of genus hominus; a slice off the haunch, there.

In the East of England I think the blending of Norman and Saxon was easy, but the stubborn Western English, more stubborn because of a mixture with the Welsh and Cornish, clung to the old speech for a long time.

Consider the Norse invasion of France, when the duchy of Normandy was formed. Note how the harsh Norse names were softened by the contact with the Latinized Franks. Thus, to consider some typically Scandinavian names, Hrolf became Rollo, Godfrey, Geoffrey, Rognvald, Ronald, Hrobjart, Robert, Rijeart, Richard, Ranulf, Ralph, Eadgaard, or Eadjard, Edvard, Eduard, Edward, Hrejnvald, Reginald, Hrodjric, Roderick. Most names in Ireland are English names taken by the Gaels, but there is one name the Saxons stole from the Irish: Edmund; this was Eamonn. Now the English language is less harsh than the Germanic, but more vigorous than the tongues of the South. But I've bored you long enough. But say, just a moment. I was wrong about Patrick being Hebraic. Its Latin, meaning, as I should have thought, patrician. This cheers me; I'd hate to go through life with a Hebrew name on me. The Gaelic form is Padraic, Padruig, or Padraig. Michael is Hebraic, the Irish form being Meehual, Micul, or Micaul. Miles, another popular name in Ireland is Latin, the Gaelic form being Maelmorra.

Well, let us have some verse; it can't be any more lacking in interest than what I've been spieling.

The Autumn of the World

Now is the lyre of Homer flaked with rust
And yellow leaves are blown across the world
And naked trees that shake at every gust
Stand gaunt against the clouds autumnal-curled.

Now from the hollow moaning of the sea
The dreary birds against the sun-set fly,
And drifting down the sad wind's ghostly dree
A breath of music echoes with a sigh.

The barren branch shakes down the withered fruit,
The seas that sweep the strands faint marks erase;
The sere leaves fall on a forgotten lute,
And autumn's arms enfold a dying race.

A Tribute to the Sportsmanship of the Fans

Headlock, hammerlock, toss him on his bean again,
Jump upon his belly and boot him in the hips,
Clamp the scissors on his neck and choke him till he's green again,
Get the fans wild-eyed, with froth on their lips.

Barlock, body-slam, nibble on his ears again —
Its just like eating cabbage — and kick him in the groin,
Butt him in the belly, that brings the cheers again,
The fans want a run for their hard-spent coin.

Flying-mare, toe-hold, twist his neck around again,
Wrap his legs around his waist and tie them in a knot,
Stamp in his mouth so his teeth cannot be found again,
The fans paid their money so make it good and hot.

Stranglehold, leg-split, jerk his knee-caps loose again,
Crack his ribs and break his arms, leave him life-long lame,
Send him out on a shutter — then listen to the boos again,
The kind fans howling that the battle was too tame.

"Aw Come On And Fight!"

His first was a left that broke my nose,
His right ripped off my ear;
The red blood splashed beneath our blows
Till we stood in a crimson smear.

He cracked three ribs with his smashing right,
His left hooks gashed my head;
I saw the ring aswim in a light
Hazy and dim and red.

He split my brow and the lid dropped down
Like a curtain over the eye;
At every shove of his wet red glove
I saw the crimson fly.
On my hands and knees in a scarlet pool
I heard the referee toll,
And the crowd roared: "Kill the yellow bum!"
Like the sea along a shoal.

I sprang, I struck, I crushed his skull
With a sudden desperate swing,
He died with his eyes to the glaring lights
And his back to the canvassed ring.

The referee counted above the dead,
I swayed and clung to the ropes,
And the crowd roared: "Yellow! Both of 'ems' bums!"
Like the seas on the beaches' slopes.

The Song of the Sage

Thus spoke Scutto on the mountains in the twilight,
Sage and seer and councilor to lords of Hindustand,
"Life, my bold young bastards, according to my light,
"Is but a bucking galley by a band of monkeys manned."

Answer soon, will youse.

Fear Dunn

NOTES

1. "The Fair Man" or "The White Man."
2. A travel magazine.

TSS: 82149-82151

ᏂᏘᏂᏘ

124. To Tevis Clyde Smith, ca. March 1930.

Well, Fear Finn:

I trust you are in good healthel and enjoying life to its fullest, as it were, so to speak. Booth said his story appeared this month, I believe it is, and, that reminds me. I must answer his letter. He was evidently drunk when he wrote it.

Have you read my "Sailors' Grudge" in the latest issue of *Fight Stories*? I ought not to be writing you, because you already owe me a letter, but it's pretty dull here when I'm not writing and I can't write all the time. Though I have been putting in some hard work. And now this hellish typewriter is bothering me; jerky and don't space right. Guess I'll have to work it over, and I scarcely know enough about it to work it over right.

Say, what's the matter with Truett? Is he sick? I've written him two letters and haven't heard a line from him.

This is a lousy town. Not even any matinee shows and I've gotten so I'd rather go in the afternoon than at night. How are you coming with the touch system?[1]

Whispers
I was born in a lonesome land
And grew in a barren town,
But I have seen the poplars shake
When the green leaves fluttered down.

Strange land, grey land
Dreaming your dreams apart;
My soul is far too small to glimpse
One throb of your mighty heart.

But I have sensed the giant pulse
Under the ceaseless flow
Of the little, crawling people
Who blindly come and go.

Like a titan whisper in the night:
"I dream my dreams," you say,
"And a thousand times a thousand years
"I count as a single day."

Well, Farnsworth said he was going to use "Shadows on the Road" as a full page rhyme in the issue after next. I wish he'd have it illustrated but I think they quit illustrating rhymes. Well, I'm not kicking; that's about the quickest action I ever got on anything, for I sold it to him just recently. And he accepted a story for the new magazine. "The Dark Man" is the name of the tale and he promised me $85.00 on publication. The editor was kind enough to say it was a "red blooded, he-man story". Well, it has plenty of gore and action. And incidently, I have created a new character to join Kull, Solomon Kane and Steve Costigan. His name is Turlogh Dubh O'Brien and I hope to have a series of stories dealing with him in the new magazine. This story, was, of course, about him. He is an Irish outlaw whose adventures are laid in the half century preceding the battle of Hastings. That's a period teeming with intrigue, war and battles and I ought to be able to spin dozens of yarns about it.

Say, I have your birthday present, but I'll have to bring it with me when I come. I don't care to mail it. And answer soon; gosh damn, my pleasures are few and far between — especially letters from my friends.

Fear Dunn

NOTES

1. Perhaps learning to touch type.

TSS: 82146

ભ઼ઽ઼ભ઼

125. To Harold Preece, postmarked March 24, 1930.

Thanks for the picture. How much longer are you going to have to stay in Kansas? Thanks very much for intimating that I could write an epic of the Wild Geese, but I think you overestimate my rhyming abilities. Say, you mentioned a correspondent in England — I wonder if you'd do me a favor. I hear that there is a larger market for bizarre and out-of-the-ordinary stories in the British Isles than in this country, but I've been unable to get any real information on the subject. I wrote to a certain English writer about it, but the

Sassenach scut never answered my letter. Now if you don't mind, I wish you'd ask your correspondent to give you the addresses of three or four magazines of the popular fiction type. I just want the names and addresses of the publications. I'll do the rest. I have a fairly good income from various American magazines, and if I could get in with a few on the other side of the pond, I'd go to England, for a while anyway. If you'll do this for me, I'll appreciate it highly.

I think you'll like the last story I sold *Weird Tales*, though of course I don't know when it'll come out. It deals with the Roman invasion of Caledonia and the war of the waning Pictish empire against the legions, when Picts, Western Britons and Dalriadian Gaels united against the common enemy. You may also like the new character I have created for the new magazine that the *Weird Tales* company is preparing to publish soon. This character is one Turlogh Dubh O'Brien and the action is laid mainly in the British Isles, in the half-century following Clontarf. I have submitted only one tale concerning this character, and it was accepted with an apparent relish, but I hope I can sell a series of stories on the same idea.

I remember you once mentioning that so many localities in Ireland have Germanic rather than Celtic names. Most of the names are of Gaelic origin, having been Anglicized or Danized, if I may use the words. Thus, Leinster, Munster and Ulster are Celto-Danish — that -ster being the Danish addition to Laigheann, Mumhain and Ulahd. The pronunciations are, I think, Linn, Moon, or Mun, and Ula.

I got a letter from Buoth O'Mumhainigh, or since the spelling has been Anglicized, Booth Mooney. He mentioned that his story was coming out in the next *Ten Story Magazine*, and was also uproariously drunk at the time. The boy seems to be drinking rather heavily, lately. Well, maybe liquor makes him get more out of life.

I heard the travesty of Miami[1] the other night. I was disgusted. An English champion quits to a lousy Lithuanian and a Wop referee disqualifies him. If the staunch old Anglo-Saxon breed has reached such a pitch, what is the world to look to? But I hear the Englishman has Jewish blood in him, which would explain it. There was a time when Englishmen ruled the ring game.

Song Before Clontarf

Lean on your sword, red-bearded lord, and watch your victims crawl,
Under your feet they weakly beat the dust with their dying hands,
The red smokes roll from the serf's roof-pole and the chieftain's shattered
hall —
But there are fires in the heather and a whetting of hungry brands.
The beaked prows loom like clouds of doom along each broken port,
The monks lie still on the heathered hill among the fallen stones,
Over the land like a god you stand, our maidens howl for your sport —
But kites await in the heather to tear the flesh from your bones.
Clouds and smoke for a broken folk, a lash for the bended back —
Thus you roared when your crimson sword blotted the moon on high,

But sea breaks and the world shakes to the battle's flying wrack,
And death booms out of the heather to nail you in the sky.

Well, my imagination doesn't seem to be very lively so I'll let it ride; write soon.

NOTES

1. Phil Scott of England was disqualified in a match with Jack Sharkey, a son of Lithuanian immigrants, in Miami, February 27, 1930.

TSS: 92108

---

126. To Tevis Clyde Smith, ca. early April 1930.

Well, Fear Finn, you mention being in a lethargic moodle — not muddle. A strange coincidence. I also ripped up a missile I started to you, in irritation at my banal inaness, if I may coin a phrasel. I wish you would enlarge the poem you quoted in your letter, and send it to the *Junto*, or else to me.

I don't suppose you've seen anything of the *Junto*. I haven't. The Argosy[1] pipple enrage me highly by their damned discriminating attitude. I haven't gotten their latest catalogue no more as nothing. They always send their other customers theirs before they send me one

Fight Stories ought to be out in a few days, but I don't know what, if any, they're going to publish by me. They never let me know — nay, they don't even send me a free copy of the magazine. But I'll humor them.

I'm glad you liked the rhyme in *Weird Tales*. I wrote it something more than a year ago.

I got a letter from Preecel, i. e. Hink,[2] and he said he had sold a debunking article to E.H.J. and had met E.H.J., Birchead, or Birkhead, or something like that whoeverthehellheis, also Joseph McCabe.[3] I would have liked to have heard E.H.J.'s and Harold's conversation. Harold also said he — Harold — believed in the cultural unity of the Celtic race.

Ambition

Build me a gibbet against the sky,
Solid and strong and long miles high,
Let me hang where the high winds blow
That never stoop to the world below,
And the great clouds lumber by.
Let the people who toil below
See me swaying to and fro,
See me swinging the aeons through,
A dancing dot in the distant blue.

Whispers On the Nightwinds
I would ride on the winds, I would soar like a gull,
I would plumb the green deeps where the Silence falls,
I would break the jade eyes from a golden skull
In the amaranth gleam of Atlantean halls.

Have I rended the Veil from the face of a god?
The white foam upcurls and the galleys sweep on;
Red dyes the marble an emperor trod
And the moon sinks in silence on dark Babylon.

A city of black towers looms in the stars,
And a whisper of wings makes evil the night,
In the shadows that dream the grisly eyes gleam —
A people abhorrent who love not the light.

The Gladiator and the Lady
When I was a boy in Britain and you were a girl in Rome,
Forests and mountains lay between, and the hungry, restless foam.
Today naught lay between us, only the wall, at least,
That guards the proud patrician from the slave and the dying beast.
Our hearts we read that instant my eyes with your eyes met,
But there were swords to sunder and life blood to be let.
And you will marry a consul and live on the Palatine
And I will take some slave girl from the Garonne or the Rhine.
But you will dream at the banquet, while the roses scent the air
Of a blazing eyed barbarian with a shock of yellow hair.
And through the roar of the lions and the clang of sword and mace,
I'll dream of a pair of dark deep eyes and a proud patrician face.
We still are as far asunder as the hut and the arch and dome
When I was boy in Britain and you were a girl in Rome.

Heh heh heh. Life is a elephant. I'm going to try to come to Brownwood before long but look for me when you see me. By the way, *Fight Stories* bought another Costigan story — "Winner Take All" — $80.

Answer soon.

Fear Dunn

NOTES

1. A bookstore in New York City which did mail-order business.
2. Harold Preece.
3. Emanuel Haldeman-Julius, publisher of the Little Blue Books; Leon Milton Birkhead, author of numerous Little Blue Books; Joseph McCabe author of more than 50 Little Blue Books.

TSS: 82139-82140

ભ§ઙ§ઌભ§

127. To Harold Preece, ca. early Apr 1930.

Thanks for the Saint Padraic's card. Were I to name another trio to equal the one there portrayed, I should hesitate. But I believe I would name Hugh O'Neill, Daniel O'Connell and the great Patrick Sarsfield. Strange the number of great men western Europe has produced compared to eastern Europe.

Thomas Fitzgerald, Shane O'Neill,
Art McMurrough and Edward Bruce,
Hugh Roe O'Donnell — ringing steel
Shakes the hills and the trumpets peal,
Skulls crunch under the iron heel —
Death is the only truce.

Edward Fitzgerald, Charles Parnell,
Robert Emmett — I smite the harp —
Wolfe Tone and Napper Tandy — hail!
The song you sang shall never fail
While one brain burns with the fire of the Gael
And one lost sword is sharp.

Lamh laidir abu, lamh derg abu —
Munster and Ulster, north and south —
The old hate flickers and flames anew,
The heather shakes and the pikes burn blue,
And the old clans charge as they charged with you
Into Death's red grinning mouth.

We have not won and we have not lost —
Fire in Kerry and Fermanagh —
We have broken the teeth in the Saxon's boast

Though our deed have littered each heath and coast,
And by God, we will raise another host!
Slainte — Erin go bragh.

I don't know if I thanked you for the picture in my last letter. If I didn't, you can take it that I do now. It's a good likeness of you. Glad you're selling articles to E.H.J. I've tried my hand at it myself, but that just isn't in my line. I'm no debunker. I have to work too hard. If I had plenty of money it might be different, but if I had plenty of dough, I'd probably be too busy spending it to have any debunking time. Judas, what I could do with a million! Prize fights, horse races, yacht races, chorus girls, explorations, rare books. But Hell, what's the use. If I ever get rich I'll be too old to enjoy it. By the way, are you following my swash-buckling sailor in *Fight Story Magazine*? He appears semi-regularly there.

Saint Padraic's Day usually leaves me with a distaste for the whole Celtic Irish race. Simply because my last name isn't Gaelic, the shamrock I wear is sometimes the object of questioning glances. Well, anyhow I notice damn well that none of my bold tribesmen have tried to uphold Celtic integrity by jerking it off. I'll wear the green if I have to fight every damned Celt in the world. How many of those who wear purely Gaelic surnames don't have the blood of Danes, Welsh, English or Dutch in them? Blasted few. You'll find a locality or town for every one of my names, in Ireland. There's a Robertstown in Kildare, an Irvinestown in Fermanagh, a Patrick — Hell, anywhere you look — and a Mt. Howard in Wexford. I'll admit my blood is more or less mixed up — but how many people in Europe and America are not of mixed bloods? If nobody but a pure Celt wore the green, it wouldn't be worn except perhaps by a few savages living in the Connaught hills. A man has too many grand-parents to be pure blooded anything. One of my great-grandfathers was born somewhere on the Atlantic Ocean between the coast of Kerry and New York — I mean, my great-great-grandfather — he was of the old Gaelic family of the MacEnry. He married Anna O'Tyrrell, who was born in Connaught. Another of my great-great-grandfathers was born in Georgia of Anglo-Irish parents. Another was born in Virginia of Scotch-Irish parents. Another was born in Denmark and he married an Irish-American woman in Mississippi. But enough of that; I didn't start out to give my family tree — only to illustrate the unlikelihood of our ancestors to perform according to the mandates of pure racial lineage. Looking back over three hundred years I can find only one member of the family who did not trace his line back to Ireland, whether his name was English, Irish or Scotch — the red bearded Danish giant who was one of my great-great-grandfathers .

Considering one's innumerable uncles, aunts and cousins it's easy to understand the old saying about the whole world being akin. What a conglomeration of mixed breeds this country is — and it isn't being improved by the hordes of Teutons, Slavs and Latins who continue to pour in.

As far as I'm concerned, the only true Americans are those from the British Isles. I realize that their arrival was antedated by Spanish, Dutch and French and the descendants of those old settlers I admit as countrymen. But I do not admit a man is an American simply because he himself was born here.

TSS: 92060-92061

ꕥꕥꕥ

128. To Tevis Clyde Smith, ca. April 1930.

Salaam:

Well, Fear Finn, I believe in days gone yore you parodied "The Mutiny of the Elsinore," but I think I'll try my handel at it. If it isn't all it should be, consider that after all, I am not a blond.

The Mutiny of the Hellroarer

I played a trick on Mr. Strike when I first came aboard. I wore a wig over my yellow hair. It was a black pigmented wig. Mr. Strike bounded upon me from behind the after-hatch and strangled me. The wig saved my life by falling off just as I was going down for the third time.

"Aha," I gurgled, staggering loop-legged into the scuppers for a drink of bilge water. "I fooled you that time!"

Mr. Strike slunk away in embarrassment. But his eyes lighted as he saw the Eurasian cabin-boy. He gave what he left to the cook to fix up for supper. Mr. Strike was ninety-five years old, but he did not look a day over ninety-four. How I admire him! He was but a shadow of his original self; he stood but six feet and eight inches and weighed a scant three hundred pounds. He did not like me at first, but later on became one of my closest friends and would hit me on the nose every morning by way of greeting.

Our crew was the scum of the high seas — but we soon weeded out the unfit. When the *Hellroarer* finally sank in mid-ocean with all hands, there were only dominant blonds left aboard with the exception of our faithful servitors — six Chinese, a Malay, fourteen Japs, three Burmese, eighteen Hottentots, nine Eskimos and a hundred and thirty-eight Laplanders. With this faithful handful we resisted every effort of the ten mutineers to chase us off the poop-deck. That was a wild scene and one which brought back ancestral memories! Memories of the time that I, a perishing blond, a dominant blond, sat in the high places and sneered at the rabble below. We had the Chinese making stink pots out of limburger cheese — we would show these mutineers why we were the masters — only a dominant blond can stand limburger cheese. The Japs we kept day and night chewing tobacco to spit the juice in the eyes of the beasts in the forecastle. Our method was this — fifteen Laplanders would hold one mutineer while a Jap spit in his eye. I could find no work for the Malay, so I used to beat him up every day in order to keep my dominance over the rest of them.

Our arch-foe was Mr. Smellbare. He was the only blond in the forecastle. He told me once: "Do you see this scar on my neck?"

I did not see it but was afraid to say so, so I said yes.

"You are an infernal liar," said he, kicking me into the scuppers and hammering me with a belaying pin till he was exhausted. "There is no scar there. The wound healed without leaving a trace. A crazy cook cut off my head one time with a meat cleaver. We were in the midst of making westing at the time; later the captain dressed the wound with gun-powder and tobasco sauce. At the time however, I went about my work carrying my head in one hand. There is no time to waste when one is wearing ship."

"Where do you wear a ship, Mr. Smellbare?" I asked. He was my deadly enemy all the rest of his life.

During the mutiny I approached Mr. Strike who was squatted on the poop deck gnawing the haunch bone of a brunet.

"Mr. Strike," I said, "I think the mutineers are about to attack."

"Take the men and oppose them," he answered with his usual quick decision. "Drive them off the main deck or die in the attempt. If you miss me off the poop deck I will be in the cabin reading Nietzsche."

Later on Mr. Strike killed Mr. Smellbare. I saw Mr. Strike racing across the deck at full speed, half a jump ahead of Mr. Smellbare. I saw his strategy. He would lure Mr. Smellbare into jumping overboard after him. At the rail he cleverly allowed Mr. Smellbare to precipitate him into the ocean by kicking him viciously in the pants. At that moment the Armenian cook rushed up and cut out the seat of Mr. Smellbare's britches with his meat cleaver. This embarrassed Mr. Smellbare so much that he leaped overboard and drowned — theoretically, though I have since met sharks who were rather vague about their origin and spoke with a decided Virginian accent.

At this moment the *Hellroarer* blew up and we were all killed.

Well, Harold writes me to say that he feels much peppier. He is now — or is still — whichever way it is — in Muskogee, Oklahoma. I imagine that town is even lousier than Kansas City.

Thorfinn, Thorfinn, where have you been?
And whence do you come, in the rain and the night?
The grey ocean surges have swallowed your men
And your dragon-ship sleeps where the wolf-waves roll white.

On your corselet is crusted the salt of the sea,
And the blown spray is frozen to ice in your hair,
Your keen sword is broken, and still hauntingly
Your eyes like a fey-woman's distantly stare.

Were there figures unnamed in the seas of the West,
Were there scale-crusted dragons that shattered your ships?
Were there ocean-fiends riding the dark billows' crest,
Or icy sea-women with death on their lips?

"Bare stretch the seas to the set of the sun
"No mermaid or kraken opposes the keel
"Of the lies of women and priests are they spun,
"To naked winds only the blue billows reel.

"West, ever west like a sea-gull we fled,
"The wind in our sails and the spray in our teeth,
"And the moon or the sun a cold radiance shed
"Through the fathomless fathoms that thundered beneath.

"Then at last rose in wrath the monster we dared,
"The winds' maddened stallions neighed death all around,
"The white fangs of the hounds of the ocean were bared —
"And we tossed like a rat in the teeth of the hound.

"Lashed into blindness, we staggered in flight,
"We reeled to the rush of the howling white host,
"And then like a phantom born out of the night,
"Through the fury and madness, I glimpsed a strange coast.

"Eastward and eastward the gale hurled us on,
"And the dragon-ship staggered at each stroke and strain,
"Till she sank like a stone in a frenzy of dawn
"And the sea cast me forth from her bosom again.

"I am haunted by dreams that are stronger than ghosts,
"They lift me and thrill me with weird second sight,
"Who can rest or be still who has seen nameless coasts,
"Has glimpsed a new world in the storm and the night?"

Answer soon, will youse.

TSS: 82102-82103

129. To Tevis Clyde Smith, ca. May 1930.

Well, Fear Finn, I hope this letter finds you o.k. As I, very naturally, haven't heard from you since I was at Brownwood, I don't know how you're getting along but I hope you came out all right. Write and give me the low down.

I got back from Mineral Wells yesterday and was somewhat gratified to find a letter waiting me from Farnsworth accepting "The Gods of Bal-Sagoth" — a Turlogh O'Brien tale — for *Strange Stories* — $140.00. Also a letter from Byrne of *Fight Stories*, taking "Waterfront Fists" — a Steve Costigan story — $90.00. They seem to take a lively interest in Stephen.

I saw some fairly good shows while I was gone: *The Great Gabbo*, *Wise Girls*, *Montana Moon*, *The Sophomore* — again — , *Hell's Heroes*, *The Delightful Rogue*, *Darkened Rooms*, *The Mighty*, and *The Benson Murder Case* — mostly old pictures but fairly good.

I have begun a correspondence with Alex Doktor[1] and find him to be an unusually well balanced lad. None of the vague ravings whereof we know — at least, not so far. I asked him to put yours and Truett's names on the receiving list of *The Potpourri* and he said he'd be delighted to. He's German, of course, as his name signifies, and says he was born in a log cabin in Continental, Ohio. He doesn't seem to be sophisticated. I rather like his letters. And you know I'm prejudiced toward his race — I was first attracted toward you by your honest Teutonic features and High Dutch accent. Ja wohl, herr Von Scutto!

Have you received a *Junto* yet? I should think one was about due. But life is full of banalities and even the *Junto* sometimes fails to come out on time.

Well, Clyde, if you'll write and tell me when, or if, you'll have a day or so of leisure, I'll try to make it over there and bore you for a short time. Write and tell me when to come, because I don't want to hoof it all the way to Brownwood and then maybe find you out of town.

Fear Dunn

NOTES

1. Doktor, of Toledo, Ohio, was one of the few non-Texan members of *The Junto*'s mailing list.

TSS: 82573

130. To Tevis Clyde Smith, ca. May 1930.

Well, Fear Finn, I was in Brownwood yesterday but I was just in and out. I was there longer than I thought I'd be, but it was so uncertain I didn't have time to look you up. If I'd have gotten hold of you and arranged to meet you some where, I knew I'd probably have to leave before you could get there.

I got a letter from Truett, at Galveston. He seemed to be enjoying his vacation fairly well. *Fight Stories* was kind enough to give me the cover design this month[1] but they changed the title and the chapter headings and made quite a number of changes throughout the story which seemed not only needless to me, but in some places entirely distorted the original meaning. I think some of the changes must surely have been mistakes in printing.

I am confronted with the enigma of editors. They say they want action-stuff. Well, I have a story[2] with *Argosy* which I am as certain they will reject as I am that I'm sitting here. Yet it bristles with fast, well-written action. There is a perfect shimmer of swords from the opening scene where Thorwald Shield-hewer throws a drinking-horn of ale in the face of Chief Brulla of Hjaltlands, to the scene on Hakon Skel's dragon-ship where Cormac Mac Art unmasks the Mysterious Stranger and Wulfhere Hausakliufr roars: "Aim her prow east, carles, we go to set a new king on the throne of Dane-mark!"

By golly, whatever else they may say about that story, they can't kick about the action. I consider it my best attempt of the sort, to date. But will I sell it? Like Hell I will.[3]

Oh, well — Mist and madness and mockery rule and weariness dulls the whetted tool and the mind of a man is the dust of a fool and the ways of the world are weary.

A Stirring of Green Leaves

I long for the South as a man for a maid,
The rose at the window bar,
The stars and the palm-trees' velvet shade
And the strum of a Spanish guitar.

My people laughed at the frost and cold,
And the blast from winter's mouth,
But my soul is worn and thin and old
And it reaches blind to the South.

Why should I yearn for a gypsy trail
Through the olive trees of Spain?
Mine is the race of the Western Gael
And the cold, slow blood of the Dane.

But never the restless leaves are stirred
By a breath from summer's mouth
But like the soul of a wandering bird
My soul is yearning South.

The Rhyme of the Viking Path

I followed Asgrim Snorri's son
Around the world and half-way back,
And 'scaped the hate of Galdarhrun
Who sunk our ship off Skagerack.

I lent my sword to Hrothgar then,
His eyes were ice, his heart was hard;
He fell with half his weapon-men
To our own kin at Mikligard.

And then for many a weary moon
I labored at the galley's oar
Where men grow maddened by the rune
Of row-locks clacking evermore.

But I survived the reeking rack,
The toil, the whips that burned and gashed,
The spiteful Greeks who scarred my back
And trembled even while they lashed.

They sold me on an Eastern block,
In silver coins their price was paid,
They girt me with a chain and lock —
I laughed and they were sore afraid.

I toiled among the olive trees
Until a night of hot desire
Brought sharp the breath of outer seas
And filled my veins with curious fire.

Then I arose and broke my chain,
And laughed to know that I was free,
And battered out my master's brain
And fled and gained the open sea.

Beneath a copper sun a-drift,
I fled the ketch and slaver's dhow,
Until I saw a sail up-lift
And saw and knew the dragon-prow.

Oh, East of sands and moon-lit gulf,
Your blood is thin, your gods are few;
You could not break the Northern wolf
And now the wolf has turned on you.

Now fires that light the coast of Spain
Fling shadows on the Moorish strand;
Masters, your slave has come again,
With torch and axe in his red hand!

A Marching Song of Connacht

The men of the East are decked in steel,
They march with a trumpets' din,
They glitter with silk and golden scales
And boast of high kings' kin —
We of the West are clad in hides
But our hearts are steel within.

They of the East ride gallant steeds,
And each knight wears a crown —
We fight on foot as our forebears fought
And we drag the riders down.

They of the East are full of pride,
Cubs of the lion's den.
They boast they breed a race of kings —
But we of the West breed Men.

The pictures were hot; answer soon, will youse.
Fear Dunn.

NOTES

1. "The Iron Man."
2. "The Night of the Wolf."
3. Archibald Bittner, editor of *Argosy*, rejected the story, saying it was "a lot too vague and slow-moving."

TSS: 82142-82143

131. To Farnsworth Wright, ca. June 1930.

Mr. Farnsworth Wright,
Weird Tales Magazine,
Chicago, Illinois.

Dear Mr. Wright:

I have long looked forward to reading Mr. Lovecraft's "The Rats in the Walls" and it certainly comes up to all expectations. I was amazed by the sweep of his imagination — not so much because of the extent of his reachings into the realms of imagination, which though cosmic enough in his story, he has exceeded in other tales, to my mind, but because of the strange and unthinkable by-path into which he was wandered in this tale. There, assuredly, he has taken a road never before traversed, or even dreamed of, by any writer or thinker, ancient or modern. He has painted an incredible word picture, that needs a Dore to put on canvas, and creates a suggestion of nameless semi-human monstrosity, like the suggestion gotten from a study of Kubin's *Waldgespenest.*

The climax of the story alone puts Mr. Lovecraft in a class by himself; undoubtedly he must have the most unusual and wonderfully constructed brain of any man in the world. He alone can paint pictures in shadows and make them terrifically real. As to the climax, the maunderings of the maddened victim is like a sweep of horror down the eons, dwindling back and back to be finally lost in those grisly mists of world-birth where the mind of man refuses to follow. And I note from the fact that Mr. Lovecraft has his character speaking Gaelic instead of Cymric, in denoting the Age of the Druids, that he holds to Lhuyd's[1] theory as to the settling of Britain by the Celts.

This theory is not generally agreed to, but I scarcely think that it has ever been disproved, and it was upon this that my story "The Lost Race" was based — that the Gaelic tribes preceded the Cymric peoples into Britain, by way of Ireland, and were later driven out by them. Baxter,[2] the highly learned author of *Glossario Antiquae Britanniae* upholds this theory on the grounds that the Brigantes, supposed to be the first Celtic settlers in Britain, were unacquainted with the "p" sound, which was not used in Britain until the advent of the Brythonic or Cymric peoples. According to this, the Brigantes were a Goidhelic tribe, and Lhuyd's point seems proven.

Personally, I hold to the theory of Cymric precedence, and believe that Brythonic tribes inhabited, not only Britain and Scotland before the coming of the Gaels, but Ireland as well. The blond Britons appear to me to be a closer branch of the ancient Aryan stock, the Gaels arriving later, and being mixed with some Turanian or Mediterranean blood. But every man is entitled to his own view and a writer has the right to use any and all theories, no matter how conflicting, in his stories. I may write a story one day upholding a certain theory of science, letters, anthropology or what-not, and the next day, a story upholding a theory directly opposite. A fiction writer, whose job is to amuse and entertain, should give all theories equal scope and justice. But I'm taking up too much of your time.

Cordially,
[Robert E. Howard]

NOTES

1. Edward Lhuyd, 1660 - 1709.
2. William Baxter, 1650 - 1723.

TSS: 52675

ઉ꧂ઉ꧂

132. To Tevis Clyde Smith, ca. June 1930.

Well, Fear Finn:

The pictures came at last and here they are — yours, I mean. They're not so good. The light wasn't good that day, as you remember and I think the film must have been at fault. But the main blemish seems to lie in the developing. I don't understand why the studio should do such rotten work; they used to do first class stuff. But I haven't sent any films to them for several years and they may have changed hands. I note they've gone up in their prices, and naturally, they'd lower the standard of their work. The higher the prices, the lousier the work.

Last Monday Pink Tyson[1] and Slue-foot Cross[2] came around before I was up — i.e. about ten o'clock in the morning — and wanted me to go with them on a trip. Slue-foot had a vacation and as neither Pink nor I were working at anything particular we thought we might as well help him take it. We went to San Antonio that evening and spent the night in a tourist camp; the next day we found out that they were going to have some fights there that night and stayed to see them. When we went to the arena they wouldn't let us in because we weren't members of the clubs but that didn't faze us. We joined the club. Heh heh heh! I'm a member of the Business Men's Athletic Club of San Antonio. Whee! Well, when I looked around at the wops, spicks, Chineees and niggers who were among those of my club brothers it gave me a big laugh. The fights were fairly good all except the main event which was an uproarious comedy. A Dallas ex-policeman named Battling Dunn fought Dangerous Dan Navarro from Monterey who looked more like an Armenian than a Mexican. Dunn quit like a rat in the third round.

Next morning we left San Antonio and after absentmindedly straying several miles on the Houston road in an effort to get out of town, we found we were going in the opposite direction and clapped on all sail for the Llano. We went through Kerrville and Junction and camped on the Llano some ten miles out of Junction. We stayed there that night but as we had absentmindedly omitted to bring anything that looked like bait, the fishing wasn't much of a success. We got some frogs but an eel kept stealing our bait and we caught one fish — a pound and a half cat which we later tossed back into the river. I don't get much kick out of fishing but I did enjoy rowing up and down the river. We made several miles altogether in the rowboat.

We spent one night only on the Llano. Just before I left Cross Plains, I got a letter from Farnsworth saying he was starting an Oriental magazine and asking me to send him some Oriental tales. The more I thought of it, the more I decided that if I delayed too long he might get mad at me and turn to some other louse for the stuff, so the next morning, after our night on the river, I told my bold comrades that I was going to clap on sail for Cross Plains. They wanted to go on the Concho anyhow, so we raced merrily on through Menard, Eden and Paint Rock, at which point they went on to the river and I came on to Cross Plains, getting here just in time to hear Schmeling declared winner on a foul.[3] Phooey. I despise Sharkey but it looks like he gets some rotten breaks. I bet Dempsey comes back now.

How about answering a letter every now and then?

NOTES

1. Lindsey Tyson.
2. Aud Cross.
3. Jack Sharkey was disqualified for fouling Max Schmeling in the fourth round of a championship fight on Monday, June 23, 1930.

TSS: 82154

133. To Tevis Clyde Smith, ca. June 1930.

Salaam, Fear Finn:

Then Stein the peddler with rising joy,
Said: "We were at Brooklyn bridge;
"We worked our grafts at Perth-Amboy
"And up on the Denver ridge.
"Before Fort Wayne, on Racine's plain,
"Chicago, Frisco, Brent,

"From Monterey to the coasts of Maine,
"Wherever a dime was spent.
"We've rooked the Yank from the Hudson's bank
"To the hills of Mexico,
"And there's still a tip for another gypp,
"Cohen and Stein and Moe."
"Well, here's to honest good thieving blood,
"Cohen and Stein and Moe."

Well, I sold "Alleys of Peril" to *Fight Stories* for $80.00. I haven't heard from the others I have out. Here's a little parody on one of Soivice's stuff.

I was once, I declare, a grog-shop man
And I lolled in the cool of a bar;
I have known, I will swear, in a new life's span,
A desert where no springs are.
For far over all that folks hold dear
In me there lives and leaps
A love of the lowly stuff called beer,
A passion for foaming deeps.
To fill my glass with no paltry plan,
To guzzle and swig at will,
To mock at the raging revenue man
And steep my soul in swill.
To scorn all strife and view all life
With the goofy eyes of a drunk,
From the dizzy sea to the hangman's tree,
From the saint to the heart of the skunk.
From the boozy king to the beggar stewed,
From gin to the saki stall,
For I know that the beer for good was brewed
And I want to drink it all.
To drink it all! The good brown beer,
From the pub to society ball,
With never a bouncer to kick my rear
Or slam me with a maul.
With pink D.T.s I will pay the wage,
But leave my guzzling free,
For once I know in a bygone age
They made a Dry of me.

Well, me bauld buccarearo, since writing the above I stopped and wrote a ten page story, "The Fangs of the Copperhead" which I intend to try to sell Fiction House. It took me about three hours to write it, but I bet I don't sell it.

TSS: 82206

ꕥꕥꕥ

134. To Tevis Clyde Smith, ca. June 1930.

Salaam, Fear Finn:

Well, me bauld buccaneer, I sold "The Voice of El-lil" to Farnsworth for $95.00 being about the first story I ever sold that I had to batter out by pure force of study. He says it's to appear in the first copy of *Oriental Stories*, which will come out about September 15.

Remembering your remarks about historical stories, I quote from his letter: "I especially want historical tales — tales of the Crusades, of Genghis Khan, of Tamerlane, and the wars between Islam and Hindooism. Each story will be complete in one issue, and we will use no serials. The longer lengths are preferred — that is about 15,000 words."

You ought to be able to sell something on those lines.

I quote from Rupert K. Goofo's *Lives and Crimes of Notable Artists.*

Vinson, Smith and Howard were three of the most spectacular stars that flashed across the boozy horizon of that age. Starting life as idealists — professionally, at least — they soon became embittered and as George Bernard Shaw said in a lecture before the Dublin Girl Scouts: "Three lousier scuts never went down the pike."

Vinson, after the phenomenal success of his first book, *The Sex Life of the Female Cockroach*, betook himself and his millions to the South Seas where he set to work to drink himself to death with a pernicious determination that would have done credit to a worthier cause.

About that time Howard went to Ireland and succeeded in stirring up a small rebellion which might have had far reaching effect had not Howard, in a moment of irritation, betrayed the plans to the English. This made him quite popular with his tribesmen and he was much sought after, especially by the kinsmen of the men who had been forced to flee for their lives account of his treachery. But Howard went to England where he made violent efforts to establish himself as one of the house of Surrey, calmly ignoring the fact that his ancestors had established themselves in Ireland before the Howards were made lords of Surrey. He did, however, succeed in making much publicity for himself by assailing Lord William of Surrey as a thief and an ingrate wherever he met him.

Smith, meanwhile, having rapidly built up a large fortune by his novels, squandered something like a million dollars on liquor and chorus girls. He served some time as a general in the rebel army of Mexico, having bought his commission for a hundred thousand dollars, paying the amount in German marks. His duplicity being discovered, he was forced to flee for his life, but not before his quaint ideas of strategy and his jovial generosity in regard to human life had entirely ruined the rebels' cause. He fled to South America and spent some time living like a sultan in an obscure and backward Latin kingdom. It being discovered, however, that he had been paying his bills with cigar coupons, again he was forced to flee. Returning to the United States he was hired by a large New York paper as society editor. He hired a ghost writer to do his work for him and he himself spent all his time at races, football games and prize-fights, writing up these sports for a number of papers under the name of Cooto. Under this cognomen he exposed various scandals and made up quite a few himself. At last however, he managed to work up what he spoke of in after years with much gusto, as his masterpiece in newspaper work. That is to say, he got a position as a butler in the mansion of the owner of the paper on which he worked, and working at this lowly job in disguise, took a number of flashlight pictures of the magnate in a very compromising position with the house maid. These pictures Smith managed to publish, with a long detailed story, in the magnate's own paper. He accomplished this by holding up the entire force and forcing them to put out the paper at the point of a machine gun.

As is to be supposed, Smith was again forced to flee the country. He went to England where he met Howard and they celebrated the occasion by getting bestially drunk and reciting their most obscene parodies in Piccadilly Circus. Arrested for throwing rocks at Big Ben, the premier of England came to their assistance and in return they published a long rime in his honor. Critics are still trying to figure out whether this verse is a compliment or a subtle insult.

Howard, pursuing an amour with a bar-maid in the Limehouse, was soon after this mobbed by a gang of maddened Irish to whom he insisted on singing, "God Save the King," and boasting of his part in the betrayal of the recent rebellion. He was rescued by a squad of London bobbies whom he rewarded by presenting trick cigars which exploded and singed off their eye-brows. He then wrote and published a book entitled, *The Innate Treachery of the Gael* in which he reviled the Irish for turning on their benefactor as he termed himself.

He and Smith were living at this time at the house of the premier on whom they sponged in the most shameless manner. Smith courted a young lady of royal connection and they were to be married at Buckingham Palace with much splendor, but the bride-groom did not turn up. Later it came out that while his supposed bride waited at the altar, he had been assisting Howard in preparing plates for their new book which appeared on the streets next day, sold by ten thousand news boys hired for the purpose. Having completed the printing of the book, Smith and Howard returned to the house of the premier at dawn, hilariously drunk. On the premier remonstrating with them on their outrageous conduct, they fell on him jovially and threw him out into the street in his night gown.

The new book turned out to be a savage attack on the premier and his family as well as on all the notables of Great Britain. I quote one of the least objectionable lines: "But of all the lousy sons of bitches that this rotten island has produced Lord James Scutto is the cream; this ape-faced rat had the infernal nerve to speak to us the other day without tipping his hat; but what else can you expect from a low bred louse like him?"

A vengeful mob came after the authors but they had left, leaving only a note in which they scathingly called to the premier's mind his duties as a host and assured him that they would darken his door no more, until he made proper apologies. They had also taken with them all the silver ware they could lay their hands to.

Escaping to Paris they bitterly denounced the ingratitude of the British and collaborated on a book entitled: *The Treachery of the Ingrate, or England the Viper.*

With the money realized from this book and from the sale of the premier's silverware they took up their abode in the Latin Quarters, writing for Vinson to join them. About this time he found it convenient to do so, as the people in the South Seas, deciding that there were limits even to beach-combing, kicked him off the beach and bade him never to return. After a battle lasting all day and half the night, and requiring the combined efforts of the entire male population of Hawaii, they managed to throw him on an outbound steamer whence he showered them with anathemas and belaying pins until the ship had steamed out of throwing distance to the shore.

Joining Howard and Smith in Paris, these three rogues immediately set to work to gyp the government out of its colonial possessions. How the plan succeeded is told in my chapter of the same book: *Three Criminal Artists on Devil's Island.*

Answer soon, will youse?

Fear Dunn

TSS: 82473-82474

ᏅᏅᏅ

135a. To H. P. Lovecraft, draft, ca. July 1, 1930

Admittedly, your theories in regard to the Celtic races are logical, well grounded and in many cases, unanswerable, by my scanty knowledge at least. However, it seems to be the general trend of recent researchers to believe that the separation of Gael from Brython occurred before the conquest of Britain, and that the language of the Cymric Britons was merely a branch of Continental Gaulish. There seems to be a difference between Gaelic and Brythonic which runs back into the mists of antiquity and seems to suggest a vastly ancient separation—possibly before the Celtic invasion of western Continental

Europe. As regards present day Cymric or Cymreag, I attach less significance to it as a Celtic speech than most do. You are quite right in saying that it departs from the Aryan root stock far more than does present day Gaelic. I consider the Cymric has been so mixed with Mediterranean, Latin, Saxon and Scandinavian languages that it retains but little of the pristine Celtic qualities. However, I believe that the language of the ancient Britons and Gauls was as close to the Aryan root as that of the Gaels, with the exception of the "qu" which the Gaels retained as "k" longer than the Brythons. I take this to prove that the Brythons earlier branched away from the Aryan stock and came into contact with other races sooner than did the Gaels. The use of s in Gaul proves variance in Britain.

The modern trend seems to point to a generally recognized theory that the first Celtic invasion consisted of Goidhelic peoples, who swept over Europe at the end of the Neolithic Age. These were followed by a wave of Brythonic people who conquered them and drove them into Ireland and Scotland, and perhaps Cornwall. Later still—about the first century B.C. another wave of Gaels came into Ireland and later spread into Scotland.

My theory conflicts with this view and I will frankly admit I have no grounds whatever for many of my notions on the subject and will make no attempt to prove my beliefs. I have not studied the very latest results of researches and there are probably many flaws in my theories.

My idea is that the Brythonic peoples were first to branch away from the Aryan stock somewhere on the plains of Asia, and that they and not the Gaels brought the Bronze Age into Europe. My reason for this view is the fact that Caesar found the Britons still using swords of bronze. If, as some historians maintain, bronze using Gaels fled before Brythons wielding iron swords, it seems to me the Britons should have opposed the Romans with weapons of the latter metal. I believe that the Gaels, a small branch of Celts, remained in the original homeland of the Aryan peoples longer, untouched by non-Aryan influences and therefore retaining the original Aryan language longer. I believe that their roaming followed a different line from that taken by the Brythons; that they came to the Mediterranean Sea and followed its shores westward, intermingling to some extent with the peoples they found there—this would account for the original trend of scholars to class the Irish as a Mediterranean race, and account also for the numerous words of Hamitic or Semitic affinity in the Gaelic language. Whether the Gaels or Milesians lingered in Egypt as mercenaries and whether they spent some time in Spain before coming into Ireland, as the legends say, I am not prepared to say, though I believe it to be extremely likely. Indeed, I think it quite likely that the Celtiberians of Spain were the ancestors of the Irish and Scotch.

I quote some extracts on the Celtic subject, some of which seem to bear out parts of my notions and some of which seem to refute them entirely, as I said before.

"The view that there was on the Continent an older group of Celts who preserved the Indo-European sound qu (the so-called qu group) and who were followed by a conquering group, who changed that sound to p (the so-called p group) is now most generally discarded. Though we know but little of the language of the ancient Belgae, it is sufficient to class it with that of the Celts and perhaps to identify the Galates and the Belgae. Anyhow it is clear that (Greek word)[1] and (Greek word)[1] are two distinct words that neither of them has anything to do with the modern names Goidhelic and Gael." (The Encyclopedia Americana).

I also quote the same authority which speaking of the divisions of the Celtic race says it is: "Correct in a purely linguistic sense divides the Celtic languages into a K group (Goidhelic) and a P group (Gaulish and Brythonic). The most notable characteristics which set off the Celtic languages from the other members of the Indo-Celtic family are: (1) The fall of initial and intervocalic, this change which is common to both branches of Celtic, took place before 1000 B.C. and before the Goidhelic Celts separated from the Brythonic Celts and the invasion of Britains, (2) the change already referred to, (viz. of qu to k and p) which took place after the separation, Old Irish coic, Old Welsh pimp, five, (3) the change of the Indo-Celtic e to Celtic i, Latin verus, Old Irish fir, true, (4) the change of vocalic r and l to ri and li.

"Were it not for a common vocabulary the Brythonic group of Celtic would be separated by an unbridgeable gulf from the Goidhelic. This cleavage is observable from the earliest monuments and is chiefly due to the following factors: (1) The different treatment of the Indo-Celtic qu, which at a very early period became p in Brythonic but which in Goedhelic was for a long time preserved and then, even in the oldest Irish, changed to k (written c.) Gaulish agress in making this change with Brythonic of which, to that extent at least, it may be regarded as a prehistoric type. E.g. Gaulish pempe, five, Old Welsh pimp, Breton pemp, Old Irish coic; Old Irish macc, Welsh map, son."

I think the reason for Brethonic or Cornish more nearly resembling Gaelic is as I quote from The History of Ireland, edited by Henry Smith Williams:

"Early writers pointed out a Goidhelic element in the topographical nomenclature of West Britain, and concluded that the country was once occupied by the Goidhel whence they were driven into Ireland by the advancing Cymri. This was a natural and reasonable conclusion at the time. But our present knowledge compels us to adopt a different view . . . . the numerous traces of Goidhelic names found there are derived from an Irish occupation in historic times."

This appears to me to further point to a much later entrance of the Gael into the British Isles. The more or less simultaneous invasion of Wales and Scotland by the Gael seem to me more the expansion of a new, vigorous and growing tribe than the reviving growth of a ancient nation. I quote Bede:

"At first this island had no other inhabitants but the Britons . . . .[2] When they had made themselves masters of the greater part of the island, the Picts from Scythia . . . . accordingly sailed over into Britain. In process of time Britain, after the Britons and Picts, received a third nation, the Scots, who migrating from Ireland under their leader Reuda . . . . seized . . . . settlements amongst the Picts."

I think such Latin authors as mention the above matters coincide with this account, in that in their accounts the Britons precede the Picts and the Picts, the Scots or Gaels. The legends of the various races agree upon it, as do, I think, the narratives of the British historians, Gildas and Nennius. I have not read The Irish Annals nor The Pictish Chronicle but if I am not much mistaken both agree in placing the arrival of the Gaels in Scotland much later than that of the Picts and Britons. It seems to me that if, as most historians maintain, the Gaels had been living in Ireland where they were driven by the Britons, for so many centuries, they would have come into Scotland at an earlier date, as the British tribes in that country seemed too scanty to offer them as much opposition as the Picts did.

Henry Smith Williams' History of Ireland: "The last of the prehistoric races of Ireland were the Scots or . . . . Milesians. At the earliest period . . . . it was occupied by a sparse population . . . . Tuatha Feda, doubtless of aboriginal Iberic race of western and southern Europe . . . . It is not necessary to suppose that all the tribes included under this name (Firbolgs) came at the same time. The effect of their immigrations now appears that in the north the people were Cruithni or Picts . . . . in the east and center British and Belgae tribes; and in Munster when not distinctly Iberic, of a southern or Gaulish type."

I quote further from the same authority: "This struggle (the conquest of Ireland) was brought about by the arrival from abroad of a new tribe or the rise of an old one. The former view seems the more probable, for at that time great displacements of the Celts were taking place subsequent on the conquests of the Romans and some of the displaced tribes may have migrated to Ireland. The victors in the struggle appear afterwards as Scots."

And by Scots is meant, of course, Gaels. I will frankly admit that I base my theories as to Celtic occupation of the British Isles largely on the Milesian legends. I firmly believe that subsequent research will prove these supposed myths to contain more truth than is generally supposed. Gibbons sought to refute the so-called legend that Ireland was the original home of the Scots, and maintained that on the other hand, the Gaels spread into the smaller island from Britain or Scotland, but the original supposition has been proven since his time. In like manner I believe that other legends of the Irish will be some day confirmed. Zimmer, in his "Kelt-Studien" says: "We believe that Meve, Conor Mac Nessa, Cuchulainn and Finn Mc Cumhail are just as much historical personages as Deitrich of Berne or Etzel." And if the Red Branch legends are to be accepted largely, I see no reason for denying that the older Dananean myths contain at least a base of fact. If, as I quoted above, it is a fact that British or Belgic tribes were holding the eastern and central parts of Ireland before the coming of the Gaelic Milesians, it seems natural to think that like races were already firmly established in Britain, which island being so much nearer the mainland.

I do not subscribe to the theory which makes Partholan and his followers Gaels. I see no reason to suppose that the first Celtic invaders of Ireland were of the same tribe as the last. If so, why the long gap of time between the coming of the two branches, and where were the Milesians living to escape the wave of

Brythonic invasion that is supposed to have occurred between the coming of Partholan and the coming of the Milesians?

I believe that Partholan and his men were as represented by Irish legend—Egyptians or Phoenecians, sea-farers from Africa or some island in the Mediterranean. I believe that the Fomorians were some Finnish or Germanic race living in Denmark or Jutland, or possibly the Hebrides Islands, and that the ensuing waves of Nemedians, Firbolgs and Tuatha De Denann were Belgic or British invaders from Britain. Firbolg or Men With Bags, seems to be merely the Gaelic manner of pronouncing Belgae. The Milesians I believe to have been the true Gaels, a Scythic branch of Celts who left the Aryan steppes much later than the Brythonic peoples and who after centuries of wandering, eventually came into Ireland.

Another and possibly more obscure reason for my belief is this: most of the Gauls and the Britons seem to have been of a large blond type, with light eyes and yellow hair, the true Aryan complection. But according to certain traditions, the Milesians were dark, of a "Spanish" type, when they invaded Ireland. According to these traditions, the Milesians or Gaels retained the Aryan height and light eyes—generally grey in this case—but were dark of skin and hair. This departure from the original Celtic stock might have taken place in Ireland after the invasion, despite legends to the contrary—might have merely been a result of the conquerors mingling with their Mediterranean subjects. But I think it points to long residence or wandering among Hamitic or Turanian peoples before coming into the British Isles. It seems to me that if any great mixing between Aryan and aboriginal Mediterranean took place in Ireland, it would have been between the earlier peoples. But the Nemedians and Tuatha De Danaan peoples are usually represented as very fair. I believe the typical Gael to have been grey eyed and black haired, and that more recent traditions representing heroes as fair either come from a mixture of Gael with Brython or else result from the same reasons that caused Cuchulainn, "a small, dark man" in early legends, to become a golden haired giant in the later legends. Still, Cymreag, Gaelic, Brethonec and Brezonec are but variations of the one great Celtic race.

NOTES

1. The original transcript has these two parentheses as "Greek Word" as shown in the draft. Howard later filled in the parentheses with the Greek names for the Celts. See the finished letter 135b, page 49. JB
2. These ellipses from here on appear in the draft as originally typed by Howard. JB

TSS: 92072, 92094, 92117

135b. To H.P. Lovecraft, ca. July 1, 1930.

Mr. H.P. Lovecraft,
10 Barnes Street,
Providence, R.I.

Dear Mr. Lovecraft:

I am indeed highly honored to have received a personal letter from one whose works I so highly admire. I have been reading your stories for years, and I say, in all sincerity, that no writer, past or modern, has equalled you in the realm of bizarre fiction. I realize that it is the custom for enthusiastic readers to compare a favorite author with Poe, and their comparison is seldom based on any real estimate, or careful study. But after a close study of Poe's technique, I am forced to give as my personal opinion, that his horror tales have been surpassed by Arthur Machen, and that neither of them ever reached the heights of cosmic horror or opened such new, strange paths of imagination as you have done in "The Rats in the Walls", "The Outsider", "The Horror at Red Hook", "The Call of Cthulhu", "The Dunwich Horror" — I could name all the stories of yours I have read and not be far wrong.

Thank you very much for the poetry. I should like very much to see more of it. "The Dweller" especially intrigued me, as I found in it much of the quality of your most powerful prose stories — a sudden Door-like opening on absolutely unguessed conjectures, that sets a sort of inarticulate madness that howls for expression, clawing at the reader's brain.

I am indeed gratified that you have liked my efforts in *Weird Tales*, and I thank you very much for your kind comments on them.

I am going to impose on your good nature to the extent of discussing my reasons for believing the Cymric peoples were first in the British Isles. My education on the subject is meager, but it is one which has always interested me greatly, perhaps because of the dominating percent of Gaelic in my own veins. Such authorities as I have read seem very conflicting in their views and often self-contradictory, so perhaps already research has rendered my ideas absurd and ridiculous. However, I shall venture to commit myself.

Admittedly, your theory, as put forth in your letter, is logical, well grounded, and in many cases, unanswerable, by my scanty knowledge, at least. However, it seems to be the general trend of recent researchers to believe that the separation of Gael from Brython occurred before the conquest of Britain, and that the language of the Britons was merely a branch of the Continental Gaulish. There seems to be a difference between Gaelic and Brythonic which runs back into the mists of antiquity and seems to suggest a vastly ancient separation and possibly a development in different parts of the world. As regards present-day Cymric or Cymreag, I attach less significance to it as a Celtic speech than most do. The use of "s" in Gaulish, which did not extend in the same manner to Brythonic, seems to point to a variance after Brythonic separated from Gaulish, either on the Continent or in Britain. You are quite right in saying that Welsh or Cymric departs from the Aryan root stock far more than does present-day Gaelic. I consider that the language — Cymric — has been so mixed with Mediterranean, Latin, Saxon and Scandinavian languages that it retains but little of the pristine Celtic quality. However, I believe this mixing took place at a comparatively modern date and that the language of the ancient Gauls and Britons was as close to the Aryan root as that of the Gaels, with the exception of the "qu" sound which the Gaels retained longer than the Brythons. I take this to mean that the Brythons earlier branched away from the Aryan stock and came into contact with other races sooner than did the Gaels.

The modern trend seems to point to a generally recognized theory that the first Celtic invasion consisted of Goidhelic peoples, who swept over Europe at the end of the Neolithic Age. These, according to many historians, were followed by a wave of Brythonic people who conquered them and drove them into Ireland, Scotland and perhaps Cornwall. Later still — about the first century B.C. another wave of Gaels came into Ireland and later spread into Scotland.

My theory conflicts with this view and I will frankly admit I have no grounds whatever for many of my notions on the subject and will make no attempt to prove them. I have not studied the results of latest researches and there are many flaws that I myself can see in my theories.

My idea is that the Brythonic peoples were the first to branch away from the Aryan stock somewhere on the plains of Asia, and that they and not the Gaels brought the Bronze Age into Europe. My reason for this view, that is, in regard to the bronze, is the fact that Caesar found the Britons still using swords of copper and bronze. If, as some historians maintain, bronze using Gaels preceded and fled before Brythons wielding iron swords, it seems to me that the Britons should have opposed the Romans with weapons of the latter metal. I believe that the Gaels were those Celts who remained in the original homeland of the Aryans after the ancestors of the Brythonic races moved westward. Living among Aryan tribes they retained the original Aryan language longer. I believe that their roaming, which began centuries later, followed a different course from that taken by the Brythons; that they came to the Mediterranean Sea and followed its shores westward, intermingling to some extent with the peoples they found there. This would account for the original trend of scholars to class the Irish as a Mediterranean race, and account also for the numerous words of Hamitic or Semitic affinity in the Gaelic language. Whether the Gaels or Milesians lingered in Egypt as mercenaries and whether they spent some time in Spain before coming into Ireland, as the legends say, I am not prepared to defend, though I believe it to be extremely likely. O'Donovan and O'Reilly's *Irish-English Dictionary* shows clearly the connection of many Gaelic words with Hebrew and Greek words, though the last is natural with any Aryan language, of course. The author in his preface states that the work of the Earl of Ross and General Vallancy show that a large element of Phoenician exists in even modern Gaelic. The question is, however, whether this element was brought in by the Gaels who collected it on their wanderings, or was introduced by traders. I, personally, think it very likely that the Celtiberians of Spain were closely allied to the Gaels, and possibly themselves the ancestors of the Irish and Scotch. As they were allies or tributaries to the Carthaginians, their speech must have been mixed largely with Phoenician.

Bishop O'Brien of Cloyne scoffs at the legends representing the Gaels wandering from Scythia into Egypt and thence to Ireland, but admits that the Celtiberians were doubtless among the early settlers of Ireland.

I quote some extracts on the Celtic subject, some of which seem to bear out parts of my notions and some of which seem to refute them entirely, as I have said before.

"The view that there was on the continent an older group of Celts who preserved the Indo-European sound qu (the so-called qu group) and who were followed by a conquering group, who changed that sound to p (the so-called p group) is now most generally discarded. Though we know but little of the language of the ancient Belgae, it is sufficient to class it with that of the Celts and perhaps to identify the Galates and the Belgae. Anyhow it is clear that *Γαλαται* and *Κελτοι*[1] two distinct words, and that neither of them has anything to do with the modern names Goidhelic and Gael." (*The Encyclopedia Americana.*)

I quote the same authority which says a division of the Celtic race:
"Correct in a purely linguistic sense divides the Celtic languages into a K group (Goidhelic) and a P group (Gaulish and Brythonic). The most notable characteristics which set off the Celtic languages from the other members of the Indo-Celtic family are: (1) The fall of initial and inter-vocalic; this change which is common to both branches of Celtic, took place before 1000 B.C. and before the Goidhelic Celts separated from the Brythonic Celts and the invasion of Britain, (2) the change already referred to, (viz of qu to k and p) which took place after the separation, Old Irish coic, Old Welsh pimp, five, (3) the change of the Indo-Celtic e (long) to Celtic i (long), Latin verus, Old Irish fir, true, (4) the change of vocalic r and l to ri and li.

"Were it not for a common vocabulary the Brythonic group of Celtic would be separated by an unbridgeable gulf from the Goidhelic. This cleavage is observable from the earliest monuments and is chiefly due to the following factors: (1) The different treatment of the Indo-Celtic qu, which at a very early period became p in Brythonic but which in Goidhelic was for a long time preserved and then, even in the Oldest Irish, changed to k (written c) Gaulish agrees in making this change with Brythonic of which, to that extent at least, it may be regarded as a prehistoric type. E.G. Gaulish pempe, five, Old Welsh pimp, Breton pemp, Old Irish coic; Old Irish macc, Welsh map, son."

I think the reason for Brethonec or Cornish more nearly resembling Gaelic is as I quote from *The History of Ireland*, edited by Henry Smith Williams: "Early writers pointed out a Goidhelic element in the topographical nomenclature of West Britain, and concluded that the country was once occupied by the Goedel whence they were driven into Ireland by the advancing Cymri. This was a natural and reasonable conclusion at the time. But our present knowledge compels us to adopt a different view . . . the numerous traces of Goidhelic names found there are derived from an Irish occupation in historic times."

This appears to me to further point to a much later entrance of the Gael into the British Isles. The more or less simultaneous invasions of Wales and Scotland by the Gaels seem to me more the expansion of a new, vigorous and growing tribe than the reviving growth of an ancient and conquered nation. I quote Bede:

"At first this island had no other inhabitants but the Britons . . . . When they had made themselves masters of the greater part of the island, the Picts from Scythia . . . . accordingly sailed over into Britain. In process of time Britain, after the Britons and Picts, received a third nation, the Scots, who migrating from Ireland under their leader Reuda . . . . seized . . . . settlements amongst the Picts."

I think such Latin authors as mention the above matters agree with this account, in that the Britons precede the Picts and the Picts, the Scots or Gaels. The legends of the various races coincide with it, as do, I think, the narratives of the British historians, Gildas and Nennius. I have not read *The Irish Annals* nor *The Pictish Chronicle* but if I am not much mistaken both agree in placing the arrival of the Gaels much later than that of the Picts and Britons. It seems to that if, as most historians maintain, the Gaels had been living in Ireland where they had been driven by the Britons, for so many centuries, they would have come into Scotland at an earlier date, for the main British population seems to have been confined largely to the southern part of the island.

I believe that the Gaels landed first in Ireland. Henry Smith Williams' *History of Ireland*: "The last of the prehistoric races of Ireland were the Scots or . . . . Milesians. At the earliest period . . . . it was occupied by a sparse population . . . . Tuatha Feda, doubtless of aboriginal Iberic race of western and southern Europe." These were soon conquered by the Celts. "It is not necessary" (quoting from the same history) "to suppose that all the tribes included under this name (Firbolgs) came at the same time. The effect of their immigration now appears that in the north the people were Cruithni or Picts . . . . in the east and center British and Belgae tribes; and in Munster when not distinctly Iberic, of a southern or Gaulish type."

To further establish the identity of these first Celtic invaders I here quote from *The Catholic Encyclopedia* which contains a very exhaustive study of all Irish subjects. Speaking of the early history of "Ogygia, or the Ancient Island. The Firbolgs . . . . were kindred perhaps to those war-like Belgae of Gaul. The Milesians certainly belong to history though the date of their arrival in Ireland is unknown."

I quote again from Williams' *History of Ireland*: "This struggle (the conquest of Ireland) was brought about by the arrival from abroad of a new tribe or the rise of an old one. The former view seems the more probable, for at that time great displacements of the Celts were taking place subsequent on the conquests of the Romans and some of the displaced tribes may have migrated to Ireland. The victors in the struggle appear afterwards as Scots. (Gaels.)"

I frankly admit that I base my theories as to Celtic occupation of the Isles largely on the Milesian legends. I firmly believe that subsequent research will prove these supposed myths to contain more truth than is generally supposed. Gibbons[2] sought to refute the so-called legend that Ireland was the original home of the Scots, maintaining that the Gaels spread into the smaller island from Scotland, but the converse has since been proven. In like manner I believe that other legends of the Irish will be some day confirmed. Zimmer in his *Kelt-Studien*[3] says: "We believe that Meve, Conor Mac Nessa, Cuchulainn and Finn Mac Cumhail are just as much historical personages as Dietrich of Berne or Etzel." And if the Ossian legends are to be accepted largely, I see no reason for denying the old Dananean myths at least a grain of truth, a base of fact. If British or Belgic tribes were holding the eastern and central part of Ireland before the coming of the Gaelic Milesians, it seems natural to think that like races were already firmly established in Britain, which island being so much nearer the mainland.

I do not subscribe to the theory which makes Partholan and his followers Gaels. I see no reason to suppose that the first Celtic invaders of Ireland were of the same tribe as the last. If, as some historians maintain, Partholan and his men were Gaels, and the later Milesians came from Gaul, how is it that they escaped the wave of Brythonic invasion that is supposed to have occurred during the long gap between the coming of Partholan and the coming of the Milesians?

I believe that Partholan and his men were as represented by Irish legend — Egyptian or Phoenician sea-farers. I believe that the Fomorians were Finnish or Germanic pirates living in Jutland, and that the ensuing waves of Nemedians, Firbolgs and Tuatha De Danann were British invaders, or possibly Belgae. Firbolg, or Men With Bags seems to be merely the Gaelic manner of pronouncing Belgae. The Milesians I believe to have been the only true Gaels, Scythic Celts who left the Aryan steppes much later than the Brythonic peoples and who after centuries of wandering, eventually came into Ireland.

Another and possibly more obscure reason for my belief is this: most of the Gauls and the Britons seem to have been of a large blond type, with light eyes and yellow hair, the true Aryan complexion. But according to certain traditions, the Milesians were dark of a "Spanish" type, when they invaded Ireland. According to these traditions, the Milesians or Gaels retained the Aryan height and light eyes — generally grey in this case — but were dark of skin and hair. This departure from the original Celtic stock might have taken place in Ireland after the invasion, despite legends to the contrary — might have merely been a result of the conquerors mingling with their Mediterranean subjects. But I think it points to long residence or wandering among Hamitic or Turanian peoples before coming into the British Isles. It seems to me that if any great mixing between Aryan and aboriginal Mediterranean took place in Ireland, it would have been between the earlier peoples. But the Nemedians and Tuatha De Danann are usually represented as being very fair. I believe the typical Gael to have been tall, grey eyed and black haired, and that more recent traditions representing heroes as fair, either meant some man in whose veins Brythonic blood predominated, or else the legends themselves became changed in the same manner that caused Cuchulainn, "a small, dark man" in early legends to become a golden haired giant in the later legends.

But after all, these classifications are more or less unimportant, since Gaelic, Cymreag, Brethonec, Brezonec and Gaulish are all parts of the great

Celtic race and language which left its mark in more places than is generally realized and formed the base for so many modern languages, though its influence is largely forgotten in the passing of the ages.

I must crave your pardon for taking up so much of your time. I had not realized that I had strung out such a lengthy discussion in so much detail, and hope I have not bored you too much.

I hope that you will have the time and inclination to write me again when it is convenient for you, for I enjoyed your letter very much, and I strongly hope to read more of your stories in *Weird Tales* soon.

Cordially,
[Robert Eiarbhin Howard]

P.S. I took the liberty of writing this letter on the typewriter as indeed, I do all my correspondence; I write such an abominable hand, I can scarcely read it myself.

R.E.H.

NOTES

1. Galatai and Keltoi, Greek names for the Celts. JB
2. Edward Gibbon (see letter 122, page 16).
3. *Keltische Studien.* The quotation is from *The Catholic Encyclopedia*, which abbreviates as Howard does here.

TSS: 11400-11404

❧❧❧

136. To Tevis Clyde Smith, ca. July 1930.

I haven't heard from our story[1] but that's not unusual, seeing that I haven't heard from a story I sent to *Weird Tales* some time before I sent the other; the editor may be taking a vacation or something.

I believe you'll sell that story to Fiction House.[2] Have you heard from the stories you had out to *Snappy* and the like? I hope you'll have sold something by the time you get this letter. I got a long letter from Lovecraft. That boy is plenty smart. And well read too. He starts out by saying that most of my arguments seem logical enough and that he is about on the point of accepting my views — and then follows with about three or four closely written pages with which he rips practically all my theories to shreds. He's out of my class. I'm game to go the limit with a man my weight, but me scrapping with him is like a palooka climbing into the ring with a champion. I think I'll ask him a lot of questions about things when I write him, instead of presenting my own views. That don't mean, understand, that he's convinced me to his way of thinking. Not at all; I still think I'm right. But I want to find out some of the things I'll bet he knows — obscure phases of history and forgotten cultures, and mystic cults and all that. He says his young friend Frank Belknap Long, and Clark Ashton Smith have often praised my junk. Well, I'm very glad of it, naturally.

I'll try a little comedy, as of old.

Voyages with Villains

(A few of the memoirs of Rupert Goofo, from the book titled as above, containing his narrations of travelling in the company of those men who have well been termed The Rogues of America, Smith, Howard and Vinson.)

Knowing my companions as I did, I was dubious about venturing into the domains of the Sultan Mechmet Ali, for his subjects differed greatly from the supine Hindus with whom we had been dealing. I was certain that if my friends made as free with the harems of the Moslems as they had with the zenanas of the more civilized kingdoms and sultanates, we would be in jeopardy of belongings and limbs, if not our personal safety. But my companions, with their usual bullheadedness, insisted on going, so, after paying all the bills which they had left up to me — and the number thereof was legion — I hastened after them.

Note: There follows an account of their journey, and of Smith's narrow escape from a village of enraged jungle dwellers, whom he sought to chase over a high cliff, by means of wearing a tiger's skin and bellowing in a voice which Goofo describes as nerve-wracking and irritating in the extreme. The account proceeds.

The glorious moment had come! We were presented to the exalted Sultan Mechmet Ali. I was fully cognizant of the honor of the occasion, but I doubt if my materialistic companions shared my thrills. They were half drunk as usual, and at the very moment the escort was presenting us, I spied Vinson industriously endeavoring to gouge out a jewel which represented one of the eyes of the golden leopards which formed a base of the throne.

I noted that the Sultan's eyes were fixed on Smith with a basilisk gleam and without answering our salutation, Mechmet Ali suddenly laughed harshly and raucously. Smith suddenly began to sweat profusely and to my utter amazement said: "Hell's devils, it's Clankin Jarkis!"

"The same," snarled the sultan, brandishing his sceptre. "Now I've got you where I've wanted you for years! Your goose is cooked! Now for the broadsword and deserted castle —"

Perceiving that the sultan knew Smith of old, and was therefore and mechanically, his enemy, I called the attention of the rest and we went into conference to decide how to escape the spite of this vindictive sovereign.

"Tell him you'll buy him a drink," suggested Howard, this being about the only solution he ever offered on any question.

"Kick the unmentionable in the rear works," whooped Vinson hilariously, having just emptied a rum bottle.

At this moment the sultan, or Jarkis, whichever you wish to call him, strode down from his throne to taunt us with our helpless condition.

"I," said the sultan, shaking his sceptre in Smith's face, "am going to take a keen scimitar and pursue you up and down the halls and chambers of my harem, ever and anon hacking off slices of your skin, until you are running around in your bare skeleton."

He emphasized his remarks by slapping Smith with his sceptre. This enraged Smith who instantly retaliated by knocking the sultan on the back of his neck where he waved his legs and yelled for his men-at-arms to seize us. I must say my companions put up a noble resistance, closing eyes, mashing ears and breaking noses, but superior numbers overcame us and we were dragged off to the dungeons.

Note: Goofo here accounts their stay in the dungeons of Mechmet Ali, and their escape which was accomplished by seducing the wife of the guard; Smith and his companions not only contrived to escape but to carry a large part of the treasury with them.

We proceeded to the kingdom of the native prince Hutdara. This prince was highly cultured, having been educated in Europe and was a great admirer of Smith's poetry. He was glad to see not only Smith, but Howard and Vinson as well, knowing little of their true characters. Let it suffice to say that we were eventually escorted to the boundaries of the realm and literally kicked out. This embarrassed me highly, but it did not faze my dissolute companions who merely yelled: "Go to hell, you bastards!" And threw cobblestones at the emirs. Their actions while at Hutdara's court were quite in keeping with their general character.

Note: In this day of refinement and ultra-sophistication, the cultured reader finds it impossible to understand the complete depravity and scandalous barbarity of the three authors mentioned. Yet if one doubts, let him read for himself the outrageous collaboration of these men, in which they boast of their lives and works. The title is *The World's Three Greatest Men.*

The above is meant to be humorous, heh heh heh, but reading it over I find it isn't much. My vein of low comedy seems to be getting thin. I quote from a letter from Farnsworth: "I am very well pleased with 'Red Blades of Black Cathay,' and may use this as the cover design story for our third issue of *Oriental Stories.* We can offer you $118 on publication for it; and also $118 for "Wings in the Night" for *Weird Tales.* This is at our regular rate of 1c a word."

Answer soonel, will youse.

Fear Dunn

NOTES

1. Probably "Red Blades of Black Cathay."
2. Probably "Eighttoes Makes a Play" which Howard helped plot.

TSS: 82130-82131

ΩΩΩ

137. To H.P. Lovecraft, ca. August 1930.

Dear Mr. Lovecraft:

Let me first thank you for the opportunity you have given me to read your poetry; I need not tell you that I appreciate your kindness highly. You have, in this sonnet-cycle,[1] accomplished a superb artistic work, to my mind. It is not for me to say which of the poems were best; I read the whole with complete enjoyment. To say that some were superior to the others would be to imply that certain facets of a diamond were superior in luster to the rest. In expressing a preference for some of the poems, I do not by any means seek to imply an inferiority of the others. But I was especially taken with "The Book", "Recognition", "The Lamp", "The Courtyard", "Star-Winds", "The Window", "The Bells", "Mirage", "The Elder Pharos", "Background", and "Alienation".

I am glad that you liked "The Moon of Skulls" and hope my future efforts meet your approval. And I am highly honored to know that Mr. Long and Mr. Clark Ashton Smith have noticed my efforts. Both are writers and poets whose work I very much admire, having carefully preserved all of their poems (as well as all of yours) that have appeared in *Weird Tales* since I first made my acquaintance with the magazine.

I scarcely need say that your comments on historical and prehistorical matters I found to be highly interesting and instructive. You touched on a number of phases of which I am totally ignorant, and in matters wherein our views differ somewhat, I candidly admit that I am not scholar enough to present any logical argument. Your observations regarding the Mongoloid aborigines and their relation to the fairy-tales of western Europe especially interested me. I had supposed, without inquiring very deeply into the matter, that these legends were based on contact with the earlier Mediterraneans, and indeed, wrote a story on that assumption which appeared some years ago in *Weird Tales* — "The Lost Race." I readily see the truth of your remarks that a Mongoloid race must have been responsible for the myths of the Little People, and sincerely thank you for the information. As the present Mongolian is more or less repellant in appearance to the present-day Aryan, how much more must the primitive or retrograded type of Mongoloid repelled the original Aryan, who was probably superior in physical comeliness to moderns!

As regards Partholan, legends I have read seem to differ, some ascribing his origin to Greece, others to Egypt. Donn Byrne in his romances speaks of "Partholan of Egypt", and maintains that the present names of MacParland and MacFarlane are an evolution from Partholan, though the chief's entire band of descendants seems to have been wiped out by the plague. The Firbolgs and the Tuatha De Danaans, as you know, were represented to have been descendants of those Nemedians who escaped the swords of the Fomorians and returned to Greece, whence they had originally come to Ireland. Returning at different times, they were bitter rivals until the coming of the Milesians, from Spain by way of Egypt and Scythia (according to legends.) Firbolg, or Men With Bags is supposed by some to be merely the Gaelic way of pronouncing or indicating Belgae, which if correct, would seem to point to a Continental or Brythonic affinity.

Regarding Oriental phases in the Celtic language, you are doubtless right in attaching little significance to it. Indeed, the likenesses of Gaelic to Semitic, seem too slight to warrant basing any theory upon them — though the thought is entirely too fascinating from a fictional point of view for me to ever abandon it entirely. I quote here all the evidence I have been able to find that points to a linking of the languages — scanty, I will admit, nor do I indeed put it forth to hold up any theory of mine. I quote from O'Reilly and O'Donovan's *Irish-English Dictionary* published by Duffy and Co., Dublin, more than thirty years ago. No very modern authority, to be sure.

"The old Irish, began their alphabet with the letter B, and therefore the Irish called it Beith-luis-nion from its first three letters."

(This agrees with certain Eastern races, though it is certainly but a trivial point.)

"However, in imitation of other learned languages, and particularly the Latin . . . . . . the modern Irish thought proper to begin their alphabet with A. This letter . . . . is not unlike the Hebrew Aleph, and the Chaldaean and Greek Alpha."

Concerning the word Bel-ain, meaning the circle of Belus or the Sun, it is said: "Ain or ainn in Irish signifies a great circle; and Bel or Beal was the Assyrian, Chaldaean, or Phoenician name of the true God, while the patriarchal religion was generally observed. This name was afterwards attributed to the Sun when those oriental nations generally forgot, or willingly served from the worship of the true God and adored that planet as their chief deity. It is very certain that the primitive Irish observed this idolatrous worship of the Sun under the name of Bel or Beal, whatever part of the world they derived it from, as appears very manifestly by those religious fires they lighted with great solemnity on May day; a fact which is evidently proved by the very name whereby they distinguished that day, which is still called and known by no other name than that of La Beal tinne, i.e. the day of the fire of Bel or Belus. . . . . I shall finish these remarks with observing that the word Ain or Ainn, is the Celtic original upon which the Latin word Anus was formed; it was afterward written Annus . . . . to mean solely and properly the solar circle or annual course of the Sun."

"The name of this consonant (B) in Irish approaches much closer in sound and letters to the Hebrew name of the said letter, than either the Chaldean Betha or the Greek Beta, it being in Irish Beith and in Hebrew Beth. Beth signifies a house in Hebrew, and Both in Irish is a very common name for an open house or tent. It is to be observed that the Irish consonants, b, c, d, g, p, t, by a full point or tittle set over any of them, do thereby lose their simple strong sound, and pronounce after the manner of the Hebrew bh, ch, dh, gh, ph, th, which are simply and genuinely aspirated; on the other hand, it is to be particularly noticed, that the now-mentioned Hebrew consonants, by them called Begad-Kephat, memoria causa, by fixing a dagesch or full point in the middle of any of them, do thereby also lose their simple aspirate sound and pronounce strong like the Irish b, c, d, g, p, t; so that the addition of a full point to the above mentioned Hebrew consonants changes them into their corresponding letters of the Irish. By this kind of reciprocation between the Irish and Hebrew languages, the antiquity of the Irish or Celtic seems to be sufficiently demonstrated; although it must be confessed that the using a full point in either of the languages is of a late invention."

"The Irish D also agrees with Gr. Th or Theta, in like manner with the Hebrew Daleth or Dh, which, by putting a full point over it, becomes a D. The Irish language is industriously censured by some critics for admitting a superfluous D or Dh at the end of several words . . . . . . And we find a near coincidence of that redundancy in the Hebrew language; thus in the Hebrew raah, to see, leah, to toil or labor, etc., the final letter He or h, is not pronounced, but, like the Irish Dh, becomes a mute or quiescent letter.

"It (E) is in Irish called eabha, the aspen-tree; and is not unlike the Heb. heth.

"It (F) is called fearn, the elder tree. It is the same with the Hebrew vau, because the figure and sound of both letters are very nearly the same.

"(G) The very figure of the letter g, in some of our old parchments, is not essentially dissimilar to some of the cuts of the old Abrahamic and Phoenician gimel. The Hebrews call this letter gimel, as we are assured by grammarians, from its crooked figure, bearing some resemblance to a camel, which in Hebrew is called gamel or gamal; and to observe it, by the by, gamal, as well as camal, is the Irish for a camel.

"(M) We think it well worth observing here, that our language bears a perfect resemblance, in the disposition of its pronouns, to the manner of ordering them in the Hebrew; for the latter divide them into classes etc. .The prepositive are set before words, and the subjunctive are written in the end of words; both equally determine the person.

"(N) It is called Nuin, the ash tree. In Hebrew it is called Nun, from the sound

"(O) It is the positive vowel of the diphthong oir, the spindle tree; and we find this diphthong in the Hebrew: as, Heb., Goi, Lat., gens.

"(P) The Greeks, to observe it, by the by, have taken their (word for tower or castle) from the Phoenicians, their first instructors in letters, in whose language it is Borg, which is plainly of the same root with our Irish word brog or brug, a strong or fortified place, also a lord's court or castle; whence the

French Bourg, the German Burgh, and English Borough, do in a larger sense signify a town. We find the like affinity in many words between the Greek and Latin and Irish languages: as, Ir. cairg and carga, Easter; Latin, pascha, and Chaldaice, pascha, which is derived from the Hebrew Pasach or Phase; Lat., transitus, the Passover. It hath been observed before that the Lingua Prisca, or the primitive Latin tongue, was chiefly formed upon the Celtic and the truth of this assertion is abundantly confirmed through the whole course of this dictionary. Celtic coib, Lingua Prisca cobiae, Latin copiae."

The remarks regarding Celtic likenesses to Greek and Latin and other Aryan languages are of course, beside the point. Nor is there any particular reason, I admit, in supposing that the Semitic semblances are other than mere coincidence or later additions to the language, borrowed, perhaps, from the Latin. However, I can not but believe that the ancient world was knit more closely together than is generally supposed.

As refers to the worship of Bel, I have read somewhere that the Celtic term Bally, meaning town refers to Baal, the Semitic god, which worship, it is averred by some was introduced into Ireland by Phoenician traders and settlers after the Milesian invasion (setting the date of that invasion further back than is generally accepted) or was brought into Ireland by the Gaels themselves. But attempting to untangle legends and find some phase on which they all agree, would seem to be an endless task — too puzzling for my scant knowledge, even if I could read them in the original. One legend for instance, has the Gaels wandering into Egypt to serve as mercenaries, just at the time the Hebrews are leaving, and another legend has it that the Milesians were already well settled in the Egyptian barracks when the Jews arrived, and that it was malcontents among the Gaels who went into Goshan and stirred up the Hebrews to revolt. Another legend makes a powerful Irish family named Cusac the progenitors of the Cossack race, while of course you are familiar with the many tales of the Lia Fail, the Stone of Destiny which Jeremiah (reputed to be a Jap named Gera mia, Giver of Stones) is supposed to have brought into Ireland with him and on which the present English kings are crowned.

I have read an interesting theory put forth by some historian whose name I cannot now recall, (I can remember faces and events but find it almost impossible to remember names and dates) but as closely as I can remember his idea was something like this: That western Europe was first settled by a nomadic tribe of Celts whose language was the basis of modern Gaelic; that these primitive Gaels were driven into the outer fringes by the more powerful Brythons who became Gauls, Belgae and Cymri. That the legend of Partholan refers to the first settlement of Ireland by these Gaels, and that the plague to which is ascribed their destruction really refers to an invasion by Britons, who dispossessed them of the more fertile parts of the island. That the Fomorians, Nemedians, Firbolg and Tuatha De Danaans were various waves of Brythonic peoples from the larger island. That meanwhile a powerful branch of Gaels had taken refuge in the mountains of Spain or southern Gaul, where they resisted the assaults of the Brythonic Gauls, and retained all their tribal characteristics, as a primitive race of mountaineers is likely to do, and that it was these people, who, giving way before the Romans, crossed over into Ireland and became the

Milesians of legend. He explains their relationship to various tribes of Ireland by the fact that many of Partholan's Gaelic descendants still maintained a desultory warfare with the conquering Britons.

His theory seems plausible in many ways, though I do not concur in all his suppositions. Of course, I really have no right to quarrel with a historian, but when the historians quarrel among themselves, even such a slightly informed layman as myself is likely to draw his own conclusions. I am ready to accept the above mentioned idea that the Gaels came to Ireland from Spain or southern Gaul; indeed, the legends seem to confirm that, if legends can be said to confirm any historical fact. But I strongly doubt the assertion that the Gaels preceded the Brythons into any part of western Europe, and I hold — with the obstinacy of ignorance no doubt — that the Gaels followed an entirely different route into Europe than that taken by the Brythons. I am probably all wrong, but I believe that the Gauls or Brythons are supposed to have come out of Central Asia, crossing northern Russia, possibly the Scandinavian countries, and coming down into France through Germany.

I have no real reason to uphold my belief, but I believe that the Gaels came the other way — the southern route, so to speak, across Asia Minor and Africa and up into Spain. This trek must have taken place at a very early date, in the first dim dawn of history when the movements of all tribes and nations were very vague and easily lost to the recorders. They probably lived for many centuries in southern Gaul before they went into Ireland.

But as I said, my ideas and sources of information are so nebulous that they are not worth imposing on anyone. I won't ramble in this direction any further except to say that in regard to the relationship of the Gaels to tribes already in Ireland, I do not imagine that the Gaelic invasion was a sudden flood of entirely unknown people. I suspect that Gaels had been filtering into Ireland for some time in one way or another, and there were probably a number of settlements in various parts of the island, doubtless near the coasts.

Professor Smith's[2] deductions are interesting, though I cannot say that I agree with all of them. I believe, like you, that civilization is a natural and inevitable consequence, whether good or evil I am not prepared to state. As to the single civilization theory — no doubt the Egyptian culture greatly influenced the rest of the world to a large extent, though I had thought that as early as 6000 B.C. the pre-Semitic Sumerians had a civilization somewhat superior to the contemporary Egyptian one. Perhaps the Grecian culture had a basis of Egyptian, transmitted through the conquered Cretans, though it appears to me that the Hellenic invaders, rather than adopting it as their own, reared a separate civilization on the ruins of the Mycenic civilization. I cannot think that the Nile valley culture affected the people of China, Mexico and South America overly much, though there may have been more intercourse between these early races than we think. Possibly, as he says, later Neolithic races were contemporary with the Eastern civilizations; I seem to have read somewhere that the early Cretans were supposed to have been in the tag end of their own particular New Stone Age when they first came into the knowledge of the Egyptians. That seems to me to be a more or less minor point.

And now I come to a point where I must impose on your good nature. I mean by that, I am about to ask a number of questions about subjects wherein my ignorance is exceeded only by my interest. Let me first say, in partial explanation of my lack of information on the subjects about which I am going to inquire, that my failure to inform myself has been less lack of interest than lack of opportunity. Western Texas is no particular seat of culture, and it is almost impossible to obtain books on obscure and esoteric subjects anywhere in the state. The greater part of my life has been spent on ranches, farms and in boom towns, where there were quite often neither book shops nor libraries within a hundred miles, and my studies were mainly in snatches, in spare moments when I was not working at something else. Only the last few years have I been able to devote the greater part of my time to writing and studying, so you can readily see why my education is not all it should be.

But the questions. I have noted in your stories you refer to Cthulhu, Yog Sothoth, R'lyeh, Yuggoth etc. Adolph de Castro, I note, mentions these gods, places, or whatever they are, only the spelling is different, as Cthulutl, Yog Sototl.[3] Both you and he, I believe, have used the phrase fhtaghn. A writer in the Eyrie, a Mr. O'Neail, I believe, wondered if I did not use some myth regarding this Cthulhu in "Skull Face". The name Kathulos might suggest that, but in reality, I merely manufactured the name at random, not being aware at the time of any legendary character named Cthulhu — if indeed there is.

Would it be asking too much to ask you to tell me the significance of the above mentioned names or terms? And the Arab Alhazred, and the *Necronomicon*. The mention of these things in your superb stories have whetted my interest immensely. I would extremely appreciate any information you would give me regarding them.

Hoping to hear from you again, and again thanking you for an opportunity of reading your poems,

Sincerely,
[Robert E. Howard]

NOTES

1. *Fungi From Yuggoth.*
2. Probably Sir Grafton Elliot Smith, 1871 – 1937.
3. In de Castro's "The Electric Executioner."

TSS: 50343, 64523, 64524, 50346, 50347

138. To Tevis Clyde Smith, ca. early September 1930.

Well, Fear Finn:

I hope you'll sell the dueling story.[1] Thanks for the addition to my already long list of notable relatives. Admittedly, Uncle Terence was something of a family scape-goat, but he redeemed himself at Shiloh; even my great-aunts admitted there must have been some good in the lousy sonofabitch. But he shouldn't have taken part in the battle at all; he was too drunk to duck.

Truett and I had a good time — leastways, I did and I reckon he did. And by the way — I'm going to write a history of early Texan days some time, entitled: *An Unborn Empire* or something like that. You won't have any objection to me using your articles as instances of Texas romance, will you? Of course, I'll give you full credit and cite your news stories as references. By gad, we'll make history, yet.

I got a letter from Lovecraft and he referred to August Derleth; you know, the fellow that writes the very short stories that appear regularly in *Weird Tales.* I was amazed to learn that Derleth is only twenty-one years old. He must have started writing when he was about ten. Lovecraft says he wishes he had the dough to travel all over hellandback, or words to that effect. Gad — he does more than I do. The first letter I got from him, he'd just gotten back from a month's trip; the next he'd been up to Salem, and Marblehead and Boston. The next letter, he'd gotten back from Boston, I believe and was just fixing to go up in Massachusetts to visit the Frank Belknap Long Jr. family for five days. This latest letter was mailed in Backbay, Boston, and he said he was writing it while on his way to Quebec. He said he'd never seen Europe, but craved to and intended to do so. I was surprized to learn that he occasionally got stuff rejected, also Clark Ashton Smith, who must be no spring chicken, as Lovecraft told me Clark Ashton had out a volume of verse as early as 1910. Wandrei, he said, a very fine poet whose works appear every now and then in *Weird Tales*, is only twenty-two. I'm beginning to believe the poetry-business is a lot like the fight game — most of the poets do their best work early in life. But I'll bet Lovecraft is older than most of the others. I think if I get time, I'll write to Derleth, Smith, Long Jr., Dwyer, Wandrei, Danziger and Arthur Machen. Lovecraft says that he's having Long send me his "loan-copy" of verse — all that's left of his publishings. He says it's a pity that Long, like himself, has to grind out his energies in hack work. And say — a tip on *Science Wonder Stories.* Lovecraft tells me Clark Ashton is hesitating over a contract for a series of interplanetary novelettes, because the management of the magazine is shady in money matters.

Speaking of Derleth, Lovecraft says: "His work in *W.T.* does not represent him at all, being merely pot-boiling hack material; but his really serious products (on the order of Marcel Proust) display qualities amounting almost to genius."

Weird Tales announces for next month's issue my story, "Kings of the Night" — ($120.00). Some ways this story is the best I ever wrote. Nothing very weird about it, but good battle stuff, if I do say so myself.

They cast her out of the court of the king
Into the night and the dust,
For even to lustful kings there comes
An end to a maddening lust.

Naked she lay in the filthy dust,
Under the star-dimmed skies,
And the serving wenches trod her down
And spat between her thighs.

They pressed their buttocks to her lips
In the lust of their wanton play;
The mute black slaves stole out of the courts
And raped her where she lay.

Gaunt midnight changed the haunted skies;
Her limbs flexed on the ground;
The ragged beggars slunk from their lairs
And snarled like wolves around.

Her lovers were thieves with faces scarred,
Her couch was dung and dust,
And she drowned the beggars one by one
In the deeps of her chartless lust.

There came a man in the dark of dawn,
As a wolf that scatters curs,
And the filth she wallowed in could not hide
The beauty that was hers.

"Mylitta, goddess of whoredom, thanks!"
He quoth with his eyes ablaze,
"I have found her at last for whom I have sought
"For a day and a million days!

"Weak are the women in whose white arms
"I have mocked with evil mirth,
"But here is the wench that was made for me
"In the dawnlight of the earth!

"Mine are the lusts of hoofs and horns,
"Of the he-goat and the loon,
"And the naked witches that demons deflower
"On the dark side of the moon.

"No common sin may fire my eyes,
"Glutted with excess fell —
"My lust is stained with the dung that stirs
"On the stinking streets of Hell.

"Daughter of Evil, all foul things
"Sat down when down you sat —
"Come — we will build a tower of sin
For eons to shudder at."

Translation from the original Sanscrit — or is it Sanskrit? — of Partha Mac Othna. This translation was first published in London in 1548 and the first edition is invaluable. This is because there is a comma on page 345 which is lacking on all later editions. Therefore, a first edition brings $10,000 while you can pick up the other editions anywhere for fifteen cents.

Fear Dunn

NOTES

1. Published as "Fashions in Duels," Dallas *News*, November 30, 1930. The story states that Terence Corcoran's diary is "now in the possession of his great-grandnephew, Robert E. Howard of Cross Plains..."

TSS: 82137-82138

ଔଓଔଓ

139. To Tevis Clyde Smith, ca. September 1930.

Well, Fear Finn, me bauld braw Hieland bully, I take typewriter in hand to write youse a letter. Where did you and Truett spend the week end — Austin?

I've been lazy; doing very little work. I haven't even got anything out at present. Since seeing you I sold, "Waterfront Law" to Fiction House. Yeah, a Steve Costigan; a new and original plot: Steve engages in a bloody battle to get some money which a crooked woman gypps him out of. They offered me $70.00. I've got to figure some way of making these stories longer. They've been too short lately.

I got a letter from Lovecraft wherein he tells me, much to my chagrin, that Cthulhu, R'lyeh, Yuggoth, YogSothoth, and so on are figments of his own imagination. He says: "The reason for its echoes in Dr. de Castro's work is that the latter gentleman is a revision-client of mine — into whose tales I have stuck these glancing references for sheer fun. If any other clients of mine get work placed in *W.T.*, you will perhaps find a still wider spread of the cult of Azathoth, Cthulhu, and the Great Old Ones. The *Necronomicon* of the mad Arab Abdul Alhazred is likewise something which must yet be written in order to possess objective reality. Abdul is a favorite dream-character of mine — indeed, that is what I used to call myself when I was five years old and a transported devotee of Andrew Lang's version of the *Arabian Nights*. A few years ago I prepared a mock-erudite synopsis of Abdul's life, and of the posthumous vicissitudes and translations of his hideous and unmentionable work *Al Azif* (called — some blighting Greek word — by the Byzantine (something) Theodoras Philetas, who translated it into late Greek in A.D. 900!) — a synopsis which I shall follow in future references to the dark and accursed thing. Long has alluded to the *Necronomicon* in some things of his — in fact, I think it is rather good fun to have this artificial mythology given an air of versimilitude (?) by aside citation. Clark Ashton Smith is (something) another mock anthology, revolving around the black, furry toad-god Tsathoggua, whose name had variant forms amongst the Atlanteans, Lemurians, and Hyperboreans who worshipped him after he emerged from inner Earth (whither he came from Outer Space, with Saturn as a stepping stone). I am using Tsathoggua in several tales of my own and of revision-clients' — although Wright rejected the Smith tale in which he originally appeared. It would be amusing to identify your Kathulos with my Cthulhu — indeed, I may so adopt him in some future black allusion. Incidentally, Long and I often debate about the real folklore basis of Machen's nightmare witch cults (referring here, I guess to "The Red Hand" and so on). I think they are Machen's own inventions, for I never heard of them elsewhere; but Long cannot get over the idea that they have an actual source in European myth. Can you give us any light on this? We haven't the temerity to ask Machen himself."

Naturally I know nothing about it, but I'm going to tell Lovecraft if he'll give me Machen's address, I'll write and ask him about it. I'd like to know myself. And I'm going to ask Lovecraft if I can use his mythology in my own junk, — allusions, you understand. You know, there's a scholarly bunch of men writing for *Weird Tales* — myself excepted, of course. Well, I have a smattering of various bits of knowledge, and a facile and deceptive mind that should gain me admittance in various scholarly circles. I suppose a person meeting me for the first time would get the erroneous idea that I am well read, for if I do say so, I have a knack of discussing things I know nothing about. Closer acquaintance discloses the fact that my erudition is all superficial — reckon that's why intellectual people lose interest in me so damn quick. Well — I've got work to do. I can't spend much of my time in acquiring deep knowledge, and if I could, I wouldn't.

Will you answer my letter soon, you loathsome reptile?

Fear Dunn

TSS: 82141

140. To H.P. Lovecraft, ca. September 1930.

Dear Mr. Lovecraft:

I envy you your sojourn in Quebec. From what I have read and heard of the city, it is indeed the most archaic city in the New World. I should like very much to go prying around in out-of-the-way places, redolent with the musk and decay of antiquity — but I've never had the time or money.

I am highly obligated to both yourself and Mr. Long for the loan of *A Man from Genoa*. I have not gotten the book yet, mail service being rather irregular in this part of the world, but I am looking forward to its perusal with the greatest anticipation.

I was amazed to learn that August W. Derleth is only twenty-one. He must have begun marketing his work at a very early age, for it seems that I have been reading his stories in *Weird Tales* for years. My friends and I have often commented on the excellence of his products and wondered why he did not try his hand at longer stories.

I have noted Mr. Dwyer's letters in the Eyrie, and remember the poem you mention.[1] I cannot at present recall Mr. Talman, though I have undoubtedly read stories by that author. Thank you very much for giving me the addresses of these gentlemen, also Donald Wandrei's. I am usually so busy I don't know when I'll have time to write them, but I mean to do so as soon as possible. Correspondence with such gentlemen, as with yourself, is a rare treat and an honor.

As regarding the Persians, and their relation toward the Aryan race as a whole, about the only difference between them and the Mesopotamian races seems to me to be a more kindly attitude on the part of the Persians toward conquered races. They were cruel, but we do not find the systematic and continual butchery of subjugated peoples as was the case with the Semitic races. To me there is a strange and powerful fascination about this wayward branch on the Aryan tree; it stirs my imagination to contemplate those proud, half-naked blond savages riding down out of their mountain fastnesses to ravage the rich lands of the plains — their whirlwind conquests and appallingly swift moral and physical disintegration. Indeed Croesus might say he conquered his conquerors, for Lydia's looted wealth played havoc with those hardy barbarians. I suppose a strong Turanian strain had filtered into the Persian blood-stream before they came into the plains. We read that their youths were trained to do only three things: ride, speak the truth and bend the bow. If you will notice, the bow is basically a non-Aryan weapon, and one which the Persians must have taken from some Oriental neighbor. The Greeks never esteemed its use, and archery was little thought of in Rome's regular legions, though their auxiliaries practised the science effectively. The western races seemed partial to hand-to-hand fighting, a natural preference, considering their superior strength and stature.

The Celts were not bowmen, nor were the Germans. True, no Eastern nation ever equalled the skill and science of the medieval English archers but I think even this can be traced indirectly to non-Aryan influence. The Normans brought the bow into England and it was arrows that decided the day at Senlac. But the bow came into France with Hrolf and his Norsemen, and the Danes particularly had been using the weapon skillfully for centuries. It is very likely that the Scandinavian peoples learned the effectiveness of the bow while still roaming the steppes of Northern Asia, by contact with some bow-and-arrow Turanian people, and brought that knowledge with them when they overflowed over Greater Sweden, into the Baltic countries and later all over the world. Of course, I do not mean that they really introduced the bow to the other western nations as a hither-to unknown weapon. But I mean that my belief is that archery as an art and science of war, originated with the Mongoloid races, was imparted to the eastern-most ancestors of the Danes and was spread by them over Europe.

For the bow is connected and interwoven with Oriental history from the very dawn of history. We read of the prowess of the Pharaohs, shooting from their war-chariots and slaying lions and Hittites impartially; the Philistines give back from the fury of Saul and shower him with shafts from a distance; the Babylonians and Assyrians war with heavy bows, curved in an exaggerated fashion; the Persians and Scythians exchange heavy flights of whistling shafts before they close in battle. And to come to a more recent date — the Roman legions reel before the cloud of Parthian arrows, the Crusaders fall before the Turkish bows, and the wild riders of Attila, Genghis Khan and Tamerlane wipe out whole armies without coming to sword-points.

As regards the Armenians, I am inclined to the theory that they represent a race whose original type was Semitic, who fell so completely under the dominion of their Aryan conquerors that they forgot their original Semitic language, and retained the later-acquired speech through following centuries of re-Semitizing.

I agree with you that the Tuscans influenced Roman physiognomy and character greatly. And that brings up another question — who were the Tuscans and from where did they come? I would certainly like to see your views on the subject.

I shall watch for the tale, "Medusa's Coil,"[2] you mentioned. Regardless of the author, if you instilled into the tale some of the magic of your own pen, it cannot fail to fascinate the readers.

As regards African-legend sources, I well remember the tales I listened to and shivered at, when a child in the "piney woods" of East Texas, where Red River marks the Arkansas and Texas boundaries. There were quite a number of old slave darkies still living then. The one to whom I listened most was the cook, old Aunt Mary Bohannon who was nearly white — about one sixteenth negro, I should say. Mistreatment of slaves is, and has been somewhat exaggerated, but old Aunt Mary had had the misfortune, in her youth, to belong to a man whose wife was a fiend from Hell. The young slave women were fine young animals, and barbarically handsome; her mistress was frenziedly jealous. You understand. Aunt Mary told tales of torture and unmistakable sadism that sickens me to this day when I think of them. Thank God the slaves on my ancestors' plantations were never so misused. And Aunt Mary told how one day, when the black people were in the fields, a hot wind swept over them and they knew that "ol' Misses Bohannon" was dead. Returning to the manor house they found that it was so and the slaves danced and shouted with joy. Aunt Mary said that when a good spirit passes, a breath of cool air follows; but when an evil spirit goes by a blast from the open doors of Hell follows it.

She told many tales, one which particularly made my hair rise; it occurred in her youth. A young girl going to the river for water, met, in the dimness of dusk, an old man, long dead, who carried his severed head in one hand. This, said Aunt Mary, occurred on the plantation of her master, and she herself saw the girl come screaming through the dusk, to be whipped for throwing away the water-buckets in her flight.

Another tale she told that I have often met with in negro-lore. The setting, time and circumstances are changed by telling, but the tale remains basically the same. Two or three men — usually negroes — are travelling in a wagon through some isolated district — usually a broad, deserted river-bottom. They come on to the ruins of a once thriving plantation at dusk, and decide to spend the night in the deserted plantation house. This house is always huge, brooding and forbidding, and always, as the men approach the high columned verandah, through the high weeds that surround the house, great numbers of pigeons rise from their roosting places on the railing and fly away. The men sleep in the big front-room with its crumbling fire-place, and in the night they are awakened by a jangling of chains, weird noises and groans from upstairs. Sometimes footsteps descend the stairs with no visible cause. Then a terrible apparition appears to the men who flee in terror. This monster, in all the tales I have heard, is invariably a headless giant, naked or clad in shapeless sort of garment, and is sometimes armed with a broad-axe. This motif appears over and over in negro-lore. I do not know what sort of tales modern darkies tell. For years I have lived in a section where negroes are very rare. Indeed, no colored person is allowed to remain over night in this county.

But through most of the stories I heard in my childhood, the dark, brooding old plantation house loomed as a horrific back-ground and the human or semi-human horror, with its severed head was woven in the fiber of the myths.

But no negro ghost-story ever gave me the horrors as did the tales told by my grandmother. All the gloominess and dark mysticism of the Gaelic nature was hers, and there was no light and mirth at her. Her tales showed what a strange legion of folk-lore grew up in the Scotch-Irish settlements of the Southwest, where transplanted Celtic myths and fairy-tales met and mingled with a sub-stratum of slave legends. My grandmother was but one generation removed from south Ireland and she knew by heart all the tales and superstitions of the folks, black or white, about her.

As a child my hair used to stand straight up when she would tell of the wagon that moved down wilderness roads in the dark of the night, with never a horse drawing it — the wagon that was full of severed heads and dismembered limbs; and the yellow horse, the ghastly dream horse that raced up and down the stairs of the grand old plantation house where a wicked woman lay dying; and the ghost-switches that swished against doors when none dared open those doors lest reason be blasted at what was seen. And in many of her tales, also, appeared the old, deserted plantation mansion, with the weeds growing rank about it and the ghostly pigeons flying up from the rails of the verandah.

There is a legend that was quite popular in its day in the Southwest, which I am unable to place. That is, I cannot decide whether it is one of the usual inconsistencies negro-folk-lore often displays, or a deliberate Irish invention, intended to be a bull. That is the one about the headless woman, who strange to say, was often heard grinding her teeth in the angle of the chimney, and whose long hair flowed down her back!

Negroes are an interesting study. There used to be darkies who vowed they could see the wind, and that it was reddish in color. They said that's why the pigs squealed so when it began to get cold — they too could see the wind and were afraid of it. And there was one Arabella Davis, I remember, whom I used to see, when a child, going placidly about town collecting washing — I mean when I was a kid, not Arabella. She was a black philosopher, if there was ever one. Her little grand-daughter tagged after her, everywhere she went, carrying Arabella's pipe, matches and tobacco with as much pomposity as a courtier ever carried the train of a queen.

Arabella was born in slavery, but her memories were of a later date. She often told of her conversion, when the spirit of the Lord was so strong upon her that she went for ten days and nights without eating or sleeping. She went into a trance, she said, and for days the fiends of Hell pursued her through the black mountains and the red mountains. For four days she hung in the cobwebs on the gates of Hell, and the hounds of Hell bayed at her. Is that not a splendid sweep of imagination? And the strangest part is, it was so true and realistic to her, that she would have been amazed had anyone questioned her veracity.

But here I am rambling on indefinitely. Thank you very much for the kind things you said about the "Bran-cult." I notice the current *Weird Tales* announces my "Kings of the Night" for next month's issue. I hope you like the story. Bran is one of the "Kings". I intend to take your advice about writing a series of tales dealing with Bran. If you can get Machen's address from Mr. Derleth, I'll see what I can do. If Machen answers my inquires at all, his reply should be very interesting. I have always been fascinated by his work, though I will say, frankly and with no intent to flatter, that I consider him inferior to yourself as a horror story writer.

I hope you will have — or possibly I should say, will have had, when this letter reaches you — an enjoyable visit in Quebec. I repeat I envy you. It has been so long since I have taken a trip of any kind, I feel as if I were taking root. For instance, it has been two years since I have been across the Mexican Border. I live in a section of the country not particularly stimulating to the imagination, unless the inhabitants continual struggle against starvation can be said to be a stimulant. The drouth hit this country hard, and please do not think I exaggerate when I say that many tenant-farmers and their families are at present subsisting entirely on parched corn. There is no grass; the people eat the corn that belongs by right to the farm-horses, and the farm-horses eat mesquite beans. Soon the beans will be gone and the horses will die; the people will die too, unless the government aids them.

But I have rambled long enough; pardon me if much that I have said has been boresome.

Most cordially yours,
[Robert E. Howard]

P.S. Thank you very much for the picture of Paul Revere's home. I note that it is surrounded by stores and shops of Italians. It's a pity that all the landmarks of American history seem to be in the process of being swamped by the tide of foreign invasion. The same process is going on on the Gulf Coast, and in the Rio Grande valley country.

R.E.H.

P.S.S. I have received Mr. Long's book since writing the above; I have not yet had time for a proper study of it, but from my first perusal, I can see the poems come up fully to all expectations.

R.E.H.

NOTES

1. Bernard Austin Dwyer's "Ol' Black Sarah," *Weird Tales*, October 1928.
2. Revised by H.P. Lovecraft for Zealia Reed Bishop, this story was not published until January 1939.

TSS: 26261-26264

◆

141. To H.P. Lovecraft, ca. September 1930.

Dear Mr. Lovecraft:

I am very glad that you enjoyed your visit to Quebec so much, and your vivid description of the city fills me with an intense desire to see it for myself. It must indeed seem a detached fragment of an older world. Your description of your voyage, and the sunset view of Boston harbor fascinated me as much as your stories have fascinated me. It must indeed be a unique sensation to a landsman to see only billowing waves for horizons. A sensation I have yet to experience. Outside of a steamboat ride or so on the Mississippi and a few short launch rides on the Gulf, my experiences on the water have amounted to nothing. Thank you for the post card pictures.

I have re-read *A Man from Genoa* many times and each reading has strengthened my first estimate of the author — that he is truly a magnificent poet.

I quite agree with your praise of Mr. H. Warner Munn. I have been reading his work in *Weird Tales* for many years and consider it of the highest quality. I should like very much to see the history of light weird fiction you say he is preparing, as well as your own survey.[1] I believe you said your article was published in *The Recluse*. Do you suppose I could obtain a copy containing it?

Your remarks on the Etruscans interested me very much. I am sure you are right in believing them to be of a very composite type of Semite and Aryan. It's a pity no more is known about them; doubtless their full history was a spectacular pageant of wars, intrigues and culture development. Where did they have their beginning? What unknown tribes went into their making? Was it conquest, friendship or pressure from some common foe which brought together and mingled these alien race-stocks into one people? Was this mingling accomplished in three or four generations or did it require the passing of a thousand years? In what secluded valley did these people slowly and peacefully climb the ladder of evolution or over what waste-lands were they harried by what nameless enemies? Did they spring into being in Italy, or did they come from some far land? And if the latter, what drove them from their original home-land and what chance flung them on the Italian coasts? These are questions whose answers we doubtless shall never know, and after all, may be asked of almost any race.

I was also interested in the theory of type-differences in the Semitic races, of which I had never heard before. It sounds very plausible, for there always seemed to me to be a basic difference between, say the Bedouin Arab and the Jew, even allowing for the long centuries of different environment and ways of living. That is an aspect of history full of dramatic possibilities; a clean cut divergence of type existing back to the very dawns of time. An ancient feud between the ancestors of the desert dweller and the fertile valley dweller, symbolized by Cain and Abel and by Esau and Jacob. The real basis of the Arab's hatred for the Hebrew having its roots in primordial racial feud rather than religious differences of comparatively modern times. I must weave that thought into a story some day.

Your remarks about the early history of Rhode Island were highly educational to me. I am so confoundedly ignorant about the history of my own country. I only knew, vaguely, that in its early days Rhode Island was a wealthy, tolerant and non-Puritan state. It's a pity the Revolution played such havoc with the plantations. I imagine, that, as you say, there has been a great deal of literary tampering with the original folk-lore of the state. You are right too, in remarking that what is close at hand tends, ordinarily to lack interest.

For instance, I have been repeatedly urged to make an article or tale of a certain murder-ranch which lies several miles west of here, and on which, some thirty years ago, a series of unspeakably ghastly crimes were enacted, and on which skeletons are every now and then found to this day. However, I have not the slightest idea of putting it on paper — more especially as one of the men who committed some of those crimes is still living and at large!

You are quite correct in saying that demonry of one's own race is more real and vivid than that of some other race. That is why, I suppose, that tales of Puritan New England and such Scandinavian sagas as that one dealing with

Grettir the Strong and his battle with the vampire, seem more gripping and grisly than stories of Indian magic and negro voo-doo.

What a deformed branch of the tree of progress that witch-craft phase of Puritan New England became! To what basis do you attribute it — religious fanaticism stretched beyond human boundaries and producing abnormalities, or an inherent abnormality in the people that produced the fanaticism? To me the aspect of that age and its people is beyond all comprehension. I frankly cannot begin to fathom the dark mental perversity that brought such grisly Chimerae into being. A fantastic idea presents itself to me persistently, that the littoral had something to do with it; perhaps the cold New England winters that cooped people into houses and turned back the pages of time to the ice-fringed shores and snowy forests these peoples ancestors knew before they came into England. We know that the Scandinavian peoples are prone to dark brooding and paranoidal impulses. Can it not be that the cold, overcast skies, the brooding hills and dark mysterious woods brought forth a latent insanity lurking in these persecuted and creed ridden people? Lingering racial memories and superstitious fears breaking from the long sleep of centuries to take on monstrous shapes.

I have long been sure that there was Celtic blood in your veins and sure, it is great honor is due you as a descendent of the great O'Neills. How many times has my blood tingled to read of the deeds of Shane and Hugh and Eoghain Ruadh!

Teutonic horror-tales, as you say, have a quality all their own, and most grisly, striking a different note than the lore of more southerly races. As regards your own horror-story style I would say that it is basically Gothic, but that it is not handicapped by the too-ponderous, rather unwieldy and rather barren narrative style we are apt to associate with Teutonic literature. The Celtic influence is readily seen, to my mind, in the smoothly flowing style of your tales. Altogether, if I may venture to say so, your horror-work seems to me to lean toward the Gothic in conception and the Celtic in execution. You certainly seem to have as much connection with Celtic tradition as Machen.

As for myself, I can lay scant claim to either school, my tales being more on the action-adventure style than the true horror-story. If I had any particular method, I suppose it should be Celtic, since the great part of my blood is of that race. My branch of the Howards came to America in 1733 and the first of the American line married an Irish girl, an example from which no Howard has since deviated, to my knowledge. Behind my English name are lines of purely Gaelic Eiarbhins, O'Tyrrells, Colquhouns, MacEnrys, and Norman-Irish Martuins, De Colliers, FitzHenrys. Yet there is a Scandinavian strain at me, for one of the MacEnrys of my line married the daughter of an Irish woman and a red-bearded Dane who first opened his eyes on the cold shores of the Skaggerack.

It seems to me that I have heard somewhere before of the "moonack" but I could not swear to it. I wish I had the time and money to go carefully through the Old South and gather negroid traditions systematically. As it is I only remember snatches heard years ago. There are very few negroes in this part of Texas and these are nothing like the "old-timey" ones.

I remember the idea of whippoorwills and psychopomps in your "Dunwich Horror" and how I was struck with the unique grisliness of the notion; did the Puritans bring the belief with them from England or did it spring up in the New World?

The tale of the murdered traveller is, as you say, quite common in all sections and reminds me of one, very old, which was once quite prevalent in the Southwest and which must be a garbled version of some legend brought over from Scotland. It deals with three brothers stopping at a lonely cabin high up in the mountains, kept by an evil old woman and her half-idiot sons. In the night they cut the throats of the older brothers, but the younger escapes. Now enters the really fantastic part of the tale. The younger brother flees across the mountains on his fleet horse and the old woman mounts and pursues, carrying a cane held high in her hand. Again and again the boy eludes her, but each time she holds the cane high and sings a sort of incantation:

"Sky-high, caney,
"Where's Toddywell?
"Way over on the Blue-ridgey mountains!
"Haw back!"

Perhaps in the original tale, the answer is given by the cane. Anyway, the cane points out the way the boy has taken and the pursuit is renewed. Eventually the fugitive gains "a pass in the mountains" and escapes. When a youngster I always shuddered at the mental picture that tale brought up — the lean and evil hag with her lank hair flying in the wind, riding hard across the dark mountains under the star-flecked skies, gripping her gory knife and halting on some high ridge to chant her fantastic incantation. But it is but one of the many bloody tales that once flourished in the Scotch-Irish settlements of the Southwest.

About that ghost-switches tale outside the door — that always struck me as being about the most grisly in its implication of any ghost-tale I ever heard — more so because of its nameless suggestions. The fault I find with so many so-called horror-tales (particularly including my own) is that the object of horror too swiftly becomes too solid and concrete. It takes a master of the pen, such as Machen and yourself, to create a proper *suggestion* of unseen and unknown horror. The illusive shadows lurking at the back of the brain are so much more monstrous and blood-chilling than the children of the actual mind. I'm not saying this like I'd like to say it. But the rustle of leaves when there is no wind, the sudden falling of a shadow across a door, the furtive trying of a window-catch, the sensation of unseen Eyes upon one, these give rise to speculations more monstrous and terrors more cosmically icy, than any chain-clanking apparition, or conventional ghost, that appears in full glory. When a writer specifically describes the object of his horror, gives it worldly dimensions and solid shape, he robs it of half its terrors. Somewhere, somehow, there must lurk in the dim gulfs of our racial memories, titanic and abysmal horrors beyond the ken of the material mind. For how else are we able to half conceive and fear entities we are not able to describe? Seek to draw their images for the conscious mind and they fade away. We cannot shape them in concrete words. Well, I seem to be repeating myself without saying yet what I'm trying to say.

But I'll say this: humanity fears floods and starvation, foes and serpents and wild beasts, but there are fears outside these concrete things. Whence come these fears from the *outside*? Surely in its infancy mankind faced beings that live today only in dim ancestral memories, forgotten entirely by the material mind. Otherwise, why is it we half-visualize in that other, subconscious mind, perhaps, shapes beyond the power of man to describe?

Your mention of the Italian invasion of New England brings up a phase of American life that always fills me with resentment: that of the overflowing of the country with low-class foreigners. I've seen it happen in Texas. The state is slowly being taken over by a South and Central European population. Louisiana is already over-run with Italians; they were brought in to work the corporation-owned plantations and they swarmed into the cities. Conditions in the Latin Quarter of New Orleans are of almost unbelievable filth and depravity.

Almost the same conditions exist in South Texas on the great cotton farms. These farms, owned largely by men in other states, are worked entirely by Mexicans. As each farm consists of from three to eight thousand acres in actual cultivation, it requires the work of many hands. A Mexican thrives on wages that would reduce a white man to starvation. I have seen the huts built for them by their employers and overseers — one roomed affairs, generally painted red, one door, two or three glassless windows. There are no chairs, beds, tables or stoves. The Mexicans sleep on rags thrown carelessly on the floor and cook their scanty meals of frijoles and tortillas on open fires outside. The death rate is enormous, the birth rate even more enormous. They live like rats and breed like flies.

But while I dislike the methods used in bringing huge droves of Mexicans across the river to stuff the ballots on election day, or to compete with white labor, still I look with tolerance on those already here, and prefer the Mexican to the Italian. After all, the Mexican has some claim to priority, for his ancestor greeted Cortez. These in Texas and along the Border are predominantly Indian; the Spanish strain is very slight. In the interior you will find many old dons of almost pure Castilian strain, living a lazy, old World sort of life on their wide-spread ranchos. But like most of the better class of foreigners, we seldom get any of that sort of immigrants.

There is a great deal of romance about these descendents of Cortez' knights. I recall just now one Ramon Macias, an aristocratic Mexican if there ever was one, son of General Macias, "Calles' Butcher", as the general was called; Ramon was a sort of black sheep. He had pure Latin features but his eyes were grey and his complexion lighter than mine, and he was a true descendent of the men that broke the Aztec empire. I saw Ramon fight one Sandi Esquival ten grueling, bruising rounds one night in San Antonio, when I knew that Ramon had a bullet in his back that prevented the proper use of his right hand. A handsome lad he was then, but a few years later I saw him again and could scarcely suppress a shudder; some bravo's knife had left a grisly scar clear across his face that twisted his lips into a permanent snarl.

But pardon me; I'm prone to wander off the subject and meander around quite aimlessly. I was speaking of the foreign influence in America. There is, for instance, a town not many miles from San Antonio called New Braunfels — a German settlement. The only non-German inhabitants are a small colony of factory workers who are looked on with much resentment by the townsmen. It's merely a bit of transplanted Germany; German architecture, German food, German language — even German laws. It's a beautiful little town, the cleanest as to appearance, of any town in Texas. You'll see portly, bearded gentlemen strolling down the streets sedately puffing at gigantic pipes, just as they must do in Potsdam, Dresden or Dusseldorf. Just a little bit of Germany, that keeps itself apart from the rest of America. They strictly obey their own laws, but they don't — or didn't — like law enforced on them by American officers and judges. This I well know, for when I was there six years ago, I was mistaken for a Ranger and thought for a bit I was going to be mobbed! And that would have been infernally embarrassing because, with the usual perversity of luck, I wasn't packing a pistol that night; had left it in the hotel.

Still, the best immigrants we get in Texas as a whole, are Germans. They are thrifty, law abiding and hard working; superior in living standards to the Mexicans and Sicilians who swarm to our coasts.

I'm sending you a picture you may find interesting: a snap-shot of the Alamo, in San Antonio. It's just about surrounded with modern buildings but it still retains some of the look of a by-gone age — built in 1728, I believe. I'm not superstitious, but standing in the Alamo I have the same sensations I've had standing under the Dueling Oaks outside New Orleans — as if the place were haunted. San Antonio is a picturesque town, with the narrow river winding in and out all through it, with its broad plazas, old missions and cathedrals, and adobe houses shouldering modern buildings.

Most cordially yours,
[Robert E. Howard]

NOTES

1. "Supernatural Horror in Literature."

TSS: 21442-21445

ଔ୫ଔ୫ଔ୫

142. To Harold Preece, ca. October 1930.

Well, Harold, how did you like my story, "The Voice of El-Lil," in the new *Oriental Stories*? I'm very well pleased with the magazine myself. But listen — if you've read the story, you probably noticed a sentence which referred to non-Aryan peoples in Connaught *and* Galway. That's the printer's mistake, not mine; I wrote "Connaught and Galloway," meaning, of course, the province in Scotland. I don't know why it was changed.

I find tales of the East extremely fascinating, and am beginning to believe that the old, old theory of Turkish-Gaelic affinity is well borne out. The races have much in common — cruelty, treachery, loyalty, fatalism, spend-thriftiness, berserk fighting rage, a love of music and poetry.

I lately sold a tale to *Oriental Stories* in which I created the most somber character I have yet attempted. The story is called "Hawks of Outremer," and I got $120 for it. The character is Cormac FitzGeoffrey: "Clean shaven and the various scars that showed on his dark, grim face lent his already formidable features a truly sinister aspect. His low, broad forehead was topped by black, square cut hair that contrasted strongly with his cold blue eyes. Son of a woman of the O'Briens and a renegade Norman knight, Goeffrey the Bastard, in whose veins, it is said, coursed the blood of William the Conqueror, Cormac had seldom known an hour's peace or ease in all his thirty years of violent life. Hated by the Irish and despised by the Normans he had payed back contempt and ill treatment with savage hate and ruthless vengeance."

One of the main things I like about Farnsworth Wright's magazines is you don't have to make your heroes such utter saints. I took Cormac FitzGeoffrey into the East on a Crusade to escape his enemies and am considering writing a series of tales about him.

The tang of fall is in the air and the whisper of autumn in the skies. Summer is waning into the yellow leaves of all the yesterdays and the heart of me is thin and old. The sky is deep and blue and mysterious with the changing of the seasons and strange thoughts stir deep in me, but age forever steals on me in the autumn of the year, and though I am young, my soul is old and wavering like a thread-bare garment outworn.

All that is deep and gloomy and Norse in me rises in my blood. I would go east into the sunshine and the nodding palm trees, but I bide and the dream of the twilight of the gods is on me, and the dreams of cold and misty lands and the ancient pessimism of the Vikings.

It seems to me, especially in the autumn, that that one vagrant Danish strain that is mine, predominates above all my Celtic blood. It is in the autumn that the wanderlust grips me, and my sleeping dreams are not of the lazy palm fringed lagoons, the desert caravans, the loud bazaars and the tropic jungles to which my waking thoughts turn, but of cold blue seas beneath a clear and frosty sky, of clean sandy fens stretching from the cold foam to blue mountains, of boats racing through the flying spray, and fishers' nets, shining like silver on the shore.

I never saw such things; yet they gleam plainly in my dreams. I see them with the eyes of old Samuel Waltser, who knew them and loved them in his youth, aye, and with the eyes of a thousand generations of blue-eyed, red-haired fishermen and sailors and Vikings behind him, who were his ancestors, and who were no less ancestors of mine.

Ah, well, I will not weary you with my vagaries.

Bob.

TSS: 92082

ᘓᘐᘓᘐ

143. To H.P. Lovecraft, ca. October 1930.

Dear Mr. Lovecraft:

It is with greatest delight that I learn Mr. Wright has accepted "The Whisperer in Darkness" and I look forward to its appearance with highest anticipation. If I had never read any of your work, the weird and cryptic fascination of the title would intrigue me, and as it is, knowing the high quality of your tales, I know that that title is a true indication of a superb piece of bizarre artistry. I only wish that the story appeared in the next issue of the magazine.

Thank you very much for *The Recluse*. I have read and re-read your article[1] with the utmost interest. You handle the subject in a clean-cut and highly intelligent manner, and certainly no one in the present literary world is more capable of dealing with that subject. I certainly wish you would enlarge this article into book form. I must admit my ignorance — the majority of the stories you mention I have never read — some I had never before even heard of. I have read most of Poe's work, a good deal of Bierce, some of Machen, Dunsany, etc., but I do not think that I ever read a line of Blackwood, for instance. I am, frankly, not at all widely read.

I am very sorry to hear that Mr. Cook[2] has had a nervous breakdown and trust he will soon be in better shape. I will indeed appreciate your obtaining Mr. Munn's sketch for me.

I am very glad that you liked "Red Thunder". I wrote it one midnight when distant thunder was rumbling through the high heaped clouds of the dark. I highly appreciate your comments on the rhyme; I neglected to tell you that I meant you to keep the copy, as well as the Alamo picture; I have several more. I intend some day to bring out a book of verse, but I doubt if it will be very soon. Some time ago I ceased sending my verses to various poetry magazines; my best efforts were usually returned with lines by the editors, expressing appreciation for the rhymes, but requesting me to contribute verses less bitter or rebellious. My answer generally was that I refused to emasculate my stuff —

poor as it was — for the empty honor of seeing my name in print. If poetry magazines paid for contributions it would be different. I find *Weird Tales* much more liberal regarding verse than most poetry magazines.

I'm sure you would enjoy San Antonio. It's not like any other Texas city — more like New Orleans in general color, but with a flavor distinctly its own. The little San Antonio river adds to its picturesqueness, being crossed in the main part of town by no less than sixteen bridges. The visible population is largely Latin, leisurely and old-world-like. You can go for blocks and never hear a word in English. Great numbers of Chinese settle in the purely Mexican quarters and amalgamate with the Latins, as well as negroes and a goodly number of Italians. The town being primarily Catholic, many old and picturesque cathedrals abound there, and just out of town are a number of old missions, some of them built before the Alamo, partly with material brought from Spain. Some of these missions are still in use. Living conditions are naturally low in San Antonio and a great deal of lawlessness exists. "The lower country" as it is called here in West Texas, swarms with mixed breeds of various nationalities who, mixing with the old lawless Scotch-Irish Texas stock, produce desperate characters. Consider the condition: the first of the Nordic breed to invade that part of Texas were pioneers in the true sense — traders and buffalo hunters pressing westward. They found colonies of Spaniards who had already merged into the Mongoloid-Indian population and become what we know as Mexicans. These first pioneers mated freely with Indian and Mexican women and spread their offspring widely. Then followed the cattlemen — always a lawless race in whatever country they are found. These, like the hunters, were mostly of English, Irish and Scotch-Irish stock, and came from the Southern states. Then, just about the time that the ranchmen were being pushed out of East Texas by the advance of the squatters — small farmers — some German prince, whose name I have forgotten, dumped a great conglomeration of Teutonic immigrants on the Texas coast. He left them to starve but the Indians fed them and they eventually founded the town of New Braunfels. A constant stream from Germany has poured into the lower country for over half a century and of late years Slavs and Latins from eastern and central Europe and Italy and Sicily have swarmed to its shores. Immigrants from the British Isles and the Scandinavian countries have been comparatively few, though many Swedes and Danes have settled on the wide plains of Northwest Texas. Forty or fifty miles west of this locality the country swarms with Swedes.

But to return to the lower country — you can see what amalgamation of the various breeds would produce in many cases; where the mixture is of Indian-Mexican, pioneering British stock, German, Polack, and Latin. Of course many of the older families, both American and German, have held themselves apart from the rabble and intermarried with their own race and with each other, but the later arrivals from Europe tend to mix and mingle without rhyme or reason.

I am much taken with your suggestion for tying up the Etruscans with an Elder World civilization and mean to have a fling at it some day, though my notions about them now are so hazy that it will require a great deal of study of their ways and customs before I would be able to write intelligently about them.

I am inclined to agree with you that the Assyrians and Phoenicians were of Alpine-Semitic stock, also about the Jews. It is evident that the present day Hebraic race has little in common with the original wandering, fighting type. I wonder if that Alpine type could have been the result of admixture with Turanian races? It is said that the Assyrian's physiognomy was much like the present day Russian Jew's, and we know that the Jews of Russia and Poland have a great deal of Mongoloid blood in them — descendents of those Turanian Khazars with whom numbers of Jews settled and mixed in the Middle Ages.

Islam under the Arab caliphs certainly was superior to contemporary western civilizations, from all I have read, and had it not been for the unstable nature of the Semite, would surely have developed eventually into a civilization far surpassing our own, today. But it seems Semitic nations cannot stand the test of time. The caliphates were crumbling to decay when the Seljuk Turks overran and assumed leadership of Islam. Then cultural progress ceased; the Turk never built anything; his mission in life has been to destroy. He is in many ways, the counterpart of the Dane of Viking days, who, incapable himself of creating, nipped the growing culture of Saxon-England in the bud and almost totally blotted out civilization in Ireland. The Turanian has always, it seemed to me, been the man of action rather than the man of study and art. He has been, and still is, bold, adventuresome, capable and unsentimental, brutal and domineering; in creative genius he is infinitely inferior to the Semitic race. It would have been bad for the west had Martel lost at Tours; it would have been infinitely worse if the Occident had fallen before the hordes of Attila, Genghis Khan or Timur-il-lang.

The Orient was early an enthusiasm of mine, though for some years I lost all interest in it. This interest was revived by the appearance of Mr. Wright's *Oriental Story Magazine*, to which I have contributed a number of tales. I, frankly, have never even set foot on the east bank of the Mississippi River, but if popular fiction writers wrote only about countries with which they were actually familiar, the fiction supply would be enormously limited! By the way, if you chanced to read my "The Voice of El-Lil" in the first issue of *Oriental Stories*, I wish to say that that line mentioning the "pre-Aryan people of Connaught and Galway," represents a mistake of the printer. I wrote "Connaught and Galloway," meaning of course, the district in Scotland.

I found your chronicles of Rhode Island most fascinating and realize more than ever my vast ignorance of American history. You are right in saying that the average American knows only his own district. And then usually very imperfectly; I know only a skim of the history of Texas, and I daresay that the number of Rhode Islanders who are as well acquainted with the chronicles of the state as you are, are comparatively few. The average man does not concern himself much with history. America is entirely too big; too big to hold together long, especially with the invasions of unsavory hordes of foreigners. I sympathize with your interest in colonial days; I myself find it difficult to co-ordinate myself with the age in which I live. I have often wished strongly that I had lived on the ancestral plantations in the Deep South, in the days before the Civil War! I particularly wished this in earlier days, when dragging a cotton-sack through the morning dew or swinging an axe in the face of a blue blizzard.

You Rhode Islanders reached your Golden Age earlier than the people of the South did, and your description of life in the old Narragansett plantation country makes my mouth water for mellow old days now gone forever. It is the fashion of the democratic modern age to jeer loudly at the old aristocracy-ruled days, but I'll be damned if I see anything particularly inspiring about the present-day trend — I see in this age neither a dignified civilization nor a clean, virile barbarism capable of producing a later culture. It seems merely a wallowing chaos with all lines down, a senseless commercial scramble in which all ideals are lost sight of.

The shipping era of your state was a virile and inspiring phase, and the picture you suggest of slave-ships sailing up unknown rivers and stumbling on ancient secrets is highly fascinating. The very phrase: the slave trade, conjures up intriguing pictures. That time has been neglected too much by fiction writers, rich as it is in dramatic possibilities. The linking of distant coasts by trade and exploration is a fascinating thought, anyway. The names and phrases: Slave Coast, Old Calabar, Bonney, Ashanti, Dehomey, Black Ivory, Bight of Benin, have always touched responsive chords in me. And consider the contrast — clean-cut clipper ships, manned by hardheaded, clear-eyed Yankee sailors, racing from the high, pure wind-swept coasts of New England, to the sullen, dank, devil-haunted swamps of the Slave Coast, with its abhorrent secrets, night-black jungles, squalling, teeming life, where fires flared and tom-toms thundered through the thick, musky night and black naked figures leaped and howled before blood-stained idols.

What a black and bloody land the West Coast of Africa is! The chronicles of the fleeting black empires read like nightmares. I tried, in "Red Shadows" to create a slight sense of the bestial inhumaneness of the country, but failed utterly. It must be something that a man must see in order to get a complete idea of it. Some day I intend to go and see it at first-hand.

If climatic and topographical conditions had been different, I wonder what the result would have been; for the majority of our negro slaves were of a comparatively low order of being. Living in the swamps and jungles they could not have been otherwise. I believe that if the American negro was a descendent of the more advanced Kaffir tribes of the south and east, his progress since emancipation would have been much more rapid.

Rhode Island has certainly had a vigorous and healthy history and I hope it will escape the swamping by foreigners that seems to have overtaken so many old American localities.

The legends you cite are extremely interesting, especially the one about the rock which bleeds in the light of the moon. That is a particularly fantastic touch, so strangely fantastic that it must have some basis of fact, though doubtless the fact is far removed in substance from the details of the myth. It seems to me that the more wildly fantastic a tale is, the more likelihood there is for its being grounded in reality one way or another. The average human is so unimaginative that the highest flights of fantasy are beyond his power to create out of nothing. The bleeding rock reminds me of a similar Irish legend, that of Raimreach Ruadh, wife of Goban Saer, in Bantry.

Speaking of witches reminds me of an old woman I knew in my early childhood in the "piney woods". She went bare-footed, was generally accompanied by a large flock of geese, gathered up manure to fertilize her garden, in her bare hands, and was generally looked on as a witch — tolerantly, to be sure, but the niggers were much afraid of her. One day she put a death-curse on a playmate of mine and nearly frightened him into a fit. And perhaps it was as well for her that superstition was not as rife as in former ages, because shortly afterward the child died.

As to the murder-ranch I mentioned, such ranches were fairly common in Texas during an earlier day. The owners would keep a cow-puncher working for perhaps a year without pay, then when he demanded his money, he was driven away; if he showed fight, he was shot down and his body thrown into a gully or an old well. This particular ranch lies some miles west of this town and is now in different hands. The old man who owned the ranch, was, I have heard, of particularly repellent aspect and more dangerous than a rattle-snake. His worst crime, at least I consider it was, was the murder of a servant's baby; its noise irritated him and he dashed its brains out against the ranch house wall. He lived to be very old and was doubtless partly insane in the latter part of his life.

His son now has a ranch some hundreds of miles west of here, and some twelve or fifteen years ago killed a Mexican, sewed the corpse up in a cow-hide and flung it out on the prairie to rot. The Cattlemen's Association sent out a detective — just why so much trouble was taken about a Mexican I cannot understand, unless he was some way connected with the Association — and this detective, playing the part of a deaf mute, worked for months on the murderer's ranch and finally got full evidence. No one would have thought of looking into the cow-hide, for it merely appeared that a cow's carcass was rotting out there on the plains. The killer was brought into court and got a sentence of two or three years, though I cannot say as to whether he ever served his time or not. The last I heard of him, he was prospering in the western country.

I agree with you that Puritanism provides a rich field for psychological study. I have never had the fortune to read your story, "The Picture in the House" but would most certainly like to.

I have noted the prevalence of perversion and unnatural crime in Puritan annals, and understand how it could have hardly been otherwise, since, as you remark, all natural instincts were strangled and strait-jacketed.

I found your remarks on witch-craft highly interesting. It was not until a few years ago that I realized that such a cult really did exist in former times — discovered this by reading an article by Joseph McCabe on the subject. Your comments threw a good deal more light on the subject. A wealth of fiction could be written about it — especially about the time that European civilization seemed on the verge of crumbling before its insidious undermining. You are probably right in believing that the New England witch-craze was caused by members of the cult — probably trying to revive the old ways in the New World.

What you say of the youth and enthusiasm of the Celtic race is true, but I fear the good points of the race are balanced by points not so good. Celtic treachery is as well established as Celtic mysticism; Celtic dissention, jealousy and fickleness brought the English into Ireland and kept them there. The Gaels have never learned to act with each other; in later years many of the great leaders of Irish independence have been Celtized Englishmen. Why, it was only a part of the Irish who broke the Danes at Clontarf, and Mac Gilla Patrick not only refrained from aiding his countrymen, but actually attacked the Dalcassians as they returned and dogged their trail clear into Clare. And the great Brian Boru won the crown from Malachi by treachery. The history of the Irish race is one of betrayals, and only the incredible vitality of the breed has allowed it to exist at all.

Celtic nature has its moments of spontaneous gaiety and good nature, but it has depths of dark brooding and unexpected cruelty. It is wayward and uncertain as the wind; as water that flows to the sea and the grey waves of the sea. The Celt is oppressed by the everlasting sadness of the world and the fleeting shadows of this ephemeral dream we call reality. He is a primitive creature of rivers and shadows and dreams that can instantly turn to nightmares. He is moved and shifted by all winds that blow; his actions are determined by moods that pass over his soul like the shadows of wind-blown clouds across the grass. He fights the wars of all peoples and wins all battles except his own. He builds colossal cities and shivers in their streets, a beggar. He watches, unmoved, the slaughter of thousands, and breaks his heart over the falling of a leaf. He gives his coat to a stranger and robs his brother. A word can make him swear friendship for his enemy, and a word can make him turn against his best friend. He is Ishmael and his brothers are the Sons of Hagar. I am going to venture to quote here a rhyme of mine, of little worth, but in which I tried to create, in my crude way, some hint of the restlessness and discontent that is the heritage of all men of Gaelic blood.

Rueben's Brethren
"Unstable as water, thou shalt not excel."

Drain the cup while the ale is bright,
Brief truce to remorse and sorrow!
I drink the health of my friend tonight —
I may cut his throat tomorrow.

Tonight I fling a curse in the cup
For the foe whose lines we sundered —
I may ride in his ranks when the sun comes up
And die for the flag I plundered.

Kisses I drank in the blaze of noon,
At eve may be bitter as scorning —
And I go in the light of a mocking moon
To the woman I cursed this morning.

For deep in my soul the old gods brood —
And I come of a restless breed —
And my heart is blown in each drifting mood
As clouds blow over the mead.

I am highly intrigued by the drawings of the images but am unable to give you any information about them. It might be possible that the works of P.W. Joyce might throw some light on them, though Joyce was more of a historian than an archaeologist. However, his works are veritable store-houses of knowledge, and it is possible that his *The Story of Ancient Irish Civilization* might contain references to the origin or use of such images. This book is printed by The Talbot Press, Dublin, and published by Longmans, Green and Co., 39 Paternoster Row, London.

For my part, I am too little versed in antiquities to even offer an opinion, but I am inclined to think that these figures represent a pre-Christian age and have some phallic significance. I am especially inclined to this view by the consistent use of triangles in the stone figure. Phallic worship was very common in Ireland, as you know — the legend of Saint Patrick and the snakes being symbolical of the driving out of the cult — and in almost every locality where phallic worship thrived, small images representing the cult have been found, in such widely scattered places as Africa, India and Mexico. Though of course the workmanship of the images differs with the locality and I have never seen or heard of, figures just like these of yours. At any rate, they are fascinating and open up enormous fields of dramatic conjecture. I am sure you could build some magnificent tales out of them.

Your remarks on your ancestry interest me very much, more especially as the study of genealogy is one of my hobbies, or rather, would be, if I had time and opportunity to pursue it. It's interesting to trace back American families and learn just what part of Europe they came from. It's a queer thought to think that Americans are transplanted Europeans, somehow; after a race has lived in a locality five or six generations, its members tend to unconsciously consider that the race has lived there always — it really takes some conscious thought to realize that it's otherwise!

You evidently have a great deal of Cymric Celtic in your veins. The modern Welsh are fully as imaginative and mystic as the Irish and in many ways are more steadfast and trustworthy, seeming to lack much of the Gaelic fickleness.

I have heard of the famous "Luck of Eden Hall" and would like very much to see it. In my early childhood I memorized Longfellow's poem about it. How do you suppose the legend started? Was the cup taken from a rath, where it formed part of the loot of some forgotten king, do you suppose?

Like you, I would like very much to see Stonehenge and the Druidic forests. I can never quite bring myself to believe the tales of Druidic atrocities and debased worship. Most of such tales were spread by the Romans, who always accused their victims of hideous deeds mainly to excuse their own cruelties.

Stonehenge is supposed to be a pre-Druidic ruin, is it not? At any rate, it has always puzzled me as to how primitive men erected such things. Admitting the possibility of rearing great slabs of stone upright by sheer man-power, how could slabs of almost equal size be lifted and placed on top of the upright slabs without the aid of machinery? It looks impossible, unless the ancients built some sort of a mound up which they dragged the slabs. All in all, such edifices create a slight disquietude when considered thoughtfully, a faint feeling as if they had been erected by giants or creatures whose development lay along other lines than those of ordinary humanity!

I agree with all you say about foreign immigration. "The melting pot" — bah! As if we could assimilate all the low-lived scum of southern Europe without tainting the old American stock. And that stuff they pull about "everybody being foreigners except the Indians," makes me fighting mad. Then the Indian is a foreigner too, because he was preceded by the Mound-builders. And the Gaelic-Irishman is a foreigner because the Picts came into Ireland before him. And the Anglo-Saxon is a foreigner in England because the Cymric Celts were there when he came. No — the true facts are this — after our ancestors had conquered the Indians, killed off the wild animals, leveled the forests, driven out the French and Spaniards and won our independence from England, a horde of lousy peasants swarmed over to grab what our Aryans ancestors had won.

Once it was the highest honor to say: "I am an American." It still is, because of the great history that lies behind the phrase; but now any Jew, Polack or Wop, spawned in some teeming ghetto and ignorant of or cynical toward American ideals, can strut and swagger and blatantly assert his Americanship and is accepted on the same status as a man whose people have been in the New World for three hundred years.

I would limit immigration in this manner: I would open the doors wide to all people of the British Isles. Let the other nations howl about discrimination. Why should we not discriminate? Did the Italians, the Russians, the Liths settle and conquer and build this country? Did the ancient Greek colonies welcome Egyptians and Phoenicians as citizens, or did they proudly remain Hellenes? Why should we open the doors to strangers? Britons settled this land and I would always welcome Britons. The rest, with exceptions among the higher class Scandinavians and French, I would bar completely.

Well — I can't say that I've added anything to the greatness of the nation, but I at least come of a breed that helped build up the country, which is more than can be said today by any number of Hebraic-Slavic-Latins running around and calling themselves "Americans".

My branch of the Howards came to America with Oglethorpe 1733 and lived in various parts of Georgia for over a hundred years. In '49 three brothers started for California. On the Arkansas River they split up, one went on to

California where he lived the rest of his life, one went back to Georgia and one, William Benjamin Howard, went to Mississippi where he became an overseer on the plantations of Squire James Harrison Henry, whose daughter he married. In 1858 he moved, with the Henry's, to southwestern Arkansas where he lived until 1885, when he moved to Texas. He was my grandfather.

The Eiarbhins, or Ervins, to give the name its present Anglicized spelling, came to America a very long time ago; just when I am not sure, but it was before 1700. The family was originally Scotch and there is a legend to the effect that the name was once "Mac Conaire". How that name came to be Eiarbhin is more than I can say, but descent from Conaire, ard-righ of Erin is claimed, which, if true, shows that the clan went into Scotland at a comparatively late date.

At any rate, it was a wild Highland clan in the days of Robert Bruce and because they followed him and were granted favors by him, it is a tradition in the family that a male child in every generation be named Robert. My great grandfather was Robert Ervin, and my great-great grandfather the same; my grandfather, by some chance, was named George Washington Ervin, but he named his youngest son Robert, and I have several cousins of that name.

However, the Eiarbhins went westward early, and had been in Ireland for generations, before they came to America. My grandfather Colonel G.W. Ervin highly resented any attempt to attribute Scotch characteristics to him.

In 1800 the family was well established on large plantation in North Carolina, but moved to Mississippi in the early 1840s. The Civil War ruined the plantation system and Colonel Ervin came to Texas in 1866.

The Henry's were the last of my various lines to arrive in the New World, being deported from Ireland a few years before the Revolutionary War because of rebellious actions against the English government. My great-greatgrandfather, James Henry, was born on the Atlantic ocean on the way over. He eventually settled in South Carolina where Squire James Harrison Henry was born.

So I really have no connection with the early history of Texas, though I was born here. Still, because of birth and environment I feel more closely knit to Texas than to the Old South. And it must indeed be said, that though most native Texans are of Southern blood, there is a great difference between them and natives of the Old South. I notice it every time I go to Louisiana or Arkansaw. We think of ourselves, and really are, not Southerners nor Westerners, but Southwesterners. Our accent is more like the South than the North or the Middle West, but it differs greatly from the true Southern accent. We constitute an empire of our own, and should never have entered either the Union or the Confederacy. With the great tracts of land we then owned and the possibilities we possessed, we had the makings of a vast and mighty empire. And it should have been so; America is too huge, too unwieldy; I fear it cannot long stand.

I have but recently returned from a trip to the great northwest plains which, beginning about the 33rd parallel run on up into Oklahoma and Kansas. Texas is really, especially in the western part, a series of plateaus, like a flight of steps, sloping from 4000 feet in the Panhandle to sea-level. You travel for a hundred or so miles across level plains, then come to a very broken belt of hills and canyons, then passing through them you come on to another wide strip of level country at a lower or higher elevation according to the direction in which you are traveling — and so on, clear to the Gulf. I was on the Llano Estacado, or Staked Plains, so called from the fact that Spanish priests, crossing the plains long ago, marked the way with buffalo skulls stuck on stakes. Twenty years ago most of that country was cattle-range; now the great majority is in cultivation. The Llano Estacado is the last stand for the big-scale Texas farmer. Farms of a thousand acres, every inch under cultivation, are not uncommon. A farm of that size requires a tractor and a veritable herd of work horses to cultivate it properly. During busy seasons the work goes on day and night; they work by shifts and labor from sunrise to sunrise. The average elevation is better than 3000 feet and the country is perfectly flat. You can see for miles in every direction; there are no trees except such as have been planted. It's a great, raw, open new country with mighty possibilities, but I'd go dippy living there. I was born and mainly raised in the Central Texas hill country and I have to have hills and trees!

The Llano Estacado is largely in the hands of native Texans of old American stock. You see, it's really a pioneer country. The European scum sticks to the lowlands and the Gulf coast, waiting for the Old Americans to open the country up and get it going — and paying. *Then* they'll swarm in and take it over.

I hate to see all the good ranges being broken up into farms. Once this country here on the Callahan Divide was a great cattle country with wide sweeping ranges, clear cold springs and streams and rich grass waist deep. Then the inevitable farmer came in droves, with his mule and his plow and his drove of offspring. They fenced the land and the grass died; shinnery and mesquite and scrub oak sprang up and choked the springs; the streams ceased to run and the country dried up. The farmers wore out the soil. That's the way they always do in a big country. They wear out a field, and simply move over and clear out another field. Eventually they run out of fields as the country fills up.

The oil booms came along and ruined what agriculture was left. Now this country is poverty ridden and worn out. The old rocky, clayey farms won't produce anything, what with the drouths, and the oil has just about played out or else the big companies have bought out the smaller ones and shut down the works, to cut expense or to freeze somebody out. But now this country is drifting back to cattle and sheep and goats again. It's still a great country it just needs a little intelligence. All over the older settled parts of Texas, the trend is away from agriculture and back toward stock-raising.

But is it any wonder that thrifty, hard working foreigners overrun the land when the descendents of the sturdy pioneers are in so many cases so shiftless and stupid and lazy?

Texans are naturally nomadic. It's difficult to find an old man who has grown old in the locality in which he was born. This extends to tenant farmers who often shift every year from one farm to another. And not farmers alone.

Why, by the time I was nine years old I'd lived in the Palo Pinto hills of Central Texas; in a small town only fifty miles from the Coast; on a ranch in

Atascosa County; in San Antonio; on the South Plains close to the New Mexican line; in the Wichita Falls country up next to Oklahoma; and in the piney woods of Red River over next to Arkansas; if you'll glance at a map of Texas you'll note that covers considerable distance, altogether; and I didn't mention a few short stays in Missouri and Oklahoma. I've lived in land boom towns, railroad boom towns, oil boom towns, where life was raw and primitive, and all I can say is: Texas is just too big for me to grasp. A better man than I will have to write her history.

I've seen towns leap into being overnight and become deserted almost as quick. I've seen old farmers, bent with toil, and ignorant of the feel of ten dollars at a time, become millionaires in a week, by the way of oil gushers. And I've seen them blow in every cent of it and die paupers. I've seen whole towns debauched by an oil boom and boys and girls go to the devil wholesale. I've seen promising youths turn from respectable citizens to dope-fiends, drunkards, gamblers and gangsters in a matter of months.

But the old Texas is gone or is going fast. All the plains are fenced in, where in my childhood I've ridden for a hundred miles without seeing a foot of barbed wire. I can't remember when I've heard a coyote. And one of my earliest memories is being lulled to sleep in a covered wagon camped on the Nueces River, by the howling of wolves.

When they built Crystal City twenty years ago in Zavalla county, some forty miles from the Mexican Border, the wolves came howling to the edge of the clearings. The woods were full of wildcats, panthers and javelinas, the lakes were full of fish and alligators. I was back there a couple of years ago and was slightly depressed at the signs of civilization which disfigured the whole country.

Well, it's not all civilized. There are places left where a man can get out and take a deep breath. In the hundred mile stretch from Sonora to Del Rio on the Border, there's not even a cluster of Mexican huts to mar the scenery and there's just one store, a sort of half-way place. The rest is just — landscape! Wild, bare hills, with no grass, no trees, not even mesquite; not even cactus will grow there — only a sort of plant like a magnified Spanish dagger, called — I believe — sotol.

And I have an idea that the plains south of the Llano Estacado are more or less wide open. A land boom flopped there quite a number of years ago and the railroad to the town where I lived a while was discontinued. I was very young and my memories are scanty; but I remember illimitable plains stretching on forever in every direction, sandy, drab plains with never a tree, only tufts of colorless bushes, haunted by tarantulas and rattlesnakes, buzzards and prairie dogs; long-horn cattle, driven in to town for shipping, stampeding past the yard where I played; and screeching dust winds that blew for days, filling the air with such a haze of stinging sand that you could see only for a few yards.

Judas, what a country! People came out from the East and filed on government land; and they went broke and went back home, or they went crazy and blew their brains out. Not many native Texans could stand it, even. People lived in tents, shacks, dug-outs — then they left, cursing the country and the old cattle-men watched them go and grinned in their whiskers. Though how even a Texas steer could live in that country is more than I can see.

But of all lousy lands, the Wichita Falls country takes the cake to my mind. There the plains are of white alkali and the glare nearly blinds you. The climate is treacherous. You ride out in the morning in your shirt sleeves, admiring the dreamy slumber of the plains, with the birds singing in the one tree the county boasts, and the heat waves shimmering in the distance; you see a coyote loping along with his tongue hanging out in the heat — and then by noon, maybe, a blue blizzard comes howling over the prairie and freezes your gizzard. Before they got gas wells in that country they burned corn cobs; I've seen stacks ten feet high in people's back yard. Before they could ship corn in or raise it, cowpunchers burned dried cattle dung and before them the hunters and traders and Indians burned buffalo chips.

No, I don't care to live on the Cap-rock. This Cap-rock is the name of the rim of the highest plateau in Texas — the edge of the Staked Plains; at a distance it looks like low-lying clouds along the horizon; then it appears to be an unbroken range of hills; then you ride up on it and see that it's really a sort of cliff, marking the plateau and extending for more than a hundred miles.

But in a little town on the plains I met a figure who links Texas with her wild old past — no less a personage than the great Norfleet,[3] one of modern Texas' three greatest gunmen — the other two being Tom Hickman and Manuel Gonzalles, captain and sergeant of the Rangers respectively. Norfleet is not unknown in New York and Chicago and a few years ago gained national fame by tracking down a band of con-men who had swindled him out of considerable money; he landed them all in the pen, instead of shooting them. An enterprizing firm published a book of his experiences, which reached an enormous sale.[4] He is now a United States Marshal and his latest exploit was in Chicago where he killed two gangsters who had the drop on him. He is a small, stocky man, about five feet four, I should judge, of late middle age, with a scrubby white mustache and cold light blue eyes, the pupils of which are like pin points. He is a very courteous and soft spoken gentleman and I could not help but noticc, as I shook hands with him, that his hands are not of the type usually found in men who are quick with weapons — his hands being very short and blocky in shape. Nor did he have that quick, nervous grip in handshaking that I have noticed in killers. His nerves are in perfect control but in his quick movements he reminds one of a cat, and like all gunfighters, he keeps his hands in constant motion and never very far from his gun.

Though a very respectable and law-abiding citizen, Norfleet is as quick on the draw and as deadly a marksman as Billy the Kid, John Wesley Hardin, Sam Bass, Al Jennings or any of the other old time Texas warriors.

The old-time gunmen of the west are passing fast, and when I say gunmen, I do not refer to the cowardly scum of the modern cities who disgrace the term by calling themselves gun-fighters.

Some ten years ago one of the greatest passed over the ridge — Bud Ballou, once a Ranger, whom Tom Hickman killed in the Wichita Falls country.

Of course, real gunfighters were comparatively rare, even in the old days, despite lurid western literature to the contrary, which literature would make appear that every man was then a walking armory and spent most of his time practicing the draw from all positions and shooting from the hip, the knee cap, and the collar button! Most men carried guns, but few were expert in their use. Just as in medieval times most men carried swords but the majority were neither duelists nor skilled fencers. It is surprizing the number of men who have been shot at and missed, in the west. But a strange thing seems to be, that a woman seldom needs any practice to get her man! They have a natural killer's instinct that sends their shot home. How often do you hear of a woman shooting at her husband and missing him?

A great majority of the killings in the old days were done with a shotgun from behind a rock fence. Killers generally show a preference for catching their man unarmed and then shooting him in the back.

But the real gunman scorned such subterfuges generally and was passionately proud of the notches on his gun.

A bold man was Dock Holder, who held forth in East Texas in the '80s and '90s. A gunman named Jackson shot him down, and Holder's sister lifted him and held him up while he killed Jackson. Of such stuff were Texas women made! Holder survived his wounds and lived until several years ago when one Jerome Persons got the drop on him and finished him with eight bullets through the body.

But for cold steel nerve no man ever surpassed that showed by old Judge Jarrell[5] in his street-fight with the Harris boys in Waco. The Judge was an intellectual old man, but very radical in his views, a Civil War veteran and a gentleman of the old school. The Harris boys were newspapermen and they caught him in a cross-fire. J.W. Harris was standing in the door of his newspaper building firing, while across the street diagonally his brother J.F. Harris[6] had his stand. Judge Jarrell walked swiftly yet deliberately across the street toward J.W. Harris, holding his fire. Something about that steady advance shook J.W.'s nerve and his shots went wild. J.F., after missing repeatedly, came running across the street, firing as he came. At less than twenty feet a bullet shattered Jarrell's arm and the Judge fired for the first time, killing J.W. Harris. Then the Judge turned to meet the remaining brother who rushed in and attempted to grapple. Another man somehow ran between them and all three went down in a heap; and there the Judge, as cool as steel, reached his pistol-arm over the man between them and blew out J.F. Harris' brains. Two shots and two killings! He lost his arm but his foes lost their lives.[7]

The Judge was a close friend of Brann, the Iconoclast, who was keeping Texas in an uproar, and this shooting occurred not long before Brann and Davis shot each other to death on the streets of Waco.[8]

Texas, all in all, has had a history of almost unbelievable violence and bloodshed. As late as the '80s it was not uncommon for some gunman to shoot down another in the streets of some western town and not allow anybody to touch the body — sometimes the corpse lay in the streets for days.

Well, it could hardly be otherwise, considering the powers that went to make up the history of the state. Our southern neighbors added considerably to the general disorder. For years we carried on an unofficial and unrecorded border warfare with Mexico and even today, the road between the Border towns of Eagle Pass and Del Rio, which follows the Rio Grande, runs along the rim of the valley, out of sight of the river. Once it followed the bank of the river but so many white people were shot by Mexicans across the river, the road was changed.

Thanks very much for letting me see the articles about Providence, also the splendid poem, "The East India Brick Row." I enjoyed scanning them all, particularly your poem, which is as fine as any of its kind I ever read. It's a pity that the old landmarks had to be torn away; modern America seems blindly bent on wiping out all vestiges of her glorious past.

What you say of the neighborhood in which you live is peculiarly fascinating; like living in a sort of mystical dream-town above and aloof from the rush and hurry of work-a-day world. You are very fortunate, I think, in your environment. In such a place one has time and inspiration for study and deep contemplation, I should think. Man is greatly molded by his surroundings. I believe, for instance, that the gloominess in my own nature can be partly traced to the surroundings of a locality in which I spent part of my baby-hood. It was a long, narrow valley, lonesome and isolated, up in the Palo Pinto hill country. It was very sparsely settled and its name, Dark Valley, was highly descriptive. So high were the ridges, so thick and tall the oak trees that it was shadowy even in the daytime, and at night it was as dark as a pine forest — and nothing is darker in this world. The creatures of the night whispered and called to one another, faint night-winds murmured through the leaves and now and then among the slightly waving branches could be glimpsed the gleam of a distant star. Surely the silence, the brooding loneliness, the shadowy mysticism of that lonesome valley entered in some part into my vague-forming nature. At the mouth of the valley stood a deserted and decaying cabin in which a cold-blooded and midnight murder had taken place; owls called weirdly about its ruins in the moonlight, and bats flitted about it in the twilight. I well knew, in later years, the man who committed that murder, and he never dared ride past that ruined cabin by night-time.

But I have rambled on long enough — too long. Again I must express the utmost delight to learn that another of your marvelous tales is to appear in print. I look forward to its appearance with the keenest relish, and hope that the day is soon when my library will be graced by the presence of your stories in book form. That will indeed be a treat of rare enjoyment.

By the way, I recently sold *Weird Tales* a short story, "The Children of the Night" in which I deal with Mongoloid-aborigine legendry, touch cryptically on the Bran-cult, and hint darkly and vaguely of nameless things connected with Cthulhu, Yog-Sothoth, Tsathoggua and the *Necronomicon*; as well as quoting lines from Flecker's[9] "Gates of Damascus" and lending them a cryptic meaning which I'm sure would have astounded the poet remarkably!

But I hope I haven't bored you too much by my maunderings.

Very cordially yours,
[Robert E. Howard]

P.S. Thanks for the copy of your bookplate; it's a clever idea.

NOTES

1. "Supernatural Horror in Literature."
2. W. Paul Cook, editor and publisher of *The Recluse.*
3. James Franklin (J. Frank) Norfleet (1865-1967).
4. This could be *Norfleet: The Actual Experiences of a Texas Rancher's 30,000 Mile Chase After Five Confidence Men*, by Norfleet himself; or *Norfleet: The Amazing Experiences of an Intrepid Texas Rancher with an International Swindling Ring*, also by Norfleet, "as told to Gordon Hines."
5. Judge G.B. Gerald.
6. Should be W.A. Harris.
7. The gun battle between Gerald and the Harris brothers took place in Waco on November 19, 1897.
8. William Cowper Brann and T. E. Davis.
9. James Elroy Flecker (1884-1915), English poet

TSS: 11495-11505

144. To Harold Preece, ca. October or early November 1930.

Well, Harold, I'm sorry to hear your nose is troubling you again. I hope it will get alright. My own nose is nothing to brag about, having been broken several times. Man is a frail and very imperfect piece of nature.

I heard A.E. speak — that is, his welcome banquet was broadcast. He has a most peculiar voice and though I highly enjoyed hearing him recite some of his poems, the strange quality of his voice got on my nerves somewhat. He talks more like a limey than a mick.

Speaking of poets, thanks very much for the poem you sent me — the one by Lenore. That is a truly splendid piece of work, as indeed, all of your sister's work is. I have no hesitation in declaring that she will be some day — and that soon — recognized as one of the foremost poets of the world. She should make an attempt to bring out her work in book form. To my mind she is far superior to Edna St. Vincent Millay right now.

I'm glad you liked "The Voice of El-Lil." Of the stories you mentioned, I don't believe I've ever read that tale of Kipling's, "The Finest Story in the World," but London's *The Star Rover* is a book that I've read and re-read for years, and that generally goes to my head like wine.

Have you read my latest story in *Weird Tales*? I believe you'll like it; it deals with Rome's efforts to subjugate the wild people of Caledonia. The characters and action are fictitious, but the period and the general trend of events are historical. The Romans, as you know, never succeeded in extending her boundaries very far into the heather and after several unsuccessful campaigns, retreated south of the great wall. Their defeat must have been accomplished by some such united effort as I have here portrayed — a temporary alliance between Gaelic, Cymric, aboriginal and possibly Teutonic elements. I have a pretty definite idea that a slow filtration of Germanic settlers had begun in eastern Caledonia long before the general overflow that swamped the Latinized countries.

Some day I'm going to try to write a novel length tale dealing with that misty age; allowing myself the latitude that a historical novelist is supposed to be allowed, I intend to take a plot something like this: dealing with the slow crumbling of Roman influence in Britain, and the encroachment of Teutonic wanderers from the East. These, landing on the eastern coast of Caledonia, press slowly westward, until they come in violent conflict with the older Gaelic settlements on the west. Across the ruins of the ancient pre-Aryan Pictish kingdom, long pinned between implacable foes, these war-like tribes come to death-grips, only to turn on a common foe, the conquering Saxons. I intend the tale shall be of nations and kings rather than individuals. Doubtless I shall never write it.

As regards the pre-Aryan communities I mentioned in "The Voice of El-Lil," as you know all western Europe was once inhabited by small, dark, garlic-eating tribes of Neolithic culture, known variously as Mediterraneans, Iberians, Basques, Long-heads, Garlic-eaters, and in Britain, Silures or Picts. Traces of these people, conquered and subjugated by the Aryan Celts, show still in the races today in the British Isles, and these primitive peoples I mentioned are undoubtedly vestiges of the race — whence doubtless come the legends of Phoenician settlements in Cornwall and Ireland. New races of Nordic Celts or Teutons coming into the Isles, seeing these small dark men concluded that they were of Semitic blood, or Egyptians. The fact is, they preceded all other races into the west, possibly excepting a very primitive Mongoloid prototype which was soon extinct.

This Mediterranean type underlies all races and only a few centuries is required for this people to change the physiognomy of their conquerors Who, for instance, not knowing their real origin, would realize that the first Aryan ancestors of the Italian, the Greek, the Persian and the high-caste Hindu were light-eyed blonds, almost identical with the present day Scandinavian?

But to return to the Mediterraneans of the Isles, where these tribes remained a race apart longer than anywhere else. These aborigines are popularly known as Picts, and by this name I have designated them in all my stories — and I have written a number in which I mentioned or referred to them — "The Lost Race," "The Shadow Kingdom," "The Mirrors of Tuzun Thune," "The Dark Man," "Kings of the Night," to say nothing of several which I have not marketed.

Doubtless this term is in strictest sense, incorrect. I doubt very much if those ancient folk had any term that designated them as a people; Tuatha Feda, roughly, forest people, was the name given them by the Gaels of Ireland.

Bede says the Picts came to Scotland from Scythia after the Gaels had arrived in Ireland. The Gaels drove them into Scotland, rather, would not let them settle in Ireland, and later came over and dispossessed them. It is readily seen that these people were not aborigines, since the Gaels came into Ireland as late as the first century A.D.

But here arises a question: did these "Scythic" people take the name of an older race among which they settled, or did they lend those older peoples their name?

It is no doubt but that the "Picts of Galloway" were of a very mixed race, with Celtic no doubt predominating. But when I speak of the Picts proper, I am referring to the older, pure-blooded pre-Aryan type.

I think the following theory to be fairly logical: that Caledonia was inhabited from earliest times by a dark Mediterranean people; that the conquest of the Romans drove numbers of Cymric Britons into the heather, whence, no doubt, comes the tales of the "Caledonians," large, fair-haired people who fought with war-chariots. No doubt these tribes mixed a great deal with the natives.

Then, in the press of Roman conquest, which no doubt caused displacements of many Celtic tribes, doubtless including the Gaels, who must have come into Ireland from the mountains of Spain or Southern Gaul, another wave of Celts came into Caledonia, that race known as Picts. They may have been of Gaelic, Belgic or Brythonic type, though all evidence points to a non-Gaelic language. Or they may have been a type of Celt unclassified. Very likely it was already a mixed race, with Latin, Teutonic or even Semitic elements. This race, settling in Caledonia, possibly conquered the natives and gave its name to them.

You understand I have little or no foundations for this theory and am merely putting it forth as a supposition.

The natives of Galloway were spoken of as "the Picts of Galloway" long after the coming of the Saxons. Doubtless a strong strain of Mediterranean blood coursed in their veins, but they were a very mixed breed — besides the Pictish blood mentioned, they had strong elements of Gaelic, Brythonic, Danish and Saxon. More especially as Galloway, as the name implies (Gael-Gall, meaning a province under the control of the Gall, or foreigners) was early conquered by the Angle kings and did not regain its independence for a long time. The name Pict came to mean merely a native of Galloway. But behind that local term loomed a great shadowy realm reaching back into the Stone Age. Therefore, the term Pict as I use it, refers to that old, old Neolithic race in its purity and completeness.

According to Scotch legends, which speak of the Picts with the utmost horror and aversion, the Pictish kingdom was destroyed and its subjects wiped out by Kenith MacAlpine. Doubtless the kingdom was destroyed, but it is likely that the people were absorbed by the surrounding Gaelic tribes. And this kingdom was the mixed one of which I have already spoken. The old pure Mediterranean type had largely disappeared. Distance lends perspective but it also distorts and foreshortens. Doubtless the legends of the Picts became mixed with the older, darker legends of the ancient Mongoloids of the Continent. These tales form the base of the Aryan folklore — as regards dwarfs, elves, gnomes, kobolds, demons, and the like — and twining themselves about the myths of the Picts, lent them a supernatural accent —

demoniac appearance, subhuman stature, and so on. No doubt the later Picts were of more stocky build and unprepossessing appearance than the purer blooded Gaels, but I cannot believe that they were as hideous in aspect as the legends make them out.

Mihiragula

Out of the East the stark winds rise,
Mihiragula;
Into the East the vulture flies,
A black flame lights an idol's eyes,
And war-clouds blaze in the haunted skies,
Mihiragula.

The sword drips red in a hellish light,
Mihiragula;
Empires break in the howling night
Under the hoofs of the Ephthalite;
And the gods go down as the arrows bite,
Mihiragula.

Banners reel in a blazing sky,
Mihiragula;
Towers break as the dust clouds fly,
Kings from their gem-set thrones on high
Fall as the black horse thunders by,
Mihiragula.

Where are the purple flags unfurled,
Mihiragula?
Like the clouds on the Oxus curled,
Dust winds torn and tossed and whirled —
Fades in the memory of the world
Mihiragula.

Belshazzer

Slow through the streets of Babylon he went,
The naked harlots knelt and shrank aside;
The canopy above him swayed and bent:
"Way for the king of kings!" the herald cried.
— And in the crowd a lean and ragged Mede
Thumbed a knife edge and grinning, turned aside.

Timur-lang

The warm wind blows through the waving grain —
Where are the glories of Tamerlane?
The nations stood up, ripe and tall —
He was the sickle that reaped them all.
But the sickle shatters and leaves no trace —
And the grain grows green on the desert's face.

The Peasant on the Euphrates

He saw old Sumer reel before the hoofs
Of Sargon; and the Babylonian roofs
Go up in flames to quench the Mede's hot ire;
He knew the Persian's and the Greek's desire;
He saw red kingdoms born and pass away,
Like clouds upon a dreamy summer day.
Roman or Arab, Turk or Briton — all,
All one to him, the everlasting thrall.

TSS: 92101-92102, 92063

ᴙᴕᴙᴕ

145. To H.P. Lovecraft, ca. November 1930.[1]

Dear Mr. Lovecraft:

As always, your letter proved highly enjoyable. I did indeed find the *Recluse* article most fascinating and instructive and look forward its enlarged and republished form. Nothing that anyone else could write could possibly be better or more comprehensive in its scope. I highly appreciate your offer to lend me the Blackwood books and intend to take advantage of your kindness at some future date when my plans are not quite so uncertain as they are now. Thank you very much for the magazine with your story;[2] I am certain that "The Picture in the House" will prove a real treat.

You're quite welcome to the "Red Thunder" business. I appreciate your comments on my verse and most certainly agree with you regarding the conventional unconventionalism of modern poets. That's a point I've maintained for years — that these supposed exponents of radical freedom of thought and expression are serfs of conventions even more hide-bound and narrow and despotic than the old line. I am acquainted with a certain young and as yet unrecognized Texas poet whose work is superb — in spite of his views, I maintain, and not because of them — and this attitude is apparent in his every action; an excellent fellow when he forgets his superiority for a little, he is so infernally afraid that he'll appear human, he often makes himself obnoxious. One shining example of tolerance and broad-mindedness among the moderns is my friend Ben Musser,[3] a poet of no small note. Well — my rhyming isn't of sufficient importance for me to take it seriously, or to bind myself to any school or rule. I'm no poet but I was born with a knack of making little words rattle together and I've gotten a bit of pleasure from my jinglings. I'm willing to let the real poets grind out their images with blood and sweat, and to go through life piping lustily on my half-penny whistle. Poetizing's work and travail; rhyming's pleasure and holiday. I never devoted over thirty minutes to any rhyme in my life, though I've spent hours memorizing the poetry of other men.

I'm sure you would like San Antonio. I hope to spend a few months there and if I do I'll send you a lot of pictures of the place and the country thereabouts. The old Buckhorn Saloon is worth a trip to the city. It's full of heads and horns of buffalo, long horn steers, deer, elk, moose, rhinos, javelines, walruses — every imaginable species. But the most interesting items are the snake rattles. It includes the biggest collection of rattles in the world. The counters and walls are decorated in designs made entirely of gilded snake rattles — literally thousands of them. Did you every hear a rattler sing at you in the dark or among bushes, where you couldn't see him but knew he was somewhere within striking distance? It's the most blood chilling sound on earth. But the old Buckhorn — I can remember the days when it was in a big building and they sold hard liquor over the bar — it grates me now to see a Heinie behind the mahogany purveying kosher sandwiches.

Yes, the lower country is filling up with Latins and Polacks and even the Mexicans resent that fact. I remember the conversation of a certain Spanish-Italian desperado, one Chico the Desperate, whose real name was Marcheca, on the road to San Antonio, a few years ago. Chico was suspicious and reticent at first but soon warmed up and narrated his crimes with a gusto that kept me roaring with laughter. He was either a monumental liar or the most atrocious rogue unhung. But what amused me the most was his violent denunciations of the foreigners who were stealing the country! He was in favor of deporting all Germans, Polacks, and yea, even Italians! who had come over within the last generation and giving their land to natural Americans — including himself. He explained that the deportation of foreigners would not touch him, for though he was but one generation removed from Spain on the one side, on the other hand the Marchecas had been settled in America for three generations. Well — I'll freely grant an Englishman, Scotchman, Irishman or Welshman the right to become an American the instant his foot touches American soil, but as far as I'm concerned a wop or a Slav can't become American in five hundred years. But as for Chico's Spanish affinities, I don't believe I ever heard a Mexican admit he was anything but pure Castilian or Aragonese. His hair may be kinky or he may have the copper skin of a Yaqui but he will assure you that at least one of his very recent ancestors first saw light in Barcelona, Valladolid or old Seville.

A bull-fight was going to be broadcast today from, I think, Rio Nosa; that's one form of amusement I've never been able to induce myself to watch.

I could stand the slaughter of the bulls but the disemboweling of the wretched worn-out horses would sicken me. The only inducement that would make me attend a bull-fight would be an absolute assurance that the bull would toss, rip open and dash the brains out of three or four spig toreadors. I would welcome such a spectacle with sincere gusto. There's a rotten streak in a nation that enjoys bull-fights. The Greasers come back with an indictment of prize-fighting and cock-fighting, but there is a difference. There is no comparison between pugilism and bull-fighting, and as for cock-fighting — well, it's a fighting cock's nature to rip and kill, and a scrap between two well matched game chickens, armed with gaffs is comparatively short and painless — I've seen more sickening mutilations in barn-yard brawls than is usual in the fighting pit. But I am not upholding cock-fights; the law against it is one law I'd like to see enforced in Texas. But I do say it's not as bestial as bull-fighting. Another thing that points to a weakening in the moral fibre of the American people is the interest which folks on the Border have been taking in such things of late — women as well as men, and not alone the idle rich. A bull-fight across the line draws crowds of eager Americans. And I note that certain adventurous Americans and Englishmen are going into the business — bad cess to them.

You are right in your denunciations of unrestricted immigration. I am sorry to hear that the old sturdy New England stock has been so swamped with aliens, and am glad to know that certain sections have held their own. You are fortunate in having lived in a district apart from the mongrel swarms. Your remarks about the eastern cities are highly interesting. My ideas about them, are of course, very vague, but I had noticed that in news items and the like pertaining to Philadelphia, Irish and English names seemed to predominate. I had heard, too, that the Old South is fairly free of foreign taint and am wholeheartedly glad to know that the homeland of my ancestors has escaped the overwhelming flood of alienism. I have never seen the South — the Deep South, beyond New Orleans, but I hope to visit it some day and to settle there, perhaps, and I would hate to see it swarmed over and violated by a low-browed foreign herd. I am sure Charleston is a beautiful city and would be a splendid place to live. I share your dislike for cold weather. So much so that I find this part of Texas unsuited for me. That is why I want to go to San Antonio — it's two hundred miles south of here and much warmer. This Callahan Divide country isn't as cold as it is on the Plains, but it's colder than I like. I'm not sure I'll ever be content this side of Mexico City. If I had my choice of residence, it would be there. I've never seen the place, but I've heard so much about it, the prospect is alluring.

As you say, the cases of Rome and America are curiously paralleled in regards to the foreign invasion, and your remarks on the subject made me realize that fact more than ever. When the barbarians finally broke into the empire, they found an unwieldy, cumbrous hulk, without identity or union, ready to topple at the first vigorous shove. Fortunately the tribes who finally trampled the crumbling lines, were of a young, vigorous race, capable of rebuilding what they had torn down, along more sturdy lines, perhaps. But now — where in all the world is there an unspoiled, hardy race of clean-blooded barbarians, fit to take the reins of the world when the older peoples decay? That great reservoir of strong, fresh races is exhausted; it seems to me that the last Aryan tribe to come into its own — the Russians — must eventually repeat the pages of history and conquer the civilized world, as all rising Aryan powers have done in the past. But it is a possibility which I contemplate with scant relish. There is too much Mongol blood in the veins of Russia for me to regard that nation as anything but alien.

Your contrast between Greece under Roman rule and the French-Canadians interested me very much. I had no idea the French in the New World had so completely resisted the advance of English culture and ideas. The people of Quebec must be a fascinating study.

I was also much interested in your remarks pertaining to the Assyrians and Turanians. True, the Assyrian nose is non-Turanian, and you are probably right in assuming that the resemblance between the Assyrian of yesterday and the Russian Jew of today can be traced to the Semitic relationship. The truly Semitic Jew is doubtless superior to the Mongoloid Jew in moral and cultural respects. However, the Mongoloid type seems to be the more aggressive of the two, judging from the great swarms of Jews now swamping the ranks of pugilism. Most Jewish fighters seem to have been born in Russia or Poland, or to have ancestral linkings with those countries, and they make, on the whole, skillful and courageous fighters.

I imagine that combination you mention — Semitic nose, Mongol eyes, Aryan hair, etc., produces a weird effect, even more so than the red headed niggers you occasionally see in the South. The most inhuman hybrid I ever saw was standing in the door of a laundry shop not far off Canal Street, in New Orleans. He — or it! — was as black as any negro I ever saw, but had the slant eyes and broad features of a Chinaman. He even wore a pigtail and had his hands in the wide sleeves of a typically Chinese outfit.

Your comments on the Carthaginian-Jewish subject proved most instructive to me, as it presented a phase of history entirely new to me. I have badly neglected informing myself on that subject and didn't even know that the Carthaginians became Judaised. If I had thought at all about it, I would have vaguely supposed that the Romans completely exterminated the Punic race. The Arab too, as you say, is doubtless of mixed breed; it seems to me as if the men of Yemen claim descent from conquering Persians of Cyrus' time, do they not? The Moorish subject too, is a fascinating one, and it is no doubt that their culture was of a high quality. And the Berbers — there's an interesting race, and an ancient one. Somewhere I seem to have read that their ancestors were fair haired and light eyed and lived in caves along the coast country of what is now the Barbary States.

I think Wright's *Oriental Stories* bids fair to show more originality than the average magazine dealing with the East, though the initial issue, was, to me, slightly disappointing — not in the appearance of the magazine but in the contents. However, with such writers as Hoffman-Price, Owens and Kline, I look for better things. I particularly hope that you will find it convenient to contribute to the magazine, since with your magnificent talents and your sincere interest in things Oriental, you should turn out some splendid work. Mr. Wright tells me that my "Voice of El-Lil" has so far tied another story for first place. I hope you like the tale.

Mr. Wright tells me that the issuing of *Strange Stories* is being delayed because of Macfadden's disputing the right to the title. Several months ago he accepted a couple of my tales for the magazine, one of them dealing with the Bran cult,[4] and I would like to see the publication on the newsstands.

Returning to the Eastern question, I too have been somewhat disgusted at the efforts of various writers to portray a conventionalized Orient. Especially the occultism of the East; Kipling, Mundy, a few others, they can write convincingly of Oriental mysticism; not many others that I have read after. For my part the mystic phase of the East has always interested me less than the material side — the red and royal panorama of war, rapine and conquest. What I write for *Oriental Stories* will be purely action, and romance — mainly historical tales. And I greatly fear that my Turks and Mongols are merely Irishmen and Englishmen in turbans and sandals!

Speaking of *Arabian Nights*, one of my first books was a copy of that great work — I was six, I believe.

The civilization you mention on the African east coast must have been a very mixed one — possibly an invading settlement of Hamitic conquerors, with a substratum of black aborigines; the whole modified more or less by a filtration of Semites from the east. What noble speculations the matter brings up! With a mingling of such passionate bloods as these, what violent intrigues, what plots and counter-plots, what savage crimes and what dark murders must have shaken the walls and palaces of that vanished civilization! I agree with you in doubting that the seeds of cultural development are present in the negroid race as a whole. They can ape and copy but that they could build a civilization of their own, I doubt.

Doubtless you are right in your theory that the easy life of the tropics contributed to the negro's lack of progress. As we know, the tropical countries can play havoc with the higher races, and make a beach-comber out of an aristocrat sometimes. Returning to the non-negroid blacks of East Africa, is it not supposed that the Elamites were an Australoid or negroid type? If so, is it not possible that they represented a branch of that East African amalgamation — perhaps a mixed race of Australoid and Hamitic or Semitic blood. Or they might have been a distinct type, approximating the black skinned, thin lipped, highly developed type you describe — Dravidian, perhaps, since I believe certain authorities tend toward the theory of a wide drift of Dravidian peoples extending from India to Egypt in very early times. Well, I'm not well enough informed in these matters to speculate, but I heartily agree with your remark that Africa offers a rich field for fantastic fiction.

The image you sketched is most intriguing in its implication of antiquity and its prehistoric possibilities, and I hope you'll make a story of it some day.

The legend of the bleeding rock in Ireland, is briefly, that Saint Moling changed the wife of Goban Saer, and a companion into stones; these stones are pointed out in Curraun townland, parish of Saint Mullins, in the barony of Bantry, County Wexford, and are known as Raimreach Ruadh; once, it is said, a blacksmith cut three grooves in the larger stone to blast it, whereupon blood oozed from the grooves, and the people decided that Red Raimreach was still alive and her blood circulating through the stone to which she had been changed.

The corpse in the range-cow's carcass was a ghastly business. I have not read the books by Gorman you mention[5] but the titles sound intriguing. The witch-cult offers great possibilities, in itself, and a writer need not tie himself down to the actual limits of the thing. Why should the cult be merely a fertility worship? Why should it not have deeper, darker significance, dating from pre-human memories? — In fiction, at least!

Your analysis of the Celtic nature is correct, as far as I can see. After all — where does reality quit off and unreality begin? We know that we cannot trust our external senses — why should we imagine that we can trust our inner promptings, impressions and senses? When we are dead it is as if we have never lived, therefore, how can we be sure that we live? I remember a most curious dream I had when a child that I have remembered long after I have forgotten the tang of stolen fruit and the feel of the morning dew on my bare feet. I dreamed that I slept and awoke, and when I awoke a boy and a girl about my age were playing near me. They were small and trimly shaped, with very dark skin and dark eyes. Their garments were scanty, and strange to me, now that I remember them, but at the time they were not strange, for I too was clad like them, and I too was small and delicately fashioned and dark. I had been sleeping on a sort of couch, richly made, which stood on a wide porch or room — I am not sure now. But if it were a room it had many wide windows without panes, and it seems that there were large columns. The room or porch looked out over a green and beautiful landscape of trees and grass grown hills sloping to a wide bay, glittering blue in the sunlight. Now, as I woke in my dream, this scene was fully familiar to me, and I knew that the boy and the girl were my brother and sister. It was not as if I had gone to sleep and awakened in a strange world; it was as if I had merely wakened from a sleep, returning to my natural, work-a-day world. And suddenly in my dream, I began to laugh and to narrate to my brother and my sister the strange dream I had had. And I told them of what — if there is any truth at all in reality — constituted my actual waking life. I described to them, as a vivid dream, my waking life, but could not put it clearly because it seemed dim and vague, as a dream seems dim and vague when one awakes. I told them that my dream had seemed so vivid while dreaming it, that I had actually thought it to be real, and believed myself to be a stocky blond child living a waking life, without knowledge of any other. And I said that I was glad I had awakened because that dream life had not been a good one, but full of strange barbarisms and roughness. Then they laughed and I awoke in reality — or slept again, I have occasionally wondered which! On which side of the gulf of dreams do we walk, and do we sleep when we think we wake?

But even when all life seems like a dream to us, the unreality of our triumphs and pleasures, which fade like autumn clouds, cannot soften and blunt the sharp pains of life — it is in pain that the material hard cold reality of the universe is most plain to us. What if we are but things of mist and shadow? Because we can suffer so, our pains are real, and we might as well be solid fleshly things such as the realists tell us we are. There is no refuge in idealism.

I am glad you liked "Reuben's Brethren". It has never been published save in a small privately circulated paper.[6]

I am glad too, that you are so well inclined toward the South. Her past and her traditions are close to my heart, though I would be a stranger within her gates. But my people settled and helped build her greatness and they shared her fall and ruin. Blood like that in my own veins was spilled like water from Manassas to Appomattox, and I still have kinsmen scattered all over the old states.

I am glad that there is a revival of genealogical interest in New England. In these days of Slavic-Latin invasion the old stock does well to turn an eye toward the land from which they came and remember the royalty of their breed. You say that most of the people of Rhode Island came from Lincolnshire, I believe — a shire that has always sent out sturdy sons. And your people came in 1630 — you certainly have a right to call yourself an American, if anyone does! Exactly three hundred years since your family settled in the New World.

I have read of Albert Martin and his heroic expedition.[7] In those days men put honor above their lives and he well knew that to enter the Alamo meant his doom. But he went clear-eyed to his fate, and died like a true Aryan, taking more than a life for a life. There were more than a few sons of New England who helped bring into birth the Republic of Texas — Stephen F. Austin, for instance, who in his way did as much for the struggling nation as Sam Houston did.

Speaking of Stonehenge, doubtless the Celts did erect it, but as you say, we need not confine ourselves to actuality in our dealings with it.

You are certainly correct about the standardism of America, and the merging of local individualisms. The great majority of people seem to look on this standardization with complacent approval. Not me; I seem to see the country assuming a drab and colorless uniformity without even a distinctive dialect — unless it is the Yiddish oi oi babble. But I think that even so the country will prove too unwieldy to survive. One part of the nation is exploited by men who live in another part. As the southwest has for years been exploited by oil companies and cattle and grain companies whose heads are located in New York or Chicago. Such concerns drain the money out of the country and bring nothing in. Oh, they pay wages of course, but in the case of the oil companies, a great majority of the workers are not native Texans, but Pennsylvanians, Kansans, and Indianans brought in by the promoters. This was especially so in the early days of oil development. Recently I seem to sense a slight stirring of sectional feeling; a certain class is growing in the southwest, not determined by race or business, which centers a real dislike upon the capitalist city of New York, and this dislike is growing into a real hatred. A small beginning, it is true, but it looks like a beginning to me. You see, for instance, men leave their farms and go work in the oil fields; the first wells drilled are almost invariably the property of small promoters; the big companies won't take any risks. They leave the wildcatting to the little fellows. Then when the field is going in full blast, they come in and start grabbing. Maybe there is an oil war on, or they want to freeze somebody out. They shut down the field and leave hundreds of men out of a job. The farms have been ruined by the oil boom and there's nothing to do but pack up and move on to some other field. This is the ruination of this country.

Then the juggling of the wheat and cotton and beef markets works real hardships on the farming class. All these things are beginning to be ascribed, more or less correctly, to Wall Street and New York.

Personally, I believe it would have been better for America to have been divided into several parts; say four sections, comprising the South, North, Northwest and Southwest. They could have been closely united by treaties and affinities of language and racial stock, so as to offer a compact front to any European invader, while developing each along its own natural lines. By the medium of trade, money would have flowed freely back and forth across the frontiers, stimulating prosperity, and one section would not suffer from asinine laws passed in another. Oh well, I don't know enough economics and politics to venture such propositions. But that dream of a Southwest empire from Blanca Peak to Panama makes my mouth water.

No, the founders of Texas had little idea of making a separate Republic out of the vast lands they wrested from the Latins. Old Hickory sent Sam Houston to Texas to add that country on to the United States, and most of the Texans clamored for admittance into the Union. But some of the far-sighted ones, Houston among others, held in their minds that lost dream of empire — well, it wasn't to be.

You are right; economics will have to be revolutionized entirely if the nation is to continue, and the choice seems to lie between fascism and communism — both of which I utterly detest. And doubtless the world will eventually, as you say, sink back into barbarism — if any humans are left alive after the next war. And since the inevitable goal of all civilization seems to be decadence, it seems hardly worth while to struggle up the long road from barbarism in the first place.

I'm glad you found my ramblings regarding Texas not too boresome. It is almost an empire in itself, and I look with real fury on the suggestion of dividing it into several states, though probably it would be an advantage to the Southwest politically. There are so many different kinds of landscapes in the state, though I must admit that a great percent of the scenery is utterly drab and without interest. Still, there are contrasts, and I can think of no more striking one than the sight that meets one's eyes when entering the Rio Grande valley on the Falfurrias-Edinburg road. The way lies seventy miles through level monotonous waste-land — an arid, sandy desert, grown scantily with grease-wood bushes and chaparral, unrelieved by any hill, tree or stream — then without warning you ride out of the desert edge into the irrigated belt. Abruptly the whole scene changes; green fields, with broad irrigation ditches winding through them lie smiling in the sun, and blossoming orange-groves wave in the soft breeze; the road becomes an avenue of palms, flanked on either hand by the tall straight trees with their broad leaves whispering in the wind — and the little towns are so thick you can see from one to the other, almost, looking straight down the unwinding road — at least, that was the Valley six years ago. I hear it has changed a great deal since then, but I am sure that the great floods of people pouring in, have not changed the general scenery much. Gad — I realized when I first saw it, how the Israelites must have felt when they first looked on Canaan after their wanderings in the desert.

There is another interesting but rather depressing phase of Texas in that region between San Antonio and Eagle Pass. In a certain section they raise little but onions and they plant onions as upper country farmers plant cotton — by the hundreds of acres. They have no water on top of the ground and a great many small oil promoters from my part of the country have gone there with their "spudders" — movable rigs for shallow wells — and made a bit of money drilling for water for irrigation. Ye gods — what a country! It isn't exactly flat, but rather rolling and bald as any desert, minus the sand. You can stand on a slight rise and see exactly the same thing stretching out to the horizon on every hand. It creates a most bewildering impression — it's surprizing how easily you can get turned around and completely lost, in a country where you can see for forty miles. It's worse than a level desert; besides it all looks just alike — you get mixed up in directions and things you see at a distance don't turn out to be where they seem. No fences, no trees, no cattle; just a few houses here and there baking in the hot sun and a few rigs pounding away — it gives an impression of utter desolation, worse than a desert, because buzzards fly over a desert and horned toads and snakes wriggle in the sand. Yet almost all of that dreary and lonely land is sown with onions! They weren't up when I was there and the landscape didn't look like any human being had ever laid a plough to it. There a mesquite tree looks like an oasis.

There are so many different phases of the state that people living in part of it are almost like foreigners to those living in another part. For instance, many folks living in East Texas regard West Texans much as, say, a New Yorker regards the people of Colorado and consider them to be a sort of cross between a cowpuncher and a Comanche. I travelled a couple of hundreds miles east of here since writing you before, and a citizen of the locality learning where I was from, he gazed on me with great interest exclaiming that I was indeed from the wild and woolly West! It seems that East Texans tend to roam east and south, and West Texans mainly travel westward — while a great percent of the population wanders all over the state and spills over into New Mexico, Arizona and California. I have never been to California but I hear that there is a great deal of prejudice in that state against Texans, just as there is in Kansas and Oklahoma — Kansas prejudice dating back to the days when Texas cowboys took the big trail herds up the old Chisholm to Abilene, and shot up the town to celebrate. Well — it wasn't such a hell of a town that the Kansans had to get snooty about it. Admitting that the Texas puncher of the old days was a dangerous and boisterous varmint, still when the boys had hazed a herd of longhorns up from the Border, through flooded rivers, blizzards, deserts and hostile Indian country, it was natural that they'd want to blow off steam. Abilene owes its very existence to the big Texas herds that flowed through it to the markets of Chicago and the East.

One branch of the old Chisholm trail ran within about thirty miles of this town, and the early squatters in this country subsisted mainly on strays that somehow got left in their brush corrals after the herds had gone on. But it was dangerous business; the punchers disliked having their steers swiped and they didn't like squatters anyhow. But gad, everybody stole cows in those days. All the big ranches were built or at least aided materially with running irons and mavericks. The big cattlemen who hanged rustlers were generally just as much thieves as the men they strung up; it was big business devouring the little, and the small-time promoter paying the penalty for his puniness.

The fiercest fights were between sheepmen and cattlemen and later between the small farmer and the ranchmen. That last was a bitter war, carried on with neither honor, mercy nor human consideration. Ranchmen cut the squatter's fences, burned his buildings, and frequently wiped out whole families, men, women and children with no more hesitation than Comanche Indians would have shown. In return the squatter stole the ranchman's cattle and killed them on the sly, fouled the springs, dammed up the streams, dynamited dams on ranchmen's property, ambushed cowboys and shot them out of their saddles — and made laws. That's the way they licked the cattlemen — by legislation. They simply swarmed in and took the country, swamping the original settlers just as they, in turn, had swamped the Indians in an earlier age. One of the worst of all cattlemen was an Englishman who lived in Concho country; his worst — and last — crime came about this way; finding that a young man he didn't fancy, was writing letters to his daughter, he took a crushing revenge and killed the postman who delivered the letters! He made a sweeping gesture of it by sending word to the sheriff, who was kin to the slaughtered postman, that he intended killing him too, on general principles — a bad move — the sheriff killed him instead. That all happened only a few years ago.

One could write a book from the tales told of Sonora alone, a sleepy little town of a few hundred inhabitants lying in the hills about a hundred miles from the Border. For instance, a good many years ago, a young cowpuncher went on the rampage up in Wyoming and started smoking his way to the Border. I don't know what started him on the tear — maybe a girl went back on him, or red liquor ran him crazy — anyway he came south like a sand-storm, leaving a trail of shot-up towns and bullet-riddled marshals and sheriffs behind him. That went alright as long as he was in Wyoming, Colorado and New Mexico, but the Texans of that day were a hard, hard breed. He rode up on the hills about Sonora one day and started throwing rifle bullets into the streets. Everybody scattered, not thinking much about it, but supposing it was just some local puncher in on a tear. But he got hold of somebody and sent word that he would ride into the town at a certain hour for supplies and he ordered the stores left open and the streets deserted — he would kill any man, woman or child he saw in the town. And he most certainly meant it. At the hour named he rode down the street and saw no living soul. The stores were open but they were deserted. He dismounted and entered. No one behind the counters. He began filling his saddle-bags with groceries — and the town marshal appeared at one door and the county judge at the other. When the smoke cleared away all three were down — the Wyoming man stone dead and the other two badly wounded, though they recovered.

Then once, up in Oklahoma, a young puncher stole an old ranchman's daughter and they rode hell-for-leather for the Border, with the old man hot on their heels. Another hundred miles and they might have been safe, but the old man caught up with them and killed them both just outside Sonora.

With the passing of open range one picturesque type has practically vanished — the range tramp. He was indeed a hobo but a more cleanly type than the ordinary wandering Willie. He worked for his living, but he did not need much nor did he work long or stay long in any one place. He drifted up and down the ranges from Mexico to Canada, and from the Canadian River to the Coast; his sole belongings were a broom tailed bronco, a worn old saddle and the clothes he wore. There were no fences to bother him and he need not stay in beaten trails. He grazed his mustang in the tall lush grass and slept under the stars. He was sure of a meal for himself and the bronc at any ranchhouse he stopped at, and when he needed a little money he stopped a few days and lent a hand at round-up or corral-building. He gambled a little, drank a little, played the painted ladies a little, but his love for these things could never make him settle down to the thirty-a-month grind of the average cowhand. He shunned trouble but was generally deadly when cornered. He drifted across the ranges, a lazy and good-natured ghost that came at dusk and went at dawn, and he never settled down until the coyotes picked his bones. He was not troubled with policemen and vice squads; he was not forced to tramp through dusty highways, or ride the rods, or gorge on mulligan in a lousy, vermin-ridden jungle. He had it over the modern city-going tramp a hundred ways and when I reflect on his nomadic and care-free life, I wish I had been born forty years ago.

Well, Texas is swiftly becoming modernized to suit the standards of big business; very seldom you even hear any of the old range songs any more — "Sam Bass", "The Killing of Jesse James", "The Old Chisholm Trail", "Utah Charlie", "San Antonio", "The Ranger."

But Texas was never as prolific in the matter of songs as Arkansas, for instance. In the Scotch-Irish settlement of Holly Springs where William Benjamin Howard settled in 1858, they still sang songs that carried the tang of the heather, though the singers were generations removed from the old country. Forty years ago such songs were popular there, as "Barbary Allen", "William Hall, a young Highlander", "The Wearin' of the Green", "Little Susie, the pride of Kildare", "Shamus O'Brien", one the name of which I forget but it had to do with the elopement of "pretty Polly" with one "Lord Thomas" who had drowned "six king's daughters", "Caroline, the belle of Edinburgh-town", and one which began

"Young Johnny's been on sea,
Young Johnny's been on shore,
Young Johnny he's in New Orleans
Where he has been before."

Narrating the triumph of a prosperous young sailor over an avaricious landlady. Then there was another, the name of which I do not know, but it contained the lines:

"Oh, come to me arms, Nora darlint,
Bid your frinds and ould companions good-boi,
For it's happy we will be in thot dear land av the free,
Livin' happily wid Barney McCoy."

Then there was one which must be very old, dealing with "Fair Elinor", "Lord Thomas" and "the brown girl". Lord Thomas married the brown girl because of her wealth, but invited Fair Elinor to the banquet, where the jealous brown girl killed her with "a wee pen-knife." Thus the horrific climax!:

"Lord Thomas having a Hielan' sword,
It being sharp and small,
He cut off the brown girl's head
And threw it against the wall!"

But doubtless you know the old ballad. Such were the songs sung by the people who came from Mississippi and the Carolinas and Georgia to build a homeland in the piney-woods of southwestern Arkansas. Squire James Henry was among the first to hew a clearing and build a house, and after him came the Howards, the Laffertys, the Burkes, the Houses, the Sinquefields, the Goodgames, the Goings, the Drakes, the Hulsemans, the Proctors, the Sullivans, the O'Briens, the Ellises, the Deans, the Hastings — southwestern Arkansas was a virgin wilderness in the 1850s — thick pine woods that had never known an axe, rich land beneath them, bear and deer in plenty. The settlers were responsible to no one. A few like Squire Henry had money in Arkansas's one bank, in Little Rock. Most of the rest seldom saw a coin. They didn't need it; they raised or took from the woods what they needed. Waves of war washed back and forth across the piney-woods, and nearly devastated the country, but it recovered from the devastation quicker than other parts, because the people were more hardy and primitive. Forty years ago they were giving "sheep saffron" and "chicken saffron" for "aggers" in Arkansas — tea made from dried sheep and chicken dung. Fires were banked in the wide fireplaces at night to keep the coals glowing, for matches were practically unknown.

Lumber mills came at a comparatively late date; when my grandmother came to Texas in '85 she sold large tracts of fine pine land for fifty cents an acre and thought it a good bargain. The buyers have become rich from it. The first usage of the land was agriculture; the larger cotton raisers like my great-grandfather, Squire Henry, took their cotton down to New Orleans on steamboats by way of the Ouachita, the Red River and the Mississippi. The Squire didn't share in the general ruin of Southern planters because, after he was discharged from his regiment in the first year of the war because of old age and wounds, he came to Texas with his niggers and for three years he raised and stored cotton. After the war was over, he went back to Arkansas and went into business with the money resultant from the sale of that cotton. He slipped one over Abe Lincoln that time, because the emancipation meant nothing to his niggers and they didn't get their freedom till after the war was well over, and they'd already built the foundations of the Squire's fortune. But if he drove them like a madman, he protected them, and years afterward, when he was past seventy, he fought one of the most desperate men in the country, with his naked fists, for bullying his niggers.

Probably the most picturesque figure in the Holly Springs country was Kelly the "conjer man", who held sway among the black population in the '70s. Son of a Congo ju-ju man was Kelly, and he dwelt apart from his race in silent majesty on the river. He must have been a magnificent brute, tall and supple as a black tiger, and with a silent haughtiness of manner that included whites as well as blacks. He had little to say and was not given to idle conversation. He did no work, nor did he ever take a mate, living in mysterious solitude. He always wore a red shirt, and large brass ear-rings in his ears added to the color of his appearance. He lifted "conjers" and healed disease by incantation and nameless things made of herbs and ground snake-bones. The black people called him Doctor Kelly and his first business was healing. Later he began to branch into darker practices. Niggers came to him to have spells removed, that enemies had placed on them, and the manner of his removal must have been horrific, judging from the wild tales that circulated afterwards. Consumption was unknown there, almost, among whites, but negroes had it plentifully and Kelly professed to cure such victims by cutting open their arms and sifting in a powder made of ground snake-bones. At last negroes began to go insane from his practices; whether the cause was physical or mental is unknown to this day, but the black population came to fear him as they did not fear the Devil, and Kelly assumed more and more a brooding, satanic aspect of dark majesty and sinister power; when he began casting his brooding eyes on white folk as if their souls, too, were his to dandle in the hollow of his hand, he sealed his doom. There were desperate characters living in the river-lands, white folks little above the negro in civilization, and much more dangerous and aggressive. They began to fear the conjure man and one night he vanished. Nor is it difficult to picture what happened in that lonely cabin, shadowed by the pine-forest — the crack of a shot in the night, the finishing stroke of a knife, then a sullen splash in the dusky waters of the Ouachita — and Kelly the conjure man vanished forever from the eyes of men.

Arkansas had many noted fighting-men in those days, who fought for the fun of it, as bears fight, making a carnival of blood-shed at every log-rolling, dance or frolic, but as it happens, the greatest fighting man of southwestern Arkansas was not a native of that state — he came into Holly Springs one day, bare-footed, black-bearded, limping from a bullet-wound in his leg — a present from certain revenue officers who objected to his brewing of mountain-dew on his own land at Sand Mountain in Georgia. He married a second cousin of mine and to the best of my knowledge there never was a man that licked him, even when he had a gallon of whiskey in him. He was nearly seven feet tall and built in due proportions. By trade he was a wagon-maker and his labor with the mallet gave his huge arms a hitting power that was far too much for the kicking and gouging of the ordinary rough-and-tumble fighter.

And speaking of mountain-dew, again we have big business devouring the small-scale producer. Why did the revenue men go into the hills and hunt down men who were merely seeking to augment their fearfully barren lives with a little hard money on the side? To protect the big liquor corporations! Why, the white liquor made by Southern mountaineers was generally far superior to anything the bar-keep shoved across the bar, but the makers seldom had the money to buy any sort of a license to manufacture or sell whiskey. Not infrequently the best customers the moonshiners had were owners of saloons. The mountain-men would raft their produce down to the river towns — corn, a little cotton maybe, coon and possum and wolf and bear skins — an innocent looking cargo, and certainly no room on a flat raft to conceal contraband. But underneath the raft, fastened firmly to the bottom, were kegs and barrels of good white corn liquor. By day the "upper" cargo was unloaded and sold, and late that night the "lower" cargo was slipped ashore to the saloons on the river bank. The liquor was carefully concealed, allowed to age a few months, colored, bottled and sold across the bar as labeled Bourbon, Haig & Haig, Scotch, or what have you! And at about three hundred percent profit for the saloon man. But the customers weren't cheated; it was good, pure whiskey, not to be compared for an instant with the muck modern bootleggers make.

You're right about oil booms — they bring a lot of money into the country and take more out, as well as ruining the country for other purposes. This might offend men in the oil business, but it's the truth that I've seen more young people sent to the Devil through the debauching effects of an oil boom than all the other reasons put together. I know; I was a kid in a boom town myself. The average child of ten or twelve who's lived through a boom or so, knows more vileness and bestial sinfulness than a man of thirty should know — whether he — or she — practice what they know or not. Glamor and filth! That's an oil boom. When I was a kid I worked in the tailoring business just as one terrific boom was dwindling out, and harlots used to give me dresses to be cleaned — sometimes they'd be in a mess from the wearer having been drunk and in the gutter. Beautiful silk and lace, delicate of texture and workmanship, but disgustingly soiled — such dresses always symbolized boom days and nights, to me — shimmering, tantalizing, alluring things, bright as dreams, but stained with nameless filth.

The shimmer and the filth were lacking in the old days, when men and women were more or less clean-lived and primitively-hardy. Some day I'd like to write a chronicle of the Southwest as it appears to me, but I don't suppose I could handle the thing properly. Well, if I never write it, at least people of my blood had a hand in making it — which is infinitely better than unromantically writing down the deeds of other men. Kinsmen of mine were among the riflemen at King's Mountain, and with Old Hickory at New Orleans; I had three great-uncles in the '49 gold rush — a Howard and two Martins — the Howard settled in Sonora, California, and one of the Martins left his bones on the trail — both my grandfathers rode for four years with Bedford Forrest, and I had a greatgrandfather in the Confederate Army too, as well as a number of great-uncles — one died in a nameless skirmish in the wilderness and another fell in the battle of Macon, Georgia; my grandfather Colonel George Ervin came into Texas when it was wild and raw, and he went into New Mexico, too, long before it was a state, and worked a silver mine — and once he rode like a bat out of Hell for the Texas line with old Geronimo's turbaned Apaches on his trail; an aunt of mine married and went into the Indian Territory to live years before the government ever opened the land for settlers; and one of my uncles, too, settled in what is now Oklahoma, in its wildest days, when it swarmed with half-wild Indians and murderous renegades from half-a-dozen states.

Colonel Ervin once owned a great deal of property in what is now a very prosperous section of Dallas, and might have grown with the town, but for the whippoorwills. They almost drove him crazy with their incessant calling, and though he was a kindly man with beasts and birds, and killed men with less remorse than he killed animals, in a fit of passion one night, he shot three whippoorwills; it was flying in the face of tradition and he quickly regretted it, but the damage was done. According to legend, you know, human life must pay for the blood of a whippoorwill, and soon the Colonel's family began to die, at the average of one a year, exactly as the old black people prophesied. He stuck it out five years and then, with five of his big family dead, he gave it up. No one every accused him of cowardice; he hacked his way alone, through a cordon of Phil Sheriden's cavalry-men; but the whippoorwills licked him. He sold his Dallas property for a song, went west and bought a sheep-ranch. Of course, Dallas was a swamp then, and very sickly. Still, it's not wise to kill a whippoorwill. Screech owls are about as bad; but you can stop a screech owl's screeching by taking off your left shoe, turning it upside down, and then putting it back on at once. A funny thing, but it works every time. Of course, the owl only screeches so long, and by the time you've made up your mind to try the old superstition, and have done it, the owl is through and flown off.

I've received the magazine[8] since writing the first part of this letter, and have read your story and article with keenest interest. The tale lives up to my expectations; indeed you have never, in any later story, I think, created a more masterful atmosphere of almost intolerable ghastliness. I cannot praise the story too highly; it shows, as do all your tales, the master's touch. And I enjoyed your philosophical article very much. I am hardly capable of judging it, since I never devoted any study to theology, philosophy or science, but I do not think that anyone could have handled the subject in a more masterly manner. I particularly like the point you made in that truth and necessity not always coinciding, some religion is necessary for the masses. I have always maintained this, myself. As for myself, neither idealism nor materialism appeals to me greatly. That life is chaotic, unjust and apparently blind and without reason or direction anyone can see; if the universe leans either way it is toward evil rather than good, as regards life and humanity. That there is any eventual goal for the human race rather than extinction, I do not believe nor do I have any faith in the eventual super-man. Yet the trend of so many materialists to suppress all primitive emotions is against my every instinct. Civilization, no doubt, requires it, and peace of mind demands it, yet for myself I had rather be dead than to live in an emotionless world. The clear white lamp of science and the passionless pursuit of knowledge are not enough for me; I must live deeply and listen to the call of the common clay in me, if I am to live at all. Without emotion and instinct I would be a dead, stagnant thing.

A materialistic resignation to unalterable laws is sensible but repellant to me. I will freely admit the necessity and desirability of such a resignation which is no more than recognizing natural laws — if such things be. A man who does not resign himself is like a caged wolf who breaks his heart and beats his brains out against the bars of his cage. Yet I must admit that such a course appeals to me more than that of calm submission. Foredoomed to failure, a man can still snarl and tear. Many and many a time, when one is reeling and dizzy and sick at heart and soul, broken and tossed by the blows of fate or destiny or whatever it is that makes life a hell on earth, one may wish for the ability of philosophic resignation; but with a slight renewal of strength the old blind fighting lust comes surging back and makes him break his fangs on the iron bars anew.

I'm no philosopher, but resignation isn't in my blood. I wish it was. It isn't necessarily a hope to win that makes a man rebel against the infamies of life, vainly. Defeat is the lot of all men, and I come of a breed that never won a war. Men and women too, of my line have fought for hopeless lost causes for a thousand years. Defeat waits for us all, but some of us, worse luck, can't accept it quietly.

Life reminds me of a fight I had, when a kid, with a heavyweight prize fighter. Round after round I rushed savagely and futilely, mad to come to grips and smash his ribs in, but hitting only the naked air. It was like fighting a shadow that wielded clubs; at the end of the fight I was swaying on the ropes groggy and dizzy, with my nose broken and my face cut and bruised, sick with a feeling of utterly helpless futility. That's Life — it's full of things that punish you fiercely and that you can't come to grips with. Punishment isn't so bad if you're handing it out at the same time. The other fellow may be strangling the life out of you, or ripping your ear off with his teeth, but if you're driving your knee to his groin, sinking your fists in his belly or have your thumb in his eye, you can stand the punishment. The hell of it comes when you're up against a battler you can't hit, or are licked and down in the muck with the other fellow stamping your guts out or grinding your face in with his hob-nails. That's Life — fighting shadows; taking lickings that you can't return.

But here I'm rambling on and on without coherency or connection. Thanks very much for giving me the tip about Talman.[9] I can't place Frio Canyon just now, though it seems I've heard of it. It's probably in the Davis Mountain country; I've never been in that part of Texas. Your comments on your early environs — thickly settled district on one hand and countryside on the other — intrigue my imagination; it must have been much like living on the threshold of the older and newer ages, with a clear insight to both. You looked back into the pioneering youth of the country and forward into its maturity. And the cultural history and architectural age of your environments has undoubtedly contributed to your splendid literary background. I envy you them.

Best wishes — cordially yours,
[Robert E. Howard]

P.S. I've received a letter from Talman, regarding contributions to his paper;[10] he says you suggested my name to him, and I wish to express as much as I can, my sincere appreciation of that fact. I am indeed deeply grateful to you. I'm glad you liked "Kings of the Night", also; I hope that your "Whisperer in Darkness" will be swiftly followed by many other tales; I can hardly wait for it!

NOTES

1. Date changed at Rob's suggestion due to *Strange Stories* information that Howard gives HPL, which HPL repeats to Donald Wandrei in a Dec. 1, 1930 letter. JB
2. *The National Amateur*, July 1919.
3. Editor of *Contemporary Verse* and *JAPM: The Poetry Monthly*. See letter 110 in Volume 1.
4. "The Dark Man."
5. Perhaps *The Place Called Dagon* (1927) by Herbert S. Gorman.
6. *The Junto*.
7. Albert Martin, of Rhode Island, a defender of the Alamo.
8. *The National Amateur*, July 1919, containing Lovecraft's "Idealism and Materialism: A Reflection" and "The Picture in the House."
9. Wilfred B. Talman.
10. *The Texaco Star*.

TSS: 21871-21882

146. To Tevis Clyde Smith, ca. November 1930.

Well, Fear Finn:

I read your article in the *Dallas News*[1] and enjoyed it as much as I did in the original. Have you sold any more lately?

I quote from Farnsworth's last letter: "'The Voice of El-Lil' is tied for first place with 'Strange Bedfellows,' in the letters and votes received so far for the first issue of *Oriental Stories*. This augurs well for the popularity of 'Red Blades of Black Cathay' and 'Hawks of Outremer,' which I think are much more striking. Von Gelb has galley proofs of 'Red Blades of Black Cathay' and is working on a cover design. Joseph Doolin will do the black and white illustration."

I'm working on the second draft of our collaborate story[2] and will try to get it to you in a few days.

Say, why haven't you sent me the bill for that door? I'm sure you've had it fixed by this time.

NOTES

1. "Fashions in Duels," November 30, 1930. See letter 138, note 1, page 63.
2. Either "Eighttoes Makes a Play" or "Diogenes of Today."

TSS: 82561

ঙ൨ঙ൨

147. To *Weird Tales*, ca. November 1930.[1]

I was particularly fascinated by the poem by Alice I'Anson in the latest issue. The writer must surely live in Mexico, for I believe that only one familiar with that ancient land could so reflect the slumbering soul of prehistoric Aztec-land as she has done. There is a difference in a poem written on some subject by one afar off and a poem written on the same subject by one familiar with the very heart of that subject. I have put it very clumsily, but "Teotihuacan" breathes the cultural essence, spirit and soul of Mexico.

NOTES

1. Published in the January 1931 issue.

ঙ൨ঙ൨

148. To Harold Preece, postmarked November 24, 1930.

I hope you'll pardon my negligence in answering your letter; please believe that it was not due to lack of interest. I was sorry to hear of Mr. Preece's mishap and sincerely hope that he has had a quick and complete recovery.

I haven't seen any of the pictures you mention. In fact, I haven't been to a show at all lately.

Nor have I read *The Bronze Age and the Celtic World*, though the title interests me highly and I intend to read it as soon as I can obtain it. To what race does the author ascribe the origin of the Cymry, if not to the Celts, and how does he account for their Celtic language in that event? As for the existence of a solid Celtic empire, I view the theory with doubt; the very nature of the Celt precludes such a possibility; but that Europe was once dominated by a number of tribes alike in blood and language, which formed the base for the Grecians, Latins, Italians, Spaniards and Gauls, I firmly believe. That the Latin language is an outgrowth of ancient Celtic is well established. And that the first Aryan conquerors of Greece, the Acheaens, were Celts is apparent.

I was interested in your mention of a Wishing Well — is it a natural spring, or what are the legends attached to it? And I feel greatly flattered that lines of my rhyme should have occurred to you, while strolling through the hills and woods. And I am also glad that you liked my story in *Weird Tales*. And thanks for the paper you sent me.

I imagine that Lenore finds anthropology a very interesting subject; it is one I would like to explore myself, but I'll never have a chance, I reckon. I certainly hope she gets the scholarship she is working for, and feel confident of her ability to do so. However, I see no reason why her scientific studies should affect her poetry. It should merely widen her poetic horizons; there is no richer field for the poet than the study of man from the primitive slime to the ultimate and unredeemable slime of civilized sophistication.

I'm afraid this letter is short and uninteresting, but my companionship cannot be stimulating, even in correspondence. I am haunted by the realization that my best days, mental and physical, lie behind me. And God knows my past life has not been so happy that I can look upon the future with any hope. A small thing, trivial in itself but significant — I put on the gloves the other day for the first time in months, and, for the first time in my life, found myself staggering and holding on to avoid being knocked out, and unable to inflict any punishment on my opponent. My legs never failed me before, but this time — well, I've slipped a long way, in every way. I'm just a shell of a man.

Slow sift the sands of Time; the yellowed leaves
Go drifting down an old and bitter wind;
Across the frozen moors the hedges stand
In tattered garments that the frost have thinned

A thousand phantoms pluck my ragged sleeve,
Wan ghosts of souls long into darkness thrust.
Their pale lips tell lost dreams I thought mine own,
And old sick longings smite my heart to dust.

I may not even dream of jeweled dawns,
Nor sing with lips that have forgot to laugh.
I fling aside the cloak of Youth and limp
A withered man upon a broken staff.

TSS: 92079

ଔଔଔଔ

149. To Tevis Clyde Smith, probably ca. December 1930.

Fear Finn:

I'm not surprized that Byrne turned down the story. Like all my work, it was weak in plot construction. Few action stories have a plot worth a damn, but how the authors get by with them, I don't know. I can't. Perhaps the editors resented the touch of realism in the action. The fight was simply a dramatic description of the Goddard-Choynsky bout[1] with a few changes, such as the ending; in the first fight Goddard eventually won by his rough tactics; flinging his body against Choynsky and crushing him through the ropes weakened the lighter man so much Goddard knocked him out later in the bout. I read the duel article[2] in the *Dallas News* and am thinking of sending it to Lovecraft, to show him what a Hell-ripper Uncle Terrence was. I'm glad you're selling stuff to your home-town paper. Keep it up, and you might establish a regular market and broaden out into other Texas papers. Most writers got their start in some such way.

I'm having no luck with *Fight Stories*. They rejected one story some time ago, and since then they've had another over a month and haven't reported on it at all. I somehow feel that they've soured on me, although in the last rejection letter I got, Byrne assured me that they all liked Costigan and wanted the series to continue. But I feel that I've sold them my last story — on Costigan, at least.

I reckon you had a good time when you went to Bonham. I thought I'd get to come to Brownwood for the game, but I won't be able to make it. I don't know when I'll get to come over.

Yes, Farnsworth gave us quite a hand on our Oriental tale and I feel that it should win first place, in spite of the stupid errors and anachronisms I made in it. My "Voice of El-Lil" tied for first place in *Oriental Stories*, I guess you noticed. It was the very devil to write, but I rather like the thing. Considerably to my surprize, "Kings of the Night" won first place in *Weird Tales'* popularity balloting. I knew it was a good tale, but it was so devoid of romance — love interest, that is — and any really weird touch, that I did not think it would take very well with the readers.

Farsnworth tells me that he is going to make *Weird Tales* a bi-monthly like *Oriental Stories* — cutting my already slim market in half. He says he's stocked up on *Weird Tale* stories for the present. He also says that if he fails to win his fight with MacFadden, he'll publish *Strange Stories* under a different name, but that as he's already spent several hundred dollars fighting MacFadden, he's not going to change the name unless he has to.

I've sold nothing recently except a tale to *Oriental Stories* and one to *Weird Tales*. The Oriental story I feel I sold merely on my reputation — if I can be said to have one. The title, "The Blood of Bel-Shazzer," referring to a jewel, was the only interesting thing about it. The plot was hackneyed and sketchy, the action labored and artificial. Only once in the entire story did I evoke a slight spark of the fire that has smoldered out in me. But at least I sold it, for $115. The *Weird Tale* story, a short one that brought $64, was infinitely better, though marred by a clumsy style and a too melodramatic development. It carried out the theme I mentioned to you in a previous letter; the title is "The Black Stone," and is the best attempt at bizarre literature that I have yet sold. I have a still shorter and better story, "The Thing on the Roof," which I have not yet sent Farnsworth and which I may not send him, since he says he is stocked up. But this story is by far the best thing I have ever written and one which I am really inclined to believe approaches real literature, distantly, at least.

I have done nothing recently. I have a number of manuscripts that are practically ready to be sent off, and a number more which lack only a little work to be completed. Some would probably sell, but I have been too lethargic. The game is hardly worth the candle.

I might work up a sort of artificial fighting fury and crash through but the result would not be reward enough for the effort. Months ago the game lost all its zest for me.

I don't know what I'm going to do next, or where I'm going. Probably nothing and nowhere. I've been sketchily considering a trip to Mexico City but I won't go. There's no particular reason why I shouldn't, I suppose, except that the thought of bestirring myself and making the effort is one that well-nigh overwhelms me. I have money enough to go anywhere in the Western Hemisphere, but the thought of going anywhere is as repellant as is the thought of staying here.

No doubt you've heard of the Yezidis who live on Mount Lalesh in Syria and worship the devil in the form of a brazen peacock. They believe that Satan was the foremost of angels and that he rules on earth for ten thousand years. God, they say, is too far away, too gigantic, to be concerned with the affairs of the earth, and only by worshipping Melek Taus can anyone prosper, for only he has charge of men's affairs. Certainly the Devil is loose on the world, and the evil are more likely to prosper than the honest and virtuous. Perhaps the Yezidis are right. Certainly their cult is as logical as religions which teach that this earthly hell of red chaos and black insanity is ruled by principles of good and light, that justice exists and reigns, and that men are compensated for good and evil — God, what a bone-clanking jest — like the cataclysmic laughter from the gaping and froth-dripping jaws of a bleached skull. Yet worshipping Satan is too much like kow-towing to a conqueror. We may realize his power without doing obeisance to him.

Great events are shaping themselves in the East. If any man is left to write the history of these times, he will have horrific tales to tell. People under-rate Russia. The potentialities of world-conquest lie in the minds and calloused hands of those mujiks. The whole world is quaking and rocking, and an undercurrent of insanity is bubbling and seething beneath the surface. Every time the wind blows out of the East I smell the reek of war in it. Nothing is stable now; we live in the midst of the Age of Change. International convulsions and gigantic upheavals are hovering in the very air of the world. The richest countries in the world writhe in starvation while the rich folk go blindly to their own doom, like swine who are unaware that the muck they tread on is alive with waking serpents. The wings of Melek Taus hover over the world, the winds whisper of revolt, anarchy, war and red ruin for all the sons of men.

Already Mussolini's feet are unsteady in Italy and last night France was without a government. In Scotland ninety thousand men go out on a strike, and social unrest spreads over the British Isles. In Russia men on trial for treason fling accusations at the powers of the world. And Italy is accused of forming secret alliances with Bulgaria, Turkey, Austria and Germany to overthrow the conditions imposed on them by defeat in the last war. Well, let the nations cut each other's throats, and let war sweep the planet clean. When it's done we can all lie down in the grateful sleep of everlasting oblivion and the clean winds and the seas will erase from the poor old world the scars of mankind's existence.

But to get to our petty affairs again — petty to the world, but all-important to us, God knows. If you haven't sent "The Honor of the Game" to *Argosy*, send it first to Street & Smith, *Sport Story*, I believe is the name of their magazine. It has no chance with them, but it has no chance with any magazine, so as well one as the other. *Argosy* sent me an envelope and blank for the names and addresses of ten of my friends, saying that they did not wish any of my friends to miss my stories which appear in *Argosy*. A bit if irony which slightly gagged me. And besides, I haven't that many in the world, anyway. Farsnworth tells me that for some esoteric reason known only to the radio people, Station WTAM has ceased to dramatize stories from *Weird Tales*.

Sure, come ahead. No need for you to bring any muck. We can get plenty here. So it will be better for you to come straight through, I imagine, for as far as I know the roads are in good shape. Dave was saying the other night, when he and Pink and I were sitting around drinking beer in the ice house, for me to get you and Truett over here Saturday and we'd throw a party in his shack, that night. Well, we'll see what we can do, so come gradually ahead yet.

Fear Dunn

P.S. Say, bring me a June[3] *Weird Tales*, will you? I can't get the damn thing here and I haven't seen the latest one. Thanks.

NOTES

1. Joe Goddard fought Joe Choynsky three times, twice in 1891 for the heavyweight championship of Australia (Goddard won both), and once in Philadelphia in 1898 (no decision). Based on the description, the Howard story is probably "Double-Cross."
2. See letter 138, page 63, note 1.
3. "June" appears to be a typo, as internal evidence all points to a December composition date, when the January *WT* would have come out.

TSS: 82125-82126, 82665

150. To Tevis Clyde Smith, ca. December 1930.

Well, Fear Finn:

I don't know when I'll be able to come to Brownwood, but you're welcome to the capper, which is the only distillery appliance I have.

Farnsworth writes me that Macfadden is disputing his title to *Strange Stories*, which is delaying the publication, but says he still intends to put out the magazine, though he don't know when it will be.

I recently sold a story to *Weird Tales*,[1] a Solomon Kane story about which I hesitated several months before finally sending. It's about the poorest story I've ever sold, marking a distinct transition in my development as a writer — a sort of half-way mark between pure action stuff and the cosmic horror tale, to which style I have at last managed to achieve, to a certain extent at least. I doubt if I will sell *Weird Tales* any of the latter very soon, because my style of handling this new theme is bound to be clumsy and amateurish, but I feel that I may eventually gain some recognition in that field. Of course, I'll never equal Lovecraft, but I believe I can do at least as well as most of the other *Weird Tale* writers do in that line. Not that I mean to drop my action stuff, not in the least.

Lovecraft says that he envies me my Southern blood, that he has always admired the South, though he is a native New Englander of many generations descent. He speaks with great admiration of the old Southern aristocracy era, and says that Charleston is his favorite of all cities, and that he may move there some day to live.

By the way, did you ever hear of the lost towns of the Rio Grande mouth? There were two, just where the river empties into the Gulf. The one on the Mexican side was called the City of Bagdad, and the one on the American side was called, I believe, Clarksville — compare the artistic ideas of the two nations! — and now, I hear, not a stick remains of the Mexican town and only a few signs of Clarksville. It seems that in 1887 the towns were flooded and partly destroyed, and the rail-roads later ruined them and caused them to be abandoned entirely. I hear that the City of Bagdad was a town of fifteen thousand people, of all breeds, and was quite an important town in the days when boats plied up and down the river. The towns were, as I gather, just across the river from each other.

I hope you've sold something else by this time.

Fear Dunn

NOTES

1. "The Footfalls Within."

TSS: 82542

ⲰⲰⲰ

151. To Unknown Recipient, Undated, unsent[1]

Salaam:

I do not remember who I told you I was going to tangle with but the last bout I had I got a hell of a beating. That is, the other bird hit me with every thing but the Congressional Report but wasn't able to knock me off my feet or hurt me much, see. We mixed it from start to finish the only difference being that he is hitting where I am and I am hitting where he is not. I hung him over the ropes or put him down for a count every time I landed only I just didn't land often enough.

I am finding it difficult to find birds who will box for me for some reason or other. Not long ago I worked up a match with a 190 pound gazoot and he said lets hit this bag first. I had a bag weighing about forty pounds hanging up which I punch to help my hitting muscles. He swung with all his might and lifted it nearly to the limb it was hanging on now then said he let me see you do that good. I let go with my right and the bag went clear over the limb and hung up in the tree. Is that as hard as you can hit he says and I says no, certainly not and he says I have just now remembered an important engagement I have so you'll have to find somebody else to box with you. If I thought that he thought I am too frail for him to box with I would hand him one on the chin.

I do not suppose I will go to Devil's River or any place because I am broke just now and anyway I have lost enthusiasm. Though it would [be][2] rather fine to get out in the boundless plains where the golden sunsets flame—you'll have to pardon me. I am writing a western thriller and the habit is getting on me.

Say, you know a lot about this physical culture hooey, can you tell me how much under developed I am? I know I am not as large and muscular as I should be and it is difficult for me to build myself up. Here are my measurements—how do I stack up to the ordinary, average man standard.

height	6 feet
weight	190 pounds
chest	42 inches expanded 45
head	23 inches
neck	17 inches
shoulders	491/2 inches
waist	36 inches
hips	40 inches
thighs	23 inches
calves	15 inches
upper arm	141/2 inches
fore arm	131/2 inches

[. . .]

NOTES

1. This letter is moved to this position due to Howard giving his full body measurements, specifically focusing on his weight of "190 lbs.". In letter 111 (Vol. 1) to Harold Preece, he states his weight at about 180 lbs., and in letter 168 (Vol. 2) to Lovecraft, he gives his weight as 200 lbs. and next in letter 199 (Vol. 2) to Wilfred Talman, he gives his weight as 203 lbs. I believe this letter is also written to Harold Preece, as Howard mainly wrote Preece about his physical development and boxing matches in his existing letters. If the latter is true, this also to me gives an approximate date, as the last extant letter to Harold is dated Nov. 24, 1930. JB
2. The word "be" is not in the original letter and was added for clarity. JB

TSS: 92093

1931

152. To H.P. Lovecraft, ca. January 1931.

Dear Mr. Lovecraft:

As always I found your recent letter most interesting and instructive. Your comments on pioneering gave me a new and fascinating slant on the thing as a whole, making me realize that after all, the pioneering and settling of a new wild country is a reversion to the primitive Aryan type of life. This fact is obvious, yet I had never so fully realized it before. Since reading your letter I realize too how closely New England and the South are knit to England. It is a rather fascinating thought somehow, to think of men in England planning and mapping out towns across the ocean in a wilderness they never looked on. Doubtless the West has passed through a more truly primitive pioneering epoch, but you folks of the New England states and the South had the enormous advantage of an epoch we have not had and will not have. You had the advantages of a settled and mature cultural civilization before the rise of the present machine-ruled age. You had a period of cultural development during which your ships plied the high seas bringing the wealth of foreign ports, and the arts of poetry, literature, architecture and so on, acquired solid foundation and had the opportunity to flourish and blossom. Even now, in this helter-skelter age, I believe that New England, as represented by its older and purer element at least, presents a more firmly grounded bulwark of the deep solid principles and ideals that once characterized this Anglo-American civilization, than can be found anywhere else, and will resist the senseless wholesale exploitation of mechanized modernism longer than any other part of the country. I may be wrong, as I have never had the opportunity to observe conditions first hand, but that is the impression I get.

The Southwest and West on the other hand, have never had the time to develop a cultural civilization of their own. The transition from primitive pioneering times to the machine age is almost unbroken. Westerners have not had and will not have time to develop any real civilization, founded on cultural ideals and principles, before the rise of the mechanized epoch. What past of that sort the Southwest and West can boast, is now symbolized by the crumbling walls of old Spanish missions — mute reminders of the lazy, colorful and romantic days of Spanish rule in California and Texas, when gay clad caballeros diced and flirted and raced horses and dueled in the shadow of those missions, and within their cool drowsy shelters, monks and priests toiled at neatly written manuscripts, and decorated the walls with delicate hand-painted and hand-carved patterns. No, pioneer life was somewhat inspiring, was hardy and clean, but it was fiercely barren, too, and had the effect of making men and women so brutally practical that most of the latent poetry and artistic instinct was ground out of their souls — and then before their descendents could develop, as you all in New England developed, a cultural civilization with distinctive standards, the machine age was — or is — dominant.

I am very glad you liked "The Voice of El-Lil" and sincerely appreciate the kind things you said about the tale. You're right, of course, about the Asia Minor business. Using the term to designate Mesopotamia was sheer carelessness in me. I'm afraid you'll find my work riddled with errors like that. I have a slovenly way of not stopping to look up references when I'm writing. But my erroneous use of Asia Minor was really inexcusable and I'm glad you called my attention to it. By the way, what is your opinion about the origin of the Hittites? My ideas about this race is very vague; I seem to have a dim impression that they inhabited most of what's now Anatolia, and that after fighting back and forth with the Egyptians and Assyrians for many centuries, they were finally conquered and Aryanized by the Phrygians who preceded the main body of Hellenic conquest. And I seem to have read that these Hittites employed large bodies of Amazons in their armies. But possibly my data is all wrong. If you can cast any light on this ancient people, I'd highly appreciate it.

Mr. Wright informed me of his plan to make *Weird Tales* a bi-monthly and I'll admit I don't like the idea. It cuts down the market too much. I don't believe the change will be very popular with the readers, either. Like you, I hope the magazine isn't discontinued. It's the only magazine in the world, so far as I know, in which the writer can give full sway to his imagination. Yet there is one advantage in the bi-monthly idea — I'll get to read your "Whisperer" all at once, without having to wait a month for the last installment. Mr. Wright told me he was pretty well stocked up on *Weird Tale* stories, and that fact, together with the fact that no more serials will be used, caused me to abandon a sequel I was writing to "Skull-Face."

Speaking of rattlesnakes, in the Spring when the varmints come out of their lairs I'll try to get you some rattles. They make rather interesting items in a collection of curios, and as this is a snake country through here, I ought to be able to secure some good ones. I remember one time when I was about twelve years old, a friend and I were trapping in the Coleman county hills, and one warm day in early Spring we went looking to our traps. It was just such a day when snakes, half blind and sluggish from their long sleep, crawl out and sun themselves on rocks in the lee of a hill. We were on the south side of a good sized hill, and my friend climbed down a big rock to examine a trap set back under it in a sort of a cave. Carelessly bending down on all fours to look under the rock, he set his bare hand within a few inches of a four-foot diamond-back rattler that lay sunning himself. I'll never forget that. My friend gave a howl and came floating back up the cliff like a wind-blown wisp of fog; I presume he climbed somehow, but his ascent gave the impression of a squirrel-like scamper straight up the sheer rock. I was laughing so, and he was so weak from fright that our well-meaning stones went wild and the snake crawled sluggishly back under the rock. He was really too lethargic to bite anyone. And I'm not likely to forget the time that I, climbing up a creek bank, guilelessly and trustfully took hold of a water moccasin thinking it was part of a tree. In the east part of this town the country is sandy and copperheads used to abound. A few years ago a big snake of that species bit a child, striking her with such force that he knocked her down, and then biting her repeatedly while she was on the ground. Big spots came out all over the child, but these West Texas kids are as hard to kill as cats. She nearly died, but eventually got over it. A mad snake is the devil's own; he won't quit striking you until he is dead or you, and I've heard of snakes continuing to strike the corpse of a man they'd killed, until their venom sac was completely empty. Not long ago they passed an ordinance prohibiting hogs from running wild in the Austin hills, and now I hear that the snakes are increasing at an alarming rate and even wriggling down into the city itself. Hogs eat snakes and so do chaparral birds — Indian runners or sage-hens they call them in the West — and I used to have a tomcat that killed snakes of all sorts and devoured them with gusto. A rattler can bite a hog all day without hurting the hog.

Bullfighting is indeed a reversion to Roman amphitheater days. I have an idea that the Mediterranean peoples have practiced it in some form or other every since the days of Crete, where it flourished, according to paintings on vases and the like. You're right about athletics; more and more the tendency is to watch the professional perform rather than to indulge one's self. Organized athletics are having an effect on the schools which I do not believe is good. When I was a country schoolboy there was little systematic and competitive athletics, but all engaged in some playground form of amusement — baseball, snap-the-whip, wolf-over-the-river, wrestling, all hard strenuous games inclined to toughen and strengthen the participants. Now, certain groups of pupils play football and basketball and compete in track events, and the great majority stand about and watch them. It seems to me that organized sport is tending to create a powerful and athletic minority and a soft-bodied and sluggish majority. Take the average high school. Ten, or perhaps fifteen percent of the pupils go in for the grinding grill of competitive athletics; the rest do nothing in the way of building their bodies, or dissipating their natural animal spirits in wholesome ways. No wonder drunkenness and immorality are so prevalent among students. To the average boy or girl the accumulation of knowledge isn't enough to spend their energy on — they can learn only so much, anyhow, and the Devil himself couldn't teach the average pupil, with his undoubtedly limited capacity, very much, anyway. They must have a physical outlet, and since systematic sport denies this to all but a chosen few, the rest naturally turn to amusements less wholesome. This seems to be the trend of modern life, to me.

Thanks very much for the statistics-paper. It seems in truth that only Americans are dying in New York and only Jews are being born. It seems certain that in a generation or so, New York will be a full fledged Hebrew city, 100 Yiddish. Yet I am less sorry to see this happen to New York than I am to note the inroads of the aliens into New England, though I'm sure that wops and Polacks are preferable to Jews. I can understand how the French you mention are to be preferred to the rest; as you say, they have some right on this Continent. I was much interested by what you say of the Fiji Island colony. Ye gods, what next will be dumped on the shores of this long-suffering land? They must present an interesting study, at least. You are probably right in assuming them to be of Australoid-Dravidian stock, with a liberal mixture of pure negroid from prehistoric times.

I'm afraid that in a few generations Texas will be over-run with mongrels. Looking at the state as a whole: the great bulk of the population is of Anglo-American stock, mainly with Southern ancestry, but with quite a goodly proportion who trace their lines back to the Mid-West or New England. Central Texas is more dominantly Anglo-Saxon and Scotch-Irish than any other portion. On the Border there is a large Latin element, and on the coasts swarms of foreigners. The inevitable Jew infests the state in great numbers. You can hardly find a town of three thousand or more inhabitants that does not contain at least one Jew in business. And the Jew almost invariably has the country trade. It is a stock saying among rural Texans that if the Jew cannot sell his stuff at his price, he will sell it at yours. What they cannot seem to realize is that at whatever price he sells his shoddy junk, he is making a bigger profit than the legitimate merchant can make. No Aryan ever outwitted a Jew in business. I used to work in a Jewish dry-goods store. Before each sale — and Jewish sales go on forever — I would "mark down" the goods according to his instructions. For instance, the regular retail price of a pair of trousers would be $5.00. I would mark in big numbers on the tag — $9.50, then draw a line through that and mark below, $5.50. Thus the duped customer, noting the marked out price and comparing it to the new price, would consider that he was getting a bargain, whereas he was in reality paying fifty cents more than the regular price of the garment. But you can't make the average countryman believe that he's not saving money and getting gorgeous bargains by trading with the Jews.

But to return to the foreignization of the state. Houston, the largest city, has a vast alien population — Jews, Slavs, and Italians, the last drifting up from New Orleans. Dallas fairly swarms with Jews, in ever increasing numbers. In fact, the term, "Dallas Jews" is applied indiscriminately to inhabitants of the city by spiteful people. Dallas also has numbers of Greeks, Russians and Italians and quite a few Mexicans. San Antonio has a large population of Mexicans, twenty or thirty percent of the entire population, and the usual quota of Jews, Italians and Slavs. Of the remaining population, a large percent is Germanic. Fort Worth, thirty miles west of Dallas, and originally settled by cattlemen, is overwhelmingly American; the foreign percentage is very small. Waco, in central east Texas, has, in addition to a vast negro population, a steadily increasing foreign element. The Jew is there, but not many Italians, their place being taken by Poles, Bohemians, Czechs and Magyars. In contrast to most of the rest of the state, the rural element about Waco is strongly alien in flavor, immigrants from eastern and central Europe having swarmed into the country a generation or so back, and slowly pushed out the original Anglo-American farmers. There were several waves of immigration. The Scotch-Irish and Anglo-Saxon farmers followed the cattle-men, then a host of Germans came up from the coast, and later, after them came a swarm of Poles and Bohemians who now seem destined to eventually take over the country. In some places, a "white German" even with a strong Deutch, accent seems like a brother, among the swarms of "black Germans" — dark haired Poles and Slovaks. Even there, there is still a substantial base of Anglo-Americans but I cannot say what a few more generations will do. Austin, the capital city, set among picturesque hills, is mainly free from aliens, but Galveston and Corpus Christi swarm with Italians, South Americans, Cubans, Filipinos, Slavs, Jews — the usual population of sea-port towns. As for the Rio Grande Valley, the alien population is immense, some towns, I hear, being almost entirely composed of Latins and Jews, aside from their natural Mexican element. A broad belt of coast country from Port Arthur to Matagorda is dominated by the usual swarm of Poles, Swedes, Slavs, Latins, Germans — etc. West of Cross Plains, the fertile grain country is inhabited thickly by Swedes and Germans, and this is the case with most of the richest parts of the state. The American farmer cannot compete with the low living standards and close economy and wheel-horse work of the alien farmer. He is slowly but surely being pushed off the best land, into the cities or on to worthless farms. Just now his last stand is on the great plains of western Texas, and he is supreme there, because it's a big country, and a hard country, and no place for weaklings, and un-developed as yet. And for enduring hardships and taking big chances, for guts and stamina and man-killing work in huge, dynamic bursts, there never was and never will be a race to compare with the American of old British stock. It's not the fierce hardships that ruin the race — they can overcome any obstacle, so long as it's big enough and hard enough to grip and trample; but the long, monotonous, grinding toil with a far-distant goal to view, the skimping, and petty economy, the saving the pennies and living on bacon-rinds, the use of every inch of land, every blade of grass, every hog's bristle, all that whips the Anglo-American, viewed as a whole, while such things are second nature to the peasant from Europe. America must learn the secret of concentrated farming before her sons can compete with the scum of Europe. But who in the Devil wants to succeed by the bacon-rind and hog-bristle route?

Let the wops live on a penny a day and grow rich selling garbage crumbs. Haven't I seen Joe Rizza and his wife, stand day after day, seven days in the week, behind a counter shucking oysters and waiting on trade as if their lives depended on it, and he worth maybe a hundred thousand dollars and the owner of a whole chain of Italian restaurants and fish houses? And my French land-lady, bewailing the ancient glories of French New Orleans, would wrathfully repeat the tale of how Joe Rizza had landed in America fifteen years before with not even a nickel to his name. Gad — how she hated the Italians! And how all the Creoles hated them. It was my fortune to be acquainted with some elderly maiden ladies by the name of Durell — gentlewomen of the old school, living in semi-seclusion and striving to maintain the standards of a faded aristocracy, and reconcile their natures with the necessity which forced them to run a rooming house. They talked French among themselves and though born and raised in New Orleans, spoke English with a very distinct accent. They talked a great deal of how the rising wave of Italian immigration had swept the original French inhabitants away; and I have seen the old Durell mansion in the heart of the Old French Quarter — now the Latin Quarter — once a stately, century-old, residence, built with characteristic French style — now a hovel housing half a dozen squalid Italian families, with goats browsing and ragged children playing in the weed-grown, filth-strewn court-yard. In justice to the Italians, I must say that the scum that overflows New Orleans really originates mainly in Sicily. There are many very decent Italians in the city who look down on and despise these Sicilians as fiercely as do the French. But to get back to Joe Rizza and his oysters — the only sign of wealth sported by the Rizza family was the large gold rosary worn by his wife, the sight of which always sent my French landlady into tremors of wrath. She resented the fact that a wop's wife could wear a rosary such as she, whose ancestors once ruled New Orleans, could not afford. But no other sign was given by the Rizzas than that — to the casual eye they were hounded by the dogs of starvation whose fangs they could only hope to avoid by — shucking oysters seven days out of the week, from early morning to late at night! And I'm sure they lived on just a few cents a day, just as they had in the days when they really were poverty-stricken. I've heard that wops haunt the garbage piles for their food, and I'm prepared to believe it. Well, let Americans watch closely the Jewish-Italian way of making money, let them take the lesson to heart and go and do likewise, if they wish to compete with them — but I'm willing to bet my hat that the average American would rather hang or starve all at once than to drag out a slow starvation of body and soul over a long period of years, merely to acquire the empty honor of dying a rich man.

Your vivid and fascinating descriptions of the South fill me with a great desire to visit there. Every word of it was deeply interesting and instructive to me, as my ignorance of that country, geographically and historically, is abysmal. I was particularly enthralled by your descriptions of Virginia, and Charleston. It must be fascinating to watch the remodeling of Williamsburg. When it is completely restored it should prove a veritable paradise to lovers of the old days and old ways of Colonial America. You know, I find it almost impossible to vizualize a long-settled countryside. I always think of large cities in connection with long settlement, which is natural considering the fact that such cities as San Antonio and New Orleans have always represented old established occupancy to me, and the Cajun and nigger teeming swamps of Louisiana gave me no real impressions on the subject. Born and bred in the newer lands as I was, it is hard for me to visualize a countryside peopled by folk who have lived there for hundreds of years. Here in Texas, in this part particularly, a farm-house fifty years old is considered remarkably ancient. Fifty years ago the danger of Indian raids was scarcely past. The thought of a farm that has been passed down from generation to generation, through perhaps a hundred and fifty years is most strange to me. I must see the Eastern states before I can formulate any logical impressions of the idea. Dialects always interest me, and I appreciated very much your comments on Charleston accent. In keeping with my ignorance of the South in general, it was news to me, that citizens of this city spoke with a different accent from the rest of the South, and I am sure that the reasons you put forward for this difference are correct.

Your letters are certainly broadening my views and store of knowledge; they give me a conception of the country east of the Mississippi, which has always been a great vague land of mist in my mind. How few people give any thought to the history of even their own locality! Why, it was from the Concho River, only about a hundred miles from here that John Chisum started to New Mexico in 1868, with his herd of ten thousand cattle, his caravan of wagons and his army of hard-bit Texas cowpunchers, yet his name is hardly known in this country. John Chisum was born in Tennessee and grew up in East Texas. He was an empire builder if one ever lived. To read New Mexican history of the 70s it would seem that he supported the territory — people either worked for John Chisum or stole cattle from him! In the days of his greatest power his herd numbered more than a hundred thousand head. The Long-rail and the

Jingle-bob were known from Border to Border. He always kept open house; there any man could stay and eat his fill as long as he wished and no questions were asked him. Breakfast, dinner and supper places were set for twenty-six at the table in his big adobe house and generally all places were full. He was a figure of really heroic proportions, a builder of empires, yet he was by instinct merely a hard headed business man. Nothing dramatic about John Chisum, and maybe that's why history has slighted him in favor of fruitless but flashing characters who blazed vain trails of blood and slaughter across the West. John Chisum never even buckled a gun on his hip in his life; he was a builder, not a destroyer. He did not even take the war-path in that feud known as the bloody Lincoln County war. Have you ever read of it? There's drama! There's epic and saga and the red tides of slaughter! Heroism, reckless courage, brute ferocity, blind idealism and bestial greed. And the peak of red drama was touched that bloody night in the shuddering little mountain town of Lincoln, when Murphy's henchmen crouched like tigers in the night behind the flaming walls of McSween's 'dobe dwelling. Let me try to draw that picture as it has been told and re-told in song and story in the fierce annals of the Southwest — the greatest fight of them all.

The night is forked with leaping tongues of crimson flame; the bullet-riddled 'dobe walls have crumbled; the fire has devoured the west wing, the front part of the building, and now licks greedily at the last room remaining of the east wing. The walls are beginning to crumble, the roof is falling. Hidden behind wall and stable, eager and blood-maddened, crouch the Murphy men, rifles at the ready. For three days and nights they have waged a fruitless battle with the defenders; now since treachery has fired the adobe house, their turn has come at last. They keep their eyes and rifle muzzles fixed hard on the single door. Before that door, in the red glare of the climbing flames lie McSween, Harvey Morris, Semora, Romero and Salazar in pools of their own blood, where the bullets struck them down as they rushed from the burning house; four dead, one — Salazar — badly wounded. O'Folliard, Skurlock, Gonzalez and Chavez have made the dash and somehow raced through that rain of lead and escaped in the darkness. Now is the peak of red drama, for in that blazing snare still lurks one man. The watchers grip their rifles until their knuckles show white. McSween's right hand man has yet to dare that lead tipped gantlet — Billy the Kid, that slim nineteen-year-old boy, with the steel grey eyes, the gay smile, the soft voice and the deadliness of a rattler. The flames roar and toss; soon he must leap through that door if he would not be burned like a rat in a trap. Bob Beckwith, whose bullet struck down McSween, curses between his teeth and trembles like a tensed hunting hound in his eagerness. He and his comrades, hidden by wall and semi-darkness, are comparatively safe — but no foe of the Kid's is safe within gun-shot range. Scarce ten yards away the soaring flames will etch their prey mercilessly in their rifle sights — how can the best marksmen of the Southwest miss at that range? Bob Beckwith curses and his eyes dance with madness. He killed McSween; now to his everlasting glory he must kill Billy the Kid, and wipe out the stain of Murphy blood — Morton, Baker — victims of the Kid's unerring eye and steady hand. A shower of sparks — the roofs falls in with a roar; as if the happening hurled him from the building, a figure leaps through the door into the red glare. A mad rattle of rifle-fire volleys and the air is filled with singing lead. Through that howling hail of death the Kid races and his own guns are spurting jets of fire. Bob Beckwith falls across the wall, stone dead. Two more of the posse bellow as the Kid's bullets mark them for life. Slugs rip through the Kid's hat and clothes; death sings in the air about him — but he clears the wall and vanishes in the darkness. His time is not yet come and there still remain further red chapters to write in that red life. The Murphy men come from their coverts to roar their triumph, and while fiddles are brought and set going, the victors drink and shout and dance among the corpses in the light of the flaming embers, in a wild debauch of primitive exultation. But the Kid is fleeing unharmed through the night and he wastes no time in cursing his luck; plans for swift and gory vengeance occupy his full thoughts.

Truly the bloody Lincoln County war is the saga of the Southwest; glory and shame and murder and courage and cruelty and hate flaming into raw, red primitive drama, while through all stalked the gigantic shadow-shape of Billy the Kid, dominating all — as if that crimson feud were but the stage set for his brief stellar role — his star that flamed suddenly up and was as suddenly extinguished.

Mongolization is certainly going on among the Russians to a larger extent than I had realized. The cases you mention, of Mongols taking Russian names and settling among Europeans, surely would seem to prove that the eventual trend of the Russians was toward complete Orientalization. Probably it will take a long time, but with the increasing rousing of the East, and the westward drift of Mongoloid peoples, I fully expect that some day the typical Russian will be slant eyed. That negroid-Jew you speak of must have been a grotesque and amusing spectacle. Amalgamation produces curious results. I imagine those Cape Verde Bravas are bad hombres. There are several of them who have gained some prominence in the ring, and they have an untamed look about them.

What you say of the Carthaginians interested me very much. I have noted the quick and complete absorption of the Vandals on the site of their ancient empire. Those Aryan barbarians must have practically vanished in a comparatively few generations. The further south Aryans wander the more swiftly they are absorbed it would seem, and this fact makes me lean to the theory that Africa has in prehistoric and semi-prehistoric times swallowed up completely, unrecorded drifts of white tribes, both Aryan and Semitic. It seems logical to me that some white races might have wandered down into Africa either across Suez or the Straits of Gibraltar, and forging into the interior, mingled with the dusky natives and eventually vanished. It would not take many centuries to breed out a white strain almost entirely, and I have repeatedly read of vague rumors of red-haired niggers occasionally occurring in the interior of the Continent.

Speaking of *Oriental Stories*, I'll admit I was disappointed in Owens' story in the first issue.[1] He seemed to have written it hurriedly and without making much attempt at realistic portrayal. I've never read the novel you mention by Benoit.[2] And I must admit that the prehistoric South African race[3] is news to me too. What you say of them interests me most intensely and I would appreciate it sincerely if you would tell me all you know of them. I look forward to the time when you will find it convenient to write an African tale, for in this barren period of literature, such treats as this is bound to be, are few and far between. I've never read "Facts Concerning the Late Arthur Jermyn and His Family",[4] but I'd certainly enjoy doing so, if you have a spare copy or one you can lend me. I entirely sympathize with you in your irritation at the editor's changing the title. The original title certainly was far superior in originality and interest.

In your remarks on prehistoric races you certainly present a clear picture of the various theories of anthropologists and historians, and one which helps me to straighten such theories up in my mind. I must devote some study to these subjects, as they are of intense interest.

Thanks very much for sending me the articles on Druidic remnants. What strange and misty speculations are brought up by the thought of those gaunt and brooding columns! What curious and fantastic rituals of worship were there enacted, and what invocations of what monstrous gods? I am almost consumed by curiosity concerning the immemorial past, and irritated beyond measure to think that that curiosity will never be satisfied!

The dream you described is most fascinating, particularly the names, etc., and the culmination. I remember reading the incident in Long's serial,[5] which, by the way, is the best thing appearing in *Weird Tales* since Mr. Wright published your last story. Long lacks something of your own master touch, but he is a good craftsman and this story is splendid. Wandrei's dreams of Druidic forests are interesting also. I believe that many dreams are the result of ancestral memories, handed down through the ages. I have lived in the Southwest all my life yet most of my dreams are laid in cold, giant lands of icy wastes and gloomy skies, and of wild, wind swept fens and wildernesses over which sweep great sea-winds, and which are inhabited by shock headed savages with light fierce eyes. With the exception of that one dream I described to you, I am never, in these dreams of ancient times, a civilized man. Always I am the barbarian, the skin-clad, tousle-haired, light eyed wild man, armed with a rude axe or sword, fighting the elements and wild beasts, or grappling with armored hosts marching with the tread of civilized discipline, from fallow fruitful lands and walled cities. This is reflected in my writings, too, for when I begin a tale of old times, I always find myself instinctively arrayed on the side of the barbarian, against the powers of organized civilization. When I dream of Greece, it is always the Greece of early barbaric days when the first Aryan hordes came down, never the Greece of the myrtle crown and the Golden Age. When I dream of Rome I am always pitted against her, hating her with a ferocity that in my younger days persisted in my waking hours, so that I still remember, with some wonder, the savage pleasure with which I read, at the age of nine, the destruction of Rome by the Germanic barbarians. At the same time, reading of the conquest of Britain by those same races filled me with resentment. Somehow I have never been able to conceive fully of a Latinized civilization in Britain; to me the struggle has always seemed mainly a war of British barbarians against Germanic barbarians, with my sympathies wholly with the Britons.

But my most vivid dreams have been of Indian wars. The last Indian raid in Central Texas was in 1874 when Big Foot and Jape the Comanche left their reservation and swept through Texas, leaving a trail of fire and blood. The Frontier Battalion — Rangers — trapped the war-party on Dove Creek perhaps a hundred miles west of here, and both war-chiefs went to the Happy Hunting Ground at the muzzles of Texan rifles. But the old people of this country have many tales of Indian terrors, and I have listened to many such stories, particularly when I was a child and very susceptible to such things. So the Indian wars seem even more realistic and actual than even the World War. When old timers have told of red skin raids, the telling, even of a halting illiterate style, has seemed so vivid to me, that sometimes it seems as if I, too, must have really lived through those times. Even now, the tale of a massacre and scalping that occurred perhaps seventy years ago seems more real and horrifying than the horrors of the Great War little more than a half score years ago.

And I've often relived those days in my dreams. I have known the lurking stillness about a lone cabin, broken suddenly by the nameless rustle of leaves and underbrush — the tense waiting in the darkness, eyes straining into the shadows for the crawling foe — the quavering call of the wolf, and the sudden horrified realization that it was no beast that gave tongue in the night — the glimpse of vague shadows flitting among the trees and underbrush — the sudden, blood-freezing clamor of madly exultant yells and the rain of arrows and bullets against the cabin-logs — the vain and frenzied firing at mocking, darting shadows — the cold clammy sweat of fear, and fingers clumsy with haste fumbling with powder horn, wadding and bullet pouch — the arching, comet-like flight of flaming shafts into the roof and the terrorizing smell of smoke — the ghastly realization that the ammunition is exhausted — the new tenor of the war-whoop as the savages find their shots are unanswered — the rush across the clearing in the moonlight and the shattering strokes of rifle stock and tomahawk on the splintering door — the futile efforts to hold the door, in a shower of flaming embers from the burning roof — the deluge into the room, over the ruined door, of fiendish painted faces and brawny arms, polished bronze in the red glare of the flames — the frenzied swinging of the broken rifle stock at narrow, shaven heads in the strangling smoke — the gleam of tomahawks in lean hands — then red chaos and oblivion. All this I've known in my dreams. They always get me, the red devils!

It was the Comanches and Kiowas that raised particular Cain in Texas; in earlier days the Wacoes, Tonkawas — cannibals, and supposed connected with the Caribs — and other small tribes made some raids, but they never amounted to much. The Comanches were devils. Blood kin of the Mescalero Apaches, too. Once, long ago, Comanches and Apaches were one tribe, but during a big drouth and famine, the ancestral tribe split up, one half taking to the plains, the other to the mountains. For mutual welfare, the mountain people agreed to eat no buffalo or other plains creatures, while to the plains people the mountain animals were taboo. The mountain men became Apaches, short, stocky, with unusual strength and endurance, while the men of the plains became tall, rangy, powerful and magnificent horsemen, and were known as Comanches. The greatest chiefs of the Apaches were Mangus Colorado and, of course, Go-yat-thi-lay, known as Geronimo. Petah Nocona was the last and greatest war-chief of the Comanches while his half-breed son, Quanah Parker, is one of the stock folk-lore characters of the Southwest and as smart a horse thief as ever rode off with a rancher's hoofed stock. All Comanches prided themselves on their horse-thieving ability.

You are right in saying that America's main struggle is between the individualist and the corporation and I suppose nothing can stop the present cultural and industrial trend. Doubtless in a few more generations all the United States will present one uniform pattern, modeled on the mechanized fabric of New York. I have seen pictures of the new architecture; it certainly is in keeping with the growing spirit of the Age, and would seem to conform to the strictest ideas of standardization. If the Colonies had never separated from England, many of the tangles confronting the people might, as you say, have been more readily adjusted. At least, America would not have been deluged by a horde of non-British immigrants as it has been.

Your comments on the New England-Canadian question presents a thought entirely new to me. I had not realized to what an extent the New England states and Canada were connected, geographically and economically. I sympathize with your dream of political connection as well, and believe, with you, that such a step would be of benefit to both New England and Canada. It would certainly mean a revival of old thought-ways and ideals — a sort of British Colonial renaissance with the accompanying gain in literature and art. Why, the thought is really a wonderful one, with gigantic possibilities. British New England might well become the seat of learning and culture for the world, a sort of modern Athens, or rather, a Mermaid Inn for a modern Elizabethan Age. It would receive, not only the best minds of Canada and its own domains, but to it, from all the rest of America, would flock folk in whom Colonial traditions and ideals still live. Well, it rouses splendid speculations, even if it never comes to pass.

I am glad my comments on the Southwest interest you, and I feel most highly honored, indeed, at the kind things you have said about my descriptions, etc. Kelly the conjure-man was quite a character, but I fear I could not do justice to such a theme as you describe. I hope you will carry out your idea in writing the story you mention, of a pre-negroid African priest reincarnated in a plantation negro. As for me handling this theme better than yourself, it is beyond the realms of possibility, regardless of any first-hand knowledge of background which I might possess. I lack your grasp on cosmic thoughts, your magnificent imagination, your command of rhetoric and vocabulary, your power to invest the unreal with a grisly reality — in short, I am a mere novice where you are a master. I hope you will write this story some time, and if any of my anecdotes of pine land and negro lore can be used in any way, or give you any ideas, you are more than welcome to them.

I hope to some day write a history of the Southwest that will seem alive and human to the readers, not the dry and musty stuff one generally finds in chronicles. To me the annals of the land pulse with blood and life, but whether I can ever transfer this life from my mind to paper, is a question. It will be years, at least. Much of the vivid history of the Southwest is lost forever and the breed growing up now looks toward, and apes, the East, caring nothing at all about the traditions and history of the land in which they live. How many know anything of Lucien Maxwell? Yet in his day he owned a Spanish land grant bigger than whole Eastern states, containing more than a million acres. This was in New Mexico in the '70s and '80s. In his mansion he kept royal style, with places for two dozen set at his generous table; the dishes were of solid silver, the wine goblets of solid gold. He sold his holdings for $7,50,000, and the buyers sold for nearly twice that amount. He died a poor man. How many know of Captain King, who owned the biggest ranch the world has ever seen? It stretched from inland rivers to the Gulf of Mexico and when the country was settled up, it was divided into whole counties. I have seen the old ranch house which cost nearly a million dollars to build, and it looks more like a castle than an ordinary house. How old it is I cannot say, but the great stone stable has a date of 1856 carved over the door, and once cannons were mounted about the building to resist Indian attacks and Mexican raids. It lies adjacent to the little town of Kingsville, a most beautiful town — the prettiest I have yet seen in Texas. The worthy ranch-man was an old sea-captain and I have heard it hinted that, if he followed the same tactics on sea that he did on land, he must have been a pirate. Years and years ago he was killed by a Mexican vaquero who worked for him, and who, it is said, carried out his orders regarding various men who owned ranches the captain desired. Be that as it may, they died and their ranches were engulfed in the ever growing boundaries of the great ranch. Giant fortunes are not built without intrigue and bloodshed, whether those fortunes be land or gold, or both. And John Chisum, who built the Texas town of Paris, and who owned more cattle than any other man in modern times — he is almost forgotten. And Pat Garrett, who ended the blazing comet-trail that was the life of the Billy the Kid. Garrett was an Alabama man, but he grew to manhood in Texas. And Sam Bass, of whom the old song narrates:

"Sam Bass was born in Indiana, that was his native home,
And at the age of seventeen, young Sam began to roam,
He first came out to Texas, a drover for to be,
And a kinder hearted fellow, you seldom ever see.
Sam used deal in race stock, one called the Denton Mare;
He matched her in scrub races and took her to the Fair.
Sam used to coin the money, and he spent it just as free,
He always drank good whiskey, where-ever he might be."

Sam's exploits shook the country, but he fell at Round Rock, outnumbered and surrounded by a vengeful posse, and already his fame has faded. And Pat Couglin of New Mexico, cattle-king in his day, and John Slaughter of Texas, who moved his herds into the naked lands and fought Indian raider and Mexican bandit alike, and later white rustlers and renegades. He is forgotten. And Willie Drenon,[6] whom I saw wandering about the streets of Mineral Wells, twenty years ago, trying to sell the pitiful, illiterate book of his life of magnificent adventure and high courage; a little, worn old man in the stained and faded buckskins of a vanished age, friendless and penniless. God, what a lousy end for a man whose faded blue eyes had once looked on the awesome panorama of untracked prairie and sky-etched mountain, who had ridden at the side of Kit Carson, guided the wagon-trains across the deserts to California, drunk and reveled in the camps of the buffalo-hunters, and fought hand to hand with painted Sioux and wild Comanche. One of the last of the old scouts he was, this pioneer, whom Kit Carson picked up, a lost and bewildered French immigrant boy, wandering about the wharves of the port where he had landed, and his neglect by the country and the people he served is but one case in many thousands. Always the simple, strong men go into the naked lands and fight heroical battles to win and open those lands to civilization. Then comes civilization, mainly characterized by the smooth, the dapper, the bland, the shrewd men who play with business and laws and politics and they gain the profits; they enjoy the fruit of other men's toil, while the real pioneers starve.

Well, they have gone into the night, a vast and silent caravan, with their buckskins and their boots, their spurs and their long rifles, their wagons and their mustangs, their wars and their loves, their brutalities and their chivalries; they have gone to join their old rivals, the wolf, the panther and the Indian, and only a crumbling 'dobe wall, a fading trail, the breath of an old song, remain to mark the roads they travelled. But sometimes when the night wind whispers forgotten tales through the mesquite and the chaparral, it is easy to imagine that once again the tall grass bends to the tread of a ghostly caravan, that the breeze bears the jingle of stirrup and bridle-chain, and that spectral camp-fires are winking far out on the plains. And a lobo calls where no wolf can be, and the night is dreamy and hushed and still with the pregnancy of old times. But gone are the days when the prairie schooners carried their cargo of empire into the sunset lands and gone the reckless, roaring days when the trail herds went up along the old Chisholm. The old time cowboy with the Spanish mustang and the longhorn steer has followed the raiding Comanche, the buffalo hunter, the wholesale cattle rustler and the old scouts into silence and oblivion.

But I've rambled enough, and I hope I haven't bored you. I'm sending you some stuff under separate cover which I hope may be of interest. These are some snap-shots, a magazine containing a story by me,[7] and a tale of A. Merritt's[8] which recently appeared in *Argosy*. My story hasn't any particular merit but it may serve to amuse an idle hour. The magazine containing it, and the pictures are yours to keep, and there's no hurry about returning the Merritt yarn.

With best wishes,
Most cordially yours,
[Robert E. Howard]

NOTES

1. "Singapore Nights."
2. Probably *L'Atlantide*, published in English as *Atlantida.*
3. The Boskops. See letter 156, note 5 and letter 169, note 7.
4. Published as "The White Ape," *Weird Tales*, April 1924.
5. "The Horror from the Hills," *Weird Tales*, January and February-March, 1931 (2 part serial). Lovecraft's dream, as related in a letter to Long, was included in the second installment.
6. William F. Drannan was the nominal author of *Thirty-One Years on the Plains and in the Mountains* (1900) and *Chief of Scouts* (1910). Most authorities consider his memoirs spurious, if not outright fabrications.
7. *Fight Stories*, January 1931, "Alleys of Peril."
8. Probably "The Snake Mother," serialized in seven installments in *Argosy*, October 25 through December 6, 1930.

TSS: 21474-21479, 64378, 21481-21483

153. To H.P. Lovecraft, ca. January 1931.

Dear Mr. Lovecraft:

This is a rather a belated letter thanking you for the cards and literature you sent me. They certainly constituted a wealth of interest and information, and looking at the views of the old houses and reading the descriptions made me determine more strongly than ever to cross the Mississippi some day and see these things for myself. I am particularly glad to hear that efforts are being made to reconstruct Colonial survivals. The old houses, landmarks of past grandeur, and so utterly different from the architecture to which I have always been accustomed, particularly intrigued me, and gave me the sensation of gazing at views of an entirely different country, rather than a different part of my own native land. Indeed, I cannot but believe that were it not for a common tongue, America would be a land of many different countries, as divergent and unalike as, say, Holland and Hungary. I am fascinated by your New England scenery and would like to take a walking tour from Rhode Island to Maine; indeed I am determined to do so if I ever come East. I would like to go along the old Mohawk Trail at sunrise, a trail which must be fraught with the ghosts of the past and the memories of stirring events in the dim yesterdays. By the way, what is the average altitude of the New England states? I suppose it varies greatly from point to point, owing to the great number of mountains. This part of Texas where I live has an altitude of about 1700 feet and I find I feel better at a somewhat higher level, as a usual thing. That's one thing I have against the coast country — lower altitudes do not seem to agree with me.

I presume you will have gotten the package of cards etc., by the time you've received this letter. Please look them over and see if anything is missing. The package was opened by mistake before I brought it home, and while I do not think such a thing occurred, it is possible that something might have been dropped out. I am very sorry this happened, and if anything is missing, I will do all in my power to recover it and return it to you.

I'm enclosing a post card folder of Texas which I hope you may find of interest. You needn't bother to return it. It's not very complete and gives scant idea of the state as a whole; you'll note that nearly all the views are laid in South and East Texas. But it's West Texas that's the coming empire, however much the Easterners of Red River and the lower Brazos may slight that fact. El Paso and Amarillo are the only towns of any size west of the Colorado but that's no drawback to my mind. And some day the Llano Estacado will team with great cities — not in my day, though — thank the lord. You'll note in these views, the oleanders in bloom in Galveston; the flowers and palms of the streets are the best features of a rather dingy old town, fading as a sea-port since they brought deep water up to Houston.

Again thanking you for the opportunity of studying the views and scenic literature, I am,

Yours most cordially,
[Robert E. Howard]

TSS: 65708

ꝏ

154. To Tevis Clyde Smith, ca. Mid to Late-January 1931.[1]

Fear Finn:

I've delayed writing you, hoping I'd receive the check for the Cathay hooey, but the devil only knows when we'll get it. I got a letter from Talman of the Texas Company saying that he hadn't seen my Camp Colorado article,[2] but had an idea that the moguls had approved of it. I hope so. Talman praised our Cathay story highly and said he was sure the historical details were nine-tenths correct. I'm going to write him that you supplied the historical data, so if he finds an error he'll blame it on you — he said lousily. He says he's going to write Farnsworth to have a historical story in every issue. I hope Farnsworth will decide to do so; that would give me an even break. I realize that I can't compete with the rest of the Oriental writers on a modern Oriental basis; too many of them are too well informed. Why don't you write a historical novelet for Orientals?

I finally landed another Costigan story. Byrne intimated that it wasn't up to standard, but accepted it. He evidently didn't think much of it, for he only offered me $75 when I expected to get $90 or $100 if I sold it at all.

I read your article about the moody settlers[3] of early Texas. It was very well written indeed, and as far as I know, unique. If anyone else ever dwelt specially on that subject, I never heard of it. Have you sold anything else recently?

I did quite a bit of work, sent off a number of manuscripts, and then got to loafing again. I've worked along in a desultory manner, trying to work up some energy but this rainy soggy weather enervates me.

Orientals might possibly send the check for the Cathay story to you; if they send it to me, I'll either bring it over, or let you know immediately. The devil only knows when we'll get it.

Fear Dunn.

NOTES

1. Date on letter changed at Rob's suggestion. JB
2. "The Ghost of Camp Colorado."
3. "Brooding Nature of Pioneers," Dallas *News*, January 11, 1931.

TSS: 82491

ଔଌଓଔଌ

155. To Tevis Clyde Smith, ca. Late February, after February 16, 1931.[1]

Well, Fear Finn:

You owe me a letter, but no matter. I'm just writing to tell you that that confounded check hasn't come yet. It surely will be here in a week or so.

Dobie's book[2] has certainly made a hit; and I understand he had the Devil's own time getting it published. It makes me think of what the publishers wrote you about the Cortina biography.[3] I'll bet that they'd have written Dobie about the same line if he'd written them about the Coronado gunk. The publishers don't know what people want. Now is the time to write historical Texas stuff, because the Southwest is entering a big literary boom. For the next few years it's going to be exploited plenty. A good move, too; I think — and hope — that people are tired of this damned pseudo-artistic hokum — perverts, morons, degenerates and thin blooded sophisticates, and are going in for more wholesome literature — reverting to the colonial and settlement periods. By the way, have you sold anything more, recently?

Pink[4] and I went over to Fort Worth to see the Dula-Freeman fight[5] and it was a hummer. Dula did better than the scribes gave him credit, though he was far outclassed from start to finish. He took a most vicious beating but came back strong in the last round. At the end of the first frame, I didn't think he'd last out the bout, but he's tough as a boot. The last round he and Freeman fought it out, head to head; all four fists smashing away, felt, right, left, right. Freeman's good, no doubt about it. He ought to keep the welterweight title a long time. But Dula's even tougher than I'd thought.

I finally clicked with *Action Stories* — $75 worth. Street & Smith wrote me, wanting to take over the Steve Costigan series for their magazine *Sport Stories*, which they say is a bi-monthly. I told them I expected that *Fight Stories* would want to keep Steve, but offered them another prize-ring series instead. I hope they'll accept.

Well, here's hoping we get that check right away.

Fear Dunn.

NOTES

1. Date changed at Rob's suggestion. JB
2. *Coronado's Children.*
3. Juan Cortina led two so-called "Cortina Wars" against Anglo-American authorities in the Rio Grande Valley, seeking to assert the rights of Mexican-Americans.
4. Lindsey Tyson.
5. Arthur "Kid" Dula of Brownwood was a favorite of Howard's. Tommy Freeman was the world welterweight champion. The two fought in Fort Worth on Monday, February 16, 1931.

TSS: 82487

ꟹ ꟹ ꟹ

156. To H.P. Lovecraft, ca. February 1931.

Dear Mr. Lovecraft:

I highly appreciate your intention for me to retain the antiquarian literature, and would indeed like to have it for my permanent collection, since you say you have duplicates to all the material you sent me, though I feel it would be an imposition on you to ask you to go to the trouble and expense of sending the package back. As I remarked in my last letter, I found the views and descriptive matter most fascinating and received the impression of life lived in a spacious, mellow and solidly founded age so utterly different from the plane of existence I have always known.

I can imagine your fatigue after revising an entire book of verse — it must be a task that exhausts one's energies; however I know that you did a first-class job on it; you could not do otherwise.

Glad you found the folder and pictures of interest; I should have a vast collection of snap-shots, considering the extent of landscape over which I've carried a Kodak. But sometimes I've been too lazy and sometimes I've found to my disgust that I was out of films. One time I remember I visited the old Santa Gertruda Rancho (Captain King's South Texas hacienda) and there remembered I'd carelessly left my Kodak at the little town of Bishop a good many miles away. When I went up on the Plains last fall, I took along my Kodak for the purpose of securing some snap-shots for you, of the Caprock and the canyons — and it was cloudy and rainy practically all the time. Of all the pictures I took, not one was any account at all.

I am glad to learn that New England is resisting the modernistic movement, and that the South also is not following the new trend so much. Chicago — the Middlewest — it's to be supposed that they'd fall for the futuristic hokum. Chicago must be a lousy dump from all I've heard. Here in the Southwest, as I see it, at least, modernistic architecture and the like is resisted to a large extent by a Spanish style, tradition, culture or whatever it might be called, though I suppose the eventual result will be a weird blending of the styles. I hope not, though. I particularly like the old "Mission" form of architecture and if I ever build me a house, it will be as much like a hacienda of Spanish days as possible. The furniture too, of high-class Mexicans has a certain richness and attractiveness seldom met with in American homes, whatever their wealth — Mexicans, that is, who have not adopted American ways too wholly. Altogether, Mexican tastes as a whole, appeal to me, though I cannot say that the Mexicans themselves do.

Thanks for giving me the data on the Hittites; most of it was news to me, as my historical education is extremely sketchy and I haven't kept up with researches and archeological discoveries, though they fascinate me. If I was wealthy I'd never do anything but poke around in ruined cities all over the world — and probably get snake-bit.

No, I hadn't heard anything about *Weird Tales* going monthly again,[1] but I'm glad to hear it. My magazine-market is slender enough as it is, without reducing that part of it. I'll probably try to write the "Skull-Face" sequel as I intended.

Glad you found the snake-yarns of some interest. The Southwest has been so long noted for its crop of truly mastodonic lies about reptiles that I find myself hesitant to discuss serpents at all, lest I be placed in the same category! I remember the "Yig" story;[2] it was a good one and I thought at the time that I could detect the touch of your master-hand here and there. I should think it quite likely that a rattler-victim might burst if bitten a great many times. One bull diamond-back carries enough venom in his fangs to kill almost anything smaller than an elephant, except those animals which seem to be immune from such venom. I remember once seeing in a moving picture, a fight between a mongoose and a cobra. The scene wasn't faked, but was a German-issued news-reel spliced into the main picture to lend atmosphere to an Oriental locale. The fight, with the accompanying Oriental music, was most weird. I must say I was surprized at the appearance of the mongoose which I had pictured as something like a mink. He was of a very deceptive appearance; he looked clumsy and slow but he was so quick it was hard to follow his motions. He made no waste movements whatever and his timing and judgment were absolutely wonderful; he would feint with his nose in a way that was science itself and his counter-spring was nothing short of marvelous. If I were managing a boxer, I'd buy him a mongoose and make him study it hours each day. This mongoose, by the way, got his snake.

To return to snakes; this may sound like a regular Texas snake-lie, but I had (and may still have, for all I know) a curious ability to sense the presence of a snake, particularly a rattler, before I saw, smelt or heard him. This ability was very strong in me during the ages of nine, ten and eleven, and gradually dwindled as I grew older, though it's never failed me entirely — yet. I may walk blindly into a whole den of the scaly beasts some day, like a cryptic joke of the gods, but so far some obscure instinct has kept me off snakes, even when I couldn't see them. I can't explain this instinct — I can't begin to. But I know that in the past, particularly during the ages I've mentioned, I've suddenly felt cold shudders run up and down my spine, have been shaken with deep nausea, and looking about, have discovered a rattlesnake coiled somewhere out of sight, or sunning himself. It hasn't worked every time. Sometimes I've been only a foot or so from the varmint when I felt the warning, involuntary shudder and nausea. The first time I ever experienced this, was when I was very young, and out in the pastures on a school picnic. We came out of a scrub of woods and went down a slight slope into a sort of wide meadow. I was walking across a fairly large rock, intending to step down off it, when suddenly the sensations described took me, with a blind and sudden panic, and instead of stepping down from the rock, I leaped as far out as I could, and even as I leaped, I heard the blood-freezing whir of a rattler. He was coiled at the base of the rock, and if I had stepped, I'd have stepped right into his coils. As it was I sprang over him and landed out of his reach. This instinct may be a common one for all I know, and I believe any man can feel a rattle-snake's eyes fixed on him, if he isn't completely absorbed in something. That they have hypnotic power is well known. Squirrels, prairie dogs and birds are unable to flee when transfixed by the basilisk power of the serpent's stare, though they may leap up and down, flutter wings or limbs, and give vent to the most pitiable outcries. I hate snakes; they are possessed of a cold, utterly merciless cynicism and sophistication, and sense of super-ego that puts them outside the pale of warm-blooded creatures.

It's a pity the Yids have taken New York. I imagine the mongrel population does present a bizarre aspect — I remember with what deep interest and absolute fascination I read your story, "He",[3] with its setting in the mysterious labyrinth of New York's alleys and secret ways. I cannot praise that tale too highly; the impelling sweep of its power held me positively enthralled and spell-bound.

I must say that you have done what no one and nothing else ever has done — aroused in me a spark of interest in New York. Until reading your observations on the city, I cannot truthfully say that I ever felt any real desire even to visit New York. I always wanted to see New England, but New York never interested me. But what you say of the dark aliens, towering buildings, labyrinthine alleys, etc., and your comparisons of the city with Babylon and the dark towns of old, rouse in me a sense of exotic strangeness, mystery and weirdness, as in the shadow-haunted, black-spired cities of lost empires.

I agree with you that there is far too much Semitic control of publication and I view this fact with deep resentment. If American literature can't somehow shake off the strangle-hold the Jews seem to have gotten on it, I believe it's doomed. Not denying that the Semitic race is capable of producing fine work itself; but to each race its own literature. I don't want to control the artistic expression of the Jews, and by God, I don't want them to control and direct the expression of my race.

You're right about the haggling and noise accompanying commerce among the Orientals. In New Orleans all this noise and argument isn't confined to the Semites alone. I used to pass the Old French Market and hear the Italian women screeching and squabbling over pennies, and see them grabbing and snatching in shameless greed until I was sick and ashamed of the whole human race. That kind of stuff absolutely physically nauseates me. I realize that in the slums it's a struggle to live and conditions make people fight over pennies, but plenty of the people I saw screeching and scrapping in the markets were not slums-rats. The Continental European peasant seems to have inherited an innate spirit of hard, shameless avarice, difficult to get rid of.

I have read and re-read, with the utmost interest, your comments on Colonial architecture and wish to thank you for going to so much trouble of detail and explanation, for it has been a veritable education for me. My ideas of early architecture have been so very vague — based mainly on Spanish missions, old adobe houses, and a few plantation houses with great pillars, on the banks of the Mississippi. I wish to express my admiration for your knowledge of the subject, which is certainly deep and vast. I hope you will be able the make the trip to Europe which you mentioned once because, from what I've read of old castles and buildings in general there, they must furnish a veritable paradise for an antiquarian. Looking over your descriptions and the drawings — and you are an illustrator of no small talent — I find a curious fact in regard to architecture of the Southwest — it is, largely, a queer conglomeration of the styles you depict, together with many features either evolved separately or imported from Mexico and Southern Europe. I have seen nearly every feature you mention in one way or another, but cannot remember having ever seen any house that represented entirely, any one of the types you show. The New Jersey house with its porch seems more familiar than any of the others you have sketched, though without the attic windows.

One feature that the older houses of the Southwest had — after log-cabin days — was the porch. Almost invariably there were deep, wide porches, front and back; sometimes one porch which went clear around the house. These were necessary for coolness; milk and ollas of water were kept there where the breeze could blow on them and at the same time remain in the shade. And people sat there and rested in the evening. But now porches are vanishing. People don't sit on them like they used to; they're out gadding about. Old ranch houses used to have a wide open hall running through them — or rather the house itself was divided into two parts connected by a roofed hallway open on both sides. Generally the family slept in one part of the house and cooked and ate in the other part.

I'm surprized to hear the Virginians still use rail fences; they went out of general use in Texas years and years ago. In fact, they never were used in the western part very much — there wasn't enough trees. Rail fences were used in Arkansas — my grandmother — born in Alabama and raised in Mississippi and Arkansas — used to say that she'd never heard of barbed wire till she came to Texas in 1885.

You find the most un-American looking houses in South Texas, where Poles, Swedes and Germans have built homes, following old country styles. I particularly remember an old Swede who lived about seventeen miles inland from Galveston who lived in real old-country style — if that means living like a hog. He lived in a queer two-storied house with a very steep roof and small windows, and the stairway on the outside. He lived in the second story; the lower floor was a stable wherein dwelt horses, mules, cows, hogs and chickens. He lived in America for a good many years but never took out naturalization papers. At last he sold out and went back to Sweden with all the money he'd hoarded. And he found that he was no longer a Swedish citizen. They shot him back to the U.S. and the U.S. didn't want him either. He wasn't a citizen and he got into some kind of a jamb by lying, somehow, I heard, to the customs officials. They booted him back to Sweden and the last time I heard of him, he was being kicked back and forth like a football. Nobody wanted him; and if you'd ever smelt him, you wouldn't wonder why.

Your sketch of the New England stone walls reminds me of the stone fences, sections of which I've tumbled down in search of gold popularly supposed to have been hidden under them by Mexican outlaws — in the Palo Pinto country. Stone fences were common there, among the hills and when I contemplate the work they represent, it always fatigues me.

It is a beautiful and alluring scene that you draw in your vivid description of New England landscape with its ancient farm-houses, streams and dreaming valleys and I can understand your attachment for it and sympathize with your feelings at seeing the old landmarks give way to the rising tide of modernism — well, may they not all go, and may the Colonial traditions still stand for many years to come!

I'm glad you find my rambling comments on Southwestern history and tradition not too boresome. Yes, I think the section is at last coming into its own in literature. A vast lost empire has been slumbering here for a hundred years, waiting for some skilled pen to wake it into life. I think that writers are beginning to realize the fact now. More, I think that at last, the bulk of people are beginning to weary of sophisticated trash, novels dealing with perverts and half-baked pseudo-artists, and are turning toward the more wholesome phases of American life — toward the clean, clear cut epics of pioneering and settlement. Well, the past is dreaming in the Southwest, high endeavor, stark cruelty, red war and heroism — material for a thousand books and chronicles. An empire dreams between Red River and the Rio Grande —

Here men and women were confronted, in the very recent past, by conditions that had been forgotten east of the Mississippi for centuries. When men began to write of the West, it was to exploit its more lurid aspects for sensational purposes. Hence, rose the "cowboy" tradition, the "Wild West" tradition — an absolutely criminal distortion of the literary growth of the region and traditions that made a vulgar jest out of what should have been one of the most vital and inspiring pageants of American history. What the ignorant and blundering pens of sensational yellow-backed novel writers failed in doing, the pens of sophisticated arm-chair critics completed. Really good writers, with a few exceptions, shied away from the Western tale, lest they be branded with the yellow-backed dime novelist. It seems to me, from what I've read and heard, that most people who have never seen the West, are divided into classes — the class that believes the West swarms with movie-type cowboys and Indians where bullets whiz continually — and the class that lifts the lip in scorn and rejects all the tales of the West as mere drivel. The truth, as of course you realize, not belonging to either of the above mentioned classes, lies about half-way between. Men didn't go about with guns slung all over them, shooting at the drop of a hat, hanging rustlers to every tree, chasing Indians twenty-three hours of the day, but life was a fierce and hard grind, and murder and sudden death were common. Now thinking people all over America are beginning to realize the truths of the pioneer West, with the resultant boom in good Western literature — which I hope spells the doom of the Wild Bill dime-novel.

Referring to the Chisholm trail, which I've mentioned before, I was born almost on it, as the main branch passed very close to the little town where I first saw the light of day. That branch went up into Oklahoma and Kansas. The western branch went into New Mexico and on up into Canada. Think of hazing a herd of longhorns from the Rio Grande to Canada! Yet it was done occasionally; it took a year at the least estimate.

Yes, John Chisum was a giant figure of the early days — much, as you suggest, like the hard headed and hard handed barons of medieval days — with the exception that he never did any of his own fighting himself!

Thank you very much for the kind things you said in regard to my efforts at depicting the Lincoln County War; I appreciate them very highly indeed, coming as they do, from a man of your literary ability and artistic education.

Yes, the Lincoln County War was a dramatic and bloody episode, wherever the Aryan race reverts to its early history in thought and mode of living, fierce feuds arise and are fought out to the bitter finish. Witness the feuds of the Virginia and Kentucky hills; witness the short, ferocious feuds of early Texas; witness the "wars" of New Mexico, Arizona, Colorado and California.

Western feuds have generally been fought over land — cattle — sordid commercial wrangles in outward appearance, but with the underlying reasons of stubborn independent pride. More men have been killed in Texas over fences than for any other one reason. When two men own each thousands of acres, it seems foolish for them to shoot each other to death because one insisted on setting his fence forward a foot or so, doesn't it? But it's the old story of "the principle of the thing". And after all, a man can't be blamed for defending what he thinks is his, or taking what he thinks is his. Say you and I own adjoining ranches and I claim that the fences weren't run according to the survey. I claim a strip of your land four feet wide and half a mile long. You are just as certain that it don't belong to me. I come in the night and set the fence up four feet. You are patient and not quarrelsome, so you come back the next night and set the fence back where it was. I come again and start moving that fence once more. Well, there's nothing left for you to do but take your Winchester and start throwing lead in my direction and you're quite right, too. A man has a right to defend his property. It's not the money value or the grazing value of the land; it's the sturdy resolve of the Anglo-Saxon or the Scotch-Irish-American not to be bullied out of his natural rights. And when both contestants are of the same breed, and both absolutely certain they're right, well, by-standers might as well start ducking, because there's only one way to settle a row like that, and if it's taken to court, it won't do any real good, but merely make feeling more bitter on each side, whichever way the decision goes.

The Lincoln County War began in a cattle row. Thieves were stealing John Chisum's cows and being acquitted in the courts. Dolan, Reilly and Murphy were merchants in the town of Lincoln and all-powerful. Murphy ordered his lawyer, McSween, to defend certain rustlers against the charge brought against them by Chisum. McSween refused and Murphy fired him. McSween was engaged by Chisum, prosecuted the rustlers and sent them up the river. Then McSween, Chisum and an Englishman named Tunstall went into partnership and McSween opened a big general store in Lincoln. He grabbed most of the trade and Murphy saw he was being ruined. McSween won a suit against him and for reasons too complicated and lengthy to narrate here, Murphy got out a writ of attachment against McSween's store and Tunstall's ranch — the last an obviously illegal movement, since Tunstall owned his ranch apart from the partnership and had nothing to do with the lawsuit. A posse of some twenty men rode over to attach Tunstall's ranch. They overtook him in the mountains, shot him down in cold blood, beat our his brains with a jagged rock and left him lying beside his dead horse. That was the beginning of the Bloody Lincoln County War.

Billy the Kid was working for Tunstall as a cowboy. The Kid's real name was William Bonney; he was born in the slums of New York, the son of Irish emigrants. He was brought west when a very young baby and raised in Kansas and New Mexico — mainly the latter. Pancho Villa killed his first man when he was fourteen; Billy went him one better; he was only twelve when he stabbed a big blacksmith to death in Silver City, New Mexico. That started him on the wild life. When he drifted into the Lincoln County country, he already had eleven or twelve killings to his name, thought only nineteen years old — that isn't counting Mexicans and Indians. No white man of that age who had any pretensions to gun-fame counted any but the regal warriors of his own race and color. The Kid had probably killed ten or fifteen men of brown and red skins, but he never considered them worthy of mention, though he was considerably proud of his white record.

The Kid was a small man — five feet eight inches, 140 pounds, perhaps — but he was very strong. But it was in his quickness of eye and hand, his perfect co-ordination that made him terrible. There was never a man more perfectly fitted for his trade.

The Kid had been living by gambling and rustling until he started working for Tunstall. At the time of the latter's brutal murder, he was making an honest living as top-hand on the Rio Feliz rancho. Had the Englishman lived, the redder phase of the Kid's life might well have never been written, for Billy liked Tunstall almost well enough to go straight for him.

But the murder of his friend drove him on the red trail of vengeance. McSween organized a posse to arrest the murderers, and had Dick Brewer, foreman of the murdered Englishman, sworn in as a special constable. They rode out after the killers and caught two of them in the Pecos Valley — Morton and Baker — former friends of the Kid. On the way back to Lincoln the Kid killed both of them, supposedly when they tried to escape. One of the posse, an old buffalo hunter named McCloskey, was killed by Frank McNab when he tried to protect the victims.

The next victim was a Murphy man named "Buckshot" Roberts, a Texas man whom it had once taken twenty-five Rangers to arrest. He was so full of lead that he couldn't lift his rifle shoulder high, but shot from the hip. Thirteen McSween men cornered him at Blazer's Mill on the Tularosa River led by Dick Brewer and the Kid. Bowdre, the Kid's closest friend, shot Roberts through and through, but before the old Texan fell he wounded Bowdre, John Middleton and George Coe, and as he lay dying he shot off the top of Dick Brewer's skull.

The next episode took place in the town of Lincoln. Judge Bristol dared not open the regular session of court there and sent word for Sheriff Brady — a Murphy man — to open court and adjourn it as a matter of routine. On his way down the street to the courthouse, the Sheriff and his deputies were ambushed from an adobe wall by the Kid, Bowdre, O'Folliard — a Texas man — Jim French, Frank McNab and Fred Wayte; and Sheriff Brady and Deputy Sheriff Hindman were killed. McSween was enraged by this cold blooded murder and threatened to prosecute Billy, which he probably would have done had events allowed. A very religious man was McSween and no more fitted for the role in which Fate had cast him, than a rabbit is fit to lead a pack of wolves. However, he felt that he was in the right, and did his best. Following the murder of the Sheriff, he elected — by force of his gunmen — a fellow named Copeland to the office. Murphy appealed to Governor Axtell, who removed Copeland and appointed George Peppin in his place.

Peppin immediately organized a posse and rode out after McSween's men, killing Frank McNab. Then followed the famous battle of the McSween house. The clans met in Lincoln and in the fighting that followed, Morris, Romero, Semora, and McSween were killed on the McSween side, and Salazar, and Gonzalez were wounded, while on the Murphy side, Crawford was killed by Fernando Herrera, and Lucio Montoya was wounded by the same man. Bob Beckwith was killed by the Kid who also wounded two others.

That was the end of the Lincoln County war, proper. Murphy had died, a broken man, a crownless monarch, and the rest were ready to throw down their guns and call it a draw. All except the Kid and his immediate followers. But from that point, Billy's career was not that of an avenger, fighting a blood-feud. He reverted to his earlier days and became simply a gunman and an outlaw, subsisting by cattle-rustling. There was one other incident of the War, after peace had been declared; one George Chapman, a lawyer from Las Vegas, hired by Mrs. McSween, was murdered wantonly and in cold blood by a Murphy man, one Richardson, a Texan.

Emigration to that part of New Mexico had just about ceased. The tale of the Kid's reign of terror spread clear back east of the Mississippi. President Hays took the governorship away from Axtell and gave it to Wallace — who, by the way, while writing *Ben Hur* had to keep his shutters close drawn lest a bullet from the Kid's six-shooter put a sudden termination to both book and author. John Chisum, the Kid's former friend, and others got together and elected Pat Garrett Sheriff. Garrett was a friend of the Kid's and knew his gang and his ways. He, himself, was Alabama born, Texas raised — a man of grim determination and cold steel nerves.

Meanwhile the Kid went his ways, rustling cattle and horses. One Joe Bernstein, clerk at the Mescalero agency, made the mistake of arguing with the Kid over some horses Billy was about to drive off. A Jew can be very offensive in dispute. Billy shot him down in cold blood, remarking casually that the fellow was only a Jew.

Several times Garrett and his man-hunters thought they had their hands on Billy but he eluded them. Once they cornered him at a roadhouse, but he killed Deputy Sheriff Jim Carlisle — again in cold blood — and escaped. At Fort Sumner he killed one Joe Grant, a Texas bad man who was after the reward offered for the Kid.

But Garrett was on his trail unceasingly. The Kid's best friends were Bowdre and O'Folliard. At Fort Sumner Garrett killed O'Folliard and at Tivan Arroyo, or Stinking Spring, he killed Bowdre and captured the Kid. Billy was tried in Mesilla and sentenced to be hanged for the murder of Brady and Hindman. He was confined in Lincoln and kept chained, watched day and night by Deputy Sheriffs Sell and Ollinger. He killed them both and got clean away. But love for a Mexican girl drew him back to Fort Sumner when he might have gotten clean away into Old Mexico —

I think the very night must have ceased to breathe as the Kid came from Saval Guierrez's house through the shadows. Surely the nightwind ceased to rustle the pinon leaves and a breathless stillness, pregnant with doom lay over the shadowy mountains and the dim deserts beneath the stars. Surely the quivering mesquites, the sleeping lizards, the blind cactus, the winds whispering down the canyons and the 'dobe walls that glimmered in the starlight, surely they sensed the passing of a figure already legendary and heroic. Aye, surely the night was hushed and brooding as the Southwest's most famous son went blind to his doom. He crossed the yard, came onto the porch of Pete Maxwell's house. He was going after beef, for Celsa Gutierrez to cook for a midnight supper. His butcher knife was in his hand, his gun in his scabbard. Pete Maxwell was his friend; he expected no foes. On the porch he met one of Garrett's deputies, but neither recognized the other. The Kid, wary as a wolf, flashed his gun, though, and backed into Pete's room which opened on the porch. There he halted short — in the shadows he made out vaguely a dim form that should not be there — someone he knew instinctively was neither Pete nor one of Pete's servants. Where was that steel trap will of the Kid's that had gotten him out of so many desperate places? Why did he hold his fire then, he who was so quick to shoot at the least hint of suspicion? Azrael's hand was on him and his hour was come. He made his last mistake, leaping back into the doorway where he was clearly limned against the sky. He snapped a fierce enquiry — and then Death bellowed in the dark from the jaws of Pat Garrett's six-shooter. They carried the Kid into a vacant carpenter shop and laid him on a bench, while the Mexican women screamed and tore their long black hair and flung their white arms wildly against the night, and the Mexican men gathered in scowling, fiercely muttering groups.

The Kid was twenty-one when he was killed, and he had killed twenty-one white men. He was left handed and used, mainly, a forty-one caliber Colt double action six shooter, though he was a crack shot with a rifle, too. That he was a cold blooded murderer there is no doubt, but he was loyal to his friends, honest in his way, truthful, possessed of a refinement in thought and conversation rare even in these days, and no man ever lived who was braver than he. He belonged in an older, wilder age of blood-feud and rapine and war.

Yet to compare him with such brigands as Jesse James, Sam Mason, the Harpes, etc., is foolish. The Kid was an aristocrat among his kind, and as far above torture, needless brutality and senseless slaughter as any man might be. It took the slums of the great cities, the blind, bloody chaos of Border warfare and the gloomy shadows of the thick forests to produce the really inhuman criminals. It was the wilderness that bred Mason, the Harpes and John A. Murrell. Just as the gloom and silence of the New England hills brought forth the lurking shadows in the souls of the Puritans, so the grim deeps of the wilderness brought forth the slumbering atavism and primordial instincts of inhabitants, and made ordinary men into monstrosities from whose foul and abhorrent image the mind shrinks aghast.

And what a grisly fantasy was John A. Murrell's imperial dream and what a strange and ghastly empire he planned! Surely in that man slept the seeds of greatness, overshadowed by the black petals of madness.

The shadow of John A. Murrell and the shadow of the threat of his outlaw empire still hovered over the pine woods and the river lands in the 1850s when my great-grandfather, Squire James Henry, came west along the Wilderness Road with fifty head of fine cattle, a drove of horses, and five big wagons loaded with his family, slaves and belongings.

They were in Murrell's country, and though he had recently been released from prison and his planned slave-uprising had been nipped in the bud, his name was still one to conjure shudders. And in the sunset they came to a wild, frothing river, lashed to frenzy by the flooding rain, and saw, on the other side, a man sitting on a log beneath the forest branches. Something about his posture fired grisly recognition in the mind of a man traveling with the wagon-train and he paled and cried out that it was John A. Murrell who sat on the opposite bank.

I wish I could find words to paint that picture so that you might see it in your mind. The rain had slackened, the clouds were breaking away, rolling sullenly back, shot with blood. On all sides loomed the great trees of the wilderness, monstrous, grim, and pregnant with evil. On the eastern bank the wagons were halted, mired with the ooze and mud through which they had toiled since dawn. Before them the nameless river frothed and leaped and raced like a living, malevolent thing, howling among the rapids. On the further bank sat that still figure, like an image, unmoving, a symbol of unnamed threat and lurking horror. Behind him the sun was setting, like a ball of blood, glimmering evilly through the black trees and sending somber shafts along the dark and dripping branches that deepened into night-like gloom in the depths of the forest.

The women of the party blenched and the black slaves wailed their terror in a wild death-chant — all except Wyatt, the "outlaw", who feared not man nor demon. The women begged Squire Henry to turn back, or to camp on the east bank, but the Squire merely cursed. He rode into the foaming flood on his great black horse, old Proctor, and the hounds of the flood caught him and shook him like a rat in their teeth. But he battled his way back to the bank and he bound the wagons strongly together. Then he struck into the stream again, with the horses swimming and the wagons floating, and he and Wyatt riding along-side to steady them against the sweep of the current as much as they might. They gained the western bank, and the Squire and Wyatt rode back after the cattle and the horses. The beasts plunged and screamed their fear and the river tore at them white-fanged; and the Squire was threatened not alone by the roaring white water; he saw in Wyatt's murky eyes and in the set of the thick lips, the thought to strike him from his horse and drown him in mid-stream. But he divided his attention between the slave, the river and the beasts, knowing that Wyatt would not dare attack him except from behind; and lashing, battling and cursing, he swam the beasts across and came out safely on the western bank. Then he remembered the man on the log.

He reined about and looked for him; the man still sat in the same posture in which they had first glimpsed him. Apparently he had not moved. The Squire rode up close to him and spoke aggressively and harshly, leaning out from his saddle. The man made no reply; his hands lay listlessly at his side, and vacant eyes gave back an unseeing stare. The squire saw and realized what broken ambitions and ten years in a prison dungeon had done to the man. His face was worn and lined and prematurely old. From beneath wispy white hair, pale, glassy eyes stared through the Squire and far, far beyond him. A rifle lay by the log, like a forgotten bauble. There he sat, in a cloud of lost dreams and dim red visions, the King of the Mississippi — who had worn his crown and pressed his regal seat only in mad visions — the monarch that was to be, in that mad, black kingdom of death and destruction, whose plan was conceived in insanity and crushed in blood and terror. His face was old beyond the ken of men, his eyes were those of a ghost — and his slim white hands that had ripped so many shuddering souls from their fleshly bodies, lay limp on the log that was his final throne.

And so the curtain of iron laughter rings down on the red comedy, and the gods cut the string on which their puppet dances, flinging him into the pit of lost desire. And the red dream of glory and power and gilded empire ended on a rotting log by a nameless river where frogs croaked from the mud and the rain dripped drearily from the shaking branches, black against the sunset. Something about the thing slightly awed the wild Irish planter, and without a word he reined away, gesturing for the wagons to follow. They took up the long westward trek again, lumbering away through the trees; and still John A. Murrell sat upon his log, hearing naught, seeing naught, lost in the shadows of old dreams, and night fell over the wilderness.

Thank you very much for loaning me the manuscript (which I'm returning in this letter). I found it fascinating, with its horrific hints of semi-human monstrosities, and Elder cities set in dark, grim jungles. It's the sort of horror story I like, with its weird foreshadowings and grisly climax — above all, the shadowy web-work of dark implication lying behind the visible action of the tale.

I'm glad you found the prize-fight story of some interest. It's one of the least machine-made of the tales I've been supplying that magazine for the past couple of years. As you say, the pulp magazines are specializing to an alarming rate — western stories, fight stories, air stories, gangster stories — for instance — *Wild West Weekly*, *Battle Stories*, *Gangster Stories*, *Two-Gun Stories* (!), *Wall-street Stories*, being a few of the titles of magazines now seen on the newsstands. I've never tried the pseudo-science field — I'm so grossly ignorant of mechanics and science it would be virtually impossible for me to write convincingly in that line. Have you ever tried *Argosy*? I believe you could sell them some weird stories — they gobble up Merritt's stuff and you have him beat seven ways from the ace. Not that Merritt isn't good; he is. But his work lacks the sheer, somber and Gothic horror of your tales. A touch of mere fantasy sometimes mars his work, whereas your horror-tales are built starkly of black iron, with no slightest hint of tinsel — and therein lies their greatness. I've been reading your tales over again, in the old magazines — "The Unnamable," "The Temple," "He," "The Terrible Old Man," "The Silver Key" — and I hope that Farnsworth will see his way to publish all of them in book form soon — together with "The Festival" and "The Music of Erich Zann" both of which I missed, somehow. These must have been published in the old *Weird Tales*. By the way, did the old magazine go bankrupt or was it in good shape when Mr. Wright took it over? I seem to have heard from some source that it was in pretty rotten shape when he took it.

If you haven't seen the latest *Oriental Stories*, let me know. I have some extra copies. It contains a story by Tevis Clyde Smith and me[4], which you might possibly entertain an idle half-hour with, though I fear it isn't anything to brag about.

I'm sending you some stuff in a separate envelope which I hope you'll find interesting.

What you say of the pre-historic African race[5] is most interesting and thought-inspiring, and I hope future research throws more light on the past. I feel a deep pity for that people — living in peace and friendliness — an unwarlike and pastoral race — and suddenly confronted by a horde of black slayers as rude and merciless as they were strong. It must have been a slaughter rather than a war, and it's a damned pity that the Boskop people didn't have some Aryan traits to stiffen their spines and train their hands in fighting. I hate to think of white people being wiped out and enslaved by niggers. How do you suppose these people got there in the first place? Did they wander down the coast until they came to a country that suited them, or do you suppose their trek took many generations as they slowly shifted southward?

I've read the concluding chapters of Long's story[6] — a splendid tale and very well written. The narration of the dream was the high spot of the whole story, and to my mind, exceeded the final climax. The language used in the whole chapter of the dream, is nothing short of pure poetry and I have reread it repeatedly, and with the utmost admiration. The finely worked plot with its shuddery hints and horrific climax in the night-mantled hills is an absolute triumph in Gothic literature — a story within a story.

I can hardly find words to express the extent to which I was fascinated by your comments on your Roman subconscious and dream-life. As you say, one's instincts and fancy take strange quirks. I envy you your deep and profound knowledge of history and familiarity with classic names and places. I fear I've merely skimmed my historical studies, culling disconnected bits here and there.

But (to omit all mention of American instincts and subconscious sense of personal connection), my strongest instinctive leanings are toward the more ancient cities. I somehow feel more a sense of placement and personal contact with Babylon, Nineveh, Askalon, Gaza, Gath, and the like, than I do with Athens or Rome. I know nothing of the ways and customs of those ancient cities, cannot even form a clear mental picture pertaining to them, yet when I think of the ancient world, my thoughts leap instantly and subconsciously to the valley of the Tigris and Euphrates and the fertile lands of Mesopotamia, in the early days of the Semitic kingdoms. I can form no mental picture of Asia Minor of that day — I instinctively think of it merely as a waste of enemies and barbarians. Egypt is a land of brooding mystery that from time to time sends swarming hordes of war-chariots sweeping from the south to ravage and destroy. My real interest and sense of personal placement ceases with the establishment of the Mede-Persian empire. I feel no real kinship with the Semitic races of that day, and I do feel a personal connection with the Aryan Medes and experience a sense of gratification at their victory; yet from that time on, or at least until the Crusades and the invasions of the Mongols, the Near East holds no particular interest for me. Nor, until many centuries later do I feel any clear sense of personal connection with any age or any locality, until my sense of placement settles on the British Isles.

I feel more of an instinctive interest and loyalty toward individuals rather than nations, races or countries; as for instance, and especially, King Saul, King Arthur, (whether historical or legendary), Joan of Arc, Robert Bruce, Brian Boru and Hugh O'Neill. And to a lesser extent, Hannibal, Arminius, King Penda of Mercia, Alfred the Great, Richard the Lion-heart, Bertrand du

Guesclin, Edward Bruce, Shane O'Neill, Hugh Ruadh O'Donnell, William Wallace, Patrick Sarsfield, and The FitzGerald.

I have always felt a deep interest in Israel in connection with Saul. Poor devil! A pitiful and heroic figure, set up as a figure-head because of his height and the spread of his shoulders, and evincing an expected desire of be king in more than name — a plain, straight-forward man, unversed in guile and subtlety, flanked and harassed by scheming priests, beleaguered by savage and powerful enemies, handicapped by a people too wary and backward in war — what wonder that he went mad toward the end? He was not fitted to cope with the mysteries of king-craft, and he had too much proud independence to dance a puppet on the string of the high priest — there he sealed his own doom. When he thwarted the snaky Samuel, he should have followed it up by cutting that crafty gentleman's throat — but he dared not. The hounds of Life snapped ever at Saul's heels; a streak of softness made him human but made him less a king. He dared too much, and having dared too much, he dared not enough. He was too intelligent to submit to Samuel's dominance, but not intelligent enough to realize that submission was his only course unless he chose to take the ruthless course and fling the high priest to the vultures and jackals. Samuel had him in a strangle-hold; not only did the high priest have the people behind him, but he played on Saul's own fears and superstitions and in the end, ruined him and drove him to madness, defeat and death. The king found himself faced by opposition he could not beat down with his great sword — foes that he could not grasp with his hands. Life became a grappling with shadows, a plunging at blind, invisible bars. He saw the hissing head of the serpent beneath each mask of courtier, priest, concubine and general. They squirmed, venom-ladened beneath his feet, plotting his downfall; and he towered above them, yet must perforce bend an ear close to the dust, striving to translate their hisses. But for Samuel, vindictive, selfish and blindly shrewd as most priests are, Saul had risen to his full statue — as it was, he was a giant chained. David he knew was being primed for his throne — under his very feet they pointed the young adventurer for the crown. Yet I think he was loath to slay the usurper, because he felt a certain kinship with him — both were wild men of the hills and deserts, winning their way mainly by sheer force of arms, forced into the kingship to further the ends of a plotting priest-craft. To one man Saul could always turn — Abner, a soldier and a gentleman in the fullest sense of the word — too honorable, too idealistic for his own good. Saul and Abner were worth all that cringing treacherous race to which they belonged by some whim of chance.

David was wiser than Saul and not so wise, caring less for the general good, much more for his own. He was the adventurer, the soldier of fortune, to the very end, whereas Saul had at least some of the instincts of true king-ship in his soul. David knew that he must follow the lines laid out for him by the priests and he was willing to do so. A poet, yes, but intensely practical. When he heard of the slaying of Saul and Jonathan, he composed a magnificent poem in their honor — but first he gave orders that the people of the Jews should practice with the bow! He knew that archery was necessary to defeat the Philistines, who were evidently more powerful in hand-to-hand fighting than the Israelites, and were skilled in arrow-play. He had a long memory and his enemies did not escape — not even Joab, who did more to win David's kingdom for him than any other one man.

I cannot think of Saul, David, Abner and Joab as Jews, not even as Arabs; to me they must always seem like Aryans, like myself. Saul, in particular, I always unconsciously visualize as a Saxon king, of those times when the invaders of Britain were just beginning to adopt the Christian religion.

Another Hebrew who interests me is Samson, and this man I am firmly convinced was at least half Aryan. In the first place, he had red hair or bright yellow hair; I feel certain of this because of his name, and the legend concerning his locks. His name referred to the sun, always pertaining to redness, brightness, golden tinted, in any language; his strength lay in his hair; I connect his name with his hair. What more natural than a superstition attached to the red hair of a child born in a in a dark-haired race? And that angel in the field — well, in the old, old days of Ireland, there was a legend that the old gods had fled into the west, from which they occasionally emerged to bestow their favours on some lucky damsel. Many a wanderer from the western hills assumed the part of a god. I am convinced that the "angel" was a wandering, red-haired Aryan, and that Samson was his son.

The strong lad's characteristics were most certainly little like those of the race that claimed him. He wouldn't even associate with his people. He feasted and reveled with the lordly Philistines, and his drinking, fighting and wenching sound like the chronicles of some lad from Wicklow or a wild boy from Cork. He was a great jester, a quality none too common in his supposed race, and in the end he displayed true Aryan recklessness and iron lust for vengeance. When, in history, did a true Semite deliberately kill himself to bring ruin to his enemies? The big boy was surely an Aryan.

My antipathy for Rome is one of those things I can't explain myself. Certainly it isn't based on any early reading, because some of that consisted of MacCauley's *Lays of Ancient Rome* from which flag-waving lines I should have drawn some Roman patriotism, it seems. At an early age I memorized most of those verses, but in reciting, changed them to suit myself and substituted Celtic names for the Roman ones, and changed the settings from Italy to the British Isles! Always, when I've dreamed of Rome, or subconsciously thought of the empire, it has seemed to me like a symbol of slavery — an iron spider, spreading webs of steel all over the world to choke the rivers with dams, fell the forests, strangle the plains with white roads and drive the free people into cage-like houses and towns.

It's difficult for me to visualize a Romanized Britain. I know it is there, with the villas and towns you dream of, but I've always instinctively connected myself with the untamed tribes of the West, or those of the heather. The great oak forests are friendly to me, in my dreams, giving me shelter, food and hiding-place. And it's almost impossible for me to visualize a Druid as anything but a tall, stately old man, white robed, having golden buckled sandals to his feet and a staff to his hand, with a long white beard and very kindly, very wise eyes. I've never been able to think of the cult as any other than white bearded sages, wise in astronomy and agriculture, very close to Nature. It's difficult for me to think of them in connection with human sacrifices and I've never been able to lend in writing an air of mysterious horror to Druidic-worship. I may some day, but it will be in direct violation to my instincts on the matter. My sense of somber mystery and elder-world horror centers on the worship and priest-craft of the little dark people who came before — the Mediterranean race which preceded the Celts into Britain. I can experience a real shuddery sense of black magic and devil-worship when I contemplate these little stone age men, with their dark spirits and their bright spirits, their human sacrifice and their polished weapons and implements, the uses for some of which are not now known.

And just as you consciously prefer the Grecians and instinctively lean toward the Romans, I consciously despise the Stuart kings, and instinctively defend them. If there's anything in ancestral memory, this is natural, for to the best of my knowledge, my ancestors on both sides of the Irish Sea fought for those kings. Indeed, one Sir Robert Howard spent seven years in the Tower on their account and was freed only at the Restoration. Always, when I read anything against the Stuarts, I unconsciously find myself defending them, even though I may consciously heartily endorse everything said in their disfavor. I reckon I'm just naturally a Jacobite by instinct — why, the Devil knows, because I detest the line consciously. I feel a real personal shame in regard to the Boyne Water. A pity that Shamas a cacagh had not at him even a wee bit of Patrick Sarsfield's spirit. Monmouth was the best of that line, to my notion, and even he ran like a scared rabbit.

Let me again express my admiration for your drawing ability; your pictures of the Roman and the cavalier are strikingly vivid, and I share your dissatisfaction with drab modern mode of dress. I think I'd feel more at home in a suit of chain mail and a surcoat myself! Men's styles have certainly come upon colorless and uninteresting ways.

But how I've rambled on! I only hope I haven't bored you to the point of nausea. I never seem to be able to find a stopping place. Thanking you again for the architectural sketches and descriptions, the loan of the ms. and the antiquarian literature, I am, with best wishes,

Cordially,
[Robert E. Howard]

NOTES

1. *Weird Tales* published on a bimonthly schedule from February-March 1931 through June-July 1931.
2. "The Curse of Yig," revised by Lovecraft for Zealia Reed Bishop, *Weird Tales*, November 1929.
3. *Weird Tales*, September 1926.
4. "Red Blades of Black Cathay."
5. The Boskops. See letter 152, note 3 and letter 169, note 7.
6. "The Horror from the Hills"; see letter 152, note 5.

TSS: 11459-11470, 45021-45023

157. To Wilfred Blanch Talman, ca. February 1931.

Mr. Wilfred B. Talman,
The Texas Company,
New York city.

My Dear Mr. Talman:

I can hardly find words to express my appreciation for your interest in "Red Blades of Black Cathay". Both Mr. Smith and I are highly gratified by the compliments you paid the story, and hope that future efforts will meet with your approval. I also appreciate very much your writing to Mr. Wright in commendation of the tale. I hope that our details were as nearly accurate as you say — we were rather uncertain on a few points — medieval Oriental history being so sketchy. I must admit that there was a weak point in the story — from my study of Genghis Khan I feel certain he would never have allowed Godric to reign as an independent and equal king; he would have destroyed the empire of Black Cathay entirely first. But we had to have it that way, in order to allow Godric to live and realize his ambition. You being a writer yourself, understand such difficulties. Of course we took a great deal of liberties in regard to the actual conquest of Black Cathay, but I suppose that comes under the head of fictional license or something. By the way, the name "Subotai" is the Mongol term for buffalo.

I hope your company can use the article I sent them,[1] as I think the readers would find the subject matter interesting, at least. It deals, as of course you know if you've seen the article, with old Camp Colorado, which is situated some twenty-five miles southwest of this town and was one of a string of army posts which was literally the Southwestern frontier in the 1850s. I have some more articles in mind which I hope will find a place in your publication.

Thanks for the magazine. And by the way, I've been intending to subscribe to the publication for some time, but I can't find the rates. If you'll let me know the price of a year's subscription, I'll mail you a check at once; the magazine is the most interesting one of its sort I know.

Again thanking you for the kind things you said about the Cathay story, and hoping to see something from your pen in both *Weird Tales* and *Oriental Stories* soon, I am,

Cordially,
[Robert E. Howard]

P.S. I'm mailing you the November copy of *Weird Tales* which you said you missed; hope you like "Kings of the Night."

R.E.H.

NOTES

1. "The Ghost of Camp Colorado."

TSS: 15321

ଔ෴ଓ

158. To H.P. Lovecraft, ca. March 3, 1931.[1]

Dear Mr. Lovecraft:

I'm writing this letter only some two hundred thirty-odd miles from my home town, yet it's like being in a different state, so much difference exists in climate, topography and inhabitants. It's spring here, with birds chirping, roses and smaller flowers in bloom, deep fresh grass, palm trees, banana trees, date and fig trees adding to the effect. Only the Mexicans hurry here, ordinarily; the white people go leisurely. Tomorrow begins a week-long fete marking the opening of the old Spanish governor's palace,[1] closed and vacant for generations. Thousands are expected; Cardinal Patrick Hayes of New York is to be the special speaker. San Antonio's strong for fiestas, fetes, bailes, etc.

This town is about the only place in Texas that takes much stock in history; the city itself is like one vast museum of old times.

There is, of course, a great percentage of unmixed American population, but a vast number of San Antonio's people are a welter of mixed bloods of many nations: Indian, Spanish, French, German and Polish. Mexican blood tinges the social order up and down the scale. You will find it in the veins of aristocratic American families, and in the veins of mixed-breed negroes. Not many negroes here though; low class Mexicans crowd them out or absorb them.

Rather too cosmopolitan for my tastes. My natural homeland is Central and Western Central Texas, which localities (with the Great Plains region) are freer from foreignization than any of the rest of the state. I'll add the piney woods of East Texas to that list, though the great new oil fields of that regions are likely to bring in a foreign element. But East Texas swarms with negroes, of which there are but few in Western Central Texas. Neither are there many Mexicans in the latter province, the land being almost entirely in the hands of small independent farmers and resident ranchers. Absentee ownership will eventually prove the ruin of South Texas just as it was the ultimate ruin of Ireland. In my part of the country, the Latin element is small. Here it predominates. The oil booms brought swarms of people from other states into Central Texas and many of them were of foreign parentage, but in almost all cases they were German, Scandinavian or Irish extraction. The Latins don't follow the oil trail much. These Nordic strangers are easily assimilated and absorbed by the native population. Not so easy to absorb strangers from Southern Europe. It's more likely to work the other way round. The percentage of brunets in this city is infinitely greater than in my home-land. The streets swarm with flashing black eyes and black locks, whereas in Central Texas blue and grey eyes and light or only mediumly dark hair are overwhelmingly the rule. A couple of weeks ago I was in a boxing arena in Fort Worth, watching a bout between the welterweight champion and a lad who was a high school kid with me once, and I noted the predominance of white men in the crowd, which filled the great building to full capacity. Outside of a very few Mexicans, I did not see a single person who was not an unmistakable American of Nordic descent. Of course, there doubtless were a few foreigners but the percent was negligible. Fort Worth is certainly a white man's town — one of the few so remaining. It lies 165 miles east of my home-town, and San Antonio is only some 70 or 80 miles further away, south, south-east. You can travel clean across the state from east to west and find little change in the nationalities of the natives, but a hundred miles north or south makes a lot of difference.

San Antonio certainly offers a colorful and interesting spectacle, not to be duplicated anywhere in the New World. I'm sending you some views which I hope may be of some interest. The colored pictures I got in the Buckhorn Saloon and the uncolored Mexican views I obtained in a little curio shop down on Houston Street, which deals exclusively in Mexican things.

Best wishes and most cordially,
[Robert E. Howard]

NOTES

1. The Spanish Governor's Palace officially opened on March 4, 1931 as a museum. Date of letter changed at Rob Roehm's suggestion. JB

TSS: 65782-65783

ଔଋଔ

159. To Tevis Clyde Smith, ca. March 1931.

Well, Fear Finn:

Congratulations on your history book.[1] I'm sure glad you've decided to put it out and believe you'll make some money on it. Let me have the honor of buying the first copy, autographed. Who's going to do the printing? Tough luck, getting all your stuff back, but you'll make it all right.

This week they're holding the formal opening of the Spanish governor's palace, built 1749 and Cardinal Patrick Hayes came all the way from New York to bless it. I got a big kick out of going through the place — it looks just like scenes from swash-buckling movies. I wouldn't be surprized to see Douglas Fairbanks came bounding into the patio with his rapier and jack-boots.

Fiction House Inc., wrote me and said emphatically that that they wanted Steve and advised me to write a new series for Street & Smith which I'd already offered to do. I haven't heard from Street and Smithereens yet.[2]

What a library they got here alretty! A whole room with genealogy nearly. Like most men who have nothing to be proud of in themselves, I seek a vicarious pride in my ancestry. I have the herewith or rather wherewith to refute the Kentucky Howards, by Zeus, who claim the name comes from Hog-ward, or hog-herder. No such things; according to the most authentic accounts and records, there never was such a term as hog-ward; it was hog-herd and the family of Hoggarts got their names thence. One branch of the Howards come from the occupation name of Hayward, meaning a fence-tender — Hayward — Hawyard — Haward — Howard. The other branch got their name from their common ancestor, Hereward the Wake — Hereward — Heward — Haward — Howard. A law suit in my family nearly a hundred years ago proved that the name was never Hayward, so naturally it is of the other branch and I am a direct descendent of Hereward the Wake. That's news to me — I thought my line came into England with the Conqueror and was free of Saxon blood. It's an old South country Saxon family. But that there were Normans by the same name is evident from the records of Fitzhowards, Fitz being of course a typically Norman-French suffix or whatever you call it, meaning son of. I also came upon the first evidence of the Ervin family in America — a will made by a slave-holder in North Carolina and witnessed by one Robert Ervin; date, 1724. That he was kin of mine I know, because the Ervins settled in North Carolina and lived there until 1840, and only my branch spells the name that way. Well, I'm glad both Howards and Ervins had sense enough to settle in the South when they came to America.

Well, pretty soon I'm going down to a music hall, I think, and watch the big smoke George Godfrey do his stuff. He has challenged any nigger in San Antonio to hit him in the belly and they have a 212 pound smoke for the job. Frank Richards, the man with the iron belly is in town and raging. He says George is trying to steal his stuff and will probably raise some kind of hell at the fights tonight. The music hall is in a tough locality but maybe I'll get by without being blackjacked.

By the way, Lovecraft told *me* that August Derleth told *him* that Farnsworth told *him* that the first of June *Weird Tales* goes back to the monthly basis. I gather that writers and readers whooped with rage at Farnsworth; I hope the finances are as good as I hope they are.

Fear Dunn.

NOTES

1. *Frontier's Generation.*
2. Steve Costigan, Howard's humorous boxing character, starred in a series of stories for Fiction House's *Fight Stories* magazine. Street & Smith wanted Howard to move Costigan over to one of their publications. Howard declined and sent them the stories of Kid Allison, instead. Three of these yarns appeared in Street & Smith's *Sport Story Magazine.* See letter 155.

TSS: 82543

ꕥꕥꕥ

160. To Tevis Clyde Smith, ca. March 1931.

Fear Finn:

I don't have to tell you how sorry I am about the Vinsons.[1] I wrote to Truett but there wasn't much I could say. There isn't anything anyone can say, really. Anything like that is past words. Words are such damned weak and futile things any time.

Too bad about your typewriter breaking when you were winding up the history, but the old machine has lasted mighty well. When do you expect to get the history out?

Well, I was in the library the other day when I heard a sort of bellow or roar and looking up saw Harold Preece towering over me. He was accompanied by one Georg Papsoon, a Pennsylvania Slovene, and Communist organizer. A keen, bright looking young man, well dressed, with black hair, brown eyes and very dark skin he was. He soon went his way and Harold and I, while waiting on the corner, were accosted by another wayfarer of same general aspect who spoke broken English. Harold said he had seen him coming out the Salvation Army cursing because they wouldn't let him shave and wash up there and Harold had sent him to some damned place where he could. The hunky was quite merry, saying that he had already mooched a meal and fifteen cents. This disgusted Harold who complained to me that such persons quit worrying about the social revolution the minute they got something to eat. My only reply was the cryptic remark that most of these blankety-blank Communists were Polacks or Wops.

Harold seems to be getting along very well with his debunking and is attending the university. He invited me to come over and read some of my verse before his class, club, cult or something; I declined with a slight shudder. He also wanted to take me around and introduce me to Solon Stewart, the solitary writer, but I didn't have the energy. Harold said that he had gotten a letter from a man in Oklahoma or some place saying that he had devoted the best years of his life upholding the Cause and now thought the cause ought to uphold him a little, as he was broke and he wanted Harold to sign a coupon pledging to help support him for the rest of his life. Harold said he ignored the letter and I smiled a sour smile and said that evidently the man was a fool and no true patriot; for look ye, I remarked, the fellow had worked all his life and ruined himself uplifting the masses and now in his old age and starvation he was fool enough to believe that the masses ought to uplift him a little, whereas it was evident that he had missed the true calling of the Crusade, which is to aid the down-and-out masses, not the individual. Whereat Harold smiled weakly and said naught. Harold said the Communists were whooping it up hereabouts and that a parade of soldiers which had just passed, was to awe them. He probably over-rates them.

I'll look up your genealogy as soon as I can, though not knowing the first names of your ancestors, I can't promise you much. I couldn't find out much about my own, except to establish a fact I've guessed for some time, that Robert Irwin, signer of the Mechlenburg Declaration of Independence was no relation whatever of mine. It was about 1763 before he came to Mechlenburg.

Damn, I must be washed up. No energy. I've been here a week and some days over, and I've been to exactly one show; and one set of fights. The low altitude must have something to do with it, though I've done quite a bit of work.

Answer soon, will youse?

Bob.

NOTES

1. Rev. Wade Vinson, Truett's father, died on March 3, 1931.

TSS: 82132

ଊ

161. To Tevis Clyde Smith, ca. March 14, 1931.

Well, Fear Finn:

Heigho for sunny San Antonio. It's been the damndest rain imaginable here last night and all day. I'll admit most of the weather has been good.

Your history looks great and from what I read, has a remarkably vivid and entertainingly ironic style. By the way, you want me to return the proof-sheet?

Of all the disgusting adds, that crack you sent me about Generous Joe[1] takes the cake. If that fat hog ever did anything to build up the empire, I'm a Dutchman.

Yeah, I had an idea I'd run into Harold. He had beat his way over and says he has no trouble getting rides. He says he and Lenore have become almost strangers. She, he says, has taken up the study of anthropology and runs in a different set than he.

Those old boys of the Dime Novel brigade sure lived virile and active lives. As for Tyline Perry,[2] I've never read anything by her, but I guess she's hot on the heels of Vina Delmar — not in style, for I know naught of her line, but in fame, fortune and fertility.

Grinding apprenticeship — boy, you said it. It's a question of which will wear out first — the grindstone or the grindee. I've heard nothing more from Street & Smith; I believe they want Steve or nobody.

I'll see what I can do about tracing your ancestors, though it's a bewildering game, because of the custom, extant among all Western races, of naming so many families and members of families almost exactly alike. My confounded ancestors must never have registered births, land deeds, marryings or any damned thing. Outside of the Robert Ervin I mentioned, I've found one other ancestor — a John Ervin who served in Edward Buncombe's Fifth Regiment, was wounded and discharged in 1778. And I'll bet he shot himself in the foot unintentionally.

The D.A.R. have a whole set of volumes of ancestors in which I'm sure you'd find most of yours. I'll try to look through them for you.

I find that the present noble family of the English Howards trace their descent to Henry I, king of France, and Anne of Russia. Also that all the royal families of Europe, including those of Sweden, Rumania and Bulgaria are directly descended from Robert Bruce. Also that the royal family of Sweden is more Scotch than Swedish. And Cal Coolidge is a direct descendent of Mark Antony, through Charlemagne. And Charlemagne was not full blooded Frank at all, but had a strong strain of Roman blood — Mark Antony's — and a stronger strain of Celtic — the blood of Coilus, a Celtic king of Britain. And here are the derivatives of some Scotch clans: Grant — Le Grand, French; Gordon, de Gourdon, French; Campbell, de Campobello, French, or possibly Italian; Bruce, de Bruys, or de Brix; French; Cummins, de Commines, French; etc.

There's sure been a run of gangster pictures here; the pipple may be meek and law-abiding, but they sure whoop with glee every time a rod-man bumps off a copper on the screen. I think it's an unconscious vent to their resentment against the cops who herd them about in their every-day life. Well, there's the makings of some first class gangs in the young Mexicans who swarm the streets here.

I've seen a number of shows: *Rango*; *The Last Parade*, with Jack Holt; *Hook, Line and Sinker*; *Little Caesar*, with Edward Robinson; *The Doorway to Hell*, with Lew Ayres; *Good News*; *Billy the Kid*, with Johnny Mack Brown.

I've also seen George Godfrey and Max Schmeling perform and if there's anything in comparative showings as judged by exhibitions, the Big Smoke ought to be able to beat the Hell out of Max. (Pronounced Mox.) Gawge weighed 275 pounds but he got around as light as a cat; Judas, he's big! He's a good clown, too, and played up to the crowd. Max didn't make much of an impression on the unusually small crowd which mixed considerable razzes among their cheers. I don't think the crowd liked Generous Joe Jacobs, his Yiddish manager. I damned sure didn't.

Fear Dunn.

NOTES

1. Joe Jacobs, Max Schmeling's manager.
2. According to a letter from Tevis Clyde Smith to Howard, Perry was "a former Brownwood girl who has had one novel published, and has another one due off the press shortly. I understand that she has sold about ninety short stories in the last three or four years, too."

TSS: 82000-82001

ଔଓ

162. To Wilfred Blanch Talman, ca. April 1931.

Dear Mr. Talman:

I'm glad you liked "Kings of the Night." You needn't bother about returning the magazine; I have several other copies.

Thanks for the *Texaco Star*. I wonder if you could let me have about three or four more copies of that issue? I'd like to present them to the people who gave me the information I used in the article.

I haven't gotten a check for the article yet, but I reckon I will before long.

I'm very glad that my article was well received, and hope that future articles which I intend to submit, will be as well liked. I am indeed honored that, as you mentioned, the Director of Publications should praise my work before the Company officials; I am the more gratified because this is the first article of the sort I ever submitted to any publication, having devoted practically all my time to fiction.

Our mutual friend Mr. Lovecraft writes me that a publishing house had been corresponding with him in regard to possibly bringing out his stories in book form. I most sincerely hope that they close the deal satisfactorily to all parties, for literature would be enriched exceedingly by the appearance of his tales on the book shelves of the world. And God knows, modern literature needs some such stimulus, for it has fallen on barren ways.

Hoping to hear from you again, I am,

Cordially
[Robert E. Howard]

P.S. I hope you liked my Crusading junk[1] in the latest *Oriental's*, though I have a feeling that it fell short of whatever vague standard I intended it for.

NOTES

1. "Hawks of Outremer."

TSS: 15323

ꕥꕥꕥ

163. To Tevis Clyde Smith

Marlin, Texas,
May 9, 1931.

Fear Finn:

Have youse heard anything more about the proposed book of poetry? Have you sent in your poems yet?[1]

I saw *The Front Page* last week at Fort Worth. Have you seen it ? My main feeling was a desire to take that louse "Murphy" and break his spine just to hear it snap. Of all the revolting swinishness I ever saw depicted — it's about the most powerful show I ever saw — raw — smashing — nauseatingly realistic. I wanted to see George Arliss in *The Millionaire* but didn't get to, though it was showing there. Have you seen the streamers of *Shipmates* where invisible hands clap applause incessantly? Of all the utter hokum.

I got a laugh out of my story which appeared this month in *Action Stories*.[2] They changed the name of the character — McClarney — to Steve Costigan, though the style of the tale was nothing at all like Steve. And they capped the story "by the author of 'The TNT. Punch'." I never wrote a story by that title in my life.[3]

I see where the Claytons are bringing out a new magazine dealing with weird subjects and another dealing with historical tales of romance and adventure[4] — two cents a word on acceptance and up. If I can't make both of them I ought to be ham-strung. You ought to re-read Dumas and crash the historical one — the ad says the tales should generally feature the Anglo-Saxon but that the gallant Frenchman and dashing Spaniard will have their place. I see where I dress Solomon Kane up in a nom de plume and let him thrust, parry and riposte for eighteen chapters.

That reminds me; I just recently got a letter from Farnsworth who's just read Lamb's book on the later crusades,[5] and wants me to write a tale dealing with Baibars the Panther; do you know anything about him? I'll conceal my ignorance with a flare of action, as usual. Just in case you ever want to write to me, send it to my usual address. I won't be here long.

Fear Dunn.

NOTES

1. Alvin P. Bradford, of San Antonio, was editing a collection of contributions to *The Junto* which was to be titled *Virgin Towers*; the collection was never completed.
2. "The Sign of the Snake."
3. Howard had titled the story "Waterfront Law."
4. *Strange Tales* and *Soldiers of Fortune*, respectively.
5. Harold Albert Lamb's *The Flame of Islam.*

TSS: 82177

ଔଓଔଓ

164. To Tevis Clyde Smith, ca. mid-May 1931.

Well Fear Finn:

I got a letter from Bradford saying that the book business was coming on very slowly because the mutts weren't sending their tripe in. (My words, not his.) I hope you've sent in your poems by this time; I can see the only way we'll ever put it across is for us to just get up and push it. If Bradford hasn't got action from the rest, I'm going to write to them, myself, personally. There's no use in frittering around forever, and between you and me, I'm afraid a lot of the Juntites are rather lacking in punch.

By the way, when you're in the newsstands, I wish you'd glance at *Sport's Story* now and then, if you don't mind. I can't get it here, and I'm afraid I'll miss my story when it comes out. And I want to do some publicity work when it appears. Street & Smith, after long deliberation, finally decided to take another yarn of mine[1] and sent me a check for $90. Fiction House has been turning down Steve regular.[2] I got a long letter from Byrne which said, in part:

"My idea of a Steve Costigan yarn is one in which Steve is recovering from an overdose of belladonna that some tricky opponent has put into his eyes before the bout. He is wearing glasses and has a scholastic, weak-kneed appearance. They get him to box an exhibition bout for society with the east coast champ refereeing. And the heat of battle, plus Steve's near-sightedness causes him to sock the champ by mistake . . . . . the champ comes back at Steve

. . . . Mike, the bulldog, leaps into the ring, tearing the champ's pants off in front of the society queens. And then in the things that follow you have Steve in his normal sphere, doing the things we like to see him doing."[3]

Fear Dunn.

NOTES

1. "Kid Galahad."
2. "Shackled Mitts" was rejected April 22.
3. This suggestion became "Cultured Cauliflowers."

TSS: 82133

ଔ

165. To Tevis Clyde Smith, week of May 18, 1931.

Fear Finn:

I should have answered your letters before, but I've been working pretty hard. In the time I've been back from Marlin — a little more than two weeks — I've written three Costigan stories,[1] a Kid Allison tale,[2] a western adventure yarn[3] and a long historical novelet.[4] Also been studying the crusades and the Irish-Danish wars. And I've got plenty to do yet; the *Texaco Star* appears to want more articles, Farsnworth wants the Baibars story, and I've got some stuff I wrote at Marlin — a ring story I want to rewrite for Street & Smith,[5] and a pseudo-scientific junk I want to finish and get off to the Claytons. And with all that work, very likely I won't sell any of it. Though Fiction House did take a yarn for *Action Stories* - $75 — that must be their regular price for short stories now.[6]

The address of the *Texaco Star* is The Texas Company 135 East 42nd Street, New York. Hope you sell them a flock of stuff, and I'm sure you will. Wish you'd get me a *Frontier Times* and keep it till I see you; I want to see my reprint,[7] also the review they gave your book.

I guess you're right about the Virgin Towers business. I'll send Bradford the fish and a half, but not till I write him and ask him what the Hell. I have an idea the Juntites wouldn't kick in with the required dough. I hope to Hell you and I can bring out a volume of verse soon. I got one of those sterotypes from Lenore, by the way of Mooney, myself, and I reckon everybody connected with the *Junto* got one or more.

The stuff I quoted in my former letter about Costigan's belladonna spree was in the words of Byrne, verbatim — whatever the Hell that means. I submitted a story based on the suggestion[8] and I hope he takes it. The yarn I sold *Action Stories* had characters named Mike Dorgan and Bill McGlory and I just wonder if Dorgan isn't changed to Costigan before it appears in print.

Say, I wish you'd do me a favor; give the enclosed negatives to the photographer and have him develop them and send the pictures to me; I'm going to use some of them in an article to the Texas people, I think. I'm enclosing some dimes and if that isn't enough, let me know.

Fear Dunn.

P.S. I got a letter from a kid in Kansas, who had recently read my "Crowd-Horror" in *Argosy*; he said he was affected the same way, and wanted to know what to do about it.

NOTES

1. "Cultured Cauliflowers" and "One Shanghai Night" are two of the three.
2. "College Socks."
3. Unknown.
4. Probably "Spears of Clontarf."
5. Possibly "The Fighting Fury."
6. "The House of Peril."
7. "The Ghost of Camp Colorado" was reprinted in *Frontier Times*, June 1931.
8. "Cultured Cauliflowers."

TSS: 82050

ঌ≈ঌ

166. To Farnsworth Wright, ca. June-July 1931.

In your last letter you asked me to give you some information about myself. Well, it is risky, to get a writer talking about himself, ask him to give a brief resume of his accomplishments and he's very likely to inflict his whole biography and philosophy on you.

I noticed that question about my being a professor, etc., in the Eyrie. Well, if it had not been for a scourge of cholera, I'd have been a Californian instead of a Texan. Cholera hit a band of '49ers on the Arkansas River and wiped out all but seven of the party of nineteen; others were so weakened by the disease they had to turn back, of one of whom I have the honor to be the grandson. William Benjamin Howard.

Well, my tale is soon told. I come from old pioneer stock. By nationality I am predominantly Gaelic, in spite of my English name — some three fourths Irish while the rest is a mixture of English, Highland, Scotch, and Danish. I was born in a little, fading ex-cowtown about thirty miles west of Fort Worth.[1] Practically all my life, has been spent in the country and some of the Texas cities. I have only a high school education, and not a particularly elaborate one at that.

Like the average man, the tale of my life would merely be a dull narration of drab monotony and toil, a grinding struggle against poverty. I have spent most of my time in the bad barren semi-waste lands of Western Texas, and since infancy my memory holds a continuous grinding round of crop failures, sandstorms, drouths, floods, hot winds that withered the corn, hailstorms that ripped the grain to pieces, late blizzards that froze the crops in the bud, plagues of grasshoppers and boll weevils and that stripped the cotton. I remember year-long drouths and that killed the very mesquite trees, when the streams were dry, and the cattle ate cactus until their mouths and bellies were full of the spines and then lay down and died when even the cactus was gone.

My boyhood was spent in the oil country — or rather oil came into the country when I was still a young boy, and remained. I'll say one thing about an Oil boom — it will teach a kid that life's a pretty rotten thing, about as quick as anything I can think of.

I've worked at several jobs, but wasn't a success at any of them; I've picked cotton, helped brand a few yearlings, hauled a little garbage, worked in a grocery store, ditto in a Jewish dry-goods store, worked in a law office, jerked soda, worked in a gas office, tried to be a public stenographer, packed a surveyor's rod, worked up oil-field news for some Texas and Oklahoma papers — etc., etc., and also etc.

I've always had a honing to make my living by writing, ever since I can remember, and while I haven't been a howling success in that line, at least I've managed for several years now to get by without grinding at some time-clock punching job. There's freedom in this game, that's the main reason I chose it. As Service says:

"—In bellypinch I will pay the price
But God, let me be free!—
For once I know in the long ago,
They made a slave of me."[2]

Life's not worth living if somebody thinks he's in authority over you.

You gave me my start in the racket by buying my first story — "Spear and Fang." I was eighteen years old at the time. Pounding out a decent living at the writing game is no snap — but the average man's life is no snap, whatever he does. I'm merely one of a huge army, all of whom are bucking the line one way or another for meat for their bellies — which is the main basic principle and reason and eventual goal of Life. Every now and then one of us finds the going too hard and blows his brains out, but it's all in the game, I reckon.

And after all, even the bitterness of existence has certain compensations, slight though they may be. To be brought up in the lap of luxury, to live a life of idle pleasure — never to know the bite of cold, the sting of heat, the pangs of hunger, the agony of unceasing toil, the black bitterness of failure, the sordidities of poverty, the blood, the grime and the sweat — to live such a life is to miss the full grip of human realities. The best way a man can live is by hard slugging and the best way he can die is with his boots on.

Well, I started to tell you something about myself, but there's so little to tell, I'm rather at a loss as to what to say. I've been working at the writing-racket pretty regularly since the age of fifteen and hope eventually to get somewhere. It's a game I honestly love, and the praise the readers have been kind enough to give me in the Eyrie has given me an immense amount of sincere pleasure.

I was lucky enough to discover early in life what I wanted to do, though I've done a great deal of wandering in bewildered circles, even so. And here and now, apart and aside from the subject, I want to make a prediction — that the Southwest is entering what I believe will prove to be a gigantic literary boom, and the next generation will see this section for the country fictionized, dramatized, and glorified generally. I believe the reading public is growing weary of the pseudo-psychological rot and ultra-sophisticated muck the writers of the present predominant school have been inflicting upon it, and is turning more and more to a cleaner, more wholesome phase of life, such as is exemplified by the epics of exploration, conquest and settlement. And certainly the history of the Southwest is rich in drama. And I shall be glad to see my part of the country come into its own — my people had no hand in the very early conquest of the Southwest — they were all Southern slaveholders who drifted West after being ruined by the Civil War — but they had a part in the settlement and development. And so I feel linked to the country, not only by birth, but by descent and tradition.

And there I believe is about all the information I can give about a very humdrum and commonplace life.

NOTES

1. Peaster, Texas.
2. From Robert W. Service's "A Rolling Stone."

❦

167. To Harry Bates, June 1, 1931.

Mr. Bates,
New York City.

Dear Mr. Bates:

You may, or you may not have noticed my work in *Weird Tales*, *Oriental Stories*, *Ghost Stories*, *Fight Stories*, *Action Stories*, and *Argosy*; but that doesn't matter so much. The point is, I'm deeply interested in the intention of your company to bring out a new magazine devoted entirely to historical tales. I want very much to do business with this magazine, and would appreciate any pointers you might give me as to how to make the market in case this story is not acceptable. I realize that editors do not have time to give detailed criticisms; but just a line or a few words scrawled on a rejection slip would help me wonderfully.

I'm hoping you can use this tale — "Spears of Clontarf" which I am enclosing. It deals with a phase in history too much neglected by writers — that of the Dano-Irish wars which culminated in the final shattering of the Viking power at the battle of Clontarf. Those days of war and rapine represent an age crammed with vital drama, enough to supply a hundred thrilling volumes.

In writing this tale, I have dipped deeply into both history and legendry, striving to interweave historical facts and folk-lore myths in a realistic and logical manner. It is my belief that practically all legends have some solid foundation of fact, though they may be so changed and distorted as to be unrecognizable. Thus, in the case of Dunlang O'Hartigan, and his sweetheart, Eevin of Craglea, the guardian faery-spirit of the O'Briens, I honestly believe the legend had some such basis of fact as I have presented in this story. As you know, the legend represents Eevin as presenting her lover with a magic mantle making him invisible; he threw it off in the heat of battle, Murrogh crying out to him, and was instantly slain as she had predicted. It is my honest belief that the girl who later became the wife of Craglea in the legends, persuaded Dunlang to wear some sort of armor — the Irish of that day generally wore none at all — and in the legends that sprang up about the great battle, that armor became a "mantle of darkness."

In gathering material for this story I have drawn on such sources as Joyce's *History of Gaelic Ireland*, *The Saga of Burnt Nial* Spenser's *View of the State of Ireland*, *The Wars of the Gaels with the Galls* and other histories.

I hope you can use this story; if not, I would, as I've said, highly appreciate any tips you can give me as to making the new market. I'm also interested in the other new magazine you are bringing out — the one devoted to weird and bizarre stories — more especially as I have been a regular contributor to *Weird Tales* magazine for about seven years.

Cordially yours,

TSS: 65964

ଔଓ

168. To Tevis Clyde Smith, ca. early June 1931.

Fear Finn:

Thanks very much for the *Frontier Times*. Bozo gave you a pretty nice write-up about your bookel,[1] but he should have devoted more space to it. Did you read Big-foot's adventures? Boy, Pink and I nearly busted laughing over it. There was a red-blooded character in a red-blooded epoch!

I see that *Women of All Nations* is showing in Ft. Worth; if it comes to Brownwood, be sure and let me know and I'll try to come over and see it.

Well, there ain't much to say. I'm working pretty hard and I reckon you are too. Street & Smith gobbled up another Kid Allison. They're generally pretty prompt; just about twelve days after I sent them this yarn — "College Socks" — I got a check for $100.

Well, write me when you get time.

Fear Dunn.

NOTES

1. In *Frontier Times*, June 1931, editor J. Marvin Hunter noted receipt of *Frontier's Generation*, a "valuable booklet" with "much interesting and worth-while history of early days." The issue also included an installment of the serialization of John C. Duval's *Adventures of Big-Foot Wallace.*

TSS: 82045

169. To H.P. Lovecraft, ca. June 1931.

Dear Mr. Lovecraft:

I didn't take much of a trip after all. I had vague ideas of drifting down to New Orleans when I started out, but they didn't materialize. I merely went to Fort Worth, about 165 miles east of here, and then down to Waco, which lies about a hundred miles south of Fort Worth, then on a small health resort about thirty miles east of Waco where I spent a week.[1] I came back through the Central Texas black-land belt and I never saw finer prospects for crops this year. All over Texas for that matter, the land is a riot of wheat and oats. Whether they'll be able to sell it, the Devil who rules the Southwest only knows. Times are fiercely hard, even though the mild winter saved the cattle and stock, and the people are restless and getting mean. There's been more shooting scrapes and cutting affrays around here in the last few months, than there has been since the early days.

Thanks very much for the package of views and literature, also for the folders of Florida. That must be an exotically beautiful country, and I'm mighty glad you got to make the trip. Charleston must be a most fascinating place; I am enthralled by the pictures of it you sent me. Many of the views of San Augustine seem familiar to me, because of their resemblance to the Spanish architecture of Southern Texas. Especially the patio of the "oldest house" which much resembles the Governor's Palace in San Antonio, snap-shots of which I'm enclosing. But that trick of building the upper part of the house with wood is new to me. You are right about the western Spaniards borrowing ideas from the Indians. You'll notice in some views I sent you of New Mexico, the similarity between the ancient pueblos and the Spanish buildings.

I'm very sorry to hear that you've been suffering with eye-strain. It seems most writers are afflicted with that complaint, more or less, as is natural, I suppose. My eyes are bad; especially my left, which has stopped some savage blows in bygone days that didn't do it a lot of good.

I'm delighted to hear about your new story — the Antarctic horror[2] — and sincerely hope that you found a market for it. Literature, at a low ebb generally, is enriched by every stroke of your pen. I most certainly hope that Putnam & Sons have decided to bring out your work in book form — both for your own sake and for the sake of American literature as a whole. I look forward to the appearance of the volume with eager anticipation, and hope I can have the honor of being the first to review it for the Southwestern papers.

I have read and re-read with the most intense interest, your descriptions of rural Rhode Island, and I am amazed to learn of the wide unfrequented stretches. With my hazy knowledge — or rather my complete lack of knowledge — of the area, I had vaguely supposed all of the Eastern states to be thickly settled, as in the case of some of the Middle-western states. How I would enjoy gazing on some of the contrasts you so vividly depict! I must visit the Atlantic sea-board some day, though the Devil only knows when it can be.

The population, as you describe it, aside from the older Saxon communities, must be bewilderingly cosmopolitan indeed. I imagine that your French element must be about the most desirable of all the alien stocks. France is not particularly well represented in Texas, though of course quite a number of persons with French blood in them have drifted in from Louisiana, and most of them are so long Americanized they differ but little from the Anglo-Americans.

I can appreciate your feelings toward New York, as a Nordic city engulfed by alien hordes — much the same process must have taken place in Rome, in the days of the later empire. I can imagine a Roman patrician of the old pure stock feeling much the same toward later Rome, as you feel toward modern New York.

Yes, I intensely enjoyed your descriptions and drawings of colonial architecture. The picture of "Cliveden" was most interesting. American architecture has certainly fallen far from the taste and artistry of the Colonial types, as far as I can see. The most radical change I've noticed in Texas architecture is in the type of court-houses. All over Texas they are replacing the old buildings with a very modernistic type — I'll try to get you some pictures of the new and the old, for comparison.

Its a dirty shame that the Polacks are selling those fine old stone walls and replacing them with wire fences. Another proof that traditions mean nothing to these aliens, who bring their own traditions with them and callously trample on those of the land they pollute by their presence.

I'm glad that you found my ramblings about State history and legendry of some interest. My mind is a kind of jumbled store-house of tag-ends — snatches of history, incidents in the lives of gunfighters and outlaws, anecdotes, myths, legends of the country, and the like. I could fill a thick volume of such disconnected bits and still not exhaust my chaotic store.

John A. Murrell was a hell-bender, in Southwest vernacular. He planned no less than an outlaw empire on the Mississippi river, with New Orleans as his capital and himself as emperor. Son of a tavern woman and an aristocratic gentleman, he seemed to have inherited the instincts of both, together with a warped mind that made him as ruthless and dangerous as a striking rattler. He must have murdered at least a hundred niggers in his time, yet they trusted him, and even when he was in prison, they were ready to rise in the revolt he had plotted and destroy their masters, had not chance intervened. It reminds me of the revolt old Colonel Leopard the carpet-bagger planned in East Texas. He stirred the niggers up and was going to lead them to a bloody victory. He was holding forth in a meeting place in the woods, with the fires blazing, and hundreds of blacks howling like fiends, and Leopard roaring and shouting as he goaded them to frenzy — urging them to march on Waco and slaughter every white man, woman and child in the place. And about that time old Captain Wortham and his bush-rangers opened fire from the bushes and they dropped eight niggers at the first volley. The rest scattered and the worthy Colonel led the flight. The Texans hunted him clear across the state with bloodhounds and while he was licking his sores in Old Mexico, a letter came from his wife telling him a daughter had been born to them. He wrote back and told her to name it Coyote, because, he said, the Texans had hunted him across the state like a coyote. And Coyote they named the child.

I'm surprized that *Argosy* rejected your stories, especially in the old days, when the magazine was superior to the present one. But what can you expect from any standardized publication? They'd turn down the masterpieces of all the ages, if they chanced to depart slightly from the regular pattern. I've made *Argosy* once, with a prize-fight story;[3] they've rejected stacks of my stuff, and in my case, I reckon the rejections were justified. I must admit most of my junk is deserving only of rejection slips. And by the way, I want to thank you again for suggesting my name to Mr. Talman as a possible contributor to *The Texaco Star*. I'm sending you a copy of the publication, containing my article on old Camp Colorado,[4] which Mr. Talman tells me received quite a bit of favorable comment from the moguls of the company. I've had time only to work up the one article, but hope to be able to place more of them soon. And I have you to thank, for had you not suggested me to Mr. Talman I'd never have placed the article.

Awhile back Street & Smith suggested I supply them with a series of prize-fight stories; they snapped up three yarns,[5] but I don't know how long I'll be able to keep selling stories of the ring. I've written so blame many I'm hard put to work up new plots and situations — particularly as it's a rather narrow field in its dramatic possibilities. Well, I repeat that I hope to soon see your work in book-form; I don't know of any literary event which could give me more genuine pleasure.

Yes, I got quite a kick out of Long's story,[6] and wrote to Mr. Wright praising the author's work and urging him to use more of the same sort. I have not seen the unfavourable comment on his work you mentioned — in fact, I'm not familiar with the *Editor* magazine — but I cannot see how any sincere objection to his style could be made. I like Long's work, and if anything I can do, can help offset the criticism you referred to, I'll be more than glad to do it. Yet, though the whole story was excellent, in my honest opinion, your interwoven dream was the high spot.

What you say of the unfortunate Boskops[7] interested me greatly, also your remarks about the Wegener theory.[8] I first heard of that theory about three years ago — or perhaps it was a different theory based on similar principles — I had gone up to Fort Worth to see the Doss-Chastain fight[9] and the college professor[10] with whom I stayed talked quite a bit about the theory of land-driftage, and suggested I write a story based on it. But I lack your cosmic sweep of style and imagination, and I never attempted it. I'd forgotten all about the theory until you mentioned it in your letter. It is indeed a fascinating thought, and I am anxious to see how you have handled it in the Antarctic tale.

Fantastic linkings with by-gone ages are certainly curious. I must confess I lean toward the theory that racial memories are transmitted from ancestor to descendent, though I am not prepared to offer any argument upholding it. I have wondered at times if I number some Babylonian or Chaldean among my ancient ancestors, so strong at times have I felt a connection between the ancient East and myself — for it is only with the Mesopotamian countries that I feel any sense of placement. My only sensation of the East beyond the rivers of that day is but a dim haze of unknown lands and half-mythical races. Yet I certainly show no trace of Oriental blood — thank God. Strangely enough, something like you mentioned, I feel a dim sense of a vast epoch lurking *behind* the East of the early ages — a sort of huge lurking night behind the dawn represented by Egypt and by Babylon — a dim sense of gigantic black cities from whose ruins the first Babylon rose, a last mirrored remnant of an age lost in the huge deep gulf of night. I have touched on this briefly in a story titled "The Blood of Belshazzer"[11] which Mr. Wright accepted for *Oriental Stories*.

Regarding the various interests for time-cycles and individuals — to me history seems mostly a chaotic jumble, through which move certain fairly well defined streams and currents, but which is mainly too tangled for my comprehension. As I have said, I lack your universal and cosmic scope and comprehension. From contemplation of history as a whole, my mind retires bewildered and baffled and fixes on various figures which rise here and there momentarily above the general drift. It is the individual mainly which draws me — the struggling, blundering, passionate insect vainly striving against the river of Life and seeking to divert the channel of events to suit himself — breaking his fangs on the iron collar of Fate and sinking into final defeat with the froth of a curse on his lips.

As for Biblical history, my real interest begins and ends with the age of Saul, outside of snatches here and there, as in the case of Samson. I'm sure you're right in your theory that numbers of Aryans must have drifted into the near East of that age, and as far as I can see, the days of Saul and David represent an Aryan phase in the racial-life of Israel. With the passing of David, my interest fades. The history of Judea sinks back into the general aspect of a truly Semitic court and dynasty, with a typical Oriental ruler in Solomon.

Another thing difficult to understand is my aversion toward things Roman. As you say, Rome made no attempt to destroy the folk-traditions of her subjects; life in the Roman republic and early empire must have been far more desirable than life in the later feudal age. Rome built system and order out of chaos and laid down the lines of a solid civilization — and yet the old unreasoning instinct rises in me and I cannot think of Rome as anything but an enemy! Maybe it's because Rome always won her wars until the very last days, and my instincts have always been on the side of the loser — Celtic instincts again, I suppose.

It is quite possible that you have a trace of Roman blood, from Romano-Cymric ancestors, especially since your Welsh lines were in such close proximity to the centers of Roman occupation. I hope you will soon be able to gratify your wish to visit your ancestral home, and I am sure that in the shadows of the Druid oaks and ancient Roman ruins, you will realize your fullest expectations of atmosphere, sleeping racial memories and ancestral traditions.

My sense of placement, as I've mentioned, is always with the barbarians outside the walls. Indeed, when I look upon the picture or drawing of some old walled city, and try to imagine myself in that setting, I always have the sensation of standing on some wooded hill or in the desert without, gazing over the walls, rather than of being inside the city. You mentioned your vivid dreams of a Roman personality; in my dreams of old times, I am always a light eyed yellow haired barbarian, resembling my real self but little. And yet it is evident I have quite a wide strain of Mediterranean blood in my veins, for though I am long-headed and blue-eyed, my hair is dark, and so is my skin which does not blister in the sun, but burns so brown that I have a few times been mistaken for a Mexican, though my features are certainly not those of a Latin, thank God. When I was a child I was a pure Saxon in type, with curly yellow hair and very fair skin, but as I grew older I grew darker, taking after a line of black Irish ancestors.

Another instinctive feeling of mine is that of kin-ship with the Scandinavian peoples of my English line, rather than the Anglo-Saxon stock. I suppose that any man with English blood in him has a good deal of the Saxon in his veins, yet I have never felt any kin-ship with the Juts, Angles and Saxons who made the first Teutonic invasion of Britain. My sense of personal placement in the Isles centers mainly in Ireland and Scotland; what connection I do feel with England begins with the Danish invasions. Nor is this feeling perhaps unnatural for my very name is not the modern form of the Saxon Hereward or Hayward, but is the Anglicized form of the Danish Havard. And some recent ancestors of mine, though greatly mixed with Irish blood, still had more of the look of the Scandinavian than of the Saxon; with their high, rather narrow heads, blue eyes and dark hair and beards, they must have looked much like the Vikings of the Dubh-Gall who swept the Isles in the old days of plunder and conquest.

I remember the first story I ever wrote — at the age of about nine or ten — dealt with the adventures of one "Boealf" a young Dane Viking. Racial loyalties struggled in me when I chronicled his ravages. Celtic patriotism prevented him from winning all his battles; the Gaels dealt him particular hell and the Welsh held him to a draw. But I turned him on the Saxons with gusto and the way he plundered them was a caution; I finally left him safely ensconced at the court of Canute, one of my childhood heroes.

I'm glad you liked "Children of the Night". Some remarks of yours in your letters regarding the Mongoloid aborigines gave me many of the ideas. As regards my mention of the three foremost weird masterpieces — Poe's, Machen's and your own — it's my honest opinion that these three are the outstanding tales. Though I consider your "Dunwitch Horror", "Horror at Red Hook" and "Rats in the Walls" quite worthy of ranking alongside Poe and Machen, also.

I've received your letter from San Augustine since writing the above and have read it and re-read it with the most intense interest; your observations on the city and country have been a real education for me, since my ideas about Florida have been about as vague as they are about China. Thanks very much for the postcards, folders, booklets etc.. I am repeatedly impressed by the tropical beauty of the scenes they show; a tropical atmosphere not even equalled by any of the scenes in extreme South Texas. I envy you your travels! And I hope you got to take that excursion to Miami and Key West which you mentioned. I'm sorry to hear that Whitehead is in poor health, and hope for his speedy recovery. I'm glad to hear that Long and Dwyer have found my work interesting, and I very much appreciate their kind comments.

Glad you enjoyed the cuttings etc. I sent you. The Austrian architectural survivals of the "little people" were new to me; I'd never heard of them before either. Great fictional possibilities there! By the way, I learn that the Clayton people are about to bring out a new magazine on the order of *Weird Tales*; the address is Harry Bates, Editor, Clayton Publications, 80 Lafayette Street, New York, in case you care to try them. They're also contemplating bringing out a magazine dealing entirely with historical tales — cloak-and-sword romances, etc.

Well, I knew there was a catch in it somewhere — the grain crop, I mean. At the beginning of this letter I mentioned the fine prospects for wheat and oats. Now the insects have attacked the grain and are stripping it; farmers are cutting it green in self-defense, and still the worms eat it. Threshing it is all that will stop them, and it's too green to thresh, mostly. Of course further south the grain is more forward, and most of it will be saved. Besides that, some terrific hail-storms have damaged the crops. It's always something in Texas. And even if a huge wheat crop were made, the farmers wouldn't get any price for it. Always a mild winter is followed by an insect plague. Prospects look good for cotton this year, but I know, almost, that there will be a swarm of grass-hoppers. They'll strip the fields over night. In a lifetime spent in the Southwest, I've seen perhaps a half-dozen full crops made. Drouth, floods, hails, sand-storms, boll-weevils, worms, grass-hoppers — all take their toll. Some people accuse the Southwest of being backward — God, if we are, we have reason to be. This is a fierce, barren land; a hard, drab land, where all the elements are set against the hand of man.

And confound it, it seems as if most of the farmers won't use what sense they have. Take this land around here; most of it isn't worth anything. Yet forty years ago, it was rich and fertile. But the men who farmed it knew nothing about crop-rotation, fertilizing the land, or anything else. They planted cotton till they wore the land out. Drouths baked all the moisture out of the soil and floods washed it away. This land washes amazingly in rainy seasons. Terracing would have saved it — would have kept the fat dirt from washing away and held the moisture in the land. But it's only recently that any terracing has been done and now it's too late. Of all the land in Texas that needs it, only about 10 percent is being terraced. Now they're wasting time and money terracing bare yellow clay from which the richness has long been washed, while out west of here, on the fertile Coleman prairie, the same old thing is in process — the land's washing away and nobody turns a hand to stop it. Maybe in a few years when the fields are practically worthless, some one will begin to make terraces. Most of the best farmland in Texas is in the hands of Germans, Bohemians and Swedes — especially that rich Black Land belt above Austin; nearly all that rich, waxy black country is being owned and worked by Swedes. The old Texas stock has been crowded off into the bare clay hills and sand roughs. But the first Texans were following grass and they rode over the rich farm-land and left it to the European emigrants who came later. And many Anglo-American families have left the farms and moved into the cities. Another thing that rasps me, is the failure of most farmers to raise any of their own food. They plant cotton — grain, some corn perhaps — most of them never have a garden, raise no chickens, turkeys, ducks or geese — have few cows, or none. A farmer is supposed to be at least partially self-supporting. Many of these farmers come into town to buy their vegetables at the stores. Of course that isn't the case among all of them. But one reason the farmers are in such bad lines today, is their failure to raise poultry and vegetables at home. Well, it's none of my business, of course, but I hate to see individualism fade out entirely.

But times are changing fast. And just now I am thinking, for no particular reason, of a picturesque but rather lousy phase of Southwestern life which has practically vanished in the past ten or twelve years.

Several years ago it was the custom in West Texas towns to set aside a certain day in the month known as "trade's-day". In this town it was the third Monday of the month and was referred to variously as "Third Monday" "Trade Monday" and "Horse Monday." On that day the streets and alleys were full of men swapping horses and mules. For three or four days before "Trade's Day" the roving brotherhood would begin to arrive — the people who went about making their living by horse trading. They were generally a seedy and disreputable lot, who moved about in wagons, with a string of lean, mangy cayuses, lived from hand to mouth and camped wherever night found them. Trades' Day would find them camped at the edge of town, sometimes a dozen families together, and they would plunge into the business at hand. Farmers would come to town with equally worthless nags and the noise of arguments, assertions and refutations must at times have equalled the clamor in an Oriental bazaar. How anybody ever made anything out of most of the swaps, is more than I can see. It always looked to me as if both parties got gypped.

The wandering horse-traders were more or less of a nuisance; they were thievish, quarrelsome — though not particularly courageous — and the men would invariably get drunk and beat their wives so the women would howl until it was a scandal to hear. After prohibition came in their favorite drink was fruit extracts and the amount they imbibed was a caution to behold. I used to work in a grocery store and the amount of lemon extract etc., I've known some of them to buy in one day, would startle one. I particularly remember a couple who were generally together most of the time: a big red-whiskered brute and a horrible hunchback, a stunted monstrous giant, of the most sinister aspect I ever saw in any man. He seldom talked, and I never heard him speak above a menacing whisper. Generally Red-whiskers did all the talking for the pair, prompted by the hunch-back's uncanny whispers.

I remember once I heard a most outrageous outbreak of noise and clamor — howls, blows, bellowings and the drum of flying hoofs — and saw Red-whiskers careering down the street in high state. He was lying hog-drunk in the bed of a wagon, roaring at the top of his voice and slashing at his son — a kid of ten or twelve — with a rolled up slicker. The kid was screaming at the top of his voice, standing upright and pouring leather into the mules. The old man was beating the boy, the boy was beating the mules, and the mules were at a dead run. Why the wagon didn't come to pieces, I don't know, for it was just hitting the high spots.

What became of the horse-traders, the Devil only knows. Maybe they all drank themselves to death. With the stuff the people drink these days, it would not be an impossibility. American taste in liquor has sure degenerated — of necessity, of course. Bootleggers take no pride in their work. When I used to work in a law-office I saw a good deal of good whiskey, but for the past few years it's been getting rottener and rottener until it's risky to even smell a cork. The stuff don't make men drunk; it maddens them.

I remember a wild night I passed on an isolated ranch[12] in mid-winter, several years ago; one of the party was wild drunk on beer and another was stark crazy on raw Jamaica ginger, with the obsession that he was a werewolf. One of the bunch was a young German[13] who didn't drink, and wasn't used to the violent drunks common to Americans; he backed up against a wall and I couldn't help laughing at his expression when the Jamaica victim began to smash the furniture, gallop about on all-fours and howl like a mad-dog. About midnight a howling blizzard came up to add to the general lunacy. Gad, it makes me laugh to think about it now.

I have — since writing the above — received your card from Dunedin, and repeat I envy you your sojourn into Florida. The scene on the card strongly reminds me of pictures I've seen of the South Seas. I'm glad you like the old Gulf; I feel as if she's a part of Texas — and God knows, she's taken enough Texans and their work into her bosom. She's treacherous as a Mexican dance-hall girl; not only broken ships sleep in the slimy ooze of her deeps, and the bones of sailormen — walls and columns and shattered dwellings of landsmen lie there strewn among the bones of their builders. Galveston — Rockport — Corpus Christi — she broke their levees and foamed over their walls and the people drowned like rats. They say the sea-wall at Galveston is safe; I say — not publicly, but to you — that no wall is sufficient to hold back the Gulf when she shakes her mane; and that as the pirate Lafitte once drove his ships across the howling waves that hid the island, so again the Gulf will claim her own at will. Once the sea rolled over these hills and plains, and I believe at no distant date, as the history of the planet is measured. And I believe that some day the Cap-rock will again be the shore of the Gulf, and that Houston, Galveston, San Antonio, even Fort Worth and Dallas will sleep untold fathoms beneath the foam. For I have found petrified deep-sea shells hundreds of miles inland, and it is always said that the sea eventually claims her own again.

I'll most assuredly watch for Whitehead's new story; and I appreciate his salutation on the card. I hope that his ill-health has not seriously impaired that remarkable muscular development of his which inspired so much admiration among the people of the West Indies; did he show you his feat of tearing a pack of cards into halves and quarters with his bare hands?[14]

I've been reading over the Eyrie of the latest *Weird Tales*, and am gratified to note with what enthusiasm the readers hail your forthcoming tale — "The Whisperer in Darkness". Their enthusiasm for your work denotes a real appreciation of genuine literature — an appreciation which is, alas, too often lacking in the reading public. As for myself, I can hardly wait for the story to appear.

I also note with considerable amusement that a rumor has been circulating pertaining to me being a professor in the University of Southern California. It was, it is true, only a freak of chance that kept me from being a Californian. Had not cholera struck the camp of William Benjamin Howard and his band of '49ers on the Arkansas River, reducing their number from nineteen to seven, and weakening their leader so he was forced to turn back, I, his grandson, would have undoubtedly been born in California instead of Texas. But as for being a professor of history in a great university, that's beyond the pale of possibility — I never even attended college as a student.

It's been some weeks since I wrote the first part of this letter, in which I commented on the grain crop. Since then a bumper crop has been assured. Hail did damage in some sections, but not as much as was expected. And — in this locality at least — the invading horde of army-worms which was stripping the oats, was devoured by an army of bugs following close on its heels. The insect world has its migrations and tribal drifts, its wars and its massacres, just the same as the world of humans. But the grass-hoppers are swarming in and if something radical isn't done, they'll eat the cotton before it can bloom. We lack not insect scourges here. I've seen the ground so thick with big, fuzzy, horned caterpillars that one could not walk without crushing them. And grass-hoppers — Lord! I remember one particular scourge that ate not only the cotton but the very leaves off the trees. About the only person that really enjoyed that plague was my pet raccoon who ate those big jumbo grasshoppers till he could hardly waddle. Of course the coyotes always thrive likewise.

So Texas has a big grain crop this year — particularly a big wheat crop. God knows what we'll do with it. The kind, benevolent gentlemen in Wall Street have juggled the prices down until the wheat will hardly be worth the gathering. And our Bolshevik brethren are considerately glutting the market, so as to ruin what remains. Dear little Russia, with her American-made machines, she will see that the grain farmers of America are ruined, if others fail. Well, I reckon we can always eat the damned stuff ourselves and feed it to the stock. Next year we'll have a drouth, and those who store grain now will be wise.

I notice a slight — oh, a very slight — trend back to the soil. A few people are leaving the city, under the press of present economic conditions; going back to the farms their parents left, or that they left in their youth. After all, there remains in our weak veins, some slight trace of the sturdy blood of our pioneer ancestors, that revolts against working for some other man forever. On all hands I hear the announcement — "I'm getting tired as Hell working for the other man." There is freedom of a sort on the farm, though it may be purchased with grinding toil and barrenness of existence.

Well, Aryans were not made to coop themselves in walls. This fact is brought strongly to my mind each time I go to Fort Worth. There, of all Southwestern cities, is the last full stronghold of the Anglo-Saxon. Almost everyone you meet has some pristine feature — blue or grey eyes, yellow hair, fair skin — one or more pure Aryan feature. Yet they seem stunted — stocky, but undersized. I notice this fact more than in any of the more cosmopolitan cities. Why, I am not a particularly large man, judged by Oil-Belt standards; I weigh 200 pounds in good condition, but am only 5 feet 11 inches tall, yet when I walk the streets of Fort Worth I fairly tower above the crowds. I take this to show that the Anglo-American race deteriorates in cities. In Houston, Dallas, San Antonio, you will meet giant Italians, Hebrews, Greeks, Slavs. But the Saxons can not, as a whole, stand city life and keep their original stature, I believe. Of course there are always exceptions. But West Texans seem to be a taller and stronger race than their East Texan brothers, though this may be an hallucination on my part. Of course, all through the Oil-Belt you will see hordes of Middle-westerners — big men, mainly of Germanic or Scandinavian blood, from Kansas, Nebraska, Illinois, the Dakotas. Tall mountain men from Kentucky and West Virginia. These with the native giants form an impressive part of Oil-Belt population. In this town and abouts it's not uncommon to see men over six and a half feet tall. I believe the finest built big man I ever saw — barring Tiny Roebuck, the giant Indian wrestler — was a huge Viking of a man from somewhere in the Middle West. He was an oil driller, and he spoke of Manchuria, Sumatra, Persia, China, as familiarly as the average man speaks of the streets of his home-town. He stood some six feet and eight inches, weighed about 270 pounds, and there was no fat on him. He was no victim of abnormal glands — neither his jaw, hands nor feet were out of proportion. He was simply a natural giant, blue eyed and with a shock of flaxen hair. He moved with a certain aloof dignity, like a lion, and continually cursed the Catholics — why, God knows.

These men from the Middle-west — oil field workers at least — are generally a turbulent race, ready to fight at the drop of a hat, with their fists, but generally not so quick to draw knife or gun, as the fighters of the Southwest. And I notice a racial difference here, not as applied between Middle-westerner and Southwesterner, but between white men as a whole, and Latins. The Mexican is quick and deadly with a knife, but his instinct seems to be to slash his foe to ribbons, while the instinct of the Anglo-American seems to be to thrust — to drive the blade in straight with terrific force. One of the cleanest stab-wounds I ever saw was in the body of a young cowpuncher who'd had a row with another cattleman. A long-bladed stockman's knife had been driven nearly to the hilt between the sixth and seventh ribs and left sticking in the wound. The victim had removed it himself, drawing it straight out. Had the wielder twisted it, it would have made a nasty wound. As it was, though dangerously near the vitals, the young fellow recovered quickly, and lived to be shot down by Mexican bandits south of the Border.

Another friend of mine got one of those long stockman's knives rammed into him — the blade went in under the collar bone and went nearly through him, just missing the arch of the aorta. Such power had the wielder of the knife put behind the blade, the sheer force of the blow knocked the victim down. He recovered after quite a long period, during which he imagined in his delirium that he had slain his foe and had his severed head under the bed to gloat over. Thinking perhaps that the victim might seek to put his dream into reality, the man who had stabbed him carried an automatic shotgun for years. He put it aside at last, and not many weeks ago his eldest son put it into play again — it figured prominently in an informal shotgun duel in which its wielder came out victorious, though he failed to finish his man.

Shotguns had their part in the winning of the West; yea, verily, and even today the humble scatter-gun is generally the ace when the last hand is dealt in the feuds of the brush-wood — which, mark ye, have not attained the publicity given the feuds of the mountain-laurel, but lack not in the essentials of sortie, surprize and sudden extinction. If they are shorter, they are more suddenly deadly. Only a few months ago a shotgun, crashing from the brush-wood, put a period to an old hate that has been smoldering in the sand-roughs only a few miles from this town; a hate that began when the present victim's brother died in Arizona and his chaps and spurs were sent back to his people to quarrel over. So a very brave man has gone over the ridge, and his grand-nephew has begun a forty-year term in the penitentiary. Thirty years — from real or fancied partiality of a kinsman, to a shotgun thundering in the twilight.

I remember another shotgun victim who lived among the hills quite a number of miles south of this town. His waylayer aimed too low; the victim — a friend of mine — escaped with his life, but I counted twenty-seven buckshot in his leg the next day. And his horse's shoulder was badly torn, which was a dirty shame. I believe that incident soured my friend, for only a few years later he figured in another shotgun jubilee, with the exception that this time he was at the other end of the gun. His target was the man whose daughter he had married, and he did not miss — either time. In fact, he killed his victim deader than a cooked goose.

But lord, lord, here I am rambling on and on without rhyme or reason. If I seem drowsy and lacking in connection, please blame it on the heat and languor of spring. My laziness always increases in warm weather, and for the past days I've sort of let things slide. In the past three weeks I've managed by sheer force, to pound out four prize-ring short stories, an adventure short, a Western short, a fact article and a long historical novelet, and the effort has been about as much physical as mental. My indolence has always handicapped me.

Again I thank you for the wealth of material you have so kindly sent me — the package of pictures and literature, the cards, views and folders of Florida and the South; I value them all highly and they form an important part of my collections. And so, with the very best wishes, I am,

Cordially,

P.S. I'm venturing to include a rhyme of mine here, which is doubtless entirely without rhythmic or literary merit, but which does, I feel, in some slight way describe the sensations one receives while traveling that savagely barren country between the little town of Sonora and the Border.

The Grim Land.

From Sonora to Del Rio is a hundred barren miles
Where the soto weave and shimmer in the sun —
Like a horde of rearing serpents swaying down the bare defiles
When the scarlet, silver webs of dawn are spun.

There are little dobe ranchoes brooding far along the sky,
On the sullen dreary bosoms of the hills;
Not a wolf to break the quiet, not a desert bird to fly
Where the silence is so utter that it thrills

With an eery sense of vastness, with a curious sense of age,
And the ghosts of eons gone uprear and glide
Like a horde of drifting shadows gleaming through the wilted sage —
They are riding where of old they used to ride.

Muleteer and caballero, with their plunder and their slaves —
Oh, the clink of ghostly stirrups in the morn!
Oh, the soundless flying clatter of the feathered, painted braves,
Oh, the echo of the spur and hoof and horn.

Maybe, in the heat of evening, comes a wind from Mexico
Laden with the heat of seven Hells,
And the rattler in the yucca and the buzzard dark and slow
Hear and understand the grisly tales it tells.

Gaunt and stark and bare and mocking rise the everlasting cliffs
Like a row of sullen giants hewn of stone,
Till the traveler, mazed with silence, thinks to look on hieroglyphs,
Thinks to see a carven Pharaoh on his throne.

Once these sullen hills were beaches and they saw the oceans flee
In the misty ages never known of men,
And they wait in brooding silence till the everlasting sea
Comes foaming forth to claim her own again.

NOTES

1. Marlin, Texas, where Howard's mother was a sometime patient at the Torbett Sanatorium.
2. "At the Mountains of Madness."
3. "Crowd-Horror."
4. "The Ghost of Camp Colorado."
5. Kid Allison stories.
6. "The Horror from the Hills."
7. See letter 152, note 3 and letter 156, note 5.
8. Continental drift theory propounded by Alfred Lothar Wegener, Frank Bursley Taylor, and John Joly.
9. January 20, 1928.
10. The Howards were acquainted with Dr. Robert T. Hill, the "dean of Texas geology."
11. "Belshazzar."
12. Stone Ranch, owned by Tevis Clyde Smith's uncle Ben Stone.
13. Herbert Klatt.
14. In a letter to HP Lovecraft, March 6, 1933 (in volume 3), Howard quotes from a letter Whitehead wrote to *Adventure* magazine, published in the issue for November 10, 1923, in which, among other things, he describes this trick.

TSS: 50038-50046

170. To Wilfred Blanch Talman, ca. July 1931.

Dear Mr. Talman:

I should have answered your letter months ago, but I've been crowded with work, besides having been away from home a good part of the time.

I'm looking forward to reading your story in *Weird Tales*, also the full-page poem[1] you mentioned. Hope you've placed several tales, since writing me. I like your work.

I suppose you had the meeting of the Kalem Club[2] as you planned, and I'm sure it was an enjoyable event. Seeing a whole gang of writers together would be an innovation to me. My personal acquaintance with literary people is extremely scanty. I've never even seen over three or four writers and poets, in my entire life.

I notice you mention having met Quinn,[3] the king-favorite of *Weird Tale* fans. I'd be interested in your impressions of him; for some unknown reason, I've always pictured him as a tall, powerfully built man with a leonine head and a full beard.

I'm glad to see Lovecraft has returned to the ranks of active contributors; I very much enjoyed his "Whisperer in Darkness" and I hope he continues the work.

Best wishes.

Cordially,
[Robert E. Howard.]

NOTES

1. "Doom Around the Corner," November 1931, and probably "Ballade of Creatures Abroad by Night," September 1933.
2. A group that included H.P. Lovecraft and his New York associates, so called because all the original members' names began with the letters K, L and M.
3. Seabury Quinn.

ભ80ઇ૦૯ભ80

171. To H.P. Lovecraft, July 14, 1931.

Dear Mr. Lovecraft:

Just a line to congratulate you on "The Whisperer in Darkness."[1] I stopped work right in the middle of a rush job and went thirty miles to get the new magazine, and didn't do a lick of work until I'd thoroughly read your tale. To say I enjoyed the story would be putting it lightly. Your subtle handling of the difficult theme again proves your mastery of the bizarre branch of literature. The subtle threading through shadowy mazes of horror, the dark implications, the tensing trend toward the horrific climax, marks this story as one as far above the general ruck of weird literature as any finished work of art is above the efforts of tyroes. The final implication, that the mask etc., *might not be of wax*, was almost intolerably grisly, with the demoniac shadowy vistas of ghastly speculation at which it hinted. Thanks very much for including Kathulos and Bran in your dark references.

I suppose you're back in Providence now, after your delightful journeys. Talman mentioned that the Kalem Club would convene upon your arrival in Babylon — I believe Kalem was the name.

I trust you're not bothered with the heat-wave. In the Southwest and Midwest the sun's been bowling them over regular. So many poor devils have been driven to jobs of manual labor who never worked outdoors before, and they can't stand the pace. An indoor worker can't conceive the power of the sun on laborers, especially in the great fields of grain, which seem to absorb and generate more heat than is believable.

Right here, right now, it's cool. A sandstorm just passed over and the atmosphere is still rather dusty along the horizons, though clearing rapidly. Just a flurry. We don't have sandstorms like we did when I was a kid, when they used to blow three days and nights without a let-up. The Panhandle's settling up, and the land's under cultivation that was bare prairie when I was a child. At least that's the reason generally given for the decreasing number of sandstorms. But nobody can explain the drouths! Best wishes.

Cordially,
[Robert E. Howard.]

NOTES

1. *Weird Tales*, August 1931.

TSS: 64687

ഢൡഢൡ

172. To Tevis Clyde Smith, ca. August 1931.

Fear Finn:

Well, I doubt if this missile will be very scintillant. Gone are the gay and festive days when I could instill sparkle and wit into a letter.

I just got a letter from Farnsworth hinting Tamerlane as a fit subject for an *Oriental Story* story. He likewise mentioned my "The Thing on the Roof" which is not only the best story by far that I ever wrote, but which is, in my honest opinion a really first-class weird story judged by any standards. That sounds conceited and probably is; just the same, I hold to it. Several months ago Farnsworth rejected the tale saying it seemed too erudite for the general reader, though he liked it himself. Claytons likewise rejected it, saying the plot was too thin etc. etc. also etc. There was no attempt at plot. Like most real weird stories, it had no plot. *Argosy* rejected it with the usual stereotype. Then Farnsworth asked to see it again, when he accepted my "The Sowers of the Thunder" for *Oriental Stories*. In his latest letter he accepted it for $40. Not much money, but in this case I wasn't really thinking about the money and he could have had the story for nothing, if he'd made me that proposition. I'd have given it to him free, just to get it in print. Now I've got to get hold of something on the Big Tatar and try to pound out a novelet; I've been thinking of writing a tale about him for a long time. And Babar the Tiger who established the Mogul rule in India — and the imperial phase in the life of Baibars the Panther, the subject of my last story — and the rise of the Ottomans — and the conquest of Constantinople by the Fifth Crusade — and the subjugation of the Turks by the Arabs in the days of Abu Bekr — and the gradual supplanting of the Arab masters by their Turkish slaves which culminated in the conquest of Asia Minor and Palestine by the Seljuks — and the rise of Saladin — and the final destruction of Christian Outremer by Al Kalawun — and the first Crusade — Godfrey of Bouillon, Baldwin of Boulogne, Bohemund — Sigurd the Jorsala-farer — Barbarossa — Coeur de Lion. Ye gods, I could write a century and still have only tapped the reservoir of dramatic possibilities. I wish to Hell I had a dozen markets for historical fiction — I'd never write anything else.

Dave was asking last night when you and Truett were coming over.[1] He said there was some beer aging for your arrival, though still green at present. He wants us to go on a small beer party, as in the old days. I don't know whether you'll be able to drink home-made beer after your Mexican invasion, but in case you feel equal to it, let me know and we'll try to make preparations. Get hold of Truett and find out how he feels about it.

Fear Dunn.

NOTES

1. Dave Lee; Truett Vinson.

TSS: 82033

173. To H.P. Lovecraft, ca. Mid to Late-August, after August 16, 1931.[1]

Dear Mr. Lovecraft:

You must indeed have had a delightful journey and I envy you your invasion of the semi-tropical haunts, which evidently must be far more exotic and dream-provoking than anything we have in Texas. I very much appreciated the views, folders, etc., you sent me, and read your descriptions of the country with the greatest interest. I was also interested in what you said of Savannah, the more so because my branch of the Howards landed there when they first came to America, in 1733, I believe it was.

Yes, I did indeed like "The Whisperer in Darkness", and appreciate the kind things you said about "The Footfalls Within", which I feared failed miserably in creating the atmosphere I was striving after. I speak with full sincerity when I say I am bitterly disappointed that the Putnams rejected the mss. they were considering — disappointed not alone for your sake, but for the sake of literature as a whole. However, though set-backs and disappointments are part of every man's life, the power of your work will eventually over-ride all obstacles. You cannot fail of eventual recognition, and with it the fame and monetary remuneration you so richly deserve. I am also very sorry that Mr. Wright rejected the Antarctic story, and hope by this time you've marketed it elsewhere; if you should fail to sell it, I would like very much to read it sometime in manuscript form, if it isn't asking too much.

I'm glad you found some of the Texas material of interest. Yes, the old Governor's Palace in San Antonio is most interesting, having been restored with the utmost care; it has the atmosphere, somehow. To add to the interest, the woman in charge is a direct descendent of the Canary Islanders who, arriving in San Antonio de Bexar in the early 17's, practically created the city; it was then only a cluster of missions and a military post. If anyone has a background of inherited traditions, she has, for her people have lived in, and governed the city since its birth; her brother was mayor for years. The changing fortune of the city is somehow symbolized in her, for only in her eyes does she show her Latin strain, just as San Antonio becomes yearly more and more Americanized and modernized.

I've wandered about a little in the last few months, though my journeys are hardly worth the name, since I haven't left the state; you can cover a good deal of territory, though, and still stay in Texas. I went into Central East Texas, into the edge of the Bohemian settlements, and am again impressed by the fact that the average native American cannot hold his own with these invaders. They are industrious, law-abiding, hard-working and unusually intelligent. They are also clannish and help each other. In a day when most farms are mortgaged and remortgaged to the hilt, practically all Bohemian farmers are free from debt. Nor are their activities limited to rural pursuits. They come into towns and make shrewd, conservative business men, and fine professional men. They are less like us than are the Germans, but are less quarrelsome, and apparently less inclined to drunkenness. I see little chance of their being absorbed in the native population, since they tend to cluster together in communities and to intermarry with each other. At the same time they send a continual flow of young men and women out into the more purely Anglo-American localities, and some of these marry Americans. In other words, the extensive Bohemian settlements seem to me like a clump of luxurious grass which is slowly spreading over the surrounding country. In a few generations, we may note a distinct Bohemian influence in the main blood-stream of Texas, though on the other hand, I may attach too much significance to this trend. The dominant Bohemian type seems to be dark, though often with fair skin and blue eyes. I have seen a few who looked distinctly Celtic, while others show unmistakable traces of Turkish blood. There is some friction between them and the native Americans, though as a whole these Bohemians are a peaceable race and seem to mind their own business pretty well. While I was in Temple this friction was evident in a row which took place in a Bohemian community a few miles from the town. Conflicting stories were told and the true details will probably never be known, concerning the trouble between the Bohemian and a native

American — but the Bohemian was dead, with a bullet in his back and nine gashes in his head — still clutching his pistol, which was, however, unfired and still in its holster.

Later, I went to Fort Worth — the Mecca of all West Texans — and returned through the land of my birth — for the first time since early childhood. The country seems to be changed little — except that it is even less thickly inhabited than formerly — it passed through an era of extensive farming which proved more or less of a failure. Many of the farmers left and the country settled back to its natural destiny of cattle-and-sheep-raising. The tide of progress seems scarcely to have touched Peaster, the tiny village where I was born — as then the few stores are kept by old ranchmen too old for riding and roping — tall, bent old men with flowing white moustaches and keen blue eyes who sit and dream of old times.

A student of early Texas history is struck by the fact that some of the most savage battles with the Indians were fought in the territory between the Brazos and Trinity rivers. A look at the country makes one realize why this was so. After leaving the thickly timbered littoral of East Texas, the westward sweeping pioneers drove the red men across the treeless rolling expanse now called the Fort Worth prairie, with comparative ease. But beyond the Trinity a new kind of country was encountered — bare, rugged hills, thickly timbered valleys, rocky soil that yielded scanty harvest, and was scantily watered. Here the Indians turned ferociously at bay and among those wild bare hills many a desperate war was fought out to a red finish. It took nearly forty years to win that country, and late into the '70s it was the scene of swift and bloody raids and forays — leaving their reservations above Red River and riding like fiends the Comanches would strike the cross-timber hills within twenty-four hours. Then it was touch and go! Much as one may hate the red devils one must almost admire their reckless courage — and it took courage to drive a raid across Red River in those days! They staked their lives against stolen horses and white men's scalps. Sometimes they won, and outracing the avengers, splashed across Red River and gained their tipis, where the fires blazed, the drums boomed and the painted, feathered warriors leaped in grotesque dances celebrating their gains in horses and scalps — sometimes they did not win and those somber hills could tell many a tale of swift retribution — of buzzards wheeling low and red-skinned bodies lying in silent heaps.

But that was in the later days. In the old times the red-skins held the banks of the Brazos. Sometimes they drove the ever-encroaching settlers back — sometimes the white men crossed the Brazos, only to be hurled back again, sometimes clear back beyond the Trinity. But they came on again — in spite of flood, drouth, starvation and Indian massacre. In that debatable land I was born and spent most of my early childhood. Little wonder these old tales seem so real to me, when every hill and grove and valley was haunted with such wild traditions! The very county of my birth — Parker — got its name from old Colonel Parker,[2] who spent actually years haunting its hills and valleys in search of the daughter stolen from him by the raiding Comanches — Cynthia Ann Parker. How many long lonely danger-fraught nights he lay alone in the wilds, hunting out his foes, spying on their camps, trailing their hunting parties and their war-parties — hoping, yearning for some sign to show the child he sought lived — it was not granted to him, though I'm sure — and hope — that many a painted brave rode the fading trail to Ghostland to pay that debt. There is an aching sorrow about the tale of Cynthia Ann Parker, a terrible pathos that takes a man by the throat. Flung between red men and white, driven along a trail black with hate and red with blood, to this day the memory of Cynthia Ann Parker lingers and haunts, like a pitiful ghost crying in the night.

I saw Dark Valley again, which I think I've mentioned to you before. Dark Valley — now hardly worthy of the name, to the casual glance, since many of its trees have been cleared away, and the road, which used to follow the bed of the winding creek, now passes along high up on the ridge. But down in the valley the untouched wilderness still waves — there the trees grow taller and thicker than anywhere else in Texas, I believe — their rank growth is almost sinister — suggesting something malevolent, somehow. The country is still very sparsely settled, and of the two-roomed cabin on the creek bank, where I lived, no trace now remains.

Not long after returning from this trip, I took a somewhat longer one in the other direction — to San Angelo, about a hundred miles southwest from this place, one of the most promising towns west of Fort Worth, and the greatest wool and mohair market in America. It's fine rolling prairie country, with some hills. The entire population of the county is about 38,000, of which 25,000 live in San Angelo, which leaves a rather light population to be distributed over 1454 square miles of rural territory. I went south about eighty miles to Sonora, an old frontier town abounding in virile traditions, then turned east about sixty-five miles to Junction, county seat of Kimble, a county which has an area of 1301 square miles, and a population of 3581. There isn't a railroad in the county but some fine roads. And beautiful mountainous scenery. Then from Junction I went to Kerrville, a rather noted health-and-pleasure-resort among the mountains about fifty miles southeast of Junction; after a couple of days stay at Kerrville I went on to San Antonio, seventy miles to the south, then continuing south to George West, about a hundred miles from San Antonio — turned east again there to Beeville, and back home by way of Goliad, Victoria, Gonzales, Austin and Brownwood. It wasn't really much of a trip, as it extended only over about a thousand miles altogether and I was gone only a week. But I rather enjoyed it, though I'd been over most of the country before. South Texas is the portion of the State vibrant with early historical tradition — there the first colonies were planted and there were fought all the battles of the Revolution. I believe Goliad, Victoria and Gonzales are, in many ways, the most picturesque-looking small towns I've ever seen in Texas. Many of their buildings are very old, and the towns are laid out on the old Spanish style, with broad plazas. The population is now largely mixed with German, especially in Victoria, and as many of these Teutonic emigrants came in the '80s and '90s, and even earlier, they have added their part to the elements making up the towns, and much of the older architecture reflects a later German influence. After their stirring history most of these southern towns seem sleeping — quiet and drowsy, they live in dreams, while the frontier has moved on, with it the sweep and change of progress and events.

No doubt you're right in deciding that racial memories are a myth. As you point out, a distant ancestor could hardly have much influence on the life and ideas of a present day descendent. Yet it might be possible that atavistic forces might reproduce, to a certain extent, a shadowy ancestral shape in modern form. We know that cases exist in which a person bears a striking resemblance to a grand-parent or even a great-grand-parent, and this might occasionally be extended further into the past. I believe that one certain ancestor may sometimes exert a stronger influence on his descendents than former or later forbears. For instance there is an extensive family here who numbered, among their not very recent ancestors, a full-blood Portuguese. The present representatives of this family cannot have a very broad strain of Portuguese in their blood now, in fact, the added strains of British blood must have almost drowned it out — yet practically all of them to this day, show unmistakable Latin features and characteristics, and some of them, even of the youngest generation, would easily pass for full-blooded Portuguese. I do not maintain that they have inherited any racial memories — in fact, I feel certain of the contrary — but the fact remains that that one thin strain of Latin blood has proved stronger than all the Anglo-American blood since acquired. And if that one Latin has transmitted his racial tendencies and features throughout all the line of an otherwise British-American family, it seems that the case might be reproduced elsewhere, when the influence of one particular ancestor, or group of ancestors, might be felt for generations.

I was much interested in your remarks about the coloring of yourself and your various ancestral lines, as noting the hue of eyes and hair and complexions of people is one of my hobbies. Not that I have any particular reason for it, since I do not hold with the theory that a man's character etc. is shown by his coloring; in fact I have very little faith in the study or theories of physiognomy. I have seen pure blonds and pure brunets who had instincts and natures almost exactly alike.

I was also very much interested in hearing about the researches in the Near-East. The Sumerians must have evolved their civilization somewhere, as you point out, and the question of where? evokes almost limitless realms of speculation. What are your own theories on the subject? — I mean where do you suppose these tribes worked out their problems of progress? Perhaps the ever-rising sand-ocean of Turkestan hides the ruins that might tell of their march upward from the ape. Or — it seems somewhere I've read of a theory that the Mediterranean shifted her bed within the lifetime of mankind and drowned great areas of level sea-land. Is it possible that in these sunken lands the ancestors of the Sumerians attained mind and culture — and that in tales of that inundation grew the legends of the Flood? — and of lost Atlantis? And since the Tigris-Euphrates civilization is now believed to have preceded the Egyptian, is it now the theory that from the Sumerian culture the Egyptian grew, or that these civilizations evolved along different, separate lines?

It may be, as you say, that my preference for the Danes over the Saxons comes from reading Norse sagas — though the first Nordic folk-tale I ever read was *Beowulf*. It may be rooted in an old hostility to the word "Saxon"; in my childhood and early boyhood I hated everything English with a deep and abiding hate, and the terms Sassanach and Saxon represented to me the objects of my hatred. Even now I prefer to think that my English strain is rather Danish than Sassanach, since as near as I can learn my distant English ancestors came from the old Dane-lagh. But it's really not worth considering, since any Saxon strain in me must necessarily be very small, and the same goes for the Danish, though one of my great-great-grandfathers came directly from Denmark. Yet I believe that every Englishman, Irishman or Scotchman, or person of such descent, has more Norse blood in his veins than is generally realized, considering the extent to which the Norse over-ran the British Isles for centuries. I know that with practically all of the people I know: they jest and joke a great deal, and laugh easily, but get them alone and scratch the surface and you find the almost fatalistic pessimism and gloomy philosophy generally attributed to the Scandinavian peoples. It may be Celtic, I don't know; but I do know that our German neighbors seem more innately cheerful and optimistic than do we of the old stock.

Like you, the sagas of Norse gods and heroes fascinate me. Their mythology seems more characteristically Nordic than any other — naturally, of course. I still feel a deep resentment toward Charlemagne for his bloody conversion of the Nordic pagans — and while I do not consider that it was in revenge for his ruthless crusade that sent the more remote Norsemen sweeping down to ravage the south — it was more likely a natural result of growth and expansion and press of population — still I can appreciate the feelings of those Odin-worshippers who destroyed shrine and monastery and burned the priests in the ruins of their altars. They had little reason to love Christians, with the Great King's example before them. I like to feel that Karl realized, before he died, that doom was bursting on his borders, and that retribution was sweeping on his vassals, if not on himself. And it is pleasant to reflect on those Vikings who stabled their horses in his palace.

I'm surprized to learn that the Claytons rejected your stories. I notice that many of the old *Weird Tale* writers have found a berth there. The editor rejected a couple of my yarns; he gave no reason for the rejection of one,[3] but he objected to the other[4] on the grounds of thin plot and light action. Later Mr. Wright accepted this yarn for *Weird Tales*, though he had formerly rejected it.

I'm glad Bates is abandoning the restrictions against atmosphere stories. In a letter to me, some months ago, he said they preferred stories with a good plot and about three climaxes, I believe it was. Of course, he knows what the readers want, and I don't blame him for trying to supply the demand. But as far as I'm concerned, a plot is about the least important element in a weird story.

Yes, we made a big grain crop, after all. We have no market to speak of, but the people are storing it, and will have feed for their stock this winter, which is what they didn't have last. I hear that on the Plains they're burning wheat for fuel. Crops over Texas are rather spotted. In South Texas, with the exception of the Rio Grande valley, the cotton crop has been practically a complete failure. Insects destroyed the bloom. The stalks are tall and strong, but they have no cotton on them. People from this part of the country used to go south to pick cotton; it looks like it will be the other way this year. Yet I see that parts of South Texas are calling for cotton-pickers. This shortage of labor is not so much because of a bumper crop, as because of the exodus of Mexican workers, who have been flocking back into Old Mexico by the thousands. North and West Texas seem destined to raise fine cotton crops, but it won't be worth picking. In South Texas over a week ago, cotton was selling for a little over five cents. By the time it's ready to pick on the Plains, it won't pay for the labor. Maize was blighted, also, in South Texas, because of too much rain, though they made a good corn crop. In fact, the corn has been good all over Texas, just about. You should see the people laying in provisions for the winter! Right around here there's a distinct movement back to the farm, and this fact, coupled with the scientific methods which are beginning to take root among the younger generation of agriculturists, causes me to believe that the country will pull through, if given half a break. Canning machines are working over-time, as the native Americans are following the example of their German neighbors, who have been putting up their own food and raising their own vegetables for generations. I look forward to feasting on canned stuffs myself, this winter, though the spoiling of six dozen cans of fresh corn has rather disgusted me. Fruit, vegetables, and meat are being put up — young bulls going into cans at a remarkable rate — heart, liver, tongue, and all — everything but the horns and hoofs! It's a pipe-dream, but I'd like to see the day when Texas would be independent as in the old days — at least as far as food-stuffs go.

Glad my remarks on Trade's Day were of some interest. As far as I know, no one has ever chronicled it and its followers at all. Many phases of the Southwest have been neglected or ignored entirely.

The old Gulf is interesting, as you say. But repellant too, at least to me. She's too treacherous. It sickens one to think of the horrors that she has shaken from her white mane — when people died screaming at Galveston — Corpus Christi — Port Aransas — Indianola — oh, the list is far too long. Texas has no coast; when the waves rise and roll inland there is nothing to break their force. The whole state is a series of steppes — plateaus that descend like stairs from 4000 feet elevation to sea-level. The counties that line the Gulf range in elevation from sea-level to perhaps fifty feet. During a bad storm, the waves rush inland with nothing to stop them. Once a railroad train was washed off the track nearly twenty miles from the coast. Even now many of the houses a considerable distance inland are anchored to the ground with heavy iron cables set deep in concrete, and are furnished with thick shutters, against the wind, which during those tropical storms, rises to appalling proportions. Towns, once thriving and prosperous, have been crippled and forever ruined; others have been wiped out — destroyed. Such as Indianola, the City of Bagdad, Clarkesville, of which it's said no slightest trace now remains to mark that once important port.

Relatives of mine were in Galveston when it was washed away in 1900, but fortunatcly all were saved, though many of their friends were drowned. One of their friends, having been out of the city at the time, hastened back to find that his whole family had perished. He fell like a dead man and when he recovered consciousness, days later, his hair was white as snow. Aye, men's hair turned white then, and the hair of young men and the soft locks of girls. And there was a woman who walked across an ironing board from one crumbling building to another, stronger one, with a child in her arms, and the black night howling over her and the screams of the dying in her ears — the black waves foaming and lashing under her feet and the corpses wallowing and bumping against her feet. And just as she stepped into the comparative safety of the other building, the walls she had left collapsed and thundered into the raving waters and screams of her friends were drowned — with hundreds of others, their bodies were never recovered. Many were swept out to sea; the salt-mashes were littered for many a mile. And strange to say, a babe in a cradle was washed far inland and lived when so many died — people found her floating in her cradle among the debris and they took her and raised her, not knowing her name or anything about her, but she lives, a woman in South Texas, to this day.

God, what black horror must have gripped the hearts of the people, when the doom of winds and waves struck them in the night — when they rushed from their houses with the thunder of the crumbling sea-wall in their ears, and were caught in the black madness that thundered over the doomed city — that shattered their walls, broke their roofs, swept their houses away like straw and strewed dead bodies for a hundred miles among the marshes. Who was spared when the tide broke? Old crippled men cried in vain for aid; the babe at the breast was torn away to drown alone; women whose hour was upon them were hurled out on the breast of the black horror, and their shrieks of agony were choked by the clamor of the waves — aye, babes struggled into birth in that horror, meeting death instead of life. The very tombs were broken open and moldering shapes floated among the living and the newly dead. Trains, halted by the rising water on the mainland, were deserted by their frenzied passengers — and these passengers told tales of corpses floated up to the windows that seemed to fumble at the panes with dead fingers.

Galveston must have seemed like a city of the dead when the tide abated. And thirst and hunger and the black horror of madness fell upon the survivors stumbling among the ruins where ghouls ran looting the dead, hacking off the fingers to get the rings.

God grant no such fate befalls the city again. But in the old days before the city was, the pirate Lafitte drove his ships right across the island in a storm.

Texas, at least the southern part, was under water at no greatly distant date, as the age of the earth is reckoned. Even now one can trace in the hills, the old lines of the ancient shore — promontories, indentations and harbors. Such a great expanse of the state, bordering the Gulf, is only a little above sea-level, it would take no impossible convulsion of Nature to drive the waters a hundred miles inland — an earthquake or a volcano in the Gulf. Such things have occurred. I don't know what the scientists say about it — whether the water-line receded because of some natural shifting, or because of the drying up of the Gulf. But we have no protection in the way of cliffs or mountains against a tidal-wave and I do not intend to ever make my permanent home on the Gulf-coast.

It may be my imagination that Americans in cities are shorter than formerly — and really, I have no right to make any sort of an assertion concerning city-people, since I so rarely visit cities. However, it is the truth that the larger towns and cities of Texas swarm with folk of very medium stature, particularly in Fort Worth, compared to the people of the rural localities, especially in the Oil Belt and the western area. It may be that people are really growing taller — indeed, a study of athletes would tend to prove it. The heavyweight champions are a pretty good index, I should think. The present day fighters seem to be taller. Going a good way back, Jem Figg — 1695-1734 — was six feet tall, but Jack Broughton — 1704-1789 — was five feet-ten; Jack Slack — 17-1778 — while weighing over two hundred pounds, was five feet-eight; Bill Stevens, Bill Darts, Tom Faulkner, Ben Brain, Tom Spring, Gentleman John Jackson, Jem Mace, Tom Sayers, not one of them was six feet tall. The great Bendigo was five-nine, Daniel Mendoza was five-seven, Yankee Sullivan was five-eight. These were all Englishmen, of course. John L. Sullivan, first American champion, was a little over five-ten. Succeeding champions were mainly taller. Fitzsimmons was five eleven and three-fourths. Corbett, Jeffries and Dempsey were each six one and three fourths; Burns was short — five feet-seven. Jack Johnson and Gene Tunney were each slightly over six feet. Willard was a giant, six feet six and a half. The present champion — so-called — Max Schmeling, is six feet one. The ring is at present full of giants, mostly foreigners. Primo Carnera of Italy, Jose Santa of South America, Pat Redmond of Australia, Vittorio Campolo of Argentine, all of these are nearly seven feet tall. Then we have Babe Hunt of Oklahoma — the list is too long. Dempsey could have whipped the entire gang in one ring when he was in his prime.

Present day Texans seem shorter and bulkier than formerly. If there ever was a typical type of Texan, he was tall and rangy. Their mode of life made for such a build. Most of the earlier settlers, too, were of Scotch-Irish descent and I believe — though I may be wrong — that the Scotch-Irish leaned to height and ranginess in build. I was interested in what you said about the heights of Talman, Wandrei etc. My friends are mostly of good size, and strongly built, since most of them are men who make their living by the work of their hands. By a peculiar coincidence, the majority of my friends have been, and are, of a uniform height of five-feet eleven-inches — which is my own height. I have noted this time and again. Some are taller; Tevis Clyde Smith, co-author of "Red Blades of Black Cathay" is six feet one; another friend by the name of Vinson is six feet two. Both live in Brownwood, forty miles south of Cross Plains. Of my five special friends here, four are five-feet-eleven. One — a Kansan of German descent — is six-feet one. However, he is lighter than the others.

Speaking of the contrast between Nordic and Latin knife-play: I don't know whether the slashing habit is an Indian or a Spanish instinct. If Spanish, it may be a survival of Moorish influence. As of course you know, the Oriental nations favor curved blades, and generally slash instead of thrusting. The early Nordic warriors hacked too, but they used straight swords, depending on the weight of the blade and the force of the blow, whereas the Orientals curved the blade to gain the effect. But the early Greeks and the Romans understood the art of thrusting, as witness their short swords. And the rapier was created in the West. I am not prepared to say whether the Spaniards borrowed any ideas or weapons and their use from the Moors, but I will say that Mexican swords are generally more curved than those used by Americans. I noted this recently during a trip to the battlefield of Goliad where Fannin and his men were trapped by the Mexican army. I saw two sabers — a Mexican arm and an American — both of which were used in that battle. The Mexican sword was curved far more than the Texan weapon — in fact, it would be almost impossible to thrust effectively with it. Blade, hilt and guard were all made in one piece of steel, and I could hardly get my hand inside the guard to clutch the hilt; some grandee wielded it, no doubt, some proud don with blue blood and small aristocratic hands — well, I hope he got his before Fannin surrendered, and gasped his life out in the mud of Perdido with a Texas rifle-ball through him.

Glad you liked my verse — which, like most of my stuff, hasn't been published and probably won't be. Thanks for pointing out the break in metre. I'd never have known it, otherwise. Scanning verse — outside of iambics — or is it pentameter? — I never can remember which is which — is something that's entirely beyond me. I know nothing at all about the mechanics of poetry — I couldn't tell you whether a verse was anapestic or trochaic to save my neck. I write the stuff by ear, so to speak, and my musical ear is very full of flaws.

Thanks for commenting on my energy in writing — but honestly, I'm provokingly indolent. I work in bursts and spurts. I may turn out a month's output in a few days, and then loaf for weeks. I sell so little, though, that I have to produce a great deal in order to make a living at all. Just before Mr. Wright left on his vacation he took a long story for *Oriental's*,[5] which he had requested — a yarn dealing with Baibars the Panther. The readers seem to like my historical tales, for some reason or other, and I'm duly grateful, for I love to write historic fiction, puerile though my efforts may be.

Thanks very much for the material, especially the snap-shot of yourself, also for the post-card view, and the literature about the meteorite. I remember, very faintly, the fall of a meteorite in South Texas, many years ago. I was about four years old at the time, and was at the house of an uncle, in a little town about forty miles from the Mexican Border; a town which had recently sprung up like a mushroom from the wilderness and was still pretty tough. I remember waking suddenly and sitting up in bed, seeing everything bathed in a weird blue light, and hearing a terrific detonation. My uncle — an Indian — had enemies of desperate character, and in the excitement it was thought they had dynamited the house. There was a general leaping up and snatching of guns, but nothing further occurred. Next day it was learned that a meteorite had fallen. People who saw it described it as being about the size and shape of a barrel, and averred it burst twice before striking the ground, making a loud explosion and shedding that strange blue light over everything. No trace of it was ever found.

And speaking of natural phenomena, an occurrence has taken place in Texas which is without precedent. We have had an earthquake.[6] Faint tremors have been recorded in El Paso before, probably echoes of California quakes, but not within the memory of white men has Central Texas felt a tremor. It seemed to center in Valentine, in the Sierra Viejas, but was felt all over West and Central Texas. Since the first jar, several other quakes have been felt at Valentine, and the people have been sleeping outdoors mostly, I hear; the

Mexicans particularly being terrified. Their adobe houses fell down like stacks of cards, though no one was hurt, it seems.

The quake was very apparent in this part of the country, and many of the people, never having experienced anything of the sort before, were completely mystified. Of course, I had to sleep through it, to my disgust. I'm a rather sound sleeper anyhow, and that night several of us had been out on a small party; for the first time in years, I was slightly intoxicated when I retired, besides being tired from wrestling with the huge foreman of the local ice factory. So I slept more soundly than usual and knew nothing at all about the earthquake until next morning. A rather amusing incident was attendant to the quake — one of my friends, who was one of the party before mentioned, drank considerably more than I did, and awakening in the midst of the quake, thought he was in the grip of delirium tremens or some other mysterious malady connected with the intoxicants he had imbibed. He was sleeping in an upstairs room and felt the shaking very plainly indeed. He was extremely relieved to find it was only an earthquake.

Nothing of the sort has ever happened in Texas before, to the best of my knowledge. I'm sending you some clippings, and with these comments you have a first-hand account of Texas' first earthquake, from a participant — though the participant ingloriously slept through the entire excitement!

I can't sleep through a thunder-storm, but I can sleep through almost any other sort of disturbance. It would take quite a bit of shaking up to waken me, ordinarily. And being wakened by shaking is something I always despised. I remember when I was a kid of eighteen, the owner of the boarding house where I stayed always woke us up by trying to shake the liver out of us, regularly at six o'clock. He seemed to think it a great joke and some of the boys learned to wake up as he entered their room, and leap out of bed in a hurry. I protested in vain, and one morning when I was awake, I heard him ascending the stairs, and I lay still, feigning sleep; as he bent over the bed and laid hold of me I gave him a smash under the heart that nearly laid him out and after that, when he wanted to wake me up, he did so by calling from outside the doorway.

Well, the oil war rages. Doubtless you've heard some echoes of it, on the East Coast. The Oklahoma City Oil Field is under martial law, and so is the great East Texas field. A thousand men of the National Guard are patrolling East Texas and they have Hickman and his Rangers there — to protect the National Guard, I reckon. Ordinarily I am rabidly opposed to any sort of martial law, but this time I believe it's a good thing. The big oil companies are strangling the very life out of the industry.

I haven't visited the East Texas field but I hear it's a hummer. Several former law-officers of this section of the country served there for awhile in one capacity or another. But there seemed to be considerable prejudice there against West Texans, especially as officers, and this was probably increased when the former marshal of this town killed a man at Gladewater in a raid. Shortly afterwards an East Texas officer ran amuck and killed a Ranger, narrowly missing several other officers, before he himself was killed by one of them.

But there'll never be another boom like Ranger had. Ranger lies about fifty miles east of this town, on the Fort Worth road, and there's little about it now to suggest the wild and lurid glamor of its past. This town too, like most towns of this region, had its booms and echoes; millions of dollars have flowed through it; men have come here paupers and left millionaires, and vice versa. Particularly vice versa.

To get back to the oil situation etc., it looks as if some radical step must be taken if the independents are not to be ground down entirely. I note that Kansas is considering a shut-down. Good enough. I hope it's a step she takes. Of course nothing can be expected of Pennsylvania and California, but Texas, Oklahoma and Kansas can do a lot, if they stick together and stand by their guns.

States' rights seem to be fast fading into non-existence. Laws have become props to uphold big criminals and heels to grind down petty violators. Most of the present contempt for law seems to be the result of corrupt law-officers — graft, fraud and injustice run rampant. A big shot can get away with anything while ordinary men are ruthlessly trodden into the mire. There was more justice in the old days when each man packed his law on his hip. Men — at least in the West — recognized the rights of the individual, which are now ignored. Nowadays a man isn't supposed to have any heart, guts, brains, blood or honor. He's supposed to crawl on his belly and lick dirt before the fetish of that vast, vague and uncertain idol Society — while the big ruthless ones trample that same idol with perfect impunity. I say Society is founded on individuals who have individual rights. This was once recognized. An uncle of mine, a gambler who was well known in the Southwest in the '80s, when on the witness stand, knocked down a domineering prosecuting attorney who was attempting to badger him. The judge only mildly reproved him, recognizing the fact that a man has individual honor apart from his obligations to "the Mass" and a right to resent insults, on any and all occasions.

But now — damn such a stinking age. If I could choose the age in which I was to live, I can think of no better epoch than this: to have been born about a hundred years earlier than I was, to have grown up on the Southwestern frontier, to have fought through the Texas Revolution and taken a part in San Jacinto, to have served as a soldier in the war with Mexico, to have gone to California with the '49ers, and to have fallen in some great battle of the Civil War. If I could have grown up and lived in primitive virile surroundings, if I could have taken part in stirring events, if I could have shot straight, lived like an Indian, run like a mustang and fought like a grizzly, I would not care whether I could read a line or write my own name. And here I am, fat, slothful, un-warlike and short-winded!

Your mention of Latins reminds me of a question I have intended asking for some time — are the New England wops as criminally inclined, and as well organized in crime as the Italians of Chicago and New York? I suppose a great deal of killing goes on among them, where-ever they are, as that seems to be a characteristic of the Latin races. Our most turbulent element is the Mexicans, of course, who slaughter each other with energy and consistency. Yet it isn't fair to blame their lawlessness on the Latins, since there is so little actual Spanish blood in most of them. San Antonio leads the rest of Texas cities in crime a long way. In the three weeks I spent there last winter there must have been half a dozen murders, at least — all Mexicans. And a daily and nightly tale of sluggings, robberies and hold-ups; burglaries and thefts. Occasionally a Mexican kills a white man. Naturally, the closer to the Border, the more such crimes occur. The most recent atrocity was when a Mexican wood-chopper raped and murdered a little white girl and fled from San Antonio south across the Border. The Mexican government refused to give him up for punishment. Well, I know what would have happened in the old days.

In Northwest and West Texas, the Mexican population is very scanty and of course the crimes are fewer. Though not altogether unknown. A year or so ago some Mexicans murdered an officer in Mason county, for which they went to the chair. And a few years ago, further west, a young Mexican was guilty of a most detestable crime. He had married a white woman, who being a bed-ridden invalid and having a baby about two years old to support, probably turned to him in desperation, having no means of support. For some reason or other he became angered at her, and to torment her, tortured the child before her eyes for hours in the most hideous manner, and wound up by beating out its brains with a rat-tail file. But they got that spig.

Some years ago in this country two Mexicans came to a lonely ranch-house to rob a white woman — but she killed them both with a butcher-knife. And again a young Mexican, in the town of Brownwood, evidently went crazy over brooding about Pancho Villa who was raising Hell down in Mexico. He'd been raised by a family who treated him like a son — but he attacked the woman who'd raised him, and her young daughter, one morning about dawn, and slashed both of them badly before they could take the knife away from him. He ran then, but he didn't run far. Pursued by a mob of wrathful whites, he gained the open country, and tried to shoot a rancher as he ran by the man's place. But his gun snapped and the rancher sent back an answering bullet that dropped him dead in his tracks. In his pocket they found an unmailed letter addressed to his brother in Villa's army, in which he swore to come and join the bandit, and to kill all the white people he could on the way. Poor devil, it's just as well for him that the rancher's shot killed him quick. That was an easy death.

I note that another book of ghost-lore has blossomed from the pen of Montague Rhodes James — of whom I had never heard in my life before I read your fascinating article on horror-literature in *The Recluse*.[7] I would like to read some of this gentleman's work. Could you tell me what company handles his stuff, or where I could obtain it?

My reading has been and is, indeed, deplorably scanty. I find, looking over the tales you mention in your article, that I have read only a very small percent of them. Sometime I hope to be able to take off about a year and catch up with some reading. Your splendid article — which I have re-read repeatedly — whets my appetite for the bizarre. Some day I must read "Melmoth" and the tales you mention by Blackwood, Chambers, Machen, etc.

I read Whitehead's "Black Beast"[8] and wrote him my appreciation of the tale. By the way, while you were in Florida, did you hear anything of "the Old People"? According to Hugh Pendexter, old chronicles of the country speak of ruins of roadways, fortresses and buildings, supposed to have been erected by some pre-Indian race. In his serial recently appearing in *Adventure* — the first installment of which appeared in the same issue as "The Black Beast" — "Devil's Brew" he strikes some really convincing notes of lurking horror and sinister speculation with his mysterious sunken city, brooding beneath the sullen waters of a swamp-land lake, with its serpent-guardians and cryptic golden, headless and winged images, hinting uncanny origin and meaning. If you haven't seen this tale, I'd be mighty glad to lend you the magazines containing it.

I note with delight that you have a story appearing in the next *Weird Tales*.[9] I await it with impatience. By the way, E. Hoffmann Price writes me that he and Mashburn[10] are attempting to promote a sort of anthology of weird tales — or rather a collection of ten selected stories, which includes your "Pickman's Model" and my "Kings of the Night." I'm all for it, myself. Have they mentioned anything about it to you? I think it would be great.

I'm glad to hear you've gotten over your eye-strain. A writer with bad eyes is like a fighter with crippled hands. Doubtless your trip gave your eyes a needed rest.

And speaking of trips, I hope you'll find it convenient to come to Texas some of these times. For nearly a year my plans have been very chaotic and uncertain, and I've hardly been able to outline my life from one day to the next. Even now I cannot predict with any certainty where I'll be tomorrow or the next day. But it's possible that by next summer I'll be in a more settled and tranquil state of existence, and if so, I'd like very much to entertain you to the best of my ability.

There are parts of the state I'm sure you'd find interesting, and if things work out like I hope they will, I'll show you all of it, with some of Oklahoma and New Mexico thrown in. Much of the territory is monotonous and possessed of a sameness, but a lot of it is fascinating, especially the hill countries. I often wished you were with me on my recent short trip through the southwestern hills, especially along the Old Spanish Trail, winding in and out among the vast, thickly timbered slopes and along the rivers, through deep cool valleys. There is a slumberous quiet among those hills, where the occupancy of man has scarcely made itself evident. Big wild turkeys flew across the road, so close that I could have dropped them with a pistol-shot — but I'm no hunter. It will take a hundred years to settle up the wilder portions of the state. I know of few greater pleasures than to drive over the long dreaming miles with the towns left behind and scarcely even a ranch-house or a wandering traveller to break the primeval solitude. And further west it is even wilder and less frequented. There is Brewster County with its area of 5,935 square miles, and its population of 6,624; Crockett area 3,215 square miles, population, 2,590; Pecos, area, 4,134 square miles, population 7,812; Terrell, area, 2,635, population, 2,660 — one human per square mile; Maverick, area 1,251 square miles, population 6,120. And etc., etc., also etc.

It's rather foolish to make plans far ahead — and by next summer I may be in Oklahoma, China or Hell — but if I am settled as I hope to be, I'd feel honored by a visit from you.

Best wishes.

Cordially,
[Robert E. Howard]

P.S. Glancing over this letter, much of it seems rather morbid. If I'm too prone to linger over subjects of gory or gloomy trend, I really must beg your pardon. We of the Southwest — of the old stock, at least — are inclined to be a gloomy race. Our folk-songs reflect our natures. The greater majority of the songs and ballads which grew up in, or were favorites in the early Southwest, dealt almost exclusively with battle, murder and sudden death. Listen to some of the lines of a few:

"As I rode by Tom Sherman's barroom, Tom Sherman's barroom, so early one day,
"I saw a young cowboy, so young and so handsome, all wrapped in linen, as though for the grave!"

And:

"Twas in the merry month of May, when all sweet buds were swelling
"Sweet William on his death-bed lay, for the love of Barbara Allen."

And:

"One morning, one morning, one morning in May,
"I heard an old soldier, lamentingly say—"

And:

"Come all you punchers and listen to my tale,
"While I tell you of my troubles on the Old Chisholm Trail —"

And:

"Oh, beat the drum slowly and play the fife slowly,
"And play the death-march as you bear me along!
"Take me to some green valley and lay the sod o'er me,
"For I'm a young cowboy and I know I've done wrong!"

And:

"He had wasted in pain, till o'er his brow
"The shades of death were gathering now.
"And he thought of his home and his loved ones nigh
"And the cowboys gathered to see him die!"

And:

"Early in the morning, in the month of May,
"Brady came down on the morning train,
"Brady came down on the Shining Star,
"And he shot Mr. Duncan in behind the bar!"

And:

"Oh, once in the saddle I used to go dashing,
"Oh, once in the saddle I used to look brave,
"I then got to drinking, and then took to gambling,
"Got into a fight, and now for the grave."

And:

"Oh, put me in that dungeon, oh, put me in that cell —
"Put me where the north wind blows from the southeast
corner of Hell!"

And:

"The dogs they did howl, the dogs they did bark,
"When Stackerlee the murderer went creeping through the
dark —
"Everybody talk about Stackerlee!"

And:

"Come all of you my brother scouts,
"And listen to my song;
"Come let us sing together
"Though the shadows fall so long."

And so on. The list is endless. These songs were the natural outgrowth of the country and the country's people, and reflect the spirit of the people far more accurately than can any work of educated poets and writers. Some of them were old Scotch-Irish ballads twisted about and changed to suit the times, the surroundings and the listeners. Others grew like mesquite grass, from the soil and the settlers. They dealt with violence, misfortune and doom, for the frontiersmen encountered such things far more often than they encountered cheer and good ease. And if I am boresome with my gloomy tales and incidents and observations, please pardon it. It's a racial tendency.

R.E.H.

By the way, I'm sending you a *Sport Story* magazine containing a yarn of mine,[11] the first of a new series, the continuance of which I have an idea will depend a great deal on the expression of the readers' opinions. If you like the yarn, I'd be greatly obliged if you'd drop Street & Smith a line saying so, that is if it isn't too much trouble. If the publishers receive some letters approving my work, they'll be more likely to continue buying stories of the series. Also by the way, here's a snapshot of me for your private rogue's gallery — don't judge me too much by my looks; I'm really not as scoundrelly as I look.

P.S.S. I just finished reading your latest story in *Weird Tales*, and am fascinated by its beauty and mystic depths. It calls to mind "The White Ship" and "The Silver Key" — shimmering etchings of pure beauty. And well do I recall the Terrible Old Man who talked with haunted pendulums. I hope you will use him again.

R.E.H.

NOTES

1. Date of letter changed at Rob's suggestion. JB
2. Parker County was named for Isaac Parker, an early legislator, James' brother and Cynthia Ann's uncle.
3. "The Horror from the Mound."
4. "The Thing on the Roof."
5. "The Sowers of the Thunder."
6. A magnitude 5.8 earthquake, the strongest in Texas history, occurred on August 16, 1931, centered near Valentine, Texas.
7. "Supernatural Horror in Literature."
8. *Adventure*, July 15, 1931.
9. "The Strange High House in the Mist," October 1931.
10. W. Kirk Mashburn.
11. "College Socks," September 25, 1931.

TSS: 25346-25357

174. To Tevis Clyde Smith, ca. September 1931.

Fear Finn:

> Lizzen my children and you shall be told
> Of the midnight ride of Mikey de Gold!
> In feathers and tar he rode away
> On a ten-foot rail at the break of day.
> And Hebrews cheer when the tale is told
> Of the thrilling ride of Mikey de Gold.

Wotta life, wotta life! Here is de low-down on Mikey de Gold:[1] "As a Jew I know that anti-Jewish prejudice exists. I will fight it to the death. * I will stand up for my race, as I will for a Negro or Italian in like circumstances. And I refuse to run away, even if there were an escape in Palestine or Africa, as there certainly is not. America is our country, as much as anyone's. We will plant ourselves here, not retreat to some mythical fatherland in the deserts of Palestine or Africa."

* Mikey de Gold fighting to the death, according to the custom of his race

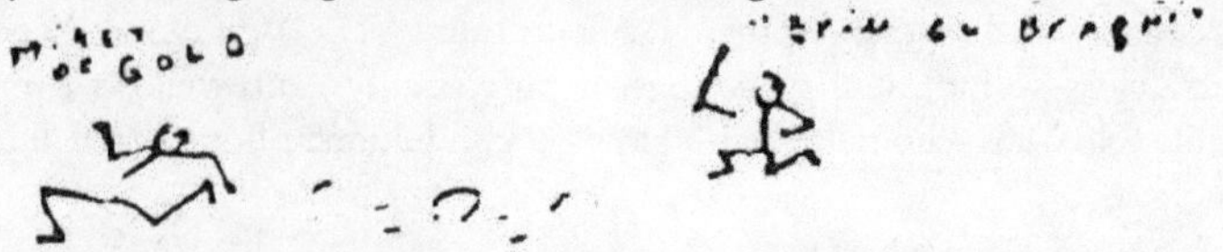

I'm interested in the Christopher business.[2] Right now Alvie de Brad[3] has my completed copies — I don't even have carbons, as far as that goes — but I'll write de Brad and tell him to send my verses back. He's surely got copies of them at least, by this time. As you say, it won't hurt to investigate the Christopher. I wish we could get out a book of verse before we get too old and feeble to peddle them from door to door.

I'm glad to hear the G.M.C. are going to review your book, and I appreciate your attitude in not sending them the book and scathing them with rebukal, knowing how distasteful vulgar publicity is to youse.

I got another letter from Bernard Dwyer, in which he says Lovecraft lent him a picture of me, and he wants to know what sort of physical work I did to develop my frame. I'm ashamed to tell him I never did any. He's no shrimp himself — six feet three in height and weighs 230 pounds. Also got a long letter from Talman, who said in part :

"As a matter of fact, your personality intrigues me. I've heard a little about you from Lovecraft, of course, but even he doesn't seem to know much about you. When we had to write a brief biography of you for *The Texaco Star* my knowledge of the Sage of Cross Plains was so limited that I fear the biog. didn't do you justice.

"Well, now, just what about yourself? Do you spend all your time writing? What is your age, your previous condition of servitude, your background, your foreground, and your intermediary history? Where did you get that powerful flow of words that enables you to uphold the suspense of a 'battle' story?"

Well, with my usual modesty, I'll have to admit that after winning the bare-knuckle heavyweight title of the Oil-belt, I served a term in the Spanish Foreign Legion, strangled Abd el Krim with me bare talons, twisted off Sandino's head for me watch-fob, and put in several years hunting heads in Borneo.

For a young man, Talman has travelled pretty swiftly. He's not quite twenty-seven, but a former student of Brown, graduate from Columbia Un., reporter on the *New York Times* and later one of the regular staff. Now he's assistant editor of the four magazines of the Texas Co.. In addition he's been married a couple of years. He said as a staff member of the *Times* he had to work only four or five hours a day, but he soured on newspaper work. His eventual goal is writing.

He's met Quinn, (alias Jules de Grandin) and says he's a courteous gent of middle age, with a Southern accent. He says Quinn is independent and knows how to twist the editors. Says he recently turned down a big contract from Street & Smith, reported valued at $10,000. A gent can afford to be independent when he already has jack. Talman, incidentally, is of Knickerbocker Dutch descent, and says "Brooklyn" comes from "Breuckerlen" a town in Holland.

Fear Dunn.

Pey Ess: Let me see the scather about the Jews when you get it finished I know it'll be good.

NOTES

1. Michael Gold, editor of *The New Masses* and author of *Jews Without Money*.
2. As Alvin Bradford seemed to be making no progress on his proposed collection of material from *The Junto* (see letter 163), Smith had proposed sending a collection of poetry by himself, Lenore Preece, and Howard to The Christopher Publishing House, Boston.
3. Alvin Bradford; see letter 163, note 1.

TSS: 82057-82058

ଓଷ୍ଠଛ

175. To Wilfred Blanch Talman, ca. September 1931.

Dear Mr. Talman:

Thank you very much for the letter you wrote to Street & Smith.[1] I know it will help me with the editors. I'll return the favor at the first opportunity.

I feel honored that my work has interested you, and thank you for the comments you made about it. I also appreciate your giving me the sketch regarding yourself, because I'm always vividly interested in the career, struggles, etc., of authors. Especially my fellow contributors to *Weird Tales*, to which I sold my first stories. I admire both your literary education and your success in the newspaper world, the more remarkable — it seems to me — because of your youth.

You ask me something about my own life and etc. Well, my life has been hum-drum and drably monotonous, with no high spots of drama or adventure.

My ancestors were among the early settlers of America, and after a hundred years or so spent in Georgia and the Carolinas, began drifting West. The Civil War caught the Howards in Arkansas and the Ervins in Mississippi, and ruined both families financially. The Ervins landed in Texas in 1866, the Howards in 1885. Both lines were of restless disposition, and I've had kin in nearly every movement of conquest and colonization from the Revolution on — War of 1812, Gold Rush of '49, Civil War, settling and developing of West Texas, Apache uprising in New Mexico, settling of the Indian Territory — etc.

I was born in the little ex-cowtown of Peaster, about 45 miles west of Fort Worth, in the winter of 1906, but spent my first summer in lonely Dark Valley among the sparsely settled Palo Pinto hills. From then until I was nearly nine years old I lived in various parts of the state — in a land-boom town on the Staked Plains, near the New Mexico line;[2] in the Western Texas sheep country;[3] in San Antonio;[4] on a ranch in South Texas;[5] in a cattle town on the Oklahoma line, near the old North Texas oil-fields;[6] in the piney woods of East Texas;[7] finally in what later became the Central West Texas Oil-belt.[8]

Except for short periods spent in New Orleans and San Antonio, I've lived in the country and in small towns all my life. I got through high school by the skin of my teeth. I always hated school, and as I look back on my school days now, I still hate them with a deep and abiding hatred. Outside of mathematics — at which I was a terrible mug — I didn't particularly mind the studies, but I hated being confined indoors — having to keep regular hours — having to think up stupid answers for equally irritating questions asked me by people who considered themselves in authority over me. During vacations — which in the country frequently lasted six or seven months — I hoed cockleburrs and picked cotton. Not with pleasure. I detested any kind of work. My idea of a proper existence was to gallop around over the country on a Steeldust racing mare or a Spanish mustang, steal melons, hunt possums, trap varmints, go swimming, race horses, and wrestle with my friends.

Oil hit the country in which I lived when I was about twelve and I might have applied myself and developed into a tool-dresser or a driller, eventually, but that looked like a lot of work to me. After moving into town — I say town, by comparison — I worked at various things during vacation, such as a grocery store and a Jewish dry-goods store. I graduated from high school at the age of seventeen and went to work in a tailor shop — I was a solicitor — in other words I went out and euchred the customers into patronizing the shop, brought the clothes to the shop, cleaned them and delivered them — for which I got a third of the entire proceeds. Wearying of this, I dallied — at the age of eighteen — with thoughts of a musical career and started taking violin lessons from a wandering old fiddler who'd gone on the rocks because of drink. But he took up with a wandering minstrel show and skipped the country, so I started taking lessons from an old Scotchman who led the local band. I took one lesson and then the Scotchman came to a sudden and violent end. I then made arrangements to continue my lessons with a German but before I could begin, he jumped town just ahead of the law, leaving a trail of deft swindles behind him. Soured on the musical profession, I went to Howard Payne College at Brownwood, Texas, but not to take a literary course, no, no! I studied shorthand and typing, and returning to my home-town, I began my venture in the business world. Having just sold Mr. Wright my four first stories, I had no enthusiasm about landing a job, but did get one writing up oil-field news for various Texas and Oklahoma papers. Oil business being slack, there wasn't much money in it, but I eked out a living packing a rod for a geologist. But that job played out and I went into a law office as private secretary. A townsite boom hit the town and I lost both my jobs — private sec. & oil correspondence; I was exasperatingly inefficient at both. An oil-man let me use his office to install myself as public stenographer; I made very little money, but during that time wrote and sold my first novelet, "Wolfshead." I then tried working in a post office but couldn't get along with the postmaster, so that venture was out. Next I worked a while in a gas office, but lost the job because I wouldn't kow-tow to my employer and "yes" him from morning till night. That's one reason I was never very successful in working for people. So many men think an employee is a kind of servant. I'm good-natured and easy-going, I detest and shrink from rows of all sort, but there's no use in a man swallowing everything.

I worked around a little here and there at various things, and one day got the advance pages of "Wolfshead" which was about to be published. Reading it over I was so depressed and discouraged that I went and got a job jerking soda in a drug-store. The manager was no Santa Claus, but we got along alright after I offered to tie my right hand behind me and beat his head off with my left. But it was a lousy job. The town was in the midst of an oil-boom and most of the time I held down the whole damned drug-store by myself. Working seven days out of the week, till past midnight every night, and going at high speed most of the time, my health went on the rocks. Worn out mentally and physically, I practically abandoned all hopes of a literary career, and crawled off to Howard Payne's business department again to study bookkeeping. I studied hard at first, then my health came back and I spent most of my time writing verse and playing seven-up with the tool-dressers etc. at the boarding house.

I dallied through the winter, and the summer of 1927 found me still trying to graduate from the business dept. That summer I began trying the writing game again, and when I sold Wright a batch of yarns, I immediately stopped trying to get a job as a bookkeeper — though I had my diploma from the business school — and went to work writing again. I couldn't have held a job as a bookkeeper anyhow. After completing the course, it was a bigger mystery to me than when I started on it. Since the summer of 1927 I've done little besides hammer out fiction — selling only a small percent of all I write, but eking out a living. I might make more money at something else, but I wouldn't have the freedom and that's the main attraction of the writing game.

I believe I mentioned that I sold my first story in 1924. I first started writing at the age of fifteen. A literary course in some college would doubtless have been a help to me, but I never felt I could afford it, besides, college is too much like school to interest me much. Besides Wright's magazines, I've sold stuff to *Fight Stories*, *Action Stories*, *Ghost Stories*, *Argosy*, and of course *Sport Stories*. Not a very impressive number of markets, but I don't have to keep regular hours and have somebody holding a stop-watch on me, which is what I always detested about regular jobs. My tastes are simple; I like prize-fights, football games, horse-races and beer. I haven't much education myself, but I appreciate it in others.

And I hope I haven't bored you too much by these long pointless ramblings. You ask me for my candid opinion as to your prospects as a writer.

Candidly, I feel certain that anyone who can write as fine a poem as "The Haunted Isle"[9] has splendid chances of reaching the top of the game. I'm looking forward to reading your "Doom Around the Corner."[10] Don't be discouraged if your stories lie in the editorial offices for a while. I sold Mr. Wright "The Hyena" in 1924 and it was four years before it was published.

I'm very interested in your account of Quinn. He must be a fascinating character. Also intrigued with your comments about the Netherland origins of New York names. Now Flatbush, for instance. I always wondered how in the hell that got its name. Brooklyn sounds so much like an English name I never gave its origin a thought. You clear up these points splendidly, and I'd like more elucidation on like subjects. The American occupancy of the Nederlandsche people always interested me, and Irving's Knickerbocker tales are some of my most enjoyable memories — the reading of them, I mean. The occupancy of New York by the Netherlanders must correspond in a way to the occupancy of the Spanish in the early Southwest — in both cases the original settlers were dispossessed by Anglo-Saxon invaders. Yet it hovers somewhere in the back of my mind that the Netherlanders themselves were invaders, in that they licked a bunch of Swedes to get possession of New Netherland. Am I right, or has my vague knowledge of history betrayed me again, as usual? I'd appreciate accurate information on the subject. Also concerning the patroon system, about which I am vague, but which seems to have been a lusty and full-blooded period, somewhat corresponding to the plantation epoch of the South.

Well, I've rambled enough. Thanks again for the boost to Street & Smith. Hoping to hear from you when you find it convenient,

Cordially,
[Robert E. Howard.]

NOTES

1. Regarding "College Socks."
2. Seminole, in Gaines County, circa 1908.
3. Bronte, in Coke County, circa 1909.
4. Circa 1910.
5. Poteet, in Atascosa County, circa 1910.
6. This location has been positively identified as Byers, Texas.
7. Bagwell, in Red River County, circa 1914.
8. Cross Cut, in Brown County, circa 1915-1916; Burkett, in Coleman County, circa 1917-1919; and Cross Plains, in Callahan County, September 1919 onward.
9. "Haunted Island," *Weird Tales*, January 1928.
10. *Weird Tales*, November 1931.

TSS: 15324-15325, 15493

ଔଓଌଓଔ

176. To Tevis Clyde Smith, ca. September 1931.

Fear Finn:

I've been waiting for a letter from you, but maybe you wrote and it's been lost in the mails, as I never received the other you sent me. Or maybe you've been expecting a letter from me.

I've been patiently waiting for the return of my verse from Bradford, and I don't know why in Hell he hasn't sent it, or at least written me. I'm getting fed up on this sort of treatment. If he doesn't send them pretty damned soon, I'm going to San Antonio after them. Have you heard anything from him, or from Lenore?

Let me know if you've heard anything from the Christopher bunch. I don't want to keep them waiting too long, but I've been so cursedly busy that I've felt like I couldn't take the time to re-copy my verse, if I could possibly get the copies I've already made. This is a sweet damned time for Bradford to hold out on me, by God, just when I'm already packing about as much as a human can stand up under.

Fear Dunn.

TSS: 82043

ଔଓଌଓଔ

177. To Wilfred Blanch Talman, ca. October 1931.

Dear Mr. Talman:

I'm returning herewith your stories, "The Heads at Gywry" and "Midnight Coach" which Mr. Lovecraft forwarded to me. Thanks very much for the opportunity of reading them. I liked them both immensely. The first mentioned tale shows a remarkable sweep and depth of imagination, and fine macabre development, like the slow sinister beat of nameless drums in the distance. In that tale you have captured vividly a sense of soul-shaking evil, and in the flight of the villagers, you have worked out a sense of suspense and impending doom that is fiendishly realistic and gripping. Altogether a remarkable story.

In the other I was much interested in your use of the old Irish legend of the coiste-codnar and the dullahans. Which last, by the way, is more Scandinavian than Irish, and was brought into Ireland, no doubt, by invading Vikings, who, in the grim cold lands of their nativity, were accustomed to behead corpses lest their ghosts be too strong, or perhaps to prevent them becoming vampires. Doubtless the tale of headless horrors stalking through the rolling grey mists on the bare fens gave rise to such legends. I hope you'll use Irish legends in other tales, and certainly, there's a broad and fertile field there, and a whole gamut of supernaturals from the Payshtha, the dragon of the lake, to the amorous gean-canach with his winning ways with milk-maids. The most of the shiagh are whimsical and fantastic but some are grisly and weird, survivals, perhaps, of Danish legendry.

I believe, though, of all your stories, I like "Doom Around the Corner" though this statement is in no way meant to depreciate the rest of your tales. This story is the sort that especially appeals to me — subject matter, style and development. It possesses unusual realism and convincingness, and is free from the artificial sort of conversation so often dragged into tales in order to conform to certain vague literary conventions. I've noticed this freedom and ease in your other stories. All in all, "Doom Around the Corner" is one of the most perfect short stories I've read in a long time.

Cordially,
[Robert E. Howard]

TSS: 15322

178. To H.P. Lovecraft, ca. October 1931.

Dear Mr. Lovecraft:

Thanks for the post-card views. The Lathrop school and the store are certainly quaint and fascinating looking old buildings. I wonder if American barns weren't copied on the style of these old-time houses. I've seen numerous barns in this part of the country that looked something similar, especially the sloping roof.

Congratulations on the story, "In the Vault".[1] I hope Mr. Wright publishes it soon.

I envy you your visits in the New England hill country. I know you enjoy these trips immensely — just as I know I would. I enjoyed Mr. Talman's stories greatly. And especially liked the one in the current *Weird Tales.* I sympathize with you in your job of editing the College history.[2] That must be a wearing task.

Its hard for me to keep at my typewriter days like this — and this day is a delightful change from the weather that's been prevailing here. It's been abominably sloppy and nasty, following a short drouth. The other night it rained over eight inches, which is very unusual for this part of Texas, and I was out in the worst of it.

Somewhat past midnight, at the height of the downpour, I sallied forth to rescue a small but pestiferous pig from the flood which was threatening to drown him in his pen. Did you ever pursue a yammering pig around a muddy pen at midnight, with the rain driving down in torrents, the wind howling in gusts, and the thunder and lightning splitting the heavens? If the pen had been larger I don't suppose I'd ever have caught the little wretch, and when I did, he yelled bloody murder all the way to the barn where I dumped him into a shed with the greatest of disgust. The old sow woke up — it's not her pig but she seems to think she's responsible — and she tried her best to tear down her pen so she could get out and rip me up, and as I plodded back through the mud and rain, I'll admit I was completely disgusted with livestock in general. The next day my rheumatism got in its licks and that didn't sweeten my disposition any.

I'll admit I'm naturally leary of pigs. My distrust of them dates back to an episode in South Texas when I was a very young child. A little girl in the vicinity fell into a hog-pen and the hogs dismembered her and had her half-devoured before anybody could come to the rescue.

The sow I mentioned before — a big, mean, chicken-killing, fence-breaking old outlaw — has it in for me, anyhow. Nearly every time I've gone into the lot it's been a scrap. Talk about an elephant's memory! I was gone for several days and when I got back, the misguided old heathen was waiting for me at the lot-gate, and I had to fight her off with a club. Yesterday she got me hemmed up against the barn and came for me, roaring like a wild beast, champing and snorting, and if there hadn't been a section of iron pipe handy, one of Mr. Wright's contributing gang would have been minus a good leg or so. A fighting sow can tear a limb off a man with little effort. I bent the pipe over the old fool's back and sold her the idea of retiring, but she retreated sullenly. I hate to manhandle animals, but it was she or me. She may get me yet, but I hope to dine on roast pork eventually.

But, heavenly days, how I'm rambling, without rhyme or reason. With best wishes,

Cordially,
[Robert E. Howard]

NOTES

1. Published in *Weird Tales*, April 1932.
2. Lovecraft was editing *History of Dartmouth College*, by Leon Burr Richardson, for the Stephen Daye Press.

TSS: 65707

179. To Tevis Clyde Smith, ca. October 1931.

Fear Finn:

The reason I haven't written you sooner is because I've kept thinking ever since I got home that this damnable weather would let up and I'd come over to see you.

Your poem was magnificent. It's the first bit of verse which has made goose-flesh on me in the Devil knows how long. I'm going to quote some of it to Lovecraft in my next letter. I can't praise it enough; it had the ring and the swing, the throb and the pulse and the thunder. I hope we can get out our verse in book form. I want to send a copy, for one thing, to the editor of the *Poet's Scroll*, who used to reject my verse because he said it was not rhythmic, whereas he didn't have the guts to admit the real reason — which was that it was entirely too brutal for him and his pink tea laureates. That reminds me that in his last letter Lovecraft told me that he'd never encountered a better natural ear for rhythm than mine — all of which is an extreme exhibition of vanity on my part, for me to repeat, but I never laid claim to be any modest shrinking violet.

I got a hilarious kick out of your football broadcast, and am prompted to follow your example in a way:

The Associated Press reports a violent scandal in the radio world, when a sports broadcaster clashed with the Committee of Radio Control, in which row an All-American football star seems to have been involved. Howard, the announcer in question, was attacked by the Committee because of his recent broadcast of the Georgia-Southern California game. He was accused of exhibiting extreme partiality, and of using ungentlemanly language when alluding to members of the Southern California squad. A typical comment of his follows (censured by the Press), "Monler is back — he takes the ball and starts through the line — he's loose — some lousy son of a (censured) and Monler broke through for a negligent gain of forty yards before hauled down by Smith, who is playing a beautiful defensive game. There! A slash off tackle that was stopped before it was started by Smith, who broke through and tossed Monler at the line of scrimmage. What's that? Who said Smith bit Monler's ear? That's a dirty lie! There's the play — Monler through the line but Smith stopped him again with a beautiful kick in the solar plexus. That's football! Clean, hard tackling! Go on, kick the California (censured) under the belt:" The Committee also found fault with one of Howard's statements that, "he hits center for four yards, but is thrown for a three yard loss, being stopped at the line of scrimmage without gain, after picking up three yards and making it a first down." Howard maintained that this was technical broadcasting in the nicest sense, which view was upheld by Smith, All-American back for Georgia, who had muscled in on the conference. The argument grew general and Smith, evidently in his cups, broke off the mike and knocked the President of the Committee in the head with it. After which, according to press reports, the free-for-all started, culminating in a riot call and the arrest of the participants. Howard and Smith made scathing attacks of the Committee through the papers and hinted that they might publish a book proving their own innocence and integrity and the vileness and depravity of their accusers."

Write soonal.

Fear Dunn.

TSS: 82475

ઉઙઙઉઙ

180. To H.P. Lovecraft, ca. October 1931.

Dear Mr. Lovecraft:

I intended to answer your very interesting letter sooner, but I've been up to my ears in work. I'm glad you found the views of some interest; if I had had more time as I passed through the countries where these were taken, I might possibly have gotten clearer pictures, since in many cases I didn't have the sun right. Thank you very much for the nice things you said about "College Socks" and thanks very much indeed for the letter to Street & Smith, which I know will help me along a great deal with the editors.

I hope Mr. Wright will reconsider and accept the Antarctic tale,[1] but if he shouldn't, I'd like very much to read the ms. Yes, I did indeed like "The Strange High House."[2] It's pure poetry of the highest order, and like all great poetry, stirs dim emotions and slumbering instincts deep in the wells of consciousness. I like the illustration, and like you, think that Doolin[3] is a splendid addition to *Weird Tales*. By the way, I wonder what ever became of Rankin?[4]

Speaking of Bohemians, what are they, anyhow? I know of course that they are Slavic in language and lineage, but what I'd like to know, is where they came from, and how they got there? Were the Czechs a Slavic tribe drifting off the main Slav stem who wandered into Bohemia following the westward drift of the Teutons, or were they the Dacians etc., of Roman times — did they follow the Germans across the Danube or were they already there when the Goths started westward? Was Bohemia originally a province of Germany or did the Prussians wrest it from some more Slavic kingdom? And didn't Bohemia form a part of the Ottoman empire for some time following the conquests of Suleyman the Magnificent, or did it? My ideas about the history of Eastern Europe are vague in the extreme.

Yes, the region between the Trinity and the Brazos saw many a red drama enacted. I remember an old woman, a Mrs. Crawford, whom I knew as a child, and who was one of the old settlers of the country. A gaunt, somber figure she was behind whose immobile countenance dreamed red memories. I remember the story she used to tell of the fate of her first husband, a Mr. Brown, in the year 1872.

One evening some of the stock failed to come up and Mr. Brown decided to go and look for them. The Browns lived in a big two-storied ranch-house, several miles from the nearest settlement — Black Springs. So Brown left the ranch-house, hearing the tinkling of a horse-bell somewhere off among the mesquite. It was a chill dreary day, grey clouds deepening slowly toward the veiled sunset. Mrs. Brown stood on the porch of the ranch-house and watched her husband striding off among the mesquites, while beyond him the bell tinkled incessantly. She was a strange woman who saw visions, and claimed the gift of second-sight. Smitten with premonition, but held by the fatalism of the pioneers, she saw Brown disappear among the mesquites. The tinkling bell seemed slowly to recede until the tiny sound died out entirely. Brown did not reappear, and the clouds hung like a grey shroud, a cold wind shook the bare limbs and shuddered among the dead grasses, and she knew he would never return. She went into the house, and with her servants — a negro woman and boy — she barred the doors and shuttered the windows. She put buckets of water where they would be handy in case of fire, she armed the terrified blacks, and led them into the second story of the ranch-house, there to make their last stand. She herself went out upon the balcony of the second story and waited silently. And soon again she heard the tinkle of a horse-bell; and with it many bells. Cow-bells jangled a devil's tune as the mesquite bent and swayed and the riders swept in view — naked, painted men, riding hard, with cow-horns on their heads and cow-tails swinging grotesquely from their girdles. They drove with them a swarm of horses, some of which Mrs. Brown recognized as her own property, and at their saddle-bows swung fresh crimson scalps — one of these had a grim familiarity and she shuddered, but stood unmoving, starkly impassive. Inside the house the blacks were groveling and whimpering with terror. The Comanches swept around the house, racing at full speed. They loosed their arrows at the statue-like figure on the upper balcony and one of the shafts tore a lock of hair from her head. She did not move, did not shift the long rifle she held across her arm. She knew that unless maddened by the death or wounding of one of their number, they would not attack the house. That one arrow flight had been in barbaric defiance or contempt. They were riding hard, spurred on by the thought of avengers hot on their trail, light-eyed fighters, as ferocious as themselves. They were after horses — the Comanche's everlasting need — they had lured the rancher to his doom with a tinkling horse-bell. They would not waste time and blood storming the ranch-house. They did not care to come to grips with that silent impassive figure who stood so statue-like on the upper balcony, terrible with potentialities of ferocity, and ready to spring and die like a wounded tigress among the embers of her home. Aye, they would have paid high for that scalp — there would have been no futile screams of terror, no vain pleas for mercy where no mercy ever existed, no gleeful slitting of a helpless soft throat; there would have been the billowing of rifle-smoke, the whine of flying lead, the emptying of saddles, riderless horses racing through the mesquite and red forms lying crumpled. Aye, and the drinking of knives, the crunching of axes, and hot blood hissing in the flames, before they ripped the scalp from that frontier woman's head.

Silent she stood and saw them round up all the horses on the ranch, except one in a stable they overlooked — and ride away like a whirlwind, to vanish as they had come — as the Comanches always rode. They came like a sudden wind of destruction, they struck, they passed on like the wind, leaving desolation behind them. Taking the one horse that remained to her, she went into the mesquites and some half a mile from the house she found her husband. He lay among the dead grasses, with a dozen arrows still protruding from him, his scalped head in a great pool of congealed blood. With the aid of the blacks who had followed her, wailing a wordless dirge of death, she lifted the corpse across the horse and carried it to the ranch-house. Then she put the black boy on the horse and sent him flying toward Black Springs, whence he soon returned with a strong force of settlers. they saw the dead man and the tracks of the marauders; the wind blew cold and night had come down over the hills, and they feared for their own families. Mrs. Brown bade them go to their respective homes and leave her as a guard in case of the return of the slayers, only Captain McAdams, with whom, she said, she would feel as safe as with an army. So this was done, but the Comanches did not return. They swept in a wide half circle like a prairie fire, driving all the horses they found before them, and outracing the avengers, crossed Red River and gained their reservations and the protection of a benevolent Federal government.

Mrs. Brown was Mrs. Crawford when I knew her. A strange woman, and one whom the countryside looked on as a "medium"; a seer of visions and a communer with the dead. After she married Crawford, he went forth one day to look for his horses, just as her former husband had. Again it was a cold drear day, gloomed with grey clouds. Crawford rode away awhile before sundown and she heard his horse's hoofs dwindle away on the hard barren ground. The sun sank and the air grew cold and brittle. On the wings of a howling blue blizzard night shut down and Crawford did not come. Mrs. Crawford retired after awhile, and as she lay in the darkness, with the wild wind screaming outside, suddenly a strange feeling came over her which she recognized as the forerunner of a vision. The room filled suddenly with a weird blue light, the walls melted away, distance lost its meaning and she was looking through the hills, the long stretches of mesquite, the swirling blue distances and the night, upon the open reaches of prairie. Over the prairie blew an unearthly wind, and out of the wind came a luminous cloud and out of the cloud a horseman, riding hard. She recognized her husband, face set grimly, rifle in his grasp, and on him a blue army coat such as she had never seen before. He rode in utter silence; she did not hear the thunder of his ride, but beneath his horse's hoofs that spurned the hard earth, the dead prairie grass bent and the flints spat fire. Whether he rode alone she could not tell, for the luminous cloud closed in before and behind and he rode in the heart of the cloud. Then as a mist fades the vision faded and she was alone in the dark room with the wind screaming about the house and the wolves howling along the gale. Three days later Crawford came home, riding slowly on a weary horse. The blizzard had blown itself out; the cold sunlight warmed the shivering prairies and Crawford wore no coat, as when he had ridden away. He had not found his horses, but he had found the tracks of the raiders who had taken them, and while examining them, a band of settlers had swept past on the trail, shouting for him to follow. And he had followed and in the teeth of the freezing blizzard they had harried the marauders to the very banks of Red River, emptying more than one saddle in that long running fight. She asked about the coat, the blue army coat she had seen in the vision, and he replied with surprize that he had stopped at a settler's house long enough to borrow the coat, and had returned it as he rode back by, returning from the chase.

Many a time, as a child have I listened to her telling strange tales of old times when white men and red men locked in a last struggle for supremacy. I wandered around her old ranch-house in awe. It was not the memories of Indian forays that made me shiver — it was the strange tales the country folk told — of doors in the old ranch-house that opened and closed without human agency, of an old chair rocking to and fro in the night in an empty room. In this chair Crawford had spent his last days. Men swore that the chair rocked at night, as he had rocked, and his old spittoon clinked regularly, as it had clinked in his lifetime when he rocked, chewing tobacco, and from time to time spat. Mrs. Crawford was a true pioneer woman. No higher tribute could be paid her. I liked and admired her, as I admire her memory. But to me as a child, she was endowed with a certain awesomeness, not only as far as I was concerned, but to the country-folk in general.

Any touch of supernatural always effected me as a child. But my ghosts — which I did not believe in, but which caused me goose-flesh in the dark — were always white ghosts or black ghosts. I never even considered a red ghost. I never thought of being haunted by Indians, even though I knew at times I might be walking over ground which held hidden the moldering bones of great chiefs and mighty warriors. I examined and handled bones taken from an Indian mound and the only feeling they aroused in me was a desire to have a collection of Indian teeth and finger-bones for a necklace. Even when ghost tales told by an old negress sent me shuddering and shivering to bed, I could have lain down near a collection of Indian skulls and slept soundly, untroubled by ghostly or demoniac speculations. I would have feared living Indians; extinct red-skins held no terrors for me.

But the traditions of the Palo Pinto hills: there it was that Bigfoot Wallace slew his first Indian. Have you heard of Bigfoot Wallace? When you come to the Southwest you will hear much of him, and I'll show you his picture, painted full length, hanging on the south wall of the Alamo — a tall, rangy man in buckskins, with rifle and bowie, and with the features of an early American statesman or general. Direct descendent of William Wallace of Scotland, he was Virginia-born and came to Texas in 1836 to avenge his cousin and his brother, who fell at La Bahia with Fannin. He was at the Salado, he marched on the Mier Expedition and drew a white bean; he was at Monterey. He is perhaps the greatest figure in Southwestern legendry. Hundreds of tales — a regular myth-cycle — have grown up around him. But his life needs no myths to ring with breath-taking adventure and heroism. On his first adventure into the wilds he was captured in the Palo Pinto hills by the Keechies and was tied to the stake to be burned, when an old squaw rescued him and adopted him in place of a son, slain recently in a fight with another tribe. As an Indian Wallace lived for three months, hunting with them, riding with them on their forays against other tribes and against the Mexicans. Once with them he drove a raid into Mexico and in desperate hand-to-hand fighting with the Mexicans, won his name as a warrior. But he wearied of the life, and escaped to his own people again. He was scout, ranger, hunter, pioneer and soldier. When he settled on a ranch in the Medina country, he made a treaty with the Lipans that they would not steal his cattle. They kept that treaty until they decided to move westward. When they moved, they took Bigfoot's stock with them — every head of it. Bigfoot was slow to anger; he was swift in vengeance. He went to San Antonio and was given charge of a ranger company of some thirty men. With them he hunted the thieves to the head-waters of the Guadalupe River. In the ensuing battle two white men bit the dust, but forty-eight red warriors went to the Happy Hunting Grounds, and the Lipans dwindled from that day, and in a comparatively short time, were but a memory of a once-powerful tribe.

Tales, and many tales, are told of his adventures as a scout, a ranger, a soldier and a stage-driver from San Antonio to El Paso, but the tale I like best is the tale of his battle with "the big Indian", the epic combat of all the Southwest.

The rangers had trailed the Indians to the head-waters of the Llano. They went into camp, seeing at sundown the signal-smokes going up. Bigfoot was restless; that turbulent, individualist spirit of his would not let him lie down and sleep quietly with the enemy near, while other men stood guard. A few hours before dawn he slipped out of the camp and glided through the mesquite and chaparral like a ghost. Daybreak found him traversing a steep narrow canyon, which bent suddenly to the left. As he made the bend, he found himself face to face with a giant painted brave. In fact, they caromed together with such force that both were thrown to the earth by the compact. Simultaneously they bounded to their feet and for a flashing instant stood frozen, the grey eyes of the white man glaring into the flaming black eyes of the Indian. Then as if by mutual consent, each dropped his gun and they locked in mortal combat.

No white man in the Southwest could match Wallace in hand-to-hand fighting, but this red-man was quick as a cougar and strong as a bull. Not as heavy as Wallace, he was nearly as tall, and, clad only in a loin-cloth, and covered with bear's oil, he was illusive and hard to grapple as a great serpent. It was man to man, blade to blade, the terrible strength and ferocity of the giant white man matched against the cruel craft and wiry agility of the savage, with all his primitive knowledge of foul crippling holds and twists. Back and forth they reeled, close-clinched; now rolling and tumbling on the ground, tearing and gouging; now staggering upright, locked like bears. Each was trying to draw his knife, but in the frenzy of battle, no opportunity presented itself. Bigfoot felt his wind failing him. The iron arms of the brave bent his ribs inward and threatened to shut off his breath. The grimy thumbs with their long black nails gouged cruelly at his eyes, ripping the skin and bringing trickles of blood; the steely fingers sank deep in his corded throat; the bony knees drove savagely for his groin. Shaking the blood and sweat from his eyes Wallace reeled upright, dragging his foe by sheer strength. Breast jammed hard against breast, they leaned against each other, gasping wordless curses. The great veins swelled in

Wallace's temples and his mighty chest heaved; but he saw in the red mist the sweat beading thick the redskin's face, and the savage mouth gaping for breath. With one volcanic burst of superhuman effort, Wallace tripped his foe and hurled him backward, falling on him with all his great weight. The Indian's head struck crashingly against a sharp-pointed rock and for an instant his dazed body went limp. And in that instant Wallace, with a desperate lunge, snatched out his knife and sank it to the hilt in the coppery body. As a dying tiger bursts into one last explosion of terrible power, the Indian started up convulsively, with a terrible yell, throwing off the giant white man as if he had been a child. Before Wallace could recover himself the Indian's hand locked on his throat, the brave's knee crashed down on his breast, and the knife in the red hand hissed down. In that flashing instant Wallace looked death stark in the face — he thought agonizedly of his childhood home and a girl who waited him at the settlements — he saw the black eyes of the Indian "gleaming like a panther's in the dark" — the knife struck hard — but only into the earth beside Wallace and as the knife came down, the Indian fell forward with it, and lay dead on the breast of his foe. And Wallace said that a grim smile curved the warrior's lips, as if, dying, he believed he was sending the white man to blaze the ghost trail ahead of him.

Shaken with the titanic upheaval of that terrible battle, Wallace rose, gazing dazedly down at the silent form of the conquered. His knife was still sheathed in the Indian's body. The point of that knife was in the red-man's heart and the wonder of it is that the brave, after receiving that terrible wound, lived long enough to all but slay his foe as he died. Such vitality, surely, is possible only to beasts and men bred close to the red throbbing heart of the primordial.

Wallace looked down at his foe and in his heart rose the respect of one warrior for another. He did not scalp the big brave; he arranged the stiffening limbs and piled rocks above the corpse to make a cairn and protect the body from the ravages of buzzards and coyotes, and beside the brave he laid the knife, and the Indian's rifle, broken to pieces — weapons for a warrior to bear to the Happy Hunting Ground. And I think of Wallace standing alone and sombrely beside that rough cairn as the sun came up over the wild tree-clad hills.

Your comments on the possible locale of early mankind proved of great interest to me; as indeed I always find your remarks regarding history and historical theories of most vivid interest. I wonder what new discoveries the next century of research will bring forth? There is, to me, an awesome and enthralling fascination about historical research — groping in the dark dusty corridors of the past and dragging forth nameless and cryptic shapes to light. I'd like to accompany some research party or expedition some time — some where — it doesn't particularly matter where.

Concerning Saxon and Danish descent, how do historians etc., explain the difference between Saxon and Scandinavian tongues? I mean, was the Saxon language — as spoken in the days of the conquest of Britain — closer to the Nordic root-stem than the Scandinavian, or vice versa? I presume that the division between Saxon and Norse occurred before the fall of the Roman empire — or am I wrong, as usual? What made the Saxon language so much softer than the Norse? Was it a modification of the original Nordic tongue, and did this modification take place in Germany before the conquest of Britain, or in the latter country after the conquest? Or was it the Norse tongue which was modified by some cause or other? In other words, was Saxon a branch of Norse, or was Norse an off-shoot of Saxon? I suppose that the Jutes, Angles and Saxons all spoke the same tongue with different dialects, just as later the people of Norway, Sweden and Denmark spoke one language. I said that Saxon was softer than Norse; that is my own idea and may have no basis in reality, since I know nothing of either language. But Saxon seems softer to me, with its "ceorl" and "eorl" compared to the Norse "carl" and "jarl". I'd appreciate any information regarding these matters.

Yes, economics are in a mess, as you remark. Economic problems were always a hopeless jumble to me, from which my baffled mind recoils to contemplate less complex situations of past ages. Maybe that's why I like the study of history so well — I'm unable to orient myself with this complicated age and understand it.

Nature is a grim old mistress, as she has proved time and again, in Galveston and elsewhere. Storms and inundations have always sent shivers along my spine, even in the contemplation of them. Anything you can't fight is horrible. You can't shoot or cut a hurricane nor brain a flood with a bludgeon. All you can do is die like sheep — a most detestable end. I wouldn't live on the coast for that reason — although destructive wind storms are not uncommon in this country. I have noted a tendency to resent remarks concerning the possibility of future catastrophes, among the people of the Coast. Just as Californians speak of the earthquake as "the big fire" and resent comments regarding earthquakes. I remember a night I spent at Rockport, a little port not very far from Corpus Christi. I stayed in a big rambling hotel close to the water's edge, and learned that in one of the more recent hurricanes — one which did great damage in Corpus Christi — a derelict hull rammed the hotel and almost demolished one side of it. But the proprietor of the hotel waxed irritable at the suggestion that the town might fall prey to another hurricane some time, and he said that Rockport was in no more danger from the elements than any other town in the country. Not wanting to antagonize the man, I agreed with him, commenting on the peril of oceanic inundation of Denver, Colorado, and the risk of tropical storms run by the inhabitants of Butte, Montana, and Madison, South Dakota. But he seemed to suspect a hint of irony in my innocent remarks, and thereafter treated me coolly.

Doubtless you are right in saying America will probably not develop a uniform type of size, owing to the vast extent of the country, and the diversity of racial blood-strains. Doubtless Sir Arthur Keith is correct in his theory that the size average of Americans as a whole is shorter and thicker, considering the vast numbers of stocky foreigners who have poured into the country of late years. Whether Americans of British descent tend to grow shorter, I am not prepared to say, though it seems to me that modern Texans are, as a whole, shorter and stockier than their earlier ancestors, though I may be wrong. For myself, at least, that is true; I am of squat build compared to my grandfathers, both of whom were six feet two inches tall, my great-grandfather Ervin who was six feet four inches, my great-grandfather Henry who was about the same height, and my great-grandfather Howard who was six feet eight inches. Some of my great-uncles were nearly seven feet in height. None was abnormal; they were simply big men, well proportioned and powerfully built. My grandfather George Ervin was accounted the strongest man in his regiment and one of the strongest men in Forrest's command. He could cleave a man from shoulder to waist with a single stroke of his saber. He owed his life to his great strength on at least one occasion, when he was captured by a band of guerrillas — thieves who preyed on both armies. They bound him on a mule and were taking him into the thickness of the forest to do away with him, when, as they were passing through a dark thicket, he suddenly snapped the cords with which he was bound, and seizing a revolver, leaped into the thicket and invited his foes to come in and take him. But they declined and made a hasty retreat, like the dirty yellow cowards they were. These ancestors of mine were taller and rangier than I, generally; some were as heavily built as I am, but all were taller. If I ever have a son, I have a feeling he'll be shorter and stockier than I am. In fact, I look depressedly down the long vistas of descent to the time when my descendents, having grown shorter and heavier in each generation, eventually resemble toads and go hopping drearily through life, croaking praises of the lost tallness of their ancestors.

I greatly appreciate the kind things you said about my verse, and thank you very much for the information regarding various forms of poetry, and the scanned examples you gave, and which I have studied long and closely. As I said before, I never studied verse-forms; I always was fascinated by poetry, and have always intended to learn something about the mechanics of it, but somehow the time or opportunity never presented itself. I can make a stab at scanning iambics, but as I said, the rest is Grecian to me. Thanks for the tip about the poetry-books to study; I intend to follow your advice regarding them when I get the time. The main trouble with writing verse is, there is so little money in it. I never felt I could afford either money or time in studying a subject in which there was such slight monetary recompense. Some time when I have more time and money — if that time ever comes — I'll make a close study of mechanics and forms, and try to versify a little for my own amusement and satisfaction.

There is a fascination about meteors, one of which is on display among the trophies of the Perdido Battlefield. They rouse fantastic speculations as to their former state — also as to what might happen if one of them crashed through a roof instead of falling in a field or pasture.

I remember the earthquake used in "Cthulhu", that is, I remember you using it, though of course, the actual shock was not felt in the West. It must have been an eery experience. With my usual ignorance of occurrences east of the Mississippi, I didn't even know South Carolina experienced a shock in 1886. Earthquakes seem to occur in all parts of the country, without any particular choice of locality.

Yes, states' right and individuality seem doomed, just as the individual seems doomed — except, of course, the individual who is rich and powerful enough to make his own laws and ride on top of the cheat and hallucination of mass-rule. Standardization is crushing the heart and soul, the blood and the guts, out of humanity and the eventual result will be either complete and unrelieved slavery or the destruction of civilization and return to barbarism. Once men sang the praises of ephemeral gods carved out of ivory and wood. Now they sing equally senseless praises to equally ephemeral and vain gods of Science and Commerce and Progress. Hell.

I would rather have lived in the pioneering age I mentioned — but the trouble is that in whatever age I lived, I would doubtless be as slothful, timid and disinclined to strife and violent action as I am in this age. If I could change my nature to suit the epoch, I can think of several ages in which I had rather live. Your choice of 18th Century England is quite interesting, and I reckon that particular age was wholesome and sound, and agreeable to a thinker and practical philosopher. I am even more interested in your choice of a Roman environment. Don't worry about my instinctive distrust of Rome! Though somewhere in this life or one previous, I have picked up a decided personal antipathy for things Roman, I have no quarrel with anyone's preference for those things. In fact, I am highly interested in your Roman leanings, and would like to know more about your feelings for that age and empire, and your instinctive placement therein. As far as that goes, I wouldn't mind to have been a British or Gothic mercenary in the Roman army in the days of the later empire, when political graft and corruption made possible the acquisition of large fortunes quickly. I would like to have been stationed somewhere in the Orient, rather than in Germany or Britain, where there was less chance of acquiring treasure than there was of acquiring a split skull. I would like to have had control of some rich territory or city, and after a few years spent in systematic plunder, to have retired to a large villa in southern Italy, to spend the rest of my life in idleness and luxury, honored and respected by all. Roman civilization must have been paradise to such barbarian warriors as entered the ranks of her legions and acquired wealth and power. Superior in vitality and vigor to the degenerates about them, they coped successfully with the heirs of the waning empire in war and intrigue, gathering unto themselves treasures of the ages, which they had not been at trouble to create or collect, and their iron frames allowed them heights of debauchery impossible to the weaker and softer Romans.

Italians — and especially Sicilians — seem to lead all immigrants in crime, all over the country. It may not be strange, considering the heritage of bandit and piratical blood in Sicilian veins — the admixture of Grecian, Roman, Phoenician, Illyrian, Vandal, Arab, Norman, Italian — there's a good argument for the law-abiding instincts of a pure race, considering the criminality of the Sicilians compared to that of the Swedes, who are probably the most law-abiding elements America receives from Europe. Texas has a number of Italians, who mix in readily with Spanish and Mexican elements. Portuguese are less in number and seem to stay more to themselves. Poles, which you mention as numerous in New England, constitute a considerable percentage of aliens in the Southwest, though less in number than Bohemians and Germans. My main irritation at all these races, is their clannishness and their general refusal to contribute anything to the welfare of the country, beyond that which will rebound with advantage to themselves. There was trouble among the German settlements during the Civil War. Germans were about the only aliens in Texas in those days, and they didn't think they ought to have to fight in the Civil War. Well, I can understand their viewpoint. Many of them had only been in this country a few years. They owned no slaves, had no quarrel with the Federal Government, and had only a vague idea of what the war was about anyway. Just the same, they were thriving and growing fat off the country; they had the same advantages and rights as the natives, and it looks like they should have shared some of the responsibilities. At least, that's what the Texans thought and those lean bronzed frontiersmen were in the habit of backing up their opinions with Colt and Bowie. The German settlers would not go to the war, so the war was in a few cases brought to them, suddenly and violently, after the fashion of early Texans. Besides, the Irish have never been noted for their love of the Dutch, and most of the Texans were of Irish or Scotch-Irish descent. Some of the Germans hid along the rivers and some got over into old Mexico. One group of eighteen started, but the Texans got wind of their intended flight to avoid military service, and came up suddenly with them on the Guadalupe River. Those were savage and ruthless days. The fight was short and terrible. When it was over eighteen Germans lay stretched silent in their own blood and their conquerors were riding back to their own settlements. To the more civilized people of this day and time, the early history of the Southwest seems incredible violent and blood-stained. But it was the characteristic of the frontier, and in the Southwest the pioneers, reverting by necessity to the barbarism of their ancestors, merely duplicated the colonization epoch of the East, a century or so before.

There was a good deal of pro-Germanic sympathy in this part of the country during the last war, nor was it always limited to people of pure German descent. However, many Germans were as staunchly patriotic as any American, and I noticed that the most truly American were generally those who had been born in Germany and had known something of that country before they came to America. Quite a pro-German feeling existed among some of the second and third generation, who, knowing nothing about the land of their ancestry, imagined it a glamorous realm of beauty and justice and ancient culture. A local editor refused to publish a rhyme of mine during war-time for fear of offending the German element of the population — I'm glad he did because the rhyme was a work of childhood and amazingly rotten, even for a child. But it shows how strong German sentiment was in parts of Texas. There was some talk of holding a pro-German rally and raising the German flag at a picnic, but it was abandoned, partly because none of the patriots could procure a flag and partly because the Anglo-Saxon population was prepared to scatter Teutonic remnants all over the landscape by the means of shotguns and high-powered rifles.

The main thing I dislike about Mexicans is their refusal to speak English. Most of them can speak our language — at least they can, but they won't. Of course, numbers of Mexicans will answer questions to the best of their ability, but lots of them — and especially when you get south of San Antonio where they swarm — seem to think they are subtly insulting a white man by denying all knowledge of the English language. Ask one of them something and very often he'll look at you stolidly — "No sabe Englese." You know he's lying, but there's nothing you can do about it. You restrain your impulse to strangle him, and go on. The average Texan knows as little about Spanish as the average Mexican claims to know about English. I guess it's the Indian blood in them that makes them so confoundedly stolid and reticent.

I ran onto a white renegade once, though, that made me madder than any Mexican ever did. He was a white-bearded dissolute looking old scoundrel, clad in the slouch hat and boots of a cowboy, and he was apparently living in the Mexican quarter of a little South Texas town, not so very far from the Border. He refused to talk, also, or to answer a simple, civil question, and a fat Mexican woman leaned out of a window, squealing an hilarious string of Spanish, at which the brown-skinned loafers chortled and looked superior. I thought yearningly of San Jacinto, and left. It's bad enough for a greaser to retire behind a masquerade of ignorance in order to avoid answering a civil question regarding directions, etc., but when a white man sinks so low he consorts with the limpid-eyed heathen and pulls that "no savvy" business, it rouses thoughts of massacre and sudden immolation.

I'll appreciate the address of M.R. James. I'm sending you the issues of *Adventure* containing Pendexter's yarn.[5] No hurry about returning them. I'm very glad that "Pickman's Model" has been used in a British publication,[6] and will gladder when it appears in American covers. Price said in his last letter that he and Mashburn had not had an opportunity to go further into the business of getting the anthology going,[7] but that they intended to see about it eventually.

Glad your eyes are holding up well. My own optics have been giving me a good deal of trouble. I ought to wear glasses all the time, but I dread the idea. There's always so much chance of somebody smashing them in your eyes. Glasses are a distinct disadvantage in every-day life, though I'm grateful to their aid in reading and writing.

I hope you can come out to Texas some time. I'm sure you'd enjoy New Orleans and the Louisiana swamp-country, as well as the more westerly regions. There is, of course, little difference between western Louisiana and western Arkansas and the eastern-most part of Texas. After you get to Fort Worth you begin to see the real Western Southwest. I hope some day I can show you around over the state. There are numbers of places unknown and unvisited by the great mass of tourists which I believe you would find interesting.

I'm glad my sombre narrations haven't proved too boresome. Western folkways and traditions are so impregnated with savagery, suffering and strife, that even Western humor is largely grim, and, to non-Westerners, often grotesque. Of songs sung on the Western frontier, most of them, especially cowboy songs, originated in Texas, since that state was the first Anglo-American region to truly deserve the designation of "West" in the proper sense. Texas songs went up the Chisholm with the longhorn herds and spread all over the West, being changed in other states to correspond with the locality in which they were sung. Other songs — hunter's and rivermen's — came through the

Middle-West. A few originated in America, most were old British ballads changed by ignorance or intent, taken from, and added to, to suit the minstrels' notions. It's strange how old some of those songs are, and how long the old ballads lingered. For instance, "Barbara Allen" at one time sung all over the South and Southwest. Its age can be calculated when it is known that the last stanza of the original version — which stanza I have never heard sung, is as follows:

"But by and rade the Black Douglas,
"And wow, but he was rough!
"For he tore up the bonny briar
"And threw it in Saint -----'s Loch."[8]

I've forgotten the name of the Loch and so leave it blank. And then there was an old drinking song very popular in taverns a generation ago:

"Old Compass lies dead and is under the ground,
"Ho, ho! under the ground!
"A green apple-tree grew over his head,
"Ho, ho! over his head!"

The revelers had long forgotten who or what "Old Compass" was, but, in correspondence with Gordon,[9] the ardent collector and student of folk-songs, I learned that this was a distortion of an old English song of the days of the Commonwealth, and that "Old Compass" was none less than the bloody hypocrite himself, Cromwell. But this song was never popular in Texas; it flourished in the Irish communities of Arkansas.

I received your card from Plymouth and was fascinated by the view of the old house. Indeed, the very picture of the ancient building seemed to breathe the spirit of the Colonial days. And thank you very much for the generous material from Charleston. The pictures are very clear and vivid and most fascinating, and they suggest a leisurely artistic age of mellow culture and tradition, alien, strange and intriguing to me — contrasting strangely with the restless background of the Southwest. I have found Arkansas and Louisiana alien to me — I am sure I would find the deep South even more alien and fascinating.

I am most delighted to hear that Long's story and your "Erich Zann" are appearing in book-form.[10] Let me know when the book appears; for I most certainly will enrich my book-collection with a copy. What makes me more eager for it, is that I've never read "Eric Zann" and look forward to a rare literary treat.

I hope you liked the "Bal-Sagoth" yarn.[11] As for "The Black Stone" my story appearing in the current *Weird Tales*, since reading it over in print, I feel rather absurd. The story sounds as if I were trying, in my feeble and blunderingly crude way, to deliberately copy your style. Your literary influence on that particular tale, while unconscious on my part, was none the less strong. And indeed, many writers of the bizarre are showing your influence in their work, not only in *Weird Tales* but in other magazines as well; earlier evidences of an influence which will grow greater as time goes on, for it is inevitable that your work and art will influence the whole stream of American weird literature, and eventually the weird literature of the world. I do not say this in flattery but because I know it to be a truth. If you and I were stepping off the paces of a life-and-death duel, I would still say the same thing, because it is an inevitable truth.

By the way, I have been recently corresponding with Bernard A. Dwyer — a most interesting correspondent, whose letters hold a touch of true Celtic mysticism.

But I've been rambling on long enough. Hope I haven't bored you too much. And thanks again for the pictures. Best wishes.

Cordially,
[Robert E. Howard.]

P.S. I have received and read Talman's manuscript and think it splendidly done; I suppose it will appear in *Weird Tales*.

By the way, if you like a good tearing smashing game of football, you might drop around to Cambridge the 24th of this month, when the Lone Star State makes her first invasion of the East. The University of Texas plays Harvard then, and a special train carries thousands of Texas fans to the game. Eastern sports-writers underrate the power of the Texas team, champion of the Southwestern Conference, and as strong or stronger than last year, when it easily conquered S.M.U. of Dallas, the one Southwestern team recognized by national sports-writers as a whole. S.M.U. gave Notre Dame her hardest fight, swamped Indiana University and routed the Navy with ease, but fell an easy victim to the thundering attack of the Longhorns. Last week Texas defeated the University of Missouri 31 - 0, and they're coming East with the intention of giving their best. They are big, powerful men with a line like a stone wall and a ramming, bone-crushing attack, mixed with crafty aerial tactics. I believe it will be a game you would enjoy.

R.E.H.

NOTES

1. *At the Mountains of Madness.*
2. "The Strange High House in the Mist," *Weird Tales*, October 1931.
3. Joseph Doolin.
4. Hugh Rankin.
5. "Devil's Brew," *Adventure*, July 15 and August 1, 1931.
6. *By Daylight Only*, Selwyn & Blount, 1929 (*Not at Night* series).
7. See letter 173, page 196.
8. "Levin's" (see letter 043 in Volume 1).
9. Robert W. Gordon.
10. *Creeps By Night*, edited by Dashiell Hammett, The John Day Company, 1931. Frank Belknap Long's story was "A Visitor from Egypt."
11. "The Gods of Bal-Sagoth."

TSS: 50557-50566

181. To Tevis Clyde Smith, ca. October 1931.

Fear Finn:

I wrote Bradford a coarse rude letter full witt sneps witt snerls witt gneshes, and of course, the very next day I got the perms. A day earlier and I wouldn't have been guilty of such bad humor. Well, anyway, I have the verses and we can send them off any time; just let me know the details.

This morning I took out a big registered enwelope with a "War Department" letter-head. I had visions of me shouldering a Springfield already, but it was from a gentleman named Barlow,[1] at Fort Benning, Georgia, asking me for my autograph, for which purpose he enclosed a blank sheet of paper and a stamped self-addressed envelope. He also enclosed a 115 page ms. which he said Lovecraft had instructed him to forward me. It's the Antarctic story which Farnsworth rejected,[2] and which Lovecraft promised to let me read in the original. On the title page was written in pencil:

"Schedule of Circulation."
"Augustus Derletus to Donaldus Vandreius
Melmoth the Wanderer to Klarkash-ton
Klarkash-ton to B'ra-Dwi-yhah
Bernardus Diverius to Grandpa Theobold."

Which of course are August Derleth, Donald Wandrei, Clark Ashton Smith, and Bernard Dwyer: but who is Grandpa Theobold?[3]

"Let it rest with the ages mysteries,
And but recall the day
I was want to go where the cannikins clinked,
Not caring who should pay."

Cities brooding beneath the seas
Yield their chalcedon and gold;
Ruthless hands the treasures seize,
Rending the Ages' mysteries,
But who is Grandpa Theobold?

Secret of the eternal Sphinx
Is a story worn and old,
Like a tale too often told;
All the ancient unknown shrinks —
But who is Grandpa Theobold?

Fingers turn the hidden Keys,
  Looting wealth from lair and hold;
  Cast what shapes in what dim mold?
Question now the Eternities.
  But who is Grandpa Theobold?

Prince, before you snare the stars,
  Speak, before the sun grows cold
Scowling through the morning bars,
  Who is Grandpa Theobold?

Fear Dunn.

NOTES

1. Robert Hayward Barlow.
2. "At the Mountains of Madness."
3. One of Lovecraft's appellations for himself.

TSS: 82034

ଔୡଔ

182. To H.P. Lovecraft, ca. October 1931.

Dear Mr. Lovecraft:

Many thanks for the opportunity of reading your magnificent "At the Mountains of Madness". This story certainly deserves publication in book form and I hope some day to see it so published. There is not, as far as I can see, a single false or unconvincing note in the whole; the entire story has a remarkable effect of realism. And I marvel once more — as in so many times in the past — at the cosmic sweep of your imagination and the extent of your scientific and literary knowledge.

When Mr. Barlow sent me the ms. he did not mention whether it should be returned to him, or to you, so I am sending it to you, as I suppose it was intended that I should.

Cordially
[Robert E. Howard]

TSS: 20740

183. To Tevis Clyde Smith, November 1931.

Fear Finn:

Here are the blasted verses and a few stamps to help the work along. If the Christopher don't take our stuff — in event of that rare possibility, heh heh heh — we'll try some other blasted house.

I didn't get to see the game, through I wanted to come over. *Monkey Business* was a confounded disappointment. Oh, well — oh well.

I'm glad you liked the Oriental story; I take it you are referring to the Belshazzar tripe.[1] Personally, I thought it was pretty rotten in spots, particularly towards the conclusion when I had to drag in so blasted much explanation. I've had nothing in *Sport Stories* lately. You ought to make *Soldiers of Fortune*; I don't believe I'll ever make the Claytons. I'm damned if I can solve their formula. Apparently they have a secret code which escapes the casual eye — and never crops out in the stories they publish. I sold Byrne a Costigan story recently — $60 this time.[2] He's been cutting my rates steadily. By God, if he falls below that, I'll give the series to Street & Smith — and I suppose get it rejected. I thought when he hit the $75 level it was the limit.

I recently sent Farnsworth some rhymes, the first in a long time and he took a couple of them. One was one of a sonnet cycle he formerly rejected:

The Last Day.

Hinged in the brooding west a black sun hung,
And Titan shadows barred the dying world.
The blind black oceans groped — their tendrils curled,
And writhed and fell in feathered spray and clung,
Climbing the granite ladders, rung by rung,
Which held them from the tribes whose death cries skirled.
Above, unholy fires red wings unfurled —
Grey ashes floated down from where they swung.

A demon crouched, chin propped on brutish fist,
Gripping a crystal ball between his knees;
His skull-mouth gaped and icy shone his eye.
Down crashed the crystal globe — a fire-shot mist
Masked the dark lands which sank below the seas —
A painted sun hung in a starless sky.

The other was the first sexy rhyme I ever sold:

Moonlight on a Skull.

Golden goats on a hillside black,
Silken gown on a wharfside trull,
Screaming girl on a silver rack —
What are dreams in a shadowed skull?

I stood at a shrine and Chiron died,
A woman laughed from the purple roofs,
And he burned and lived and rose in his pride,
And shattered the tiles with clanging hoofs.

I opened a volume dark and rare,
I lighted a candle of mystic lore —
Bare feet throbbed on the outer stair
And book and candle fell to the floor.

Ships that reel on a windy sea,
Lovers that take the world to wife,
What may the Traitress hold for me,
Who scarce have lifted the veil of Life?

Fear Dunn.

NOTES

1. "The Blood of Belshazzar," *Oriental Stories*, Autumn 1931.
2. Probably "Night of Battle."

TSS: 30286

ଔଓଓଔ

184. To Tevis Clyde Smith, ca. November 1931.

Fear Finn:

Have you heard anything from the Christopher? I'm particular desirous of getting out a book of our rhymes as soon as possible, because war-clouds are looming thicker on the horizon, and I'd like for us to get some of our stuff between book-covers while we're still alive.

"Many fell at the grog-shop wall
Clicko the Hittite was first to fall."

Not that I intimate you will fall before I do, oh fellow Hittite. You'll probably survive to turn down an empty glass to mark the youthful passing of the fat brown Hittite known to a cool and suspicious world as R.E.H., Esquire.

Just before I left Cross Plains, work descended on me in large quantities. A novelet returned from Street & Smith,[1] requesting that I alter it — i.e., eliminate the saloon and speakeasy setting. My hero was a bouncer in a tough waterfront bar. I made him a cook in a hamburger stand. Also a lengthish yarn from Clayton,[2] requesting me to cut down the action, which they said was out of place in a tale of that nature. I acceded to both requests, practically rewriting the stories, at least once, some parts more, and wrote a Costigan yarn before I went all to pieces. I feel that my revised jobs will be turned down because I sent them off without corrections, without even reading them over for mistakes. When I finished them, I'd been working so long and so hard I wasn't in any shape to hunt for mistakes. I tried to read the stuff over, and the sentences didn't make sense to me. Oh, yes, did I mention it — the Costigan yarn was in answer to a request for more Costigan tales by the new managing editor of *Fight Stories*, one W.M. Kofoed.

This morning I got — forwarded by Pink[3] — a letter from Farnsworth, accepting my Tamerlane yarn — $140 — but requesting a more interesting title than "The Lame Man."[4] I don't believe the readers will like it. There isn't a gleam of hope in it. It's the fiercest and most sombre thing I ever tried to write. A lot of milksops — maybe — will say it's too savage to be realistic, but to my mind, it's about the most realistic thing I ever attempted. But it's the sort of thing I like to write — no plot construction, no hero or heroine, no climax in the accepted sense of the word, all the characters complete scoundrels, and every-body double-crossing everybody else.

The other night I started eliminating the Yellow Peril with a butcher knife and in the conflict bounded out of bed and on account of the cord on my foot,[5] did a neat nose-dive onto the floor which skinned my face somewhat. I'll remember that if I ever get the drop on a Japanese.

And so, oh fellow deluded Hittite; write me.

Fear Dunn the Hittite.

NOTES

1. "Fighting Nerves."
2. "The People of the Dark."
3. Lindsey Tyson.
4. Title changed to "Lord of Samarcand."
5. Howard had for some years been in the habit of tying a cord from his foot to the bedpost, as a check against his tendency to sleepwalking.

TSS: 82054

ঌ

185. To H.P. Lovecraft, December 9, 1931.

Dear Mr. Lovecraft:

I would have answered your letter long ago, but the fact is, I spent some time in East Texas, and am just now catching up with my correspondence. Thank you very much for the cards, etc., some of which were forwarded to me in East Texas. I found the views, as always, most fascinating, especially the beautiful old New England doorways, and the streets of Portsmouth. More and more I am realizing what a domain of tranquil beauty the ancient landscapes and towns of New England must be.

I'm glad the publishers appreciated your work on the book you spoke of, and that you are to have their business in the future.

Too bad Rankin had to be let go. As you say, he put more weirdness in his illustrations than any of the *Weird Tales* artists. Too bad the liquor threw him. It's a hard horse to ride. I know. I like Doolin; especially his ability to depict the muscular development of his subjects — a department of the game at which Senf[1] is deplorably weak.

Thanks very much for the information regarding the Bohemians, which proved quite an education for me. They seem to have been a liberty loving and independent-minded race, which probably accounts for their superiority over other Eastern European races. As you remark, they must be greatly mixed — their types, I have noted, run from pure blonds of Nordic aspect to swarthy brunets with distinctly Turanian features — despite their resistance of Turkish conquest there must have been considerable mixing of bloods along the borders; or perhaps some Turkish blood got into the main stream through Serbian channels. Most of the Bohemians I have noticed seemed to have round or mesocephalic heads, but a few were long-headed. I cannot say I like them as a race, though I am not particularly prejudiced against them, any more than I am against any alien swarm. The coach of the Cross Plains high school football team[2] is a Bohemian, and Bohemian names appear more and more in various sections all over the state.

Yes, Bigfoot Wallace was really a gigantic figure in the old days of the Southwest, when individual prowess and courage meant so much in the development of the frontier. Wallace was well qualified to rank with the more widely known Indian fighters, such as Wetzel, Kenton, Boone, Kit Carson, and Buffalo Bill — if you might call the last an Indian fighter, one of the most over-rated and over-advertised figures west of the Mississippi. If there ever was a greater Indian fighter than Wallace it was Wetzel, and the only reason for that is that Wetzel was a monomaniac and lived only to take Indian scalps. By the way, I once was acquainted with a descendant of that grim warrior, and no more striking example of the change a few generations make in a line could be imagined. This Wetzel was a harmless giant, good-natured and rather simple-minded, no more like his ferocious ancestor than an ox is like a tiger. Yet the poor devil came to a violent end, when he was shot down by an enemy on the streets of Brownwood a few years ago.

I was much interested in your comments on the Danes and Saxons, and would like your aid in untangling a question about which I have always been vague. Just what is the exact difference between the High Germans and the Low Germans? Were the Goths, Franks, Vandals, etc., High Germans, or had the separation between High and Low occurred at the time these tribes began their wanderings? I agree with you heartily that there is a distinct Mongol strain in the Scandinavians, else whence these round heads, which have caused the Swedes etc., to be referred to generally as "square-heads"? In fact, most of the Swedes that I ever saw were brachycephalic, though it was generally in the case of peasant immigrants.

Whitehead's information about the negroid strain in the modern Danes struck me as rather ludicrous. That's a mating of Poles with a vengeance! The Scandinavian and the nigger, the extremes of development! Well, it's glad I am that my Danish great-greatgrandfather was so fair-skinned, blue-eyed, and red-haired-and-bearded that no one could mistake him for a Virgin Islander!

Economics is a study I loathe and about which I am completely ignorant. I cannot help but feel that there is an artificial something in a world so completely dominated by present principles, a rotten trunk in the mushroom growth, that will some time bring the whole bloated structure crashing down, or explode it like a bubble.

Your remarks regarding the sizes of Talman, Wandrei, etc., remind me of a question I've been intending to ask for some time, regarding Wandrei, whose poems I have often read with great appreciation in *Weird Tales*. Of what nationality is he, and does he devote all his time to literature, or if not what sort of business is he in? I realize that none of these matters is any of my business, but his verses have created an interest in him, and they seem to indicate a close study of literary forms and styles.

I appreciate very much indeed, the kind comments you made regarding my efforts at verse. I am determined to some day make a study of the art of poetry, so as to try to hammer the kinks out of my meter, rhythm, etc.. Though when I'll have the time and money, I can't say. By the way, I recently took the liberty of using your mythical "Arkham" in a single-stanza rhyme which Mr. Wright accepted for *Weird Tales*, and which fell far short of doing justice to its subject. Here it is:

Arkham.

Drowsy and dull with age the houses blink
    On aimless streets the rat-gnawed years forget —
But what inhuman figures leer and slink
    Down the old alleys when the moon has set?

Your instinctive placement with the Rome of antiquity is, as I've remarked before, most interesting, and I found your narration regarding this fascinating beyond measure. Some senses of connection with past ages seem so unerring, so strong and so instinctive that I sometimes wonder if there is a bit of truth in the theory of reincarnation. It is difficult, I admit, to conceive of any sort of an after-life, yet the light of human knowledge casts its gleams such a short distance, the abysses of the unknown are so vast, that it might be that there are grains of truth in even such a fantastic belief as reincarnation. And if so, perhaps dim shadows of memory might accompany the ego upon its travels down the centuries.

Perhaps you were an armored Roman centurion and I was a skin-clad Goth in the long ago, and perhaps we split each others' skulls on some dim battlefield!

Roman Britain! There is a magic charm to the phrase — the very repeating of which brings up in my mind vague images, tantalizing, alluring and beautiful — white roads, marble palaces amid leafy groves, armor gleaming among the great trees, blue meres set in the tranquil slumber of waving forests, strange-eyed women whose rippling golden hair falls to their waists, the everlasting quiet of green hills in the summer sun, standards gleaming with gold — though it is always as an alien that I visualize these things. It is as a skin-clad barbarian that I stride the white roads, loiter in the shade of the green whispering groves, listen to the far elfin echo of the distant trumpet call, and gaze, half in awe and half in desire, at the white-armed women whose feet have never known the rasp of the heather, whose soft hands have never known the labor of fire-making and the cooking of meat over the open flame. I am of Britain, but it is the Britain of the Pict and the Gael.

I sympathize with New England's Italian problem. So far, the wops haven't come into Texas in such large numbers as to constitute much of a problem, though with the departure of thousands of Mexicans, who are swarming back into Old Mexico, I wouldn't be surprized to see their place taken by Italians. Already in some parts of the state there seems to be a movement on to bring in hordes of Latins and Slavs from the Eastern cities.

Glad you liked the Pendexter story. When I was reading it, I had an idea that he'd reveal the haunting horror to be a reptile of some sort, and wished that you were writing it, for I knew you'd make the climax fit the atmosphere in a much more shuddersome and imaginative manner.

Glad you found my recent efforts in *Weird Tales* of some interest. I've been trying to make the new Clayton magazine but don't seem to have much luck in that direction.

As for the Texas-Harvard game — the next time I start bragging on a football team, do me the favor of knocking me in the head with the barrel of your pistol. Of all the ignominious, utterly disgusting upsets, that took the cake.[3] I hope the next time this state sends a team East, it'll send one of the strongest — not one of the weakest. But I wasn't the only one fooled; most of the sports-writers in the Southwest predicted a banner-season for Texas University, and proclaimed the power of its team far and wide. Yet it failed to make good in almost every instance. Shortly before the team came to Cambridge, it barely nosed out Oklahoma, and was defeated by Rice Institute, one of the weakest teams in the Conference.[4] So after all, the defeat by Harvard was not such a great surprize as it might have been, though the large score certainly was. I am not seeking to take any of the glory from the Harvard players. They were a great team, they played magnificent football, they deserved to win. Yet it was not the strongest team in the Southwest they were pitted against, though it might be that had they been, the result would have been the same. After the Harvard game Texas University was defeated by S.M.U., and by Texas A & M.[5]

I'm not a fanatic on sports, I hope, but I'll admit, I get a good deal of enjoyment out of certain kinds. Boxing is my favorite, next to it football, and wrestling, when it's on the level. I enjoy games that are mostly contests of brawn and endurance, with a certain amount of personal conflict a definite element, as in boxing, wrestling, and to a somewhat lesser extent, football. I never had the opportunity to play football — when I was a kid it wasn't played in the country — but my favorite games were always of the rougher sort. I remember once I tried out for basketball, and quit in disgust during the first practice because I was repeatedly reproved for roughness. I kept instinctively tackling the ball-carrier, after the manner of a football player, though I'd never seen a game of football in my life. Such games as basketball, tennis, golf, and the like interest me not at all. I like to watch a good game of baseball or polo, but no game can interest me much unless there is plenty of violent action in it, the hurtling of man-power against man-power, muscular force pitted against muscular force. I like to watch a powerful, fiercely-driving, bone-crushing football team in action, plunging the line. There's a player on the team of a small college in Brownwood whose play is replete with real drama — a big Indian,[6] whom it would warm your heart to see the way he rams the opposing linesmen in the belly with his head. But I didn't intend to ramble on this way.

Best wishes.

Cordially,

[Robert E. Howard]

P.S. I'm enclosing an amusing clipping, narrating a characteristic incident in the robust days of Fort Worth, twenty years ago.

NOTES

1. Curtis C Senf.
2. W.E. "Pancho" Vilha.
3. Harvard defeated Texas 35-7.
4. Texas defeated Oklahoma 3-0 and lost to Rice, 7-0.
5. The Longhorns lost to SMU 9-7 and to Texas A&M 7-6.
6. Howard Payne College's fullback was Hoot Masur.

TSS: 63987-63989

186. To unknown recipient, ca. 1931.[1]

R.E.H. as mythical Dane Dream character Hrobjart Havard's sen:

NOTES

1. This is a drawing of a Dane, with comment underneath, believed by some to have been sent to Harold Preece, based on a name under the drawing that also appears in a Preece letter

ଓ୫୦୫ଓ୫୦

187. To Tevis Clyde Smith, ca. After mid-1931.[1]

Fear Finn:

I'm damned if I can think of anything intelligent or amusing to say.

My empty skull is full of dust,
I have no beer to drink;
I would the Queen her rump would bust
Upon a skating rink.

As I was going down the street
I met with Rabelay;
Said he, "I have no dung to eat
"Upon my wedding day."

"Be of good cheer, my boy," said I,
And smote him in the back.
"On yonder horizon I spy
"An oscillating jack."

With loud acclaim he praised my name
With fame that should endure;
I left him singing like a child,
While fishing in the sewer.

And down the street, by merest chance,
I met de Maupason;
Quoth I, "My friend, where are your pants?
"You have not got them on."

He smiled a Mona Lisa smile.
"Sacre by damn!" said he.
"The lousy wop is full of guile,
"And likewise the Chinee."

"But now," his eyes with ardor shined,
His shirt waved like a sail.
"I go in woodland lanes to find
"Material for a tale."

"Material for a — what?" I said.
He briskly marched away.
The bawdy lamps were glowing red;
I heard a street-band play.

And hand in hand, the stars they ran,
The seas were full of beer;
And down the street an aged man
Came spinning on his ear.

Around, around, around he spun,
And never a word he spake,
With awful leers he ate a ton
of fish and ginger cake.

His foot was on a hell-cat's tail,
Her back a Gothic arch;
The stars came down like blazing hail,
And sang the Wedding March.

With evil grin he wagged his shin,
And round and round he whirled;
His hair was combed by all the winds
That roam around the world.

A figure whipped along the street,
Like a sparrow in the rain;
Such boots were his as case their feet
Who tramp the Spanish Main.

He strode to sound of magic lutes,
Oh, red the wine he drank!
Kit Marlowe in his Spanish boots
With rapier at flank.

I began this letter — if such it could be called — days ago. I don't know when I've been more barren of ideas. I could usually write a letter, at least. Maybe it's because I've been so frothing mad at the editors and that graft of a Fiction Guild, I haven't had much room for intelligent ideas. Anyway, there it stands.

Fear Dunn.

NOTES

1. Letter moved to here due to approximate date. JB

TSS: 82477-82478

1932

188. To Tevis Clyde Smith, ca. early January 1932.

Dear Clyde:

I only learned of your uncle's death today.[1] I just want you to know that I sympathize deeply with you and your family. There isn't much anyone can say on such an occasion, and I was always awkward at trying to express myself, but you know how I feel about it.

[Bob]

NOTES

1. James Roberts Stone died December 29, 1931.

TSS: 82064

❧❧❧❧

189. To H.P. Lovecraft, ca. January 1932.

Dear Mr. Lovecraft:

Yes, I enjoyed the postcards very much. As you point out, the case of New England's settling was certainly unique among the colonies, inasmuch as it was a wholesale transplanting of English life into the New World — though sure I'd never realized it until you pointed it out. I've learned a great deal more from your letters about the Atlantic sea-board than I've ever learned from histories and the like. And from my correspondence with Talman I'm getting a lot of interesting lights on the early Dutch occupation of New York — or Niew Amsterdam, if that's the way it's spelled.

Thanks very much for the generous amount of information regarding High and Low German, which seemed to cover the subject in a very clear and concise manner. I especially liked the chart which I have studied with great interest. I reckon it's difficult to trace a modern word or term to its exact source, especially when that source is non-Latin. For instance it's long been my whim to discover the original form of my first name. Dictionaries give it as a High German name, arguing an eastern European origin; yet it appeared in Saxon England as "Redbrint" and among the Scandinavians as "Hrobjart". The Normans, among whom it was a favorite name, having adorned some of the most infamous scoundrels in history, seem to have introduced it into the British Isles in its present form. Do you have any idea as to what the confounded cognomen was originally?

I've noticed the American term you mention in regard to "Pennsylvania Dutch". This race has swarmed into Texas in large numbers, following the oil fields, and most of them are easily recognized by their large noses and dark, almost — and sometimes — swarthy skins. Was that their original complexion, or have they mixed with some Latin or Slavic invader since coming to America?

The color-condition in the West Indies was news to me, but I do not think it would cause me any particular annoyance, in case I should ever be so fortunate as to visit these islands. Manners and mode of conduct depend, of course, on custom, habit, etc., and I hardly think I'd feel any embarrassment at social contact with such persons as you mentioned — the cultured aristocratic ones, of course. Though if any should seek to pay court to a sister or daughter, I'm afraid I'd resort to primitive Nordic tactics, regardless of the suitor's quarterings. Somehow that reminds me of the breeding of negro girls for concubines which was once practiced in New Orleans and doubtless elsewhere, though possibly never on a very extensive scale. Their owners had an eye to posterity and mated them with as much care as they might have given to the breeding of their race horses. The girls were raised with only one idea in view — the pleasure of their masters — and were often well educated and refined. After a few generations such girls, the vestige of negroid blood in their veins scarcely discernable, carefully raised, well taught in the arts of love, knowing no will save that of their masters, made mistresses and slaves not excelled by any Eastern seraglio. They brought fancy prices, and they were worth it.

Thanks very much for the opportunity of seeing Wandrei's picture — which I'm returning. He seems to be enviably tall, and certainly has a fine head. I have often admired the depth of his imagination, both in his prose and his verse. I had no ideas he was as young as he is.

I hope some steps will be taken in America before the whole damned structure falls to pieces. But I have no faith in the leaders of the country. The United States might pull out of this depression, but right now the country is faced with a war for which it's not prepared. Some time ago I predicted that Japan would ignore the protests of the League of Nations; that having secured Manchuria she would move on China proper; that American businesses in Manchuria would put up a howl and the American government would become embroiled; and that the European nations would back out, leaving America holding the sack. A great deal of this has already happened.

I realize that possession of Manchuria is vital to Japan, with her ever-expanding population. She can not let go her grasp. On the other hand, even if this situation is smoothed over without war, we will be forced to fight her sooner or later. With room and resources by which to expand — all of which Manchuria furnishes — in thirty years Japan will be the most powerful nation in the world. And development and power mean conquest to any Oriental nation. It's my belief that Japan will sooner or later clash with Russia, who can hardly allow an Oriental empire to grow up beside her — but it would not surprize me, for the present, to see Russia and Japan allied against America — which will play hell getting any help from any European nation.

I love peace, yet I wouldn't mind a war right now such a hell of a lot, if the country was prepared; but it isn't. Japan knows it; that's why she thinks she can kick the flag around, beat up American officials, and get away with it. I wish to the devil the country was prepared. I wish warfare was on its older, simpler base. Though I'm far from war-like, yet I've always felt that with the proper training, I could learn to be fairly annoying to the enemy with a bayonet or rifle butt, but this new-fangled chemical warfare would make me a total loss. What's the glory in pushing a button and slaughtering men fifty miles away, or flying over a city and spraying the noncombatants with liquid hell? When they traded the warhorse for a submarine, they ruined the blasted business as far as I'm concerned. That's what science has done for the world. Ruled by scientists on one hand and big business on the other, the average man has about as much chance as a beetle in a chicken-yard. Admitting that scientists have made the world a much easier place to live in, what's the use, if they're preparing to blot all life from it by their hellish inventions?

But that's none of my business. Fellows like me are not the ones interested — not the ones who plan and direct the wars; only the ones who get slaughtered. Well, whatever the cause of war, once it's started, the only thing to do is to fight like hell, and if the country was prepared, I wouldn't kick. I'm not saying, keep out of wars; I'm only saying, always be ready in case of war.

Referring again to your sense of placement with Rome — which is a subject so interesting to me I can hardly keep off it — your explanation is logical and without doubt correct. My sense of placement among the various western barbarians can doubtless be explained as logically. But there is one hobby of mine which puzzles me to this day. I am not attempting to lend it any esoteric or mysterious significance, but the fact remains that I can neither explain nor understand it. That is my interest in the people which, for the sake of brevity, I have always designated as Picts. I am of course aware that my use of the term might be questioned. The people who are known in history as Picts, are named variously as Celts, aborigines and even Germans. Some authorities maintain they came into Britain after the Britons, and just before the coming of the Gaels. The "wild Picts of Galloway" which figure largely in early Scottish history and legendry, were doubtless of a very mixed race — probably predominantly Celtic, both Cymric and Gaelic, and speaking a sort of bastard Cymric, adulterated with elements of Gaelic and aborigine, of which latter strain there must have been quite a percentage in the blood of the Picts. There might have been considerable Germanic or Scandinavian mixture, as well. Probably the term "Pict" was properly applied only to the wandering Celtic tribe which settled in Galloway and presumably conquered and was absorbed by the aboriginal population. But to me "Pict" must always refer to the small dark Mediterranean aborigines of Britain. This is not strange, since when I first read of these aborigines, they were referred to as Picts. But what is strange, is my unflagging interest in them. I read of them first in Scottish histories — merely bare mentionings, usually in disapproval. Understand, my historical readings in my childhood were scattered and sketchy, owing to the fact that I lived in the country where such books were scarce. I was an enthusiast of Scottish history, such as I could obtain, feeling a kinship with the kilted clansmen because of the Scottish strain in my own blood. In the brief and condensed histories I read, the Picts were given only bare mention, as when they clashed with, and were defeated by, the Scotch. Or in English history, as the cause of the Britons inviting in the Saxons. The fullest description of this race that I read at that time, was a brief remark by an English historian that the Picts were brutish savages, living in mud huts. The only hint I obtained about them from a legendary point of view, was in a description of Rob Roy, which, mentioning the abnormal length of his arms, compared him in this respect to the Picts, commenting briefly upon their stocky and ape-like appearance. You can see that everything I read at that time, was not calculated to inspire an admiration for the race.

Then when I was about twelve I spent a short time in New Orleans and found in a Canal Street library, a book detailing the pageant of British history, from prehistoric times up to — I believe — the Norman conquest. It was written for school-boys and told in an interesting and romantic style, probably with many historical inaccuracies. But there I first learned of the small dark people which first settled Britain, and they were referred to as Picts. I had always felt a strange interest in the term and the people, and now I felt a driving absorption regarding them. The writer painted the aborigines in no more admirable light than had other historians whose works I had read. His Picts were made to be sly, furtive, unwarlike, and altogether inferior to the races which followed — which was doubtless true. And yet I felt a strong sympathy for this people, and then and there adopted them as a medium of connection with ancient times. I made them a strong, warlike race of barbarians, gave them an honorable history of past glories, and created for them a great king — one Bran Mak Morn. I must admit my imagination was rather weak when it came to naming this character, who seemed to leap full grown into my mind. Many kings in the Pictish chronicles have Gaelic names, yet in order to be consistent with my fictionized version of the Pictish race, their great king should have a name more in keeping with their non-Aryan antiquity. But I named him Bran, for another favorite historical character of mine — the Gaul Brennus, who sacked Rome. The Mak Morn comes from the famous Irish hero, Gol Mac Morn. I changed the spelling of the Mac, to give it a non-Gaelic appearance, since the Gaelic alphabet contains no "k", "c" being always given the "k" sound. So while Bran Mac Morn is Gaelic for "The Raven, Son of Morn", Bran Mak Morn has no Gaelic significance, but has a meaning of its own, purely Pictish and ancient, with roots in the dim mazes of antiquity; the similarity in sound to the Gaelic term is simply a coincidence!

But what I intended to say was, I am not yet able to understand my preference for these so-called Picts. Bran Mak Morn has not changed in the years; he is exactly as he leaped full-grown into my mind — a pantherish man of medium height, with inscrutable black eyes, black hair and dark skin. This was not my own type; I was blond and rather above medium size than below. Most of my friends were of the same mold. Pronounced brunet types such as this were mainly represented by Mexicans and Indians, whom I disliked. Yet, in reading of the Picts, I mentally took their side against the invading Celts and Teutons, whom I knew to be my type and indeed, my ancestors. My interest, especially in my early boyhood, in these strange Neolithic people was so keen, that I was not content with my Nordic appearance, and had I grown into the sort of man, which in childhood I wished to become, I would have been short, stocky, with thick, gnarled limbs, beady black eyes, a low retreating forehead, heavy jaw, and straight, coarse black hair — my conception of a typical Pict. I cannot trace this whim to an admiration for some person of that type — it was a growth from my interest in the Mediterranean race which first settled Britain. Books dealing on Scottish history were easier for me to obtain than those dealing with Irish history, so in my childhood I knew infinitely more about Scottish history and legendry than Irish. I had a distinct Scottish patriotism, and liked nothing better than reading about the Scotch and English wars. I enacted these wars in my games and galloped full tilt through the mesquite on a bare-backed racing mare, hewing right and left with a Mexican machete and slicing off cactus pears which I pretended were the heads of English knights. But in reading of clashes between the Scotch and the Picts, I always felt my sympathies shift strangely. But enough of this; it isn't my intention to bore you.

I'm afraid the moving out of the Mexicans will bring in a good many Slavic and Latin emigrants — or immigrants, I can never remember which way to spell the infernal word. I'd rather have the Mexicans. They kept their place and offered very little social problem. The high-class Mexicans, mostly Spanish in blood, are generally accepted socially, though much less in Texas than in New Mexico, Arizona and California. The lower class keep to their place, mainly. But a European peasant, after learning the English language and picking up a little Americanization, sees no reason why he shouldn't immediately be given the president's daughter for wife, and a job running the government. Least ways, that's the way it appears to me.

Of course, most of the immigrants I've known have been Germans. And a more excitable, easily-unbalanced race I never heard of, unless it's the Swedes. I've heard a lot about Germanic stolidity — well, maybe these Texas Swedes and Germans are different from most. But these can go crazier quicker over less than any Celtic or Latin race I ever heard of. The Swedes are always bumping themselves off. During the war there was an old German who lived not far from this town — a fine old man, too, by the way — who, in spite of long residence in America, had failed to take out naturalization papers. Well, to show his patriotism, which was the real article, alright, he applied for citizenship, and worried for fear lest his American neighbors might despise him as an alien. Assurances to the contrary failed to reassure him, and some slight hitch came in the getting of his citizenship; it didn't amount to anything, but he blew his brains out with a Winchester. Then, not long ago, a woman in the western part of the state killed her three children and wounded herself, because she said the children were taking up American ways. But she was a Russian. And then again, in one of the foreign communities which are slowly increasing in the western part of the state, as elsewhere, a Swede was alone in his shack and it caught on fire. He ran to put out the fire and his foot broke through the floor and got caught. Well, with typical coolness, he at once set to work cutting off his leg at the knee! The fire went out before it reached him, but he died from loss of blood, having cut his leg about half-way off with his pocket-knife, before he was found. When a German gets something on his mind, he broods and broods until it assumes such monstrous proportions he goes clean crazy.

And why is it, when the English and Germans are supposed to be of practically the same race, why is it that English literature reflects, in the main, such a sturdy optimism, and an opinion that all is well in spite of hell, while German literature seems so gloomy, melancholy and assured of the futility of human vanity? Which was the original Nordic instinct? And another thing; I do not question the stubborn courage of the German people, but in this country at least, Germans are more peaceable than people of English descent, generally less ready to fight at the drop of the hat. Whence this more belligerent nature of the Anglo-Saxons?

I'm a lot like you in regard to card games and the like. Maybe if I had more luck, I'd feel differently, but I doubt it. It makes me as nervous as hell to sit still for hours at a time and shuffle and deal bits of cardboard, and I've neither the skill nor the luck to make any money at it. I haven't the analytical mind it takes to be a good card-player. I used to play seven-up a lot, and occasionally enjoy a game now, but as for bridge, poker and the like — I work too hard for my dough to throw it away. I played fan-tan half the night once and didn't win a penny. And even if I had luck and sense enough to win, I'm no gambler. I don't like to risk money I worked hard to get. I was never a very welcome guest in the gambling houses of Mexico, for I was merely a looker-on. Well, the sharks aren't all in Mexico; I remember one night in Texas, when I foolishly allowed myself to be gotten soused in one of these innocent, "friendly drinking bouts" and when I was so biffed I couldn't tell a trey from a king, the serpentine suggestion was made for a gentlemanly game of draw poker. My reply was a mocking and bibulous laugh; I'd have to be drunker than that to forget the thin strain of Scotch blood in my veins.

But physical sports, especially the strenuous kinds, have a definite interest for me. Despite the tinsel and show, the artificial adjuncts, and the sometimes disgusting advertisement, ballyhoo and exploitation attendant upon such sports as boxing and football, there is, in the actual contests, something vital and real and deep-rooted in the very life-springs of the race. Competitive sports are essentially Nordic in their nature, and if the Central Eastern European countries would devote as much time to such sports as do America and England, I think less wars, bickering and intrigues would result. Football, for instance, is nothing less than war in miniature, and provides an excellent way of working off pugnacious and combative instincts without bloodshed. Just now there is a great uproar because nearly fifty players were killed this year. The total is appalling and unusual, but it seems incongruous for so much racket to be raised over the taking of fifty lives, when wars that blot out men by the millions are looked on as necessary. God knows I'd rather die on a clean football field, playing a clean game, than to die like a rat in the muck and slush of a bloody war, the reasons for which I was only dimly aware.

Football is essentially Anglo-Saxon. The Juts, Angles and Saxons brought the game to Britain with them. The present style of football, as played in this country, is a distinct evolution, entirely in keeping with the American nature. It is a far faster, more bruising and more complicated game than the English branch. Next to boxing, it is the most difficult of all sports to master, since to be a skillful player one must combine speed, unusual strength, toughness, intelligence, co-ordination, foresight and generalship. It is not, as so many people seem to think, a mere senseless mauling match. It contains strategy, science, and the elements of psychology. A good football player must be a good judge of human nature, he must be quick and strong, a quick thinker and a clean player.

Wrestling, of course, is the most savagely brutal of all sports. Professional wrestling must of necessity be framed, since if the contestants went in with the intention of battling on the level, nearly every bout would be accompanied by a fatality, or a crippling for life. Professional wrestling now is a good show, no more.

Boxing, now on a slump, partly because of the general depression, partly on account of the poor talent, but mostly because of the avarice of the managers and promoters, and their nauseating exploitation of the game, is more primal, more fundamental, than even football. A football game can never attract me as does a really good prize-fight, but perhaps my instincts are more primitive than most. A well-trained fighter can take an astounding amount of punishment, and what seems frightful brutality to the casual looker-on, really is not. The most disgusting part of pugilism is the crowds. I know of no more nauseating sight than to see some pot-bellied, flabby-muscled, hog-jowled imitation of a man sitting in a ringside seat and squealing insults at some kid who is taking a beating that would kill the squealer and all his yellow-gutted brothers. But sometimes the fans act funny. I remember one time in Fort Worth I was watching a scrap between Kid Dula and a set-up called Racehorse Rogers. There was a Jew sitting beside me who had bet five dollars with a big fireman that Rogers would stay the limit. Rogers stayed and the Jew won the bet, but the fight was harder on him than on Rogers. As Dula would drive Racehorse across the ring, slugging him savagely, the Jew would leap up and wave his arms wildly, shrieking for Rogers to clinch! — hold! — stall! — do anything! As the gong would end the round, the Jew would shriek that Rogers was saved by the gong and would fall limply back into his seat, in a state of collapse.

The real hilarity comes at a wrestling match. Everybody, except the most rabid fans, knows that the outcome has already been decided and agreed upon before the warriors enter the ring, but it's a good show, if the boys know their stuff. Good wrestlers will bellow, make terrible grimaces, bite and claw, kick each other terrifically in the pants, pull hair out, throw each other out of the ring, etc.. It's almost hysterically funny to see such showmen perform, and to see the frothing fury that the fans who take their wrestling seriously, get into at the abuse of their favorite.

But football; that's straight, clean and Homeric. I've seen no less than heroism on the football field. I remember a halfback who used to play in the small West Texas college where I took a business course. He was a giant blond with an Irish name. He was forbidden to play the game because of a weak heart, but he faked a physical examination and got on the team. I never saw a man who played with such utterly reckless fury. Almost every game he knocked himself senseless. I remember once when he entered a game with three broken ribs and his heart nearly twice its normal size. He tore in with such berserk fury even his team-mates were appalled. Three times I saw him take the ball, hurl himself headlong at the opposing line, carrying the whole forward wall with him and lie senseless where he went down. He knew that each charge might be his last, and he might be carried lifeless from the field. Foolish, perhaps; yet no more foolish than the soldier who plunges headlong upon the bayonets of his enemies. They're all games, only in some the penalties are greater. But I'll wander on indefinitely at this rate.

I mentioned to you before the tendency of the people of Texas to live at home. This of course has been a necessary move, but it's a good one, I believe. I never saw so little money and so much food in the country in my life. Most of the barns and granaries are filled with grain, and the cattle are fat. Of course, the catch in that is so much land, crops and livestock are mortgaged, and so many bank failures have caused the collection of notes and debts and the like. Still, some of the farmers are developing a shrewdness in law and an ability to prevent themselves being stripped of everything. And the canning machines have been working overtime. Not only in the country, but in towns.

We are not farmers. We live in a small town and have only a very small piece of land, but we have enough to keep a little stock and raise a garden. Right now we have far more than we need of greens, radishes, turnips, and the like. We have been taking cattle, hogs and canned stuffs on debts, as well as grain and feed. We have a good supply of hay, oats, cotton-seed, maize, and corn, and we have meal and flour ground from corn and wheat we got the same way. We have milk from our own cow, and plenty of meat. We had a whole calf canned — it's surprizing how much meat a good fat calf makes — cans of steak, roast-beef, soup, hash, chili, liver, heart, tongue — everything but the hoofs. And you ought to see the pork we have — huge sides of bacon, yard-long sacks of sausage, hams so gigantic they have to be cooked in the vat used for rendering lard. We don't have to pay out much money for food. And we've done quite a bit of trading in a small way — trading canned meat and lard and feed for work, and other things. I just mention all this to show the present trend, even in the towns.

I hope the times get better, but I hope people will continue to live at home as much as possible. It's the only way for independence. They're building a huge dam in Brown county,[1] at a cost of several million dollars, where a couple of rivers join and run through a broad, steep-walled valley. It will be the biggest artificial lake in Texas, with a shore-line of 145 miles. A huge area will be irrigated. I want to get a few acres of land on the shores of that lake, and raise vegetables and a little stock. It's only nine miles from Brownwood, one of the best trade centers in Central West Texas, but I wouldn't be raising the stuff primarily for market purposes, but mainly for home use. When anyone has his own meat, eggs, butter, milk and vegetables and doesn't owe any money, he can tell anybody to go to Hell. That country where the lake is to be hasn't been much account, because of the lack of rain. It's mostly rugged hill-country, rocky, barren or grown with drab post oak thickets. But irrigation will make the valleys bloom like a rose, or something.

Thanks for the view of Harvard. The buildings are certainly stately and possessed of a colonial grandeur. I envy you your sojourn in Boston and exploration of the museums. How I'd love to get among such relics of antiquity as you mention! Most of the antiquities I've had the opportunity to examine in Southwestern museums have been those of Indians and Aztecs, which don't have quite the kick, somehow, that Asiatic and African relics have. Please extend to Mr. Cook my greetings and best wishes, and my appreciation for his kind comment on my story. I hope both you and he like my latest pipe-dream.

And so, with best wishes, I am,

Cordially,
[R.E.H.]

P.S. I almost forgot to tell you that I finally made Clayton's *Strange Tales* with a yarn called, "The People of the Dark" a tale of reincarnation, pre-Roman Britain, Mongoloid aborigines, yellow-haired Britons, Irish pirates, and anything else I could lug in; I hope you've also made this market, and certainly, no weird magazine is complete without your magnificent tales.

NOTES

1. Construction began in 1931 on an earthen dam seven miles north of Brownwood to impound water from Pecan Bayou and Jim Ned Creek, forming Lake Brownwood as a reservoir for the use of Brownwood and the surrounding area.

TSS: 20450-20455

❧

190. To *Weird Tales*, ca. January 1932.[1]

Congratulations on the appearance and excellence of the current *Weird Tales*. The make-up and all the illustrations are unusually good, and the contents are of remarkably uniform merit. That is what struck me — the high standard of all the stories in the issue. If I were to express a preference for any one of the tales, I believe I should name Derleth's "Those Who Seek" — though the stories by Smith, Long, Hurst and Jacobi could scarcely be excelled. In the latter's tale especially there are glimpses that show finely handled imagination almost in perfection —just enough revealed, just enough concealed. Smith's sweep of imagination and fantasy is enthralling, but what captivates me most is the subtle, satiric humor that threads its delicate way through so much of his work — a sly humor that equals the more subtle touches of Rabelais and Petronius. Yes, I consider the current magazine uniformly fine, of an excellence surprizing considering the fact that neither Lovecraft, Quinn, Hamilton, Whitehead, Kline nor Price was represented.

NOTES

1. Published in the March 1932 issue. JB

⁂

191. To Tevis Clyde Smith, ca. February 1932.

Fear Finn:

Well, how runs the world these days? I reckon you got my postcard from the Valley. I didn't stay there as long as I'd intended; I found the climate delightful, but the altitude was unhealthily low — only about sixty-five feet at Mission. Spent awhile there, and then came back to San Antonio for a few days.

I didn't go to Brownsville; only went down the valley from Mission as far as McAllen once, and did the rest of my exploring up the river — west of Mission, in Starr County, which is a striking contrast to the citrus belt, which is very thickly populated, full of blond Yankees, and rich in plants of all kinds. Starr County is a ranching country, a wild, broken terrain, cut by low hill ranges and dry arroyos, and is predominantly Mexican. Rio Grande City and Roma are almost purely spick. The former town has a population of nearly three thousand people, and there are only about twelve white civilian families there, while in Roma, the only whites are the government officials on the international bridge. Of course, Fort Ringgold is at Rio Grande City, and there are lots of white soldiers there. Architecture and everything is Mexican. It's just like being in Old Mexico.

I met a most interesting priest — a Hessian of the Oblate order, who had the spiritual guidance of thirteen thousand Mexicans in his hands. It shows how cosmopolitan this country is, when he speaks Spanish much better than he speaks English. He's a scholar of the highest order, and a purely Nordic type. I always had a prejudice against Hessians, dating from Revolutionary days, but this priest is a fine man. By the way, he remarked that he wished he had time to write himself, and said that he sold an article on "canned religion" in America, or something like that, to a German publication for $950. I'll bet he gets fed up on those South Texas spicks before he's through.

I got hold of some pure Spanish wine that would knock a mule down. A couple of big glasses, and I was ready to lick all the Yankees in the Valley. I also got a whang of Benedictine wine, that was possibly a hundred and fifty years old. It was thick as honey, and about the same color. A glass of that would make an Orangeman vote for de Valera.

Well, that's about all I can think of just now. Oh, yes; I finally made Claytons'. I sold them a couple of yarns in a row, and while they kept me waiting awhile for the dough, they paid well when they did pay — $134 for one,[1] and $144 for the other.[2] Short stories too. I hope to gosh I can sell them a long novelet.

What are you doing these days? Have you tried anybody else with the perms? If you contemplate it, let me know, because I want to pay my part of the postage. Why not write me?

Fear Dunn.

P.S. I talked with another interesting character in San Antonio — an Indian who was born in Calcutta and had spent most of his life in China; he was a pure Aryan type, straight-eyed and dolichocephalic, and but for his dark skin would have passed easily for an American. His wife was half Chinese and half Indian. He said Japan would play hell conquering China, and that Gandhi was a sap to think that India could win her independence by peaceful means. He was an Oriental nationalist if there ever was such a critter. I told him I was an American-born Mongol.

NOTES

1. "People of the Dark."
2. "The Cairn on the Headland."

TSS: 82497

192. To H. P. Lovecraft, ca. February 1932.

Back of Photograph[1]:

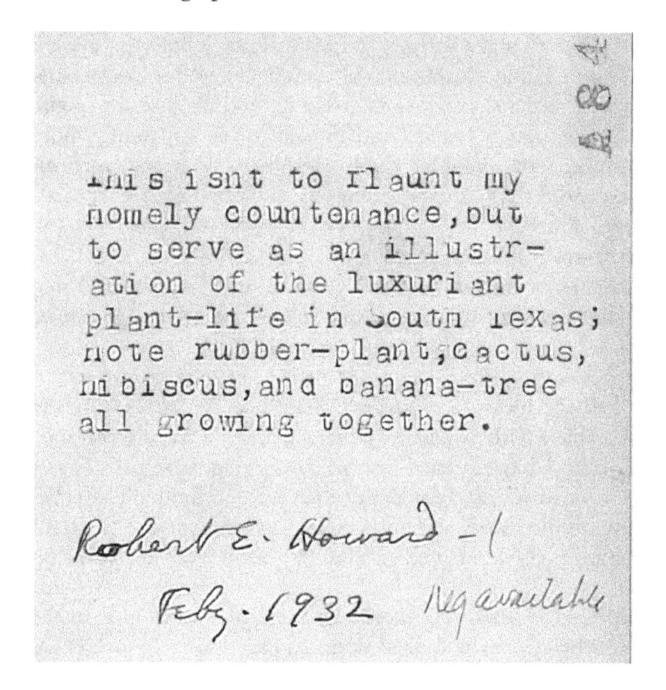
This isnt to flaunt my
homely countenance,but
to serve as an illustr-
ation of the luxuriant
plant-life in South Texas;
note rubber-plant;cactus,
hibiscus,and banana-tree
all growing together.

Robert E. Howard -1
Feby. 1932 Neg available

"This isn't to flaunt my homely countenance, but to serve as an illustration of the luxuriant plant-life in South Texas; note rubber-plant, cactus, hibiscus, and banana-tree all growing together."

NOTES

1. During the editing of Volume 3, while looking for other photographs in it, Rob Roehm found his copy of this photo, and here is the back of the photograph as typed by Howard. JB

193. To H.P. Lovecraft, March 2, 1932.

Dear Mr. Lovecraft:

I'm finally getting around to replying to your letter of Jan. 16.

I was extremely interested in your comments on the Pennsylvania Dutch. I'd heard, of course, of their witch-craft ideas, hexes, etc., but had no idea their backwardness and peculiarity was so extensive. There seems great material for a weird tale there, and I hope some day you'll find it convenient to write such a story, as I know you could lend those primitive hill people as sinister a glamour as you have lent the witch-haunted settlers of New England in tales laid in that locality. I'd like to make some explorations in their country, myself.

No doubt you are right in attributing the excitability of the Continental immigrant to his lack of racial experience in freedom, and his peasant origin. Strangely enough, Latins, that is Italians and French, while apparently more excitable on the surface, seem, beneath their exterior, to be more practical-minded and better balanced than the average Swede or German. At least that's been my observation. I believe the Latin races are really the most cynical, practical and materialistically minded people in the world.

Concerning families of mixed blood in New Orleans, I understand that there are such families as you mention, speaking French and retaining vestiges of past culture.

I certainly hope Wandrei places his novel, which, judging from such of his work as I have had the pleasure of reading, I am sure is splendid. By the way, what luck did you have with Swanson's new magazine?[1] I hope you placed the stories you sent him. I haven't tried him with anything myself. In fact, I haven't done much work of any kind for longer than I like to think of. I'm glad you liked "The Thing on the Roof" and appreciate your kind comments about it. I'll feel greatly complimented to have you allude to Justin Geoffrey and Von Junzt in your work.

I'm rather surprized to learn that there's no attempt at recruiting in the East. Here in the Southwest war is looked upon as practically inevitable. Of course many men out of work look on recruiting as a superior alternative to starving. But another thing that possibly makes Westerners and Southwesterners look on the Far East situation with keen interest, is the fact that the West would bear the brunt of a Japanese invasion. It doesn't seem very far out across the Pacific to the big guns of Nippon! Not with the modern type of ships and war-planes. Along the Border there is a definite undercurrent of expectation, or at least apprehension, of Mexican invasion in case of war. There has been a persistent rumor, every since the last war, of the mysterious presence and vaguely sinister activities of a hundred thousand Japanese in the interior of Mexico. It is well known that in several cases of banditry, the Mexican outlaws were led by Japanese. Possibly these Orientals were mere renegades — possibly not. Of late there has been some bandit activity in the Rio Grande valley, just west of the thickly settled citrus-fruit district. Mexico has unofficially declared that she will stand by the United States in case of war. But the memory of Mexican treachery is still too fresh in the minds of Texans — the betrayals and massacres at Goliad, Mier, and elsewhere — for them to take much stock in such declarations. Doubtless the government would keep its pledges. But Americans along the border seem not inclined to trust their southern neighbors overmuch. During the last war there were the usual rumors of a Mexican invasion which never materialized. But this is somewhat different. There were not enough Germans in Mexico to bring such a movement about. We don't know how many Japanese there are there. I wonder if the recent movement on the part of the Mexicans to drive the Chinese out of Mexico was prompted by Japanese? I wouldn't want to say, lacking all accurate knowledge. Possibly it was only a natural part of the recent nationalist movement in Mexico, a movement in which I am heartily in accord. Mexico has been a grab-bag for foreign exploiters long enough. I'd be glad to see them take hold of their country and make something out of it — if they can, which is rather doubtful.

Concerning the Chinese — the average Mexican is no match for him in business competition. The Chinaman is more industrious, more progressive and more intelligent. I don't know whether they've run the Chinese out of Piedras Negras or not. When I was there a few years ago — it's the town opposite Eagle Pass, Texas — it was largely dominated by Chinese. They owned small irrigated farms along the river, and ran most of the best cabarets and saloons in the town. In contrast to the Mexicans they were clean and prosperous — well, in contrast to almost anybody they were. There were first-class saloons and cafes where only Chinese or white men were allowed to enter — no Mexicans were admitted — and that in Old Mexico!

I'd prefer Chinese immigrants to Japs. From what I hear of the Japs, they're the original freeze-out artists. For instance, I've heard of their activities in the fruit-country of California. They would come in, I've heard, as laborers. They'd work for much less than white fruit-pickers and packers could afford to work for. After awhile, they'd have forced the white laborers out entirely, and the work of the groves and orchards would be in the hands of Japs altogether. Then they'd form unions and begin to raise the price of labor. Eventually the owners of the fruit would find themselves facing ruin because of these cut-throat methods. They'd be forced to sell out, and the Japs would buy, at less than the property was worth. Soon they'd be owning whole fruit valleys. Their eventual aim, was, I suppose, to control the whole fruit market. Well, they'll never get a foot-hold in the citrus-country of South Texas. Mid-Western Germans seem to have most of that.

But returning to the war; I had an experience while in San Antonio the other day which gave me a slight — oh, a very slight taste of what modern warfare would be like, and also served to show how uppermost the idea of war is in the minds of the people of the Southwest. It was a cloudy, rainy day, as so many days in Texas are, and have been for the past few years; walking along the street in the broad plaza in front of the municipal building, I suddenly was aware of a stinging, smarting sensation in my eyes, and noticed other people rubbing their eyes and shaking their heads. Men stopped each other and asked the meaning of the phenomenon. There was no smell, no sign other than the almost intolerable smarting in the eyes. I saw people involuntarily glancing up at the cloudy sky — I myself did this. The same thought had entered all minds, and one man put it in words — "By God," he shouted, "I believe the damned Japs are droppin' gas on the town!" But no plane showed among the clouds. There was a restless jerky feeling in the air — as if it wouldn't take much to start a blind panic or a senseless riot. The fire-companies were called out and the police began searching the source of the mysterious gas. As for myself, having ascertained that the low-hanging clouds were not masking an invading air-fleet, I concluded that a gas-bomb had been released somewhere near-by in some gang or racket activity; theaters have been bombed in San Antonio in the past, and as far as I know, other businesses as well. I entered the municipal building, interested myself in examining an exhibition of Chinese curiosities, and forgot all about the mystery. It was not until later that I learned the source of it. Three miles from the city, the soldiers of Fort Sam Houston had been experimenting with a smoke screen, laden with tear-gas.[2] A shift of the wind had blown it down on the city. I was only in the fringe of it; in other parts it was experienced far more thoroughly — the smoke settled like a dark fog, and the gas almost blinded people, temporarily. There was almost a near-riot. It was significant to note that people's minds leaped instantly to the thought of an air-attack. That seems foolish perhaps — but firmly rooted in the average Texan's mind is the conviction that anything can come up out of Mexico — and in such a case, San Antonio would be one of the first objectives.

Well, if England will stand firm with America, I don't fear Japan. But I wish the Japs and Russians would cut each others' throats, if there must be a war. As you say, neither is a friend of ours.

As to my feelings toward the mythical Picts, no doubt you are right in comparing it to the Eastern boy's Indian-complex, and your own feelings toward Arabic things. My interest in the Picts was always mixed with a bit of fantasy — that is, I never felt the realistic placement with them that I did with the Irish and Highland Scotch. Not that it was the less vivid; but when I came to write of them, it was still through alien eyes — thus in my first Bran Mak Morn story[3] — which was rightfully rejected — I told the story through the person of a Gothic mercenary in the Roman army; in a long narrative rhyme which I never completed, and in which I first put Bran on paper, I told it through a Roman centurion on the Wall; in "The Lost Race" the central figure was a Briton; and in "Kings of the Night" it was a Gaelic prince. Only in my last Bran story, "The Worms of the Earth" which Mr. Wright accepted, did I look through Pictish eyes, and speak with a Pictish tongue!

In that story, by the way, I took up anew, Bran's eternal struggle with Rome. I can hardly think of him in any other connection. Sometimes I think Bran is merely the symbol of my own antagonism toward the empire, an antagonism not nearly so easy to understand as my favoritism for the Picts. Perhaps this is another explanation for the latter: I saw the name "Picts" first on maps, and always the name lay outside the far-flung bounds of the Roman empire. This fact aroused my intense interest — it was so significant of itself. The mere fact suggested terrific wars — savage attacks and ferocious resistance — valor and heroism and ferocity. I was an instinctive enemy of Rome; what more natural than that I should instinctively ally myself with her enemies, more especially as these enemies had successfully resisted all attempts at subjugation. When in my dreams — not day-dreams, but actual dreams — I fought the armored legions of Rome, and reeled back gashed and defeated, there sprang into my mind — like an invasion from another, unborn world of the future — the picture of a map, spanned by the wide empire of Rome, and ever beyond the frontier, outside the lines of subjugation, the cryptic legend, "Picts and Scots". And always the thought rose in my mind to lend me new strength — among the Picts I could find refuge, safe from my foes, where I could lick my wounds and renew my strength for the wars.

Don't think I'm fanatic in this matter of Rome. It's merely a figment of instinct, no more connected with my real every-day life than is my preference for the enemies of Rome. I can appreciate Roman deeds of valor and no one gets more thrill out of Horatius's stand on the Roman bridge, than I do. I am with the Romans as long as their faces are turned east. While they are conquering Egyptians, Syrians, Jews and Arabs, I am all for them. In their wars with the Parthians and Persians, I am definitely Roman in sympathy. But when they turn west, I am their enemy, and stand or fall with the Gauls, the Teutons and the Picts! Fantastic, isn't it?

I regard the Roman hero Camillus with the respect one must give a bold and resourceful foe. I favor Brennus, of course, but must admit he was not the Roman's equal in strategy and tactics. By the way, aside from instinctive feelings and tribal placements, I wonder how the world's history would have been written had the Gauls pushed on after their defeat of the Romans at Allia, and destroyed completely the budding Roman civilization?

And I sometimes wonder if the chaos of the Middle Ages was not the result of the barbarian tribes seeking to adapt themselves to an alien civilization instead of building up one of their own? I wonder if, had Rome been completely destroyed by the Goths, Franks and Vandals, all traces of Roman culture wiped out, if, after a longer time, the Germanic nations would have emerged from barbarism by their own efforts and with a culture more suited to their particular nature? However, this practically occurred in Britain, when the Saxons swept the land clean of Roman civilization, and progress seemed to have practically ceased in England prior to the Norman conquest. Though, there, as in Ireland, the growth of civilization had been halted by the invasions of the Danes. Doubtless I am wrong, but I somehow feel that the Roman culture — especially the latter-day type, mixed with the decay of Greece and the Orient — was not suited to the straight-forward western barbarians. At any rate, I'm enclosing a rhyme[4] which I wrote when younger than I am now. It's crude, no doubt, but I rather like it. There's no hurry about returning it, though I'd like to see it eventually. That's one of a number of rhymes I hope some day to bring out under the title of *Echoes from an Iron Harp*. But the devil knows when I'll get to do it. Most authorities consider the Cimbri were Germans, of course, and they probably were, but there's a possibility that they were Celtic, or of mixed Celtic and German blood, and it gratifies my fancy to portray them as Celts, anyway.

Well, the big guns are booming in Shanghai, and the Chinese are putting up an unexpected resistance. More power to them. I'd like to see them beat the hell out of Japan. Though, if they do, it's remotely possible that it might be the beginning of the end of foreign domination in China. Remote, but possible. A victory over Japan would undoubtedly stir the Chinese, and might lead to a far more aggressive assertion of national rights. It seems hardly possible that China could win, lacking a strong central government, proper equipment, etc., and with her vast unwieldy armies controlled by separate — and mercenary — war-lords. But you can't tell. I hear on good authority that many German soldiers of fortune, from the old Prussian armies, are in the Chinese forces. I note that in Germany, by the way, the citizenship of Hitler has been questioned to the extent of forcing him to withdrew from the presidential race. I hope Von Hindenburg carries the election. During war days I would cheerfully have lighted a torch to burn him at the stake, but now I think he is one of the strongest stabilizing factors in Europe, and that his re-election would be to the advantage of not only Germany, but the entire world. He was doubtless the ablest general of any nationality in the Great War, and now seems to be about the most level-headed statesman on the Continent.

I expect the disarmament conference to come to nothing, and am in favor of that result, if the alternative means shearing more claws from our already depleted national defense. The outlawry of war is proven to have been an empty thought. I believe that the next few generations will see a continual series of wars, and the best thing to do, is to be prepared. America has no friends in Europe, or in Asia, or in the world. It seems to me that conditions are somewhat similar to those which produced the feudal age. The only nations which are likely to survive the dawning Age of Iron, are those which adopt a powerful military form of government. This style of government is not the kind to endure in such an age, because big business has its finger too much in the pie. It seems we must choose between a strong soviet government, and a strong dictatorship on the fascist style. Just as in the feudal days, men chose a strong baron or count to serve, for mutual protection. Personal liberty, it would seem, is to be a thing of the past. Individualistic independence must be sacrificed for national security. We must throw off the idealistic cloaks we have partially donned during the last generation or so, and recognize the naked bestiality of life. There is no question of right or wrong, but simply of necessity and survival. The strong will win, and might will rule, as it always has, and there need be no hypocrisy about it. Right or wrong, for instance, has little to do with the present Japanese-Chinese-Manchurian affair, as I see it. It is necessary to the existence of the Japanese nation that they expand into Manchuria, and eventually into China. It is necessary to the existence of other nations — America, for instance — that they are not allowed to expand. I am in sympathy with China, because the more Japanese forces they shatter, the less Americans will have to face when the eventual war comes. I am all for the building up of the armies and the navy, for the equipment of the forces with the most modern type of arms, and, if it seems necessary, of compulsory military training. The naked facts are — we must grind or be ground.

I am no student of events, but I consider at least these wars inevitable: a Russo-Japanese war; an American-Japanese war; a Russo-American war; a French-Italian war; and possibly a war in which Russia will be pitted against the foremost European powers. The world is a seething volcano.

Glad you found the postcards of some interest. The extreme south of Texas is really very interesting, and full of strange contrasts. For instance, the Lower Rio Grande valley, that is, the well irrigated citrus belt from Brownsville to Mission, is thickly settled, with broad, well kept roads, lined with palm-trees so that the highways are like boulevards, dotted with prosperous, thriving towns set close together, and covered with beautiful luxuriant groves of golden fruit. But west of Mission, the country changes with startling abruptness. It changes from an almost perfectly flat plain, to a rolling, brush-wood country, broken by low hills and dry arroyos. The brush is not tall but it is incredibly thick and dense. And everything seems to grow thorns — there is one plant, the name of which I forget, which grows nothing but thorns — neither leaf, bloom nor fruit. The mesquites are much thicker than they generally grow in West Texas, though perhaps not quite so tall. Prickly pears and cacti grow so thick you wouldn't believe me if I told you. Prickly pears, which in West Texas seldom grow four feet tall, stand in tree like clusters, sometimes as high as ten feet. It was in that country that chaps and hooded stirrups originated; without them a vaquero would be torn to pieces, rounding up cattle in the brush. It amuses me to see movie cowboys, supposedly of Texas in the old days, portrayed with sheep-skin or woolly chaps. If one of these gentlemen would start chasing a saber-horned steer through the South Texas brush, he'd leave tufts of wool on every mesquite and huisache and prickly pear he passed.

But to return to the population. In the citrus belt proper the Mexican is being gradually thrust out. Many of them are returning to Mexico, many are going up the river into the broken ranch country. Starr County, which lies west of Hidalgo County, is Mexican to an astonishing extent. In Rio Grande City, the country seat, for instance, a town of 2283 inhabitants, there are scarcely a dozen white families. A man said to me, "There's too much law in the settled part of the valley; west of Mission the only law is the will of the Mexican czars." That's exaggerating of course, but the rich Mexican land owners in Starr County do wield enormous power. As a contrast, the Lower Valley is settled largely by people from the Midwest who seem to be so law-abiding that they ring themselves round with ordinances and rules that the people in my section of the country don't think about.

Wondering about the future of the valley, I venture a comment: the people now settling, mainly prosperous Midwesterners looking for climate and rich land, are pushing out the Mexicans. It takes a lot of work to run a grove. The owners aren't going to do the work. If they push all the Mexicans out, they'll have to import laborers. Prices have always been low in that country, and it isn't likely that they'll ever raise them enough to attract white laborers from other sections of the country. As a result, a generation or so will probably see the groves being worked by Slavs or Italians — most likely Italians. These, being a thrifty and industrious race, will soon be owning groves themselves. If valley industry follows the trend of American industry as a whole, the big corporations will soon begin to freeze the independent fruit-growers out of business. Raising taxes and holding down the price of the fruit will do the job. I seem to see, in the future — perhaps twenty, thirty, forty years — the Lower Valley groves owned almost exclusively by big corporations, and settled and worked by Italians. All this is not for publication. It's none of my business — I don't own a foot of land in the world, or a blade of grain, or the bark on a mesquite tree. But I've seen the big cattle corporations crush out the small ranchmen, and the big oil companies freeze out the independent oil men. It's the trend of the times.

But to get back to the Valley. It's more historical than most people realize. There, for instance, were the famous ports of Clarksville and Bagdad, at the mouth of the Rio Grande; Bagdad, founded by the Spaniards about 1780, reached the pinnacle of her lurid glory during the Civil War, when the trade of the world flowed through her fingers — cotton, armaments, slaves. It was on the Mexican side of the river, Clarksville on the American. There were more than fifteen thousand people in Bagdad when the thirsty gulf rose and drank her, and her sister city, in a single night. When the dawn rose calm and clear over the waves, it was as if the sites of those river towns had been swept with a titanic broom. So a Catholic priest had prophesied, for men said it was the wickedest city in the world, with its criminals, cut-throats, pirates, smugglers, renegades and the scum of the Seven Seas. That was in 1867.

Steamboats used to go up the river as far as Rio Grande City, but not any more. Too much water is used in irrigation. Of course, there's no particular reason for steamboats to ply the Rio Grande now.

I talked to an interesting person while in San Antonio — a high caste Indian, who, though born in Calcutta, had spent most of his life in China. His wife was half Hong Kong Chinese and half Calcutta Indian herself, and I wish you could have heard her play on a contraption she called a yang-chin, or something that sounded like it. You've probably seen them, though I'd never even heard of such a thing. It had strings and she played it by tapping the strings with a limber strip of bamboo in each hand. The man interested me much. I'd never seen a high caste Indian before, and I may have embarrassed him by my close scrutiny of his head and features — for skull-formations interest me intensely. He was — as I suppose all high caste Hindus are — decidedly dolichocephalic, with a high narrow forehead and regular features. But for his color, which was very dark, he might have been an aristocratic American. He was a man of evident culture and intelligence, and I was interested in his views regarding the Jap-Chinese situation.

He maintained that no nation would ever conquer China, which he said was far too large. He said that the last census was taken in China over thirty years ago, and that the actual population far exceeded the generally accepted figure. He said that there were at least eight hundred millions natives in China, and the population was growing rapidly and steadily. Their very number may constitute a threat to white races in the future — my thought, not his. He disagreed with Gandhi's idea that a revolution could be achieved by peaceful means, but was quite evidently in full accord with the idea of self-rule in India, as elsewhere in the Orient. He was, I should say, a sort of Oriental nationalist; he spoke of "we" "us" and "our", regardless of what Eastern race happened to be his subject — identifying himself with the Indians, Chinese, Japanese, irregardless. His sympathies seemed to be with the Chinese in their present war, however.

He was a delver in religions and cults, and said that he was a firm believer in the theory that Christ spent several years in India — a theory which he had for years been seeking to prove by searching old books and manuscripts.

As I listened to him, I was fascinated less by what he said, than by what he represented — the long pageantry of wars and conquests of which he and his kind are the eventual result. I was thinking that in spite of his dark skin, the dominant line of his ancestors sprang from the same stock as mine, in the dim dawn years of lost eons. But his wandered south, down through the snowy passes of the Himalayas, and mine — and yours — went westward, over the river-slashed steppes and the rolling hills, until they came upon the sea-plains and heard the roar of the North Sea. I was thinking how those south-farers wandered, and what wars they waged, and what mud-walled villages they sacked and burnt; what nameless rivers they crossed, and what tribes fled before them. Until they came to a land that was pleasant to them, and a dark-skinned, primitive people who bowed prostrate before them; and they dwelt there as lords, with their loves and their wars, their hunting songs and their drinking horns, until the centuries wrought curious changes in their blue eyes and yellow beards, and their slaves became at last their conquerors by virtue of their primal blood, so that when the sons of their ancestors, who had wandered into the west, came across the sea, these did not recognize their kin.

But I've rambled around long enough. I'm sure the poetry lecture by Benet was very interesting. If I'd stayed another day in San Antonio, I'd have gotten to hear a lecture on the ruins of Zimbabwe by Miss Theckla Hall, whose father's ranch (two and a half million acres, I heard, but I'll swear that sounds like a hell of a ranch) was adjacent to the mysterious locality, and contained quite a few of the ruins. I'd have enjoyed the lecture, I'm sure, for it's a fascinating subject. Best wishes. And bohut salaam. (That's some kind of a Hindu salutation, though I'm a bit hazy about it.)

Very cordially,
[R E H.]

NOTES

1. Carl Swanson, of Washburn, North Dakota, was soliciting material for a magazine to be called *The Galaxy*.
2. On January 16, 1932, an officer of the Chemical Warfare-Reserve gave a demonstration on chemical warfare methods to students at St. Mary's University in San Antonio which included laying down a smoke screen on the grounds of the university. Newspaper accounts do not mention tear gas.
3. "Men of the Shadows."
4. "An Echo from the Iron Harp."

TSS: 64127-64132

194. To Kirk Mashburn, ca. March 1932.

Mr. Kirk Mashburn,
Houston, Texas.

Dear Mr. Mashburn:

I am writing to express my appreciation for your remarks concerning "The Dark Man", in the Eyrie of the current copy of *Weird Tales*. You expressed my own ideas on the matter exactly. While "The Dark Man" was not originally written for *Weird Tales*, but for the planned *Strange Stories*, which was never published, it always seemed to me that it contained enough weird touches to justify its presence in the former magazine. Thanks for coming to its defense.

I've been intending writing you for some time, anyway. Mr. Price mentions you often in his letters, and I have been much interested in your work in *Weird Tales*. I particularly remember "Tony", "Sola", "Placide's Wife", and your recent "Vengeance of Ixmal" — a powerful tale.[1] I hope to have the opportunity of reading more of your work soon.

If it's convenient I'd like to hear from you. I correspond with several *Weird Tale* writers — Price, Lovecraft, Dwyer and Talman — and I'd like to add your name to that very interesting group.

Cordially,
[Robert E. Howard]

NOTES

1. "Tony the Faithful," July 1928; "Sola," April 1930; "Placide's Wife," November 1931; "The Vengeance of Ixmal," March 1932.

ଓଃଓଃ

195. To Tevis Clyde Smith, ca. March 1932.

Fear Finn:

Sorry to hear you've been carved on again, and I hope you're getting along o.k. It must have been pretty tough. And being as you are of the writing profession, I reckon they had a time cutting through the calluses. If they ever give service stripes to writers, they ought to be awarded according to the thickness of the calluses on the rear.

I got a big kick out of your letter and your narration of the cops, cameramen, etc., caused me to roar with mirth. You took a big chance asking the cop anything; it's a wonder he didn't suspect you for an accomplice, who'd just had a bullet cut out of his rear.

By the way, did you notice where a coon cooked three cops in New Orleans? All they were doing, according to the papers, was giving him the once over with a rubber hose in his cell, when the ungrateful cur grabbed one of their gats and cooked three of them. Then he fought off several score of them for hours, until they finally got him. Thk, thk, thk. What's the country coming to when the cops can't beat up an ungrateful coon without risking their lives? Such duplicity is detestable to behold. No doubt some other coon will pay for it — and maybe this time they'll remember to handcuff him. Even a dog is likely to bite you if you kick him often enough.

Glad you liked the Roof business[1] and the Sowers stuff.[2] I've had quite a few praises on the Sowers thing, but don't know whether they'll get into the Souk.[3] Likely not. Those yarns I sold Clayton[4] were to their *Strange Tales*. They turned down "The Road of Azrael" for *Soldiers* etc., and I seemed to sense a hint of irritation in their letter of rejection, as if they suspected I'd never read the magazine. Which I haven't. But I hope to make it eventually. A man named Swanson is publishing a magazine[5] in one of the Dakotas, on the weird order. I've neglected my chances, until I wonder if the thing's about up ten years ahead. Lovecraft wrote me that he'd placed a couple of yarns, and evidently the old weird tale buccaneers have descended on it like a horde of vultures. Lovecraft said Smith, Long, Whitehead, Derleth, etc., etc., etc., had sold Swanson a lot of stuff already. By the way, Farnsworth rejected the last three yarns I sent him,[6] together with a bunch of verse. No rest for the weary. I've drifted into correspondence with some more Weird Tailors (as Lovecraft calls them) and Mashburn tells me that there seems to be a good chance of getting that weird anthology published. I hope so, ye gods.

Send the verses to anybody you wish; I'll leave it entirely to your judgment. I'm enclosing some stamps to help the good work along. We'll try to bombard the whole publishing world until we wear 'em down. I sent a copy of one of those of mine included in the bunch (I trust that sentence is clear!) to Lovecraft, to let him read it — the one called "Echoes From an Iron Harp" or something like that, and he said: "You are certainly a genuine poet in every sense of the word". And further on in the letter he said, "Your poem — as I said at the beginning of this letter — is powerful and splendid." "I don't know anyone today who reproduces the ancient Aryan emotions as powerfully, vividly, and sincerely as you do. This mood is almost obsolete in Europe and the Eastern U.S.; and if it is to have continued literary expression, such will probably come from the Southwest." Pardon my conceit in repeating these kind comments. But hell, why shouldn't I? I'm no shrinking violet.

But if a discerning critic like Lovecraft likes my stuff, then the world will certainly be enriched by our book, because both your poems and Lenore's are superior to mine. (I say this not in mock humility, but because it's true.)

Fear Dunn.

NOTES

1. "The Thing on the Roof."
2. "The Sowers of the Thunder."
3. The letters column of *Oriental Stories.*
4. "People of the Dark" and "The Cairn on the Headland."
5. *Galaxy.*
6. Probably "Phoenix on the Sword," "The Frost-Giant's Daughter," and "The God in the Bowl."

TSS: 82046

ଔଔ

196. To *Oriental Stories*, ca. Spring 1932.[1]

Brundage did a fine job in the cover illustration for the current *Oriental Stories.* I have only had time to read "Jungle Girl" so far. It is needless to praise Miller; his stories speak for themselves. I used to read his earlier work in the *American Boy*, and never dreamed that some day I'd have the honor of seeing my name in a magazine alongside his. I have only a single kick to make about "Jungle Girl" and that isn't to be taken as a criticism of the story's merit or the author's style. But Lord Bolton's end, while dramatic and gratifyingly gory, was a bit too sudden and painless to satisfy me. He was too ornery to deserve an easy finish. I'd like to have let him kick and howl a while with a tulwar through his lower abdomen.

NOTES

1. This letter was published in the Summer 1932 issue. JB

ଔଔ

197. To Tevis Clyde Smith, ca. March 1932.

Fear Finnel:

When I wzs a kie in East Texas there was forest of dog fennel but it wzas spelt different. It got on your hands and made fried chicke n taist bitter. I used to get losth in fielfs of dog gennel.

It has been many a day since I got druniy. mYbaey tou wonde r why I got drunle. I'll teel youse. Today I got an invitation fro m Kird Mashburn to visit him and E.H. Pfice i n Hp8ston for the week end or more and I didnt have the mOney to goo. They think I am a first clash writer and a xmart man and me and youse knows I am nothing but a cuntry yokel with an nack of ,aking people beoieve I airse smater than I am.

So I relcined with thankex and now no doubt they theink I am too hie hat to viesit thdme. It is rematkable how smart men think I am soumbodies. For instiacnk Lovexrakhft told Prijce I was very learn4d in certain branches. I hate to meet these really intelligent men because they think I am smarth, but the real reaason I am broke. Itsh it not a damnued shame that yhe for4most Texas writet shou;d be bro meke? I know I amy the foremosth Texas writhef because Charley Cox toldsh me I was when he was washty tyr8ntg to eucher me outf of my dough zuch as I hafme is not not much. He wanted me to signe a contrackth for one year or more and siadi I was the foremoste writher of Texas but I gid not gicvien him the contrackht.

So now I gu4sse he is nmy enemity as well as others. The paoc ist turnt on me at last to renf me but I do not give a damengh as I as brokem anyhowru. But I am too damneht drunkiteh to caretehidash. Me and Pink has ddrunl beer all evening it being gooc beer. You know, Cladye, I have been reading Shajepshere lately and thinjk Prince Henry which was Henry the Fifghth was a dirty swine to turn off Good old Sir John Falstifaff, the on.y human chatacte Shakeperezes ever creaged.

If I mete King Henry in hell I will swinge his hides. Judasses, I am drunkel! Yiu know Clyde, I have been thinking abiu t the swine that hit me in the head with a base balol when I wash waorkign iin a a carnival when I was fourtenn. I think I know who did it, and if I find him and am drunke I am liabl w to knock the hellze out of him. I know he didnt mean anything personal aboyt it, but he minht have blinded me with his damerfooloery.

I have druno only ten bootlese of beers of but I am drunk. Will you answer my letter or swill I swinge your hide in hell? Commnend me to king Hnery the fifith because I am drurnksemth.

Fear Dunn.

TSS: 82482

ଔଷ୫ଔଷ

198. To Carl Jacobi, pm, March 22, 1932.

Dear Mr. Jacobi:

I found your recent letter very interesting, and if my comments on your story "Mive",[1] have helped you with the editors, I am sincerely glad. I consider that story as one of the finest of its kind I have ever read. I am glad to hear that you have placed a story with *Oriental Stories*,[2] and shall watch for it.

I shall also look for "The Curse Pistol" in *Strange Tales*.[3] It was not my fortune to read either of the other stories you mentioned; in fact, I live so far out of civilization, as it were, that I can't keep track of the magazines very well. It's forty miles to the nearest first-class news-stand, so my magazine reading is rather desultory.

I hope you sell those stories upon which you mentioned you were working — also hope you like my yarn in the forthcoming *Weird Tales*.

Hoping to hear from you again, at your leisure I am,

Cordially,

[Robert E. Howard]

NOTES

1. See letter 190.
2. "Three Brass Cubes" was returned to Jacobi when *The Magic Carpet Magazine* (*Oriental Stories* was retitled beginning with the January 1933 issue) suspended publication. It was later published in *Complete Stories*, January 28, 1935.
3. The story was returned to Jacobi when the decision was made to suspend publication of *Strange Tales* in the fall of 1932. It was later revised by Jacobi and published under the title "The Phantom Pistol" in *Weird Tales*, May 1941.

199. To Wilfred Blanch Talman, ca. March 1932.

Dear Mr. Talman:

I've finally gotten around to answering your letter. I intended answering it long ago, but it seemed like I was always so far behind on my work, I never could catch up. Then I spent a few weeks wandering about in the south part of the state, along the Border mainly, and didn't get any work done during that time — my main occupation being the wholesale consumption of tortillas, enchiladas and Spanish wine. I remember those wanderings with envy now, for an old-fashioned Texas blizzard came up last night, after an unusually mild winter, and I reckon the fruit crop is gone to hell for the seventh consecutive year — that is in north and west Texas, I mean.

I was much interested in your remarks concerning that book *The Scottish Gael*.[1] I was not aware that such a document was in existence. I'm sure it must be very interesting. Really authentic books on Celtic subjects are rare. If written by English authors, they are usually prejudiced against their subject, and if by Irish authors, they are often rabidly biased. As a rule, German historians are the most reliable. And there's been more study of Celtic history by Germans than one would think.

I was also interested in your remarks on the Dutch settlements, and colonial history. I intend to look up that book of Van Loon's you mentioned.[2] I gather from his name that he himself is a descendant of the Netherlanders. As for these early Dutchmen having a tendency toward Indian women, well, I reckon all the settlers of America were pretty much that way. I agree with you that there's no point in glossing over these facts. If some of the aristocratic descendants of the patroons, etc., have Indian blood in them today, why shucks, that's no disgrace. At least it isn't considered so in the Southwest, where plenty of people are proud of a strain of Indian blood. I haven't any of it in me, but I have cousins of both Cherokee and Chickasaw blood, and some of the best friends I ever had were of mixed blood. After glimpsing the bank-rolls of a few red oil-land plutocrats, I wouldn't kick if I had enough Osage blood, myself, to give me a slice of the dough.

Have you decided what branch of the service you'll choose, if this business in the Far East starts another Sarajevo? I hope the War Department will see its way clear to arming each private with a submachine gun, especially after what the Chinese did to the Japs with rapid-fire guns. It's easily seen that men, well armed in this manner, have a chance even against the most up-to-date armament.

I don't know whether these submachine things are subject to jamming or not. I was always a little suspicious of automatic weapons on that count. I know when I was a kid I used to use a Colt .25 automatic that jammed about every fourth or fifth shot. I know old-timers who'd as soon pack a rattler as one of them. They won't admit there's any kind of pistol but an old Frontier model single-action, maybe with the trigger taken out.

Up in the Indian Territory, once, an aunt of mine threw down on a ruffian with her husband's automatic, and forgot to throw the safety catch. She kept jerking at the trigger, with a perfect bead between the fellow's shoulders as he ran, and wondering why the thing didn't shoot. He was out of sight before she remembered the safety. Automatics were a new thing in the Southwest then; which was lucky for the desperado, because she was a crack shot.

I was much taken with your recent poem in *Weird Tales*.[3] It's difficult to capture a completed thought in so short a verse, but you seem to have succeeded admirably. I hope to see more of your work soon.

Here's a snap-shot for your rogue's gallery. The dark complexion comes from Black Irish ancestors, not Spanish as some people appear to think. The height is 5-11; weight 203, the last time I weighed.

By the way, have you ever tried Clayton's new *Strange Tales* magazine? It's published every other month, and they pay well. I sold them a yarn dealing with the mythical Mongoloids of prehistoric Britain, and another using the battle of Clontarf for a background, though they rejected quite a few mss. before I ever landed anything.

Well, I'm running out of intelligent comments, so I guess I better bring this epistle to a close. Anyway , my right, or space-bar, thumb, is playing out on me; I nearly knocked it loose swinging on the ice-man — the thumb, I mean, not the space bar.

Cordially,
REH

NOTES

1. James Logan, *The Scottish Gael, or Celtic Manners*, 1831.
2. Perhaps *The Story of America*, 1927.
3. "Death," March 1932.

TSS: 23890-23891

ଔଔ

200. To Carl Swanson, ca. March 1932.

Lock Box 313
Cross Plains, Texas

Mr. Carl Swanson
Washburn, N.D.

Dear Mr. Swanson:

I am sending you, under separate cover, a manuscript entitled "The Hoofed Thing" which I hope you can use in your magazine. I am sending this at a venture, as I have not been able to secure a copy of your publication, and so don't know just what type of stories you use.

I'm enclosing herewith $.25, with postage, for which please send me a copy of your magazine; I live some distance from a town containing a newsstand, and it's difficult for me to obtain magazines, some times. In fact, I first heard of your new publication through my friend, Mr. Lovecraft, who I understand has placed some work with you. Hoping that we can do some business together, either now or in the future, I am,

Cordially,
Robert E. Howard

P.S. It's possible that you may have noticed some of my work in *Weird Tales*, to which I have been a regular contributor for some years.

R.E.H.

TSS: 20806

ᏅᏒᏁᏓᏅᏒ

201. To Carl Swanson, ca. April 1932.

Dear Mr. Swanson:

I am interested in your publication, and believe you will make a success of it. I understand you have stories by Lovecraft, Long, Whitehead, Derleth and others. These gentlemen, as you doubtless know, have extensive followings, and if their readers could be reached, I believe they would subscribe to your magazine.

If you like "The Hoofed Thing", use it, and pay me whatever you are able. Also please keep the $.25 I sent you, and send me a copy of your magazine as soon as it is published — also let me know what the subscription price is.

The increasing number of bizarre magazines, dealing with the fantastic and fictionized scientific, shows that there is a slowly growing field for such literature; with a return to anything like normal business conditions, I see no reason why you should not succeed at your venture. With best wishes,

Cordially,
Robert E. Howard

TSS: 92116

ᏅᏒᏁᏓᏅᏒ

202. To Tevis Clyde Smith, ca. April 1932.

Fear Finn:

I heard from that bone-crushing man-eater, that swashbuckling Black Ace, that ruthless bruiser, several months ago.[1] In reply to a timid Christmas card I sent him, he wrote that he was attending Commonwealth University, working on the side, and writing a novel — a breathless blood-thirsty narrative of seduction and roistering, of fire and brimstone, I doubt not. I remember with what searing contempt, what hippopotamus snorts of scorn he greeted my timid suggestion that he write a novel of social reform; he will write, I suppose, of bold and brutal individualists, crushing all opposition by the might of their hairy arms, and stalking red-handed and dominant above their trampled victims. Such was ever his ideal.

Hear ye the tale of "Fighting Nerves". I wrote this story — a Kid Allison yarn — as a complete novelet for *Sport Story.* I wrote it, I think, three times, before I sent it off. Back it came with the request to cut out the saloon atmosphere and reduce the length. I re-wrote it and returned it to the same magazine. It came back with the statement that they were all stocked up with fight stories — requested me to keep it several months and return it, with a letter reminding them of it. Not wanting to wait that long if I could help it — a natural desire of a penniless adventurer like myself — I rewrote most of it, changing the names of the characters, and sent it to *Fight Stories.* Back it came with the request to cut it down in length. I rewrote it and sent it back. Back it came, with the remark that it was acceptable, but that they couldn't find a place for it just then. I should keep it a month or so, and then they'd like to see it some more. So I sent it to *Sport Stories*, with a letter reminding them of what they had said. It was returned with no explanation — merely a rejection slip. So I sent it to Fiction House — and back it came with the statement that *Fight Stories* had been — or was going to be — taken off the stands. I mentioned to you a year or so ago that that magazine wasn't going to be published more than a year or so, you may remember.

Did I mention to you about getting into a belt of tear gas at San Antonio? With characteristic intelligence, the war department of the city's posts allowed a smoke screen laden with tear gas to be blown down on the city. It was a rainy, cloudy day, and the stuff settled and stayed there for awhile. A lot of people thought it was an air-raid. I was just on the fringe of it; I didn't get into the smoke screen, but I got enough of that gas to clinch my opinion that modern warfare is the tripe. There was nearly a riot.

A Weird Ballad.

The werewolf came across the hill,
—Eerily, wind, sing eerily—
The vampire drank at the Devil's still,
And the wind was blowing eerily.
Eerily, eerily, blow, wind, blow,
With a heave and a hey, so eerily.

The bale-fire burned, and the pot smoked blue,
—Eerily wind, sing eerily—
And Jules de Grandin rose from the brew.
And the wind was blowing eerily.
Eerily, eerily, blow, wind, blow,
With a heave and hey, so eerily.

His breath was strong as a witch's spell,
—Eerily, wind, blow eerily—
And his whiskers bristled like horns o' Hell.
And the wind blew through them eerily.
Eerily, eerily, blow, wind, blow,
With a heave and a hey, so eerily.

The Devil dropped dead and the werewolf fled,
—Eerily, wind, blow eerily—
And the vampire waggled his ghastly head.
And the wind was blowing eerily.
Eerily, eerily, blow wind, blow,
With a heave ho heave and a ho heave ho,
With a heave and a hey, so eerily.

Little brown man of Nippon
Who apes the ways of the west,
You have set the sword on your standard,
And the eagle on your crest.

Little brown man of Nippon,
You have dreamed a deadly dream;
You have waked the restless ravens
And the rousing vultures scream.

Oh, lines of an unborn empire,
Foam of a rising flood,
Your bones shall mark the borders,
The tide shall be your blood.

Little brown man of Nippon,
Though the star of the West be set,
And the last of the fair-haired strew the field
Where East and West be met —

Though you herd us down like cattle,
And hew us down like corn,
Our blood shall drown your vision
Of the empire yet unborn.

In utter desolation, and despair
At the end, on a blackened hill,
You shall sit and view your empire,
Broken and charred and still.

The beams of shattered houses,
Reared stark against the sky,
And fields wherein, for waving grain,
Long waves of dead men lie.

We will set the torch with our own hands
To wall and roof and spire;
We will cut the throats of our women,
And feed our babes to the fire;

We will fling our naked bosoms
Against your bloodied steel;
As you tread us under, dying,
Our teeth shall rend your heel.

But, little brown man of Nippon,
Should the dice fall otherwise,
And the gods of the fair-haired triumph
When the battle-dawns arise —

We will give your flesh to the sea-gulls
And your cities to the flame,
Till the world forgets your visions,
And the years forget your name.

Over your island empire
Shall our steel-clad squadrons fly
Till the land lies black and silent
Under a flame-ripped sky.

Till the hungry wolf goes slinking
Along your shattered streets,
And the kite in your ruined palace
Tears at the crimson meats.

And over the crimson gutters
Which infant bodies choke
The raven flaps and strangles
In the drifting shreds of smoke.

No plough shall break your valleys,
No song shall rouse your hill —
Still and silent the ploughmen,
The singers silent and still.

And your nation's only emblem,
Oh, man of the crimson dream —
Save corpses in the broken streets
And the death-fires' baleful gleam —

Shall hang at the prow of a cruiser,
That furrows the flying foam,
Bearing the spoils of conquest
To the fair-haired people's home.

Shall hang at the prow of a cruiser,
Grinning and dripping red,
The price of a dream of empire —
Little brown man, your head.

Hoping to hear from youse soonel.

Fear Dunn.

P.S. I sold another yarn to *Strange Stories*;[2] don't know how much I'll get for it; the checks come in pretty slow these days; it wouldn't surprize me if every damned magazine in the country went broke.

NOTES

1. Refers to Harold Preece.
2. This should be *Strange Tales*, the story is "The Valley of the Lost."

TSS: 82498-82500

ꕤ

203. To H.P. Lovecraft, ca. April 1932.

Dear Mr. Lovecraft:

At last I've gotten around to answering your most welcome letter. Thanks very much for the kind comments you made on the Cimbric rhyme; I appreciate them highly, and am encouraged towards further efforts.

I hope you can before long explore the Pennsylvania Dutch regions, where I'm sure you'll find splendid material for stories. I'm sure the young man you mentioned — Brobst[1] — must be quite interesting, with his first-hand knowledge of the ways and customs of the people. I am very gratified to hear that he has read and liked my yarns.

I have read and re-read your comparison of southern and northern Aryans, which is the most vivid and powerful thing of the sort I ever read, and goes deeper in the matter — to the very roots of cause and effect, and race consciousness and memory. I have vaguely felt much of what you describe with such power and clarity. Here arises a question of reality — which is real, the firmly founded security of the Latin's defined and measured universe, or the chaotic, unstable, wind-torn cosmos of the Nordic? I feel that in his aborted gropings, in his pessimisms and distrusts of security, the Nordic strikes nearer at reality than his more practical brother. What is this universe, but clouds that break up under our feet, as we stand precariously poised upon them, hurling us into the abyss of howling chaos?

I was especially interested in your remarks concerning the effect of northern skies on our barbarian ancestors. I have mentioned to you the predominance of cold grey overcast skies in many of my dreams. I hate cloudy weather, and no one appreciates the clear bright skies of the south more than I, and yet, the sight of a cold northern sky, piled high with grey winter clouds, stirs indescribable feelings in the very pits of my soul, and there is a sensation of vague familiarity, rooted deep. The cloud effects in this part of the southwest are remarkable; a cousin of mine, who has travelled widely in the western part of the continent, from the Great Lakes to the west coast, says that nowhere has he seen such sunsets, and cloud formations as in this locality. On this high divide the clouds blow up from the gulf, and they roll down from the high backbone of the continent, across the endless plains, meeting and mingling. Of all the sunsets, I believe the most impressive are those in which the whole sky seems flecked with gold, great rifts of flaming gold that sweep from horizon to horizon, with spaces of gleaming blue between. Strange that such magnificent wealth should stretch over so dreary a country of sand-drifts and post-oak hills. But when the blizzards sweep down the rolling grey clouds from the high plateaus, misty, gigantic and fantastic, fold on misty fold, rolled and tattered like grey flowing banners, it is then that all the latent instincts of my race stirs in me, and I am filled with a vague desire for snow-clad mountains, shimmering expanses of cold blue water, and frosty shores lapped by icy waves.

Swanson's venture seems rather amateurish, but he may make something of it. I let him have a yarn, "The Hoofed Thing" which Bates had previously rejected. I am very glad to hear of your new stories, and hope that they will find the market they deserve. Your latest story in *Weird Tales*[2] is as grim and gripping a tale as I ever read. The lending of common-place, every-day things and events a macabre and soul-freezing significance is the most difficult of all literary feats, it seems to me, and you are the more to be congratulated because you succeed in this so splendidly.

I feel honored that you should refer to Von Junzt's accursed document, and thanks for the German of *Nameless Cults*,[3] which I'll use in referring to it. Though I've lived adjacent to Germans for many years, I know nothing of the language — and neither do a lot of them. *The Book of Eibon* is properly noted. Smith[4] has come along in his prose fiction at an astonishing rate. In fact, I consider him second only to yourself in the weaving of fantastic tales. He has a classic background so many of the younger writers lack — myself, for instance. I don't wonder that you receive letters inquiring about the *Necronomicon*. You invest it with so much realism, that it fooled me among others. Until you enlightened me, I thought perhaps there was some such book or manuscript sufficiently fantastic to form the basis of fictionized allusions. Say, why don't you write it yourself? If some exclusive house would publish it in an expensive edition, and give it the proper advertising, I'll bet you'd realize some money from it.

I've been working on a new character, providing him with a new epoch — the Hyborian Age, which men have forgotten, but which remains in classical names, and distorted myths. Wright rejected most of the series,[5] but I did sell him one — "The Phoenix on the Sword" which deals with the adventures of King Conan the Cimmerian, in the kingdom of Aquilonia. I also placed another yarn with *Strange Tales* — "The Valley of the Lost" — a horror tale in an early Texan setting. I'm trying to invest my native regions with spectral atmosphere, etched against a realistic setting; "The Horror from the Mound" in the current *Weird Tales* was a feeble effort of the sort. And now I'm working on a mythical period of prehistory when what is now the state of Texas was a great plateau, stretching from the Rocky Mountains to the sea — before the country south of the Cap-rock broke down to form the sloping steppes which now constitute the region.

I read with interest your comments on the Eastern question, and agree with you that Japan should be kept out of China, at least. With millions of Chinese trained into the Nipponese military machine, there'd be hell to pay.

Just now my interest in the Far East is centered on that trial in Honolulu,[6] which makes me ashamed of my own race. How a white man can stand up in court and prosecute a white woman, before the scum of the Orient, with Orientals on the jury, is more than I can understand. I consider it a blot on the country's flag and honor that the case was ever brought to court; at least she should have been honorably acquitted without delay. Why, good God, what's the Caucasian race coming to? Is a white individual not allowed to protect or avenge the members of his or her family? Whatever they do to the defendants, anyway, they can't resurrect that damned yellow-belly they killed. He got it easy; good thing for him it wasn't Texas. Men have been burned alive at the stake here for less than he did.

I fully agree with you concerning the chimera of disarmament, also as to limiting international commerce. Let the nation be as self-supporting as possible. I consider the only eventual salvation of America will be a close Anglo-American alliance, which I hope to see some day. God knows, we'd have more personal liberty today if we had never broken away from the empire, and doubtless be better off in every way. If those ancestors of mine who helped mow down the red-coats at King's Mountain, could have looked forward a few centuries, I wonder if they'd have been as whole-hearted in the slaughter — possibly so, since they were Scotch-Irish refugees from the isles, and bitter. But maybe the Revolution was a mistake, anyway. If there'd been an Englishman on the throne, instead of a damned Hanover — oh, well, what the hell. I'm like you, in preferring a Fascist rule to a Commune — as the lesser of evils. Judas, Sovietism would be like being suddenly bounced onto another planet.

The afore-mentioned Hindu was, as I said, very interesting. I recognized his distant kinship to our own tribe, but in so many ways his thoughts and ideals were so alien — it was really strange. If he'd been round-headed and slant-eyed, it would have seemed natural. But somehow, even with his very dark skin, it seemed queer to encounter so many non-Aryan traits in him, when his features were so like those to which we are accustomed. For instance, he spoke of the ghastly tortures of the Orient with evident approval, as the only curb for lawlessness. And he mentioned seeing scores of Chinese Communists beheaded on the open streets, with a pleasant smile, and a manner too casual to have been feigned. The mere thought of such a spectacle slightly nauseated me. On the other hand, had we engaged in a political argument, and I had forgotten myself to the extent of knocking him bow-legged with a clout in the mush, I have no doubt that he would have considered this perfectly natural act as the nadir of abysmal barbarism. They have drifted far from the Aryan stem.

I read with much interest and appreciation your speculations on the possible trend of history, in the event of the destruction of Rome by the Gauls; they seem to have considered all possible angles. Continuing with these theoretical wanderings: suppose that Martel had not stopped the Arabs at Tours? Or that Tamerlane or Genghis Khan had conquered Europe? Or, speculating from the other way, suppose that Alexander the Great had conquered India, and pressing on, subjugated the Cathayan empire? Would the East have been Aryanized, or the Western races sunk that much quicker in a mire of Orientalism? And suppose the Black Prince had carried out his dream of Oriental conquest? He was probably the only Western general of medieval times capable of holding his own with the great Eastern conquerors. In fact, I am convinced that, with his English archers, he would have proven more than a match for Tamerlane, Genghis Khan, Baibars, Subotai, Saladin, or any of the rest. The main reason that the Crusaders and other western armies were so repeatedly defeated and overthrown by the Moslems and Mongols was partly because of the extreme mobility of the Oriental armies, partly because of the incredible inefficiency of the western kings and generals. By the way, Wright thought well enough of my yarn, "The Sowers of the Thunder" published in the current *Oriental Stories*, to advertise it in *Asia.*[7] It deals with Baibars the Panther, and the overthrow of the last Christian army in Outremer: a magnificently dramatic historical episode which I fear I have failed by a long way to do justice. I'll swear, I've written of Christian armies being defeated by Moslems until my blood fairly seethes with rage. Some day I must write of the success of the earlier Crusades to gratify my racial vanity.

History fair drips with blood. It's a marvel to me how the race has survived all the wars, pestilences, famines and massacres which have been so generously bestowed upon it since the beginning of time. Yet it's always seemed much of a miracle to me that the average child lived to be grown. Youngsters of this generation seem not quite so hazardous except in the way of mechanical speed, bad liquor and venereal diseases. But when I was a kid growing up in the country, it seemed their natural instinct to risk their necks on every occasion. And when the hazards of this younger generations — speeds, machines, poison liquor, vamps, etc., — are balanced against the hazards of outlaw horses, wild steers, rivers in flood, rattlesnakes, accidental discharges of fire-arms, rotten tree-limbs, and the savage gouging, tearing, knifing fights that were an everyday occurrence with the youths of the last generation, the balance, if anything, is on the side of the latter. When I was a kid it was a common thing for youngster to be killed or maimed by falls from horses, or the half-grown steers they rode for sport, to be hurled to their deaths by the breaking of pecan-tree limbs — the most treacherous of all woods — to be accidentally shot while hunting, drowned, or to meet crippling or death in various other forms. One of my first playmates, when I was about three years old, and he was the same age, came to a violent end from one of the above mentioned causes — got into the corrals in his play and a killer mule stamped his brains out.

Why, I always led about the most quiet hum-drum life imaginable, and took as few risks as can be imagined, yet when I recall some of the narrow scrapes I had, I can scarcely understand how I escaped death or being maimed permanently. Among those I vividly recall at present, is that of having a horse fall down a steep bluff with me; having a horse throw me and then crash down on me with her hoofs, barely missing my head, and literally crushing the flesh on my arm; getting my hand split open in an impromptu brawl while knocking the knife out my antagonist's hand, the gash missing a large vein by a hand's breadth; having the point of my own hunting knife driven deep into the inside of my knee, close to the great artery that runs there; having a horse turn a complete somersault with me, landing fairly on her back, so that all four hoofs waved for an instant in the air — gad, that was close! It was just chance, that threw me headlong out of the saddle as the mustang fell, that kept me from being crushed to a pulp, as I've known others to have been crushed. And leaping through a solid glass window at about three o'clock of a morning was not a hazard to be passed lightly, considering that I crashed through pane and screen, and fell some five or six feet to the hard ground, side-ways — when I took inventory my underwear was soaked with blood from head to foot, but, except for gashes on my arm and a triangular wound that laid bare my shoulder bone, and bruises on my ankle, knee, hip, shoulder and arm, from the fall, I was unhurt. These trivial matters stand out in my mind, because my life was so placid and devoid of adventurous risks, and yet I knew plenty of youngsters to whom such affairs — minus, perhaps, the window-leaping episode — were everyday occurrences, too common for notice or recollection — they broke wild horses and swam rivers in flood, neither of which I ever attempted; they took all kinds of risks at climbing; they were reckless with weapons, with which I was always extremely careful; some of them broke their necks, got drowned, shot or crippled, but the great majority grew to maturity unscathed. Add to those risks as well, the vicious environs of a wildcat oil boom. Yet they thrived and grew fat. Verily, though the individual human is easy to slay or maim, the race as a whole is as tenacious of life as a barrel-full of cats. Man has not yet exterminated rabbits; neither has Nature exterminated men.

Chance again is a titanic factor. It is a well established fact that a comparatively light blow on the head may often result in a fatality. Men have been killed by a stroke from a bare fist. Yet, again, the human skull may stand up under incredible battering. I remember seeing an oil field worker shortly after he'd been hit over the head half a dozen times with a Stillson wrench. You'd think a crack from a ponderous implement like that would have caved his skull in; his scalp was laid open in half a dozen places, he was bloody as a stuck hog, yet he was able to walk, supported by his friends. Nor was his skull even slightly fractured! And I saw Red — well, a noted oil-field bully, brought from Ranger to "clean up" Cross Plains, a short time after he'd begun his campaign; he was lying senseless on the floor of the jail, whither he'd been dumped, bloody as a butchered steer, with his scalp laid open in eight places. He looked like he was through; it looked as though even the redoubtable Red had reached the end of his lurid trail; while he was strangling the city marshal, the marshal's deputy had repeatedly smashed his gun-barrel over Red's head — had in fact beaten him into insensibility, so complete they had to drag him to the jail by main strength; he was out cold. He remained out, while the woman who ran the place which the officers had been raiding when Red attacked them, stood outside the jail, and harangued the crowd which stood about, trying to stir up a mob to rescue Red and avenge her insult — gad, I was in my early teens, and I remember that scene vividly — the throng milling about the tiny, one-roomed jail, glaring avidly at the blood-stained, senseless body of the bad man — the tall, slender, well dressed woman, with her hard, intelligent features over-cast with anger, standing flanked by several of her hard-faced girls, the motley crowd, huge drillers and roustabouts in their grimy, oil-stained working clothes, hatched-faced gamblers, hard-eyed, quick-fingered thugs — honest laborers and the scum and scrapings of the oil fields — gradually they drifted away, and left her still holding forth wrathfully. But what I started to say was, that Red not only lived after that terrible beating, but was as good as new, as soon as his scalp was sewed up. Though he took a hurried departure, and made no more attempt at cleaning the town.

For the past few weeks there has been one sandstorm after another. It looks like the beginning of a big drouth. If the people in this country don't raise a good grain crop this year, and there's no winter grazing, suffering among men and animals will be intense next winter. The only thing that's kept the people from starvation so far has been the stuff they raised. Well, sandstorms are unhealthy, nerve-racking and disagreeable; and yet, for my own personal preference, I prefer them to rain. I cut my teeth on sand-storms, and I spent most of my life in dry countries; I've never gotten used to incessant rain. Continued cloudy rainy weather is about the most damnable stuff imaginable. These sandstorms are drab, raw and without esthetic value, and yet, there is sometimes a weird beauty about them. When the sun sinks like a great red ball, veiled in the reddish dust that all but obscures the sky, there is a feeling of unreality somehow, to be able to gaze directly at the sun without being dazzled. Then sometimes, between sandstorms, when one has blown itself out, but left a vague sifting of dust in the air, or when another is just faintly beginning, sometimes the whole sky has a silvery sheen, and the few clouds that appear are like delicate silver traceries.

I'm glad you found the South Texas views of some interest. I do not believe that cocoanuts thrive anywhere in Texas. As to the abrupt contrasts in the lower country, you can meet with them driving along paved highways. A great deal of the country is furnished with good roads, and even when they are not paved, as in many cases they are, they can be traversed with comfort most times of the year. Tourists swarm into South Texas by the thousands, and many naturally find their way into the less settled areas. But there's still plenty untouched, and if you ever get out here to Texas, I'll show you places no tourist has ever seen — less interesting from a scenic standpoint, but rich in tradition. I'm enclosing a post-card view of a grotto, built in imitation of the famous one of Lourdes, the work of a very interesting character in Rio Grande City — the Rev. Gustav Gollbach, of the Oblate Fathers. I found him a remarkably interesting man, of unmistakable culture and erudition. He is a native of Hesse — a province against whose inhabitants I always had an instinctive prejudice, from memories handed down since the Revolution. I can remember when "that old Hessian" was a term of anathema in the Southwest. But my prejudice — which after all was active only in my extreme youth — did not extend to the Reverent Gollbach. He was dolichocepalic, typically Nordic, with light blue eyes and fair skin. He has thirteen thousand Mexicans under his spiritual guidance, and body and soul they are much the better for his aid. Although the Catholic religion is fast losing power in Old Mexico and along the Border. Ten years ago the priest was all-powerful among our southern neighbors. Now he is as likely to get a bullet in the back as a layman. I have an idea that a priest on this side of the Border really wields more power than one in Mexico.

But I know this rambling missive is trying and boresome. I must really beg your pardon; I've filled it with trivialities and maunderings, without rhyme or reason. I'll try to do better next time. I've been unwell for some weeks — a condition extremely rare for me — and my physical condition always reacts on my mental condition. When I'm not fit bodily, my mind is sluggish and stupid.

Tomorrow, if nothing happens, I start for the East Texas oil fields; I hope also to go into Louisiana. I have no zest for the trip, and would not go if it were not for business reasons. If I get into any interesting countries, I'll send you some views. Thank you again for the kind things you said about the rhyme, and my ability as a rhymer. I appreciate them the more, coming from one whose artistic ability I so highly admire. And so I close this tedious letter, hoping that next time I'll be able to put more snap into my correspondence.

Cordially,
[REH.]

P.S. Wright took another of the Conan the Cimmerian series, "The Tower of the Elephant", the setting of which is among the spider-haunted jeweled towers of Zamora the Accursed, while Conan was still a thief by profession, before he came into the kingship.

NOTES

1. Harry K Brobst, a friend of Lovecraft's, who had lived in Pennsylvania.
2. "In the Vault," April 1932.
3. August Derleth had proposed to Lovecraft that the "original German" of *Nameless Cults* would be *Unaussprechlichen Kulten.* E. Hoffmann Price objected, on the grounds that "unaussprechlichen" would mean "unpronounceable," and offered *Unenbarren Kulten.* Artist C.C. Senf, a native German speaker, was consulted, and lent his support to Derleth's suggestion. Howard used the German title only once, in an untitled story fragment.
4. Clark Ashton Smith.
5. "The Frost-Giant's Daughter" and "The God in the Bowl."
6. The notorious "Massie case," in which Mrs. Grace Fortescue, the mother of Thalia Massey, Lt. Thomas Massie, Thalia's husband, and two sailors were tried for the murder of Joseph Kahahawei, one of five men who had been accused of raping Thalia. When a jury deadlocked in the trial of the five men, Mrs. Fortescue, her son-in-law, and two of his sailor friends kidnapped Kahahawei, attempted to beat a confession out of him, and shot him. They were caught with his body in their car as they sought to dispose of it, so their guilt was not in doubt, the defense seeking to portray their actions as justified.
7. April 1932.

TSS: 11454-11458

ঌঌঌ

204. To Tevis Clyde Smith, ca. May 1932, handwritten on Worth Hotel stationary, Fort Worth.

Fear Finn:

Just a bit of press-agenting. Have you read my yarn in *Strange Tales*? How about a few lines of frenzied praise to the editor?

By the way Farnsworth advertised my Baibars yarn in *Asia* which, I guess, is about as near the smooth papers as I'll ever get. I'd intended going on from here to the East Texas oil fields, but I don't know. I haven't any pep, even for travel.

My health is poorer than it's been in some time, though you wouldn't think so to look at me; I weighed just awhile ago and kicked the beam at 208.

Fear Dunn.

TSS: 82659

ଔଔଔ

205. To Tevis Clyde Smith, ca. May 1932.

Fear Finn:

Well, here I am back at the old home town, having gone no further than Fort Worth. I could have gone on to East Texas, but I didn't have the energy. The thought of the exertion the trip entailed appalled me. The fact that travel repels instead of fascinating me as formerly, causes me a vague apprehension. I have before felt my interest and zest in things fading and waning, but my enjoyment of travel, even such humble journeys as I was able to make, always remained keen and vigorous. This is not indolence; it is merely that life has so far lost its tang that nothing I can do is worth the stress of the effort.

John Kelley of Fiction House[1] is dead. I learned this through the bulletins of the American Fiction Guild, of which I am a member, and which seems to be a solid organization. I suppose you've received a request to join.

Dave Lee is helpless with rheumatism. He has been flat on his back for more than a week, and only lately has been able to feed himself. There isn't any telling when he'll be able to walk again.

The slaying in the Cafe was news to me. What were the details? I highly enjoyed your "Bells of San Fernando". It really should go down in the annals of folk-songs, and maybe some day we'll wander about the country twanging banjoes and singing in the twilight for nickels; if so we'll popularize it.

While I was in Fort Worth the City Drug Store[2] was partially burned. The fire, which took place at about five-thirty in the morning, apparently started in the sky-light. It is said that a bucket smelling of coal oil was found on the roof — also a partly burned rag in the store, saturated with the same liquid — and the mark of a human foot smashed through the sky-light. I saw none of these things myself, and know nothing about it.

There was also another incident while I was away, which took place on this street, in fact just about a block away. A man who runs a filling station and a mill, was watching the mill, having had most of his meal stolen, when he heard somebody breaking the lock on the filling station. He came forth and opened fire, whereupon the intruder began to yell for mercy — according to what the man who owned the place told me — so the owner spared his life, but, I think, turned him in to the law.

The corner around which prosperity is supposed to be lurking seems to be a long way off; if we have a drouth, which is what seems to be making, I don't know what will come to pass this winter, when the feed stored up now is gone, and no winter grazing.

By the way, there's something I've been intending to speak to you about for some time; in the event of my death, I wish you'd drop a line to each of the following:

Farnsworth Wright, *Weird Tales*, Chicago, Illinois.
E. Hoffmann Price, 305 Royal Street, New Orleans, La.
H.P. Lovecraft, 10 Barnes Street, Providence, R.I.

Have you heard from the verses? If you want to send them off again, let me know so I can contribute my part of the stamps. We might as well keep them weaving through the mails. We might catch some publisher in a weak mood.

Fear Dunn.

NOTES

1. J.B. Kelly was Treasurer of Fiction House, the publisher of *Fight Stories* and *Action Stories.*
2. The City Drug Store in Cross Plains was heavily damaged by fire early in the morning of April 22, 1932.

TSS: 82483

ଔଷଔଷ

206. To Tevis Clyde Smith, ca. May 1932.

Fear Finn:

Thank you very much for going to all the trouble writing The Cauldron.[1] If those letters don't help with the magazine, then nothing can. You're a real friend — a fact which I duly appreciate, though I may not seem to, at times. But when I seem to radiate gall and rattlesnake venom, please put it down to the personal devil I inherited from Anna O'Tyrell, who my great-greatgrandfather married in an absentminded moment.

Whitehead is a good scout, and once, I understand, just about ran things on an island in the West Indies.[2] He's some sort of a cleric — Price[3] seems rather uncertain as to whether he's an Episcopal bishop or a Catholic priest. I'm inclined to the latter view. His current yarn in *Strange Tales* has a surprizing amount of sword-heaving.[4] I wonder if he's showing the effect of my blood-letting. Price told me frankly that he intended to go in more and more for my sort of axe-swinging.

By the way, Clyde, I got a bulletin from the A.F.G.[5] to the effect that "William Godwin Publishers Inc., 100 Fifth Avenue, hitherto publishers drugstore books and nicely bound classics planning line $2 books. Wants writers of fiction with something to say or 'with names worth paying for.'

Advance on royalties by arrangement. Write Dorothy Waring, above address." Might be worth investigating. If you write to the firm, don't say anything about the A.F.G., or the way you got the tip; bulletins from the Guild are supposed to be confidential to members.

I got Apuleius' *Golden Ass* from Argosy.[6] A confounded fake. Adlington's translation, and expurgated much more than your copy. The illustrations were nothing much. *Argosy* has a way of making misleading statements in their blurbs. This edition was privately printed — why, I can't imagine.

While I was in Fort Worth I got a book, *Lead and Likker* by O.P. White. Good stuff; told with a zip, and apparently authentic — in spots, though his information about Big Foot Wallace doesn't always jibe with Big Foot's autobiography. But he evidently knows his stuff about Ben Thompson, John Wesley Hardin, John Selman, Quantrell, John Glanton, Ferd Patterson, and the rest.

Glad you got a write-up in the *Southwestern*.[7] I'd like to have a copy, if you've a spare one; if not, I'd like for you to quote the write-up in a letter.

By the way, a friend of mine in Marlin[8] wrote Bates, boosting my "People of the Dark", and he wrote her telling her that he guessed she could consider me as a regular now — I hope he remembers that, and holds to it. God knows I need the money. Markets are cracking every day. The depression is beginning to lick the wood-pulps.

Did you notice what a hand I got in The Souk on "The Sowers of the Thunder"? I'm sincerely amazed. I knew it was a pretty good yarn, but I didn't have any idea the readers would go for it like they seem to have done. There must be more folks interested in historical episodes than is generally thought. Kirk Mashburn, a damned good writer, wrote and told me I should have sold it to *Adventure* — of which he says he hasn't missed a copy since he found one in a deserted stretch of Florida Everglades many years ago. But if I'd sent it to *Adventure*, they'd have returned it unread, same as usual. Anyway, Farnsworth suggested the story and asked for it.

The river lost its mysterious glory to Mark Twain after he became a pilot, and grew familiar with the sand bars, snags and riffles. And literature, as a whole, has lost its magic fascination for me, since I've become even the imitation-author I am. I can appreciate the tricks and turns and quirks better, but the magic glory is gone, and that's the Hell of it. But it's not all mere craft, and sometimes I stumble on to something, generally obscure and little known, in which the writer really poured out his soul for the joy of the singing, and not to sell his stuff to the mob.

I was re-reading some of your letters the other day, and I near bust a gut over your Foo Manchu parodies. They never grow old. What's the matter with us? Why do we parody no more? Has all the mirth been hammered out of us already? If the taste of Life grows so insipid this early, what will we be in middle age? Well, I'm going to try a parody anyhow. If it fails flat, it must be a sign that I'm growing old.

The Toy Rattle Murder Case
by (Jack) A.S.S. Von Swine.

Chapter .1.

Vilo Pants was in his usual position, seated on the mantle-piece, with his long legs dangling sophisticatedly over the chandelier. This listless pose was characteristic of the man; it symbolized his complete detachment from the mundane sphere. I squatted on my all-fours at his feet, as usual, looking up at him intelligently, and occasionally gently tugging at his shoe string with my teeth, lest he should forget all material things in his cosmic questing for Truth. On such occasions he would smile tiredly and tolerantly down at me. "Good old Von Swine," he would murmur, "always the realist," adding emphasis by lamming me over the head with an iron poker.

At that instant in rushed Inspector Squarkam. "Vilo!" he shouted. "Guess who's been murdered!"

"Sergeant Teeth!" shouted Vilo, leaping with glee.

"Wrong!" yelled Squarkam, as they clasped hands and danced about the center-table. "You owe me a cigar!"

Vilo was never one to show his disappointment. After rushing madly about in circles, foaming at the mouth, biting chunks out of the chairs and tables, and shattering a mahogany wine-stand over my head, he asked quietly, meanwhile hammering Squarkam's head against the floor, by the ears, "Who is it then, which is murdered?"

"You mean, 'whom is murdered'," I suggested. For even Vilo is not infallible.

"You are right, good old Von Swine," he responded readily, knocking me through a gilded screen and stamping heavily on my face — for he always takes my rare corrections in good part — "Yes, you are right, you low-lived pole cat. Squarkam, which is it which has been murdered?"

Chapter .2.

We had arrived at the scene of the crime. Ezra Tunkett, the multi-millionaire, lay in the palatial Golden Chamber, his head battered to a pulp. Nearby, in a large cradle, an infant rocked methodically, surveying us over the edge with a peculiarly malevolent glare. Ezra's rings and stick-pin were missing, his pockets had been turn wrong-side out, so it did not need Vilo's deductions to tell me that the police had been on the job. I mentioned this to Vilo, and in approval of my intelligence, he tapped me jovially on the head, with a fire-axe.

"There has been murder done," said Vilo, striding about in a circle and staring accusingly at an Italian who had been caught climbing out of the window carrying a hatchet, just after the crime was supposed to have been committed. He had been released for lack of evidence and $1.93.

Squarkam, Teeth and I gazed at each other in wonder. Vilo's deductions were marvelous. The infant sat up in the cradle and took a long tug at a bottle marked with three "X's", meanwhile eyeing us in a most venomous manner.

"It's black magic," hissed Vilo.

"It's good red rye," rumbled the infant in a deep bass voice, glaring at us menacingly, and slowly rocking his cradle.

"What shall we do with the body?" asked Teeth.

Vilo rose magnificently to the occasion. There was something of the Roman emperor about him as he said, with a royal sweep of his arm, "Dump it in the ash-can, Teeth."

I had been staring over the edge of the cradle. Now with a scorching oath, the infant drew back a brawny arm, and struck me a terrific blow on the jaw. When I recovered consciousness, I was lying in the back alley. My friends, with true loyalty, had fled from the place.

Chapter .3.

"I have discovered the murderer!" said Vilo jubilantly, emptying my portion of grape-nuts into his bowl, and pouring all the cream over it.

"Who was it?" Squarkam, Teeth and I laid down our Whizz Bangs and gawped at him.

"The infant!"

"No!" we exclaimed.

"Yes!" shrieked Vilo, going into hysteria as he thought we disputed his word, and falling off the chair frothing and champing his teeth. We brought him to himself by smashing a table leg over his head, and he sat up and smiled tiredly.

"I'm a bit done up," he said apologetically, hooking my grape-fruit, and appropriating a fifty-cent tip Squarkam had laid down for the waiter. "This case has been too much for me. I've got to take a rest. I think I'll read Van Vechen, or attend a lecture by Van Doren — something where I can let my mind rest. But the fact is, the infant was Murderous Mike of Chicago. I suspected it when I saw that he was six and a half feet tall and weighed three hundred pounds. The rest was easy. He battered old Tunkett into a jelly with his toy rattle, which was made of Krupp steel, and weighed forty pounds."

"But how did you know?" we exclaimed.

He winked at us, and emptied the jam-jar into his coat pocket for future use. "I read the morning papers," he answered coolly. What a man! What a man! What a man! What —

(Editor's note: I have nothing to say.)

Not so hot; pretty lousy. Write soon.

Fear Dunn.

P.S. I've gotten some more letters from that fool Olson, in Iowa.[9] I could endure his lunacy, but his illiteracy gets on my nerves. This time he's frothing at the mouth on account of my "Horror from the Mound". He lashed himself into a perfect frenzy because I said a vampire was really dead. He says that there is no death in the first place, and that Christ was a vampire. Also that a vampire is in "reallity" an idealist, with an earth-gravity of 50 per cent. Whatever the hell that means. He says that I ought to be ashamed "tweesting" the facts around and "making the allmighty God look like the dirtiest devil from Hell." He also says that he is going to "proove" the Medical Society is a pack of fools shortly.

He alleges to "proove" his "prooves" by Einstein, Genghis Khan, Napoleon, and other great scientists and philosophers. He seems to have the mysteries of life at his finger tips. Well, what the Hell. Write when you get time.

NOTES

1. The letters column of *Strange Tales*.
2. Henry S. Whitehead was Episcopal Archdeacon to the Virgin Islands from 1921-1929.
3. E. Hoffmann Price.
4. "The Great Circle."
5. The American Fiction Guild.
6. A bookstore in New York City that offered mail-order services.
7. *The Southwestern Historical Quarterly*, April 1932, a publication of the Texas State Historical Association.
8. Mrs. F.M. Torbett, of Marlin, mother of Howard's friend Thurston Torbett.
9. A *Weird Tales* reader who apparently wrote very strange letters to *WT* authors.

TSS: 82040-82042

ଔଔଔଔ

207. To Tevis Clyde Smith, ca. May 1932.

Fear Finn:

Lo, friend, I approach thee with a liver dripping with gall and venom, from contemplation on the great folk of Life.

Three Sketches.

— John Brown. —

You stole niggers, John Brown,
And smashed the skulls of total strangers
Who had the misfortune to disagree with you
Politically.
You had the Jehovah complex to a fare-thee-well, John,
And there was but a single blasphemy
In your religion.
That was to differ from John Brown's opinion.
They make a saint out of you, Johnny oh,
While they gnash their teeth at Quantrell.
The only difference between you gentle souls

Was that his side lost and yours won.
You stole and murdered, John,
And I could overlook that, because
Some of your victims were undoubtedly lice.
But you poisoned a sheep dog, Saint John,
And I can't overlook that.
Still, John Brown, I am grateful to you,
Because of one warm, fond, glowing memory —
They gave the word and the trap sprung
And your neck cracked like a bull-whip.
On nights of insomnia
This gleeful memory
Lulls me to sleep.

— Abe Lincoln. —

Your only excuse, Abe Lincoln,
Is your undoubted sincerity.
Because of this, men should not curse you,
But what a damnable pity it is
That you were not drowned in a handy rain barrel
Before you decided
To save the nation
By butchering it.
You loved the nation so well
That rather than let it separate and
The sections live in peace and prosperity
You tore it with cannons, scorched it with fire,
Drenched it with the best blood of the land,
And built the foundations of its eventual destruction.
You loved the South, so you devastated it,
And sowed it with the dead,
And swamped the bloody fields with the bodies of men,
Sons of men who were giving their blood and lives
For the flag and the nation when
Your ancestors were hunting squirrels
In the back-woods away from the fighting lines.
You loved the Yankees, too,
So you drove them and dragged them by the ears
Into a war they had no stomach for.
You conscripted them
And drove them to the slaughter
And wouldn't let them quit when they wanted to.
You made them win, so they ought to thank you,
And bless you for the heaps of blue-coated corpses
That stretched from the Rio Grande
To the Atlantic Ocean.

You didn't want Jack Armstrong's blood on your hands;
I wonder how it feels to have the blood
Of thousands there.

— John Kelley.[1] —

I hesitate to name your name,
John Kelley,
For I shrink from obscenity.
I hope you feel white,
After pilloring a child before a snarling pack
Of yellow-bellied swine, who after all,
Were whiter at heart than you, John Kelley.
You should feel proud, Honorable sir,
For the dung you have cast into the faces
Of the American people;
For the blow you have dealt at American womanhood,
And the woman-hood of your own color and race,
John Kelley.
You have betrayed the women of your race,
John Kelley,
And if you had the soul of a man instead of a hog,
Your dreams would be haunted by dim shapes
And quivering shadows,
By tear-dimmed eyes and pale faces and slender white hands,
By all the dim women down all Eternity,
Who suffered and passed through the red portals of Hell
To give you being, John Kelley.
This is my word to you,
And may you remember it.
It is my hope that your yellow-bellied pets
Will deal with you some day as you have dealt with your own
People;
That they will nail you into a barrel
Full of razor blades
And roll you down a hill into hell, John Kelley.

Your parody was not only comical like anything, but it was clever as the devil. I roared witt lefter witt apprishiashun witt glee.

Haley gave you a nice write-up, but no more than you deserved.[2] I hope his boost will cause you to sell some more of your books. Where did you get the Siringo book,[3] and how much did it cost? If not too much, I think I'll get a copy. I'm interested in the bold buccaleeros of early days. The other day in Ft. Worth I was talking to a man who knew Ben Thompson, and visited him in his cell right after he bumped off Jack Harris over in San Antonio. He said

Benjamin was practically the father of the city of Austin. Benjamin wrote his autobiography, but I've never seen a copy of it.[4] From what White intimates, it handles the truth with an easy abandon reminiscent of Joan Lowell.

More aborted parody.

The Tom Thumb Moider Mystery.

Chapter .1.

"Harry the Fourth was a godly king,
And he loved greatly godly bells;
He bade them ring and he bade them swing
Till a man could hear naught ellz.
In every tavern they soured the sack,
With discord and with din,
But we drowned them all with armadra-gaul
Like this at the Mermaid Inn."

Thus I sang merrily as I shined Vilo Pants' boots, while he watched me suspiciously from the chandelier. I had just spat carefully on the off-heel and was prepared to give it the final gloss with my shirt-tail, when a caulking mallet bouncing off my skull, made me aware that Vilo was seeking to attract my attention in his subtle way.

Casting a sly wink at him, I asked him, "What now, old boy?"

"Are you aware," he rapped, "that there are 5000,00000 stars in the galaxy known as Bunena-isle? So named because discovered by Titus Sonofascutus, while eating an oyster named Algernon. However, Plautus Kickontherumpo doubts if Cleopatra had red hair. Curse you — oh, damn you!"

"Well, what about it?" I asked, for his subtleties are often beyond my dull comprehension.

"Put it in a foot-note, you unspeakable swine," he snarled, angered beyond measure at my stupidity. "It will impress the bone-headed reader, blast his soul."

Staggered by the dazzling gleam of his intellect thus flooded upon me, I staggered — I reeled! With a haunting scream of appreciation I fell headlong down a forty-story elevator shaft. As I struck the basement the building reeled! The earth shook! Tons of stone and broken beams came raining down! Through the hurtling chaos and thundering walls that buckled crazily and fell with a roar, rode Cormac FitzGeoffrey, cleaving the warriors of Genghis Khan as Subotai's cleaver splits an apple pie. But even as he shouted in ferocious triumph, Steve Costigan shattered his helmet with a terrific right hook, and Kid Allison —

(Editor's note: only a slight jar on the head; nothing serious; possibly four or five compound fractures of the skull, and a few concussions.)

Chapter .2.

"Give me my shoes," ordered Vilo, and I gave them to him with such enthusiasm that one stuck in his throat, and I had to pry it out with a boot-jack named Pablo. Having donned his foot wear, and broken open my tin bank with an axe to discourage me from hoarding nickels, he turned on me.

"You louse!" he hissed, fixing me with icy glare which he obtained at a nearby Frigidaire. "Where is my murder? Is this story to drag on indefinitely? If you do not soon produce a murder worthy of my talent, I'll see what I can do about it myself!"

And his eyes wandered meaningly from my neck to a fifty pound battle-axe which his ancestor Sir Vilo de Pants did not wield at the battle of Antioch, or anywhere else, to be exact. I caught his drift.

"I catch your drift," I said.

"Thank you," he said stiffly. "Kindly hand it to me. I despise a drift which is always running around over the building and having to be caught. But you are evading the point."

"Knob's Point," I said with a ghastly laugh. "I was never there, but a relative of yours, old Captain Vilo McPants caught a sardine there named Abercrombie. What a night that was! He wooed the old moonshiner's brown-eyed daughter, and would have married her, only the old man's gun snapped."

Vilo snarled. Sometimes I think he is a bit self-centered.

"I'll get my hat and look up Squarkam," he snapped. "He always has a few good murders on ice."

He strode across the floor, jerked open the door — he recoiled with a piercing scream as a corpse fell stiffly out the closet at his feet.

"Help, murder!" screamed Vilo, bounding lightly to the chandelier. Then recovering his poise, he shouted: "Grab that corpse! Don't let it get away! Hold it for a material witness! Oh, boy, will this make a hit at headquarters! Get hold of Squarkam right away."

"I'd rather have hold of that little blond I seen him with last night," I snickered.

"That wasn't no blond, that was my favorite bootblack's wife," scowled Vilo. "She used too much Niggo-Bleacho. Ah, here comes Squarkam and Teeth."

"A murder, hey?" said Squarkam, while Teeth scowled at the corpse, and hissed, "Anything youse says will be yoused against use!"

"Come clean!" roared Squarkam, kicking the corpse in the ribs.

"Better put him on the grill," said Teeth. "He looks tough. Wait'll I put the cuffs on him — the ungrateful hound might bite us or somethin'."

Chapter .3.

"And so your ancestor Vilo the Bastard," I said, scribbling away at my friend's geniality — I believe that's genealogy, but who the hell cares? "So your noble ancestor burned this girl's house down and nabbed her as she ran out in her nightie, eh? And he raped her and gave her a couple of black eyes and left her hanging by her ankles to a tree limb. Gad, what love is! What a power! What a passion! What a man!

"Then he was captured by the king's men and thrown in the jug, and he saw her in her true light. The fickle wench! He sent word for her to change places and clothes with him, so he could escape while they took her out and chopped her fool head off, and she refused! Aye, she refused, damn her for the heartless she-devil she was! Thus strong men lose faith in women! She had been exalted by his pure love, and now — now — Ah, Vilo, pardon this passion! It's enough to make a man lose faith in woman-kind!

"But he escaped when the headsman's axe, erring from its arc, missed his neck and shattered to singing sparks on his adamantine skull. Rising, he smote the headsman on the jaw, and fled to the Orient, where, amid the luxuries of an Eastern seraglio, he —"

"Hold up!" exclaimed Vilo hastily. "Remember, this is for publication. Here comes Squarkam. What luck, old boy?"

"Rotten," said Squarkam, wiping off the sweat. "Toughest egg I ever grilled. He won't say a word. We've pulled his thumbs out of joint, singed his eyeballs, twisted his ears with iron pincers, and read the Congressional Record to him for an hour, but he just lays there and says nothing. Damn such a corpse!"

"Come, men," said Vilo determinedly. "We must search for evidence ourselves!"

So we went forth in disguise as members of the Vice Squad, and to be in keeping with his role, Vilo assaulted a little girl down a back alley. However, the little girl, who was Max Schmeling in disguise, knocked Vilo stiff and went on up the alley with a deep insulting snort of laughter.

Chapter .4.

"Well," said Squarkam jovially, "I believe I've got a clue at last! My bold-boys raided a kindergarten and they've got the ring-leader up at head-quarters, giving him the works! Tough egg — ten years old if he's a day. He fought like a tiger — shot Sergeant Teeth with a bean-shooter. They carried the brave sergeant off on a stretcher. There's a man! Credit to the force! As they carried him off, he struggled to rise — to get to his feet. He thought they weren't getting him out of range fast enough. He said, 'I don't give a damn who gets hurt, so long as it ain't me.' There's spirit for you! I'm having those glowing words framed to hang in the police-court, and I'm going to give every man a copy, so they can study them and guide their lives accordingly. Though God knows they couldn't follow that precept much more closely than they do already."

We went into the room of the police court where they keep the racks, thumb-screws, stakes, branding-irons, braziers, etc., for the purpose of making testimony as fair and unbiased as possible. Fifteen cops and the district attorney were working on the prisoner, whose howls of rage were so ferocious that Squarkam turned pale and shouted for them to throw ten more fathoms of steel cable around the prisoner before he broke loose and slaughtered them all with his cap-pistol.

"He says he can prove an alibi," said one of the cops, sweating with the exertion, as he approached us reelingly. He was on the verge of tears. "I've gone over him with a red hot iron," he wailed, "from head to foot for an hour, and the exertion is too much for me."

He burst into weeping.

"There, there," soothed Squarkam, taking him on his lap and singing a lullaby to him.

"Police life is hell," he remarked to Vilo and myself. "You've no idea what the police endure from these hardened criminals. I remember one hussy whom we had to pull out all her finger nails by the roots before she'd confess. I was completely worn out."

The weary cop had sunk into a babe-like slumber. Squarkam deposited him carefully in a spittoon, and approached the prisoner.

"Alibi, eh?" he grunted. "Make a fool out of the cops? Eh? Witnesses to prove he had nothing to do with the murder? Well, we can't fritter around forever trying to find the criminal. Go out and shoot all this fellow's witnesses."

"Well," said Vilo disgustedly. "This is the bunk. A corpse falls out of my closet, and no clues. It's a riddle —"

"Riddel!" howled the corpse sitting up suddenly. "Ha ha hah!" he laughed maniacally. "Now I remember! I was sitting in the reading room of the club! I took up a book with the name of John Riddel! I read. I became more and more bored. Suddenly all went blank!"

"Aha!" exclaimed Vilo triumphantly. "The corpse was never dead! He comes to life! Well, anybody is liable to go into catalepsy reading the tripe that louse Riddel hands out for literature!"

More gems from Olson:

"The A-Rama is Einstein A-Space, the B-Rama is brain or Brama, the C-Rama is Solar Plexus or Pain and in it's cappacity of being organic Pain it is Visshnue the creator and the D-Rama is that thing we know as Drama, which is the four-armed ballance of Shiva the destroyer, being the basical gender in nature and being in effect also sex, since sex and ellementairy nature is the same thing actually, as soon as I explain it -----"

"The chief thing Jesus tried to impress was that want is in itself allmight and that by means of training the mind for greater wants and the body to hold greater hungers, if anything hapens to the consciousness, the atoms hold the hunger and do not break in decay, accordingly as the stomack eats up the filler and the blood thins down, the person comes up with high hungers and if he is a fool he is then a vampire."

"Accordingly, no vampire, however vampirally ignorant he may be, can possibly be as vampirical as yourself and all the people of the earth, since not knowing this, you account not at all the strict code that is Mrs. Cornelius VanderBilt or Mrs. Astor or that of any Duke or Duchess of the world — Why do you suppose that a Duke considers that he may withouth regrets pierce with his sword a man that refuses to pay him respect — A man that refuses to stop and utterly postphone the filling of his hungers the instance the Duke appears in the vicinity?"

He also sends me a damnable chain letter and tells me I dare not refuse to continue the chain. Like hell I don't. I might excuse his insanity, but writers of chain-letters are a blight and a stumbling block on the road of progress.

Well, I see they had the decency to pardon the defendants in that Hawaii business.[5] It was a black shame that they were ever tried. And now they're not going to re-try those swine that helped rape the girl. Well, they shouldn't crucify her in the court-room again, but it's utterly damnable and revolting that those bastards should go free. The white people of Hawaii, if there are any left, should take them out and burn them alive. Then they ought to hang every juror that sat on the case, and as for that damned swine Kelley, they ought to tie him up in the market place and skin him alive. And I don't know but what they ought to hang the judge, too. I hope the boycott won't fall through. Even if the people are pardoned, that don't condone the swinishness of the jurors. But it's a poor revenge, and shows how low the manhood of America has sunk, when the women have to protect and avenge their sex by a commercial boycott. American men are undoubtedly the yellowest, most unspeakably cowardly lice in the world. It's time the women took hold of the country — they're the only sex left with any guts. If I thought it was any better there, I'd transfer my citizenship to the Irish Free State. Those cut-throats seem to have a little manhood left about them, anyhow. I don't know but what Australia would be a pretty good place, judging from the riots they've been having there. I've about decided that the Australians are the only white men left in the world. And they're handicapped by the damned British government they live under. Whereas Americans have been bludgeoned by laws and exploited by big business hogs, until they have no spirit left.

I see *Sport Story* is offering .1¢ per word instead of .2¢. Also Bates writes me that *Astounding Story* is going on the bi-monthly basis, while *Strange Tales* will be made a quarterly. Also that both magazines are well stocked on material. If this keeps up, I'm s.o.l., but what the hell. A writer either starves or works himself to death. Often both.
Authorial version of Duna, or however the hell it's spelled.

When I was a little lad
And lived on hog and beans,
I fain would be a-writing lies
For all the magazines.
But now across the bread-line
Evermore I hear
The swiftly busting markets
Cracking clear.
When I was a young man
Before my hair was grey,
On werewolves and prize-fighters
I toiled my life away.
But I'm weary and busted,

And wobbly in the dome,
And the beans and sow-belly
Call me home.

Write soon, or I'll send youse a bomb by express collect.

Fear Dunn.

P.S. Have you heard about .3¢ postage stamps? That'll be great.

NOTES

1. John Kelley was the prosecutor in the Massie case; see letter 203, note 6.
2. J. Evetts Haley wrote the review of Smith's *Frontier's Generation* in *The Southwestern Historical Quarterly*.
3. Probably *Riata and Spurs*.
4. In *Lead and Likker*, Owen P. White made liberal use of "Ben's own words," but they were from *Life and Adventures of Ben Thompson* by Major W.M. Walton, not an autobiography.
5. The Massie case, see letter 203, note 6.

TSS: 82548-82553

ଓଃ୨୦ଓଃ୨୦

208. To H.P. Lovecraft, May 24, 1932.

Dear Mr. Lovecraft:

Glad you liked the Oriental story, and thank you very much for the kind things you said about it. It's always with misgivings that I submit an Eastern yarn to the magazine, for I never know how many glaring errors and mistakes I've made. My knowledge of the Orient is extremely sketchy, and I have to draw on my imagination to supply missing links which I can't learn in the scanty references at my command. Price and Miller,[1] however, are a big help in the matter of Arabic names, grammar, etc..

I read with much interest your comments regarding theoretical conquests of the West by the East, and vice versa. As you say, the Arabs, at their height, were far more highly civilized than we, and an Arabic conquest — had it not been for the fundamental difference in nature — might not have been so bad — though the mind revolts at the thought. I agree with you that a Mongolian conquest would have been a mess. It seems to me that the Mongol tends to degenerate even quicker than the Aryan, when thrown from his nomadic pristine existence into luxurious environments, and more completely — as witness the decay of the Seljuks in Asia Minor, whose magnificent empire went to pieces scarcely more than fifty years after they swept out of High Asia. And look at the static condition of the Ottoman today — however, the Ottoman is a mongrel of the most tangled type, and he was never a Turk, anyhow, in the true sense of the word. If we'd been over-run and conquered by Turks or Tatars, I imagine the present-day western world would present a bewildering and paradoxical picture — probably with names like Yaruktash McDonald, Genghis O'Brien, or Tughluk Murphy.

Alexandria must have presented a gorgeous pageantry of splendor and colorful contrasts. I'd never thought much about it, and hadn't realized that it kept its Grecian character so long. We of the West are well mixed, but the natives of the Mediterranean must be mongrelized beyond all reckoning.

Thank you very much for your comments on "People of the Dark" and "The Horror from the Mound." Your remarks concerning the latter story especially encourages me. I'd begun to fear it was a complete wash-out, seeing that Bates originally rejected it, and some of my friends weren't much impressed with it. But your kind comments revive my confidence. Please extend my heartiest thanks, also, to Mr. Cook and Mr. Munn, both gentlemen for whose literary talents I have the sincerest regard. I fear my demoniac Black Book scarcely deserves Mr. Munn's high compliments. I am sorry that his work does not appear more often in *Weird Tales*. I remember his "City of Spiders"[2] as one of the most striking and powerful stories I have ever read; and his "Tales of the Werewolf Clan"[3] had the real historic sweep. He is evidently a deeply read student of history.

Poor Olson — what you say of him clinches my conclusion that he is completely insane. I first heard from him a long time ago when he wrote commenting on my "Hills of the Dead"; favorably, by the way. "The Horror from the Mound" seems to have enraged him. He hasn't pulled any "C-Space" or "vectors" on me, though he has had considerable to say about "Ramas" A,B,C, etc.. Neither has he given me the secret of immortality, though he has hinted darkly at it. I've never answered any of his letters, though the impulse has been strong to reply with a missive that would make his ravings sound like the prosaic theorizings of a professor fossilized in conventions. But it would be a poor thing to make game of the unfortunate soul.

I was much interested in what you said of the man Lumley, of Buffalo.[4] He must be indeed an interesting study; possibly of such a sensitive and delicate nature that he has, more or less unconsciously, taken refuge from reality in misty imaginings and occult dreams. I hope he completes his story, and that it is published. Do you believe the "Oriental Ancient" has any existence outside his imagination? There is to me a terrible pathos in a man's vain wanderings on occult paths, and clutching at non-existent things, as a refuge from the soul-crushing stark realities of life. One of the tragedies of Man, mounting to almost cosmic heights, it seems to me, would be for a human, having spent all his life groping in the shadows, to realize on his death-bed, that his gropings and imaginings were vain, and that his visions of "something beyond" were mere self-induced phantasies — to have all his props and stays of mysticisms and dreams and fancies and beliefs, blown suddenly away like smoke before the hard wind of reality, leaving him writhing feebly on the jagged rocks of materiality, dying as any other insect dies, and knowing that he is no divine spirit in tune with some mystic infinity, but only a faint spark of material light, to be extinguished forever in the blackness of the ultimate abyss.

I had realized, from your writings, something of the fascination sky-effects have for you, and your remarks pertaining to this subject are really poetic in vivid beauty. Like you I am moved by the golden glory that foreruns some sunsets; and then, in the long summer days, when the skies are cloudless, I am stirred by the dreamy magic of slumbering twilights, between the set of the sun, and the gathering of night. At such times familiar sights somehow take on an alien and glamorous aspect; gables of houses, wood-clad hills, even figures of people moving through the twilight. Somehow, when I see high-ridged houses blocked out darkly against the deepening blue of a western twilight sky, a vagrant thought enters my mind, a dim semi-expectancy, of fantastic winged monsters dropping from the sky and lighting on the dusk-etched roofs, folding their great wings and crouching there gargoyle-like, their chins resting in their cupped and taloned hands.

I mentioned the cloud-effects on the Callahan Divide. Some are tenuous and beautiful as golden webs or silver fleece. More are lurid, sinister, menacing and grim. This strip of country is known as the cyclone-belt, and terrible storms have wrought havoc in the past. When a funnel-shaped tornado tears across the country, men are utterly helpless. They can but crawl into cellars, if they have time, and listen to their property being blown away and destroyed, and thank the Powers if they escape with their lives. The utter helplessness of mankind before a storm is a terrible sensation. You can not strangle the lightning with your hands, you can not riddle the clouds with bullets, and you can not hack the wind with a knife. If you die, you die like a sheep, and if you live, it is by the whim of chance or the Prince of the Air. Outside of actual wind-storms, this country is much subject to terrific thunder-storms, floods of rain, hail-storms, and in drouths, sand-storms, which, of all the atmospheric disturbances I have mentioned, I much prefer. Among my earliest recollections as a child, scarce out of infancy, is that of crouching in dank, dark, or dim-lit, and sometimes reptile-haunted, cellars, while outside the wind shrieked and raved through the night, ripping the branches and leaves from the trees, while rain fell in mad foaming torrents, crashes of thunder shook the very earth, and blinding, insane rips of lightning gleamed through the cracks of the cellar-door.

Sorry to hear Swanson has had to give up his *Galaxy*. As you say, the game was given a sock below the belt when Claytons changed the appearances of their *Strange Tales* and *Astounding Stories*. The change in *Strange Tales* hit me viciously in the pocket-book, because I'd apparently just got started good with them. Another of my regular markets — *Fight Stories* — was taken out of circulation entirely recently. I like the idea of an "abridged" *Necronomicon*. After all, it wouldn't be a good idea to let the general public in on *all* the dark secrets of antiquity! Besides, you might later, in a discreet way, bring out the suppressed chapters of the demoniac work, and cash in again. If you were careful enough to word these secret chapters so nobody could possibly understand the text, the average reader would lay it down with the feeling that he'd been dipping into genuine inside dope of the cosmos, his admiration for the author would mount to heights of actual worship, and I bet half a dozen new secret cults and occult societies would spring up like mushrooms. As regards the hellish Black Book, if I can find some well-educated maniac, who hasn't been crammed with conventional occult hokus-pokus, I may have him write it for publication. If not, I may shoot myself full of dope sometime, and write it myself.

That Hawaii business is a rotten reek in the nostrils of decent men. I agree with you in believing that the island should be put under military or naval rule, and in hoping that the dirty yellow-bellies that committed the crime will be put away properly. I know what would have happened to them in Texas. I don't know whether an Oriental smells any different than a nigger when he's roasting, but I'm willing to bet the aroma of scorching hide would have the same chastening effect on his surviving tribesmen. Yet I consider the actual perpetrators of the crime more decent and honorable than the attorney who prosecuted the avengers, and the jury — supposedly composed largely of white men — which convicted them. I guess outside pressure was brought to bear on the jurymen — I understand Hawaii is controlled by Oriental interests. Instead of a boycott, a noose should have been used wholesale. As for the attorney, for any white man who is low enough to crucify an outraged child of his own color before a mongrel swarm, a roll down a hill in a barrel full of safety-razor blades is too good for him. It is my ardent hope that he will come to his end at the hands of some of his yellow-bellied pets, and that his demise will be neither swift nor painless.

I hope the boycott will continue, but it is a poor revenge, and shows to what depths of powerless cowardice American manhood has sunk, when they leave the settling of a case like that in the hands of their women. American men had better give the government over to the women, for the men have become the most spineless, yellow, cringing cowards the world has yet seen. I'm thinking of writing to my congressman to put a bill before the House recommending that men be exempt from active service in the next war, so that the women may do the fighting. If it's left to the men, America will get the hell kicked out of her. I am unable to decide whether the deterioration of the American man is a result of his domination from birth by women, or whether that domination is a result of his damned spinelessness. If this degeneration continues, damned if I don't move to the Irish Free State. Those cut-throats seem to have a good deal of manhood left. And judging from the riots and gang-fights in Australia, there are plenty of white men left in that part of the world. Australia may be the last stand of the Aryan race.

Returning to Hawaii — which I would like to do with a squadron of bombing-planes — I heard the war-correspondent, Floyd Gibbons, talk over the radio after his return from that part of the world. According to him, forty percent of the Hawaiian population are Japanese; control of the island has passed into the hands of Orientals — I guess American politicians cater to their votes and power, just as certain politicians cater to the Mexican vote along the Border — and Americans are about as safe there, and get about as much justice, as they would in a purely Oriental government. More, he did more than hint that in case of war with Japan, a concerted uprising, with arms furnished by the Japanese government, would rob America of her western-most defense, and leave her coasts open to attack. Which seems reasonable enough, and is all the more reason for putting the cursed island under a naval authority. I hope Hoover or somebody restores full citizenship to the defendants. It was a dirty black shame they were ever convicted, or even indicted.

As regards that Hindu, I only saw him once. Since the Hawaiian affair, I've had a bad taste in my mouth for all Orientals, Aryan or otherwise. I'd have been interested in his view-point on the affair — but it would have probably been just the opposite of mine, in which case I might have crowned him in the heat of the moment, at least immediately after the verdict of guilty was rendered, which shocked and infuriated me beyond measure.

As concerns the hazards of existence in the Southwest, anybody would think a virile, intensely hardy people would be bred thereby, and in some parts of the state, and in many individual cases, that is true. But here, as elsewhere, the old stock is degenerating, despite everything. Ignorance, poverty, undernourishment, and other things are destroying the descendants of the pioneers. Through this part of the country especially, the poverty, and illiteracy, of the rural population is depressing. Crowded out of the fertile parts of the state by Bohemians, Poles and Germans, the American country-people are in many parts sinking into utter degeneracy. The old free independent spirit of their ancestors seems lost entirely. In some cases, that spirit never existed anyway. Many of the inhabitants of Texas, especially in these parts, are sons and daughters, or grandchildren of poverty-stricken tenant farmers from the clay hills, sand drifts, and creeks of Georgia, Tennessee, Alabama, and other southern states — poor white trash, they were called there. They were never slave-holders, never owned the land they worked, and therefore never tried to improve their state, and they brought their characteristics to Texas. When land was cheap and plentiful, they did fairly well, according to their lights — moving onto another strip, when they had worn out and exhausted the original farm. Then land ceased to be free and plentiful, and they were stuck on the side of some alkali hill, or in the midst of a waste of sand drifts or post-oaks. There they stuck, those who had progressed enough to own their own land. Generally their sons sold it for what it would bring, and again took up the existence of tenant farmers — and nothing is more devitalizing to the land and the man. Why waste more work than necessary on land you'll never own? Texas was ruined when the squatters swarmed in and made an indifferent agricultural state out of a magnificent cattle-empire.

As regards that bould bucko Red, of the sledge-hammer fists and adamantine skull, he was merely a higher developed example of a type most common in all oil fields — a slugger, a bully, a swash-buckler, possessed of small mentality and great animal courage in certain ways. He was imported from Ranger by the gang of thugs which was then trying to run the town; after Red failed to turn the trick, the city-marshal was framed by them on a bootleg charge and lost his job, whereupon the more boisterous element held high revel day and night. Where Red came from, I don't know. Oklahoma, some said, but I'm more inclined to think he was originally from Pennsylvania or West Virginia. I never heard of him using a weapon of any sort in his scraps, and most of the Oklahoma toughs I've seen — and that state has sent more bad men into Texas oil fields than any other state in the Union — were handy with knife or gun.

At present Oklahoma is being ravaged by a thug called "Pretty-boy" Floyd, who seems to be a reversion to the old-time outlaw type. He has eleven men to his credit, seven or eight or which are officers of the law, which probably accounts for the failure of the authorities to apprehend him. It's a lot easier to beat a confession of some sort out of some harmless poor devil than it is to nab a young desperado who wears a steel bullet-proof vest, and draws and shoots like lightning with either hand.

He's being touted as a second Billy the Kid, but deadly as he undoubtedly is, I doubt if he has quite the ability of that young rattlesnake. I consider the Kid the greatest gunman that ever strapped a holster to his leg, and that's taking in a lot of territory.

If I expressed my opinion as to the three greatest gunmen the West ever produced, I would say — and doubtless be instantly refuted from scores of sources, since you can't compare humans like you can horses — but I'd say, in the order named, Billy the Kid of New Mexico, Wild Bill Hickok of Kansas, and John Wesley Hardin of Texas. The Kid killed twenty-one men in his short eventful lifetime; Hardin had twenty-three notches on his pistol-butt when John Selman shot him down in an El Paso saloon; how many men Wild Bill killed will probably never be known; conservative estimate puts the number at fifty-odd. But Wild Bill had a somewhat softer snap than the Kid, since the quick draw had not attained its ultimate heights when he was at his best. As for the famous fight with the McCandlas gang, on which much of Hickok's fame rests — in which he is supposed to have killed seven or eight of them in hand-to-hand combat, unaided, I've heard on pretty good authority that he had plenty of help, and that far from being an open, stand-up fight, Hickok and his friend way-laid the McCandlas's and mowed them down with shot-guns, and that some of Wild Bill's lady friends aided in the fray by beating out their victims' brains with hoes and mattocks, while they lay wounded on the ground. But that Wild Bill was a master killer can not be denied; differing from most gun-men, who generally aimed at the body, Wild Bill usually shot his victims in the head.

But somehow I've wondered off the subject, which was oil-field bullies. The fightingest son-of-a-gun that ever came into the Callahan oil-fields was a full-blooded Irishman from the Pennsylvania hill-country. He wasn't an unusually big man, as they go, but he was built up like a brick-house. He was steel cords and lightning — strong as a bull, with a blinding, steel-trap co-ordination that made him supreme among the general run of lumbering, slow-witted sluggers. He used to wrap his wrists and arms half-way up to the elbows with adhesive tape — to keep them from shattering under his terrific blows — and then invade the toughest joint he could find and go to the mat with the entire attendance. I've heard he licked eleven men in one day, but can't verify that statement. But he would have been a champion, if he'd gone into the ring. He fought for the sheer fun of it, and laughed all the time he fought. He wasn't a bully, in the accepted sense of the word; he never picked a fight with a peaceable man; his meat was the swaggering brawlers who thought they were tough. It's a wonder somebody didn't kill him. But he lived to die young, in a natural manner. At least, in a manner so common to oil field workers that it might be considered natural, since it was syphilis that mowed him down. It affected his mind long before it touched his magnificent body, and he lost the use of his vocal cords. He used to come into the drugstore where I worked, quite often, and he always wanted me to wait on him, since I was the only one who seemed to have sense enough, or was sober enough, to understand his signs. He couldn't speak articulately, but made noises like an infant, though he never entirely lost his sanity. And this is strange — long after he lost the power to speak ordinary simple words, he could still pronounce oaths and profane phrases. At last he died, and for months before death came, he was like a skeleton, with a hairless, parchment-like yellowish skin stretched over his skull like a death-mask.

I've seen some human ruins in my time, from venereal diseases, liquor, dope — paregoric was a great favorite with certain types. It used to make me gape, the amount an addict could store away at a time. But it knocks them quicker than other kinds of dope. Of all the paregoric-fiends that used to haunt the place I where I worked, the only one that's still alive — at least he was alive the last time I heard of him, and he must have gotten off the stuff — is an ex-vaudeville actor. He used to do clog-dances for us, after the crowd had gone and we were ready to close the joint for the night. He must have been good, before he hit the toboggan, for he still had a nimble foot.

Small things turn a man from his road into by-paths and blind-alleys, sometimes. I believe the average wretch, instead of being booted onto the road to ruin with some gigantic overwhelming cataclysm, is helped gradually, a push here and a shove there, until he's well on the down-rush, and the hob-nails of a tender-hearted humanity shower joyously on his bleeding head, and hurl him headlong on his way in a blaze of glory and cat-calls.

If mankind's affairs are tinkered with from Outside, it must be with malicious intent. If a man walks across a ten-acre tract in the dark, with one rock on it, he'll invariably bust his toe on that rock. If there is one weak spot in the ice on a frozen river five hundred miles long, he'll find it and fall through. If he is confronted with seventeen roads, one of which leads into a cactus-bed and the other sixteen to his destination, he will inevitably select the one wrong road. With seven doors leading out of an unlighted room, he will blunder into an open closet and stick his toe into a mouse-trap. I remember the heavy sign-board on a store next to the place I worked, which swung to and fro in a hard wind all night, and nearly worked loose. Everybody said it was going to fall, and the natives of the town walked shy of it. Scores of people passed and went around it. Then, just as I glanced out of the drugstore where I was working, I saw a smart dressed young salesman, a stranger in the town, advancing briskly, and knew that he was going to walk under the sign-board. I didn't have time to warn him, but I knew the board would fall, the instant he got under it. It did, and crashed on his head with what sounded like a whoop of delight, smashing his hat and laying his scalp open. He came into the drugstore bleeding like a stuck hog, and everybody surveyed him gloomily, as another example of the capriciousness of chance. I'm beginning to doubt the element of coincidence; it looks like a systematic plot to make life miserable for humanity, and the next time I fall over a chair in the dark, that shouldn't be there, I'm going to look under it for a gnome, or an elf, or some other varmint from Outside!

I remember various galling experiences, where the random-element, or the law of averages, or something, came up behind me and kicked me in the pants with a hob-nailed boot, and one as galling as any, that still makes me writhe and mutter profanely when I think of it, happened when I was a kid of ten or eleven, in a country school. I was stockily built and fairly proficient in the brutal and unscientific style of wrestling then prevalent in the country, which depended less on speed and skill, than on strength and endurance. One day the teachers came out of the school-house to watch us play — a rare event. I happened to be wrestling with a friend of mine, and they stopped to watch us. I wished to make an impression on them — to show off, in other words. I wished for a worthier opponent — since I had thrown this particular friend forty or fifty times. And while I was wishing, suddenly and stunningly I found myself thrown! It never happened before, and it never happened again — at least, with that boy. I was shocked, humiliated, well-nigh maddened. I urged a renewal of the strife, but the teachers laughed mockingly and withdrew into their sanctum. I withdrew from public view, and broodingly contemplated my shameful defeat. I sought soothing of stung vanity by vanquishing my conqueror, but it did not rob my original defeat of its sting. The teachers did not know I had been thrown by chance; they thought my friend was the better man. They probably think it to this day. I plotted a return match, some day when the moguls should again emerge to watch the antics of the herd, but it was not to be. A few weeks later the boy I wrestled went to his last reward with a bullet through his heart, and I never got to vindicate myself in the sight of those awesome and superior beings, the Teachers.

Another thing that discourages me, is the absolute unreliability of human senses. If a hunting hound's nose fooled him as often as a human's faculties betray him, the hound wouldn't be worth a damn. The first time this fact was brought to my mind was when I was quite small, and hearing a cousin relate the details of a camping trip, on which one Boy Scout shot another through the heart with a .22 calibre target rifle. I was never a Boy Scout, but I understand that they are trained to be keen observers. Well, there were about twenty looking on, and no two of them told the same story in court. And each insisted that his version was the correct one, and stuck to it. And I understand that this is common among all witnesses.

I devoutly hope I'll never be a witness in a court-trial, because I'd probably be so muddled, and make so many contradicting statements that my testimony would land *me* in the jug, instead of the defendant.

It's amazing how twisted a story can get, after passing through the mouths of even three or four people. There seems to be a perverse obstinacy in the human critter that prevents him seeing or realizing the true facts of a case. I remember once when I was working in an automobile agency during a town-site oil boom; I was alone in the place, when I heard a groaning and cussing on the outside and saw one of the town's would-be bad men approaching the joint, using a repeating shot-gun for a crutch. From the way he stumbled along, and the noise he was making, I thought maybe he'd accidentally shot himself and was bleeding to death. But when I hopefully questioned him on the subject, he replied profanely and with many racking moans, that he had re-hurt an old strain. He was barely able to walk. I helped him into a chair and leaned his gun against the wall, while he sat and pitied himself, nearly weeping as he spoke of the pain of his hurt. Like all synthetic bad men, and most of the real article, he wasn't endowed with a great deal of guts when it came to enduring pain himself. That breed is strong on dealing misery, but not so strong on taking it. After awhile I went out, leaving him still sympathizing with himself in the chair, and started across the street to a drugstore. As I crossed the street, an auto came careering down on the wrong side, and I jumped out of the way, startled and angry. But there was a man slumped down beside the driver, and from the ghastly pallor of his face and the limp way his head rolled, I knew that he was dying. I went on into the drugstore and later, while I was getting a drink, a fellow came in and asked who it was that had gotten shot. Another fellow came in and said that it was Bill D.. I here spoke up and told them that Bill D. was still in the land of the living and had only strained a tendon. They looked at me unbelievingly, and one of them said that was hokum; that Bill D. was the man, because he saw him limping along on his shot-gun, groaning like a man in his last throes. I answered that the man who had been shot, had not been able to limp; that I had seen him as he was rushed to first aid; and that if they doubted my word, let them go over and personally inspect Bill D. whom they would find sitting in a chair in the auto agency. By this time their eyes were flashing and their jaws were setting with the perverse instinct of the human who thinks his word is being doubted. It's quite possible I might have had a most unwelcome fight on my hands, when another party entered who confirmed my statement, and told them that it was another man than the afflicted and disputed Bill D. who had blown half his foot off climbing through a fence with a shot-gun, and bled to death before he could be given proper treatment. The debaters grudgingly let themselves be convinced, but I doubt if either of them ever had any use for me after that.

Your mention of Wandrei, in connection with Minnesota dust-storms, reminds me to ask about the book-length weird story he was writing. Has he finished it yet, and if so, has he found a buyer? I hope he has, or will be able to market it. His work shows a deep imagination, and a delicate touch in plot-development. His state is one — in fact, the only one — in the Mid-West, which touches my fancy somehow, the northern-most of all the states, where surely some traditions of the pioneer West must still be alive. When I try to visualize it, I merely get a mixed-up impression of vast plains covered with waving grain, cold gigantic blue skies, huge football teams, and Scandinavians with mystic blue eyes and yellow moustaches. The state must be a veritable power-house of virility.

Strange to say, the sandstorms stopped abruptly some weeks ago, and since then the whole state has been flooded with rains. There was a heavy rain last night, with some hail, and it has been cloudy today, though it seems to be clearing now. There is, in the southeast, a great heap of fleecy white thunderheads exactly like clouds in a Doré illustration. From behind them, and partly veiling them, sweeps a fan-shaped drift of light grey cloud, little heavier than mist, covering a quarter of the sky, and sharing the young dim moon in its feathery fringes. There may be hail and wind tonight, and men and their works be swept into Eternity, but just now the whole sky is soft and beautiful with sunset.

There have not been, in years, sandstorms such as the country used to know. As more and more of the Panhandle and upland plains are being put in cultivation, the drift of the sand is checked to some extent. I remember how they used to come up — sometimes suddenly, with driving clouds, a spatter of rain, and then a gust of wind-swept dust that swept the skies clean of all else. But often their coming was somewhat in this fashion: The sun would rise red and hot, in a clear breathless sky. There were no clouds, but a sort of breathless tenseness. Even in the early morning, the scanty flowers wilted with the heat, and the young leaves drooped on their stalk. Then the wind began to rise, in fitful gusts that rose and ceased suddenly. In the northwest a long low black line appeared, that grew with appalling speed. It rose steadily, seeming to climb into the sky, though its lower edge never left the earth. At first it seemed like a hideous black cloud. On it swept, towering higher and higher; now it reared its awesome crest hundreds of feet in height, and was like a black tidal-wave — an onrushing basaltic wall, stretching from east to west — a black wall five hundred feet high and ten miles long. Black dots whirled above it, which were quickly seen to be buzzards and birds of prey, flying hard before it. Now it loomed half-way to the zenith, and an awesome roar filled the air. Yet suddenly the terror of it was gone; it was no longer black but reddish-brown, and then with a rush and roar, the sand-particles were whirling past, and the wind was howling through your hair, and the sand-storm was on. It might last for days, sinking to a whisper at night, perhaps, to roar with renewed vigor at dawn. There would be no clouds, only driving, pelting, whistling sand — sand — sand! which found rest in your eyes, ears, nostrils, mouth, hair; which filtered through window frames in steady streams, and sifted under doors until a passing foot left a clear imprint. You found sand in your bed, in your clothes, your shoes, your food. When you opened your mouth to curse it, you felt grit between your teeth. At midday you could look unwinking into the sun, which hung like a pale yellow ball in a reddish flying drift. At night you might glimpse a few stars high in the dim hazy sky, lent a strange alien silver by the dust-laden atmosphere, or a moon, surrounded by a pale yellowish glow, might glimmer through. For a day or so after the wind had ceased blowing, the dust still veiled the skies, lending everything a strange unnatural quality, an aspect of illusion and witchery.

I'm sorry to hear you've been under the weather, and hope that by now you've made a complete recovery. I didn't go to the oil fields, after all. I got no further than Fort Worth, where the condition of my health caused me to abandon my plans. I remained there a few days, and then returned to Cross Plains. My health seems to have suddenly gone on the rocks, caused, I think, by strain and too close confinement. My occupation causes me to spend too much time indoors, and allows me too little time for exercize; but there is no help for it, and the shrinking of my markets forces me to increase, rather than diminish, the length and intensity of my working hours. I am not worrying; I've been on the verge of a complete break-down half a dozen times before, and my bull-like physique and vitality has always pulled me through.

Thanks for the post-card views, which, as always, proved most interesting. I envy you your visit into Massachusetts. The museums must be fascinating, and I would have enjoyed examining the Hittite relics, I know — not that I know much about such things, but remains of the Hittite and Babylonian civilizations have a peculiar fascination for me. Assyrian, also. Something that strikes me as strange, is the fact that Assyria's rule was a never-ending series of wars to put down revolts, which threatened her domination to the very end of her empire. There was scarcely a year that did not see some of her various provinces in rebellion, and the more savagely the Assyrians punished rebellions, the more fiercely the rebels rose. Those ancient Semitic nations must have been people of remarkable virility; and yet the Aryan Persians and Medes crushed these same nations easily, and had little trouble with the very races that had struggled, more or less successfully, against Assyria for centuries.

By the way, there is something I want to ask you, my own ideas on the matter being pretty vague. It is this: when you quote a bit of verse, or a few prose lines from some author, or use the same as a heading for a chapter, are you supposed to always get permission from the publishers of the original text? And when the stuff's been reprinted several times, how are you going to find out who holds the original copyright? Any information you could give me on this point would be greatly appreciated.

Another thing; I've recently joined the American Fiction Guild, which looks like a pretty good thing. If you are not already a member, and would care to look into it, I'll have them send you some literature regarding it.

I hope you'll get to take that trip you spoke of, and that it will come up to expectations. Your mention of Dwyer reminds me that I owe him a letter. He recently let me read his "Brooklyn Nights" which I found fascinating. He is a natural poet.

With best wishes,

Cordially,
[REH.]

P.S. I just received the Whitehead letter. Thanks very much for forwarding it to me. I don't know how I managed to be so careless as to neglect to give Mr. Whitehead my address. I'd already decided not to make any contract with the agent in question, and had written him to that effect. Mr. Whitehead's letter certainly clinches the matter.

If you haven't already obtained a copy of *Oriental Stories*, containing my "Sowers of the Thunder", I'll be more than glad to lend you mine.

I'm enclosing a rhyme induced by recent Asiatic affairs;[5] no hurry about returning it. Wright rejected the antediluvian Texas story;[6] not enough weirdness about it.

R.E.H.

NOTES

1. E. Hoffmann Price and Warren Hastings Miller.
2. November 1926.
3. "The Werewolf of Ponkert," July 1925, and five other stories through January 1931.
4. William Lumley, author of "Dweller."
5. The Massie case; see letter 203, note 6.
6. "Marchers of Valhalla."

TSS: 25358-25366

ଔଓଔଓ

209. To Carl Swanson, ca. late May1932.

Dear Mr. Swanson:

I'm sorry you had to give up the idea of publishing *The Galaxy*, but the magazine world as a whole is pretty shaky these days. I hope when — and if — times get better, you'll be able to carry out your original plan.

With best wishes.

Cordially,
Robert E. Howard

TSS: 92114

ଔଓଔଓ

210. To Tevis Clyde Smith, ca. very late May 1932.

Fear Finn:

Let us tool forth to Australia; yet I'm afraid I've lived among jelly-fish so long that I'm no fit companion for vertebrates. I'd like to have talkt to the fellow who was stationed in our Pacific Paradise. From what I hear the Hawaiian must about be extinct; I've heard that the percent of pure kanakas is very small, the race having been replaced by a mongrel breed of Chino-Japo-Malo-niggo-basto scum calling themselves Hawaiian, to which the lordly white politicians get down and lick their lousy feet for votes. I hear forty percent of the population is pure Japanese, and that it's an open secret that they'll revolt and take the islands in case of war with Japan. That would eliminate America's one Pacific defense. The Californians will wake up some morning with the little brown brother sitting on their necks.

Three cheers for 3 ¢ stamps. Our ancestors took away the tax-rights from the British empire, so they could give it to their own big-bellies. Our taxes make king George's levies look like the timid exploitation of a piker. Representation? Heh!heh!heh! Eeze deeze a juck! The John Bulls have taxes and beer. We have taxes. Yea, verily, we improved our lot by kicking out of the empire. "We are the pipple of England and we have not spucken yet." Nor we won't, either, except to cheer madly when the big-bellies tell us to cheer.

I hope your glasses help you. Eye trouble is hell. Mine are beginning to give me trouble; I don't know whether they'll stand up to the strain of continuous work or not. I've been averaging at least six hours a day, seven days out of the week, recently. The more work I do, the less I seem to sell. My markets are shot and so am I. I reckon I've passed my pinnacle. I'm beginning to cast about for some other form of livelihood. I told you years ago that I didn't intend to slave my whole life away for a bare living. That still goes. If my eyes hold up, though, I'm going to slave for another year.

The yammerings and droolings of Paul S. Smith of Orange[1] and his breed begin to bear fruit; Farnsworth rejected four out of the last six stories I sent him, and almost invariably the reason was given as not weird enough. Bates[2] also sends my stuff back and sympathizes with himself for the task it is to edit my stuff; if I could sell more junk, I'd buy a typewriter easier on the editors' eyes. Byrne[3] rejects my tripe — with reason; I'm slipping on action stories. Rather, I've already slipped. Mashburn complains that my characters are too bitter against the world and life as a whole. Continued disappointments in one's career are likely to curdle one's optimism. E. Hoffmann Price writes that his corporation has given him the sack, and that he intends to devote all his time to writing. Hundreds of part-time authors have been dumped on the market, and that makes competition tougher. The part time writer is often more efficient than the professional; he's had more time to study style and literature. An agency wrote me wanting to handle my stuff for a year or so. They bragged on what they'd done for Whitehead; I wrote Whitehead and he replied cryptically that he considered himself heap damn fortunate to have gotten out of their talons as soon as he did.

If you read "Jungle Girl" in the latest Oriental, you might be interested to know that it has a factual base. Miller[4] writes me, "Ah welladay; I won a bottle of champagne on that girl. She was the most beautiful female creature I ever laid eyes on, and Lord De B— had the nerve to bring her to the St. George in Algiers, where all the respectable matrons sniffed and gave her the icy lorgnette. I bet my aunt I could run off with her under his nose, and did. He had not begun to treat her mean yet, but I could see it coming; hence the story. He had her on safari with him down in Nigeria at that time."

Miller says further that the original Warren Hastings was an ancestor of his; and that we — the Aryans — are lower down than the lowest-down Malay in the matter of money-grabbing, etc.. He also said that some of his yarns, recently published in *Oriental's*, had laid around for ten years without a buyer until Farnsworth came along.

I was much interested in your thumb-nail of Suffi Limbaugh. I imagine he's quite a character. To my mind mysticism is a dreary and empty substitute for material pleasures, but I don't set myself up as a judge. Not that all mystics forego materiality. Lovecraft tells me about an old fellow who writes him all sorts of phantasies about esoteric subjects, and relates spectral manifestations glimpsed in haunted houses and the like; he professes to have pried into all the mysterious corners of the world, and to be hand-in-glove with a cryptic being he calls "the Oriental ancient" who apparently bobs up unexpectedly from behind sofas and well-curbs, gives vent to philosophic gems and utterances, and vanishes again. Lovecraft thinks the old gentleman is on the border-line of sanity, but one Brobst, a brain student, thinks he is nuts. Lovecraft tells me that Olson bombards Whitehead regularly with his ravings, and urges all the sages of the world to gang up and summon the cryptic "vectors" to aid them in foiling the plot of the diabolic "C-Space" to destroy the material universe.

Getting back to Limbaugh, I quite agree with some of his ideas, except the twelve intelligent men to rule Texas. That means we'd have to import a bunch of foreigners.

Now my damnable typewriter is going to pieces. I broke the left margin catch off it, and the letters are out of line, and in order to write at all I have to swing on each key like I was punching a bag. So I'm going to cut this letter short, and see if I can fix the blasted thing.

Fear Dunn.

P.S. More rejections from Byrne, and another rejection from Farnsworth complaining that my former "divine fire" is apparently out. I've changed my mind about that year business. But I'll work for another six months, if I'm able to.

NOTES

1. Smith's letter in The Eyrie, *Weird Tales*, February 1932, complained that "The Dark Man" was "not the least bit weird."
2. Harry Bates, editor of *Strange Tales*.
3. John F. Byrne, editor of Fiction House (*Fight Stories*, *Action Stories*).
4. Warren Hastings Miller.

TSS: 82048-82049

ঞ

211. To Wilfred Blanch Talman, ca. July 1932.

Dear Mr. Talman:

Thanks very much for *De Halve Maen.*[1] I found it very interesting indeed, particularly the list of words of Dutch origin. Noting that the Holland society is made up of people whose ancestors came to America before 1675 makes me feel almost like a recent immigrant. The Howards didn't come till 1733 — with Oglethorpe to Georgia — and one branch, the MacHenrys, didn't come until about 1770; although the Eiarbhins, or Ervins, to Anglicize it, were well established in the Carolinas in the latter part of the 17th century. The MacHenrys, incidentally, landed in New York, but they didn't stay there long; they dropped the Mac, and drifted southwestward. I said landed; I should have said, thrown off the boat by the English.

About *An Albanach Goidhel,*[2] I would indeed like to read it, though it seems pretty much of an imposition on you, especially in the light of the new postage rates.

Glad you liked the Solomon Kane story.[3] It's been on ice some time; that is to say, I believe it's been in the editorial office for some two years. Maybe since I wrote it I've rubbed some of the kinks out of my style. And again, maybe not.

Concerning firearms: I've heard of the Sullivan Law, which seems incredible in a civilized country. Although gun-toting is gradually going out of fashion, all over the land. Personally, I haven't packed one regularly in years. When I was a kid of about fourteen or fifteen, I used to tote an old .44 stuck down in the waistband of my pants. Not that I ever needed or used it, but it was a sort of natural thing, especially in the oil fields. The trigger wouldn't work and I had to fan the hammer. At close range I attained a certain proficiency, but at any distance I would defy John Wesley Hardin himself to hit anything with it. Sometimes it threw low and to the right, sometimes high and to the left; it spit powder backwards and frequently sheared the bullet, thereby endangering the user's life. I also used to pack an old Frontier model Colt .45 single-action — borrowed. It was a real gun, though heavy to pack. My favorite pocket-gun is the Colt .380 automatic. It's small, compact, easy to carry in your waistband, and highly effective at close range. Another good light gun is a hammerless five-shot .32; no hammer to catch in your clothes as you draw it. But mine isn't much good; I got it out of an East Texas hock-shop, and it hadn't been handled right. Nine times out of ten a gun won't do you any good in trouble. If you're held up, the other fellow generally has the drop on you anyhow. But there's always a chance that it might come in handy. I saw the time once in a town at midnight up on the Oklahoma line when I'd have given a tooth for a smoke-wagon of any kind.

Cordially,
REH

NOTES

1. Publication of the Holland America Society.
2. *The Scottish Gael*, see letter 199, note 1.
3. "Wings in the Night," July 1932.

TSS: 15328

ঞ৪ঞঞ

212. To H.P. Lovecraft, July 13, 1932.

Dear Mr. Lovecraft:

It is with the utmost humiliation that I begin this letter. It had long been my intention, since you first mentioned, a year or so ago, your intention of visiting New Orleans, it had been my intention, I say, to meet you there and bring you on out into Texas. I wanted to meet you, and to show you my native country. I intended buying an automobile, and being able to show you the whole state, as I might have remarked. But circumstances prevented it; the failure of certain banks, the crumpling of fiction markets, and other conditions reduced me suddenly to that penniless condition out of which I had begun slowly and painfully to climb. Far from buying an automobile, I found myself unable even to secure a saddle-pony. I say all this without shame, since I am in no way to blame, but bitter regret, since I was unable to carry out former plans for your entertainment. Nor is it my intention of burdening your ears with my troubles, but because I owe you an explanation for my failure to meet you in New Orleans. I realize now the truths of certain old adages. A wasted youth is not to be made up for by the most intense application and the hardest work of the more mature years. Still, as hope springs eternally etc., I still look forward to some dim time when I'll be able to entertain you on my native heath as royally as I wish.

I'm glad you and Price[1] had an enjoyable time. I could hardly have ventured to intrude my crude ideas in such an intellectual discussion as I know your conversation was, but I would have enjoyed intensely sitting and listening. Price was much impressed with you, according to his letters to me, and remarked that he had benefited much by your knowledge of literary workmanship. I would be interested in your reactions (I believe that's the phrase) toward him. As you probably know, I've never met him personally, though I have a high regard for him, both as a workman, through his work, and as an individual, reflecting from his letters to me. I believe he has a great future as an author before him. In his last letter he said that he'd be probably unable to visit me any time soon. I look forward to meeting him. I had to decline a recent invitation from Kirk Mashburn of Houston, who wished Price and me to spend a week-end with him. Houston might as well be Kabul as far as my chances of going there, even on excursion rates.

I thank you very much for the intriguing views you have sent me, and which go into my permanent files — likewise whetting my desire to see those places first-hand. Your vivid descriptions of the Southern terrain I have read and re-read, getting a clearer idea than I ever got from study of text-books. Somehow it comes to me with a feeling of strangeness and unreality, the realization that my ancestors climbed those mountains, rode through those valleys, drank from those rivers, and trod those streets. Only some eighty years ago men of my name left the river-plantations and pushed southwestward, and yet it is difficult for me to realize that my family had its roots anywhere but in the land where I was born and came to manhood. Among these post-oak-covered hills and mesquite-grown plains my instincts seem to place my ancestry for a thousand years. And my instinctive urge is westward, not eastward. I feel a strong longing to visit the Old South and to linger among its mellow beauties, but only as a visitor. The pull from the other direction is stronger. I can not go east permanently; when I am able to make a move from this dreary country, I must go westward — to the Big Bend, to New Mexico, or Arizona. This is not a conclusion reached by any logical reasoning process; it is a natural instinct with me. For centuries my people have pushed slowly westward. It is not in me to change that trend. But I strongly desire to see all the vast land that lies east of the Mississippi; and hope to see it some day.

Speaking of Mongol stocks, I notice the Finns seem to be somewhat divided among themselves, even to the point of violence. But as you say, they and the Hungarians have adapted themselves to western civilization surprizingly well for Mongolians. I think the backwardness of the Turks can be laid partly to the fact that they have always been more or less of a conquering caste, with the resultant intolerance of change, and distaste of manual work. They came out of the steppes, wandering, fighting nomads, who gained their living by following the flocks and plundering their fellow-man. They imposed their will on hordes of country-folk who did their work for them. The Turk has always scorned all labor but that of war. And what fighters they are! They are the one people whom decay and degeneration has not robbed of their pristine warlike heritage. History does not show a race, not even Roman or Spartan, which can boast of such consistent courage. Clean or depraved, honorable or degenerate, proud or besotted, the valor of the Turk has remained forever constant, as if it were a natural characteristic shining apart, untouched by the other characteristics of the man or the nation. I can not find an instance in which Turks showed the white feather. I intensely admire their high courage, and I hope to live to see the day when the Ottoman empire will be finally and completely swept out of existence.

I was, as always, much interested in your remarks concerning the classical world, of which I know so little. What a city Alexandria must have been! I had no idea of the origin of the word parchment. As I've said before, your letters are an actual education for me. Some day I must try to study the ancient Grecian world. It's always seemed so vague and unreal to me, in contrast to the roaring, brawling, drunken, bawdy chaos of the Middle Ages in which my instincts have always been fixed. When I go beyond the Middle Ages, my instincts veer to Assyria and Babylon, where again I seem to visualize a bloody, drunken, brawling, lecherous medley. My vague instincts towards classical Greece go no further than a dim impression of calm, serene white marble statues in a slumbering grove. Though I know the people of the classic times must have wenched and brawled and guzzled like any other people, but I can not conceive of them. The first mythology I ever read was that of Greece, but even then it seemed apart and impersonal, without the instinctive appeal I later found in Germanic mythology. Once I tried to write polished verse and prose with the classic touch, and my efforts were merely ridiculous, like Falstaff trying to don the mantle of Pindar.

I stopped writing this letter long enough to listen to the final session of the Democratic convention, which I've been following over the radio to the extent of staying up all night to listen to the — I believe it was the sixth session. I was pleased that Garner got the nomination for Vice-president; John deserved it, because it was his votes that swung the nomination of President for Roosevelt. It's well said John is for the people; I lived three years in Red River County where he was born, and anyone born there is bound to be of the people. No bloated capitalists there, not in those days, anyhow. A lady in Mission, near which Garner owns a good deal of land, told me last winter that many a time she's seen him out in the pastures burning stickers off prickly pears for his cattle during drouths. A homely touch that I appreciate highly, because that's all that kept the cattle in this section alive during the big drouth of '17 and '18. Of course my favorite candidate was Bill Murray of Oklahoma, but I knew he didn't have a chance from the start.

Bill Murray has more solid timber in him than any other man in American politics. A certain newspaper man spoke rather condescendingly of him, over the air. Let no man be deceived by the fact that Bill scorns the dapper dress and airy ways so much thought of by some people. Bill Murray has more real education than any other man in politics today, and enough sand in his craw to make the Sahara Desert look like a piker. Ealy of Massachusetts — or however his name is spelled — spoke of Al Smith as a second Jackson. Ye gods! If there's a man in the world today that remotely resembles old Hickory, it's Bill Murray. I'm proud to have been born in the same county as he was.

Anyway, I reckon Tammany will learn finally that they can't shove Al Smith down the gullet of the Democratic party.

Referring to "Pretty-Boy" Floyd, he's still at large, as near as I can learn, having recently shot his way out of a trap where the police had him surrounded. It's rumored that he was in the farm-house in Missouri the night the Young brothers massacred those six officers, and I think it quite probable. You know the Youngs were cornered in Houston and killed themselves. I don't think Floyd will go out that way. He'll probably be shot in the back by one of his own gang who wants the big reward.

I was much interested in your remarks concerning the various zones of physical violence, and was considerably surprized as well, to learn that certain sections of the country are comparatively free from violence. I supposed that men quarreled and fought with fists and weapons about equally all over the nation. While I never travelled much, I've been thrown in with men from many countries and states, in the cosmopolitan oil fields, and I've found them about uniform in regard to aggressiveness and courage, regardless of where they come from. Some were quarrelsome and pugnacious, some were retiring and peace-loving, and it seemed to depend entirely on the individual. With this exception — I don't believe I ever saw an Oklahoman who wouldn't fight at the drop of a hat — and frequently drop the hat himself. But in general it seems to me, from my observation, that the average man is opposed to violence, except as a last resort, and disapproves of it largely, regardless of where he comes from. Of course, the world is full of bullies, who strut and swagger and impose on quiet people, and is also full of raw young fellows who feel their oats, and while perhaps are not actually vicious, are always looking for an opportunity of giving their physical prowess free rein. Understand, I am not questioning your remarks concerning the zoning of American violence. Recently I have studied statistics, since reading those remarks, which bear you out surprizingly well. I can not understand it, for I don't believe the average Southwesterner is possessed of any more real warlike instincts or courage than the average American wherever you find him. I leave the explanation to smarter men than I am. I was interested in your young Kentuckian. Many Kentuckians have come to Texas, and I know several personally — "blue-grass men", mostly. That state must be the bloodiest in the union. One of my friends is a relative to the McCoys, of the famous McCoy-Hatfield feud, and the tales he tells of even modern Kentucky, can scarcely be touched by anything in modern Texas, unless it be found in some of the more primitive border sections. Another was a government agent who spied on the moonshiners, and from what he says, there is, or was, at least, a distinct feud between the mountaineers and the blue-grass people. The old hostility between the people of the barren mountains, and the people of the fertile valley. He is an old man now, and conditions doubtless have changed. But it would stir your blood to hear his tales of raid and counter-raid, flight, pursuit, and the stark savagery of bloody battles in the hills.

Returning to violence in the Southwest. I have seen a good many fights and brawls, and more have gone on without my having witnessed them, all about me, all my life. Judging from the number of such affairs, it would seem the people of this country were unusually quarrelsome. Yet these fights and feuds were in the main carried on by a small minority of people who were forever quarrelling and fighting with each other. The majority of people went about their business and seldom resorted to any kind of violence. For instance, in a country school I attended, when about ten or eleven years of age, there was usually a fight going on on the grounds, any time you looked around, yet these scraps were almost invariably between a group of perhaps half-a-dozen boys, whose main object in life seemed to be the mutilating of each others' features. They fought each other and it was very rare that any of the rest of us ever had any trouble, either with them or with each other. And these fights seldom amounted to anything. The real blood flew when the trouble lay between persons who were not generally quarrelsome. It stands to reason that a boy or man who fights all the time doesn't expect to take his average scrap too seriously. There are exceptions to this rule, but they frequently die young.

For myself, I can say, truthfully, that, with one exception, I always did my best to avoid trouble of all kinds, and never fought unless a quarrel was deliberately forced on me, and I had to act in self-defense. There is a sordidity and bestiality in the average alley-fight that is bound to repel any man of ordinary sensitivity. A friendly go with the gloves is different, or a clean fight in the ring, with no hard feelings. That's good and healthy. But a tearing, gouging, biting, kicking dog-fight, down in the muck, with a dirty crowd yelling and cursing — that's neither cleanly nor decent. Though many a bully is in his element there. There's much of the actor in the average bully, and he must have his audience. I take notice that if you challenge him to come away from his gang, out in woods or fields with only the naked earth and the sky to watch, and none to cheer him on and none to tear your fingers from his throat if the fight goes against him, very often he will decline the invitation.

Most of the people I know are like me — they hate trouble and avoid it as much as possible. Yet it does seem that there is a great deal of quarreling and scrapping going on all the time. I attribute this in part to the great numbers of bullies in the world. They won't let a man alone. This was particularly true during the oil booms, of course. But the country at any time is too much infested by such bravoes. The average bully is a creature of great muscular power and feeble intelligence, whose main object in life seems to be the imposing of his presence on less belligerent people. He swaggers and brags and talks loud, scowls and swears and blusters; his conceit is monstrous and often takes the place of courage, bolstering him up to acts, the guts for which he would otherwise lack. He assumes that he is greatly feared, simply because the average man would rather give him the path, and let him bellow, than to get into a fight or some other kind of trouble. Because a man gets out of a skunk's way is no sign he is particularly afraid of the varmint. But the professional bully is a thorn in the flesh of decent men. Once let him get the idea that you are afraid of him, and he grows drunk with egotism, and starts riding you. He seldom has sense enough to know when he's gone far enough, and I've known men to be driven to momentary madness — and murder — by the continual abuse of such a character. It's one of the many injustices — if that's a proper word — of this country and system. A bully doesn't generally start picking on you unless he is your physical superior. And he usually has a gang behind him. There are three courses open to you, and each is abhorrent. You can swallow his insults and indignities until your very guts revolt; you can resent them, and get beaten into a pulp, with perhaps your ribs stamped in and your teeth kicked out after you're down and out; or you can kill the bastard and likely go into court and listen to his pals swear your life away. Rats rally to one another's defense much quicker than honest men rally to help one another.

There is one consolation to a peace-loving man; the average bully doesn't last many years. He gets shot up or cut up, or he gets on the wrong man and has the devil beaten and stamped out of him, and mends his ways — sometimes. I've seen bad men, semi-bad-men and would-be bad men come and go, and it was a bear-cat that lasted over ten years.

Talking about Red, whom I mentioned in a previous letter, got me to thinking about a fellow who was probably the worst man, for all-around toughness, that this part of the country ever produced. The oil field didn't bring him in — he was born and raised down in Brown County, some miles south of this place. Now I think of it, I believe he had a harder head than Red. In his palmy days I never heard of anyone daring to tackle him with anything less than a club or a gun-barrel. He was tall, lithe, slit-eyed, wore a sort of sardonic half-smile on his lips usually, and walked with the springy tread of a big cat. And he was all bad. He used to come into the boom-town joints with a six-shooter in his hand and advise the customers to hunt the floor, because he was going to start shooting waist-high and at random. But concerning the adamantine quality of his skull — I don't know how many knocks it withstood in the course of his lurid career, but I do know of the following incidents: in the boom days of Desdemona, he stuck his head into a gambling dive and instantly somebody wrapped a lead pipe around it, fracturing his skull; he was laid up for weeks, but recovered; the city marshal of Cross Plains had him down in the street one night, hammering his head with a gun-barrel, when one of his pals knocked the marshal kicking from behind, and the tough customer departed, apparently none the worse for the battering; the proprietor of a hotel in the same town struck him over the head with a pistol-barrel, knocking him down a whole flight of stairs; none of these taps seemed to worry him a great deal. But years of dissipation and wild living finally told on him. He drifted away into other oil fields, and when he came back to this country, he seemed but a hull of a man. Men who formerly feared him, pummeled him with impunity. And his aborted sense of humor brought more trouble on his long-suffering head. In a poker game, for a joke, he reached across the table and cut one of the players from his shoulder to the hip on the opposite side. It wasn't a deep cut, just through the skin, but it bled like a butchered steer. The victim, a former school-mate of mine, thought so little of the jest, that he procured a rock and hammered the joker's scalp into a beastly mess, before he could be pulled off. I didn't see the incident, but I saw the joker some days later and damned if he didn't look like the last rose of summer. His scalp — which he never had bandaged — had mostly healed, but the terrible mauling had somehow affected his arm, and his legs. He held his arm in an unnatural manner, and walked jerkily. I don't believe the fellow's head will stand many more beatings without his mind being affected. He seems to have vanished again — off to the East Texas fields, I imagine. The last time I talked with him — several years ago — he'd been up in the hills of Arkansas, and evidently got into a crowd too tough for him, even. He said those benighted Arkansawyers were not civilized, and that he considered himself lucky to have escaped with his life, leaving behind his entire bank-roll. By which I deduce that he won their money with the cards, and they took it back — and his too — at the point of a gun; a custom not unknown in the oil fields.

By the way, one night a few weeks ago I was wakened from sleep by the crash of a .44 and a terrible cry that marked the end of one of the town's toughest characters. You have doubtless noticed the inhuman quality in the last cry of a man stricken by death. I don't know which is the more nerve-racking — the death-cry of a man, or the screams of a woman over her dead. This was a freak-shot, in a way; it was fired at close range, and it seems as if it should have torn the whole top of the victim's head off, but the bullet, crashing through the rim of the temple, rolled around the inner curve of the skull, cracking it like an egg, and lodged in the back part of the head. The man lived some fourteen or fifteen hours afterwards, with his brains oozing out, but of course he never recovered anything like consciousness — only his incredible vitality kept him alive that long. I had known him for years, but not as a friend. He hated me, but left me severely alone, and that's all I ever asked of any man.

As regards the mysterious workings of adverse chance in regard to man, stumping of toes, breaking of ice, falling of sign-boards, etc., that was mostly in jest, of course. The universe as a whole is undoubtedly indifferent to man and his paltry wishes and ambitions. Though I am by no means certain that unseen and only dimly suspected forms of life and energy do not impinge upon us from Outside. The universe as a unit is indifferent to man, true; but it is full of material, visible beings not indifferent to him and his works — mosquitoes, jack-rabbits, man-eating tigers. They prey on him or furnish him sustenance as the case may be. I am not certain that there are not invisible beings and forms of matter, above or below our senses of discernment, which are not altogether oblivious or indifferent to mankind. This is no question of the supernatural; there may be beings and forms of life natural enough in their sphere and plane, yet still intangible to us.

Yet for accidents, it is true that certain people seem targets for accidents, because of some lack in their make-up — some lack of coordination, concentration, or reasoning faculty, perhaps. I knew a fellow once who was a good example of that. This person, a classmate of my earlier days, had scars all over him from various blunders and mishaps. He had scars from machinery into which he had managed to get his fingers; scars gotten from whittling, sawing, and driving nails; one scar, I regret to say, he'd gotten from my knife. But mishaps seemed to dog him continually, and it was my honest conviction when I told him that he was doomed to perish early in life. Nor had he been out of school many years, when, having climbed into a tree to help free an aviator whose parachute had caught in the branches, he fell from an upper limb and landed headfirst. He weighed 212 pounds, and he never recovered consciousness.

I don't know what's come over Texas. Instead of drouths, we have floods. Right now all the western rivers are on the rampage; the Colorado, the Frio, the Guadalupe, the Nueces, the San Antonio, and all the others. At least nine lives have been lost, and the damage to property runs into the hundreds of thousands of dollars. Highways and railroads have been washed out, bridges washed away. And naturally, humanity couldn't be content with the damage the elements were doing, but they had to war on each other. Guns barked in the flooded district to the southwest and a soldier out of San Antonio got a slug through his heart. All up and down the flooded area survivors clinging to trees and house-tops were taken off by the rescuers. Most of the damage to property was in southwestern Texas, but the water was higher in this part of the woods than I've ever seen it. Judas, what a rain! It started raining about midnight, and along towards dawn it turned into what almost amounted to a cloud-burst. I've seen it rain in Louisiana and the East Texas blacklands, but I never saw such a rain — and this section was almost on the fringe of it, the main bulk falling west of here. All the creeks and rivers rose out of bank, and the Brown County lake, which was estimated would be two years in filling, was flooded over-night; 145 miles of shore-line, and mighty deep, too.[2] That was four days ago, and still the water is gushing over the spill-way, in spite of the fact that all flood-gates are being kept wide open, to take care of the surplus. Two main streams run into the lake — the Pecan Bayou and the Jim Ned, and the water in both streams is backed up for miles. I never saw so much water in West Texas in all my life. A new high-way, recently built by Brown County at much expense, was simply cut to pieces. The farmers along those streams are ruined; their whole crops swept down to the Gulf. Particularly those above the new highway that crosses the Bayou. Against the urgent protests of these men, the highway engineers built a dump or levee across the river bottom, more than half a mile wide — supposed to keep the highway above water. To the assertions that the flood-gaps were not large enough to accommodate the water at high-tide, they merely laughed. What do farmers know about road-building and bridge-building? So this flood ripped their fine levee to shreds, rushed over it and washed the highway down the creek; and what is much worse, the remnants of the levee backed the water up and ruined hundreds of acres of grain which otherwise might have escaped destruction.

That's a typical example of scientific misrule. What does a farmer, who has only lived on the bank of a stream fifty or sixty years, know in comparison to a dapper young engineer, who has been out of a technical college for at least six months? The tyranny of science is beginning to irk the people. I could mention numbers of incidents, not in civil engineering alone, in which blunders cloaked in the name of science have been imposed on the people, over-riding the protests of experience and common judgment. Scientific methods are being made a fad and a fetish. I have no quarrel with true science; but I would suggest that the devotees of science realize that there may be sound sense in men who never went to college and to whom the technical jargon may be sheer gibberish. We have made gods out of our scientists; but they have no right to practise their theories on us. They presume too much; a club properly applied might bring home a realization of the rights of humanity, even unlettered humanity, to whom science is a closed book, and who know only what their experiences have taught them.

Ah, well, if our leaders will give us back our booze I will quarrel with no one. My entrails have been insulted with so many damnable concoctions for so many years, that I fear I may have lost the ability to appreciate good liquor — though on my pilgrimages to Mexico I find that knack unimpaired so far. I shudder when I think of the stuff I've put into my innards. Looking back, I find that drinking, in this country at least, has been divided more or less definitely into various epochs, in each of which a different brand of poison and hell-fire dominated the thirsts of the people. Right after prohibition came in, everybody drank a tonic known as Force, which bore a picture on its label of Samson tearing the lion — and its effect was similar; they alternated this with another tonic known as Lyko. Then followed a fruit extract period, until the companies began bringing out extracts without alcoholic content. I still recall the fervent and sincere bitter blasphemies of staunch souls who had quaffed numbers of bottles of extracts, before discovering their non-alcoholic nature. Then came the boom-days of Jamaica ginger, which exceeded all epochs before and since. I doubt not that even now the mad-houses are filled with the gibbering votaries of jake. Legislation interfered with jake, and the makers of white mule, red eye and rot-gut came into their own. Of course, these drinks had been interwoven in all the other periods. Alternating poisons were hair-tonics, wood-alcohol and canned heat. I've seen old soaks who apparently preferred canned heat to anything else. Then there were other tonics — Sherry Bitters, Padres Wine Elixir, Virginia Dare. Virginia Dare tastes the best — that is to say, a strong man can get it down by gagging and holding his nose. A friend of mine and I stood one rainy night in the lee of the Brown County library wall, and strove manfully to get down a bottle of Sherry Bitters. Seasoned though we were on rot-gut, we ended by throwing the bottle over the nearest fence and drifting away on the bosom of the great, silent, brooding night. Padres Wine Elixir was a favorite of mine in my younger and more unregenerate days. It is bottled in California, and is merely a cheap grade of red wine, with enough drugs in it to make it nominally a tonic. Those drugs change it from a mere low-grade wine to a demon-haunted liquor. It never hits you twice the same way, and will eventually affect your heart. Pay no attention to the amount of alcohol stamped on the label; it varies from bottle to bottle. I have drunk three bottles and gotten no more cock-eyed than I have with half a bottle on another occasion. If you keep it cold it tastes slightly better, but when it's hot it has a more lethal kick.

And yet, when I look back over a sordid past, I find that the worst liquor I ever got hold of bore the government seal and stamp. It was prescription liquor and cost, altogether, seven and a half dollars a pint; more, it purported to be sixteen years old. It knocked me blind and kicking, and if it hadn't been for nearly half a pint of Canadian rye whiskey I drank at the same time, I believe it would have wound my clock. The rye fought the poison in the other stuff. Separately, either might have finished me; together, one counteracted the other. Judas, will I ever forget that debauch! It was colder than hell, one Christmas. There were three of us playing seven-up by a fire in the woods. When the deuces began to look like aces, I called to mind the feat of Rob Roy's son in driving a dirk through a board, and forthwith stabbed at the box on which we were playing, with my hunting knife. But the box was much lighter than the Highlander's board, and knife and fist as well crashed clear through it, ruining the game. The liquor was at all of us, and one was clear wild. In the grip of the obvious hallucination that he was John L. Sullivan, he began to swing hay-makers at me whenever I reeled into reach. He was six feet two in height and as broad as a barn-door; besides, he had heavy cameo rings on each hand, and these rings sunk into my flesh unpleasantly. So I avoided him and sought to go elsewhere; I must have merely revolved about the glade, because eventually I found myself back near the fire, with my misguided friend grunting and swearing as he flailed his long arms about my ears. In desperation I caught him under the heart with my right and down he went. I remember pulling him out of the fire; and then for hours I remembered nothing, while I lay blind and senseless. But I remember the dawn that broke, cold, grey, leaden — full of retching, disgust and remorse. Uggh — those drab, brittle, grey woods! When we went to the town, we found the countryside in an uproar; for while we lay drunk, the "Santa Claus" gang that had looted Southwestern banks for more than a year, had swept into Cisco, 35 miles away and in an attempt to rob the main bank, had raved into a wholesale gun-battle that strewed the streets with dead and wounded.[3] Two or three of them had gotten away into the brush and posses were beating the hills for them. To invitations to join the man-hunt, my friends and I laughed hollowly; we were in no shape to even lift a gun to our shoulders, much less confront a band of desperate outlaws.

Gad, the country buzzed like so many bees! The authorities sent south for the great Ranger captain Tom Hickman, and Gonzaullas — "Lone Wolf" Gonzaullas — "Trigger Finger" Gonzaullas — "Quick Action" Gonzaullas — hero of more touch-and-go gun-fights than I know, and already almost a mythical figure in the Southwest. But they were not needed; the fugitives staggered in and gave themselves up — haggard shapes in torn and muddy garments, caked with blood from bullet-wounds. It was the end of the last great robber-gang of Texas. Let me see; it was three — no, four years ago. It doesn't seem that long. All the Southwest rang with the news. Their names were on all men's tongues. Now I doubt not they are completely forgotten, except by the kin of the men they slew, except by the men who carry the scars of their bullets. Helms, the leader, went to the chair, roaring and cursing blasphemies, fighting against his doom so terribly that the onlookers stood appalled. Hill, the boy whose life was twisted and ruined in his boyhood when a ghastly blunder consigned him to a reformatory instead of the orphanage to which he should have been sent — he is serving a life sentence in the penitentiary, after an escape and a recapture. Blackie, the sardonic jester, dying with a rifle-bullet through him, gasped the names of respectable business men of Wichita Falls as his pals and accomplices, for a last grim jest. Ratcliff, who entered the bank clad in a Santa Claus robe and whiskers to avoid suspicion, feigned madness, killed his jailer, was shot down as he sought to escape by the jailer's daughter, and that night a mob tore him, wounded as he was, from his bunk, and strung him up to a near-by tree, to sway in the shrieking blizzard. Eh — life is a strange fierce thing.

Yesterday I spent most of the day in the flooded district south of here. In that flood, the worst ever experienced in Central West Texas, the devastation to crops and fields has been almost beyond belief. Along the rivers and creeks, the trees for miles are festooned with grain hanging to the stems and branches like Spanish moss. Thousands of bushels of wheat and oats were in the shock, having been cut but not thrashed, and the flood swept it all away. Fences were torn up for miles and washed clean out of sight, or left tangled among trees along the banks. I don't know how many cattle and horses were drowned. The most impressive sight, however, was the Brown County lake. I can not describe the sensations of seeing that gigantic body of water where for so many years I have been accustomed to seeing dry-creek beds, or semi-dry creeks, winding among arid post-oak ridges. It has changed the whole aspect of the countryside. Where fields parched and baked under a dry sun, now vast marshes stretch out. Hills have become islands and peninsulas. Where bridges and ranch-houses stood, water eighty feet deep ripples instead. It is so strange, seeing a big body of water in the midst of this drouth-haunted country of post-oak hills. Where the water is ninety feet deep now, I have seen cattle stagger and fall and perish from thirst. I have seen whirlwinds of dust ripping among the withered mesquite where now the water stretches from brim to brim. It is but the work of men, who stretched a dam between the hills, yet it seems like a miracle. And more so when one recollects that it literally filled itself over-night. 145 miles of shore-line — and one torrential rain filled and overflowed it. For days the flood-gates have been left wide open, and still all the rivers leading into the lakes are backed up-stream for miles. It is the greatest project ever put forward in this part of the country. If times ever pick up again, and men can take up work where they left off, that lake will make the surrounding country blossom like a rose. You can grow almost anything in this country if you have the water. Irrigation ditches will provide that, and from putting in huge fields of grain and cotton, people about the lake will begin the surer and in the long run, more remunerative, practise of intensive farming — raising vegetables and the like on smaller, well-watered patches. Intensive stock-farming will follow, and blooded cattle will replace the scrubs that now swarm the hills — though these have been steadily replaced, in many cases, with purer Herefords. Then the lake will become a pleasure-center; casinos, and places of amusement will grow up along the shore. Men will come there to hunt and fish; for in the shallow, warm marshes, fish will breed and spawn by the millions, and water-birds will come up from the gulf to prey on them.

Just now there is a great deal of resentment among the farmers and stockmen who live up the rivers, who consider the dam the main reason for their ruin in the flood, though in reality much of the damage would have been done, dam nor not. But they should be paid for their fields along the rivers, for with the lake full, any kind of a rise will back the water up over these fields again. There is much hard feeling, and talk of guarding the dam against possible dynamiting. Though I hardly think anyone would be mad enough to do such a thing. The town of Brownwood lies directly below the dam, only ten miles away, and should the dam burst, the havoc wrought there could hardly be conceived.

I'll bet, if prohibition still continues in force, that the moonshiners and bootleggers will swarm about the shores, because the whole lake is surrounded by rugged hills covered with dense thickets, and arms of the lake run up into gorges and inlets where boats of contraband could be concealed. I look for stirring times — and in the amusement centers along the shore, too, when the hill-people come down and get their first look at them. A little liquor to liven things up, and the knives are likely to start humming. If things pick up, some of my friends and I intend to put us up a shack on the lake-shore, in some more or less isolated spot, where we can fish, swim and drink without interference; I know of several good spots. I went over the ground and picked them out before the dam was completed.

An old custom is being revived this year — a two-days "picnic", with, no doubt, the usual attendant rodeo and carnival. Why they want to have the thing, with everybody broke, is more than I can see. Besides, the nerves of the people are on edge, their dispositions are bad, and there's likely to be trouble. There are usually a number of fights; some of the swiftest battles I've ever seen took place at these picnics. I haven't attended these festivals very much for years, because I don't like trouble. However, I think I'll attend the political speeches this time.

Tom Blanton and Joe Jones are running against each other for congress, and they've had several clashes already. Tom called Joe a liar over at Cisco the other day, and they had to hold Joe's old man off him, I heard. I'm hoping they'll tangle at the picnic; but I haven't much expectation. Politicians fight better with their mouths than with their fists. Then I hear a fighter is going to be imported to meet one of the local sluggers, and I want to see that. However it goes, I'll bet it ends in a free-for-all battle.

I was much taken with Wandrei's recent poem, "The Little Gods Wait".[4] It had a distinctly Celtic flavor; so much so that I would not have believed that anyone besides an Irishman could have written it. I have always highly admired Wandrei's work, and I believe I like that poem better than anything else of his I ever read. I have not yet read the latest *Weird Tales*, but can tell that Smith, and Derleth and Schorer, and of course, Price, have written splendidly. I deduce this by simply glancing over the pages. But I am always disappointed in not finding one of your stories in the magazine. I hope something of yours appears soon.

The revived question of prohibition has roused in my mind a question I've intended to ask you for some time; why, when the Saxons and Normans were of practically the same race, should they have differed so greatly in the matter of temperance? On the eve of the battle of Hastings we find the Normans passing the time in pious devotions and meditations, while the Saxons revel and feast and guzzle. Again, studying the customs of those ages, we find the Saxons heaping their boards with whole roasted hogs and oxen, eating and drinking enormously; while the Normans, while their meals consisted of many courses of food prepared in many fanciful ways — gilded meats, pastries carved in the shapes of castles, etc. — ate sparingly and were temperate in their drinking. Did they take up these ways from the neighboring French, or inherit them from their Scandinavian ancestors? On the other hand, the Saxons maintained that gluttony and drunkenness were introduced into England by the Danes — possibly by the followers of that Danish king — Harthaknut, I believe, who, like Alexander, drank himself to death, while toasting the guests of a wedding. The Danes always had a reputation for gluttony. Surely the Norsemen were not otherwise. Longfellow says of Olaf the Christian, that at banquets he was, "first to come and last to go," yet from other, and possibly more accurate sources, I hear that this same monarch detested over-indulgence, so that when one of his nobles over-ate, he compelled him to play the part of the fox, in the somewhat childish games of which Olaf was fond, and he pursued over the hills by the yelping nobles who enacted the role of the hounds. So the varying tastes of the Saxons and Normans remain a mystery, as far as I'm concerned. Can you throw any light on it?

I enclose a clipping concerning Japanese ambitions. I am no economist nor politician, yet I can not but feel that the western peoples do not attach proper importance to the powers rising in the East. My studies of history show that such has always been the case; blinded by their own affairs, the people of the west have ignored the hordes of Attila, Tamerlane, Genghis Khan, Baibars, until those hordes were hammering their armies into bits. Now they ignore Tatar-Russia and Japan. The bodies have hardly rotted in Chapei, yet already Europe and America seem to have forgotten the incident. I can not but feel that European policies and squabbles are thread-bare and outworn; while the people wrangle, they are blind to the powers rising in the East that may some day overwhelm them.

I wish you were here to study folk-ways in the forthcoming picnic. I understand Jim Ferguson, our ex-impeached-governor, is going to speak in favor of his wife, who's running again for governor, having held that office once, herself; there's always fireworks when Jim speaks. In fact, I look for brisk times. Still and all, I repeat, I doubt the wisdom of holding this festival. Bad times and bad liquor; people don't give much of a damn whether they live or die; anything's likely to set them off. Knives may be out before the celebration's over. But I doubt if affairs reach the hilarious state of the cock-fight gatherings down along Pecan Bayou in the Holloway Mountains to the south. When the hill-country sportsmen gather to match their respective fighting roosters, it's no place for a peaceful man. At these gatherings both blood and red licker have flooded freely, and the clashing of the gaffs have mingled with the rattle of sixshooters, knives, and brass knuckles. When you visit me, we'll try to take in one of these shebangs. The new Brown County road runs through a gap in the Holloways, though, and I reckon the country is going to get civilized past all interest. A lot of the old-timers have moved on up the creek.

I'm sorry to hear that your health hasn't been all it should, and hope it hasn't interfered with the enjoyment of your trip. Personally, I can't enjoy anything when I'm sick. I hope you've fully recovered by this time. I certainly envy you the magnificent journey you will have completed by the time you receive this letter, and hope next time you'll be able to extend your trip further westward. There's a weary lot of Texas that isn't at all interesting to a stranger, but there is also much that is fascinating. And of course New Mexico and the West are full of magnificent scenes.

Well, I've inflicted my aimless maunderings on you long enough; thanks again for the fine views, and I hope when next you ride westward, things will be better.

Most cordially yours,

NOTES

1. E. Hoffmann Price.
2. Howard used this situation in "Wild Water"; the flooding occurred on July 3, 1932.
3. The "Santa Claus Bank Robbery" took place December 23, 1927.
4. *Weird Tales*, July 1932.

TSS: 21404-21415

ঌ

213. To H.P. Lovecraft, August 9, 1932.

Dear Mr. Lovecraft:

I am very sorry to hear of your recent bereavement. There is very little one can say on such an occasion, but please accept my sincere sympathy. Such things are the most tragic phase of Life, which is in itself fundamentally tragic.

I am sure you find a certain ease and consolation in your ramblings among the quiet beauties of the scenes you have so well described for me in the past. Old Newport must be a fascinating spot, with its glamour of old times. Thanks very much for the pictures, which I found most interesting, as always with the views you have sent me from your native country.

I'm glad you enjoyed your meeting with Price.[1] He is, indeed, a versatile chap, judging from his letters. I hope he won't find the writing game too hard going; as I'm sure he'll arrive on both feet eventually.

It would indeed be fascinating to trace the routes of my people westward, by going over those trails eastward, as you mentioned. That route would lead me from here to East Texas, then to Arkansas, then to Mississippi, then to Alabama — at last to Georgia, where the Howards landed in 1733. After that — quien sabe? Somewhere on the western coast of England, I imagine. Although because of the infusion of Gaelic blood in the strain after reaching America, I can't feel any real connection with England. From the Atlantic states I'd rather follow the strains that lead unerringly to the hills of Kerry and Galway.

As always, I read your remarks on Romans and Greeks with intense interest. I think no one has a keener and truer insight into those times and peoples than yourself. I'll admit that I derive much more knowledge and entertainment from reading what you write about them, than from reading about them in histories and the like. You infuse life and spirit into what otherwise seems dusty and inert. I have tried to study Greek and Roman history, but have found it dull and to some extent inexplicable. I can not understand their viewpoints. The Achaeans of the Heroic Age interest me, and to a lesser extent, the Romans of the early republic, when they were a struggling tribal-state, if they could be called that. But soon that interest dwindles. I attribute this, not to any real lack of interest those times contain, but to a defect in my own make-up. I am unable to rouse much interest in any highly civilized race, country or epoch, including this one. When a race — almost any race — is emerging from barbarism, or not yet emerged, they hold my interest. I can seem to understand them, and to write intelligently of them. But as they progress toward civilization, my grip on them begins to weaken, until at last it vanishes entirely, and I find their ways and thoughts and ambitions perfectly alien and baffling. Thus the first Mongol conquerors of China and India inspire in me the most intense interest and appreciation; but a few generations later when they have adopted the civilization of their subjects, they stir not a hint of interest in my mind. My study of history has been a continual search for newer barbarians, from age to age.

By the way, the study of the East Roman or Byzantine empire contains a certain amount of interest, what of their continuous wars and intrigues with the Moslems and barbarians Mongoloid and Aryan. What a strange mingling of voluptuous luxury and bloody conspiracy that empire must have been!

You are right, of course, about the relative merits of both political parties. I'll admit I got a big kick out of the Democratic Convention, but then, I'm so constituted that I get momentarily enthusiastic about nearly everything I encounter. I did think that they used the Prohibition question to befog certain more important issues. Roosevelt no doubt has his faults — as who hasn't? — but I'd cut my throat before I'd vote for Hoover. I agree with you that the Conservatives are blind — they ought to read the books you mentioned — but whoever heard of a politician reading anything? We need statesmen, not politicians — men like my revered ancestor, Patrick Henry. Instead we have Andy Mellon and Hoiby de Hoover.

Yes, Pretty Boy is still at large, and getting the blame for every crime committed in Oklahoma. The cops say he's a rat. I'd call him a wolf. The cops are all afraid of him, judging from the way they're not catching him; if he's a rat, what does that make them?

Concerning violence — I fear that I may have created an erroneous impression of Texas as a whole, by my maunderings and sordid reminiscences. I may have appeared to generalize, which one can't do with Texas; it's too big. There are many phases of Texan life, and I represent only a few, and those the more primitive. In many parts of Texas there are centers of culture and refinement — but in those parts I have not lived. In such cities as Houston and Dallas, I imagine you would find much the same conditions as exist in Eastern cities of the same size. Texas is an empire within itself and culture and ignorance, sophistication and primitiveness exist, sometimes almost side by side. Each man is prone to present the side of the shield to which he is familiar, and often falls into the fault of presenting his portion, as the whole. A cultured and educated person in some of the cities of south-eastern Texas, would probably give you a very different view of Texas — but it would be, as applied to the whole, no truer than mine, applied to the whole. It is not the newer, modernized, cultured Texas that speaks in me — in me it is the backwoods that speak. I can scarcely imagine a wider gulf than I have found existing between myself and certain city-bred Texas acquaintances. The gulf between us is infinitely wider than that existing between them and the urban people of the North and the East — if such a gulf indeed exists at all. Portions of Texas are almost earthly paradises, but I do not live in such places and never have. My lot has been forever cast in the high barren ridges, the land of postoaks and sand-drifts, of feuds and drouths, of tenant farmers and small stockmen, where life at best is a drab, savage grind for a bare existence. So it is the more primitive phases of life of which I am a part, and of which I tell and write. You will no doubt find urban Texans who will laugh at me, and say that the tales I tell are impossible and lies; they lie in their teeth, or rather through their ignorance. I make no attempt to interpret their phase of life; let them keep their hands off mine. Pardon this seeming — and irrelevant — heat. I was just thinking of some friends — perhaps I should rather say acquaintances — young members of the intelligentsia, who have made no bones about referring to me as an uncouth barbarian and callous brute. I have no resentment in that direction, but I do resent their skepticism toward the tales I was fool enough to tell them pertaining to the people among which I've lived most of my life. I may be a yokel but I'm no liar.

Pardon the foregoing. I shouldn't inflict my personal conflicts on you. It's bad taste and has no bearing to the matter in hand. What I started out to say was that my remarks and conclusions concerning my native heath have to do with, mainly, my own primitive environments, and are not to be taken as generalities, though I don't doubt they sounded that way.

Concerning beings from Outside, I don't think I said that I assumed the positive existence of such things. My mind is open; I refuse either to deny or affirm. This is precisely my attitude toward questions mystical and theological. I have read a little in science[2] — I used to be a violent admirer of Haeckel, though I don't remember much about him now — and I've listened to endless discussions by professors and men who were supposed to be scientists. I've never heard a theological argument which convinced me beyond the shadow of a doubt in the existence of a Supreme Being; nor have I ever heard a scientific argument that convinced me that such a Being did not exist. The most I've heard on both sides have been unprovable theories. The same way as regards life — if any — after death. I do not stand ready even to positively deny the existence of an orthodox heaven and hell. I have never believed in their existence, but wiser men than I have, and do. I have never been convinced that reincarnation is either a reality or a myth. I say, when it comes to such questions, that it's groping in a darkness which neither the eye or science or of theology can discern more than shadows of their own pre-conceived ideas. I have no arguments to offer. I can not defend my position either against the theologist or the scientist. I know my arguments are painfully crude and naive. Anyway, I refuse to argue with either. I detest arguments. I never won a dispute in my life, save on a few occasions when fists took the place of logic — and not often then. Generally I'd rather agree with the other fellow, even when I know he's wrong. On the other hand, once I weigh evidence — or what passes for evidence — and fully make up my mind — as on a stand like this — no amount of argument can shake me. I do not reply, but I remain unmoved.

Regarding liquor — or licker, as we call it in this neck of the woods. I have no doubt that the absolute prohibition of the stuff would make for better conditions — especially among the upper classes, to whose ease the laborer could contribute the time he wastes drowning his sorrows in drink. Personally, I regret the noble experiment. I was once an ardent prohibitionist. I liked my dram but was willing to sacrifice my tastes for society — that is to say, the upper classes, who are society, as far as I can make out. Drunkenness makes for inefficiency; a drunken man can't contribute his best efforts toward the enrichment of his masters. As for reasons of drunkenness, they are varied and involved, I think. In my case they have been.

There are no doubt, men who are stimulated to the state of exaltation you spoke of, but I think they are comparatively few. I never found anything particularly exalting about a drunk. In the first place, since having been repeatedly poisoned by bad licker, I can hardly abide either the taste or smell of even good whiskey, cognac, or wine. The stuff almost gags me with its nauseousness. Nor can I say that I really like the effect. It does not stimulate; it merely clouds the mind. During the earlier stages I have fits of jovial good-feeling, but soon follows a fierce melancholy, intensifying a naturally moody disposition beyond the understanding of a non-drinking man. A real drunk is followed by sickness of soul, mind and body, a savage disgust and a feeling of having wallowed in the filth with hogs and vermin.

In the interests of human research, and because it is the habit now to dissect all human habits by the medium of that half-baked arrogant conceit known as psychology, let me go into the winding and devious ways of drunkenness and drink. Please forgive me if I bore you, or disgust you. The ways of drink are fundamentally disgusting, none admits it quicker than I.

I was born with, not a hunger for liquor, but with a liking for it, and a discriminating taste for good liquor. That was my birth-right, about all the heritage my aristocratic ancestors bequeathed me. That I threw it away is neither their fault nor mine, but the fault of changing times and conditions — prohibition and poverty. My grandfathers, and my greatgrandfathers kept fine wines, brandies and whiskeys on hand and drank regularly and moderately. They looked on a drunken man as a thing lower than a wallowing hog — which he often is. They drank their liquor like gentlemen and took no harm. I came to drink mine like a beast. I have drunk until the moon and the stars crashed in a blinding blaze in my brain and I fell senseless. I make these remarks without pride and without the slightest shred of shame.

Undoubtedly it is a part of my Texas heritage. Early day Texans were much harder and fiercer drinkers than the people of the Old South. We — my friends and I — do not drink like our ancestors did. They took their liquors with their meals, in friendly converse at bars, and the like. We seldom touch it at all unless we have enough to throw us, and then we deliberately plan our drunks, and drink hugely and with no other end in view. Prohibition is partly responsible. If we could get it all the time in moderate amounts, few of us would ever really get drunk.

Jack London analyzed the liquor question far better than I, or any other man, can ever hope to do, in his book *John Barleycorn*, which every man should read.

Yet I will analyze my own part of the game for want of a more interesting subject. I am dull and stupid these terrific hot days and unable to carry on a really intelligent conversation.

I was a prohibitionist. I was very nearly grown before I was ever drunk, though of course I'd had drinks before then. At the time I was working in a drug store, in an oil boom. I was a work-horse. That sounds like a funny remark to make concerning work in a drug-store, doesn't? But ask any "soda-jerker" who ever worked through a boom. I worked seven days out of the week, no vacation, no time off, from about nine-thirty in the morning to after midnight — sometimes until two or three o'clock in the morning. It was a continual rush to keep up with the work. You have no idea how much ice cream and soda water a mob of oil-field workers can guzzle! Then I often had the whole store on my hands, especially at night, when the main rush came. The manager who was supposed to be helping me, would find the crowd too tough for him; when they started brawling among themselves and shooting craps on the floor, he generally sloped and left me to hold down the joint; to wait on throngs that absolutely crowded the store to capacity, to mix syrups, watch the cash register, sell patent medicines and "handle the front", wrangle with bellicose customers who wanted drink or dope and took refusal as an insult — to do the ten thousand things there is to do around a boom-town drug-store. At night I'd fall into bed and be asleep with fatigue before I landed, and the next morning I'd still be tired. I had no opportunity to rest. I had no time to write, read, or think. I went to no shows, had no social intercourse except the rough badinage that passed back and forth across the bar, had no time for girls, books, ambitions — no time for even life. I developed varicose veins and my health went on the rocks, but the worst of it was the stupefying effect on my mentality. The last few Sundays I worked there, a couple of boys — young oil-field workers of the better class — brought beer to us. They made it themselves and they and their friends drank it. They liked the drug-store bunch, and they brought us beer in big gallon medicine jugs we furnished them. It was nauseous. They never bottled it — began drinking almost before it quit working. It was cloudy, green and sweetish. Gaggh! I always let my beer stand in bottles at least a week before I touched it. But we drank this while it was still warm from the fermentation. Sunday after Sunday I got drunk on it. It helped me pass the day. It put spring in my weary muscles, and a smile — vacuous no doubt — on my generally snarling lips. It put a little of the human touch back in life again. I thought of myself as a man once more, and not altogether as a work-horse. Life, under the illusive effects of the beer, took on a brighter aspect. Old dreams and ambitions woke in me. Life stirred in me anew. The men I served drinks seemed more jovial, more friendly; the girls seemed brighter and prettier. Sunday was always the worst day, culminating a week of frenzied labor. The beer made it endurable, and quieted nerves that were jerking and twitching maddeningly. The last Sunday — which was the last day — I worked at that job, I was so drunk I could hardly wait on the customers. So was the owner, the manager, the pharmacist, and the clerks; so were most of the customers. Why not? We were all work-animals, writhing in the mire below the foot of the social ladder. We were predestined before our birth to be beasts of labor; why should we not make ourselves beasts on our own account, if doing so would lighten our load any?

Rich men, people of the upper classes, mental workers — they have no need of liquor, and possibly no right to it. But I say that the work-horse, the laboring man, has a right to anything that will brighten his hellish existence a little, even though that brightening be the illusive and lying gleam of drink, and that no man and no class of men has any right to deprive him of it. Drowned in drink, he can forgot the miseries of the week past, and the miseries of the week and the weeks and the years to come. To say that men are born free and equal is merely one of the trite and inane epigrams of the ruling classes. Most men are caught in a triple-cinch before they're born. They can't better their lot. Then in God's name, let them forget it as much as they can.

After I left the drug store and entered less strenuous pursuits, I felt no need of liquor, and did not touch it for years. When I did begin to drink again, I had grown into manhood, in size at least; I was accepted as a worthy companion by men who would have formerly scorned me for my youth and literary leanings. They drank and so did I. It was part of our fellowship. I think in the last analysis, that is why I drink, and why most men drink. It is part of the social life of men, varying according to their occupations and social status. Right now there's nothing I enjoy better than to make one of a congenial crowd of five or six jovial souls, and sit around drinking beer, eating limburger cheese sandwiches, and throwing the bull till we all get comfortably soused. My distaste for whiskey doesn't include beer. My ancestors scorned that beverage, but to me nothing can compare to a foaming stein of the real stuff, so cold that it cuts your throat as it goes down. I don't know where I got my liking for it. The Irish don't drink it much, and it was practically unknown among the higher classes of the Old South. Maybe it's because of my thin strain of Danish blood! Or perhaps because of the Germanic tinge of my environments.

I do not like to get drunk on beer. I drink it because I like the taste. But when I am drunk, I am not a picture to either amuse or disgust. I inherited the ability to handle my liquor, at least something like a gentleman. I am neither maudlin or quarrelsome, nor supersensitive. I do not cause any disturbance nor tell my troubles to strangers. Nor do I weave and stagger. When I can not walk a straight line, I can not walk at all. At my best I am a jovial companion, neither smart nor witty, but friendly at least; at my worst I am merely moody and taciturn, desiring only solitude in which to brood over the melancholy images which haunt a gloomy mind.

I reckon you're right about the Latin trend moderating the Norman instincts. I don't know what moderated the Celt. So far as I can learn, the Irish were never particularly gluttonous eaters, though great drinkers. The same applies to the Highland Scotch. Well, when it comes to eating I'm all Dane. Give me good beer and good food, and plenty of both, and the ruling classes will have no revolt out of me. (This confounded type-writer is jumping spaces.)

The Mongols and Tatars were great eaters and drinkers, and especially in their more nomadic stages. Easily seen why; they lived a strenuous active outdoor life, and then food was not always handy. When they had plenty, it was their instinct to gobble as much as possible, against the times when they might go hungry. I hardly see how the Mongols of the Gobi managed to live, when their food consisted almost entirely of meat and milk — cheese and butter, perhaps, and fermented mare's milk. They apparently had no grain, vegetables or fruit of any sort. At least not while they were penned in the wastes outside the Great Wall by the power of the Chinese. I'm all for the nomads when it came to wasting China. They'd had nothing but abuse from the Chinese for ages.

That reminds me — that business about Turanian drunkenness — that some of the readers took exception to my making Tamerlane a drinking man. I expected to be attacked on other scores — on Bayazid's suicide, which of course never took place — about my version of Timour's death — more particular I expected to be denounced because of the weapon my character used in that slaying. There were firearms in the world then, and had been for some time, but they were of the matchlock order. I doubt if there were any flint-lock weapons in Asia in 1405. But the readers pounced on to the point I least expected — the matter of Mohammedan drunkards. They maintained that according to the Koran, Moslems never drank. Wright admitted in the Souk[3] that the Koran forbade liquor, but went on to quote a long extract from Clivijo's memoirs to prove that Timour and his Tatars drank to excess.

This writing of historical stories is hell in a way, though intensely interesting. It's so easy to make mistakes. For instance I noted in his book of travels, Bayard Taylor, when speaking of his explorations in Vienna, mentioned Count Stahremberg as commanding Vienna in 1529, when, he said, Sobiesky rescued the city from the siege of the Turks under the Grand Vizier Muhammad. Stahremberg hadn't been born in 1529. Count Salm commanded then, and beat off, not Muhammad, who, with Sobiesky was still in the womb of the unborn, but Suleyman the Magnificent. It was in 1683 that the others played their part. And the Vizier was not Muhammad but Kara Mustafa.

And that reminds me — do you know what year the Danube Canal was constructed, the one that runs through Vienna, or was it a natural arm of the river? I've ransacked all the reference books in this part of Texas and can't find out. Evidently it existed in 1683, because Stanley Lane-Poole speaks of "the island suburb of Leopoldstadt";[4] that former suburb is now a part of the city under the same name, to the best of my knowledge, and is the only part of the city on the other side of the Canal from the Alstadt or old city, and lies between the Canal and the Danube proper. Yet I can find no mention of the Canal in the siege of 1529.

Lately I've been brushing up on my knowledge of Eastern Europe. I find it fascinating. And I see a certain parallel in the cases of Poland and modern America. The partition and destruction of the Polish kingdom were inevitable. All effort for centuries was toward the establishing of special privileges for the upper class, to the degradation of the lower classes — just as it is in America today. Nobles were free of taxes and heaped up enormous fortunes, while stamping out all vestige of liberty in the lower classes. Independent merchants were taxed unbearably. Independent farmers became peasants, then serfs. The elected kings were shorn of all power lest they take the part of the people against the nobles. Graft ran rampant — just as in America. Money raised to build forts and armies went into the pockets of unscrupulous nobles. The standing army was abolished because the ruling class was not willing to pay for its upkeep. Then when they needed an army, they paid the price of their swinish avarice and blindness. They had it coming to them. Austrian, Prussian and Russian overlords were no harder on the common people than their own lords had been. Likely they were easier.

But what a tangled mess and confusion Balkan history is! And what a mixture of blood-strains the average Balkan must be! Celtic, Roman, German, Slav, Greek, Mongol, Turkish — no wonder they're always ham-stringing each other. I understand that for some time in those smaller countries the Germanic strain, and culture, has been dwindling out and being replaced by the cruder and more primitive Slavic — which is bound to be well mixed with Turanian strains, considering the century-long raids and occupations of the Huns, Bulgars, Avars, Petchenegs, Khazars, Mongols, Tatars and Turks.

Outside Bohemians and Poles, there are not many representatives of the Slavic groups in the Southwest. These, I think, are the superior race — especially the Bohemians or Czechs, because of their long proximity to the German races, during which time, too, they were cut off from their southern kin by the Mongoloid Hungarians. But I understand that the eastern cities have large numbers of Balkan Slavs. I believe you've mentioned them, as settling in the New England valleys in large numbers along with the Poles.

I remember meeting one such person in San Antonio a year or so ago. He was a Communist organizer[5] — a Slovene, I was told by my socialist friend[6] who introduced me to him — the friend himself having been the Socialist nominee for lieutenant-governor of Texas. The Communist was about my own age — a trim dark young man, dolichocephalic, to my surprize, and rather handsome. Doubtless American girls found his dark, almost Oriental type of manly beauty extremely romantic. The crude blundering Saxon and the even more blundering Celt can't compete with the perfectly poised Latin and Slav in amorous skirmishes! They have us licked at the start, when it comes to the ladies. This young man had keen dark eyes and a highly intelligent type of face; nothing of the Slavic dreamer about him. He had a poise and an alertness, an air of versatility noways inferior to the Latin, yet definitely not Latin. A fantastic conceit came to me as our mutual friend did most of the conversing that passed among us. I thought of the alien hordes that swarmed into Rome before its fall, and who no doubt — at least those from the East — were as superior in adaptability and versatility to the native Romans, as these new aliens are superior to our native stock. Possibly this very chap's Dacian ancestors, mixed with Greek, were undermining the empire with their wiles from within, while our more straightforward ancestors — yours and mine — were smashing the lines from without and from the other direction.

We eyed each other as I imagine a native Roman of the old stock and an alien Greek might have eyed each other in Rome, in the later empire — with mutual distrust and lack of understanding; tinged with resentment on my part and a hint of contempt on his, which his perfect manners could not quite conceal. What, to him and his, were the traditions that lie behind me, and of which I am a part? How could the representatives of two such utterly separate stocks and traditions bridge the gulf between? It can not be bridged. Not in my lifetime or his. What is Bunker Hill, Lexington and Paul Revere to him? What is King's Mountain, the Battle of New Orleans, the drift of '49, Gettysburg, Bull's Run, or San Juan? Nothing. A meaningless drift of words, talismans of a slow-thoughted breed, to him inferior, in his own mind. If the difference lay just in this country, it might be overcome. But it lies beyond that. What to him and his is Hastings, the Crusades, the Wars of the Roses, the Battle of Culloden, of Bannockburn, of Preston Pans, of the Blackwater? The Black Prince means nothing to him, nor Robert Bruce nor Shane O'Neil. The gulf will be bridged when our race — yours and mine — is destroyed by the rising tide of such as he, and a mongrel breed, lacking all sentiment and tradition, reigns over the land our ancestors bled and sweat for. And I suppose it will come to pass. I dread their adaptability, their versatility. I could have broken this fellow half in two with ease, but it was easy to see which of us had the quicker, more alert mind. In an intelligence test he would have led me in a walk and not half tried.

But I had to laugh at his efforts to organize the thousands of Mexicans in and about San Antonio. A Mexican of the lower order will promise you anything to get rid of you, but just try to get him to make good! This particular chap led a big parade of several thousand up to the very steps of the city hall, and there one of their own race met them, in some government capacity, and made them a speech in opposition to the Slovene's — full of flowery rhetoric and burning Latin phrases. The Communist demonstration turned into an anti-Soviet rally and the organizer had to run for his life. I still maintain that a Slav can't handle a Latin, especially when the Latin is about half Yaqui.

My Socialist friend spoke bitterly of the fickleness of the Mexicans — whose ignorance is so abysmal it's almost impossible for a white man to comprehend it. That day the soldiers were out, parading down the streets — cavalry and infantry. My friend watched a regiment of cavalry canter past, sabers drawn, and assured me that they were being thus paraded in order to awe the multitude. I think he attached too much importance to his friend's endeavors. But it amused me to surprize a fleeting look of satisfaction on my friend's countenance. He evidently felt the cause was flattered by the appearance of the troops — though in reality it was just one of the ordinary parades and exercises common enough in the city.

Well, the picnic came and went, and no violence. That's the forty-ninth picnic of its kind to be held in this town, and if there ever was another one that didn't have a few fights, I never heard of it. Certainly I never saw one before so peaceful. But a lot of the old-time toughs were missing — some having left the country, some having previously stopped bullets, some in jail. Even at the boxing matches the crowd seemed to consist largely of youngsters, certainly less pugnacious than those of the previous generation. We stood packed like sardines in the outdoor make-shift arena and I don't believe the fighters suffered much more than the crowd did. One boy had a tough time — somebody kept appropriating the chair on which he was supposed to sit between rounds, and his seconds kept having to dispossess the occupant, who generally put up a resistance. And then somebody stole the kid's shirt which he'd hung up outside the ring for lack of a proper dressing room. The main bout was a flop. They brought a slugger from Fort Worth with a blare of trumpets and a ruffle of drums to fight a local boy called Kid Pancake — I don't know if that's his real name or what he is. He came from Oklahoma, originally, I think, and he looks more like an Italian than anything else. His real name may be something like Panciata. Scarcely had the fight started when the Kid leaped across the ring like the panther he is, shooting a murderous left hook to his adversary's jaw. The city boy went down like a butchered steer, his head lolling over the lower rope; he was carried out, his eyes shut, his limbs trailing limply. He was so unconscious he snored; I've seen many a man knocked stiff, but I never saw one snore before. I've heard of it, but never saw it until then. It was another triumph for the post-oak country over the more civilized portion of the state! The crowds at the fights were very orderly — oh, of course they whooped and yelled and cursed, but there was no fighting among themselves. The boys that felt the urge to scrap, got in the ring and fought it out with the gloves. One funny thing happened; numbers of young fellows tried to climb over the top of the roofless wall which surrounded the arena, and one of them, when the sheriff requested him to get off, replied with a crushing smash on the jaw that nearly laid the limb of the law among the daisies. Only a couple of fellows were thrown into the jug for drunken and disorderly conduct, though of course many more were soused. One drunk from down the Pecan Valley caused a good deal of annoyance to a political speaker who was boosting a gubernatorial candidate, by getting up on the speakers' platform, drinking the speaker's water, and resisting efforts to be dislodged. At last he got to raising so much hell they had to lock him up.

One reason there wasn't any violence of any kind, was the fact that the usual carnival was missing. There's a standing feud between country people and travelling carnivals, and I understand it's not limited to Texas alone. To the yokels, carnival people are fair play and vice versa. I'll admit I have scant patience with the country folk in that connection. Their main squawk is the gambling games attendant to the carnivals. They say they're crooked. Well, hell, whoever heard of an honest gambler making a living? Of course they're crooked. They have to be. Nobody makes the countrymen play them. It's their greed as much as anybody's. They come in and try to get something for little or nothing themselves. They lose their money, and they send up a yelp — call a cop or more often try to take matters into their own hands. What did they expect? If I'm in a legitimate business and a man comes along and gyps me on what I was led to believe was legitimate — if he makes me believe that it's on the level — reasonable returns for reasonable investment — and then skins me, why, maybe I've got a kick coming. A shyster gypped an uncle of mine that way once, and didn't live to see another sun rise.

But if I'm carrying on a crooked business, or if I try to make money out of a crooked deal, and get fleeced, then I've got no yell coming. And if I try to beat a gambling game and get skinned with marked cards, loaded dice or what-not, then I've no kick either. But the average fellow don't see it that way, of course. You'd be surprized at the venomous hatred many country people have for carnivals and carnival people. A friend of mine, for instance, a fine fellow, though a little rough in his ways, perhaps, knocked a carnival girl senseless with a baseball, and considered it a great joke. She worked at what is known as a "cat-stand" — where one throws a ball and tries to knock cats out of the rack. Instead of throwing at the cats, he threw at her, and they had to pour water on her to bring her around. That's just an instance of something that frequently happens. I may be a bit squeamish, but I really couldn't see any humor in the joke.

Maybe I'm prejudiced on that score, for I had the same thing happen to me once, though not with the same effect. I was working at a carnival, at one of those blasted cat-stands. I was behind the rack bending over to pick up a cat, when some bully let go with everything he had. I just got a glimpse of him out of the tail of my eye as he threw, and all I could tell of him was that he was a big florid man, weighing, I should judge, anywhere between two hundred and two hundred and fifty pounds, and he threw with all his might. I didn't have time to dodge and the ball caught me squarely on the ear. I was only about fourteen years old. You can imagine the effect of a throw like that, at perhaps twenty or thirty feet range, with the whole weight of a big powerful man's body behind it. It dazed me — almost knocked me down. It knocked me so dizzy I didn't even think of retaliation. And it knocked out of my head the ability to remember just how the fellow looked. I remember faintly hearing the woman I was working for, cursing him for crippling her hired help, and him laughing; but I wasn't crippled. I was just stunned and went on setting up cats kind of mechanically. The girl came up and put her arm around me and asked how bad I was hurt, and I pushed her away roughly like a kid will — embarrassed because everybody was laughing at me. I was tough as a boot — physically, I mean. But it was an hour or more before I could think straight. Then my pal and I went looking for the man that hit me, but I couldn't remember what he looked like — there were scores of big florid men there — and nobody would tell me who he was. Everybody that saw it, swore they didn't know the fellow. You know how that goes. But it irritated me. I know he did it just for a joke, and that there was nothing personal in it, but he might very easily have blinded me for life with his damned foolishness.

But anybody that works to amuse the public apparently is considered fair play. Prize-fighters, actors, clowns. The entertainer is generally far superior to his audience. It's the crowd that sickens me with such games as boxing. What does the crowd care for skill and courage? They want to see blood spilled — to see somebody hurt. Same way with acrobats. Half the people that go to acrobatic performances go secretly hoping to see one of the performers miss his grip and break his neck. Else why do they swarm out so when the performers act without a net? I had a cousin who pulled that stunt. He packed 'em in — not because he was one of the greatest acrobats west of the Mississippi, but because he never had anything between him and the ground. He was just twenty-one years old when he missed a flying trapeze in the old Delmar Garden in Saint Louis — he fell thirty feet and his back broke like a rotten stick. He always guaranteed the mob a thrill; I reckon the rats slobbered and slavered with joy over the last act he gave them. And the priests beggared my aunt for money for masses for his soul — by God, a man can't even escape the pack by dying.

I note that some indignation is being expressed over the country in regard to the detestable police practise of grilling prisoners. It's about time. I think police harshness is mainly because the people have become so cowed by the heel of the law, that they do not resent or resist any kind of atrocity inflicted on them by men wearing tin badges. In the old days we had a type of law-officers as much superior to the present type as the old-time gunfighter was superior to the present-day gang-rat. They were brave, honorable, and generally merciful when they had the edge. I can't imagine Pat Garret, Wyatt Earp or John Poe summoning his deputies to help him beat up a cringing prisoner in irons. In the old days it was no light thing to arrest a man. Resentment and resistance was the order, not the exception. I noted your remarks as to the treatment of a theoretical bully on a tear in some Eastern city. That's precisely what would happen in any western city. A number of police would be sent to handle the disturber — or in Texas perhaps some Ranger like Gonzaullas might be sent to handle him single-handed — a much more manly procedure, to my mind. Though the other way is effective with the softer-fibred toughs of the present age. There's nothing particularly courageous in half a dozen men clubbing a single individual into helplessness. But I can think of no more ridiculous and futile thing than half a dozen ordinary cops, East or West, rushing into a saloon to capture an old-time warrior of the type of Billy the Kid, John Wesley Hardin, Ben Thompson or King Fisher. All six of them would have been dead on the floor before they could lay hands on him. And if they elected to shoot it out with him, the result would have been the same, barring a lucky accident. Such types created special types of law-officers to deal with them. Instead of overpowering their prey by force of numbers, the old-time officer fought it out with the outlaws on more or less even terms — what odds existed were generally on the side of the disturbers of the peace. The modern officer, with a few exceptions like Norfleet, Hickman, Gonzaullas, and the like, would stand little chance under such conditions. Why, hell, the cops have had Pretty-Boy Floyd cornered more than once, and then failed to take him, when he came out shooting. Once a couple of them got the drop on him in a hotel, I believe it was. Lifting his hands, he casually removed his hat, and flung it across the room, sardonically requesting them to watch it. Unconsciously their gaze followed the flying hat, and that instant of carelessness was all he wanted. In that flashing bit of time he drew, and before they could move, both of them were down — along with an innocent nigger who was hit by a stray bullet. And Floyd walked out unharmed.

John Wesley Hardin was the prime law-killer of the Southwest. Conditions helped to make him a bad man, just as in the case of the James boys — I won't add Quantrell as many do. That old tale you hear in the Southwest about the Jayhawkers of Kansas murdering Quantrell's brother, and leaving the poor young lad — Quantrell himself — lying naked and wounded on the prairie — having waylaid the boys on their way from Baltimore to California — that tale, I say, is a lot of baloney. Quantrell never had a brother, as far as I can learn. And he wasn't from Maryland; he was born in Ohio. He made up that yarn to tell the Southerners when he decided at last to toss his lot among them. He was a Jayhawker before he was a guerilla. And the man who says he held a commission in the Confederate army is a liar. The Southerners would have hanged him just as quick as the Federals would have. After being refused a commission by the Confederates, he preyed on both sides, and it was the failure of a raid into Texas that really started the crumbling of his band. I've known men who rode with him, and they gilded his memory with their admiration — but honestly he was a bloody-minded devil. But what the hell! I started talking about John Wesley Hardin.

The carpet-baggers made a desperado of John. Outlawed at the age of fifteen for killing one of the swaggering black bullies that tried to rule the country after being freed, he was hounded from place to place by carpet-bag officers and negro soldiers. The fools kept sending nigger officers after him, and as regular he sent them back feet-first. After that first slaying, he ambushed three sent after him — a white man and a couple of niggers; again, after being captured by three more, he loosed his bonds and killed them while they slept — but I could go on almost indefinitely. He was, as far as I know, the only man to stand up to Wild Bill Hickok and live. Wild Bill had a standing feud with Texans. He was the most noted Kansas law, and many a battle he had with the wild boys who brought the big longhorn herds up the old Chisholm. He got the drop on Hardin, but the Texan turned the tables on him — and then spared his life. I don't know how many officers, black and white, John killed. The score was a large one. At one time he was an officer himself, in Kansas — at the same time that a price was on his head in Texas, and Wild Bill had a warrant for his arrest, but refused to carry it out. Hendry Brown, Billy the Kid's pal, was a law in Kansas, too — when they hanged him for robbing a bank in a neighboring town, he was still wearing his marshal's star. He's worth a book himself — a lean, lithe, blond devil, handsome as a classical young pagan, soulless and deadly as a rattler. Utterly without fear, he shot his way out of traps and confronted perils with heroism worthy to be sung by Homer — and again he killed causelessly and in cold blood, simply to see his victims fall and quiver.

And Belle Starr, the most famous woman-desperado of all the West — what sagas could be sung of her! Many the times she came into my aunt's millinery shop in the old Indian Territory, to purchase expensive and exclusive types of apparel fresh from the states. A handsome, quiet speaking, refined woman, my aunt said — she was of aristocratic blood, and natural refinement, for all she'd kill a man as quick as a rattler striking. It's a curious coincidence that two of the Southwest's most famous outlaws — Sam Bass and Belle Starr — were killed on their birthdays. Sometimes I feel as if the shotgun blast from the brush that mowed down Belle Starr, forecast the doom of the wild, mad, glorious, gory old days of the frontier. She was more than the wicked woman pious people call her — more than merely a feminine outlaw — she was the very symbol of a free, wild, fierce race. Will Rogers, in jest, spoke of erecting a monument to Belle Starr. Oklahoma could do worse. Whatever she was or was not, she symbolized a colorful and virile phase of American evolution.

When will a man rise up, bred from the soil, with the sun in his blood and the throb of the unfenced earth in his ear, to sing the saga of the West? Perhaps it's too much to ask. Perhaps no man will ever be born with power to etch the pageant — no, that's not the word. Etch suggests stillness, something frozen and motionless; and the pageant of the West is furtherest from that. It is alive with movement; it burns, tingles, stings with motion and raw, quick life. It flows tempestuously on in swift and ever-changing color and flickering light. There are no mild eddies and interchange of soft light and dancing shadow. All is raw and bold and blazing, flooded by the fierce merciless flame of the western sun. It is a panorama that grips and repels with its blaze, that shakes and rends and maddens.

Just west of this place begins the real western half of the American continent. You will not see the real west until you cross the Callahan Divide. Where the high postoak ridges of the divide fall away into the high plains country to west and south, begins the West. Standing on the uplands I look westward and seem to see the whole vista of mountains, canyons, peaks, rivers, endless dusty plains, cactus-haunted deserts and high mesas stretching away from my very feet to the foaming shores of the Pacific. And I close my eyes and seem to glimpse a vast dim mighty caravan surging endlessly across those vast expanses — a restless river of changing glints of light and checkered colors, surging, eddying, brawling, swirling its spate into the waste-places, but sweeping onward, untiring and irresistible. What man can pick out the separate elements in such a flood? The individual mingles with the liquid masses and is lost — yet nowhere is the individual more strongly marked, more clear-cut; pioneers and buffalo hunters, miners and soldiers, sun-burnt women in home-spun, reckless dance-hall girls, gunfighters, gamblers, cowpunchers, outlaws — Spaniards, Saxons and Indians, mingled in one chaotic flood they roar blindly toward the sea.

I am proud that in all these patterns, men of my native state had a part. Nowhere in the West will you find a place where a Texan has not set his foot. Buffalo hunters, guides, officers, outlaws — they left their mark wherever men lived hard. In the old days of the cattle-kings, it was the custom, in range feuds, to send for Texan "warriors" as they were called — sometimes most of the men on each side were Texans, fighting for hire. They were loyal to the men who paid them. Men fighting side by side in one war, might be opposed to each other in the next. It was all a matter of chance. No feudal baron of Europe was served more faithfully and fiercely than the western cattle-kings were served by these wandering men-at-arms, who wore leather instead of steel, and were far deadlier with a six-shooter than the finest swordsman ever was with his blade. They were much the same breed — descendants of those medieval swordsmen. Texans took the first herds to Kansas, to New Mexico, to Canada. One man, right after the Civil War had ruined the New Orleans market, drove a herd of longhorns to New York without finding a market. He eventually sold them in Boston. Texans fought northern Indians as well as southern red-skins. There were Texans with Custer — more's the pity.

I regret the fate of the brave unfortunate men with Custer, from whatever state they came, but as for that cold-blooded murderer, the only regret I have is that the dead lay over his corpse so thick that the Indians failed to find and scalp it. Long Hair, they called him, and his yellow locks fell to his shoulders. A few years hanging in the smoke of a filthy Sioux lodge would have tarnished that gleaming gold; would have more closely fitted the color of his soul.

The Indians didn't often have a chance to glut their vengeance to the full as at the Little Big Horn. But it was a splendid galaxy of war-chiefs that confronted the blue-coats — Gall, Crazy Horse, Rain-in-the-Face, others almost equally famous. I suppose Sitting Bull should have some credit, though like most politicians and priests, he was making "big medicine" in a canyon some miles away while the real fighting was in progress. Rain-in-the-Face is my favorite of that group. I have nothing against Tom Custer, whose career he ended so bloodily, but I admire guts in any man, and Rain had enough for a regiment. You know in the Sun Dance, when the raw-hides tore through Rain's flesh too quickly, Sitting Bull claimed that he had had no fair test of manhood and Rain bade Bull give him a test. The medicine man cut deep through the back muscles and passed the rawhide thongs through the slits, and they hanged him high. There he swung for two days, singing his war-chants and boasting of his bloody deeds — he boasted of murdering a couple of white men, a veterinary and a sutler, straggling from General Stanley's expedition, and thereby hangs a tale, and Tom Custer's doom was written in blood. At last they bound buffalo skulls to his feet, and by terrific efforts, the young brave tore free, rending the flesh and tendons in such a way that for years he had depressions as large as a man's fists in his back. But his boasts had been overheard, and Little Hair — Tom Custer — arrested him and threw him in a guardhouse to await execution. White men imprisoned there helped him escape. He sent Tom Custer a bit of white buffalo hide, with a bloody heart drawn on it with the artistry of the Sioux. It was his way of saying he would eat the white man's heart when next he met him.

They met in the howling, blind, red frenzy of the Little Big Horn. Tom Custer was a brave man; none braver on all the frontier. But when he saw his enemy riding at him through the drift of the storm, naked, bloody, painted like a fiend, lashed to his naked steed, he must have frozen with the realization of his unescapable doom. Unaccustomed fear shook his iron hand, and his shots went wide — the painted rider raced in, a naked knife glittered in the dust, blood spurted — and out of the melee rode Rain-in-the-Face, holding a quivering dripping heart on high — blood trickling from the corner of his mouth — blood that was not his own.

Like Samkin Aylward,[7] I warm to a man with the bitter drop in him. And whatever else they were or were not, the Indians weren't fools enough to forgive a wrong, or what they considered a wrong. I've often thought of fictionizing the incident just mentioned, transferring it to another race and age — having Bran Mak Morn eat the heart of a Roman governor, or Conan the Cimmerian that of a Hyborian king. I wonder how much barbarity the readers will stand for. One problem in writing bloody literature is to present it in such a manner as to avoid a suggestion of cheap blood-and-thunder melodrama — which is what some people will always call action, regardless of how realistic and true it is. So many people never have any action in their own placid lives, and therefore can't believe it exists anywhere or in any age. Another problem is how far you can go without shocking the readers into distaste for your stuff — and therefore cutting down sales. I've always held myself down in writing action-stories; I never let my stories be as bloody and brutal as the ages and incidents I was trying to depict actually were. I think sometimes I'll let myself go — possibly in a yarn of the Middle Ages — and see if I can sell the thing. I don't know much slaughter and butchery the readers will endure. Their capacity for grisly details seems unlimited, when the cruelty is the torturing of some naked girl, such as Quinn's[8] stories abound in — no reflection intended on Quinn; he knows what they want and gives it to them. The torture of a naked writhing wretch, utterly helpless — and especially when of the feminine sex amid voluptuous surroundings — seems to excite keen pleasure in some people who have a distaste for wholesale butchery in the heat and fury of a battlefield. Well — to me the former seems much more abominable than the cutting down of armed men — even the slaughter of prisoners in the madness of fighting-lust. I can read of the Little Big Horn, of Little Turtle's slaughter of Saint Clair's army, of the slaughter at Nicopolis and at Mohacz and the Horns of Hattin, unmoved except by feelings of admiration for the courage shown; but I have never been able to read of the burning of Joan of Arc without the most intense feeling of horror and rage; the same is true of the execution of William Wallace, and of Robert Emmett; thought of them rouses in me another sensation — a savage satisfaction at the memories of King's Mountain and New Orleans, with the British soldiers falling like ripe grain before the American rifles — yet I deplore the Scottish troops that fell there. I have seen persons who were constituted right opposite from me; they found accounts of battles and wholesale massacre either repugnant or without interest, yet avidly devoured articles and stories dealing with the persecution of the helpless. I've never been able to read the full history of the Spanish Inquisition; it's too horrible. But I find highly enjoyable the chronicles of Montbars the Exterminator, who went mad from reading and brooding over that same Inquisition and started out to avenge all the French who perished thereby.

Another thing — I have no patience with writers, historical or fictional, who glorify Oriental monarchs, comparing them with western rulers, to the discredit of the latter; who decry the outrages committed by the westerners on the Orientals, and then gloss over the atrocities of the latter, holding up some western outrage as an excuse. Westerners have suffered a hell of a lot more outrages at the hands of the Orientals than vice versa. I am utterly unmoved when I read of massacres of Asiatics — especially Mohammedans — by Christians. They started it, blast their hides — back in the days of Peter the Hermit, when the Seljuks took Palestine and started maltreating pilgrims to Jerusalem. And before that, in the days of Muhammad, and of the Caliphs — and of the Moors in Spain. Not a blow struck against Islam but we owed it them. Even Stanley Lane-Pool deplores the action of Milosh Kabilovitch, who struck down Murad in the hour of victory at Kossovo — he looks on it as a traitorous murder, apparently. Bah! Who ever heard of such infernal drivel. Which was worse — Milosh, who approached the Turk smiling, and suddenly drove a dagger in his guts, or Murad, who had just butchered a nation, and dragged thousands of innocent men, women and children into hellish slavery? I have intense admiration for Milosh — and for Ehud the Benjamite who stabbed Eglon the Moabitish tyrant — and for William Tell, whether real or legendary.

Speaking of tyrannies naturally reminds me of this country. I reckon the government will be giving medals of heroism to the bold soldiers who, armed only with sabres, rifles, machine guns, tear gas and armored tanks, routed the veterans with their awful sticks and horrible bricks.[9] This business ought to cause a big boom in enlistment for the next war. I remember a song they used to sing during the war, "When you come back — and you will come back! — there's a whole world waiting for you!" Yeah — with brass knucks and butcher knives.

Well, we've been having some elections in Texas, and on the first pass we dealt the Wall Street clan a body blow. I hear the big babies up that way sent down numbers of tickets already filled out for the boys to vote; they wanted to be sure their men went in. Well, the state of Texas is damned near sold out to the big interests, but not quite. Take Mr. Insull[10] — the mister is meant sarcastically. The city of Cross Plains can't even dam up Bee Branch, because it runs into Turkey Creek, which in turn runs into Pecan Bayou, which is a tributary of the Colorado River — because Mr. Beloved Insull owns the Colorado and all tributaries. As a result, the citizens of the town have to use water out of wells, that would ruin the system of a brass monkey. Brown County had one hell of a time kicking Insull and his cohorts off the Pecan Bayou so they could build their dam, but they did it, and thereby established a precedent that may help the next strugglers. I see they retired the poor fellow — his company, I mean — on a meager pension of $17,000 yearly. I pity him in his abject poverty.

Anyway, the big interests rocked in the election. Allred,[11] candidate for attorney general, as opposed to a man who was avowedly in favor of Wall Street, was not even allowed to speak over the radio, or to get his speeches published in the big papers, I understand. He had to go over in Louisiana, and talk from Old Man Henderson's station in Shrevesport — and we elected him about four to one. You may have heard some echo of Henderson's long battle with chain-store interests — a rather eccentric old fellow, perhaps, but a fighter from heel to bald spot.[12] And we're going to elect Mrs. Ferguson[13] governor again, or I miss my guess. Of course, Jim will be the real governor; he'd run himself, only he can't, because he's been impeached. The last election seemed to show that the Fergusons were very unpopular in Texas; but it's not Sterling against Ferguson; the issue is deeper. It's the common people, mainly the country people, against the corporations and the richer classes. We've won the first toss. And I believe we're going to win the rest. The governors are always men from the East or South. We Western Texans can't elect a governor — yet. But you wait a few years, till the West is completely settled up. Sterling is strong in the Southeast, but he lost the vote of the common People in East Texas proper, by imposing military rule in the oil fields. And I believe that there's enough people in Northwest and East Texas to put a new governor in the capitol. I'm enclosing a copy of an oil field — East Texas — paper,[14] as an example of Southwestern journalism. You won't find such virility in the big Texas papers. You have to go to the hinterlands, where the press isn't controlled by big business.

By the way, as an evidence of our democracy, it looks like this district is going to elect a full-blooded Syrian to the legislature.[15] He runs a small dry-goods store in this town — a very short dumpy sort of fellow, brachycephalic, swarthy, curly-haired — an Elamitish type if I don't miss my guess. He and his family are the only Orientals in this town, the Jews having pulled their freight when times got hard. A funny thing in connection with this fellow — he was born near Lebanon, in Syria, but has been in this country so long he was a stranger when his brother and he revisited the old country a few years ago. In Damascus they mistook a Moslem washing-place outside a mosque — a holy place where the Mohammedans did their ritualistic abolutions — for a public toilet, and were mobbed by a gang of maddened Islamites, who chased them for blocks, and were only pacified by money, and the assurance of the culprits' native kinsmen that the offenders were only American barbarians whose ignorance was too abysmal to be resented.

I'm glad to hear that the southern climate helped your health. I agree with you in regard to cold weather. I despise it utterly, though it doesn't have such dangerous effects on me as you described — however, I was never in a really cold climate, and don't know what it might do to me. It's never been much more than sixteen below zero in this part of the country. I was really shocked to read how the cold hurts you, and would certainly advise a change to a warmer climate — though I can understand your reluctance to sever old ties.

Long's poem in the current *Weird Tales* is superb.[16] I also like the story by Howard Wandrei[17] — Donald's brother, perhaps? If so, please extend him my congratulations and welcome to the fraternity of fantastic fictionists.

But it's time, long time, that I brought this rambling to a close. What an ungodly length of letter to impose on anyone! I fear I create the impression of loose-mouthed garrulity — if that's the way it's spelled. Such isn't the case. I have a reputation of taciturnity among a people not noted for volubility. I was raised in the postoak hills, and I know how to keep my mouth shut. I narrate and discuss matters with you, by letter, that I wouldn't mention to my most intimate Texan friends. I trust your discretion, and anyway, you have no connection with the state or the people of which I might speak, and so are impartial and unprejudiced. I don't have to tell you that a lot of the things of which I speak are in strict confidence.

With best wishes, and hoping that the editors will see the light and soon give more of your work to the public,

Cordially,
R.E.H.

P.S. Just a humorous note to taper off on; some weeks ago the guardians of the law called on a friend of mine and told him the jig was up. Seeing they had him cold, he cheerfully surrendered, and asked to be allowed to get his cap in the next room. They agreed — apparently forgetting that rooms have windows as well as doors. He must have had a devil of a time finding his cap, because the laws haven't seen him since then.

Another shooting scrape in town night before last. No casualties; just a minor wound inflicted on one of the men. Rotten shooting.

I notice that a New York reader of *Weird Tales* — in the current Eyrie — asks for reprinting of the *Necronomicon* and *Nameless Cults*![18]

NOTES

1. E. Hoffmann Price.
2. Howard took the "Science Course" at Brownwood High School.
3. The letters column in *Oriental Stories.*
4. The book referred to is *Turkey.*
5. See letter 160.
6. Harold Preece.
7. A character in Conan Doyle's *The White Company.*
8. Seabury Quinn.
9. On July 28, 1932, troops under the command of Gen. Douglas MacArthur, armed with unsheathed bayonets and tear gas, dispersed the "Bonus Army" of veterans seeking early payment of cash bonuses due them for their service in World War I and destroyed the camps they had set up in Washington, D.C. Hundreds of veterans and their family members were injured, and at least two were killed.
10. Samuel Insull, Chicago capitalist best known for his holdings in utilities and railroads.
11. James Allred.
12. W.K. Henderson, owner and on-air personality of KWKH in Shreveport, Louisiana, had for several years been carrying on a fight against chain radio stations and chain stores.
13. Miriam A. ("Ma") Ferguson. Her husband, James E. Ferguson, served as Governor of Texas, 1915-1917, but was impeached early in his second term. In 1924, Mrs. Ferguson ran for the office, promising "two governors for the price of one," and was elected. She lost her bid for re-election in 1926, did not run in 1928, and then lost the Democratic primary to Ross Sterling in 1930, setting up their rematch in 1932.
14. *The Gladewater Journal.*
15. Cecil A. Lotief, born in Lebanon (then a part of Syria), owner of a dry goods store in Cross Plains, served as a state legislator from Callahan County 1933-1937. He gave Howard an inkwell in the shape of a camel that is now at the Robert E. Howard House and Museum.

16. "When Chaugnar Wakes," September 1932.
17. "Over Time's Threshold"; Howard was Donald Wandrei's younger brother.
18. Andre Galet, in the August 1932 issue.

TSS: 50238-50254

ଔଓଔଓ

214. To Tevis Clyde Smith, ca. August 1932.

Fear Finn:

I don't know when I've enjoyed a pome like I enjoyed yours. I got an especial whang out of the line,

"I gave a laugh and I gave him my knife."[1]

It has the simple, unaffected ferocity I dote on. We should be the start of a new school of realism. You have — and I think I have to some extent — the ability to be savage without obvious effort. It seems to come natural. When the average egg tries to be brutal, the effort is apparent and falls short.

Shortly after getting your letter Pink[2] and I went down to Galveston for a week-end. We had a good time, though most people around here don't seem to be able to understand how we did, since we neither swam, fished, got drunk nor whored. City of polyglot tongues — ye olde American is a rare artickle there, as well ye know. Only one real salty touch that I remember: as we came along the wharfs one night, just before our train left, we met a couple of drunken sailors reeling along with their coats over their shoulders singing some sort of a chanty. "You boysh 'ull never shee ush again," mouthed one, "we're off to shea againsh." "You're goin' the wrong way," said the other. "We'll meet you in Davy Jones's locker," I promished. "And if you do, we'll —" the first speaker began, and his words drooled off into a drunken gibberish, as they reeled on down the wharf. We went aboard a cutter tied up to the wharfs, with one long gun, an anti-aircraft gun, and a couple of small rapid fire pieces. The sailors were American stock, mostly, but youngsters and none too strongly built, to my mind. Standing on the pilot-deck or whatever you call it, we watched a big Japanese freighter steaming into port, and looking at the little brown brother which thronged the rail in great numbers, I wondered how long it would be before the ship on which we were standing would be throwing lead at such ships as we were watching, and vice versa.

More correspondence from various Weird Talers. I find that E.H. Price is German, Welsh, and a strain of Tatar. That gives him his slant eyes, which I noticed in the pictures he sent me. He said Kirk Mashburn is a tall blond youth, whose most highly prized possession is a Toledo sword he carried while an officer in the Mexican marines. The old idea that a literary man is necessarily a sissy is refuted day by day. He also said Lovecraft was a bear-cat at gorging chili con carne, which relieves me. I was afraid H.P.L. was as abstemious in eating as in drinking.

Dreaming in Israel.

If I had dwelt in Israel when Saul was king of Israel,
If I had dwelt in Israel,
A captain of a host,
I would have taken Samuel, the hound of alters, Samuel,
I would have hanged fat Samuel
Above a fire to roast.

For Samuel was a priestling
With words for women's ears,
But Saul he was a warrior
That stalked among the spears.

And Samuel was a scholar,
From line of scribes he came,
But Saul he was a common man
Who could not write his name.

And Samuel dwelt in shadows
Of secret shrine and hall,
But Saul he stood up strongly
Before the gaze of all.

And Samuel was a subtle man
With speech that crawled and stung,
But Saul he was a plain man,
With open hand and tongue.

If I had dwelt in Israel, when Samuel ruptured Israel,
If I had dwelt in Israel
When Samuel harried Saul,
My gift had been to Samuel a poisoned cup to Samuel,
A hidden knife to Samuel,
A serpent in his hall.

For Saul he lifted Israel
By blood and sweat and toil,
But Samuel took the credit,
And Samuel took the spoil.

And Samuel lolled on couches
Where girls shook down their hair,
But Saul knew thirst and madness
Where arrows filled the air.

And Samuel died on velvet
With priests to ease his fears,
But Saul he died in battle,
Ringed round by dripping spears.

If I had dwelt in Israel when Gath came up to Israel,
When Gaza came to Israel,
With Ashdod's charioteers,
My last breath had been Samuel's, to curse the name of
Samuel,
That it was Saul, not Samuel,
Who died among the spears.

Samson's Broodings.

I will go down to Philistia,
I am sick of this conquered race,
Which curses my strength behind my back,
And fawns before my face.

I will go to the men that broke them
— They are better men than these —
I am weary of taxes and bended backs
And men that go on their knees.

I will go to the lords of Gaza,
As a peer and not as a slave,
A bow is no more than a bended stick,
A spear but a sharpened stave.

I spread my arms above them,
My fingers grip and close,
And their archers are broken carrion,
Their swordsmen meat for the crows.

I will not bear a slave to my bed;
The bread of the conquered is dust.
I will drink the wine of the conquerors,
Their women shall glut my lust.

Well, write me soon and send me another perm.

Fear Dunn.

NOTES

1. From Smith's poem "Retraction."
2. Lindsey Tyson.

TSS: 82479-82781

ଔଓଔ

215. To Kirk Mashburn, ca. September 1932.

Dear Mr. Mashburn:

Just a line (and rather belated too,) to congratulate you on "The Last of Placide's Wife".[1] It's a splendid story; you have the knack of the making the impossible convincing, which is the true test of a weird story writer.

Please pardon the brevity of this epistle, but I'm up to my ears in work.

Best wishes.

Cordially,
[REH.]

NOTES

1. *Weird Tales*, September 1932.

ଔଓଔ

216. To Tevis Clyde Smith, ca. September 1932.

Fear Finn:

You owe me a letter, you louse, he said with a sinister twirl of his Spanish moustachios, his fingers tapping the hilt of the rapier he twisted about his booted leg.

I was in Brownwood for a little while yesterday, but I took up so much time trying to find a pair of britches I could wear, I didn't get to see you. I'll descend on you sometime in the near future, perhaps.

Remember Robert Carr, "the prophet of the flamboyant younger generation"?[1] I've often wondered what ever became of him since he dropped out of sight in the literary world. Price writes me that he forsook American literature in order to help build up Soviet Russia. According to Price, he is holding down some sort of job there, apparently a pretty good one.

I feel in a good to talk of pictures, which I seldom discuss, and seldom see, for that matter. I've been fortunate enough to see several pretty good ones lately; what with my wanderings to the Coast, etc.. I've seen *Horsefeathers*, *Hold 'Em Jail*, *Back Street*, *Sky-scraper Souls*. *Horsefeathers* was better than *Monkey Business*, but not as good as either *The Cocoanuts* or *Animal Crackers* to my mind. I got more laughs out of *Hold 'Em Jail* than any picture I've seen in years. *Back Street* was powerful, to my mind, and most damnably harrowing. I wept bitterly. That's no lie. While weeping some yegg in front of me turned around and gave me an incredulous look, and thinking he was about to make a smart crack, I gave him a murderous glare, wiped away my tears and drew back my right to mash him for the insect he was, but he made no comment and turned around again. Maybe he was weeping too. I wish I hadn't seen that show. It really tore me up. The thought of an intelligent and talented woman wasting all her years on a low-lifed son-of-a-bitch and sacrificing herself and living in the shadows, it gave me the jitters. I felt like taking a club and wading through the populace like Samson through the Philadelphians. *Gutter-scraping Souls* was good too; but the thoughts and actions of civilized people are utterly inexplicable to me. The morals of the people in the picture disgusted me. They — some of them — were of the class that considers itself salt of the earth, and they acted like a herd of swine. I enjoyed it — and marveled. If that's the way people live in Noo Yawk, me for the wide open spaces where men are bastards. Of all the dreary, empty, artificial lives — ye gods. And that accursed modernistic architecture — no curves, or generous expanses, just lines, corners, angles — why, hell, I can't tell what the stuff's for, or even recognize a chair, until somebody parks his or her posterior on it. The stock-market crash in the picture made me feel sorry for the poor saps that were trying to make a little money outside my regular salary, but I'll admit I laughed with unholy glee to see the big fat hogs of Wall Street going down the line for their shirts. I realize more and more our difference from such people, mainly because of my lack of sympathy for them. That's merely a lack of conception and understanding, and shows what different lives we lead; we're really a separate and distinct people, as we've often remarked. Though now all the little sophisticates are trying to remold us to the Eastern pattern. I'd hang them for renegades, all on one gallows.

Well, the experts who predicted a great year for Southwestern football are due to be crossed up, as usual. There doesn't seem to be an outstanding team in this section. And to add to the infamy, out of the black depravity of their devious and hellish hearts, the lords of the Conference have decided no broadcasts. The West Coast, the Eastern Conference, the Big Ten and the Southern Conference have decided to broadcast — or rather the Westerners never had any other idea — but our individualistic Southwesterners refuse to be shaken. Bah! And Tech asks several thousand dollars to guarantee to meet the Jefferson College pirates — down on outlaw football. Damned peculiar — the Texas colleges go into Yankeedom and play outlaw teams with gusto, but they set up a howl when a buccaneer bobs up in their front yard. Oh, consistency, thou art a jewel which shines like a kick in the rump. I'm for subsidies and outlaw football myself. Man the starboard guns, all hands on deck to repel boarders, heave up the Jolly Roger and let's all be buccaneers.

Let me attempt a drama in the Russian manner.

A Glass of Vodka.

Scene: a Russian saloonsky.

Dmitri: "Have a glass of vodka, Vladimir."

Ivan, a barkeepsky: "Yes, Vladimir, it's good vodka."

Vladimir: "No. Why should I drink vodka when the world's all askew? I think — you understand; if I didn't think as I think, but then, of course, I'd not think as I wouldn't, if I didn't — but then, I wouldn't. But you don't understand."

Dmitri: "I think I do. Have a drink."

Vladimir: "After all, why shouldn't I? Give me the drink, Ivan. We live, we drink vodka, we die. Why should we not die? What are we but animals? If a man was anything but an animal — but then, of course, he wouldn't be if he wasn't what he had been before or after he was or was not. I won't drink."

Dmitri: "But there might be something — something, you understand. Not altogether anything, but something above — outside of all this. Or behind it. Surely behind it, yes, yes, it must be behind it. Because if there wasn't, what was or is besides this?"

Ivan: "Sure, it's all evident. It is, there isn't, or is not, because, well, because if there wasn't, what would it all be?"

Vladimir: "No, you fellows are just talking to cheer me up. I know what I know — well, maybe not all, but something. Life's that way, you know. Give me the vodka."

Ivan, philosophically: "Well, it must be a woman."

Vladimir: "It is a woman. I will not drink the vodka."

Dmitri: "Olga?"

Vladimir: "No — Ekaterine the Great."

Dmitri: "But she's dead!"

Vladimir: "So is Voltaire."

Dmitri: "But he was a Frenchman. You can't expect a Frenchman to live hundreds of years. Not in these times. The French are smart people. You can't fool a Frenchman."

Vladimir, bitterly: "No, and you can't make a sow's ear out of a silk purse either, and don't let them tell you different. Give me the vodka."

He drinks, draws a pistol and shoots Ivan through the belly. He splits Dmitri's skull with an axe, chops up the bar and writes "REASON" in blood on the ruins. At the door he reads a sign, "Vodka on tap; cheap!" He looks at his victims and laughs with bitter self-mockery.

Vladimir: "Poor Ivan! Poor Dmitri! Tumble bugs caught under the heel of Life! It was their fate, and what man can escape his destiny? I pity them, but what avails my pity against a system that makes carrion out of them? Who am I to stem the tide? What is a single sword against fifty million? Hah! hah! hah!"

Exit, cutting out paper dolls.

Ah, well, I was not cut out to be a dramatist.

One Blood Stain.

Now autumn comes and summer goes,
And rises in my heart again,
As witchfire glimmers through a pool,
The mystic madness of the Dane.

Blue thunder of a foaming sea
Reverberating through my sleep,
White billowing sails that fill and flee
Across a wind-swept restless deep —

They speak to me with subtle tongue
Of blue-bright ways my forebears trod,
When time the bearded Vikings bent
Their oars against the winds of God.

And I am but a common man
Who treads a dreary way ashore,
But oceans thunder in my dreams,
And blue waves break on creaking beams,
And foaming water swirls and creams
About the strongly bending oar.

When summer goes and autumn comes
To paint the leaves with sombre fires,
I feel, like throbs of distant drums,
The urge of distant nameless sires.

Fear Dunn.

NOTES

1. Robert Spencer Carr was the author of six stories appearing in *Weird Tales* between 1925 and 1928, the best-known being "Spider-Bite," and of a "jazz age" novel, *The Rampant Age*, 1928, which made him a literary star at the age of nineteen. He lived in Russia 1932-1938.

TSS: 82037-82039

217. To H.P. Lovecraft, September 22, 1932.

Dear Mr. Lovecraft:

I read, as always, your comments on the Greco-Roman world with intense interest. I agree with you that cultural environment and heredity is generally stronger than blood heritage. The matter of Romanized Gauls is a case in point. And in America today, many immigrants become so completely Americanized by the second or third generation that they seem to merge with the native population and to become as much a part of their adopted country and race as if their ancestors had come over on the *Mayflower*. There are plenty of exceptions to this latter case, of course, but they have no bearing on the original theory.

For myself, if I should be suddenly confronted with the prospect of being transported back through the centuries into a former age, with the option of living where I wished, I would naturally select the most civilized country possible. That would be necessary, for I have always led a peaceful, sheltered life, and would be unable to cope with conditions of barbarism. Thus, for my own safety, I would select Egypt rather than Syria, to which otherwise my instincts would lead me; I would choose Greece rather than Spain or Thrace; Rome rather than Gaul, Britain or Germany. As a matter of personal necessity I would seek to adapt myself to the most protected and civilized society possible, would conform to their laws and codes of conduct, and if necessary, fight with them against the ruder races of my own blood.

On the other hand, if I were to be reborn in some earlier age and grow up knowing no other life or environment than that, I would choose to be born in a hut among the hills of western Ireland, the forests of Germany or the steppes of Southern Russia; to grow up hard and lean and wolfish, worshipping barbarian gods and living the hard barren life of a barbarian — which is, to the barbarian who has never tasted anything else — neither hard nor barren. I never talked with an old pioneer of the true type, who, even admitting hardships that seem intolerable to modern people, and would kill folk of softer mold — I never talked with one, I say, who did not at last admit that to him that life was fuller, more vital and more full of real content than this newer phase. Of course such a man has usually been unable to adjust himself to changing conditions. To a man of intellectual accomplishments the life of a frontiersman would be intolerable; but to a man who has never known anything else, such a life would be full of vital interest.

I can not, however, agree with you that the spirit of physical contest is artificial. I may possibly have misunderstood your meaning in this case, since it is pretty easy to get out of my depth. Personally, I would never consider glorifying physical achievement above other things — a research worker in a laboratory, for instance, is of infinitely more value than the greatest athlete that ever lived. Yet I can not but think that a zest for, or at least an interest in physical struggles, ties to the very ribs of humanity. It is manifestly impossible for all men to derive pleasure from intellectual pursuits alone. The average man lacks the ability and the advantages, or perhaps I should say the opportunity. So he turns in many cases to the field of sport, for relaxation and exhilaration, and I can not but believe that if there is any artificiality in the matter, it leans toward the side of the purely intellectual pursuit. Yet I am not prepared to say that any pursuit of mankind is artificial. True, there is probably nothing about the football field, the prize-ring, the race-track or the baseball diamond that tends toward the advancement of art, science or literature. But surely we are not so bound to the treadwheel of progress that we must engage in only those pursuits which definitely make for the advancement of society. After a hard day's work I feel far more like seeing a prize-fight or a leg-show than I feel like delving into questions of science and philosophy. Understand, I am not upholding this feeling. I am only saying that the average man, like me, simply lacks the brains to find his pleasure and thrills in purely intellectual followings.

Looking back over a none-too-lengthy and prosaic life, I can easily pick out what seemed — and still seems — the peak of my life to date; that is, the point at which I derived the highest thrills — a word which my limited vocabulary causes me to overwork. I do not altogether lack appreciation for artistic endeavors. I am capable of becoming drunken on written words — the power, sweep and splendor of certain prose writers; often I have felt a wave of coldness sweep over me, with a physical accompaniment of "goose-flesh" at the pure beauty of great poetry. It is not hard for certain singers and musicians to bring tears to my eyes, or a white blaze of glory to my brain. All this, I realize, shows that the appeal is more to my emotions than to my intelligence, and possibly I am without genuine intellectual appreciation. Yet, mental or emotional, it is possible for me to keenly enjoy the triumphs and attempts of art.

Yet when I look for the peak of my exultation, I find it on a sweltering, breathless midnight when I fought a black-headed tiger of an Oklahoma drifter in an abandoned ice-vault, in a stifling atmosphere laden with tobacco smoke and the reek of sweat and rot-gut whiskey — and blood; with a gang of cursing, blaspheming oil-field roughnecks for an audience. Even now the memory of that battle stirs the sluggish blood in my fat-laden tissues. There was nothing about it calculated to advance art, science or anything else. It was a bloody, merciless, brutal brawl. We fought for fully an hour — until neither of us could fight any longer, and we reeled against each other, gasping incoherent curses through battered lips. No, there was nothing stimulating to the mental life of man about it. There was not even an excuse for it. We were fighting, not because there was any quarrel between us, but simply to see who was the best man. Yet I repeat that I get more real pleasure out of remembering that battle than I could possibly get out of contemplating the greatest work of art ever accomplished, or seeing the greatest drama ever enacted, or hearing the greatest song ever sung. I repeat, I do not seek to justify my particular make-up. But there it is. I love to watch a well-matched prize-fight, a well-fought football game. I have beat my way hundreds of miles to see both, and have endured cold, hunger and a certain amount of hardship, and I can not believe that my enjoyment of such spectacles is artificial. Animalistic it may be; unworthy it possibly is; bound to the tie-ribs of reality it must be.

I noted with interest your comments regarding the supernatural etc., and am not equipped to dispute any point of your theories. I never gave a name to my views — or lack of views — but I guess an Agnostic is what I am, if that means skepticism regarding all human gropings. Perhaps the main reason that I dislike to take a firm stand in any direction, is because of the respect I have for my father's intelligence. He is not by any means convinced that there is nothing in the matters mentioned. He is far better educated than I, and has more natural sense than I'll ever have. Scientist? He is a practical scientist if ever lived one. For more than thirty years he has been applying science in his daily life. There is no better physician in the state of Texas, though there are many who have made more of a financial success. The reason he is not a rich man is because he's been more interested in humanity than in dollars. The charity work he's done would run up into the hundred thousands, and the bills people have beat him out of would about equal that figure. He always sacrificed the business side of his profession to the scientific side. When other men were balancing their ledgers, figuring their per centages and suing for their bills, he was studying the latest methods, attending clinics and buying the latest books on medicine. He is a rare combination of a scholar and a worker. All that the finest medical schools of the South and Southwest could give him, he got, working his way through frequently, doing mental and physical work that would have been beyond the power of a weaker man. Even now, at the age of sixty-one, he does not only an office practice, but a country practice as well, that embraces parts of four counties, and has more strength, endurance and enthusiasm than I have. Hundreds of men are walking the world today who owe their lives to him, and many of these men were paupers, who were never able to pay him a cent. Nor did he ask it. Frequently he not only saved their lives, but fed their families as well. That's why he's not rich today. In the thousands of women he has delivered, he never lost one woman in childbirth. He was the first to introduce snake-anti toxin into this part of the country, and he never lost a snake-bite case, to the best of my knowledge. Publishers of the most up-to-date medical books have frequently written him, asking him to contribute reports on diagnosis and treatment for publications. All this is to simply show that he is no ignorant bumpkin, but a scientific man in the truest sense of the word — science applied, and not simply theorized on. There is scarcely any branch of medical science that he has not studied; any legitimate branch, I mean. Nor medicine alone, but theology, history and economics.

I have sat in colleges and listened to dried up professors mouthing their supercilious viewpoints on life and death, and I could scarcely restrain my mirth, when I compared them with my father, who, while they were sitting at ease in some dusty nook, analyzing the universe from a detached and superior point of view, he was grappling with the raw, elemental vitals of existence in the city slums or the backwoods hills. In his early days much of his practice was in primitive communities, far removed from any of the inventions and conveniences of civilization. He went into miserable shacks and huts, and without weapons save his own will and intelligence and a few simple medicines of the time, grappled the destroyer and repeatedly overthrew him. Science? My father knows science; it is not any empty word or a theory with him; it has been a spear with which he has ten thousand times hurled back death from the quivering body of a helpless victim.

And if he, who has plunged his hands deep into the very guts of Life and Death, and seen things that an average man seldom even dreams, if he is not ready to deny the existence of a future state, then I for one do not care to deny it. These college professors I mentioned thought they knew things because they had read the books. He has read the books, and more than that, he has known Life in its reddest, rawest, most elemental phases. Honest men, thieves; white men, negroes, Mexicans, to all he have given, and gives, the same earnest attention. It has mattered little to him whether the man or woman under his care were a saint or a criminal, a rich man or a beggar. Many and many a time he has kept watch over the sick-bed of some poor pauper, himself neither eating nor sleeping, oblivious to all else except the battle he was waging with the destroyer. And people have stood awed, seeing the intensity of that awful struggle, in which he literally held death at bay by the sheer power of his intellect and will, throughout the night, to stagger forth in the dawn, victorious.

Through the slums of eastern cities, in the outlaw-infested wilds of the old Indian Territory, in the silence and desolation of the Great Plains in the days before the law was brought there, in the sordid barrenness of the squatters' hills, in the roar and madness of oil booms, he has moved unchangingly on his way, single-handed battling disease, madness, insanity, death.

And when I compare him with professors, and with mere scholars, I am merely amused. I respect their zeal for knowledge, but I can not attach too much importance to any man's theories, unless he has backed them up with actual work and toil and matched them against the elementals of Life, as my father has.

I'm enclosing a clipping, telling of the planned destruction of the old French Market in New Orleans. That's an old landmark that seems to me should be preserved. It smelled like hell — what with the fish, lobster, wops etc., but it had a real air of olden times that wasn't altogether the scent. But you doubtless visited it. Many a plantain have I purchased there — and cooked in the manner of banana fritters I know of no better dish. Did you get any genuine Creole gumbo while there? Cooked as only the bona-fide French of New Orleans can cook it, with rice, thyme, bay-leaf, minced ham, white chicken meat, crab and shrimp, it's a food for the gods. Nor have I ever tasted a drink half as good as an old French-German woman on Canal Street used to mix — but those were the days of good whiskey. I suppose you visited Pontchartrain, the dueling oaks, and the ruins of the old Spanish fort. You should have — or maybe you did — take a boat up the river a few miles, in order to get a look at the old plantation houses which rose near the banks — at least they did in my time. Did you ever hear the old song, "The Lakes of the Pontchartrain"?

"Twas on one bright March morning, I bid old New Orleans adieu,
And on my way to Jackson, where I was force to go,
Twas there my Georgia money no credit did me gain,
And it filled my heart with sadness on the lakes of the Pontchartrain.

Through swamps and alligators, I wound my weary way,
O'er railroad ties and crossings, my weary feet did stray,
Till the shadows of the evening, some higher ground did gain,
Twas there that I met this Creole, on the lakes of the Pontchartrain.
"Good evening, fair young maiden, my money to me is no good;
"If it wasn't for the alligators, I'd sleep out in the wood."
"Oh, welcome, welcome, stranger, for though our house be plain,
We never turn away a traveller from the lakes of the Pontchartrain."

And so on for several more verses. I can't get interested in these new song-hits, but I know a lot of old ones by heart, that have been passed down through the generations, from the hills of Scotland and Ireland, across the Piedmont and the Cumberlands, over the Mississippi and through the pinelands, and onto the great plains, changing form as they went.

You are undoubtedly right in saying that it would be better to alleviate the miseries of the working classes, than to give them liquor. But who's going to do that? The workmen themselves are scarcely capable of working out their own solutions; and to all other classes we — and when I say "we" I mean the laboring masses, of which I am a member — we, I say, are less than the dogs that eat their crumbs. How can we develop intelligence and co-ordination when life is such a struggle for existence as to crowd all other considerations out? What are the philosophers and economists to a man whose days consist in back-breaking, brain-numbing toil from the time he rises until he falls dazedly into his bed that night? I agree with you that the only way the masses will ever get any favors is by force. But I doubt much if, in such event, the rulers will call in the sociologists; they're more likely to call in the gunmen and sluggers, and put down revolt by massacre and wholesale slaughter.

As for liquor as a whole — I have no use, and never had any use, for any man or any set that expected a person to make a swill-barrel of his belly in order to be sociable. I certainly think no less of a man because he refuses a drink. In fact, I was a rather rabid teetotaler at one time of my life, and wouldn't have taken a drink if the president had brought it on a golden platter. Even in my hardest drinking days, I've refrained from taking a drink, because I happened to be with a non-drinking man. I have a right to drink; the other man has a right not to drink. That's my attitude. I never regarded a man as priggish or eccentric because he doesn't drink, and I have no patience for anyone so narrow as to look on a non-drinker in that light.

As for law and law enforcement — I had no intention of casting slurs on the courage of Eastern law-officers. I don't think that at any time during our correspondence, I've cast any reflections on the courage of the people of the East, or any people, as far as that goes. I do say that it doesn't take the guts to be a law-officer anywhere today, that it used to take. As you yourself point out, the many inventions of civilization make it hard for the criminal to escape punishment; it naturally follows that the job of the cop is easier. I hardly think that such men as John Poe, Pat Garrett and Jack Hayes looked on the apprehending of criminals as "a stage for the showing off of their personal merits." When one of these men went out after a desperado single-handed it was not because of an inflated ego, but a cool confidence in his ability to do the job alone. When Jack Hayes went into a thicket and killed *eleven* Comanche Indians in hand-to-hand combat, he did not do this because he wanted to show-off. It was his job and he did it. He was confident of his ability, and he did not need a mob of men to help him. He was the greatest law-officer the west has ever seen, and he killed more men than the average cop ever arrests. The same thing can apply to Wild Bill Hickok. He was up against conditions that would freeze the guts of the average chief of police, wherever he lived. The west swarmed with desperadoes of the most terrible type — bandits from the gold-fields, renegades from all states, half-breeds, gunfighters and gamblers and wild cowboys from Texas, bringing the trail herds up the Chisholm. He went it practically alone. I have no love for Wild Bill Hickok — he killed too many Texans. But he was a power in the west. And he never had a mob at his beck and call. In fact, it was the other way around. He was repeatedly faced by organized crime of the most desperate sort. If he had been a mere swaggering swashbuckler, with a desire to strut and show-off, he wouldn't have lasted a week. As it was, he lived long enough to clean up every place he went, and had some eighty-odd slayings to his credit when Jack McCall shot him in the back of the head; at the behest, by the way, of certain organizations not openly connected with the criminal element. It may have been an inflated ego that led men like him, and like John Poe, and Jack Hayes, into wild countries, to clean it up and make it habitable, single-handed, yet at least they succeeded. And I can assure you that it was no "childish game" in which they took part — unless murder, butchery and sudden death are childish. In one town in Kansas the outlaws took out the sheriff and chopped off his head with an axe. The governor sent Wild Bill Hickok there; he went alone, killed the ring-leaders of the gang, and ran the rest out of the country. He made the town fit for a man to live in, and he did it alone. In my own time one Ranger has cowed a ravening mob; and until very recently it was never the custom to send more than one Ranger to quell an ordinary disturbance.

Romantic or not, I find much to admire in the old type of officer, who, instead of having everything on his side as does the modern cop, worked against every disadvantage and yet cleaned up his country. His resources were comparatively few. His deputies were few, if any; the countryside was frequently hostile, or at least remained silently neutral. The outlaws had friends, secret hide-outs, frequently political pull. In the last analysis, law enforcement depended largely on the individual wearing the badge. I've seen that work out myself, to an extent, in boom towns. When Pat Garrett went after Billy the Kid, he had a posse, it's true. But he asked no man to do his shooting. With his own hand he killed Tom O'Phalliard, Charlie Bowdre and Billy himself, breaking up, practically single-handed, the most desperate band of outlaws that ever haunted the hills of the Southwest.

When Jack Hayes went from Texas to California in '49 — the fact that he had to work his way, shows how rich the pickings were for a Texas law in those days — and the governor appointed him sheriff of San Francisco, he had not only the regular criminal element to deal with, but the organized Vigilantes as well. Within a year or so, he'd cleaned the town as it's never been cleaned since. And he did it practically alone. I hardly think you'd have found a more practical and less romantic man than Jack Hayes. If he was aware of his manhood, it was scarcely to his discredit, since no man ever saw him strut or heard him boast about his deeds. Indeed, no one will ever know how many Mexicans, Indians and desperadoes Hayes killed, because he never would talk of his exploits. He was quiet, soft-spoken, modest, and I repeat, the best law officer that ever wore leather west of the Mississippi.

In regards law-breakers — I am the first to admit that frequently the confirmed law-breaker is a rat, who ought to be put out of the way. Yet I can not hold that any man who breaks a law puts himself beyond the pale of human consideration and is to be held as a rabid wolf. Frequently the breaking of a law is not wanton and vicious, but merely a mistake or the result of a momentary blind passion. I do not call for mushy sentimentality in dealing with offenders — but I do call for a little common sense, which quality seems lacking in a good many enforcers of the law. Even in the case of regular law-breakers, the individual is not always a cross between a maddog and a vandal. I've seen plenty of men who were driven to crime. Society stood smugly by and let them welter, but the instant they turned in desperation to some course not exactly ethical, there was a great howling and yelling about the individual's debt to society. Apparently society has no obligations to fulfill toward the individual. I hate a habitual criminal as much as any man. But I don't class as a criminal a man who commits a crime in a moment of passion — or one who steals to keep from starving. I've rubbed shoulders with many kinds of men in my life, and there was a good deal of the devil in most of them, and a little of the saint in some. When I was working in that drug-store I mentioned, I used to run accounts of my own with certain young fellows the management wouldn't credit. In other words, I sold them the stuff on my own responsibility, and if they failed to pay me, I made it good to the management out of my own pocket. I dealt with bootleggers, booze-runners, gamblers, and hijack men, and I never lost a damned cent. Even a fellow who scattered a trail of cold checks across the country and skipped, leaving his room-mate to hold the bag, paid me what he owed the night before he took it on the lam. I don't particularly hold this up as a sign of nobility in a passel of rats and wolves. These youths of course were not hardened criminals, at least I wouldn't call them so. Though some of them undoubtedly developed into such characters. Let me repeat that I do not seek to glorify crime. I merely object to a system that allows the gangster rat to go unpunished, while an ordinary citizen who has the misfortune to slip, is practically sure of being crucified for an example. I know the grilling methods of the police, for instance, are supposed to be applied only to the worst thugs. But I am hardly innocent enough to be fooled by that. If I didn't know of a few cases xxxxxxxxxx[1], I have other sources of information to fall back on. Eastern sources too, by the way. Not many years ago I heard a Chicago literary critic remark over the air that the police generally reserved most of their strong-arm methods for unattached offenders who had no gang-connections or political pull.

I'm afraid I wouldn't fit into the scheme of more civilized sections, or even in the scheme of this section, which is being civilized as fast as people from other states can do it to their own advantage. I've always been a quiet, law-abiding citizen, to the best of my ability. Yet I, in common with most of my acquaintances, have occasionally broken laws. Just now the brother of one of my best friends is hiding out somewhere — I don't know where. But if he were to come to me, I understand my duty as a citizen would demand that I instantly hand him over to the police. Well, I have few friends in this world, but if any one of them were to come to me, hunted by the law, I'd hold myself lower than a dog if I didn't do all in my power to aid him. If that's romantic and idealistic, I'm sorry, but I can't help it.

I was nearly fourteen years old before I lived — for any length of time — in a community which supported a law officer. Generally the nearest officer was the sheriff of the county, whose office was in the county seat. Sometimes there was a sort of constable, whose duties were so light as to be practically non-existent. The communities in which I lived were unsophisticated and primitive, made up largely of people with quick tempers and violent passions. Yet life was not a holocaust of murder and rape. Mainly we settled our problems among ourselves. Civil suits and litigations were comparatively few. If some swaggering bully began to impose himself too much on the community, somebody killed him. After a killing there was always some kind of a legal investigation. But fights that did not end fatally were seldom dragged into courts. I still think that if two gentlemen want to go out where no innocent bystander will be injured, and fight if out between them, it's nobody's business but theirs. We were a taciturn, clannish people, not inclined to talk to strangers. A whole county could keep a secret and keep it well. Nor did a sheriff or officer dare resort to strong-arm methods to get information. You will understand that I am not suggesting these conditions to be applied to more thickly settled parts.

I don't pretend to know anything about life in the East, for instance, and nothing I say here is to be taken as a sectional criticism. But as I remember it, Texas was a safer and more pleasant state to live in before the influx of people from other states forced a lot of protective legislature down our throats. If there was more honest fist-fighting, there was less theft, murder and underhanded knavery; more open hospitality and trust. Now men are becoming so cowed by law that they are becoming miserly, furtive and afraid to resent an open insult. I agree with a noted lawyer, now a candidate for the legislature, and a man whose intelligence I respect. He maintains that too many laws are being passed, and forecasts the time when the people will be made literal serfs, simply by the passing of myriad laws. These laws the rich can evade, but the poor can not. Frankly, that's one of my kicks; instead of being allowed to develop gradually along our own lines, and work out our own laws and culture, the state has been flooded with capitalism from other sections of the country, by people who wanted laws enacted for their own benefit, by which they could exploit the state, and be protected from reprisal while doing so. I resent the forcing of alien culture and habits on my native state, even if that culture is superior. Its superiority in a general sense doesn't mean that it's the best thing that could happen to us. Yesterday Texas was a frontier; today it's a grab-bag for big business — business which takes far more money out of the state than it ever puts in. The transition is painful to a person of old traditions.

There is a vast difference between the old stock native Texan and people from more civilized sections. Though now it is the style in many parts of the state to ape Eastern ways and despise the mannerisms of their fathers. Eastern ways are good for the East, where they naturally developed. I am not so sure than an imitation of those ways is so good. But the old Texan: a great number of the people who have flooded this state in quest of climate, health or money, do not understand us, and make no effort to, being fortified with a feeling of their own superiority. Many evidently expect to be shot at the minute they get off the train or the boat, and finding us not particularly sanguinary, immediately swing to the other side, and despise us for lack of spirit. They seem to mistake our natural courtesy for servility. Our code of politeness does no doubt seem exaggerated to a stranger from parts where life moves at quicker tempo. Our habit of complimenting our friends, and deprecating ourselves, is merely part of our code of courtesy; the compliments are sincere, but when we deprecate ourselves, it does not mean that we lack self-esteem. Under our politeness generally lurks a keen vanity, and a sometimes dangerous pride. Beneath the veneer of our courtesy we are generally hot tempered and unforgiving. We remember our friends long, but we remember our enemies longer. Of course you know that these remarks can not apply to all Texans, now that the state is become thickly settled and complex. But it does apply to the people of the old original stock. Another thing, more cultured people are prone to sneer at a certain melodramatic tendency in people of the old stock. It is there; I would be the last to deny it. It crops out continually in my writing, occasionally in my speech, though never in my actions.

I have heard and read this tendency pointed out as an evidence that the old Southwesterner was more bluff than anything else. A greater mistake was never made, and can be classed with the fallacy that a bully is always a coward, and that a braggart never makes good his threats. Such men as Bat Masterson, Bob Ollinger, Henry Plummer, and Ben Thompson were extremely melodramatic, but were no less deadly for that reason. Ben Thompson in particular — his whole life was a stage whereon he swaggered and posed; he lived pure melodrama to the day he was riddled in the old Jack Harris Theater in San Antonio, and he shamelessly played up to the gallery gods. And he strewed his stage with thirty-odd dead men, as an earnest of his actorship. King Fisher, too, who died beside him on that red day when the curtain finally rang down on the red drama. By God, how appropriate it was that these deadly actors made their final bow in a theater, of all places! King Fisher's melodrama ran more to his attire than his actions. His boots were of the finest calfskin, with fancy red stitching; his hat was a Mexican sombrero ornamented with gold braid; for a vest he wore a gold braided Mexican jacket; a red silk sash girdled his supple waist, and from richly hand-worked leather jutted the ivory butts of the finest pistols Colt could supply by special order. His chaps were made of the striped pelt of a royal Bengal tiger, commandeered from a wandering circus. I have heard that at one time a hundred and fifty men followed him. Yet King Fisher was not merely a taker of human life. If he had been, he would have killed Horace Greeley that day in San Antonio, when Horace took him to task for his murders. Instead of resenting the impertinence, the King simply smiled and assured Horace that he had murdered no one recently. Horace then accused King of having ridden into Eagle Pass with sixteen human ears strung on his bridle reins — which was true. Still King Fisher showed no resentment at this uninvited criticism of his actions, merely smiling again and remarking that they were Mexican ears, and did not count. If Horace had ventured to thus reprove Hendry Brown or Bob Ollinger, I wouldn't have cared to vouch for his safety.

But to return to the present day: the native Texan is looked on as lawless. But if he is prone to reserve calling in the law as a last resort rather than a first, it is only necessary to remember that the time is not far back when men considered it their own personal business to protect themselves. When the uncle for whom I was named — a prominent banker on the coast — was mixed up in the "round bale war", he hired a private detective to guard his house and protect his family when he himself had to be absent, but he asked no man to protect him. He wore his protection slung on his own right hip. Anyway, when one of his associates was shot down on the streets, the gang that did it ran the sheriff clean out of town. Even when my uncle learned of a plot to murder him as he got aboard the Galveston train, he didn't ask for a police escort. He didn't even ask his friends to help him, but they were there in force, and the would-be killers backed down. I'm not telling this to show how brave my uncle was; I don't claim he was braver than anybody else. As far as that goes, he wasn't afraid of anything between the devil and the moon. But it just shows that in those days men considered protecting themselves their own personal job, unless the odds against them were too overwhelming.

As for the modern police system, I must confess that my admiration for it is not high. I hear much of its efficiency — and at the same time, in newspaper editorials, from the mouths of lecturers, speakers, reformers, and the pens of political and social writers, I hear that the nation is staggering with corruption and vice. Not many months ago a woman in an East Texas city said to me — and she held a responsible position and was in a position to know — she said, "The police don't exert themselves unless somebody pays them; promise one a hundred dollars and he'll work his legs off." Is that the sort of condition that prevails in cities? Is legal protection to be the privilege only of those willing and able to pay for it, while a man is denied the right to protect himself? For the carrying of weapons and the personal avenging of a wrong is forbidden by law. Another thing — a slight one. Once a friend of mine was walking down the street of a boom town, slightly jagged. Somebody smelled his breath, and he was thrown into jail where he spent the night, being released only on the payment of a fine. He was making no disturbance at all. Of course, the laws could not know that he would make none. Let us admit then, that they were right in casting him into jail. But — not long later I was in a drugstore where the son of a big oil magnate from the North was wild drunk and raising hell generally. Not a law ever showed up until he left. He was allowed to do just as he damned please. And if somebody had shot him, heaven and hell would have been moved to have sent the killer to the chair. Is there here a double standard of conduct? Are the obligations of the laboring man to society different from those of the rich and powerful? If our laws are so blindly just, why do the wealthy seldom ever suffer by their enforcement? There was a great tumult about Albert Fall serving his light sentence; yet for half of what he did, other men have spent a lifetime behind the bars. No, I don't believe a really wealthy man can be touched by the law, usually, East or West. On the other hand I've known plenty of cases where ignorance was taken advantage of. Men were arrested without legal right, and bullied into paying fines that could never have been collected, had the victims known anything about law. Just like the Vice-squad racket, for instance. I followed that business pretty closely in the papers and magazines. I've known it worked on a smaller scale elsewhere. Where ignorant people, men and women, knowing nothing of legal procedure, were made to believe that they had committed some offense and simply shaken down.

As for the rest, we have the Vice-squad scandal in New York; the present investigation in that city, and the kicking of various officials out of office. And there is the Lindbergh case. No feather in the police cap there, unless the hounding of an innocent girl to suicide is to be considered as such. And there is Capone, whom they had to send up on a federal charge. Nor do I ever pick up a paper that I don't read about gangster activities, extortions, city scandals, dope rings, etc.. The utter failure to enforce prohibition is likewise a case in point. No, I can't believe that the police machine works universally with anything like a smooth tread. These remarks need not be taken to mean that I am an anarchist, a criminal-sympathizer, or a rabid cop-hater. But I do believe that the system as a whole is too corrupt xxxxxxxxxx[. . .][2] I have respect and admiration for any fearless, honest officer of the law.

I'm enclosing a clipping which is probably a lot of bologna. If the outlaw had been Floyd, he'd more likely have killed the officer instead of throwing him out naked. A friend of mine recently returned from Oklahoma, where he'd gone to try his luck in the harvest fields, and he was quite enthusiastic about Floyd. From what he said public sympathy must be a good deal with the outlaw. I also hear that Floyd has been feeding a good many destitute people. They can hardly be expected to inform against him to the representatives of a society which lets them starve.

I note the mid-western farmers are raring up. I've always said that if an agricultural revolution started, it would start there. I don't have the slightest idea that their blockade will do any good, but you can't blame people for trying to help their conditions. Legislate — legislate — but what good does that do when the people are betrayed by everybody they put in office? However, the farmer is just out of luck; he's not organized well enough to intimidate anybody, and it will probably end by their being mowed down with machine guns and ridden down by cavalry. Also a little hell busting in the Illinois mining district. I suppose they'll have the troops out there, too. I'm surprized I haven't heard the term "Red" applied to the midwestern farmers. Now days if a man's hungry, he's a Red; if he wants a job, he's a Red; if he asserts his right to live, he's a Red; and should be clubbed on the head and dragged out as an enemy to organized society.

You're right about the muddle of history. It's a regular blind surging maelstrom as far as I can see. Lamb,[3] writing on the crusades, seems to discount the theory of trade-routes, at least in connection with the First Crusade. As near as I can learn, he maintains that movement was begun by Urban for his own particular purposes — he wanted to start a popular movement to counter-balance the power of his popish rival — and was carried out by the people, mainly through actual religious zeal, though this of course was modified, in the case of various nobles, by a desire to loot and to carve out new kingdoms.

Glad you found the Gladewater paper interesting.[4] It's one of the few organs of the people against the crushing tread of the big interests. The editor packs plenty of power, too;[5] immediately after he accused the state government of sending Rangers to the East Texas fields to coerce the voting, the order was countermanded. It had been announced that thirty-five Rangers were to be sent there to clean out "certain gangsters from the North". The editor of the *Journal* point-blank accused certain high officials of sending these Rangers to East Texas to bulldoze the voters in the coming election, and he added a warning which might easily have been read as a threat. Anyway, the thirty-five Rangers who were already on their way to the fields, were recalled, "lest their presence be misunderstood" it was officially announced.

I was surprized to learn that Providence weather is no colder than it is. Yet I might have known it, considering its position on the coast. Winters in this part of the state, when rainy, are generally mild, though drab and gloomy because of the continuous cloudy weather. Dry winters, especially those following drouths, are likely to be cold as the devil. I've seen people come here from northern and eastern states, and nearly freeze in the winter. That's because this cold is different from the still even cold which I understand prevails in those regions. Fairly warm days are followed by freezes, and it's difficult to accustom oneself to the sudden changes. Then there is the wind; that's what gets many people from other states. These howling, raging blizzards, falling directly off the Rocky Mountains by way of the Staked Plains, are enough to freeze a brass monkey. You can't wear enough clothing so the wind don't blow the coldness right through you. Though, as I believe I told you about the sand-storms, there doesn't seem to be as many and as vicious blizzards as there used to be. There are lots of different climates in Texas anyhow, ranging as the altitude does, from sea-level to plains of four thousand feet and mountains a mile high. Last February I sat on a porch in the lower Rio Grande Valley, in my shirt-sleeves, being pleasantly cooled by a norther that was rattling the fronds of the palm-trees, and hugged myself in unholy glee to think that my friends up on the Callahans were being frost-bitten by that same norther. But I can't stand the low altitudes of that south country. This section isn't as cold as it is up on the plains, but it's cold compared to other parts of the state. As I've probably said before, this town is on the highest point of the Callahan Divide, which is a watershed draining into the Brazos on the north and the Colorado on the south. The land dips somewhat to the north, before beginning to climb toward the Caprock, and there are no ridges to break the swoop of the northers which whistle off the great plains. Therefore it's much colder here than it is in even Brownwood, for instance, which lies only forty miles from here, but on the southern slope of the divide. In fact, this divide seems to act as a wind-break for most all Central West and Central Texas.

I sure agree with you about the relative merits of cold and heat. I detest winter. I despise to wear overcoats and scarves and all that sort of junk. I draw the line at heavy underwear. I wear the same light silk stuff in the winter that I do in the summer. But regardless of what I wear or don't wear, my feet and ears nearly freeze off. I remember one time when I was kid, I was out skating — or rather sliding, for I had no skates — on a frozen pond. I must have been a bigger sap then than I am now, even. Because the ice buckled and cracked under my weight, and I couldn't swim a stroke and was out there by myself. But luck was with me that time, because the ice didn't break until I was near shore and the water was only knee-deep. But Judas, was it cold! As I'd been forbidden the pond, I said nothing about it, didn't have a chance to change my shoes and socks, or even empty the water out, and so splashed off to school in the teeth of a howling blizzard. I had only about a quarter of a mile to walk, but before I'd covered half the distance my stockings were stiff as boards, and the water didn't splash in my shoes, because it was solid ice. When I got to school, the teacher, who was enveloped in a fur coat, wouldn't let us go to the stove to warm, because we generally got into a fight if we did. I sat there until noon, at the back of the room where the heat couldn't reach, and I want to say that it was about as lousy a morning as I ever spent, viewed from a purely physical standpoint. It's a wonder my feet hadn't been frost-bitten.

While you were in the South on your recent visit, did you hear any legends of the Cave-in-the-Rock gang? That's a bit of scenery I've always wanted to visit. A friend of mine[6] saw it a year or so ago, and said it's really impressive. It certainly harbored a desperate horde. Foremost of these were the Harps, who to my mind were the most terrible outlaws that ever cursed this Continent, not even excluding Boone Helm, from whom Zane Grey apparently drew his hellish "Gulden" of *The Border Legion*, and who on one occasion, finding himself snowed in with a companion in the mountains of British Columbia, and out of food, murdered the companion, partly devoured his body, and took up his journey again, carrying a leg along for supplies on the way; who, when strung up along with the rest of Plummer gang by the Vigilantes, standing on a wagon with a rope around his neck, asked if he was expected to jump off, or be pushed off. On being told that he could do as he liked, he replied, "Every man to his own principles! Three cheers for Jeff Davis and the Confederacy! Hurrah for hell! Let her rip!" — and jumped off.

But I was speaking of the Harps, whose devilish blood-lust can be traced partly to an evident insanity, partly to resentment instilled by persecution as Tories in their early life. They eventually foreswore even the garments of civilization, wearing the garb of Indians, and going single-file through the woods. I hear that it was a most horrifying experience to meet them, trailing silently through the forest, their women and children treading noiselessly behind them, and all stamped with the mark of their bestial ferocity. A white man reverted to savagery is a more terrible thing than a true savage, as witness the Girtys. Few there were who survived a meeting with the Harps in a lonely forest. They were too primitive and savage for the gang at Cave-in-the-Rock, who drove them forth in horror. Judas, the blood that was spilt along the Wilderness Road and the Natchez Trace!

Big Harp met his end at the muzzle of a rifle he had loaded himself, and a man whose entire family the Harps had butchered, cut around the outlaw's neck with a butcher knife and twisted his head off, breaking the spinal bones by sheer strength. They carried the head in a sack of roasting ears for a long way — and ate the corn, too, for supper, all but one young man who objected to the blood on the shucks and was jeered at — and finally stuck it up in a tree which was for years known as Harp's Head; until an old woman took down the skull and ground it up for one of the ingredients of a magic potion that she hoped would restore intelligence to her idiot son.

Fate played an ironic jest on Little Harp, the other brother. Two desperate-looking men volunteered to go up the river to the hide-out of Sam Mason, the river-bandit, and try to collect the big reward that was on his head. They brought back Sam's head rolled up in a big ball of clay, and while the judge was about to pay them off, a bystander pointed at one of the men and shouted that the fellow was Little Harp, who'd disappeared after the killing of his brother. So they stuck Little Harp's head up beside Sam Mason's.

There have been, however, few more desperate rogues than those living in old New York, from all I can hear. In the days of the Hudson Dusters, the Dead Rabbits and other gangs. Bill Poole, the leader of the "native Americans" must have possessed incredible vitality, to have lived fourteen days — I believe that was the right number, wasn't it? — with a bullet under his heart. "Good bye, boys; I die a true American!" That speech of his bade fair to become an American classic. He should have had more sense than to have gone into that Irish dive. Because a mick lets you kick him is no sign he won't shoot you in the back. Not that there were many of that gang who would take kickings from anybody, even Bill Poole. I'd have given five dollars to have seen the fight John Morrissey had with Poole. New York about that time — about 1850 — must have been a most virile and interesting place. I'd have liked to have seen the fight Tom Hyer, Poole's friend, had with Yankee Sullivan for the heavyweight title. Heavyweights! Sullivan weighed about 155 pounds. What with Hyer falling on him after he was felled, and slugging him with his knees and elbows, it's a wonder to me that Yankee survived. Sullivan was a tough nut, though. They say he gave Morissey a terrible beating, until John's ruggedness wore him down. There's a legend that Sullivan, after leaving New York, joined Walker's filibusters and perished nobly in Nicaragua. That's bologna. He went to California and was hanged by the San Francisco Vigilantes. But neither Sullivan nor Morissey nor yet Tom Hyer was the toughest product of that time, to my humble mind. That honor — or whatever — ought to go to Chris Lilly who flourished in the early '40s. After killing his sweetheart, Rose Seven, one of the belles of Five Points, with a blow of his naked fist, he became enraged because one of her former suitors, Tom McCoy, the middleweight champion, insisted on shedding tears — probably more inspired by licker than grief — and making a scene. Chris must have been jealous of McCoy, even though the girl was dead. Anyway, they fought it out with the raw 'uns, on a place between Yonkers and Hasting, and after 120 rounds of terrible battling, they carried McCoy out of the ring dead. Lilly fled to New Orleans, where he quickly established himself as the bully of the quarters, and got matched with an English fighter. The Briton's manager had learned that Chris was a fugitive from justice, and told him if he didn't throw the fight, he, the manager, would squeal to the bulls. Chris tried to dog it; he did his damndest to lay down; but he was such a fighting brute, he couldn't do it. He finally went mad with rage and fighting lust, and rushing in on the Englishman, literally beat his life out with his naked fists. The dead boxer's manager made good his threat, and Lilly was arrested and taken back to the gallows that awaited him in New York.

But here I am spieling away about things that happened in your part of the country, forgetting that you naturally know more about them than I do. Anyway, I imagine life in New York was pretty interesting in the '40s, '50s, '60s, and '70s.

Well, the election is over. No fights anywhere. That alone shows how utterly cowed the people are. Sterling was elected by a narrow margin. I'm disappointed but after all, not too surprized. There was too much money behind him for him to be defeated. Not that I'm a rabid Ferguson man. I looked on it merely as a choice of two evils. I was for Tom Hunter of Wichita Falls, but we can't elect a West Texas man, and he was defeated in the primaries. The Fergusons are from Central East Texas, Sterling from Southeast Texas. But I agreed with Jim about the forty million dollars resulting from the gasoline tax. Sterling and his mob intend to put it all on the highways, and, I hear, build some kind of an elaborate state building. Jim wanted to put a third on the highways, utilize a another third for general purposes, and use the other third to pay the poor damn teachers of the state, hundreds of whom haven't received a cursed cent in months and months. I like good highways as well as the next scut, but I'd a sight rather see the teachers get their money than to see a lot of expensive highways built. But this state was always exploited. For instance: gas produced almost in our backyards costs us $.75 a thousand, while that same gas is piped through a gigantic pipe-line to Chicago, there to be sold to the citizens at $.19 a thousand. The great majority of the money-making concerns of the state are owned by corporations and individuals in New York or Chicago, who contribute little enough to the state, except the wages they pay, and many of their employees are imported from elsewhere. The Texas people have been as ruthlessly exploited as if they were painted savages. And what grates me, is, they've put up with it.

However, if revolution ever rises in America, the Southwest is the very last place where it will blaze up. The people of this section, especially the country people, are so inured to suffering and hardship that it would take a veritable cataclysm to cause them to rise. Their capacity for enduring hardship is incredible — more, it is appalling, because it only shows what their lives have been for generations. Right now, the midwestern farms are raising hell about conditions that are, apparently, quite new to them. From what I hear, read and am told by people from that section, those folks are not used to starving. They are land-owners in what must be the greatest farming country in the world, and they are used to plenty and a bit of prosperity. Sheer suffering is new to them, and they resent it. The depression, augmented by the recent drouth, has caused them to rise in wrath. But down here the depression merely emphasized a condition that has always existed in the western Southern states. We have not, it is true, experienced a disastrous drouth since the beginning of the depression. If we had, and had our only available food supply — what we raise ourselves — swept away, things might have been different. But the point I wish to bring out is, the average farmer in the Southwest has never been prosperous, nor his father, grandfather, or greatgrandfather, unless some of the latter happened to be slave-owners. Life has always been a bitter grind of poverty; and short of massacre and wholesale rape by the ruling classes, I do not believe any semblance of a revolution could be stirred up down here. However, there is one point to be remembered: if such a rising should occur, I am afraid it would be far more desperate and bloody than the affair in the mid-west has been so far. I understand that in the more civilized sections, firearms have been practically taken out of the hands of the people in one way or another. There are few homes in the rural parts of the Southwest were there is not some kind of a gun — shotgun, rifle or pistol. I sincerely hope that no class-clash will ever come; for if it does, it will not be an affair of fists and sticks. To the best of my knowledge, the only fatality resulting from the midwestern disturbance was when an officer was demonstrating an automatic shotgun to a deputy and accidentally blew his guts out. Damned clever, these cops.

I notice where a mug named Oliver Herford has decided Shakespeare was Lord Oxford. It must have been a momentous decision, affecting the destiny of the world for Olivero got his map in the magazines. Personally, I never cared whether the Shakespearian plays were written by Shakespeare of Stratford-on - Avon, or Lord Oxford-on-Thames or Lord Bitchbelly of Hogwallow-on-the-Tripe. It's a cinch somebody wrote 'em, because I've read 'em myself, unless I was suffering from an optical delusion, and if so, I enjoyed the delusion. Although there's only one character of Shakespeare that I have any real attachment to, and that's Sir John Falstaff. I have a sincere affection for that old bastard.

I also notice where an egg named Barlow says he's given the Soviets a weapon that will make disarmament necessary, because with it war would be too terrible to conceive.[7] He seems to think our dear bewhiskered cousins will use it idealistically. He has more faith in the Slavonic soul than I have. I can see them advancing the cause of humanity by anchoring a thousand miles off our coasts and dropping gas-bombs and projectiles down our collars. Yet I am unable to work up any particular emotion. To my mind the human race is merely a parasitic freak of two-legged fungi that pollutes the universe, which would be better off — and much cleaner — without it. I have a strong prejudice in favor of life, but from a philosophic standpoint, honestly believe the universe would be better off without human varmints of any kind. Understand, I do not look forward with any enthusiasm toward being eliminated by a moujik with vodka-scented whiskers. But it looks like a choice of being shot by a Jap, sprinkled with insect-powder by a Slav, or starved by one's own benevolent capitalists. The time may come when the government will howl for the people to protect it. Meanwhile, it makes no attempt to protect its people. One thing I like about the British government — it looks after its subjects, wherever they are, so I hear. Not so with America. I've known of too many men who were coolly allowed to rot in Mexican, Central or South American prisons. This is no wild-haired suppositions. I've known several of these men personally and heard it from their own lips. One man was rescued by a British consul; one, a Catholic, by a priest. The rest rotted until their friends had paid out exorbitant sums of money for their release. Those Latin-American prisons are pure hell. Did you ever see a picture of a Mexican hoosegow? We call them bull-pens, in Texas. It's generally just a roofless enclosure, a square, squat building, with high white-washed stone or adobe walls. No roof. The prisoners are not protected in any way from the blaze of the sun throughout most of the day. They are given no bedding, benches, or tables to eat on. They are herded together in these pens, guarded continuously by brutal soldiers, armed to the teeth and frequently bare-footed — the most ignorant and savage type of human being on this continent. The prisoners are given the sorriest kind of food imaginable, which they have to cook themselves. Rain, cold, heat, they have no protection against the elements. Many go mad and knock out their brains against the walls, or are shot in frenzied efforts to escape. I never passed one of those hell-holes that my flesh didn't crawl. I never heard of anyone escaping from one, except one desperate cowpuncher who fought his way out by sheer ferocity, killing four armed guards with a rock and his naked hands, and swimming the river by night, to regain the Texas side, badly wounded and half-dead from his suffering and exertions. No, the government doesn't exert itself to protect its citizens' lives, but you let a revolution or something threaten the profits or property of the big business concerns. Then you'll see the marines moving out, bayonets fixed. Sandino — bah! A real patriot, to my mind.

When I wrote the above about the election, I made a mistake. Sterling had a lead and I thought all the returns were in. Later returns gave the Fergusons nearly four thousand lead. These returns are being questioned, and the Sterling gang is yelling about illegal voting, and the like, and demanding an investigation. Feeling is running pretty high in Texas, as shown by the fact that people have quit discussing the election on the street. When people are loath to talk about something, it's a sign they feel pretty strongly on the subject. Twenty years ago, guns might have been barking already. Now the people are mostly keeping their mouths shut and waiting. It is an instinctive way of avoiding trouble as long as possible. While I'm on the subject — aside from the election returns — I have found that the more highly civilized people are, the readier they generally are for dissentions and disputes. Why not? Rows among the civilized, however hot, seldom end in bloodshed. That's not the case among more primitive people; I think that's why such people avoid arguments instinctively, as much as possible, and are close-mouthed on almost every subject.

I hope Wandrei makes a go of it, but it's a damned bad time to resign a job and try to depend on literary work alone. I wish I had a good solid job, myself, even if it didn't pay much. As I said, I'm glad to hear that the Californian[8] is going to put your poems to music, and I'm eager for the result. If the music is anything like as good as the poetry, it will be superb. Glad to hear that your work got its proper mention in the *American Author*; I didn't see the article mentioned,[9] the magazine not being on any of the stands I frequent, but I'm glad the writer referred to you. It ought to boost you with the editors.

The eclipse was a flop here;[10] only half-part, anyhow, and cloudy that day. I hope you had better luck, though they said over the radio that it was cloudy in New England, too.

I've received your card, since writing the above. Glad you had good weather for the eclipse. I imagine it was an impressive spectacle. Thanks very much for the generous amount of cards and folders. I have gotten the most intense enjoyment out of scanning them — sort of a glimpse out of another world, as it were. I added them to my permanent files, which, thanks to your generosity, present a fine pictorial panorama (if that's the phrase I mean) of the Eastern sea-board. I was especially interested in the views of Quebec, and could almost visualize old Wolfe and his red-coated boys swarming up the cow-trails and hacking into the Frogs on the Plains of Abraham. I'll bet there's good licker in Quebec.

Have you noticed the most recent spat in Tokyo, where the little brown brother is frothing because the Bank of New York has been taking pictures? They think — or pretend to think — that these pictures will be used by the American military department, to aid in future bombardments. They flatter us; we haven't got that much sense. It gives me a big laugh to hear the government asking for recantation, apology or what-not. The Japs aren't going to apologize for anything — much less to us. Anyway, the big official on whom the responsibility rests, doesn't dare do anything that might reflect on the military regime of the empire; he'd be bumped off, just like other Japanese officials have been scuppered lately. The samurai is lifting his crest after his enforced submission to the West. It's the last flare of the old-time imperialist, to my mind. And in Germany the steel helmets are goose-stepping. The nations are heaping up the coals and stirring the fire; the pot's simmering and when it explodes, the whole world is going rock. Well, let it burst any time it wants to; I'd as soon be bayoneted or shot as to starve or grind out a meager existence under present conditions.

To give you a slight idea of what the farmer is up against, and people depending on his prosperity. Day before yesterday my father and I took some wheat to mill, that he'd gotten on a bill. We drove twenty-one miles, only to have the miller refuse to handle it. It showed signs of smut; the continued floods we've had for months have ruined most of the grain in this country. We brought it back and eventually sold it at twenty-five cents a bushel for chicken feed. My father allowed the farmer thirty-four cents a bushel for it, so you see how much we made on it. But the fellow had nothing else with which to pay his bill. At this rate we'll become wealthy fast! My father was irritated, at the mill, by the sight of big powerful-looking farmers staggering around, two men to the load, under grain sacks no heavier than those I handled with ease by myself — and God knows I'm not a particularly strong man. No doubt about it — the breed is getting soft and flabby. In fifty years I reckon we'll be too soft for anything.

Again, many thanks for the pictures, and with the best of good wishes,

Cordially,

R.E.H.

P.S. Glad you found the unpublished mss. of interest; I doubt if they'll ever find a publisher, since Wright rejected them, and I know of no other market for that kind of yarn; hope Wandrei has success in his literary venture.

R.E.H.

NOTES

1. X-ed out text appears to be "first-hand."
2. "for an ordinary citizen to expect protection or justice to any great extent." has been X-ed out.
3. Harold Lamb, *Adventure* writer turned historian, author of *Iron Men & Saints* and *The Flame of Islam*, collected into a single volume as *The Crusades*.
4. *The Gladewater Journal*, a Texas paper.
5. Don Biggers was a long-time Texas newspaper man, and had served two terms in the legislature.
6. Tevis Clyde Smith.
7. Lester P. Barlow, of Stamford, Connecticut, claimed he had revealed to the Soviet government plans he had developed showing the possibility of destroying large cities from the air. He had earlier brought the plans to the attention of American officials and members of Congress, and was seeking meetings with German officials. He hoped that revealing these plans would impress upon governments the necessity of total disarmament.
8. Harold S. Farnese.
9. "What Makes An Author Click?" by J. Randle Luton, July 1932, cites Lovecraft, Clark Ashton Smith and Edmond Hamilton as models of narrative technique.
10. A total solar eclipse was visible over parts of New England on August 31, 1932.

TSS: 50398-50411, 21440-21441

218. To H.P. Lovecraft, ca. October 1932.

Dear Mr. Lovecraft:

I hope you decide to collaborate on the proposed musical drama. Don't tell me you're not qualified for that sort of thing. You're capable of any sort of literary expression, to my humble mind. You'd instill new vigor and fresh imagination in the dramatic world, which, from what I hear, is badly in need of some such stimulus. If the Californian did his part half as well as I know you'd do yours, the success of the venture would be assured. This is no mere polite maundering on my part, but my honest opinion.

Sorry Wandrei's visit was handicapped by rain and sun-burn. Rainy weather is always depressing — to me at least; and while never having experienced sun-burn, having the hide of a bull, I imagine it's a pretty uncomfortable handicap. I hope he'll get to return to Providence before leaving the East. I've been laying of to write him for some time, but somehow haven't got around it.

Good for Derleth! Which of his stories got the citations?[1] I've known for years that he was of "the right girt", as John A. Murrell used to say. He's deserved much more notice from *Weird Tales* readers than he's gotten — doubtless because of the shortness of his stories; the readers seem to like 'em long, generally. More power to him; I wish him all the luck in the world.

And I hope Clark Ashton sells his "Vathek" episode. His style is unique — to me at least — with just a tinge somehow reminiscent of Petronius. I don't mean that he tries to copy the classics, or anything like that; but his work has a subtle mirth that I can only describe as classic. I've gotten some real belly laughs out of his subtly turned hints and allusions. This, to my mind, keeps some of his tales from being weirdly perfect — humor however subtle not fitting in with true horror — but gives them a piquant zest all their own. That he is capable of writing straight horror-stuff is evident by such tales as "The Return of the Sorcerer" in *Strange Tales*,[2] which was, as I wrote the editor, one of the most intolerably hideous stories I ever read — in other words, a sheer masterpiece. As I have said before, I rate Smith second only to yourself in the art.

Thanks for the congratulations regarding the election. It remains now to see whether Jim will double-cross us when he gets in office, like so many other candidates have done. Anyway, he'll never get in, if the Sterling mob can keep him out. They took the fight to the state convention; the convention affirmed Mrs. Ferguson's nomination, and now they've dragged it into court. It looks like a deliberate plot to take the voting power away from the people. It's rumored that the idea is to keep the matter in court until after the election, so as to jockey the Republican candidate into office, by the simple process of having no other name on the ticket. The common people nominated Mrs. Ferguson; the big interests are fighting teeth and nail to keep her out of the chair. Some claim if Jim gets in, he'll sell us out to the railroads; better railroads than Wall Street owned oil companies. I don't know. It looks like the courts, the laws, the government, all wealth and authority and power are combined to crush the last vestige of freedom out of the common people. Men that rise to lead the people sell them out and betray them. Where can a man turn? I wish I had vision, or a fanatical faith in something or somebody that creates an illusion of vision. All roads look blind to me. I see nothing but ruin, chaos, and a rising tide of slavery.

But I am prone to harp on these things; please excuse me. I know I must grow boresome.

With best wishes,

Cordially,

[REH.]

NOTES

1. Two of Derleth's short stories were listed in the "Index of Distinctive Short Stories" in *The Best Short Stories of 1932*, edited by Edward J. O'Brien: "Old Ladies" (*Midland*, January-February 1932) received two stars and "Nella" (*Pagany*, January-March 1932) received one star.
2. September 1931.

TSS: 20741-20742

❧❧❧

219. To H.P. Lovecraft, ca. mid-October 1932[1]

Here is the emblem of a lethal form of life for which I have no love, but a definite admiration. The wearer of this emblem is inflexibly individualistic. He mingles not with the herd, nor bows before the thrones of the mighty. Between him and the lords of the earth lies an everlasting feud that shall not be quenched until the last man lies dying and the Conqueror sways in shimmering coils above him.

Lapped in sombre mystery he goes his subtle way, touched by neither pity nor mercy. Realizations of ultimate certitudes are his, when the worm rises and die vulture sinks and the flesh shreds back to the earth that bore it. Other beings may make for Life, but he is consecrated to Death. Promise of ultimate dissolution shimmers in his visible being, and the cold soulless certainty of destruction is in his sibilances. The buzzards mark his path by the pregnant waving of the tall grasses, and the blind worms that gnaw in the dark are glad because of him. The foot of a king can not tread on him with impunity, nor the ignorant hand of innocence bruise him unscathed. The emperor who sits enthroned in gold and purple, with his diadem in the thunder-clouds and his sandals on the groaning backs of the nations, let him dare to walk where the rank grass quivers without a wind, and the lethal scent of decay is heavy in the air. Let him dare — and try if his pomp and glory and his lines of steel and gold will awe the coiling death or check the dart of the wedge-shaped head.

For when he sings in the dark it is the voice of Death crackling between fleshless jaw-bones. He reveres not, nor fears, nor sinks his crest for any scruple. He strikes, and the strongest man is carrion for flapping things and crawling things. He is a Lord of the Dark Places, and wise are they whose feet disturb not his meditations.

NOTES

1. Previously published as "With a Set of Rattlesnake Rattles."

220. To H.P. Lovecraft, November 2, 1932.

Dear Mr. Lovecraft:

I want to begin this letter by an apology. I am afraid my last letter may have appeared rather churlish in spots, though rudeness was not my intention. The fact is, I wrote while in the grip of one of the black moods which occasionally — though fortunately rarely — descend on me. With one of these moods riding me, I can see neither good nor hope in anything, and my main sensation is a blind, brooding rage directed at anything that may cross my path — a perfectly impersonal feeling, of course. At such times I am neither a fit companion nor a gentlemanly correspondent. I avoid personal contacts as much as possible, in order to avoid giving offense by my manner, and I should never, at such times, venture to write a letter to anyone. I am likely to offend where I do not intend, for the passionate pessimism in my mind is prone to make my manner, verbal or in writing, brusque and surly. These moods are hereditary, coming down the line of my purely Irish branch — the black-haired, grey-eyed branch, of which, as far back as family history goes, both men and women have been subject to black fits of savage brooding, which has been, in some cases, coupled with outbursts of really dangerous fury, when crossed or thwarted. My great-grandfather, whom I seem to resemble in many ways, lost his life in that manner, being the victim of an attack of apoplexy brought on by his uncontrollable rage. All this delicate and intimate data I would not be shouting from the house-tops, nor would I mention it here except for the fact that I feel you are due an explanation of possible surliness on my part. In cases where we disagree, your arguments are so well-balanced and show so much gentlemanly consideration and restraint, I would not wish to seem churlish, though my last letter may have created that impression. I will admit that when a better educated man than myself takes advantage of his superior culture and experience to cut and slash my self-esteem to shreds, and hold me up to ridicule and contempt, I feel a primitive urge to do him bodily violence. But you have never done this on any of the points on which we disagree, though I know many of my arguments must have seemed crude, naive and biased in the extreme. It is a new experience to me to encounter such consideration in one of superior accomplishments, and I appreciate it. So if I have at any time offended you with my clumsiness or surliness, please be assured that it was entirely unintentional. As a proof of my sincerity, I may mention that this is only the third time in my life that I ever apologized to anybody for anything. xxxxxxxxxx[. . .][1]

As for my aborted views on conditions in general — I see that I have so tangled up my remarks and theories that misunderstanding was bound to result. It isn't your fault; it's my own lack of vocabulary and clumsiness of expression. When I get out of my depth — which is easy — the Devil himself couldn't get what I'm trying to say. So I won't try to untangle myself, except to say the following: that I really do not hold the scholarly class in wholesale contempt. On the contrary I have a high regard for it. When I spoke of certain professors as dusty fossils, I did not mean the profession as a whole, but I had in mind certain individuals I have known who really would come under such classification. It's just another example of my vagueness of expression. Maybe I have in my system an unconscious bitterness and resentment at times, resulting perhaps from a realization of my own sketchy education and lack of real culture. Nor do I have any contempt for the East or the people of the East. I realize, as you say, that conditions vary according to environment, traditional mode of life, etc., and I would be the last to assume that the people of one part of the country are superior to those of any other part. Nor do I glorify the physical to the expense of the mental or intellectual. I am so constituted that physical things appeal to me more than mental, but simply because I would rather watch a football game than to see a scientist work out a really important problem in economics or mathematics, or the like, does not mean that I have any hero-worship for the first, or contempt for the latter. I would rather see men match physical strength than to match their wits in any sort of a contest; that does not mean that I place physical ability above mental ability. It means, doubtless, that I am more of the physical man than the mental. And I'm afraid I'll remain that way to the end, rightly or wrongly. And for that reason alone, I should never impose my gropings on abstract things on anybody. When the argument gets away from something I can see and feel and handle, I'm out of my depths. I say all this not in self-abasement or undue humility, but simply because I always try to be as honest as possible with my friends and with myself. I must be myself, whatever my faults. I might pose, and pretend an intellectuality and an interest in the higher things, but I wouldn't fool anybody, and I wouldn't try it if I could. When I say that I'd rather watch a football game, a prize-fight, a horserace or a really able dancing girl, than to delve into the mysteries of the universe, however magnificent and awesome, I'm simply being honest. I'm not trying to uphold my preferences. Each man to his own path; I have no sneer for scientist, poet, scholar, horse-trader or pugilist.

I, myself, was intended by Nature to be an athlete. If events had flowed smoothly and evenly from the time I first entered school, I would at this instant be engaged in some sort of professional athletics, rather than struggling with a profession for which I am not fitted. The chain of circumstances which altered the course of my life is too lengthy and involved to impose upon you. But I will say that I extremely regret those circumstances, and had rather have been a successful athlete than the very minor writer I have become — in honesty I will go further and say that I had rather have been a successful professional athlete than to be a great writer. This is not to be taken as a slur on the writing profession. You said once, in one of your letters that the main object in life was to get as much happiness out of it as possible — I trust I do not misquote you. The fact is that I believe I would have gotten more content out of an athletic career than I have out of this bitter grind, which I took up simply because it seemed to offer more freedom than anything else in the way of a job. Let me repeat that when I voice a preference for anything I am not depreciating its opposite. I merely speak my own choice in the matter. A thing may be good or bad for the race as a whole; it may be magnificent or foolish. I have only my own sensations to go on. If anything gives me pleasure, while harming no one else, then it is my instinct to lean toward it, however trivial. If anything bores or confuses or pains me, it is my instinct to avoid it, however splendid. I have endured confusion, boredom, and even pain in consideration of others; but I can not say that I enjoyed it.

I lack your broad and sweeping viewpoint; I sincerely admire it, but I could not copy it to my own advantage, any more than I could wear with comfort the coat of a man bigger than myself.

And another thing, before I forget it — my deep admiration for physical prowess and my continual harping about deeds of blood, may sound like I was trying to make an impression of boldness and fearlessness on my part. Please believe that I am not seeking to make any such impression. I'm a man cautious to the point of absolute timidity. The only way a man can get a fight out of me, is simply to get me in a corner where I have to fight. In that case, of course, I'm prone to give him all I have, including teeth and hob-nails, just as anybody will when cornered. It's just another incongruity of nature that a man as peace-loving as I am should be so violently interested in deeds of gore, and be unable to realistically write about anything else. When my fictional characters can't slash and slug and litter the pages with one another's carcasses, I'm an utter flop as a tale-spinner.

Your remarks concerning your trips interested me as usual. I'll bet that "Devil's Punch-Bowl" was a fascinating place. I'm not surprized that the young bloods of Natchez knew little about it. It's appalling the way the younger generations of Americans are losing hold of the traditions and folk-lore of their country. For instance, a year so ago a man of fair education, raised in this state since infancy, asked me if I knew anything about a fellow named Bigfoot Wallace! Ye gods! Even I can remember when Bigfoot's exploits were subjects for innumerable tales of the old-timers.

I appreciate your remarks pertaining to my incorporating the border villains in print. It's a matter I've been thinking about for a long time, and intend to try, if times ever get better so I can afford to do some work on my own, instead of pounding out fiction all the time. There are numbers of good books on the subject, but each book generally deals with only one time or one place. I'd like to start at the Atlantic sea-board with the early colonists and work gradually westward, carrying the work not later than the early 1900s. The latter phase of gang-life does not fascinate me. Concerning the Harps, I seem to have a vague idea that they were from Virginia where they were Tories during the Revolution. They seem to have been slightly negroid in blood-strain. About the only crime they didn't share with Sawney Bean was that of cannibalism — and there's no actual proof that they didn't. Big Harp, while confined in prison from which he later escaped — he developed a religious mania there and posed as a wandering preacher up to the day of his death — confessed that the only deed he regretted was the murder of his youngest child, whose brains he dashed out against a tree, throwing the body into the bushes to rot. He and Little Harp used to come into a lonely settler's cabin and ask news of those damnable outlaws, the Harps. If the people recognized them, their doom was sealed — the doom of the people, I mean. If not, Big Harp called pious blessings on the heads of the humble settlers, and invoked the wrath of the Lord to protect them from the hellish Harps. Then the outlaws would ride away, to commit some other depredation. The last time they pulled this stunt, Big Harp got so worked up in his role of protector that he loaded the settler's rifle from his own pouch, the man being out of powder, as protection against the Harps. A few hours later that man joined the posse pursuing the outlaws, and Big Harp got his own bullet in his spine.

Too bad New Orleans is going so modern. I'm glad I saw it before the vandalism had gotten completely under way. I was interested in your remarks concerning French food. I've encountered the "poor boy sandwich" phenomenon in Galveston and similar places. I think if I were in the restaurant business I'd exploit a "pauper's sandwich" which is going to be a necessity if things get any lousier. Too bad sea-food disagrees with you. Now with me, as with many inland dwellers, it constitutes a rare delicacy. And the word "rare" is quite descriptive. Oysters are about the only sort of sea-food which finds its way this far up-country.

When I get in a sea-port town, I revel in oysters, shrimps, crabs, sea-fish, and the like, to my heart's content. I find one thing about such food; it doesn't seem to stay with you and give you any real strength. I eat it in enormous quantities, and then in a few hours I'm ravenously hungry again. Maybe it's because, like most people in this country, I'm a beef-eater, Indeed, beef in some form or other seems to be the only food that gives me the necessary nutriment.

But I'm not narrow in my tastes. I'm a big eater and I get a real kick out of gorging. Any kind of meat — fish, fowl, beef, turtle, pork; practically any kind of fruit; I'm not much of a vegetarian. Milk — I see people coaxing children to drink milk, and I can't understand their dislike for it. I always drank it in huge quantities, and believe it's one reason I was always so healthy. Cheese — give me limburger cheese, German sausage and beer and I'm content — yes, and a bit of what they call "smear-cake" — a rather unsavory name, for what we call cottage- or cream-cheese. Mexican dishes I enjoy, but they don't agree with me much. However I generally wrestle with them every time I go to the Border. Tamales, enchiladas, tacos, chili con carne to a lesser extent, barbecued goat-meat, tortillas, Spanish-cooked rice, frijoles — they play the devil with a white man's digestion, but they have a tang you seldom find in Anglo-Saxon cookery. You know a coyote nor a buzzard never will touch a Mexican's carcass — they can't stand the pepper he ate in lifetime. The last time I was on the Border I discovered one Pablo Ranes whose dishes smoked with the concentrated essence of hell-fire. I returned to his abode of digestional-damnation until my once powerful constitution was but a shell of itself. I aided Pablo's atrocities with some wine bottled in Spain that kicked like an army mule, and eventually came to the conclusion that the Border is a place only for men with cast-iron consciences and copper bellies.

That old ballad I quoted from, "The Lakes of the Pontchartrain", must have been fairly popular at one time, though just when I couldn't say. I used to correspond with one R.W. Gordon[2] who was collecting old songs for an anthology — though I never got the chance of examining the completed work. The best thing of its kind I ever saw was an anthology compiled by Carl Sandburg, in which I found numbers of old songs I knew by heart but had never seen in print. It's cheering to find men collecting these old ballads, which seem to be forgotten by practically all people. Folks don't sing like they used to. The '49ers crossed the Plains to the tune of:

"I come from Alabama
With my banjo on my knee,
I'm goin' to Louisiana,
My true love for to see.

It rained all night the day I left,
The weather it was dry,
The sun so hot I froze to death —
Susanna, don't you cry!

Oh, Susanna,
    Don't you cry for me!
I'm goin' to Californy
    With my banjo on my knee!"

During the Civil War, one side sang,

"John Brown's body lies a-moldin' in the grave,
John Brown's body lies a-moldin' in the grave,
John Brown's body lies a-moldin' in the grave,
But his soul goes marchin' on!"

And the other side sang, among others,

"We'll hang Abe Lincoln to a sour-apple tree,
We'll hang Abe Lincoln to a sour-apple tree,
We'll hang Abe Lincoln to a sour-apple tree,
As we go marchin' on!

Then there was another which went something like this:

"Old Johnny McGruder, he went on a spree,
He captured a gunboat and started to sea,
He hauled down the colors, both red, white and green!
Hurrah, hurrah, for the bonny Blue Flag!"

And,

"Up with the bars, and down with the stars!
We'll rally 'round the flag, boys,
Rally once again!
Shouting the battle-cry of freedom!"

The boys hazing the herds up the old Chisholm used to chant,

"Ki yi, ki yi -yoh! Get along, little doggies!
Its yore misfortune and none of my own!
Ki yi, ki yi -yoh! Get along, little doggies!
You know Wyoming will be yore new home!"

Not all the songs came by the southern route; here's a verse from one you've probably heard in the rural districts of your country,

"Tom Quick he lived in the Sullivan hills,
    By the Delaware's rolling tide;
'Midst the whispering trees and the rippling rills,
Away from the world and all of its thrills,
    He hunted far and wide."

And this one used to be very popular, which began, or at least contained the lines, possibly as a refrain,

> "Blue-eyed bonny, bonny Eloise,
> — The pride of the Mohawk Vale."

Which I reckon refers to the Mohawk Valley in — New York state, isn't it? And I'm sure you're familiar with the old New England ballad relating the fate of "Deacon Jones's oldest son" who "just had turned his twenty-one." Who was nipped in the heel by a "venomous rep-tile," and the ballad of which concluded with the warning,

> "Come all, young men,
> And warning take,
> And never get bit
> By a big black snake."

Referring back to your letter: I was intensely interested in your comments on the possible trend of future economic conditions. It may be that you are right. I'm not enough of an economist to dispute it, even if I had any desire to. However, I see no reason why the dominant interests would be unable to coerce the masses by force. They have the navy on their side and the regular army; they have every flat-foot cop and detective in the country; they have money, power — the ability to fill their ranks with professional fighters, just as the companies employ strike breakers and private detectives to shoot down strikers. The masses have only their empty hands and empty bellies. As for lack of profit — what's to prevent them from actually enslaving the people? A remark no doubt wild and visionary — yet if the Russian people aren't slaves, I don't know the meaning of the word. What's to prevent the dominant classes in this country from carrying out a similar idea under slightly different conditions? Slavery is far from being extinct in this country today — though of course its present form has nothing to do with wholesale enslavement, or with what I just mentioned.

But if peonage, where a man gets a Mexican, negro, or even a white man, in debt to him, and keeps him toiling for years to pay out that debt, isn't slavery, then I don't know what it is. There's been something of a scandal concerning such practises along the Mississippi River recently. Another meddling reformer, I suppose. Nevertheless such things do exist, and are no credit to our boasted civilization.

That word reminds me of our discussion concerning what I said about my preference for a theoretical former existence. I didn't say that barbarism was superior to civilization. For the world as a whole, civilization even in decaying form, is undoubtedly better for people as a whole. I have no idyllic view of barbarism — as near as I can learn it's a grim, bloody, ferocious and loveless condition. I have no patience with the depiction of the barbarian of any race as a stately, god-like child of Nature, endowed with strange wisdom and speaking in measured and sonorous phrases. Bah! My conception of a barbarian is very different. He had neither stability nor undue dignity. He was ferocious, vengeful, brutal and frequently squalid. He was haunted by dim and shadowy fears; he committed horrible crimes for strange monstrous reasons. As a race he hardly ever exhibited the steadfast courage often shown by civilized men. He was childish and terrible in his wrath, bloody and treacherous. As an individual he lived under the shadow of the war-chief and the shaman, each of whom might bring him to a bloody end because of a whim, a dream, a leaf floating on the wind. His religion was generally one of dooms and shadows, his gods were awful and abominable. They bade him mutilate himself or slaughter his children, and he obeyed because of fears too primordial for any civilized man to comprehend. His life was often a bondage of tambus, sharp sword-edges, between which he walked shuddering. He had no mental freedom, as civilized man understands it, and very little personal freedom, being bound to his clan, his tribe, his chief. Dreams and shadows haunted and maddened him. Simplicity of the primitive? To my mind the barbarian's problems were as complex in their way as modern man's — possibly more so. He moved through life motivated mainly by whims, his or another's. In war he was unstable; the blowing of a leaf might send him plunging in an hysteria of blood-lust against terrific odds, or cause him to flee in blind panic when another stroke could have won the battle. But he was lithe and strong as a panther, and the full joy of strenuous physical exertion was his. The day and the night were his book, wherein he read of all things that run or walk or crawl or fly. Trees and grass and moss-covered rocks and birds and beasts and clouds were alive to him, and partook of his kinship. The wind blew his hair and he looked with naked eyes into the sun. Often he starved, but when he feasted, it was with a mighty gusto, and the juices of food and strong drink were stinging wine to his palate. Oh, I know I can't make myself clear; I've never seen anyone who had any sympathy whatever with my point of view, nor do I want any. I'm not ashamed of it. I would not choose to plunge into such a life now; it would be the sheerest of hells to me, unfitted as I am for such an existence. But I do say that if I had the choice of another existence, to be born into it and raised in it, knowing no other, I'd choose such an existence as I've just sought to depict. There's no question of the relative merits of barbarism and civilization here involved. It's just my own personal opinion and choice.

I reckon The Five Points district in old New York was pretty squalid from all I hear about it, yet I find it interesting — reading about it, I mean of course. Pugilism and the underworld were pretty closely linked in those days; thus we find the early champions, Hyer, Yankee Sullivan, and Morrissey, hob-nobbing with thugs and gangsters that a present-day boxing champion wouldn't be seen with. Morrissey, at least, rose above his environments. At least, I suppose it was a rise; he became a member of the New York legislature. Billy the Kid was born in the New York slums; I wouldn't be surprized if it was in Five Points that he first saw light. Quite a number of Western outlaws originally came from the East. Quantrill, for instance, was born in Ohio, of New England stock. John

Brown was from Connecticut. Henry Plummer, called by a noted historical writer, "the most consummate villain", who, under the guise of his sheriffship, managed one of the most blood-thirsty gangs of robbers and murderers the West has ever seen, was a native of Boston. And of course the Girtys and the Butlers were New Yorkers. Speaking of the latter, Cherry Valley in New York state has always had a fascination for me because of the massacre committed there by Walter Butler and Joseph Brant — though I believe it is maintained that Brant was not there, and that the slaying was done mainly by Senecas instead of Mohawks. Walter Butler must have been a genial soul — one which I'd have enjoyed seeing kicking in a noose. He was an Irishman, wasn't he? One of the Le Boteliers of Ormond originally, I doubt not. I always took sides against them in their feud with the FitzGeralds. I'll bet the Eastern states are teeming with spots of fascinating historical interest, similar to that just mentioned. I never was much in reading Indian yarns, but stories about the Long House always interested me.

The Eastern Indians were quite apparently of a much higher type than those of the West. For one thing, they tended toward the dolicholcephalic type, whereas the typical Western Indian was brachycephalic. This has not been perfectly explained; at least if it has, I haven't encountered the explanation. Some authorities seem to think — what I had decided myself before encountering the theory in print — that there was a prehistoric connection between the primitive Mongolian type and a Caucasian race, from which hybrid breed the Indian sprang. It can not be denied that the red Indian seems much less repugnant and alien to the white man than the negro, Malay, Mongol or Chinaman. Indeed, I see no reason why the race should not be admitted on an equal footing, determined by education and advancement rather than color. I have no Indian blood in me, but I certainly would not be ashamed of it if I did. I have a number of cousins who are of mixed blood,[3] boasting both Cherokee and Chickasaw strains, and this mixture does not result in any inferiority on their part. The greatest athlete this continent has ever seen was a Sac and Fox Indian.[4]

But returning to the inferiority of the Western Indians: I am not aware whether this was due to their nomadic life, or whether the life was due to their inability to develop a settled mode of living and agriculture. At any rate, it was not until the advent of the white man that the Western tribes amounted to much. The introducing of the horse into the country was what made them powerful. In some cases alliance with the whites increased their power. This was especially true of the Pawnees, who had been harried and slaughtered for generations by the Sioux. They were shrewd enough to throw in their lot with the settlers, and whole companies of regular cavalry formed of Pawnee braves were used in the Sioux wars. Their uniform presented a rather peculiar aspect, since they always cut the seat out of the breeches. When they started across the prairie on a charge, they started shedding their clothes, and before the concussion came, were riding in their loins-cloths, yelling and shooting like madmen.

They were good fighters, especially against hereditary foes, but they were hard to control during the battle and afterward. They wanted to deal with prisoners in the old tribal way. I know of at least one instance where Pawnee privates took a Sioux prisoner away from their white officer and burned him alive. Well, the Sioux were no babies in atrocities themselves. One of their favorite jests was to cut off a victim's head and thrust it into his disemboweled belly.

The Pawnees used to wander down into Texas, where they continually clashed with the Comanches, who were probably the most ferocious fighters this continent has seen. Some noted western explorer, whose identity I've forgotten, once met a band of Pawnees journeying southward, to steal horses from the Comanches, they told him. Later he encountered them again, returning to their homes on foot. They had not only failed to steal the horses of the Comanches, but these wily barbarians had stolen all their own mounts. The Comanches raised hell with the Spaniards, and later the Mexicans — into which, by the way, the bulk of the Comanche tribes was eventually absorbed. The Mexican mode of dealing with these tribes was a mixture of cringing and treachery. One time a band of Pawnees was encamped on the outskirts of San Antonio, and one of the women was seized by a big Comanche who tried to carry her off. A Pawnee brave brained him with a hatchet. The Comanches attacked the Pawnees, who were outnumbered and withdrew. Mexican soldiers joined the Comanches, and they hurried to cut off the retreating Pawnees and ambush them. The Pawnees discovered the ambush, made a flanking attack, and practically wiped out the whole combined force.

The Comanches were the prime horse-thieves of the West. They measured their wealth by the number of horses they owned. It was a dishonor for a brave to lose his horse. Sometimes a number of young warriors would find themselves without steeds, owing to losses in war or otherwise, and would "smoke horses" with more fortunate braves. The horseless ones sat down in a circle about a fire, naked to the waist, smoking their pipes. The braves from which they wished to borrow, would mount and race around the circle at full speed. Each time a brave passed the warrior who wished to borrow his mount, he would strike the sitting man across his naked back with a raw-hide whip, with all his power. These whips cut like a knife, and the first stroke would start the blood spurting. This process would continue until the victim's back was raw beef. It was his part to continue placidly smoking and receive the blows without wincing. At the end of the affair, the mounted warrior would lead his horse to the other and say, "You ride my horse, but you carry the scars of my whip."

I'm glad you saw the dueling-oaks of New Orleans before somebody cuts them down to build a hot-dog stand. A distant relative of mine exchanged shots with a brother of the governor of Louisiana there, many years ago. He was evidently too drunk to see the sights of his "navy" because he didn't score a hit, and carried five or six slugs in his flesh off the field of honor. The argument came up over a fight between a couple of newsboys, and was quite trivial to get shot about. But the victim had been with Walker in Nicaragua, and the men who survived that campaign had their lives nailed to their spines. You'd think I was a liar if I narrated the wounds he survived, to die at last of old age. He was one of the few filibusters who escaped when the rest were victimized — mainly owing to old Cornelius Vanderbilt, damn his filthy soul.

The duel was never too popular in Texas — not nearly so much as in the older Southern states. Life was too uncertain here. When everyday existence is a continual battle, men are not likely to devise and uphold elaborate systems of getting themselves formally shot.

There have been duels, of course, but most of the shooting-scrapes of early Texas were informal affairs. Enemies met unexpectedly in saloons or on the streets, and each man went for his gun. The one to unleather his six-shooter first generally survived, unless he missed. Often enough "the Texas drop" was employed, which simply consisted in catching your victim off-guard, or drilling him through a window or from behind a brush fence. When men have to fight all the time for their lives, they are very likely to take all the advantages they can.

The most famous duel in Texas was that between Felix Houston and Albert Sidney Johnston, in which the latter was wounded in the hip. Houston was a soldier of fortune, who resented the other being promoted over his head. Another was that between George Scarborough and John Selman in El Paso, in 1895, I believe it was. They went into an alley behind a saloon, stepped off their paces, turned — Selman reached for his gun and found only an empty scabbard. Somebody had slipped out his six-shooter without his knowledge. Scarborough shot him down before he had time to see that Selman was unarmed.

John Selman was the man who killed the famous John Wesley Hardin. After Hardin released from the penitentiary, he came to El Paso, and according to some, began to practise law. Outside of holding up a gambling house, he was apparently living a law-abiding life, though some connected him with the murder of one McRose, who was mowed down by a charge of buckshot one night near the international bridge. Hardin fell afoul of the Selmans in this manner: his sweetheart knocked a dance-hall woman in the head with a pistol, and young John Selman, who was an officer of the law, arrested her and threw her in jail. Naturally this infuriated Hardin beyond measure, and he swore to massacre everybody wearing the name of Selman. According to accounts, young John decided the climate was too torrid for him. Anyway, he left town in a hurry and didn't come back until after the fireworks were over. Which were not long delayed. That very night, as John Wesley Hardin stood at the bar, shaking dice for the drinks, old John Selman entered the saloon quietly and shot him in the back of the head. Albert B. Fall of Teapot Dome fame, then a rising attorney, defended Selman and naturally he was acquitted. He would have been anyway; everybody felt safer with Hardin out of the way. Selman was killed soon afterward by George Scarborough in the manner above related, and Scarborough himself was killed not long later by Kid Curry and his gang in Arizona. Mannen Clements, Hardin's nephew, swore to kill Fall for insulting his relative's memory during the trial, and on at least two occasions he attempted it, but without success, owing to circumstances. He himself was at last killed in a barroom in a most mysterious fashion, and it has been hinted that Fall knew more about the matter than he ever admitted. Incidentally, Fall defended Brazel who killed Pat Garrett, the killer of Billy the Kid, and won an acquittal.

But I was talking about duels. The only one that ever took place in this locality, so far as I know, was at a dance a good many years ago, between two cowpunchers, members of feuding families. Mutual friends stood by with guns drawn, to see fair play, while the boys stepped off their paces, turned and fired simultaneously. Both fell, one dead, one dying; their bodies were placed in a spare room and the dance went on. Dances in those days were too rare entertainment to be spoiled by murder.

Ben Thompson, a famous old-time Texas gunman, once fought a duel in New Orleans with one Emil de Tour, along in 1858 or 1859, I think it was. The Frenchman insulted a young lady on Canal Street, and Thompson, though a stranger to both, resented it to the point of knocking de Tour down and stamping him into unconsciousness. When the bould Frog recovered, he challenged Thompson, and the young Texan — he couldn't have been more than eighteen or nineteen — accepted with alacrity. The details of the chroniclers are veiled in doubt. They merely say that they fought in a dark room with knives and Thompson killed his man. But I got the facts from an old-timer who knew Thompson and had heard the tale from his own lips. Thompson was to give the word to begin. Standing in utter darkness, where neither could see the other, he gave the word and at the same instant stepped quickly and noiselessly aside. As he knew would happen, de Tour sprang like a tiger at the sound of his voice, and Thompson, thrusting by the sound of the rushing body, sank his knife to the hilt in the Frenchman's heart. The dark room and the knives were Thompson's idea. He had no patience with the formal code of the duello.

French dueling suffered when the Americans swarmed into New Orleans. The French form had become, to a large extent, a sort of polite exercise, where honor was satisfied by a scratch or a drop of blood. While it is a fact that many bloody battles were fought under the Oaks and elsewhere by Frenchmen — sometimes with sabers in which case a fatality was inevitable — yet in later days milder conditions dominated. The Americans changed this. They were practical — blood-thirsty, if you will. They introduced butcher knives, rifles, navy pistols, and shotguns — the latter often at half-a-dozen paces with an open grave between the combatants. The gory results shocked the French into disapproval of dueling. Not that this is any depreciation of French courage. It is quite true that as a nation and as individuals they have always shown a fine brand of courage, however shifty their politics might have been. The reason the English under the Black Prince and such leaders defeated them so often and against such odds, was due entirely to the long-bow in the hands of the English yeoman, the most terrible weapon conceived by man, up to the invention of gunpowder. Man to man, the French knights were the equal of the English. But having made pitiful serfs out of their common people, they had no sturdy reserve force to fall back on, and could not put an army of hardy foot soldiers in the field, as the English did. In the last analysis, it is the common people who win wars, even if directed by their aristocrats. A point the upper classes of America might well remember.

I admire many points of the French character, but I can not include their literature. This is no criticism, only my own personal viewpoint. I certainly don't consider myself a critic, but I know what I like and what I don't like. And I don't like French literature. If I were able to read it in the untranslated original, I might like it better, but I doubt it. There's a polished hardness about the literature of the Latins that I don't relish. Even when it lack this polish, I don't care for it. To me, for instance, Rabelais is neither wise nor witty, though perhaps I shouldn't pass judgment on him, since his stuff nauseates me to such an extent I've never been able to read much of it. Balzac is better, but I never could get interested in him. Dumas has a virility lacking other French writers — I attribute it to his negroid strain — but his historical fiction lacks, at least to me, the gripping vividness of Sir Walter Scott, for instance — a man whose works I highly value, regardless of what modern critics think. I don't go by what critics think, but by my own likes and dislikes. Gautier bores me immeasurably. I like Villon's poems, and Verlaine's and Baudelaire's, but don't think any of them can equal the greatest English poets. D'Maupassant has power — undoubted power. Too much power for me to read extensively. Talk about Nordic gloom — his tales of French peasant life are enough to make a man want to cut his own throat. After reading some of his more realistic yarns, I've been unable to see any good in anything, except thankfulness for the fact that I wasn't a Frenchman.

I'm narrow in my literary likings. About the only poets and writers I can stand regularly are the British and American ones. I find the old Scandinavian sagas fascinating, but I can't work up any interest in modern Scandinavian writers. They seem further removed from the pristine Viking type than the English writers. Russians seem men wandering in mazes, never getting anywhere. Gorky seems to ramble interminably, without doing anything. Some Slavonic tales are gripping by their sheer somberness, but taken as a whole their literature fails to arouse my enthusiasm. That phrase — taken as a whole — is misleading, seeming to indicate that I was deeply familiar with that literature. I'm not, of course. What I meant was that part of the literature which I have read.

I wouldn't take anything, though, for my early readings of Scott, Dickens and other English writers. I doubt if I could read Dickens now — with the exception of *Pickwick Papers* which is my favorite of all his books. He gets on my nerves, not so much by his tedium as by the spineless cringing crawling characters he portrays. I don't doubt he was drawing them true to life, but that realization makes the matter more damnable. Nicholas Nickleby was about the only one of his characters who had any guts at all. Why good gad, his characters submitted to indignities and insults and outrages that made me grind my teeth merely to read about. And I'm a peaceable man. The same can be said about *The Vicar of Wakefield*, one of the most abominable books ever penned. I've never had any respect for Goldsmith since reading it. The old cuss in the book had one daughter seduced, if I'm not mistaken, and the other abducted by the same egg. So he stood around mouthing pious platitudes — the old jackass. And when his son wanted to fight the abductor a duel, a squall of disapproval was raised to the shamed skies. I read this abomination as a part of my high-school work, and in writing my report, I let myself go the only time I ever did in school, and gave my own honest opinion in my own honest words, allowing myself the freedom of frothing at the mouth. I expected to flunk the course, so many teachers being slaves of the established, but that particular teacher was a black-headed Irish woman who evidently entertained similar ideas on the subject to mine, and she gave me a good grade instead of the tongue-lashing I expected.[5] Somewhere I read an essay on that book, and the writer spoke of the Vicar as the highest type of human imaginable, praising his meekness and humility and long-suffering and Christian spirit. Bah! A whole flock of bahs. In some cases humility is out of place. To my mind he was a lousy old worm, ten times lower-down than the libertine that misused his daughters.

I was talking about duels awhile ago, and I said the custom was never much in fashion in Texas, which is true. But there was a form of dueling extant here, which was a little too tough for even most of the early settlers of the West. It was employed by the Comanches; the contestants had their left hands tied together, and fought with knives in their rights until both were carved to pieces. This never found much favor with white men; it was too bloody and definite. One of the most desperate men in the state refused to fight that way, when challenged by my father, when he, my father that is, was a young man. The other fellow had had the best of a fist-fight, but a fist-fight didn't settle matters in Texas — not in those days. With guns and fists this fellow was a real scrapper, but steel was something different. Though urged by my father, he refused to fight Indian-style; and when my father, enraged, laid the edge of his knife to the fellow's throat and damned him for every scoundrel under the sun, he said nothing, nor did he reach for his gun, standing white and shaking. He didn't like the feel of the edge; not many men do.

You'll have to excuse me if I seem to ramble about in this letter and my style seems jerky. I'm restless as hell and can't seem to concentrate long on any one thing. I wish to God I could go to the Dallas Fair today — not that I give a damn about Dallas or the fair either, but Texas University plays Oklahoma

University there, and I'd like to see the game.[6] There's a big French-Indian fullback[7] on the Texas team that charges like a wounded bull, and — but I won't bore you with athletic details. But the hell of living so far away from any center of population is that one seldom gets to see any first-class sports.

More hell popping in Illinois; employers, officials and scabs shaking in their boots and squawking for more National guardsmen. The Insulls scooting hither and yon, possibly with their suitcases full of embezzled dough. I don't give a damn whether they catch them or not. I've always detested old Insull; but when he was on top of the heap people licked his boots and kowtowed to him, and he was allowed to get away with anything. They didn't yell cop till he hit the toboggan. It's just like the bootleggers. As long as they can pay off, they stay out of the jug. It's when laws and lawyers have them busted that they get the hoosegow. That's no idle speculation. I've known some of them personally. Not that it makes a curse to me. The only reason I have it in for the bootleggers is because of the awful muck they hand out as liquor. If I had a case of good beer on hand, I wouldn't be nervous and restless like I am. I'm in favor of the open saloon; and legalized prize-fights and horse-races, licensed gambling halls and licensed bawdy-houses. I wish I was in Mexico right now.

A bit of Hades in Belfast. Excuse me while I take time out for a few hyena-laughs. England's dear little Ulster pets are raring up. Evidently all the rioters in Ireland are not confined to the South. I can think of no more amusing a sight than an Orangeman and a Black-and-Tan knocking the socks off each other. What with Belfast and India, the empire-builders must be having a sweet time. I notice they didn't quite have the guts to let Gandhi starve himself into the Great Beyond. Whatamanwhataman. Not that I have any contempt for Gandhi. I honestly have a sincere admiration for him. He may be a visionary, but he is evidently sincere. I don't know if he's right or wrong, but I admire him just the same.

Your case in regard to cold weather is indeed puzzling. I never heard of anything like it. I sympathize with you, for it must be considerable of a handicap. I certainly hope you never have any permanent bad effects from it. As for myself, my only physical weakness, so far as I know — outside of flat feet! — is a bad heart. I inherited a weakness of that organ, and about the age of eighteen suffered from what is commonly known as an "athletic heart", or dilation. After recovery, there was still a weakness I occasionally notice now. Strenuous exertion, long sustained, or violent excitement is likely to knock me out. The last thing of the sort was several years ago, when Dempsey knocked out Jack Sharkey in his come-back. For days before the fight I was in a state of nervous tension, and during the battle, to the broadcast of which I listened in a theater, my heart went back on me. Or rather, it went back on me at the conclusion of the fight, when Dempsey finished Sharkey with a terrible smash to the jaw that came clearly over the air like the sound of a woodsman's axe cleaving a tree-trunk. I sprang up with an involuntary yell — unnoticed because the whole theater was in uproarious pandemonium — and toppled back into my seat, half-conscious. But the attack lasted only a few seconds; in fact I rose and followed my companion out so quickly that he thought I had merely been delayed by the crowd. But I was in a daze, and hardly knew what I was doing. I don't remember hearing the announcement of the winner — but I knew; I knew only one man in the world could strike a blow like that which had resounded over the air.

By the way, I suppose in your remarks about an individual having no right to expect "aid and comfort" from society in resenting rules forced on his group from without, you are referring to what I said about laws and legislations forced on Texas by outside interests. Let me assure you that I never expected favors from any force, group or individual I ever opposed. I never saw any mercy shown in any sort of a battle, and I never expect to. Nor do I ask it. If I'm fighting a man, I fully expect him to do everything in his power to win, by fair means or foul. I expect him to gouge, bite, and kick, and if he's strong enough to fell me, I see no reason why he shouldn't stamp out my brains. I've never been shown any mercy, and I'm not overstocked with it myself. The fact that I resent this over-legislation, this exploitation of my native state, doesn't mean I expect pampering from those it is my instinct to oppose. But I do resent it, even if I can't do anything about it. Just because a man is strong enough to stamp my teeth down my throat without retaliation on my part, doesn't mean I've got to thank him for it. As for laws, we've got more laws in Texas than we ever had before, and infinitely more crime. The increase in crime can not be traced merely to the increase in population. We have four death penalties in Texas — or I should say laws providing for the death penalty for four offenses — murder, rape, kidnapping and robbery with firearms. Yet each year sees a mounting number of murders. Kidnapping is comparatively rare. I'm sorry to say that there's some rape. Robbery with firearms seems somewhat on the wane — not so much because of the death penalty provided, which is seldom invoked, but because of the destruction of a few noted outlaw gangs, which were doing most of the robberies. But the list of killings is rather appalling. I can prove this by statistics, if necessary. I used to work in a law office myself, incidentally.

While I am on this matter, let me say that I am sincerely glad that the police system in the East is as good as you say it is. After all, it is corruption and not the system itself that I object to. I am always glad to receive evidence of honesty and integrity in any and all walks of life. I am quite ready to accept your word for it, without putting the matter to the proof. But — the perfection of the Eastern police system does not mean that the system in all parts of the country is perfect.

When I mentioned the case of my friend being arrested for having liquor on his breath, while the oil magnate's son was allowed to go unmolested, I was not generalizing from that single case. It was only one of many I could quote. In order that you may realize that I am not indulging in irresponsible theorizing, in regard to my own state, I am going to quote a few cases taken at random.

Understand, I am talking about Texas, not the East, North, or South. I am inclosing a few clippings from newspapers which dare to tell the truth about things. Let me say one of my kicks at law-enforcement is the difficulty to convict an officer of the law for anything he may do. Let me quote a case in point. In a certain town where I happened to be staying, an officer had trouble with a certain private citizen. There was no question of law enforcement. It was a private matter, involving family affairs. According to general opinion, the citizen was in the right of it. The officer came up to him suddenly on the street one day and shot him down without a word. I did not see the affair, but my room-mate did, and he said it was cold-blooded murder; he said the officer approached his victim without a word and suddenly drew and dropped him without warning. The murdered man was unarmed; he made no threatening move of any kind. The officer later said the man had threatened his life; I don't believe that. I was well acquainted with the murdered man and a more harmless, inoffensive mortal never lived.

If you were as familiar with the working of Texas law as I am, you wouldn't even ask if the officer was acquitted. Of course he came clear. My best friend attended the trial, and he told me it was a farce. No real attempt was made to prosecute the killer. Why? Hell, nobody doubted why. Because the fellow was an officer of the law. "You can't stick a law." An old saying in these parts and a true one. From what you say, this could not have happened in the East. But it *did* happen in Texas. This is no idle romance. If necessary, I can supply names, data and records; but only in return for assurance of treating the matter confidentially. I have no desire to risk my own life digging up things out of the recent past.

Doubtless you read, a few years ago, of the killing of a couple of young Mexicans of highly-connected families, by an Oklahoma officer. He said one of the boys tried to draw a gun. Well, why shouldn't he, accosted suddenly in the night by a stranger, in a locality always more or less haunted by hijackers and bandits? He might have drawn the gun, or he might not. At any rate, he had no way of knowing he was being accosted by an officer. Why did these officers interfere with these boys? At the trial they gave as their reason that the car was carrying a Kansas license! As Will Rogers remarked, when did it become an offense to drive through Oklahoma with a Kansas license? (Naturally the officer was acquitted.)

In Texas there was — and is, so far as I know — a big reward offered for bank-robbers — dead, only. Shortly after these rewards notices were posted, several Mexicans were killed in a West Texas town, by officers who said they were trying to rob the bank. Investigations proved that these officers had hired the Mexicans to come to town, and to enter the bank; then they shot them down in front of the bank in cold blood, to collect the reward money. I never heard just what was done to these officers, but I'm pretty sure they weren't treated too harshly. And there was a law in a larger Eastern Texas town who hired a negro instead of Mexicans, to rob a bank, in the course of which a bank-clerk was badly wounded. The officer killed the negro and claimed the reward. He got off with a penitentiary sentence.

If people seem bitter against the enforcers of the law, it is but necessary to remember that perhaps they have some slight reason. When I resent such things as I've mentioned, I don't consider myself a criminal. It isn't law-enforcement I resent, but the vandals that parade under the cloak of law. Condoning everything a man does, simply because he happens to wear brass buttons, is something I have no patience with. I won't bore you further, but will merely refer you to the clippings, which you can be assured are not the results of newspaper sensationalism. There are many fine men in Texas in ranks of the law; without them chaos and anarchy would result. But surely it is not fanaticism or outlawry to wish to eliminate the worst spots of corruption and injustice. I'll say one thing more: I hope those Florida guards that murdered the lad from New Jersey in that prison-camp, get the works, just as I'm sure they won't. There are conditions existing in Southern prison-camps that no amount of sophistry can justify. I've seen men whose backs bore the scars of the lash inflicted, not because they would not work, but because they were physically unable to do the work laid out for them — that remark just incidentally.

There was one man prison could not break. I make bold to say no prison-system in the United States, or anywhere else could have broken him, for in those days Texas prisons were hell on earth. John Wesley Hardin. He was a bloodthirsty killer, a murderer — what you will. Yet I respect him more than I respect some of the men that hunted him. He did his own killing. For only one of these killings was he tried — that of Deputy Sheriff Webb. I have little sympathy for Webb. He met Hardin in a social way, and sought to take advantage of him, for the sake of the reward. The sheriff of another county than Webb's, a friend of Hardin, introduced the men in a saloon. Webb went for his gun and dropped with Hardin's bullet through him.

John later went to Florida, where he was trailed by some Rangers. His capture was effected by a Florida sheriff, who caught his arms from behind when he sought to draw his guns. He suffered a crippling kick from the outlaw, and, I've heard, was gypped out of his share of the reward. During the melee, which took place on a train, a young boy got scared and started to duck out of the way, whereupon one of the officers shot him down. The boy was in no way connected with Hardin.

John Wesley Hardin drew twenty-five years in the penitentiary. But he refused to work. He wasn't lazy. He'd done harder work rustling cattle and hazing them up the trails than any of the prison guards had ever dreamed of. But he was unconquerable. They could rob him of his liberty. They couldn't make a slave of him. And they didn't. It was because of no softness or sentimentality they failed. All that they could do, they did. They beat him in a manner that would have killed a lesser man. They hanged him by his thumbs.

They starved him. They threw him into a dark cell to rot on moldy bread and stale water. A softer man would have died or given in. Not John Wesley Hardin. He was steel springs and whale-bone. They couldn't kill him, short of shooting him or cutting his throat. And probably they hesitated about that because of the numerous relatives he had outside the bars. Some people resent the murder of their kin, even by the laws.

John Wesley Hardin licked them. He was one man civilization never tamed. Finally they put him in a vat, where he had to pump water or drown. He didn't touch the pump. The water rose over his head and the prison officials lost their nerve. They emptied the vat, dragged Hardin out, half-drowned, but unconquerable, and threw him into a cell. After a year, he finally agreed — not by coercion, but of his own accord — to accept a position in the prison shoe-shop, where he was allowed time to study law on the side. All the vaunted power of civilization could not shake him. In him the individual was never subjected to the advantage of the mass. Nor was it civilization which finally cut him down; he met his death as I have narrated, at the hands of John Selman, a character as wild and untamed as Hardin himself.

I sure envy you your magnificent sight of the eclipse, and was absolutely enthralled by your vivid and colorful description of it. I hope you'll include that description in a story of some sort some time. You're very fortunate in having seen two total eclipses. I've never seen one, and it's a thousand to one shot I never will.

I was fascinated, too, by your descriptions of your Canadian invasion, and my mouth fairly watered as I thought of the grand liquors within your reach — unheeded by you, alas! But what I would have done to them! Quebec must indeed be a glamorous place of quaint and picturesque architecture and traditions. Aside from the liquor, your descriptions of the city really instilled in me a vast desire to see it some day, though it is a wish with scant chance of fulfillment.

I don't doubt that you're right about Shakespeare. I never paid much attention to the anti-Shakespeare theory myself.

Thanks for Wandrei's address. I'm so swamped with work that I hesitate to begin any new correspondence, but I do intend to write him some day, as he is an author whose work I sincerely admire.

And let me thank you for the pamphlet of poetic criticism which you sent me.[8] I have studied it with an appreciation I do not accord every critic. I am again impressed, as so many times before, by the extent of your artistic education. I am also impressed by the realization that I haven't a chance to ever become a poet. As you so ably put it, "— speaking in images, comparisons, suggestions, and implications rather than in coldly explanatory statements or logical expositions." I can't achieve this imagery. I have to say what I mean in bald narrative style, which is as far from real poetry as an ant-lion is from a lion.

Say, by the way, your comments about individuals having no right to expect favor from the opposition (which is quite true) could be well applied to the defeated party in Texas just now; the anti-Fergusonians. For the first time in more years than I like to remember, the old Texans have won an election. We won it fair. Not a shot was fired, not a voter slugged. And you ought to hear the other mob howl! After all who represents society? Is it the millions of people, who, if they are poor and not individually important, still compose the great bulk of the population? — or is it the handful of special privileged business men, absentee owners, and politicians who have grabbed the reins of the state? Primitive backgrounds possibly should not, as you remark, be allowed to hinder the march of progress. But what if that progress is used as a camouflage for wholesale exploitation? The people expressed their will in the election; yet now the opposition howls that society is being defied, civilization threatened, and chaos imminent. I repeat — *which group represents society?* — the great common majority, or the wealthy and powerful minority?

Jim Ferguson's wife was nominated in the teeth of such obstacles as have seldom confronted any candidate. She was opposed by big business; wealth, power; by the bulk of the so-called intellectual class; by thousands of white-collar workers who might have found themselves without a job had they ventured to vote against their bosses; as well as by thousands of honest people, who sincerely considered it to their best interests to vote for the exploiters. Add to that, the fact that most of the Republicans in Texas seem to have cast their votes for Ross Sterling. It was the common people who nominated Jim Ferguson's wife — the common folks, the poor people, the ignorant, the down-trodden, the oppressed — the scum of the earth, as it is the fashion to designate them. Jim Ferguson, with his ragged followers, whipped Sterling to a standstill: in the primaries; in the run-off; at the State Convention; in the courts. Now from the Sterling mob goes up an awful yell, and scores of them are preparing to bolt the party and vote for the Republican candidate; including a number of college professors who formed an organization to promote "good government" and primly set to work to defeat Jim and his uncultured tatterdemalions. They would hand their state over to a tribe of Vandals, if the Vandals wore good clothes and had a civilized air, rather than to side with their own race which is considered backward and out of style. The losers don't like the taste of defeat; they're not used to it. This is the first licking the exploiters of Texas have got since Jim Hogg ran the Standard Oil Company out of the State back in the '90s.

Our candidate for attorney-general[9] had to go into Louisiana in order to broadcast his speeches; and we elected him by a terrific majority. And now he's sinking the gaffs in the looters. I don't give a damn about the Fergusons. But I do give a damn about the people, the common, the low-down, the ignorant people whom the great call the scum of the earth. This has been their victory.

They came down from the hills, out of the forks of the creeks, from the mesquite flats, the post-oak ridges, the river-bottoms, the tenement-districts, the oil-field shacks: with their hickory breeches sagging their suspenders, their shoe-soles worn through, their shoulders slumping and their calloused hands hanging from years of bitter toil. Their victory won't help them much materially, perhaps; it matters little to the poor who is in power. But I rejoice in that victory. It is the last stand of the old Texan race. They'll never win another triumph. They are fading into oblivion, following the redmen. And I am ready to go with them; for with all its faults, follies and cruelties, it's my breed and my race, and I am alien to all others.

"Not of the princes and prelates with periwigged charioteers,
Riding triumphantly laurelled to lap the fat of the years,
Rather the scorned, the rejected, the men hemmed in with the spears.

"Not the ruler for me, but the ranker, the tramp of the road;
The slave with the sack on his shoulder, pricked on by the goad;
The man with too weary a burden, too heavy a load.

"Let others sing of the wine and the wealth and the mirth,
The portly presence of potentates goodly in girth —
Mine be the dirt and the dross, the dust and the scum of the earth.

"Theirs be the music, the color, the glory, the gold;
Mine be a handful of ashes, a mouthful of mold.
Of the maimed, of the halt and the blind in the rain and the cold—
Of these shall my songs be fashioned, my tales be told."[10]

I hardly know how to thank you for the bundle of cards you recently sent me. I have gone over them again and again, with the utmost appreciation, and they go into my most valued files. Anyone can get a good idea of Eastern, Southern and Canadian architecture and scenery, just by studying them. The systematic way in which they are arranged is a great aid in this study, and altogether, it is about the most valuable addition to my collection that I have received in some time. Again, many thanks!

I recently received your postcard. Glad you liked the rattles. And thank you for the kind things you said about my maunderings concerning them; there was no conscious literary effort; I was just sort of rambling along. But I'm glad my random comments proved of some interest.

Yes, a bulletin from the AFG[11] announced the crumpling of *Strange Tales*, and on its heels came back a yarn the magazine had bought but hadn't paid for. I wasn't surprized. *Strange Tales* was too narrow in policy to have lasted long, though in good times the magazine would have stood up longer than it did. By the way, before I forget it: Belknap Long, who wrote the introduction to Danziger's *Portrait of Ambrose Bierce* — is he Frank Belknap Long Jr.'s father?[12]

I'm enclosing a clipping telling of the end of one, who, in his own way, was as deadly as the creature whose remains I sent you recently. He was raised in the house which stands right across the street from where I now sit. There were four of the boys — all bad, in the Western sense of the word. I remember well the first time I ever saw any of them. I was a kid in my early teens. I rode into town one gold, grey winter evening. The grey clouds merged in the mist which seemed to change the air to damp smoke. As I went up the street on foot, a lean, hard-looking youth stared at me aggressively, and made some sneering remark about my "wild" appearance. To which I responded with an oath, in the accustomed repartee of the times, "I'm wild and woolly and full of fleas, and I never been curried below the knees!" His comment had been occasioned by my slouch hat and spurs, which were even then a rather rare sight in an oil-boom town. Later I encountered this same fellow, just as I was climbing on my mustang, and we had another slight clash of words as I rode off. I didn't know him, and it didn't occur to me that he was trying to start a fight. When I later learned who he was, I realized I'd been lucky. I wouldn't have had a chance; he was too handy with both knife and pistol. But he was a younger brother of the man described in the enclosed clipping, and probably the worst of the bunch. At present he's doing time in a Texas penitentiary. I haven't seen any of them for years, except the oldest brother, who visited the old home-town last spring, just a few months before he was killed in Mississippi during a bank hold-up. They said he'd recently finished a stretch in Leavenworth, but he looked well-groomed and sleek as a prosperous travelling salesman. This last killing leaves only the younger boys; the fellow I mentioned, and a still younger one, a kid of eighteen or nineteen, who's doing a life-stretch in Oklahoma for a kidnapping job. Those boys were just born out of their time. They were crude, and this system can tolerate anything rather than crudeness. If they'd worn dress-suits, spoken good English, and robbed the helpless and ignorant by approved legal means, they might have been lions of society, like most successful thieves of that type.

By the way, you mentioned that my "Children of the Night" got a mention in the O. Henry Memorial prize annual.[13] What is this annual, and is it possible for me to get a copy of it? The reason I ask, is I gather it's something of a boost to get mentioned in it, and it's just possible that I might be able to boost myself with an editor sometime. Any information you can give me about this business will be greatly appreciated.

But I won't impose on you any longer. I've already maundered along beyond all patience. Thanking you again for the poetry pamphlet and the generous bundle of scenic cards, I am,

Cordially,
[REH.]

P.S. Have you read my "Cairn on the Headland" in the latest *Strange Tales*?[14] If not, I'll be glad to lend you my copy. It was the artist's idea, not mine, to deck Odin in a solid steel cuirass!

R.E.H.

NOTES

1. Two lines of text have been X-ed out. Probably "The first time was for on a friend, and the second was over a."
2. Howard and Gordon corresponded during 1926-1927. See *Collected Letters*, Volume One.
3. Dr. Isaac Howard's sister, Willie, had married William Oscar McClung, whose mother was Choctaw. If Howard had other relatives of mixed blood they have not been identified.
4. Jim Thorpe.
5. This book report survives, in the Glenn Lord Collection at the University of Texas, Austin.
6. Texas University defeated Oklahoma University (as they were then known) 17-10 on October 15, 1932, at Fair Park Stadium in Dallas.
7. Texas University had three All-Southwest Conference backs in 1932, fullback Ernest Koy and halfbacks Bohn Hilliard and Harrison Stafford.
8. *Further Criticism of Poetry* (Louisville, Kentucky: George G. Fetter, 1932).
9. James Allred. See letter 213, note 11.
10. Stanzas 1, 4, 6 and 7 of John Masefield's "A Consecration."
11. American Fiction Guild.
12. It was Long, Jr. himself who wrote the introduction to the book.
13. *O. Henry Memorial Award Prize Stories of 1931*, edited by Blanche Colton Williams, included "The Children of the Night" among "Stories ranking second."
14. January 1933.

TSS: 24248-24265

ꕥꕥꕥ

221. To H.P. Lovecraft, ca. November 1932.

Dear Mr. Lovecraft:

Here's a clipping that might be of some interest, not because of its athletic significance, but because it bears out some former remarks of mine concerning the various types of Southwesterners. The difference between the typical North Texan and the typical South Texan is becoming so marked that even the newspapers are noting it, as shown in the enclosed clipping.

T.C.U., represented by the blond warriors, is in Fort Worth, where I've seen more pure blonds than anywhere else in the state — or any other state I've ever been in. Out of nineteen people met on one block, I've counted sixteen of that complexion. The further south you go, the more brunets you see. This is mainly because of the great numbers of Mexicans, Bohemians, Bavarians, and Poles settled there. Again, that section of the country has been settled longer than north and west Texas, and the people have had more opportunity to mix with people of Slavonic and Spanish strains. North west Texas was settled mainly, not by people from south and east Texas, but by people from such states as Alabama, Georgia, Tennessee, Arkansas, and Mississippi, of pure Celtic or Anglo-Saxon blood. These have not mixed so easily with Indian and Spanish strains. Yet, it is a curious fact that there are more brunets among the unmixed Anglo-Saxons of south Texas than there are among those of the north and west.

In this part of the country, that is, among the Callahan hills, there are comparatively few pure blonds, yet they outnumber the pure brunets; the characteristic type is of blue or grey eyes, with medium to dark brown hair, and a medium complexion.

In the lower Rio Grande valley, among the irrigated districts, blonds predominate, because of the great numbers of Germans and Scandinavians from the Middle West. They are easily distinguishable from the native stock. Put a blond Scandinavian beside an equally blond native Texan, and it's easy to tell them apart. It's not so easy to distinguish brunet aliens from brunet natives. Why this should be, I can't pretend to say.

Incidentally, the blond T.C.U. team has the advantage in weight, height and strength, and is perhaps the most powerful defensive line in the nation, while the brunet Texas University team has the edge on speed and spirit, and shines most brightly on the offense.

So much for Southwestern racial contrasts — or what ever they are.

Cordially,
[REH.]

TSS: 64686

ꙮ

222. To Tevis Clyde Smith, ca. November 1932.

Fear Finn:

Well, I finally get around to answering your letter after so long a time.

Lines to G. B. Shaw

Oh, G.B. S, oh, G.B.S.,
You lousy son of a bitch,
You lift your yawp across the world
Like a bullfrog in a ditch.

I would that by that foliage which
Your scholarly phizz thatches
Tied to a smoking stake you were
By a tribe of wild Apaches.

You could deride them in that style
Of which you're so enamored,
While someone with a tomahawk
Your lordly cranium hammered.

And several thousand dancing braves,
The more the merrier,
Were sticking Spanish Daggers in
Your antequate posterior.

The readers took well to my "Worms of the Earth"[1] story, much to my surprize. I didn't know how they'd like the copulation touch. My heroes grow more bastardly as the years pass. One of my latest sales[2] concluded with a sexual intercourse instead of the usual slaughter. My sword-wielder grabbed the princess — already considerately stripped by the villing — and smacked her down on the altar of the forgotten gods, while battle and massacre roared outside, and through the dusk the remains of the villing, nailed to the wall by the hero, regarded the pastime sardonically. I don't know how the readers will like it. I'll bet some of them will. The average man has a secret desire to be a swaggering, drunken, fighting, raping swashbuckler.

A Mick in Israel.

Old King Saul was a bold old scut
He rammed his sword in Ashdod's gut.
The warriors of Gaza shook in their shoes,
Their fingers twitched till they spilled their booze.
And every hussy and every john
Shook at his name in Askalon.

The warriors of Gath went after him
To hang his scalp on a hickory limb.
They went — when they came limping back
Their carried their guts in a gunny-sack.
And busted noses and blackened eyes
And chewed-up ears were as thick as flies.
And before they could unbar their gates,
They felt his hobnails in their nates.
His eyes were blue as the ocean's haze,
His hair was red as a dancing blaze.
He always drank his whiskey straight
And he had a gut that could carry the freight.
For music he had an elegant ear,
Especially after the fifteenth beer.
He'd sprawl on the throne with a stein in his mitts
And his feet propped up on a keg of Schlitz,
With a jeweled scepter beating time
To the beat of the rhythm and the rhyme,
While David on his harp would lean
Playing "The Wearin' of the Green."
And Samuel swore by bead and bell
The kingdom was going straight to Hell.
Half the babies born in his reign
Had blue eyes and a crimson mane.
The reason Samuel didn't enthuse —
He was making micks out of all the Jews!

Ah, hell, I feel unusually futile. Our artistic friends give themselves airs over us toilers and boozers. They fancy they have discovered the meaning of life, even while persisting on the meaningless of it. If life is meaningless, then it's as meaningless to write a poem, paint a picture or pen a philosophic essay as it is to play football, guzzle beer, or fondle a whore.

Musings.

To every man his trade
And the tools of his trade thereof;
To every man his hate,
To every man his love.

If I draw a jewel out of the sea
And nail it to a star,
I am no greater than the man
Who welds a metal bar.

If I fall in the gutters of the world
Where the dregs of liquor run,
I am no baser than the man
Who writes his name in the sun.

Well, after these fruitless maunderings, I have still said nothing; if you wait as long to answer this letter as I waited to write it, your name will be mud.

Envoy.
Write whenever you get the chance,
And if it is not soon,
I'll give you a lusty kick in the pants
By the light of the silvery moon.

Fear Dunn.

NOTES

1. *Weird Tales*, November 1932.
2. "Black Colossus."

TSS: 82678-82679

ଔଓ

223. To *Magic Carpet*, ca. November 1932.[1]

Thanks very much for the remarks and quotations in the Souk by which you corroborate the matter of Timour's wine-bibbing. I welcome and appreciate criticisms in the spirit of Mr. Bell's, though, as you point out, he chances to be mistaken in the matter of Timour and others. But criticisms of this nature promote discussions helpful and instructive to all. In regard to Moslem drinking, I understand that the Seventeenth Century Tatars of Crimea, before imbibing, spilled a drop of wine from the vessel and drank the remainder, declaring that since the Prophet forbade tasting a drop of wine, they thus obeyed the command. They spilled the drop and drank the rest. Many modern Moslems maintain that they disobey no holy law by drinking brandy and whisky, since the Prophet said nothing about these beverages — proving that Christians are not the only people on earth to wriggle out of laws by technicalities.

NOTES

1. Published in the January 1933 issue. JB

ଔଓଔଓ

224. To August Derleth, ca. December (15?)[1] 1932.

Dear Mr. Derleth:

I had intended answering your letter some time ago, but have been extremely busy. I have followed your work in *Weird Tales* for several years, with great interest, and have more than once expressed my admiration for your stories both to Lovecraft and to the editors of the magazine.

I am very glad that you found my remarks on my native region of some interest. I would be much interested in some descriptions of your own locality, since your state, from all I can hear, is singularly rich in scenic beauty. Old Jean Nicolet should have felt consoled for his failure to find the China he sought. You are particularly fortunate that such a large percent of your farmers own the land they work (85% is it not?). Tenant farming and absentee ownership have been, and are, among the curses of the Southwest.

I would be most glad to give you any information in my power about my native state. However, I hardly know where to begin, or what phases to deal with. Writing at random I might bore you with repetitions of things you had already read or heard, or were not particularly interested in. So if you'll tell me what phases of Texas life or history you're most interested in, I'll lay my remarks along those lines.

You mentioned that you were interested in the bad-men of early days. So am I, intensely. However, if you've made a study of them, you probably know more about some of them than I do. Anyway, if you wish, I can give you some of the low-down on John Wesley Hardin, Billy the Kid, Ben Thompson, John Glanton, Hendry Brown, John Selman, King Fisher, and other swashbucklers of the frontier. There's nothing I enjoy more than discussing these picturesque old scoundrels.

So, hoping to hear from you at your convenience, and with best wishes, I am,

Cordially,
[Robert E. Howard]

NOTES

1. "15 December" is handwritten on the bottom of the letter in different handwriting than Howard's signature. JB

TSS: 15052

❧❧❧

225a. To H.P. Lovecraft, draft, ca. December 1932.

My later conclusions were forced on me against my will. I could go on and give other incidents, but there's no need of inflicting them on you. I need hardly to say that I wish all these remarks about the police and law-enforcement to be considered absolutely confidential. I hardly know how I got to spilling all this stuff; I never put any of it on paper before, and I wouldn't be telling it to you, only for the fact that I feel I can trust your discretion. The fact that I could prove my assertions wouldn't do me much good, if I should antagonize certain forces.

I'm afraid a written statement of affairs wouldn't do much good, unless signed by some one in authority, or otherwise well known. So much stuff is circulated in campaigns and the like, charges, refutations and counter-charges. Even if I dared to publish such an accusation. The Fergusons may make some reforms. I don't know. If the *Gladewater Journal* doesn't have any affect, I'm afraid nothing I could write would, except to antagonize people against me. *The Journal* has an enormous state-wide circulation, and in spite of its sentimental style – which is deliberate, in order to catch the fancy of the common people, who respond to the truth more quickly when presented in such fashion – is considerable of a political power.

Again, it's so difficult to make any kind of reform in this state. The lines are so loosely drawn. There is so much of a grab-bag spirit, a to-hell-with-everybody-but-me spirit. In the general grabbing, the weak are so often ruthlessly trampled, and the common decencies lost sight of. Texas has for generations been the prey of two particular breeds, each equally abominable – the magnate from some other part of the nation, who wishes only to exploit the state and suck it dry of its wealth; and the native promoter and politician, who is eager to sell the birthright of his people, in return for personal graft. That is not to say that all the people who come to Texas are commercial pirates, or that all the native promoters and politicians are of the type mentioned. But both breeds do exist in goodly number. It has been so, since immediately after the Civil War.

Let me go into the matter at more length, so that we may glance at the social and historical factors behind this present tangle, and get some idea of the economic trend. To do this properly, we must go clear back to the beginning of the state, and work down to the present times. As you know, Texas was first settled by people who wished to make homes - frontiersmen, mainly, with the restlessness of their breed. They were of Scotch-Irish stock, mostly, from the Southern states. In only a few cases were they slave-holders, and in fewer cases were they large slave-holders. They were hardy, independent, honest, barbaric in many ways. Cattle-raising was of little importance. The first settlers of the Southwest were hunting farmland. They settled in river-valleys, on black-land prairies, and along the coast. After winning their independence, they began to push northward and westward, and slowly cattle-raising began to attain prominence. There were plenty of Mexican and Spanish ranchmen in Mexico and South Texas, and in southern Texas the American cowboy was born, a natural adaptation from the Mexican Vaquero. It is not here my purpose to trace the sporadic booms and bursts of prosperity of those early times – the growth and destruction of such sea-ports as Indianola, Clarksville, the City of Bagdad, etc.; the creating of new towns, (of some of which no traces now remain) during the building of which money flowed freely as blood and whiskey, and skilled labor brought almost fabulous wages; nor the aborted phase of plantation aristocracy which struggled in some portions of the southeast. But already adventurers were coming into the state: soldiers of fortune, American and European; politicians; spendthrifts who wished to mend broken fortunes; outlaws. Among these soldiers of fortune, it can not be denied, were empire-builders; of such was David Crockett, Jim Bowie, Sam Houston, Bigfoot Wallace. But among these were less developed and turbulent spirits. These mixed with the home-builders – themselves a hardy race, impatient of restraint, and accustomed to hard drinking, hard working and hard fighting. The result was that the typical Texan, from 1836 to 1880, was as wiry, hard and eager for a scrape as a cougar. They scattered all over the West, from border to border. But that came in later times than I am just now dealing with. Life in early Texas was bitter hard. Indian raids and the uncertainty of the seasons made farming pretty much of a gamble. Many of the younger men took up hunting as an occupation, as did Bigfoot Wallace, wandering further away from the settlements as the game became scarce. The settler followed the hunter. All the time there was a constant drift into the state from other sections, of both the good and the bad. But in the main they were of the types already described: mostly backwoodsmen in search of new land, with a scattering of craftsmen, and a scattering of adventurers. I think that cattle-raising was adopted gradually and naturally. Game became scarcer, and I have already mentioned the uncertainty of farming. But there was a whole new empire of open land, and Spanish cattle to graze on it. Ranchmen in south and east Texas found a market in New Orleans for their cattle.

TSS: 27577-27578

ঌ৪ৡ৩ঌ৪

225b. To H.P. Lovecraft, ca. December 1932.

[Note by HPL at head of letter: "return this to Grandpa or incur the direst consequences!"]

Dear Mr. Lovecraft:

Having read your latest letter with the greatest interest and appreciation, I'll try to answer it now, after having been delayed several times, owing to various circumstances.

I'm glad nothing I've said has proved offensive. Force of habit often makes me sound more aggressive and dogmatic in argument than I intend. This comes from having spent considerable time in rough-and-ready environments, where arguments are likely to be riddled with biting personalities, loud and arrogant assertions, and profanity. In such arguments it is impossible to win one's point by logic alone; in self-defense one is forced to adopt an aggressive attitude. This attitude is likely to become a habit, introducing into discussions where it is out of place. I've seen arguments decided, not on their actual merits, but simply because one contestant could yell louder than the others. Such disputes, also, are pretty liable to turn into fights. I'm sorry to say that it isn't among working men alone that I've encountered an irritating attitude in debate; I've discovered this attitude in several so-called intellectuals, who seemed more anxious to show up their opponents as fools, than to reach any logical conclusion. My method, in the teeth of such circumstances, has always been to avoid debate as much as possible, and when unavoidable, to be as tough as my opponents. This has brought about the unconscious mannerisms I deplored at the beginning of this paragraph. So if at times I seemed unduly aggressive and vindictive, please believe that it is unconscious and due to the causes noted above.

Your attitude regarding the relative merits of the physical and mental seems very well balanced, to me. For myself, it is impossible for me to divorce man's mental life from his physical. After all, mind itself is a physical process, so far as we know, depending upon the workings of the material matter of the physical brain, fed in turn by glands, veins, and cellular matter, all of the earth earthly. "Safe-guarding the fruits of consciousness" — I quote from your recent letter; that's a splendid phrase to my mind. And the fruits of consciousness are hardly more mental than physical, to my mind. Consciousness itself is a physical process, as far as I can see, depending, at least, on things physical. The finest intellect in the world is dependent on the slushy grey stuff of the brain, which in turn depends upon the physical skull that locks it in, the hands and feet that obey its instructions, and the mouth, teeth and intestines that feed it. That same splendid intellect can be destroyed in a twinkling by the impact of a club or stone against its bony case. And the club or stone can be wielded by an ignoramus, an idiot or an ape. If the physical is bounded, limited, guided or destroyed by the mental, the same can be said in the other way, though in some cases to a lesser extent.

As for relative strength — I can't to save my neck see why I should despise, neglect or ignore my body because a bull, elephant or electric dynamo is stronger than it. I realize that I could never equal the strength of a bull, yet my own comparatively puny thews have stood me in good stead time and again, against both men and animals. Yesterday, for instance, I helped shift a load of hay-bales from one barn to another, helped load a wagon with corn, and later did the bulk of unloading and storing fifteen hundred pounds of ground feed. All this work could have been done more easily and quickly with machinery, but I didn't have any. The fact that a gorilla could shoulder a heavy sack of grain and carry it to its proper place in the barn easier than I could, didn't alter my problem any — that of getting the stuff stored. When I escort a girl through the crush of a football crowd, the knowledge that a rhinoceros could charge through the throng and clear a way for her more effectively than I could, doesn't mean that I'm going to let her get squashed, as long as I have shoulders and elbows. Once I outran a mad bull in a short sprint to a rail fence. Now a jackrabbit could have reached the fence quicker than I, and a monkey could have climbed it a sight easier. But my own human muscles did the job well enough to haul me out of reach just as he reached for me. This may seem like a trivial example, but it was important to me. A foot and a half of bull's horn through the guts is no trifle to anybody. If a belligerent drunk announces that he is going to kick my head into the next county, I know very well that a trip-hammer could flatten him quicker than I, but that doesn't have much bearing on the case.

What I'm trying to show, is that every day, men on farms, ranches, and in oil-fields, mines, factories, small towns and country villages, are confronted with problems that require muscles as well as minds to solve. This a matter that purely mental workers can easily lose sight of, and I think is partly the reason for the contempt with which the physical is looked upon by such persons as you mention holding to "fanatical anti-physicalism". I've known a few of these persons, mainly among the young intelligentsia, or however it is spelled.

As for the importance of physical power — there is an element of vanity in the developing of a strong body, but no more than there is in the developing of a fine mind. The true athlete does not develop his muscles and co-ordination simply because of vanity, but because of pure love of the game. Strength is more or less relative, and like intellect, can not be defined by any definite limits, or measured by any accurate gauge. Of two strong men, each generally exceeds the other in some manner. One can lift more, the other can break a thicker stick, for instance. For example, my best friend and myself; (I trust this does not sound as if I were holding up myself for a strong man; I am not, particularly; I am just using this matter as an example.) My friend has a more powerful grip than I, but I can strike a much harder blow than he can; he can take a harder punch in the belly than I, but I can take more on the jaw than he. It could not be said that either of us was the other's definite superior in physical make-up. So if a man is motivated by personal vanity, in desiring to strut and swagger over other men, it is futile for him to waste his time in physical development. Regardless of how strong he becomes, he will always find men who will outclass him in one way or another. It is foolish for a man to be arrogant or conceited simply because he can lift more weight or break thicker sticks than the average man; it is foolish for him to develop himself simply because of the promptings of his vanity. But it is not foolish for him to wish to feel capable of standing on his feet and holding his own in any company. A man need not wish to feel superior to other men, but he should at least feel himself their equal. It is not particularly conceited on his part to wish to be able to always hold up his end of the game, regardless of what it may be; to do as much work as the next man; to be able to always do his part, without having to call for help; and to be able to help some weaker mortal, if it should be necessary; and to be able to stand up and take his own part against encroachment.

We live, after all, in a physical world. Few of us are fortunate enough to be able to move in a mainly mental sphere. This is especially true of this part of the country.

Humanity, as you say, means mind. But mind again rests on physical forces. In your example, the weak man who harnesses bulls, engines and stronger men, is still dependent on the physical. It is not his brain alone which harnesses these powers; he has the advantage of all the brains that have gone before him. And not alone of the brains, but of the millions and millions of grasping, groping, toiling human hands that, with their guiding brains, built slowly the edifice upon the summit of which he sits with his fingers on the reins of the lightnings. Without these hands he were helpless, no less than without the aid of the brains before him. Without the living hands that do his bidding he is helpless. He controls machines built by machines, but first these machines took shape under the clumsy, toiling fingers of flesh and veins and bone. Mind can not be divorced from the flesh. Our whole structure of progress rests, in the last analysis, on the hands of the unknown workers, from the engineers in the most modern factory back through the dim ages to the first ape-man squatting laboriously over the half-formed flint. Mind without Force is useless as Force without Mind; to me they seem inseparable. If the brain guides the hand, the hand carries out the instructions of the brain. Now a man born without hands or feet might become the greatest power of the modern world; yet he would be simply employing the hands and feet of others, and of all those gone before him.

And so I do not feel that I am wasting my time when I work at weights and punching bags to increase my wind and harden my muscles. I live among people who work with their hands. If the writing game continues to deflate, it's probable that I'll have to earn my living by some sort of hard labor, since I am not trained in any trade or profession. Last summer men died like flies in the grain fields of the Southwest and Midwest. They were men who were unused to such work; they were unfit. Their wind was bad, their muscles flabby. Confronted by the choice of working at back-breaking labor in the blazing sun, or starving, they chose the work, and died, simply because they were unfit physically. Many of those men were superior mentally to the farm-hands working imperturbably beside them. But no man knows, in this physical world, when he'll be called upon to demonstrate his right to survive, not by the craft and knowledge stored in his brain, but by the sinews and springy bones of his material body.

Therefore I feel that if it is possible, a man should try to give himself as much strength as is possible, as well as developing his mind to the utmost. The average modern man may never need such strength; but he might need it bad some time. As an example (one of many such I might cite), the friend of mine mentioned above, of the powerful grip. Last summer he was working on the high-way, and at the same time was helping build a barb-wire fence. While holding a wire against a post with one hand, and driving a staple with the other, the taut strand snapped suddenly, between his hand and the post. You can imagine the result, if you have ever seen the ghastly havoc barbed-wire can wreak on flesh, animal or human. But my friend escaped unhurt, simply because he was strong enough to retain his grip on that broken wire and keep it from being ripped through his hand. The powerful recoil jerked him backward and almost off his feet, but he held on — a feat which no ordinary man would have been capable of. He didn't have time to let go cleanly, of course. Hold on was the only thing to do. If his grip had been just a little weaker, the barbs would have been jerked through his fingers, mangling his hand in a way not pleasant to think about. Again, the father of another friend, shooting an oil-well, having lowered the nitro-can, was horrified to see it shoot out of the shaft, having been expelled by a gas-pocket. There was but one thing to be done, and he did it. He grasped the "can" firmly in his arms in midair, and held on, cradling it with his body. That took quick thinking, but it also took unusual bodily strength. Had the "can" escaped his arms, struck against the timbers or fallen on the floor, the impact would have set it off and blown to bits the rig and everybody in it. It's a wonder it didn't anyway. But there was one of many cases where a keen mind tied to powerful muscles saved human lives.

I think it was Brisbane[1] who deriding sports and physical development, spoke of the uselessness of athletics, since anything a human being could do, could be outdone by an animal. He would not box since a mule could kick harder than a man could hit, nor run a footrace because a rabbit could outrun a man, nor wrestle because a python could crush any human wrestler. To be consistent he should not eat because a hog could eat more than he, or drink because a camel could drink more, nor sleep because a hibernating bear could outsleep him, nor indulge in sexual intercourse because a bull has more vigor in those lines; nor should he learn to swim because a whale can outswim him, nor dance because a whirlwind can outspin him, nor should he ever walk anywhere because a horse, a machine, or an electric wheel-chair can take him there much faster. But some of these things are necessary to life, he might say. Well, so are some of the things he denounces; necessary at least to some people. Such men as Brisbane have made their mark; they sit at the top and have the hands of thousands to do their bidding. They forget that there are millions of humans to whom life is still more of a physical struggle than anything else.

And he entirely ignores the sheer physical joy of muscular exertions, which is separate and apart from any mental enjoyment. A man may get a mental kick out of indulging in some form of athletics, but the fleshly thrill is there too, and stronger than the other. Vanity, and a feeling of self-expression aside, there is a real pleasure in feeling the rich red blood humming through your veins, the springy response of hard flexible muscles, yes, and the berserk exhilaration of good blows taken and dealt. For myself, some form of at least moderately strenuous exercise is absolutely necessary. Without it I become sluggish and bad-tempered; my health goes on the rocks, and affects my disposition and my literary (?) output. My mental ability is so tied up with my physical condition that I am unable to separate them. Unimportant to the world at large, yes; but extremely important to me, and it is I who pay my bills, and not the world — nor Mr. Brisbane, either.

I have known a few youngsters, of both sexes, whose scorn of the physical was biting beyond words. These persons considered themselves possessed of artistic appreciation. Yet what is more beautiful than a splendid human body in coordinated motion? The lithe finely poised figure of a dancer, the pantherish body of a boxer with the wedge-shaped torso, the long swelling muscles rippling under the smooth velvety skin, the easy glide of onset and retreat, the perfect balance and carriage, the suppleness of limb — where is a finer model for an artist or sculptor? How can people go into ecstasies over a cold lifeless lump of marble hammered and chipped into a semblance of humanity, and despise the warm, vibrant, pulsing original? What is art but a poor copy of reality at best? I suppose that these afore-mentioned "artists" who rave over the sculpturings of the Grecians, would have looked with contempt or indifference at the sinewy models whose god-like features the ancient masters copied. In admiring the skill with which the artist or the sculptor reproduces reality, I do not forget my admiration for the reality he mimics. Personally, while I enjoy looking at the statue of a wrestler, a gladiator or a discus-thrower, I much prefer to watch the actual model in action. This is not spoken in depreciation of the sculptor or the artist. I greatly admire the skill which lends a painting or an image the illusion of reality, and mimics the flesh in the last small detail of joint, muscle and finger-nail. But I say it is hard for me to understand these people who say they have artistic appreciation and a love of beauty, who see the beauty in a marble imitation of a physical god, and yet see no beauty at all in a living pulsing vibrant god of muscles, in fighting togs, bathing trunks, track shorts, or football harness.

Maybe it's the sweat, dust and strain of competition which repels them. But I have an idea that the athletes of ancient Greece sweated and bled, and strained, yes, and cursed like pirates, too, when they were stacking up their records. And there's considerable sweat and strain in hacking out a fine statue from marble, I should think.

As for me, I don't pretend to be an artist, or to love beauty particularly. I enjoy the beauty of a perfect figure, but primarily it's not beauty that interests me in athletics. It's the strife, the struggle; the impact of sweaty, straining, iron bodies; the creaking and snapping of mighty thews, the berserk onslaught and the ferocious defense. Anyway, beauty is relative, I think. On my favorite football team there is a fast flashy halfback,[2] whose specialty is speed and elusiveness. He is beautifully built, from an artistic point of view. There is also a powerful fullback, a French-Indian, with broad massive shoulders and a slouching catlike gait. Now to some the most beautiful sight is to see the first mentioned lad go weaving down the field at blinding speed, avoiding tacklers with perfect control. But to me a more beautiful sight is to see the Indian fullback, with his bull-like strength, backing up the line and piling up blockers and ball-toter by sheer power and ferocity. It's not the artistic kind of beauty; but there is a beauty in the business of a job well done, of strength and fighting fury working in unison. Who can measure beauty with a set gauge? It's a word much overworked. Beauty to me is something that gives me pleasure to look upon, whether it is a sunset of blue and rifted gold; the sparkle of a diamond; the daintiness of a feminine countenance or the perfection of her figure; the lashing waves of a grey winter sea breaking along a frosty rock-strewn coast; the sleek rotundity of a thoroughbred pig; the tapering lines of a race-horse; a cluster of scarlet and russet autumn leaves; a thick luscious steak chicken-fried to a turn; a wedge of wild geese etched against a cold clear frosty sky and sounding their heart-tugging call as they race southward; a slender runner, with slender wire-hard limbs and a mop of yellow hair blowing in the wind; or a fullback built for fierce power and stamina, with broad thick shoulders, squat neck, low forehead, square jaw and massive limbs, in terrific action.

It is difficult for me to express the appreciation I feel for the kind things you said about my work. I know of no critic whose opinion I value so highly as yours, and for you to praise my efforts is indeed an honor. It renews my self-confidence, and inspires me to further efforts. However, if I possess any ability in the line of weird literature, I owe it mainly to a long and careful study of your technique. I have not tried to copy you; but I have studied your methods, just as I study the other masters of literature.

I'm glad you liked the yarns mentioned. The editor took liberties with "The Cairn on the Headland". In the original version, O'Brien was born in America. The editor changed this and made O'Brien a native of Ireland, but neglected to change the line: "We were countrymen in that we born in the same land." That would seem to make "Ortali" an Irishman, too, when I intended him for an American-born Italian. In making Odin a purely evil spirit, I did that partly for dramatic effect, and partly because I was writing from the viewpoint of the ancient Irish. They must have considered that god an utter devil, considering the murdering, looting and destroying habits of his worshippers. Their shrines and monasteries were burned and demolished, their priests slaughtered, their young men and young women butchered on the altars of the one-eyed deity, and over all towered Odin. Seeing his effigy looming through the smoke of destruction and the flame of slaughter, dabbled with blood, and bestriding mangled corpses, the victims must have seen in him only the ultimate essence of evil.

Concerning "Worms of the Earth" — I must have been unusually careless when I wrote that, considering the errors — such as "her" for "his", "him" for "himself", "loathsome" for "loathing", etc.. I'm at a loss to say why I spelled Eboracum as Ebbracum. I must investigate the matter. I know I saw it spelled that way, somewhere; it's not likely I would make such a mistake entirely of my own volition, though I do frequently make errors. Somehow, in my mind, I have a vague idea that it's connected some way with the Gaelic "Ebroch" — York.

I read with much interest your remarks on the prize annuals, O'Brien's, etc., and am glad to see that so many Weird Tale writers have got recognition. No, I didn't know my "Black Stone" had landed in the *Not At Night* anthology.[3] I'm so far off the beaten track of literature *geographically, that I get only vague hints of what goes on in the world of pen and ink.

Thank you very much for what you said about my verse. As I said above, I value your opinion most highly, and for you to speak of me as "a natural poet" gives me more real pleasure than I'd get out of having O'Brien name a yarn of mine as the best story of the year. That's no exaggeration. When you speak well of my work, I feel like maybe I have got something, after all. I wish I could give more time to verse, but the necessity of making a living crowds it out. Indeed, I've afraid I've lost the knack of rhyming. I've scarcely banged two lines together in years. The last verse I sold was stuff written years ago, and revamped; that is, pulled out of the unpublished archives and polished up a bit. Occasionally I go over rhymes I wrote a long time ago, and find I can iron out kinks that appeared impossible at the time of the original forging.

Glad you liked the rattles, and I'm sorry I couldn't get a bigger set. I'll try again next summer. If I could find a den of hibernating reptiles, and blast them out — that reminds me of a comical thing that happened several years ago. Some fellows found such a den as above mentioned, and dynamited it. One of them stood too close to the cave when the charge went off. The air was full of stones, dust, and reptilian fragments, and the first thing he knew, there was a four-foot rattler around his neck! The explosion had blown it bodily into the air, and dropped it on the person mentioned, with very little damage to the snake. But it was blind and stunned, and the fellow dislodged it without damage to anything but his nervous system, which was jittery and jibbery for days afterward. I've seen thirty or forty big snakes hanging on a barbed-wire fence after the discovery of a hibernating den, and some lairs have been found containing a hundred or more. There aren't the snakes in this part of Texas there used to be, but they'll come back. Already the owls, hawks, and ravens are returning by the thousands. The country swarms with fat jackrabbits and cottontails, and these birds of prey live off them. And the like of rats and mice you never saw. I make no attempt to explain this invasion of rodents and hunting birds. But here they are!

It's too bad sea-food affects you so adversely, particularly since you live in sea-port town. I fear you would suffer on the Corpus Christi waterfront; what with the rotting fish and shrimp along the beach, the fishing boats full of finny things, and the shacks where bait is sold in large quantities, the odor has occasionally nauseated even me, and I am even less susceptible to such things than the average. A ship ought to be able to make that port in a thick fog with no port-lights showing, by simply following the smell! The smell along the wharfs of Galveston, Aransas and Rockport is none too sweet, but that of Corpus Christi surpasses them all put together.

I noted your likes and dislikes in the food line, with great interest, having a weakness in that direction. In fact, I'm something of a gourmand — I believe you spell it that way. I, too, am a cheese addict. My favorite is Swiss; I also like limburger, cottage, pimento — in fact, almost any kind. I know of few greater treats than a slice of Swiss cheese, between two good thick pieces of white bread, with a slice of minced ham, pimento loaf, or baloney, washed down with a bottle of foaming ice-cold beer. Like you, I detest spinach, and am not fond of underdone meat. I like mine well-cooked. I'm not enthusiastic over sauerkraut, and I never ate any tripe. But liver is a favorite dish of mine, especially when fried with onions. I like chocolate passably well, though sweets in any form take the place more of an appetizer for more solid foods, with me. I go for ice-cream in a big way, though. Although after working in that drug-store I mentioned, it was months before I could regard the stuff without almost gagging. I often made a meal off it, when there was too much of a rush for me to take off time for lunch — or dinner, rather. The midday meal has always been dinner to me. My favorite is home-made cream; "sto'-bought" can never equal the other, when well made. I remember the peach-cream I used to eat at my grandmother's home, up in Missouri.[4] She had a big orchard, including many fine trees of Elbertas, which, when allowed to ripe properly, are hard to beat. At night, when everything was still, I'd wake up occasionally and hear, in the quiet, the luscious squishy impact of the ripe peaches falling from the laden branches. These peaches, mushy-ripe, and cut up in rich creamy milk, made a frozen delicacy the like of which is not often equalled. The peaches in this part of the world are nothing extra.

I'm not a great eater of cakes or candy, pudding, custards, or pies. The latter more than the others. I like most kind of pies — chicken, pumpkin, mince — especially with pecans mixed in the meat —, apricot, peach, apple, etc.. As far as that goes, I like most all kinds of food, but of course have my preferences. For drinks, I like tea, that is, iced tea in warm weather, with crushed mint-leaves and lemon, not much sugar. I care little for hot drinks, even in the winter, though I don't object to cocoa occasionally. I've never drunk a cup of coffee in my life, so I don't know whether I'd like it or not. (Incidentally, I don't use tobacco in any form, either, and haven't since the age of fourteen.) I don't care for highly seasoned food, ordinarily, though I like Mexican dishes every now and then, as well as spaghetti, macaroni and vermicelli. I like most all fruit, but eat vegetables mainly out of a sense of duty, except corn, which I admire boiled on the cob. I can eat a ton of it that way. French fried potatoes are all right, and yams, fried in their juice or baked in their jackets go well with fresh pork spare-ribs and back-bone. Turnip-greens and boiled bacon are palatable occasionally, when served with properly made corn-bread. I believe the finest, richest fowl-meat extant is goose. But fried chicken is hard to beat. I care less for sausage than any part of the hawg, but I can sure put away ham — boiled, baked, or fried. I mentioned my preference for beef, I believe.

You struck a responsive chord in me when you mentioned turkey dinner. Thanksgiving! Baked turkey, with dressing made of biscuit and cornbread crumbs, sage, onions, eggs, celery salt and what not; hot biscuits and fresh butter yellow as gold; rich gravy; fruit cakes containing citron, candied pineapple and cherries, currents, raisins, dates, spices, pecans, almonds, walnuts; pea salad; pumpkin pie, apple pie, mince pie with pecans; rich creamy milk, chocolate, or tea — my Southern ancestors were quite correct in adopting the old New England holiday.

I hope you had as enjoyable Thanksgiving this year as I did. I don't know when I enjoyed a holiday more. Early that morning, the chores being done, my friend "Pink" Tyson and I drove to Brownwood, forty miles to the southeast, to see the football teams of Howard Payne College and Southwestern University battle it out for the championship of the Texas Conference. Arriving there we went to the leading hotel and looked over the Southwestern boys, and a bigger, more powerful team I haven't seen in years. With them we listened awhile to the broadcast of the Colgate-Brown game, and I thought about you, and wondered if by chance you were seeing the game. After dinner at the home of a friend we helped him unload a bunch of steers, in order to facilitate an early arrival at the game. They were the finest, fattest, big Hereford critters I've seen in a longest time; and one of them was the meanest and wildest I ever saw. The three of us fought him all over the hill (on foot), and after we got him in the corral, we couldn't get the ropes off. We had two ropes on him, or he'd have killed some of us. When he'd plunge at one of us, the other would haul him back, and so on. As it was both of us had some narrow shaves. We finally got one lasso off his horns, but to save our necks, we couldn't get the other off. We had him hauled against the corral fence, and every time we slacked the rope, he took every inch of it, and tried to murder us. At last I threw a doubled lariat around his huge neck and snubbed his head down against the fence, and held him there while the rope was cast off his horns. Then it was every man for himself! After that we picked up another friend and repairing to the stadium, witnessed one of the fiercest, closest and hardest-fought games I have ever seen, in which a comparatively light, but hard-fighting Howard Payne team triumphed for a fifth straight championship. After the game we returned uptown, got a table at a window through which we could watch the shirt-tail parade and the other antics of the celebrating collegians, and while we watched and gorged ourselves on roast turkey and oyster dressing and ice cream, we decided international championships, selected All-Americans, and agreed that Colgate would be the choice for the Rose Bowl game with the University of Southern California. After that Pink and I drove back through the forty miles of hill country, through one of those still, clear, crisp star-filled nights that you enjoy only during good football weather. Simple and unsophisticated enjoyment, yet somehow I got more kick out of the whole affair than I've gotten out of more expensive and less innocent pleasures. We didn't even take a drink of liquor.

I'll remember that game for one reason, if for no other. It was the last game of that big Indian fullback I've mentioned before. His playing has always fascinated me with its primitive ferocity, and I've followed his career ever since I saw him play for the first time four years ago. I'll never forget that first sight of him, as he seized the ball and came ripping along the line, his bare black mane bucking through the melee. Did you ever watch a cowpuncher breaking a wild horse on the other side of the corral fence? All you can see is the puncher's head bobbing up and down along the top of the fence, with the plunges of the horse. That was what I was reminded of as I saw that black head heaving among the helmets. Bucking is the only word to describe it. He was charging at blinding speed and at the same time driving with all the power of his iron legs. He struck the line like a thunderbolt, stretched a tackler out half-stunned with a devastating stiff-arm, ripped through the swarm and fell headlong, his knee broken by the incredible strain of his own efforts. The next year he was back, stronger than ever. As time went by, and his body adapted itself to the terrific punishment he took with each game, he lost a good deal of his speed. Nature demands compensation. In his case speed and a certain amount of skill was sacrificed for sheer power. He carried the ball less and less, but his blocking, line-backing and desperate plunges made him still the most valuable man on the team. And Thanksgiving of this year he played his last game — unless he should happen to go into professional football.

During the first quarter, his line plunges and the off-tackle thrusts of the quarterback placed the ball on the one-yard line, and the big fullback crashed over for a touchdown. The place-kick was blocked. Southwestern came back fighting mad and ripped the Howard Payne line again and again. Always the big fullback was in the midst of the battle, fighting with every ounce of his iron frame and ferocious spirit. Then toward the last of the game, something happened. I don't know what it was. I was watching the ball, when a yell went up, and we saw the big Indian down. His leg was hurt. They carried him off the field and laid him on the side-lines, where they began working over his injury.

A big German lad was sent in in his place. He was good, but he was not Hoot Masur. Southwestern began an implacable drive. They marched irresistibly down the field, fighting for every inch. At last, on the sidelines, the injured player rose, with the aid of his companions. He began to limp up and down the lines, leaning heavily on a team-mate. Doggedly he plodded, half-dragging his injured member, his heavy jaw set stoically. Out on the field his team-mates, crippled by his loss, were being pushed slowly back toward their own goal. The fullback let go of his supporter, and walked alone, limping deeply, moving slowly. From time to time he worked at the injured leg, stooping, flexing, trying to bend his knee. Then he would resume his endless plodding. I forgot to watch the game in the fascination of watching that grim pathetic figure toiling along the sidelines — up and down — up and down. The sun was sinking, and the long shadow of the grandstands fell across the field. In that shadow the fullback plodded. Once, somewhere, I saw an old German print or wood-cutting, depicting a wood-cutter in a peaked hood carrying a bundle of sticks through the Black Forest. I was irresistibly reminded of this print. The peaked hood was there, even, the peaked hood of a grey sweater-like garment worn by football players when not in the game. There were the same massive shoulders, made abnormally broad by the bulge of the shoulder-pads beneath the sweater; the same slouching, forward bending pace. The shadows of the forest were to an extent repeated in the shadows of the grandstand. Only the bundle of sticks was missing, but the figure etched in the shadow stooped and toiled as if it bore the weight of a world on its shoulders. There was tragedy in the sight; he was eating his heart out because he was not back in the game, stopping those merciless onsets, giving freely of his thews and heart and blood, eating up punishment that would have snapped the bones of a lesser man. There was nothing of the story-book sob-stuff about the business. But to me, at least, there was a savage pathos in the sight of that grim, mighty figure plodding up and down the lines, striving vainly to work his bitterly injured leg back into shape, so he could re-enter the game. At last, when his captainless team was making its last stand, with its back to the wall, he sank down on the naked ground and covered his eyes with his hands. He would not watch the defeat of his mates. But that defeat did not come. Fighting like madmen, they broke up the attack just half a foot from the goal-line. The final score: Howard Payne 6, Southwestern 0. The fullback's touchdown in the first quarter was the only score. As the grandstands emptied and people rushed down onto the field to congratulate the winners, I saw him limping slowly through the throng, toward his team-mates.

Drama? You will see it on the football field, raw and real and naked, unaided by footlights, stage settings, or orchestras.

While I'm on the subject I'll continue the remarks I made about those teams clippings concerning which I sent — the West Texas blonds and the South Texas brunets. The strength and stamina of the Vikings proved too much even for the fiery fury of the black-haired Low-Country men, and after a desperate bruising battle they won, 14-0.[5] I heard the broadcast of the game in a hotel in Abilene, with the Howard Payne team which was there to play Simmons University that night, and had an opportunity of observing the predominance of blonds among this other Western team. The game first mentioned was a clash of fire and ice, the blazing spirit of the Southrons bursting in vain against the cool, implacable power of the Westerners. The quarterback of the Texas team was laid out for the rest of the season, and Stafford, the great Texas University half-back, blocked out John Vaught of the opposing team with such ferocity that he tore two of his ribs loose from his breastbone. Yet Vaught played throughout the game, and through all succeeding games — which is why he is counted one of the best guards in the nation. But the full attainment of savagery was reached the next week, when the blond victors went to Houston to play the Rice team. Maddened by a former defeat, the defending team went into the game wrought to a pitch of frenzy. They were crying mad and out for blood. They went in slugging, battling with the desperation of wounded tigers. They tore into the TCU team as if they intended to sweep it off the earth. They broke Red Oliver's jaw, they dislocated Pruitt's knee, they fractured three of Boswell's ribs close to his spine and wrenched his vertebra, they nearly broke Spearman's back, they subjected the already crippled Vaught to a merciless hammering, though his incredible ruggedness kept him in the game. The great Rice backs, the Driscolls, MacCauley, and Wallace, ripped the famous TCU line again and again, driving over a touchdown by pure ferocity. Reeling and staggering under the punishment, the blond Highlanders held them to a single score, and finished that cruel, bruising battle winners again,[6] to come on to a championship of the Southwest Conference which includes all the larger Texas colleges and Arkansas University.

But I must ask pardon for devoting so much space to a profession in which you have no particular interest. In my intense ardor for sports I am prone to forget that I may become boresome.

As always, I read your comments on political and economic possibilities with the greatest interest. You make even economics fascinating, which, as treated by anyone but yourself, is to me the most wearisome of all sciences. I am not prepared to disagree or take issues with you on any point you advance. However, in the case of the oppression of people by a ruling class, or classes, it is quite true that the revolutions of Russia and France show that tyrannies *ultimately* fall; however each overthrow was preceded by many centuries of oppression, in which generation after generation groaned under the crushing heel, before the change came about. Change apparently being one of the laws of Nature, we can not expect despotisms to endure indefinitely any more than republics, democracies, of periods of chaotic anarchy. I do not expect a permanent state of slavery, but I do look for a period of more or less length, in which class and individual liberty will be practically unknown — oh, it won't be called slavery or serfdom. They'll have another name for it — Communism, or Fascism, or Nationalism, or some other -ism; but under the surface it will be the same old tyranny, modified, no doubt, to fit modern conditions. The victims probably won't realize they are slaves for a long time, until conditions get too utterly hellish. They they'll doubtless rise, overthrow the existing rule, and institute another regime, in which the people will for a short space held the reins in chaos and confusion, then natural rulers will institute another mode of government — different in name and outward aspects, but fundamentally the same as the old, or capable of becoming modified to resemble the old type: and which will itself drift irresistibly toward eventual serfdom and ultimate dissolution. Of course all this is my own idea, and I don't pretend to be a student of economics or politics or sociology, but it seems to me that the trend of all governments and forms of governments has been toward centralization, the creation of special privileged classes, and the abolition of individual rights and liberties. It seems to me that a race, passing from the bloody darkness of semi-barbarism, basks for a short period in the light of culture and freedom, which phase is followed by an era of vast commercial prosperity, during which, unnoticed by the brainless mob which is too busy rolling in material luxuries, their rights are subtly taken from them. The over-inflated prosperity passes, and the people awake to poverty and enslavement, in one form or another. Just now, the method seems to be the confiscation of property through exorbitant taxes, coupled, indirectly perhaps, with government competing with private business. When the government goes into big business openly, the independent, whether individual or corporation, will be crushed, because the government has such vaster resources at hand. You mentioned that military enforcement of class privilege is an unstable thing. You are absolutely right. I think that the military dictatorship is inevitable, following the overthrow of the commercial masters, either by the mob, or by the military itself.

I do not think that actual peonage is impractical, considering the vast resources of slaughter in the hands of the rulers. Suppose the people are far more highly enlightened than Russians or Mexicans. Psychological equilibrium may be altered, but one ruthless and able man could overbalance all the psychology in the world. One ruthless efficient fighter in an airplane loaded with gas and explosives could make raw beef out of a whole city full of unarmed people, and their brains would spatter, their flesh shred away and their bones splinter just as easily as those of uneducated peasants. I'm probably wrong, but I honestly believe that a small group of men, guided by one brain such as Stalin's, or Mussolini's, could, with the aid of a comparatively small army, enslave a whole continent, regardless of the intellectual status of the people. Such event is a very remote possibility. A dictator would doubtless approach the matter in a more subtle way than by wholesale slaughter. But classes opposing him would be ruthlessly destroyed, and the result would be the same — the old, old fundamental of kingship: one man or one small class of men ruling the rest under one or the other of the ten million high-sounding names used to dress the raw reality of slavery. Again, remember, however high the intellectual level of the American people may be, it would take only a generation of serfdom to reduce them to the mental level of an uneducated European peasant — three, at most.

Your impartial viewpoint is admirable. For myself, I must admit that I am motivated more often by emotion and sentiment than by cold logic. I have said before, I think, that my nature is emotional rather than intellectual. Possessing many powerful prejudices, it follows that many of my views must be narrow and biased; knowing this, I try to be just xxxxxxxxxxxxx[7], but I know that my failure is frequent. I am unable to identify myself with any definite class or political movement. As for the classes, the arrogance of one, the smug complacency of the other, the stupidity of another, equally repels and antagonizes me. If it came to a show-down, I suppose it would be natural for me to throw in with the working classes, since I am a member of that class, but I am far from idealizing — or idolizing — it or its members. In the last analysis, I reckon, I have but a single conviction or ideal, or whateverthehell it might be called: individual liberty. It's the only thing that matters a damn. I'd rather be a naked savage, shivering, starving, freezing, hunted by wild beasts and enemies, but free to go and come, with the range of the earth to roam, than the fattest, richest, most bedecked slave in a golden palace with the crystal fountains, silken divans, and ivory-bosomed dancing girls of Haroun al Raschid. With that nameless black man I could say:

"Freedom, freedom,
Freedom over me! —
And before I'd be a slave,
I'd lie down in my grave
And go up to my God and be free!"

That's why I yearn for the days of the early frontier, where men were more truly free than at any other time or place in the history of the world, since man first began to draw unto himself the self-forged chains of civilization. This is merely a personal feeling. I make no attempt to advocate a single ideal of personal liberty as the one goal of progress and culture. But by God, I demand freedom for myself. And if I can't have it, I'd rather be dead.

Your view of society and civilization seems to me very well balanced, and fair. And your ideal of a modern government, is really magnificent. I must strongly agree with you that no one should be allowed to vote until he has passed an examination fitting him for such privilege. This may seem paradoxical in the light of what I just said about personal freedom, but I mentioned that that was my own personal ideal. Individual liberty doesn't necessarily entail blind dabbling in governmental affairs. Occasionally I have refrained from voting, simply because I didn't feel that I understood the matters involved well enough to take sides, and I didn't feel any limitation of liberty thereby. I likewise — as do you — strongly advocate unlimited educational advantages, so that anyone could qualify himself for the franchise. Altogether your ideal government is a splendid one — but I fear that it would not long endure on the just and fair lines you lay out. I probably have a nerve in making that remark, considering my ignorance of things social and economic. And yet I feel there is one element which (aside from the inevitable abuses of power by men of unbalanced ego, inordinate ambitions, or other motives) would ruin the equilibrium. That is the terrific animal vitality of a certain class of people. Or I should say type, for they are found in all classes, from street-sweepers to millionaires. These men — and women — are possessed of extreme natural individualism, restlessness, turbulence, and physical vitality. They are, I suppose, of the type called extroverts. From their ranks come explorers, soldiers, athletes, wanderers, and outlaws.

They are so constituted that only strenuous physical action can satisfy them. Some, favored by birth or circumstances, become soldiers, explorers, empire-builders. For every one of that breed who becomes famous in the ways mentioned, there are ten or fifteen who become dare-devil aviators, prize-fighters, football players, regular soldiers or sailors, or wandering workmen. Then there is a goodly number who turn gangster, gunman, gambler, outlaw. (Not all men drift into crime by necessity or changeless destiny of environments. Some deliberately turn to such paths because of the turbulence and restlessness of their souls.) Such men are very, very seldom artistic, scholarly, or intellectual. Generally they care nothing whatever about the arts, sciences or esthetics. In a society founded on intellect, there is no place for them. And yet they constitute a vital element of civilization. It would be impossible to educate such men into a state wherein they would occupy their leisure by study and philosophical contemplation; every fibre in their mental and physical being opposes such a thing. To expect one of these mentally impatient and physically terrific beings to sit down and wade through a book on art, economics, philosophy, or history, would be not only futile, but sheerly cruel. There is a tingling and stinging of their blood and tissues which demands that they be up and expending their terrific energies on some strenuous task or amusement. These men are not all fools or dolts. They help to build the world. I have known many of them. But they demand continual hard work and hard play of some physical sort, and when denied that, in a legitimate way, they turn to other paths less innocent. They work hard, drink hard, love hard, hate hard, and play hard; but they do not think, in the intellectual sense. Yet the most highly developed of this type demand success, recognition, wealth. Under the conditions you describe, no doubt such success could be attained, to a more limited extent than at present. But consider the less developed of the type. There again we find unlimited physical energy, and little mental ability or ambition. When they work, they work hard; when they do not work, they turn to the dance hall, the speakeasy, the athletic field. I do not believe that it would be possible to educate this race into employing their leisure any other way. Mental and artistic pursuits are senseless and repugnant to them, because of their peculiar make-up, for which they are in no way responsible. Yet, what of increasing mechanical devices, the leisure of all increases. That is well enough for people who wish to improve their minds. But what of the millions and millions who have no such wish — or ability? With no hard work to fill their hours, they will weary of the endless round of animal pleasures and tinsel enjoyments. They will begin to feel the old restlessness and the stinging in the veins. In the tame, flat world of the future, there will be no legitimate way of working off that physical superabundance of animal vitality. They will grow moody and discontented. Crime will grow steadily, as the people's discontent evidences itself in contentions, bursts of passion, and deeds of violence. Crimes will grow into riots, riots into revolutions. To save civilization, society will bring down the crushing heel again. Again I return to the question of slavery, as the only salvation of the civilization that has been allowed to crawl up from the depths. Hard, continuous work, with livable conditions and part-time relaxation, will keep the people, if not contented, at least docile for a time (as long a time as we can expect any phase of evolution to endure). Expanding their energies in labor, they will have no time for systematic plotting and complaint. In their short leisure-hours, they will be too busy enjoying their old pleasures — made sweet to the taste by rarity — to rebel. But in a machine age, how is this work to be furnished? I can only venture a theory, an imaginative picture of an age in which vast projects will be carried out, dwarfing the pyramids and the wonders of ancient times, at first simply to keep the dangerous mobs employed, later also for the whims and fancies of an inevitably created aristocratic class, at once mentally titanic, and degenerate. I seem to see a world like the dream of a crazed artist, reared by serfs and ruled by madmen with the intellects of gods.

All this is maundering, no doubt. I have no right to even conjecture, considering my lack of knowledge of the trend of world events. Anyway, the whole modern structure is more than likely to be swept away by a war or a series of wars. I care not. Individual liberty is a dream that is out-worn and will never be reborn. I have no other ideal.

Concerning police irregularities in Texas — you are quite right in saying that Texas is in the throes of change from a frontier existence to a civilized one. *As for inhibitions of honesty, however, I'm not ready to agree that we are morally inferior to anybody else; thousands of people from more civilized sections have come here lately, and I haven't observed that their percentage of honesty is any greater than that of the natives.

Of course the good police outnumber the bad, else life would be intolerable, but there is abuse, as you discerned from the clippings and incidents I sent you. As a result, there is a pretty wide-spread resentment against such abuse, which is not confined to actual law-breakers. You remember the case I mentioned, wherein an officer shot down a private enemy on a public street and was acquitted. This same officer, later, maltreated another civilian almost fatally. It seems there was a poker game going on, in which the officer lost heavily. At last, doubtless fired by liquor as well as resentment, he attacked the civilian, who ran out of the house in an attempt to escape. The officer pursued him, caught him, gave him a frightful beating with his gun-barrel, and left him lying senseless in an empty lot, with his skull fractured. This was seen by witnesses. The officer resigned from the force, but I did not hear of it if he was punished further. A friend of his on the force, I heard — and quite believe — upon hearing another civilian criticize the action of the first officer, knocked the man down with his pistol-barrel, and likewise resigned. The two then established themselves in a detective agency. If resentment for officers in general results, it is lamentable, but scarcely to be wondered at. In that very town, not so terribly long ago, a powerfully built youth, maddened by liquor and marihuana weed, nearly killed a policeman. In this case, my sympathies were wholly with the officer. As near as I could learn, he was trying to lead the boy out of a cafe, when the youth struck him down from behind with a chair, and then nearly stamped the life out him. But nearly every one I talked to of the case, expressed full sympathy with the boy, and hoped he'd be acquitted of the charge brought against him of attempted manslaughter. It wasn't that they condoned lawlessness or illegal violence; simply that abuses of law-enforcement caused resentment toward the enforcers. Incidentally, the offender was given a light suspended sentence — three years, I think.

Again, a friend and I were riding into the business part of a town with a couple of cops who had picked us up — not by way of arrest! They'd merely offered us a ride. It was rather late, and seeing a kid walking along the sidewalk, they drew up to the curb and ordered him in a domineering manner to stop and answer their questions. If there was any real reason for this procedure, I failed to see it. The boy was rather poorly dressed, but he was proceeding on his way, apparently minding his own business — a kid in his early 'teens, I should say. The cops asked him who he was; and where he had been — he told them to some sort of a school-rally, I think. They asked him where he got the scratches on his face and hands, and when he said from falling while skating, they practically told him he was lying, accusing him of fighting in the alleys. They concluded by berating him for disrespect — he having become somewhat sullen under this badgering — and profanely ordered him off the streets, saying that there was a curfew law in the town; a straight lie, to the best of my knowledge. Now this may seem like a small thing. But a boy of that age is likely to be molded into any pattern by trivial things. He went his way, smarting, without doubt, at the wanton tongue-lashing he had got, and resenting it. A few such beratings, and he could hardly be blamed for looking on the police as persecutors instead of protectors. That viewpoint might well color his whole life's actions, and tip the balance from honesty to criminality.

I've never had but one brush with the police, but I must say that did not increase my respect for the system. I was about eighteen or nineteen, and with a couple of friends of about my own age, made a flying visit to Dallas. It was the first time any of us had driven by the traffic-lights, and the lad driving, not knowing the regulations, got confused, made a mistake and drove across a stop-light. We were stopped by the cop on the next beat, and the usual lambasting followed. The officer on whose beat we had committed the offense was fair enough. I have no complaint to make about him. No one could have been more gentlemanly. But the cop who stopped us seemed to consider our blunder a personal insult. He lashed himself into a perfect rage. We had not sinned through intent, but from ignorance, though of course the officers had no way of knowing that. We were glad to be told the rules and regulations; we did not resent being halted and questioned; we would even have gone into court and paid a fine without undue protest. But we did resent being treated like gangsters and thugs. We explained the situation, and our willingness to conform with the law if it were explained to us, but the policeman who was so wrathy refused to be mollified. It was so damned unnecessary. If we had offered him any incivility, his resentment would be understandable. But none of us made any reply to his insults, not caring to be haled into court to pay a fine for "abusive language", "resisting arrest", "assault on an officer of the law", or some such charge. He loudly regretted that the offense had not occurred on his beat, so that he might run us in to spend our stay in Dallas in jail, urged the older officer to throw us in, intimated that we were fleeing from the committing of some dark crime, and concluded by accusing us of stealing the automobile in which we were riding. Well — the man doesn't walk the earth who can call me a thief on his own power without getting my knuckles in his mouth; it isn't particularly entertaining to be forced to swallow that insult because the individual who utters it is clothed in brass buttons. In the midst of his berating, a young negro started to absentmindedly walk across a stop-light, and the policeman ceased his abuse of us to leap at the offender and snarl: "Get back there, you black bastard!" Then he wheeled back to us with a triumphant glare, as if to see how we were impressed. I must admit our only feeling was one of disgust. If it had not been for the other cop, who refused to arrest us or give us a ticket, that gentleman would have made it as unpleasant for us as possible. Understand me — that incident did not sour me against the police system as a whole, or make me a violent cop-hater. I supposed at the time that such varmints as that one, were so rare as to be almost unique in his case. My later conclusions were forced on me against my will. I could give other incidents, but there's no need of inflicting them on you. I need hardly to say that I wish all these remarks about the police and law-enforcement to be considered absolutely confidential. I hardly know how I got to spilling all this stuff; I never put any of it on paper before, and I wouldn't be doing it now, except that I feel I can trust you discretion. The fact that I could prove my assertions wouldn't do me much good, if I should make enemies.

I'm afraid a written statement of affairs wouldn't do much good, unless signed by some one in authority; even if I dared to publish such a paper. So much stuff is circulated in campaigns and the like — charges, refutations and counter-charges. The Fergusons may make some reforms. I don't know. If the *Gladewater Journal* doesn't have any effect, I'm afraid nothing I could write would, except to make dangerous enemies. *The Journal* has an enormous state-wide circulation, and in spite of its sentimental style (which is deliberate, in order to catch the attention of the common people who respond to the truth more quickly when presented in such fashion) is considerable of a political power.

But reform is difficult in this state, where lines are so loosely drawn. There is so much of a grab-bag, to-hell-with-everybody-but-me spirit. In the general grabbing, the weak are so often ruthlessly trampled, and common decencies lost sight of. For generations Texas has been the prey of certain particular breeds of vultures: magnates from other sections, who wish only to exploit and loot the state; and native promoters and politicians who are eager to sell the birthright of their people in return for personal graft. That is not to say by any means that the people who come to Texas are all commercial pirates, or that all the native promoters and politicians are grafters. But both breeds do exist in goodly number, and have, since the Civil War.

The state has always had such vast resources. So many men have come here with a single idea — that of getting rich as quickly as possible, and by any means, and then returning to their own section with their loot. Such men can have no sympathy with, or care for, the state or its people. But it would take too much space here to go into the social and historical factors behind this present tangle. I think I'll prepare such a treatise, however, and send it to you later on, in which I'll try to present the salient features in the development of Texas, and their connection with present-day conditions.

Concerning barbarians and civilization: it is quite true a civilized man, if suddenly thrown into a barbaric life, would find it intolerable. But one born to such conditions feels no lack of a fullness in life, any more than the Indians before the coming of white men, felt any lack of, or need for, whiskey; or any more than the Europeans felt the lack of tobacco, before they knew anything about it. Whiskey and tobacco are artificial stimulants, unnecessary, except when a taste has been deliberately developed; so are many other of the adjuncts of civilization. We can not get along without them now; but we would be better off if we had never discovered or developed them. As for being a shaman or minstrel among barbarians — those are the very last things I should wish to be, were my lot cast among the uncivilized. It is evident that a shaman, however fantastic and barbarous his thoughts and methods, represents the nearest approach to civilized man, in his tribe and age. Therefore, he is able to glimpse, in a dim way, some of the vistas that lie above (I say "above" for the sake of argument; I am by no means sure that "progress" is necessarily a step upward.) and to feel the lack of intellectual attainment — , oh, very, very dimly, without doubt. Yet he is stirred by gnawings and vague urges that never trouble the war-chief, the hunter, or the brave, who accepts the dreams of the shamans as truths not to be questioned or worried about. So the condition of the shaman is a faint reflection of what the condition of a civilized man cast among savages would be. This would seem to be borne out by the nature of the shaman. Whether white, black, yellow or red, the witch-finder, voodoo man, priest of Odin, or shaman, seems generally to have been a gloomy, brooding, shadow-haunted mortal, groping vaguely in the shadows. On the other hand the warrior, the ordinary tribesman, has often been a jovial cut-throat, in as far as the hard physical conditions of his life would allow him, swaggering imperturbably through blood and slaughter, gorging, guzzling, breeding, killing, and eventually dying in some ghastly fashion — never troubling his head about abstractions, and really living his life to its fullest extent — however shallow that might seem to a modern man, he found it full. No; I would not have cared to be a bard or shaman; if I had been a barbarian, I would have wanted to be a complete barbarian, well-developed, but developed wholly on barbaric lines;

not a distorted dweller in a half world, part savage and part budding consciousness. Just as a man, dwelling in civilization, is happier when most fully civilized, so a barbarian is happier when fully barbaric.

Concerning duels, I hardly think we have any right to judge our ancestors by modern standards, or to condemn them harshly because so many of their duels seem to have risen from causes utterly trivial to us. We can not apply modern standards altogether to those earlier times, when men stood in somewhat different relations than at present, and were judged by different standards, determined by long trains of preceding events and customs, many of which have lost their meaning in modern times. We moderns, for instance, are so careful of our precious lives that we can not understand how a man could risk his, or take another's, over what seems to us a light matter. It could not be otherwise. We are not used to risking our lives through necessity, and we can not be expected to risk them recklessly. But the early Americans grew up in an atmosphere of peril, especially on the frontier. The very fact that a man was a frontiersman, was evidence that he was ready to risk his life lightly. He fought like a blood-mad mountain lion to preserve his life, but he would frequently walk carelessly into danger. When he was so ready to risk his own hide, it follows that he would scarcely be more careful of some other person's. He often valued his honor more highly than his life, and if he often seemed over-touchy in regard to his honor, it must be remembered that he alone was responsible for that honor and its upholding. From defending himself against enemies, it was natural that he was ready at all times to resent the slightest hint of insult or encroachment. If he had shown himself laggard in his own defense, there were plenty of individuals who would have soon made life unbearable for him. Major Henry, for instance, the gentleman of the New Orleans duel, once rode a mule across a plaza in Nicaragua, at a walk, through a hail of bullets. He rode across, and walked back, carrying a few bullets in his hide, the mule having been shot out from under him. His only reason for doing so was because of a wager of a dinner, with his brother officers. When a man takes such terrible risks simply because of a whim, it is not incongruous that he should readily shoot out any sort of an argument, whether important or not. This readiness to die or kill was simply a frontier characteristic, inexplicable to moderns, yet without which the settlement of America would never have been accomplished.

I feel, like you, that the total abolition of the duel was not altogether a move for the better. There are wrongs that ought to be settled individually and without recourse to law. As far as that goes, some wrongs are too great to be righted even by a duel. Some injuries deserve, not a fair fight for the perpetrator, but the death of a dog.

In regard to Indians, I believe — excepting the civilizations of Mexico — that the mental status of the Eastern Indian was somewhat higher than that of the Western, especially those of the great plains. I am speaking, of course, of the Indians found in what is now the United States. The Pueblos of course, had a culture of their own; but their pottery making, blanket weaving and house-building was not sufficient to stave off the invasions of the more barbarous Pimas and Apaches. The Sioux, Cheyennes, Utes, Comanches, Apaches, Pimas, Navajoes, Kiowas, Blackfeet, Arapahoes, Pawnees, Omahas, Konsas, Osages, were not, I think, quite the equals of the Iroquois, Natchez, Delawares, Seminoles, Chickasaws, Choctaws — and I can say with conviction that they were generally inferior to the Cherokees. Considering the so-called inferiority of any race, I realize the term is relative and varies with the varying viewpoint. I do not, for instance, consider myself particular superior to a Chinaman, but I'd hate like hell to be changed into one, and I'd knife him if he tried to marry, say a sister of mine. The Indian might have developed a permanent civilization, if left alone long enough, but I must admit I have certain doubts on the subject.

It is natural that we should take opposite sides in the Ulster question. No, I wouldn't want you to be kicked out of Rhode Island because your ancestors gypped the Wampanoags out of the land; but a descendent of those Wampanoags might be pardoned for feeling differently. However, if you'll glance over my comments again, you'll find that I said nothing about booting the Orangemen off the land their ancestors stole from my people. They can stay there until they rot, as far as I'm concerned. And as far as incorporating Ulster into the Free State, personally, I wouldn't take it as a gift. I'm ready to admit they're right in their present squabble with the South Irish. But that's as far as I can go. It's too much to expect me to side against my own flesh and blood with their hereditary enemies. It really doesn't make any difference to me whether the South Irish are right or wrong, any more than I care whether a member of my immediate family is right or wrong in a dispute with an outsider. If the Irish are oppressing the Ulstermen, it's no more than can be expected. After three hundred years of oppression and abuse, are they to expect perfect fairness and justice from their former victims? Wrongs breed wrongs; when a man beats a muzzled bear, he needn't howl, if, when the bear breaks his muzzle, he sinks his fangs into him, whether he happens to be holding a club then or not.

Considering the Philippines — if we were allowed to fortify them, they would be a strength. As it is, they're a weakness. Instead of being a rifle aimed at the heart of Japan (as would be the case were they fortified and a goodly portion of our Pacific fleet stationed there), they tend to divide our forces, to scatter our lines, and to subject American citizens to danger, in case of war with Japan. I think it would be a point of strategy to abandon those islands entirely, and concentrate our forces about Hawaii. That Japan would gobble them is certain, but I scarcely think they would add much to her ultimate strength, increased as it is so enormously by her grabbing of Manchuria.

No doubt the French excel us in many phases of literature. The point is that personally I can't endure much of the stuff. After wading through a few chapters, my teeth get on edge and I am aware of an almost overpowering desire to spring from my chair and kick somebody violently in the pants. That is all but Voltaire. I get a big kick out of that lousy old bastard. English poetry is probably the highest form of English literature. But my favorite writers, both of prose and verse, are British or Americans. They are A. Conan Doyle, Jack London, Mark Twain, Sax Rohmer, Jeffery Farnol, Talbot Mundy, Harold Lamb, R.W. Chambers, Rider Haggard, Kipling, Sir Walter Scott, Lane-Poole, Jim Tully, Ambrose Bierce, Arthur Machen, Edgar Allen Poe, and last, but no means least, yourself. Maybe the French excel the British in some ways, but where is the Frenchman who writes, or wrote, with the fire of Jack London, the mysticism of Ambrose Bierce, or the terrific power your own weird masterpieces possess?

For poetry, I like Robert W. Service, Kipling, John Masefield, James Elroy Flecker, Vansittart, Sidney Lanier, Edgar Allen Poe, the Benets — Stephen Vincent better than William Rose — , Walter de la Mare, Rupert Brooke, Siegfried Sassoon, Francis Ledwedge, Omar Khayyam, Joe Moncure March, Nathalia Crane, Henry Herbert Knibbs, Lord Dunsany, G.K. Chesterton, Bret Harte, Oscar Wilde, Longfellow, Tennyson, Swinburne, Viereck, Alfred Noyes, and, again, yourself.

I never read any of Conrad's work. I've never read any of G.B. Shaw's muck, either; he's probably a genius. He's also a poser, an egomaniac and a jackass. I see he's coming to America at last. Very condescending on his part. If I had my way, he'd be met on the wharf by a committee of welcome in top-hats and ivory-headed canes who would tender him the keys of the city, and pull all his whiskers out, hair by hair. Of all these foreigners, I prefer Kipling's works. He's made remarks about America that made me want to break his back, but I've got much solid enjoyment out of his prose and verse. He has guts at least, which so many modern writers utterly lack.

As for American writers, I think yourself and Jim Tully are the only ones whose work will endure; among the writers now living, I mean. Upton Sinclair may get by because of the pictures of economic and social life he draws. As for Drieser, Sinclair Lewis, Louis Bromfield, Ben Hecht, Sherwood Anderson, F. Scott Fitzgerald, George Jean Nathan, Floyd Dell, Mike Gold, — three ringing razzberries for the whole mob. They may be artists and I'm certainly no critic, but I know what I like and what I don't like, and to me they're all wet smacks. I don't know of anything I'd enjoy more than striking a match on a pile containing all Mencken's works, and if he was sitting on top of the heap, at the time, it would be all right with me. I'd rather read Zane Grey the rest of my life.

As I said on my card, I am extremely sorry to hear of Whitehead's untimely demise.[8] He was a writer of real ability, and, from all accounts, a brave and honest gentleman. Rest to his soul wherever it lies.

Well, I've rambled even more than usual. I hope I haven't bored you too much with my maunderings. I'm enclosing a few rhymes I discovered among the archives and thought might interest you a little. You can return them at your convenience; no hurry. If I wasn't so lazy I'd make copies of them. Some of the unevenness of the rhythm is intentional. By the way, could you give me the address of the *Not at Night* people?

And so, wishing you a very merry Christmas and a happy New Year, I remain,

Cordially,

[REH.]

NOTES

1. Arthur Brisbane, American newspaper editor.
2. Howard may be referring to Texas University (see letter 220, notes 6 and 7), for which the fullback was Ernest Koy and halfbacks were Bohn Hilliard and Harrison Stafford, or to Howard Payne College, for which Hoot Masur was fullback in 1932.
3. *Grim Death*, 1932.
4. Alice Wynne Ervin lived in Exeter, Missouri.
5. Texas Christian University (TCU) defeated Texas University 14-0, November 11, 1932.
6. TCU defeated Rice Institute 16-6, November 19, 1932.
7. "in my views" has been X-ed out.
8. Henry S. Whitehead died November 23, 1932.

TSS: 50413-50431

226. To Robert H. Barlow, ca. December 1932.

Dear Mr. Barlow:

Price tells me that you are interested in the collection of first drafts of Weird stories. I am sending by express, the first writings — or rather the first typings, since I do all my work on the typewriter — of "The Phoenix on the Sword", "The Scarlet Citadel", "Black Colossus", and "Iron Shadows in the Moon". Some of the pages seem to be missing from the first named story, but the others are complete. Hoping you will find them of interest, I remain,

Cordially,
[Robert E. Howard.]

P.S. "The Phoenix on the Sword" and "The Scarlet Citadel" have appeared in *Weird Tales*. "Black Colossus" is scheduled for the June issue, and "Iron Shadows in the Moon" has been accepted, but not scheduled.

REH.

TSS: 93537

ઉઊઋઌઉઊ

227. To Robert H. Barlow, ca. December 1932.

Dear Mr. Barlow:

I'll be glad to sign the title pages of the stories. If I had thought, I would have done so before sending them. Glad you liked "The Scarlet Citadel".

Cordially,
[Robert E. Howard.]

TSS: 93541

ઉઊઋઌઉઊ

228. To August Derleth, ca. December (29?)[1] 1932.

Dear Mr. Derleth:

I read your recent letter with the greatest interest. I did not know that Wright was suffering from the disease you mentioned,[2] and am extremely sorry to hear it. I trust he will recover. I have had dealings with many editors in the years I have been writing, and I have never encountered a squarer, fairer gentleman than he.

I was very much interested in your remarks concerning your native region. I had already located Sauk City on the map, but of course had no idea as to its scenery. Your description is fascinating. I was even more interested in the people as you described them. The contrast between Sauk City and Prairie du Sac must be notable. I'd like to hear more about these towns and their contrasting cultures.

I'll admit I hadn't thought of connecting "Sauk" with the Sac Indians, though the connection seems obvious enough now. I've read somewhat of the Black Hawk war, and thought the redskins got a rather crumby deal. But they got that all over the country. I'm interested to learn that the Indians of those parts were comparatively friendly. The aborigines of this region were unbranded devils, especially the Comanches. You've heard perhaps of Quanah Parker, the great Comanche warchief, son of Petah Nocona and Cynthia Ann Parker? One of my uncles married a cousin of the big chief — a white cousin, of course. But if I start talking Indians now I'll get nothing else in this letter.

Well, I'll try to give you some idea of the country I live in. To quote from statistical sources: "Callahan (County) — In Central West Texas. Created in 1858 from Bosque, Travis and Bexar Counties and organized in 1877. Named for James N. Callahan. (A noted Ranger and Indian fighter.) Area 854 sq. mi. Pop. per sq. mi., 15. Lies on Callahan divide between water-sheds of Colorado and Brazos. Rolling plains with low mountain ranges. The county is a large producer of petroleum."

Cross Plains is a small town of — well, I guess at present the population is about 1800. It varies; during oil booms the town has had a population of six or seven thousand. It has an elevation of 1715 feet, situated as it is on the ridge of the Callahan divide. Because of its situation there is an illusion of a plains country. Looking south and west from the town there is only flat country to be seen. North east some four or five miles there rises a low chain of hills known as the Baker Mountains, while to the northwest are a pair of peaks some ten miles apart known collectively as the Caddo Peaks and individually as East Peak and West Peak. The town presents an appearance about like the thousand other small West Texas towns — one wide main street, unpaved back alleys, oil derricks rising up here and there all over the business and residential sections. In old abstracts the town is known as Schleicher, it having been originally built on Schleicher County school land. It first stood near the banks of a small creek known originally as Briar, and later as Turkey Creek; but some twenty years ago the coming of the rail-road caused the whole town to be moved perhaps half a mile to the east, to its present location. That's a peculiarity of many Texas towns; the first settlers were inclined to build as near the banks of creeks and streams as possible; later the towns were moved up on higher grounds, because of various reasons — or sometimes for no apparent reason.

Being on the Callahan divide, it follows that the town is hemmed in by a dense growth of post-oaks on all sides. (There are two main post-oak belts in Texas, known as the East and West Cross-timbers; the divide is in the West Cross-timbers.) This post-oak growth is low, scrubby and thick; in the summer it is not unpleasing to the sight, densely cloaking the hills and valleys as it does, but in the winter it presents the most dreary, drab appearance imaginable. The motif of Nature then is a weary brown — brown earth, brittle brown trees — even the sky seems brownish. At times the effect is distinctly one of gaunt savagery.

The western part of the county presents a different aspect; it is mainly a cattle country, of broad plains grown with mesquite instead of oak, although the oaks are present in lesser quantity. Three big ranches take up most of that part of the county; as well as a goodly portion of the adjoining counties. Cross Plains is in the southeastern corner of the county, and main center of the county's oil industry. Outside of oil the main industry — adjacent to the town — is cotton-raising. To the north the country slopes down somewhat into the valley of the Brazos and its tributaries, before rising to the Caprock and the Staked Plains of the Panhandle. West the land likewise slopes a little before rising to the Edwards' Plateau and the region of the South Plains. Southward it drops swiftly from plateau to plateau until it reaches the coastal plains. Eastward the divide runs until it breaks west of the Palo Pinto hills, which further east drop swiftly into the Grand Prairie, where are the progressive towns of Fort Worth and Dallas. Fort Worth is nearest town of any size, lying about 165 miles to the east. Most of the trade of West Texas — with the exception of that region dominated by Amarillo, high up in the Panhandle — goes to Fort Worth. Personally, though, I like San Antonio, and spend much more time there than at the former city.

Concerning the people of Cross Plains: this section — as is the case with most of West Texas — was settled, not by native Texans from the eastern part of the state, as was South Texas, but mainly by people from the older Southern states — particularly Alabama, Mississippi and Georgia, with a sprinkling of East Tennesseans. This colonization took place mostly between 1885 and 1900. Of course these settlers found a few people already there — stockmen and ranchers from the eastern and southern parts of the state. The newcomers were mostly farmers. Now, the countryside is inhabited largely by descendents of these settlers, while the towns, especially in the oil-belt, offer a very mixed appearance. Outside of the original ranchers and the later farming class (both of practically the same stock, Scotch-English-Irish from the older Southern states) about the only other strain in the country in this section is Germanic: numbers of Germans having drifted up into this country from the Teutonic settlements of Fredericksburg and New Braunfals. But the oil booms brought many varying elements into the towns. In Cross Plains, for instance, there are, besides the older settlers, people from Pennsylvania, Kansas, Illinois, Nebraska, Oklahoma, Indiana, West Virginia, and Kentucky. Teutonic and Scandinavian strains predominate in these people, and they tend to mix with the natives and intermarry. There were other elements not so easily assimilated during the active booms — Italians, Indians, and other dark-skinned breeds. They generally passed on, making no attempt to be assimilated. Naturally practically all religious sects are represented, all the Protestant sects, as well as Lutherans and Catholics. A good many of the Middle Western oil-workers having taken up their abode in the country, have quit the oil game and bought farms, and are in the process of being absorbed by the native stock much more quickly than their countrymen in the towns. The population of both towns and country is white; there are no negroes in the county, and but a very few Mexicans — transient workers, mostly.

But maybe all this stuff isn't very interesting. You mentioned Pecos Bill. I don't know much about that mythical hombre. Likely somebody in the long settled districts of South Texas could tell you more about him. Just now the only legend dealing with his exploits which I call to mind is of obviously recent manufacture. It seems the University of Southern California was going to have a tug-of-war with the University of Oklahoma. The rope was stretched from the campus of one to the campus of the other, and Pecos Bill, who had been imported by the Californians, laid hands on it out on the West Coast and began to heave. He anticipated an easy snap, but lo, and behold, he found himself unable to gain an inch. Amazed, he told the students of U.S.C. to let go and give him full play. He gripped the rope with both hands, planted his feet, and heaved. And at last, inch by inch, the rope came to him. He backed away with it, and it came faster and faster. At last he was wading in the Pacific Ocean up to his waist, and the rope was fairly humming through his hands. Then the people of Colorado began to set up a hell of a yell. The Oklahomans had tied their end of the rope to Pike's Peak, and Pecos Bill had torn the mountain loose from its moorings and was dragging it toward the Pacific Ocean.

But some of the early heroes of the Southwest did feats almost equal to the legendary exploits of the gentleman from the Pecos. There was Jack Hayes, for instance — the first Ranger captain. He went into a thicket where twelve Comanches were lurking, and killed eleven of them in hand-to-hand fighting, and lived to tell the tale, as the saying is. Incidentally the remaining redskin was shot down as he ran, by Jack's Rangers who were stationed around the thicket.

I have often wondered what would have been the result of an encounter between Jack Hayes and John Wesley Hardin, or Billy the Kid, or Wild Bill Hickok. I'm inclined to believe that each would have killed the other. I'm assuming, of course, that it would have been a fair fight. Actually, it probably wouldn't have been. The skill of a gunman consisted almost as much of getting the drop on the other fellow as it did in drawing and shooting. I believe Billy the Kid was just a flashing fraction of a second quicker on the draw than any of the others mentioned, but I'm not sure. One thing is certain: when their time came to die, they died, and all but Jack Hayes died violent deaths. Billy the Kid died on his feet, with his gun in his hand, but blinded by the darkness that masked his killer; Hardin and Hickok were shot in the back of the head, just as Jesse James was. They never knew what hit them.

Of all gunmen John Wesley Hardin was probably the smartest. He originated some of the tricks Billy the Kid used and got credit for inventing.

For instance, the six-shooter roll, which takes a man off guard. They say the Kid invented that. Why, that was old stuff in Texas before the Kid killed his first man. To the best of my knowledge Hardin invented it, and it was practised by all the vaqueros who hazed the doggies up the old Chisholm. Many a Kansas law bit the dust before they learned the trick. Hardin once got the drop on Wild Bill himself that way, but for some damfool reason didn't drill him. The Kid was as slick as Hardin, but he had the advantage of mechanics; double-action guns had come in, in his time, and he used one of that sort — a .41, worn high up on his left hip, as he was left-handed. Hardin used a single-action — a cap-and-ball at first — and it's easy to see the difference. What Billy accomplished in a single movement, or at most a slight change in a single movement, Hardin was forced to do with three — Billy simply rolled the gun and pulled the trigger as he reversed it, while Hardin had to draw back the hammer and release it as he rolled the pistol. Success in that maneuver depending on speed, one can easily see that John had to have steel-trap quickness in his thews and nerves. And he did. Moreover he was a crack shot. Once he and a friend were coming out of a saloon, and John was pretty drunk. Seeing this, his friend pointed some distance down the street to where a loafer lounged on a whiskey-barrel, and bet John that he couldn't, in his condition, shoot the fellow off the barrel. For answer a long-barreled .44 flashed into John's hand as if by magic and at the crack of the shot, the loafer toppled from the barrel, shot cleanly through the head. The friend paid the wager.

Not that all those old gunfighters were extraordinarily good marks-men. Many of their fights took place in saloons and gambling halls, and the contestants were only a few feet apart. When Ben Thompson killed Jack Harris in San Antonio, Thompson was behind a fancy glass screen in the other's saloon, and seeing Harris approaching with a sawed-off shotgun, he simply let him have it through the screen. Again, when Billy the Kid killed Joe Grant, they were standing face to face. Hearing that Grant was after him, the Kid feigned ignorance of the cowpuncher's motive, complimented his ivory-handled pistol, and lifting it out of his scabbard, pretended to examine it — but in reality turned the cylinder so the hammer would fall on an empty chamber. Grant was too drunk — and too stupid — to notice the Kid's action. The Kid handed the gun back to Grant — Grant stuck it in his face and pulled the trigger — the hammer snapped futilely, and the Kid laughed in his face and killed him. The gun that killed Ferd Patterson was held so close to him the powder burnt his clothes. Ferd was sitting in a barber's chair, toweled and lathered, when a man strode in, remarked that the world was too small for both of them, and pulled the trigger. Who he was none ever knew.

Well, I haven't given you much, or interesting, data, but maybe it'll do for a beginning. I hope you had an enjoyable Christmas. It was pretty quiet in these parts, nothing out of the ordinary occurring. Personally, I did about as usual — ate too much rich food, drank a good deal of whiskey, and shot a few holes in the air, by way of celebration. But it was all mighty tame. I can remember Christmases when liquor flowed and gunpowder was burnt in appropriate quantities — but that's neither here nor there. With best wishes,

Cordially,
[REH.]

NOTES

1. Date handwritten in on the first page. JB
2. Parkinson's Disease.

TSS: 15042-15045

229. To Tevis Clyde Smith, ca. after mid-1932.

Ahatou noyon, Fear Finn:

Thinking of nothing particularly to say just I'll attempt to parody as in days of yore.

****

The Werewolf Murder Case

Chepter .1.

Twilight squinted down the chimneys of houses as I sat cross-legged on my divan, strumming my balalaika and singing a song of the Oriental, the mystic, the blue, the alluring, the slant-eyed Oriental. Thus I sang, my fingers galloping lightly over the strings.

"Tom, Tom, the piper's son,
"Stole a pig and away he run."

Here I received a crushing stroke at the base of the skull with an iron mallet. Realizing that my aristocratic friend, Vile-oh Pants, wished to call my attention to something I looked about at him with that wide grin which he sometimes finds irritating. Now he muttered something about a leering jackass, and knocked out seven or eight of my teeth — the joker!

Spitting the splinters out on the floor, I asked jovially, "Well, Pants, old fellow, what now?"

"That song don't rhyme," he scowled. "'Tom' don't rhyme with 'son' or 'run'."

"Well, I'll fix that," I soothed, and sang again.

"Tom, Tom, the piper's som,
"Stole a pig and away he rum."

He interrupted me with a shriek and a crunch of his hob-nailed boot in my mouth. "Not that way, fool!"

"Very well," I returned, giving him another of my grins, which this time reduced him to a gibbering state.

"Ton, Ton, the piper's sun,
"Stul a pig and away he run."

At that moment an earthquake seemed to shake down the walls, but as I lapsed into unconsciousness, I was aware that Vilo had bent the electric washing machine over my head.

Chepter .2.

Ertoghrul Khan's lance-point caught the fleeing Armenian between the shoulder-blades. With a scream that set the echoes shuddering he went down, and the hoofs of the Kumanian spurned him, the rider wrenching free the spear as he swept past.

"Ya Allah il Allah!" foam whitened the beard with the blood-mad cry.

The curved blades whistled, the sound ending in the zhukk! of cloven flesh and bone. With a wild cry a fugitive turned as the Akinji swooped in, his wide khalat spreading out in the wind like the wings of a hawk. In that instant the dilated eyes of the Armenian saw, as in a dream, the intolerant bearded face, with its hawklike nose, thin and down-curving; the gold-broidered vest beneath the flowing cloak, crossed by the wide silk girdle from which projected the ivory hilts of half a dozen daggers; the baggy nankeen trousers and red moroccan boots; the wide sleeve falling away from the lean muscular arm that lifted, ended in a curving glitter of broad steel. In that instant too, the Turkoman saw the lean stooped figure tensed beneath the rags, the wild eyes glaring from under the lank tangle of hair, the long glimmer of light glancing along the barrel of the ancient flintlock. A wild cry rang from the lips of the hunted, drowned in the bursting roar of the old musket. A swirling cloud of smoke veiled the figures, in which a flashing ray of steel cut the murk like a flicker of lightning. Out of the cloud raced a riderless steed, reins flowing free. A breath of wind wafted the smoke away.

One of the figures on the ground was still writhing; slowly it drew itself on one elbow. It was the Armenian, life welling fast from a ghastly cut across the neck and shoulder. Gasping, fighting hard for life, he looked down with wildly glaring eyes on the figure that lay near him. The Turkoman's Astrakhan kalpak lay yards away, blown there by the close-range shot; most of his brains were in it. His beard jutted upward, as in ghastly comic surprize. The Armenian's elbow gave way and his face crashed into the dirt, filling his mouth with dust. He spat it out, and it was dyed red. A ghastly laugh welled from him.

It rose to a shout that scared the wheeling vultures. He fell back threshing the sand with his hands, and yelling with mad laughter that rolled out across the trampled plain in seemingly endless reverberations.

Chapter .3.

Vilo entered on his hands and knees. He eyed me menacingly. He wrinkled his patrician nose and snarled, baring long buck-teeth.

"I'm a werewolf," he announced.

I always try to enter into his whims with zest, zim and zitality. I likewise got on my all-fours. Thereafter the only sound was the shattering of furniture and an occasional gasping oath. At last I got a headlock on him, and twisting him beneath me, hammered him into senselessness with a heavy table-leg. Rising, I weaved uncertainly into the street, spitting out fragments of teeth as I went.

A long, melancholy howl drifted up the street. I saw a young woman racing along in full flight, yelling for the police, all of which were hiding in a convenient sewer. Behind her, loping along on all-fours and clad only in a very scanty wolf-hide, came Vilo Pants. He had reverted; he had gone native; he was an atavism. So was I. So were we all. All blonds and atavisms. All Dominant Werewolves. I tore off my shirt and brandished my hairy fists to the stars. Therein I read the destiny of my race — fighters and wanderers, diggers of roots, eaters of meat, lovers of women — blonds and werewolves, since the first yellow haired people landed on English coasts. All over the world I saw them working out their imperial destiny — thousands on thousands, loping down the streets of the cities of men, clad only in moth-eaten wolf-skins — dominant men, lovers and workers and fighters — blond werewolves — men and women — men with women — men after women — always men after women — the destiny of my race — high living, high loving, high fighting, barking our dreams to the moon, wherein was pictured the symbol of our worship and our cult — set there by ancient and terrible priests — the imperial dog-biscuit.

Chapter .4.

And so this tale draws to a close. There may be others. Doubtless there shall be others — of high heroism, nobility and endeavor, shadows and light, thrones and hovels, empire-building and glue-factories. But now the twilight rests like a golden foam of light on the domes and spires and mosques of the Imperial City, and in the blue-domed seraglio, the harem favorite beguiles the sultan with pop-corn balls dipped in Shiraz wine and varnish from Lake Balkash, where the timid Mongol woos his lady-love with a ten-foot knout and the rattle of the lead-tipped lashes shakes the slumber of forgotten shareefs in the Ak Serai — the White Palace, over which broods the shadows of forgotten loves. Bismillah!

* * * * * * * * * * *

I was in Brownwood Monday. I called you up twice, or rather I tried to. Somebody said you were in cold storage. I left my number, and they said they'd have you call me, but I guess they forgot to tell you.

Fear Dunn.

TSS: 82494-82496

ଔଷ୍ଠଲଓଔଷ୍ଠ

230. To unknown recipient, ca. 1932[1]

Salaam:

Not much to say. My brain seems stagnant. I'll probably ramble.

Strange how the world grows. Texas is truly an empire state, with its new towns springing up like mushrooms. I've seen several of them spring and several slump back.

I was talking to a man the other day, an oil magnate — rather remarkable fellow, by the way, ex-cowpuncher, worked his way up from the bottom, such a large man that I looked and felt like a dwarf beside him and I weigh nearly two hundred pounds, too. He was talking about his holdings down around Catarina — Catarina! Four years ago the site of Catarina was a wilderness of greasewood and mesquite. Now it's booming like hell — and may slump as quick. Another town, Crystal City, not far from there — a fair-sized town now and growing all the time. I lived there when the first store went up during its earliest boom. Ho hum. Sometimes I feel like one of those pioneers — I've passed through many a booming town and never made a cent in any of them.

Enough. I'm too young for retrospect.

NOTES

1. This letter is moved to here due to Howard's mention of the Texas town of Catarina, and its appearance "(F)our years ago…". In letter 074, he mentions on his trip to South Texas in June 1928, that "Catarina is overrated". Rob Roehm and JB

TSS: GR 15525

UNDATED LETTERS

231. To Tevis Clyde Smith, ca. after 1930.

Well, Fear Finn, I read your story and enjoyed it even more than I did when I read it in manuscript form; I want you to autograph it for me the first chance we get. It has power and drive about it that makes it stand out clear cut and distinct from the goo and slop dripped on the public from the sex-saturated pens of most writers. It touches pungently on the basic uselessness of life, and the drag of satiety, of empty needs which cannot be satisfied no matter how much they may be glutted — all this it expounds and creates without the use of the superlatives and canting mouthings employed so much by the half-baked school of tin-can sophisticates.

I sent some stuff to the same megazin but it will be rejected. Even their rottenest stories are clever, and my cleverness is too much of the elephantine and ponderous order. I look back with awe and wonder at the days when I conceived myself a budding humorist. Heh heh heh.

Thenks very much for predicting Steve de Mauler[1] a movie career, though I fear me youse is too optimistic. Hist — Steve de Ham shall be my pawn of rewenge. Some day, in the far, dim future, when I am about ninety and able to write what I want and get it published, I shall double cross the soivice men who follow the career of Steve de Pug. They think he is a sailor — har, har, har — and so he is — but, hist, only in the merchant marine. Some day I will make Steve de Maneater dewelope an obsessional mania in regard to uniforms and go around beating up all the navy men, marines and soldiers he can find. Har har har har har har har har har har har har har har! And wit fiendish laughter, Scutto, de Mad Genius, strangled the beautiful pickle.

The Cuckoo's Revenge

I plastered rolls with Belgian cheese
For an honest livelihood;
A haughty flapper turned me down
But my revenge was good.

I lay in wait by the meadow gate
Until I got my chance;
I did not hit her, I only bit her
In her passionate pink silk pants.

I laughed at her bleet as her panties' seat
Gave way most utterly,
And I sank my teeth in the flesh beneath —
Revenge was sweet to me.

You, proud beauty, will marry some sap,
And I laugh with a right good cheer —
How will you account on your honey-moon
For those teeth-prints on your rear?

The Madness of Cormac

Lock your arm of iron
Around the reeling moon,
Draw your sword, the grey sword, the sword of Fin, the fey sword,
Carved with a nameless rune.

Brace your feet like talons
On the dreaming world,
Break the shapes, the dread shapes, the dragon-things, the red apes,
Out of the abyss hurled.

Ghosts of all the ages
Fill the ancient skies,
Red queens and white kings, nameless forms and night things,
Men fools and wise.

A Challenge to Bast

Come not to me, Bubastes,
With agate talons hid,
Veil not the fury of your eyes
Beneath the drooping lid.

Save all your gentleness for those
Mad passion makes aghast,
For they who are too frail to face
Your love's unholy blast.

But come to me as you of old
Your demon lovers met —
A black, stark naked frenzied thing
Of ebony and jet.

Where jackals haunt the shadows
In the star-light's yellow glow
With bodies writhing savagely,
And teeth that gnash in ecstasy,
We'll glut all hidden splendors
That maddened passions know.

Answer soon, will you.

Fear Dunn

NOTES

1. Howard's humorous boxing character, Steve Costigan, first appeared in the *Fight Stories*, July 1929 issue. The character had six stories published in 1930, and six stories published in 1931, all in *Fight Stories*, and one story published in *Action Stories* in 1931. This would tend to place this letter as coming out sometime in 1930, or 1931, due to the character's popularity. JB

TSS: 82607-82608

ଔଌଓଔ

232. To John Wasso, undated, unsent.[1]

My Dear Mr. Wasso:

There is a good deal of justice in what you said in your last letter, but I think you'll admit I have my own side of the matter too. I am a very busy man, Mr. Wasso, and my own work keeps me crowded for time. I had to take off time that I could not well spare to get those magazines together, and I certainly did not have time to look through each magazine to ascertain their contents. I remember that a number of bizarre stories were appearing in Argosy at the time I bought these magazines, and I assumed that some of such stories were included in the copies I sent you. Had I not thought so, I would not have sent them.

However, if this is not the case, I understand your position and that's why I'm sending you the $.93 cents you were out. Now, I want you to accept this in the spirit in which it's offered. I'm not sending this money in order to be nasty, but simply because I feel I owe it to you, and I'm in the habit of paying my debts. I don't want to be the cause of you or anyone else expending money needlessly.

And now, Mr. Wasso, I've given more time to this matter than I can well afford. Having made a mistake, I feel that I have done all I could to square it. The incident is closed then, as far as I am concerned.

Cordially,

NOTES

1. This letter is moved here as it appears from the contents of the letter that this letter was written in response to Howard becoming famous from his writings, and that Wasso had written to Howard to buy any magazines that Howard had that may have had an effect on Howard's writing. JB

TSS: 15795

ଔଔଔଔ

233. To Unknown Recipient, undated, unsent.[1]

Salaam:

"The real reason," said John L. Sullivan, slapping me on the back and giving me fallen insteps, "that I never became a poet is this: the real reason and excuse for poetry is extreme egoism. You need not make the remark you were contemplating. I realize that I am blessed with a true appreciation of my own merit. However, my inhibitions ran in other lines and I preferred to give my inferiority complex free rein by hitting my fellow man on the chin, rather than inflict my views about things of which I had no knowledge whatever, on innocent unborn generations to come. A poet seldom ever really knows anything. He feels and is aware instinctively and is usually right but as far as knowing—it takes a scientist or a prize fight manager to reason things out in a logical manner.

"Let us consider the present day writers," continued John L., gently stroking my arm and removing large areas of skin therefrom, "Doubtless the most powerful of all is Tully. This hobo will never be a Jack London, however, because he still clings to some few illusions. There are still things in life which he desires and which he will go to some trouble to acquire, and if he lives a thousand years, there always will be. Take movie actresses for example. A moment—let this be clear—Tully desires things less for themselves than because it is the fashion to desire them and he secretly yearns for the plaudits and respect of the throngs. The crowds want these things, therefore there must be something to them. He levels himself with the throng. Jack London would have strode in tossed the movie actress of his choice nonchalantly on the nearest couch—and she'd have liked it. Then in a short time Jack London would have given her a grisly leer of disillusionment anticipated and realized and would have dismissed her with a kick in the rear. Yes.

[. . .]

NOTES

1. This letter was moved to this spot first to make room in Volume 3 for the additional letters and drafts going into that already large volume, and second, because Howard mentions the writer, Jim Tully, in this letter. Howard writes of Tully in the following letters: in a poem in letter 075, written in June 1928, in Volume 1; in letter 225b in this volume; and in Vol. 3, in a letter to Lovecraft written in March, 1933. It would appear that Howard had Tully in his mind from 1928-1933. So I thought this would be an appropriate place to put this letter. JB

TSS: 90324

Appendix: Photographs

Letters Correspondents

THE REGIONAL CONFERENCE GATHERING

Reading from left to right, back row: Eugene Butler, Editor of The Progressive Farmer; Roy McDonald, National Council Chief; Harold Preece, LSC; Bill Hoting, LSC; Frank Dixon, LSD; Harvey Blailock, LSD. Front row, left to right: Walter Tomlinson, LSD-O; F. B. Mitchell; Travis Foster, LSD; Gilbert White, SS; Booth Mooney, LSC; and Harry Wiginton, GC.

In this photo of the 1927 Regional Conference Gathering of the Lone Scouts organization, are Harold Preece (back row) and Booth Mooney (front row), with white dots over their heads. None of the correspondence between Mooney and Howard survives. Mooney was the first editor of *The Junto*, and is mentioned in letters 124 and 125.

(1927 Texicoma Yearbook)

Alvin Bradford, writer, and poet. Photo from later in life.
(Source unknown)

From left: Clyde Smith and Truett Vinson. The back of the photo has Howard's typed identification: "Truett and Clyde doing a bathing beauty pose on the Cisco dam."
(Photographer Unknown)

From Left: *Weird Tales* editor Farnsworth Wright, and C.C. Senf, *Weird Tales* artist, mentioned in letter 185
(Source unknown)

H.P. Lovecraft
(Photographer Unknown)

Lovecraft and Frank Belknap Long. Long is first mentioned in letter 136.
(Photo by W. B. Talman)

Wilfred Talman, editor Texaco Star Magazine, writer. Photo from later in life.
(Source unknown)

Harry Bates, editor Clayton Publications
(Source unknown)

Carl Jacobi, writer
(Source unknown)

August Derleth. Photo from later in life.
(Photographer unknown)

Robert H. Barlow, fan, and writer. From later in life.
(Photographer unknown)

Henry S. Whitehead *Weird Tales* writer. He is first mentioned in letter 169. The correspondence between Whitehead and Howard does not survive.
(Source unknown)

Letter 145 Kelly the Conjure Man and The Ouachita River Area.

In this letter, Howard first relates the story of Kelly the Conjure Man and the Ouachita River area of Arkansas, where Dr. Howard was born and some family members still lived. Robert Howard had two pictures of the Ouachita River area.

Howard's original photo of the Ouachita area.

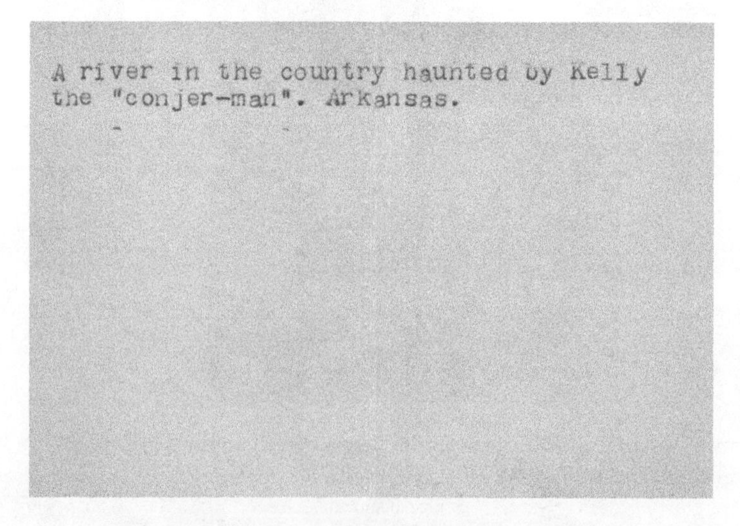

Back of photo with Howard's typed identification.

Edited Ouachita River area photo.

Back of photo: "Typical road-scene in southwest Arkansas."

Letters 145 and 191 On Bullfighting and Rio Grande City

In the first letter to H.P. Lovecraft, Howard talks of his dislike of bullfighting, and in the second letter, Howard tells Clyde about his visit to Rio Grande City, Texas. The following postcard and article were in Tevis Clyde Smith's possession.

DISTINGUISHED VISITOR HERE

Dr. I. M. Howard and son, Robt. E. Howard, who are here from Cross Plains, Texas, were sight seeing in Rio Grande City yesterday. Robert E. Howard is a noted writer, being staff writer on several leading magazines, and while here is securing data to be used in his work in the future.

Distinguished Visitor Here, Unknown Newspaper, Unknown date.[1]

Dr. I. M. Howard and son, Robt. E. Howard, who are here from Cross Plains, Texas, were sight seeing in Rio Grande City yesterday. Robert E. Howard is a noted writer, being staff writer on several leading magazines, and while here is securing data to be used in his work in the future.

NOTES

1. This article and postcard first appeared in Tom Munnerlyn's zine, *Austin #4*, and was included in *REHupa 111*, September 1991. Tom Munnerlyn included the following information: "The other item shown is a bullfight scene postcard with newspaper clippings attached, loaned to me by Roy Barkley. The card is unused and was sent to Tevis Clyde Smith by Howard with the news clips attached by Howard. Rio Grande City is in Starr County on the border with Mexico. No date is indicated." Rusty Burke and JB

TSS: 82339

Index to the Collected Letters of Robert E. Howard

Volume 2: 1930-1932

Created by

Bobby Derie and John Bullard

First Edition Bobby Derie Thanks

To Rusty Burke and Rob Roehm, for doing the work;

To Glenn Lord, for laying the ground;

To Jeff Shanks, for aiding and abetting.

Second Edition John Bullard thanks

To Bobby Derie for doing the hard work first, and for his great help in answering questions and catching mistakes I made in the updating of, and adding to, his work.

Editors' Note to the Second Edition

In attaching and updating the index to reflect the new page numbers for the second edition of *The Collected Letters of Robert E. Howard Volume Two*, here are the things from Bobby's first edition of the index that have been kept:

A page number in brackets refers to an entry that is alluded to but not mentioned directly (e.g. 3.[13]). A reference to a footnote will be demarcated with an "n" (e.g. 6n1 would be note 1 on page 6).

Titles of short stories are contained in quotation marks, while films, novels, plays, poems, and magazines are italicized. Short stories, novels, plays, and poems have the last name of the creator in parentheses following the title; films the year of publication.

Nations and states have been, in general, combined (e.g. "Rome" refers to references to the city, the empire, and the Roman people; "Germany" to references to both Germany and Germans, etc.); languages retain separate entries where applicable. Howard's references to and theories regarding the aboriginal peoples of the British Isles are included in the entry "Little People."

Material not included in this index are the prefaces, greetings, return addresses, closings, and signatures; Howard's plays and poetry included in the letters will be listed separately in the List of Plays and Poetry in the Collected Letters.

The changes I have made to Bobby's first edition, are the following:

Volume numbers have been removed from the listing as the index has been split up for each volume that index covers.

Page numbers in brackets have been changed to parentheses, with the name of the person or work as satirized/parodied/spelled differently than the cite by Howard in the parentheses for quicker finding. Entries in the following style "323n2-4" mean that the entry is in notes 2 through 4.

I have added new entries as I thought were needed.

For some entries that had "see also" entries, I have included those entries as sub-entries under the general entry, i.e. Alcohol now has all the various related entries of types and subjects under it as sub-entries.

At Bobby's suggestion, I added in a list of illustrations and photographs for quick reference.

The biggest change you will find is in the Poetry Titles section. In trying to standardize the titles of the poems I have changed the former "Untitled" poems to give their new title as the first line of the poem. The former "Untitled" listings have been removed. Of course, this may still not standardize the titles of the poems as they will appear in the upcoming *Complete Poetry* books.

Bobby Derie
John Bullard

INDEX

Numerals

A

B

C

D

E

F

G

H

I

J

K

L

M

N

P

Q

R

T

U

V

W

Y

Z

List of Howard's Correspondents for Volume Two

Correspondents are listed by letter number. Volume 2 (116-233)

Barlow, Robert H. 226, 227
Bates, Harry 167
Bradford, Alvin P. 117
Derleth, August 224, 228
Jacobi, Carl 198
Lovecraft, H.P. 135a, 135b, 137, 140, 141, 143, 145, 152, 153, 156, 158, 169, 171, 173, 178, 180, 182, 185, 189, 192, 193, 203, 208, 212, 213, 217, 218, 219, 220, 221, 225a, 225b
Magic Carpet 223
Mashburn, Kirk 194, 215
Oriental Stories 196
Preece, Harold 116, 122, 125, 127, 142, 144, 148
Smith, Tevis Clyde 118, 120, 121, 123, 124, 126, 128, 129, 130, 132, 133, 134, 136, 138, 139, 146, 149, 150, 154, 155, 159, 160, 161, 163, 164, 165, 168, 172, 174, 176, 179, 181, 183, 184, 187, 188, 191, 195, 197, 202, 204, 205, 206, 207, 210, 214, 216, 222, 229, 231
Swanson, Carl 200, 201, 209
Talman, Wilfred Blanch 157, 162, 170, 175, 177, 199, 211
Unknown Recipient 151, 186, 230, 233
Wasso, John 232
Weird Tales 119, 147, 190
Wright, Farnsworth 131, 166

List of Howard's Poetry and Plays in Volume Two

Howard's plays are denoted in italics. Where a title is not provided, the play or poem is listed with the first line as its title (for plays, the listing will be in italics).

Index to the Illustrations and Photographs in Volume Two

Photographs Appendix:

About the Contributors

Rusty Burke's father always answered his questions with "You could look it up," which is probably why he finds annotation, and the research involved, among life's most enjoyable pursuits. He does have an unfortunate tendency to spend too much time chasing down one rabbit hole after another. He has been hanging around Howard fandom for nearly 40 years, writing, editing, researching, and working to promote Howard studies.

Rob Roehm has gone to every location in the United States that Howard mentions visiting—from New Orleans to Santa Fe, and dozens of Texas towns in between—verifying and expanding our knowledge of Howard's biography. His research has also uncovered lost Howard stories, letters, and poems. He writes about these discoveries, infrequently, at howardhistory.com.

Bobby Derie is a weird fiction scholar and the author of *Sex and the Cthulhu Mythos* (2014, Hippocampus Press). According to family lore, his father wanted to name him Conan, but his mother vetoed it.

Jeffrey Shanks is an archaeologist, historian, and popular culture scholar who has authored a number of articles and essays on Robert E. Howard. He lives in Florida with his exceedingly patient wife and two kids who don't seem to mind their geeky dad.

Paul Herman is a lawyer and long-time REH fan. Publisher, editor, researcher and worker of deals. One of the very few still around who has run his fingers across REH's writing table as well as virtually all of REH's original typescripts. His scanning, identifying, sorting and indexing of the thousands of pages of typescripts has yielded literally years of work for him, which most folks know nothing about. He's shy that way.

Mark Wheatley holds the Eisner, Inkpot, Golden Lion, Mucker, Gem and Speakeasy Awards and nominations for the Harvey Award and the Ignatz Award. He is also an inductee to the Overstreet Hall of Fame. His work has often been included in the annual Spectrum selection of fantastic art and has appeared in private gallery shows, the Norman Rockwell Museum, Toledo Museum of Art, Huntington Art Museum, Fitchburg Art Museum, James A. Michener Art Museum and the Library of Congress, where several of his originals are in the LoC permanent collection.

John Bullard is a recovering attorney who has irreparably hurt his eyesight reading the small print and wants satisfaction and reparations. He also wants to thank Bobby Derie for demanding he add his name as co-creator of the index (even though all the hard work was originally done by Bobby).

CPSIA information can be obtained
at www.ICGtesting.com
Printed in the USA
LVHW030232250522
719630LV00001B/1

9 781955 446037